AF330046

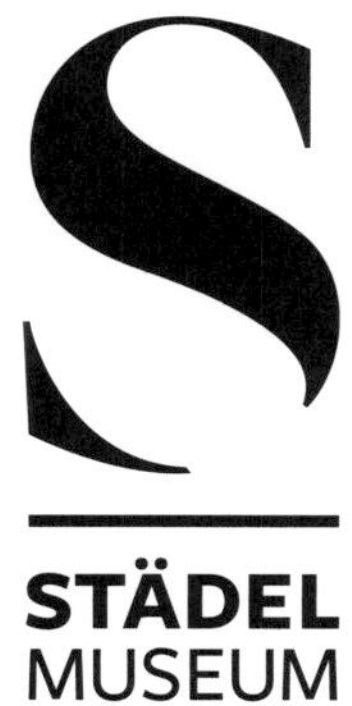

STÄDEL
MUSEUM

en passant

IMPRESSIONISM IN SCULPTURE

Edited by
Alexander Eiling and
Eva Mongi-Vollmer

in collaboration with Juliane Betz and Fabienne Ruppen

PRESTEL
Munich · London · New York

Table of contents

Authors of the catalogue texts:
AE – Alexander Eiling
EM-V – Eva Mongi-Vollmer
FR – Fabienne Ruppen
JB – Juliane Betz
SB – Stefano Bosi

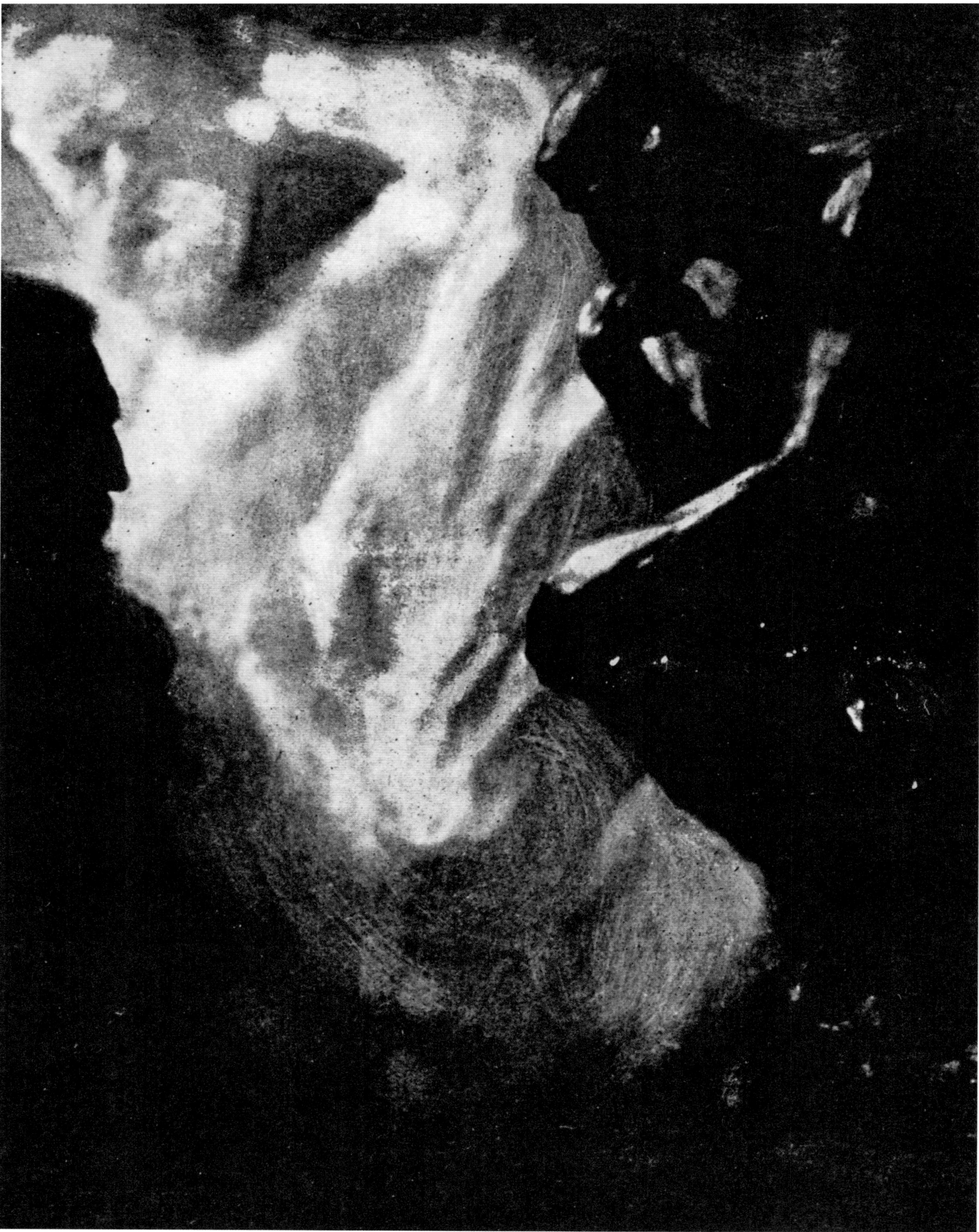

Greetings

DZ BANK AG

The Städel Museum in Frankfurt am Main and the DZ BANK AG are bound by a long-standing partnership. As early as 2008, our institute transferred a body of 220 works of photographic art to the museum from the DZ BANK Art Collection. These have been part of the permanent exhibition programme in the Garden Halls since 2012. For more than 27 years now, we have been pursuing the aim of making artistic photography accessible to a broad public and placing it in a scholarly discourse. With the ART FOYER in our Frankfurt headquarters, the DZ BANK therefore has its own presentation space, in which alternating exhibitions featuring works from our collection take place and in which an extensive art education programme is offered. Thus, at first sight it may come as somewhat of a surprise that the DZ BANK is supporting the exhibition *en passant. Impressionism in Sculpture* at the Städel Museum, which deals with Impressionism in general and with outstanding artistic positions in Impressionist sculpture in particular. As a subject, light has naturally played an important role in cross-genre artistic examination. Yet it only became a formative element in Impressionism. In much the same way that light leaves traces on photographic film, sculptors such as Auguste Rodin, Edgar Degas, Medardo Rosso, Rembrandt Bugatti or Paolo Troubetzkoy developed their sculptural works out of materialising light reflexes, out of positive and negative forms. In the nineteenth century, photographic images exercised a substantial influence on the evolvement of the arts. One of the reasons that the fundamental scrutiny of stylistic devices became possible in the modern era is that photography liberated artistic production as a whole from its supposed task of having to provide a mimetic representation of reality.

The Städel Museum's exhibition addresses a further basic aspect in the connection between the artists being presented and photography, since it became more than just a tool for documenting and presenting one's own artworks. The artists' oeuvres include not only sculptures, paintings and drawings, but also their photographic interpretations in that the visual axes, detailed views and distribution of light of each artist obtained a content-related dimension.

These illuminating cross-connections between photography and sculpture at the turn of the nineteenth to the twentieth century convinced us of the relevance of the subject, also with a view to our own promotional aims. We are therefore delighted to be supporting the exhibition and, in doing so, to be setting an example once again for our long-standing ties with the Städel Museum. We are confident that each and every visitor will have the opportunity to gain new perspectives and have stimulating encounters.

The Board of the DZ BANK AG

Kulturfonds Frankfurt RheinMain gGmbH

The Städel Museum in Frankfurt am Main is appreciated worldwide for its prestigious collection of Impressionist works of art. As early as at the beginning of the twentieth century, the museum purchased exceptional paintings by Claude Monet, Édouard Manet and Auguste Renoir – and many more. These have justifiably counted among its most well-known works ever since. However, the fact that the collection also includes a fine selection of sculptures produced within the context of Impressionism is less commonly known. This finding is not an isolated case: Impressionist sculpture is generally not nearly as well known to the public as Impressionist paintings or works on paper. To this day, research has likewise rarely directed its attention to these three-dimensional artworks. And yet it was famous artist figures such as Edgar Degas, Auguste Rodin and Medardo Rosso who shaped Impressionism in sculpture. Like their painter colleagues, they also chose motifs from the sphere of modern life. At the same time, they constantly eschewed materials such as marble or bronze – highly valued at the time – and instead favoured wax and terracotta, for example, which had hitherto primarily been used for producing preparatory sculptural works. However, they not only increasingly distanced themselves from the "perfect" with respect to their choice of material, because even the extent of the figures' completion was frequently called into question: surfaces stayed rough, traces of work were left behind as visible proof of authenticity, and the figure itself remained a torso. In addition, the sculptors played in a variety of ways with the traditional practices of viewing sculptures in that plinth heights or the distribution of light, for instance, commanded unexpected attention.

The opportunity, therefore, of being able to comparatively consider Impressionist sculpture and its innovative potential for twentieth-century art certainly holds the promise of making a number of discoveries! It is excellent to see the Städel Museum addressing this subject for the very first time in such depth – as always, thinking and acting based on its own collection.

We, the Kulturfonds Frankfurt RheinMain gGmbH, are delighted to be accompanying this exhibition project and hope that all who visit it and read the accompanying catalogue have an interesting and stimulating time doing so.

Karin Wolff
Managing Director
Kulturfonds Frankfurt RheinMain gGmbH

Lenders and acknowledgements

Lenders

Rijksmuseum Amsterdam; Museo Medardo Rosso, Barzio; Staatliche Museen zu Berlin, Nationalgalerie; Staatliche Museen zu Berlin, Kunstbibliothek; Staatliche Museen zu Berlin, Kupferstichkabinett; Staatliche Museen zu Berlin, Museum für Fotografie; Museum of Fine Arts, Boston; Richard Borek Stiftung, Braunschweig; Museum of Fine Arts, Budapest; Amgueddfa Cymru – National Museum Wales, Cardiff; Museo Civico e Gipsoteca Bistolfi, Casale Monferrato; Staatliche Kunstsammlungen Dresden; National Galleries of Scotland, Edinburgh; Museum Folkwang, Essen; Collection Jean Bonna, Geneva; Hamburger Kunsthalle; Staatliche Kunsthalle Karlsruhe; Ny Carlsberg Glyptotek, Copenhagen; Tate Modern, London; The Sladmore Gallery Ltd., London; Musée des Beaux-Arts de Lyon; Museo Thyssen-Bornemisza, Madrid; Ufficio Musei e Monumenti, Mantua; Galleria d'Arte Moderna, Milan; Musée Ingres, Montauban; Gilgore Museum, Naples, FL; The Metropolitan Museum of Art, New York, NY; Musée Camille Claudel, Nogent-sur-Seine; CNAP – Centre national des arts plastiques, Paris; FNAC – Fonds National d'Art Contemporain, Paris; Musée Bourdelle, Paris; Musée des Arts Décoratifs, Paris; Musée d'Orsay, Paris; Musée Rodin, Paris; Petit Palais, Musée des Beaux-Arts de la Ville de Paris; Galleria d'Arte Moderna Ricci Oddi, Piacenza; Musée Sainte-Croix, Poitiers; La Piscine – Musée d'art et d'industrie André Diligent, Roubaix; Réunion des Musées Métropolitains Rouen Normandie, Musée des Beaux-Arts; Mart, Museo di arte moderna e contemporanea di Trento e Rovereto/Collezione VAF-Stiftung; Segantini Museum, St. Moritz; Musée d'Art moderne et contemporain de Strasbourg; Staatsgalerie Stuttgart; Museum Ulm, Ulm; Albertina, Vienna; Belvedere, Vienna; Kunst Museum Winterthur; Woburn Abbey and Gardens; Von der Heydt-Museum, Wuppertal; Collection Museum de Fundatie, Zwolle and Heino/Wijhe; Collection PCC, Switzerland; Private collection, Courtesy of Galleria Bottegantica, Milan; Private collections in Berlin, Frankfurt am Main, London as well as in Europe and the USA, and other private collectors who do not wish to be named

Acknowledgements

Dirk Boll; Stefano Bosi; Richard R. Brettell; Birgit Brunk; Maraike Bückling; Pieter Coray; Stefanie Dathe; Roland Dorn; Alma Egger; Patrick Elliott; The Europe Trust; Spencer Ewen; Walter Feilchenfeldt; Evelyne Ferlay; Anne-Birgitte Fonsmark; Frances Fowle; Véronique Fromanger; Guendalina Giannini Mochi; Ulrike Christina Goetz; Katie Hanson; Björn Harres; Sharon Hecker; Bernd Hettinger; Edward Horswell; Flo Horswell; Christine Horwitz Tommerup; Elisabeth Jaubert; Isabelle Kneip; Mauritius Korfmann; Paul Lang; Ludwig Lichtenthal; Michael Loulakis; Bernhard Maaz; Danila Marsure; Christof Metzger; Henrike Mund; Astrid Nielsen; Joachim Pissarro; Marie-Anne Poniatowski-Krugier; Monique Rival; Dorit Schäfer; Julietta Scharf; René Scharf; Dirk Schönfeld; Dieter Schwarz; Jean-Michel Seguin; Helen Smailes; Christine Stauffer; Margret Stuffmann; Beat Stutzer; Alain Tarica; Michael and Yvonne Uva; Karsten Weber; Julia Wallner; Christoph Weigand; Wolfgang Wittrock; Oliver L. Wootton

Supported by

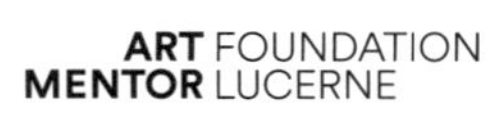 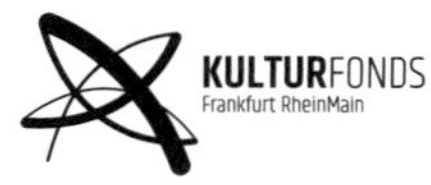 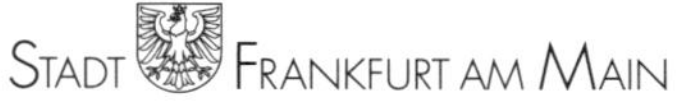

Media Partner   Cultural Partner

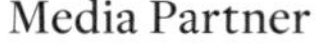

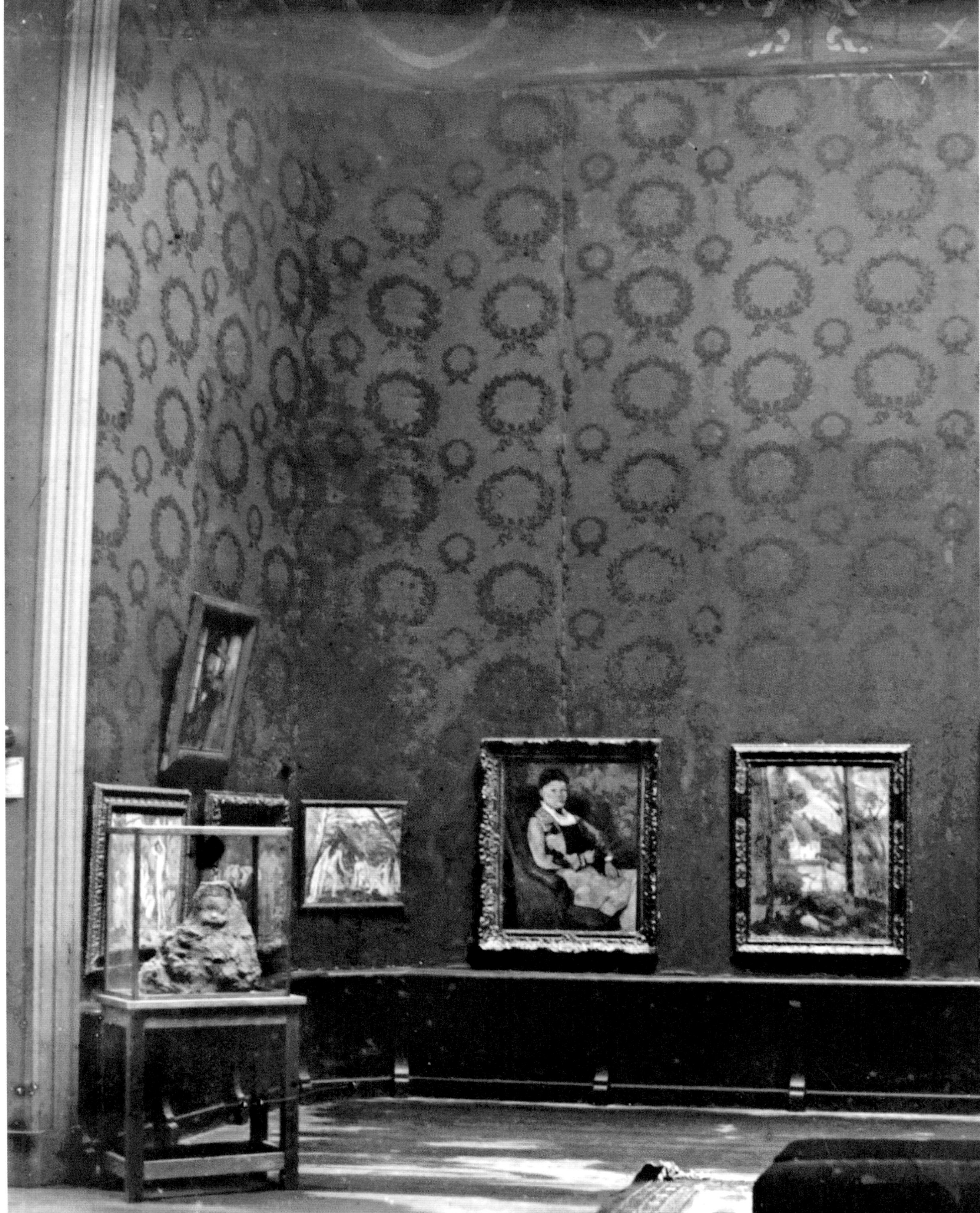

Foreword

Remarkable though it may seem, there are truly some "blind spots" in the extensive international research on Impressionist art. Whereas numerous studies have meanwhile been carried out on the participating painters and graphic artists as well as their motifs, techniques, gallerists and collectors, we must admit that investigations of sculpture in Impressionism are few and far between. Nor do publications on the sculpture of the late nineteenth and early twentieth centuries shed much light on the topic. To this day, rather, our conception of sculpture in the final decades of the nineteenth century is still dominated by the veritable excess of monumental statuary that had spread through the major cities of Europe at the time. In Paris alone, for example, the number of monuments increased from a mere eleven in 1870 to some 900 after 1900. Yet the innovative potential of the genre did not keep pace with its quantitative growth. Such a monument typically followed a simple pattern: it consisted in most cases of a man (or a bust of the same) standing atop a pillar or pyramid. What is more, numerous technical innovations had made it possible to produce downsized copies of these figures and busts at affordable prices, leading to their massive entry into bourgeois households. And the latter clients were equally fond of small-scale sculptures whose subjects were not so much dramatic or heroic as sentimental in nature. Yet whether its height was measured in metres or centimetres, sculpture followed the classicist or baroque traditions for the most part – in some cases with a hint of realism.

In view of these circumstances, Paul Lafond's critical résumé of 1919 was as little surprising as it was singular. The author lamented the fact that sculpture exhibited neither the courage nor the will to reflect the character of the modern age or lend it expression by depicting contemporary themes.[1] Indeed, in late nineteenth-century sculpture, there are but few correspondences to the paintings of the time with regard to motif. After all, didn't strolls across poppy fields and boat parties on the Seine defy three-dimensional depiction? Nor did scenes of the opera, the cafe concert or the Parisian emporia lend themselves much better to sculpture. In comparison to painting, the medium of sculpture seemed more limited in scope, which earned it the accusation of anachronism already expressed by Charles Baudelaire in his famous review of the 1846 Salon.[2]

As a closer look reveals, the assumption that the medium of sculpture was incapable of modernity and inaccessible for new themes did not apply to all three-dimensional artworks of the late nineteenth century. Alongside the sculptures for the masses, a refined and extremely nuanced sculptural current developed and sought new paths within the context of Impressionism from the 1870s onwards. There were sculptors who deliberately emancipated themselves from the corset of academic premises and experimented with new subjects, materials and modes of working and presentation, pursuing an aesthetic that was surprisingly radical from the present-day perspective. They did not, however, proceed according to any common or established formula – quite to the contrary.

The artists featured in the exhibition *en passant. Impressionism in Sculpture* as representatives of this development – Edgar Degas (1834–1917), Auguste Rodin (1840–1917), Medardo Rosso (1858–1928), Paolo Troubetzkoy (1866–1938) and Rembrandt Bugatti (1884–1916) – differed from one another, in part quite substantially, with respect to their goals and approaches. Degas drew on the themes of the opera and the boudoir to produce his primarily small-scale dancers and bathers and, apart from one prominent example, never showed his sculptural work outside his studio, if at all. Rodin made portraits and monuments for the public, but broke new ground in that area in such a way as to challenge his viewers. Rosso captured his figures "en passant" from amidst the anonymous hustle and bustle of the metropolis, aiming for the most part at more intimate contemplation. Troubetzkoy, for his part, created opulent portraits in which he succeeded in suspending the heaviness of the material by making the play of light his true subject. And the sharp observer Bugatti, with his impressive animal portrayals, brings up the rear of this procession of sculptors referred to as Impressionist during their lifetime. Yet however different their ways and means, these artists were unanimous in their efforts to renew the visual experience of sculpture with their work – and in that respect shared the concerns of the Impressionist painters.

Our visitors will accordingly have ample opportunity to view the special characteristics of sculpture in juxtaposition with Impressionist paintings, works on paper and photographs. Indeed, the exhibition creates a dialogue similar to that initiated on many occasions by the artists of the period in question.

The realisation of this comprehensive exhibition on a field that has been little investigated to this day – the sculpture that emerged in the Impressionist milieu – would not have been possible without the help of dedicated sponsors. I would therefore like to extend my sincere thanks to our long-standing partner DZ BANK, which has once again lent us its generous support for a project of programmatic importance to our institution. I am especially grateful to the two chairmen of the bank's board of directors, Uwe Fröhlich and Dr Cornelius Riese, for the confidence they place in our work and their vibrant bond to the Städel Museum. I am also indebted to the Kulturfonds Frankfurt RheinMain gGmbH, in particular the board of trustees under the chairmanship of Professor Klaus-Dieter Lehmann, the culture committee under the chairmanship of District Administrator Ulrich Krebs and the executive board with Karin Wolff and her deputy Dr Julia Cloot, for contributing substantially to the realisation of this internationally oriented project. The ART MENTOR FOUNDATION LUCERNE likewise supported our large-scale exhibition with great generosity, and I thank the foundation council as well as the executive board for their interest in our curatorial and institutional work. My thanks also go to Dr Ina Hartwig, Frankfurt's Deputy Mayor of Culture, for her devotion to our endeavour on behalf of the city's municipal administration.

The exhibition moreover received extensive media support through our collaboration with the *Frankfurter Allgemeine Zeitung* as well as our culture partnership with hr2-kultur. I am indebted to them for their commitment and close accompaniment within the context of the show.

The exhibition is the product of close cooperation between all our museum departments. I would like to express my gratitude to the various staff of the exhibition service, the conservation workshops, the in-house technical services and exhibition graphics, the museum education, marketing, graphic design, press, sponsoring, fundraising, events, catalogue management and IT departments, the administration, museum shop, library and office of the director as well as our external partners for their committed and highly professional dedication to making this exhibition possible.

We have Bach Dolder GmbH, and in particular Daniel Dolder, to thank for the exhibition's excellent architectural design. For the attractive design of the catalogue, I am grateful to Alexander Horn, Lukas Schmidt and the entire team of Studio Tonique of Frankfurt. For the publication of the accompanying catalogue, we had Prestel Verlag as a reliable partner, and to this extent I would like to thank Katharina Haderer, Markus Eisen and Cilly Klotz as well as the copy-editor Ariane Kossack.

One year before the exhibition opening, we had the opportunity to discuss the theme of our exhibition with a number of experts – some of whom also went on to contribute to this volume – within the framework of the Passavant Colloquium entitled "Impressionistische Skulptur: Flüchtigkeit in Wachs und Bronze" (31 January to 1 February 2019). I would like to extend my appreciation to Juliane Betz, Stefano Bosi, Dominik Brabant, Yvette Deseyve, Alexander Eiling, Eva Mongi-

Foreword

Vollmer, Astrid Reuter, Dietmar Rübel, Fabienne Ruppen and Nina Schallenberg for the lively discussion conducted on that occasion and the enlightening contributions to this catalogue that came about as a result – as well as to Bernhard Maaz for his memorable evening lecture.

The highly informative audio guide to the exhibition was once again in the experienced hands of Linon; here I would especially like to mention Christian Hillengass. I am moreover indebted to Björn Harres and also to Bernd Hettinger of Kunstguss Kastel, who together succeeded in replicating a figure after the manner of one of the Degas dancers in the Städel Museum collection. The exhibition film, realised for us by Christoph Weigand, provides the visitors insights into this process.

In all the many facets of the preparations for the show, the curatorial team had the dependable and creative support of Marie-Luise Geißler, Ira Haller, Alina Happ, Eva Höllerer, Kristina Lemke, Elena Schroll and Philipp von Wehrden of the Städel Museum at its disposal. I am very grateful to all of them.

And finally, my sincerest thanks go to the exhibition curators Alexander Eiling and Eva Mongi-Vollmer as well as the curatorial assistants Juliane Betz and Fabienne Ruppen. This team succeeded in realising an idea that has been close to my heart for many years – an exhibition on Impressionist sculpture – in an argumentatively and visually convincing manner. Maraike Bückling was initially also involved until the wonderful acquisition of the Reiner Winkler ivory collection demanded her undivided attention and energy at the Liebieghaus. The curators applied great expertise, curiosity and inventiveness so as to develop a highly interesting concept and bring together an impressive selection of works. We have their connoisseurship as well as their outstanding negotiation skills to thank for this exhibition in its final fascinating form.

Philipp Demandt
Director, Städel Museum

1   "La statuaire n'a pas le courage, la volonté de saisir le caractère de notre époque, elle ne sait pas le voir là où il se trouve. Ne peut-elle donc être revivifiée par des idées, des sentiments, des thèmes nouveaux? Pourquoi ceux qui manient le ciseau et l'ébauchoir s'acharnent-ils à répéter des groupes et statues vieillots, à l'aide d'anciennes formules qui n'ont plus de raison d'être? Pourquoi la sculpture ne s'adapterait-elle pas à la vie moderne? Ne peut-elle rendre des sujets contemporains?" Lafond 1918/19, vol. 2, p. 66.
2   Baudelaire [1846] 1977.

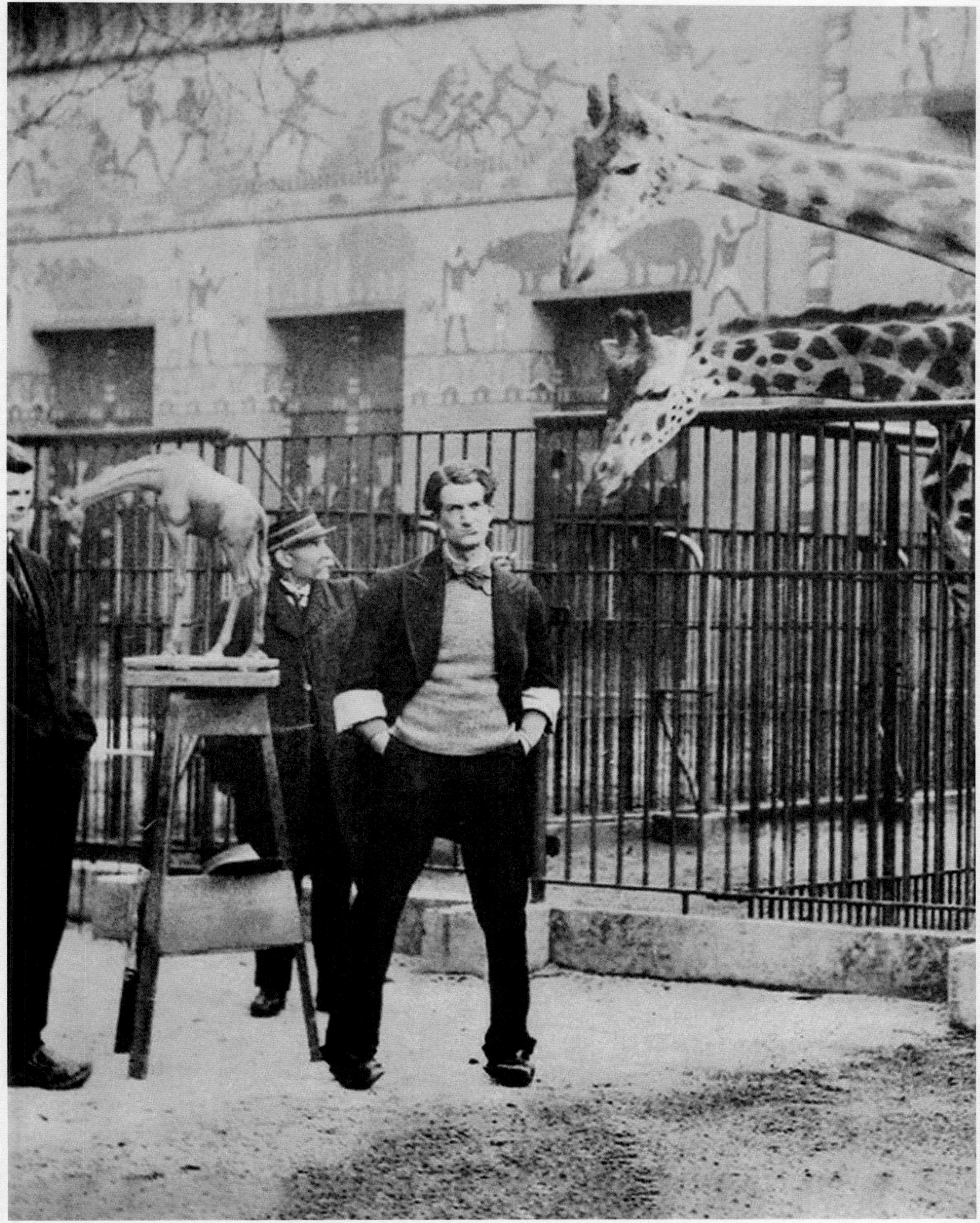

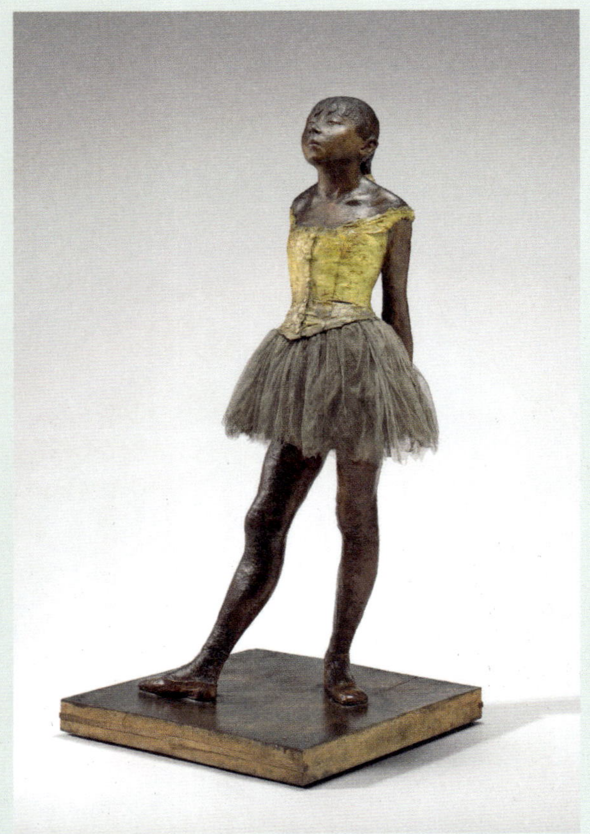

1 Edgar Degas, *Little Dancer Aged Fourteen*, 1878/1879–1881, pigmented beeswax, clay, metal armature, rope, paintbrushes, human hair, silk and linen ribbon, cotton faille bodice, cotton and silk tutu, linen slippers on wooden base, 94.4 × 35 × 35.8 cm, National Gallery of Art, Washington D.C.

Alexander Eiling and Eva Mongi-Vollmer

en passant.
Impressionism in sculpture

An approximation

In Paris of the 1880s, there was no question as to the existence of Impressionist sculpture.[1] It was proclaimed as a fact, cautiously defined and emotionally discussed. Less than four decades later, the matter was no longer quite as clear. In 1919, the French art critic André Salmon referred to the idea of Impressionist sculpture as simply "inane".[2] The collective silence on the subject that set in at the end of World War I was less harsh but more enduring. When we endeavour to pick up the threads again today, we find ourselves confronted with a series of questions: what was understood by the term "Impressionist sculpture" when it first emerged in 1881, and – contrary to Impressionist painting – why did it not become firmly established in art historiography? Moreover, which sculptors and/or works have even been labelled as Impressionist since the 1880s?

Our research drew our attention to five artists whose artistic approaches were all once discussed under this heading. Edgar Degas (1834–1917), Auguste Rodin (1840–1917), Medardo Rosso (1858–1928), Paolo Troubetzkoy (1866–1938) and Rembrandt Bugatti (1884–1916) – members of three different generations – all worked in Paris at least for a time, but otherwise shared only rather loose commonalities. This catalogue devotes an in-depth essay to each of them written by Alexander Eiling, Dominik Brabant, Eva Mongi-Vollmer, Yvette Deseyve and Philipp Demandt, respectively.

Of the sculptors cited, the only one to take part in the eponymous Parisian exhibitions between 1874 and 1886 was Degas. He showed a sculpture in public only once – the famous *Little Dancer Aged Fourteen* (fig. 1; see cat. 4) at the sixth Impressionist exhibition of 1881. It was this work that gave rise to the first references (in the press) to "Impressionist sculptors" ("sculpteurs impression[n]istes").[3] Several reviewers subsequently spoke of Degas as an Impressionist sculptor, or of his works as Impressionist – albeit always with respect to that sculpture and that exhibition only.

To understand the discussion of Impressionist sculpture that took Degas's presentation of his dancer as its point of departure, we must go back to 1846. It was in that year that Charles Baudelaire wrote a critique of the Salon in which he voiced a devastating blow to sculpture in general. In his text "Pourquoi la sculpture est ennuyeuse" (Why sculpture is boring/tedious), he denied the medium a rank equal to that of architecture and painting and categorically demanded that it subordinate itself to the other two.[4] He thus declared sculpture a decorative and complementary art. A lot of things about the medium bothered him, presumably

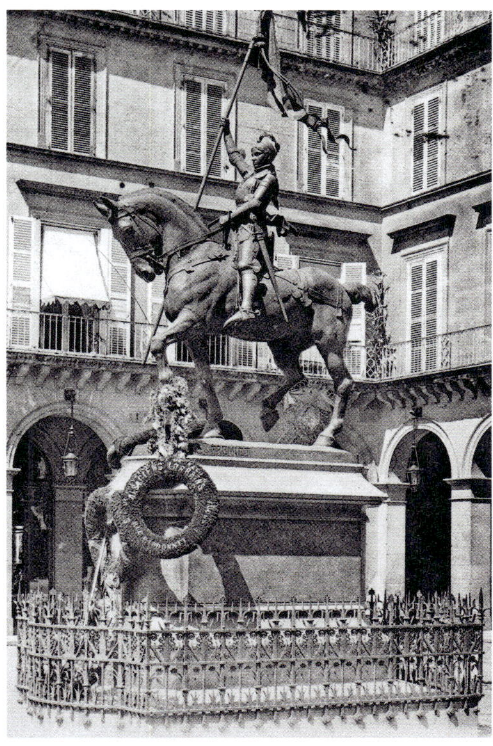

2 Emmanuel Frémiet, *Jeanne d'Arc,* 1874,
Place des Pyramides, Paris, historic postcard

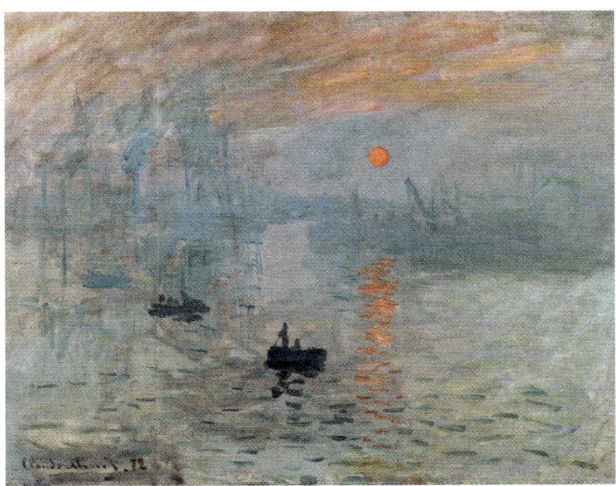

3 Claude Monet, *Impression, soleil levant,* 1872, oil on canvas,
48 × 63 cm, Musée Marmottan, Paris

first and foremost this: "Sculpture has several disadvantages which are a necessary consequence of its means and materials. Though as brutal and positive as nature herself, it has at the same time a certain vagueness and ambiguity, because it exhibits too many surfaces at once." The painter, on the other hand, decided on a single "exclusive and absolute" viewpoint, and his expression was accordingly much more forceful. In Baudelaire's opinion, sculpture was too close to nature per se, and the sculptor developed too little initiative to bring forth autonomous art. The contemplation of sculpture therefore did not require any imagination.

These provocative statements were still echoing decades later when, from the purely quantitative point of view, the medium of sculpture was in excellent shape. Around 1880, the spectrum ranged from the widespread phenomenon of the public monument to the countless objects that had found their way into upper-class homes and gardens as manifestations of a new collecting culture and, occasionally, also as status symbols.[5] In the public space, on the other hand, sculpture was assigned the task of conveying political or moral ideas in monumental form – heroes and gods gazed down from high pedestals (fig. 2).[6] At the same time, these works adhered for the most part to a conservative classical aesthetic increasingly regarded as oppressive. Modern sculptors in the period around 1880 were thus called upon to position themselves against both the fundamental Baudelairean accusation of missing artistic sensibility and the complete lack of innovation – with regard to form and content alike – encountered in mass-produced sculpture. At issue here, no less, was a renewal of sculpture and thus of a medium that, in the eyes of many present-day viewers, is far less accessible than two-dimensional art.

Impressionism in sculpture – the debate

It was primarily the artists participating in the Impressionist exhibitions mounted in Paris who set out in search of radical approaches to modernisation. The label "Impressionists" jeeringly introduced in 1874 by the art critic Louis Leroy had its origins in the term "impression" that had already been under discussion for some time. As chance would have it, Claude Monet adopted it for the title of his famous work *Impression, soleil levant* (fig. 3), which he presented in the first Impressionist exhibition. The reviews by such critics as Jules-Antoine Castagnary and Émile Zola emphasised that, like the other artists taking part in the show, Monet was no longer interested in the reproduction of a given subject, but in the conscious individual visual sensation it elicited.[7] Representational depiction now faded into the background as the focus of the artworks shifted to the act of perception. Under these conditions, sculpture – as the prototypical representative of objectness – came under fire from all sides. It seemed essentially to be the pure antithesis to the impressions so fleetingly and sketchily captured by the painters. After all, painting was incomparably better at conveying the constant fluctuation of modern-day motifs seemingly perceived in passing (*en passant*) than sculpture, with its oppressive heaviness and immobility.

Yet if our exhibition discusses the existence of Impressionist sculpture, our first step must be to clarify what is meant by the highly ambiguous term "impressionism". The studies of the past decades have adopted a wide range of different viewpoints in the attempt to formulate a definition. Apart from the pure fact of an artist's participation in the Impressionist exhibitions,[8] they have taken a number of other aspects into account. Sociohistorical factors such as society's urbanisation and embourgeoisement[9] have been as much part of the debate as deliberations on the relationship between the academy and the avant-garde. Scholars have looked into the connection between the then-new artistic practices, on the one hand, and the history of physiological optics and scientific study of visual and perceptive processes[10], on the other hand, but also the role played by art criticism.[11]

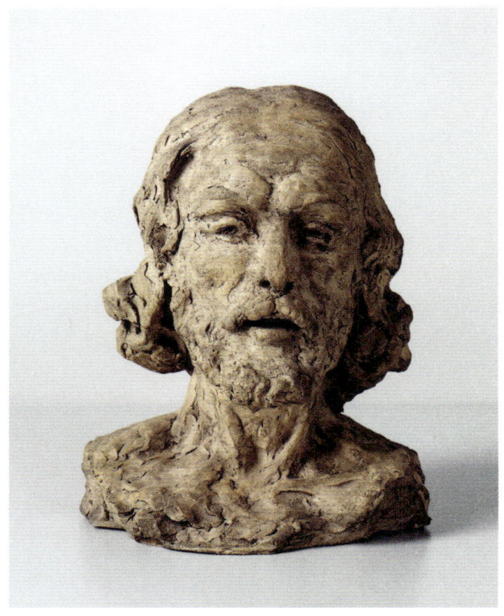

4 Auguste Rodin, *Head of Saint John the Baptist,* 1877/78, terracotta, 30.5 × 23.7 × 21.1 cm, Staatliche Kunsthalle Karlsruhe (cat. 102)

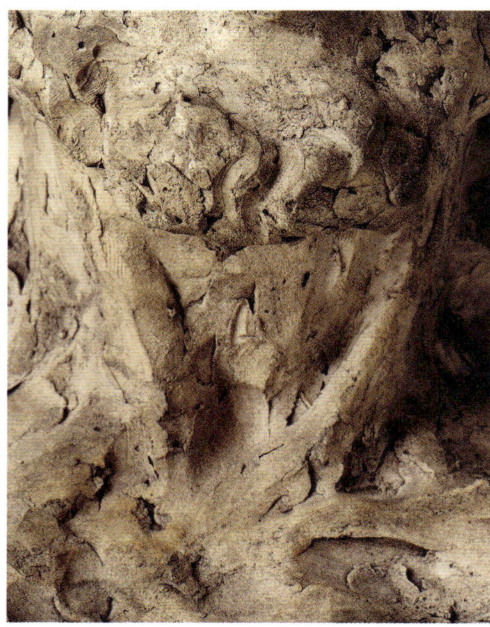

5 Auguste Rodin, *Head of Saint John the Baptist* (detail), 1877/78

And not least importantly, they have carried out analyses of the painting techniques that have shed light on the special characteristics of impressionism, for example the *non-finito*.[12] As the contribution by Fabienne Ruppen in this catalogue shows, however, by the time Impressionism reached its heyday, there were a wide range of criteria underlying the definition of the term – even if many of them later lost currency and were replaced by others.

As was already the case back then, impressionism is today perceived primarily as a two-dimensional art, making the question as to what constitutes Impressionist sculpture all the more complex. Sculptures were already on view in the first Impressionist exhibition, albeit far outnumbered by other mediums. The spectrum of the sculptures presented between 1874 and 1886 is as remarkable as it is heterogeneous. It ranges from neoclassicist examples by Auguste-Louis-Marie Ottin (1811–1890; cat. 1–2), a sculptor meanwhile all but forgotten, to pieces by Paul Gauguin (1848–1903; cat. 3) in marble and wood, and even a figure in wax: Degas's *Little Dancer Aged Fourteen* (p. 12, fig. 1). Hardly any of these works exhibits the ephemerality we associate with Impressionism today – quite the contrary. When the critic Jules Claretie responded to Degas's sculpture of a dancer on display at the sixth Impressionist exhibition in 1881 with an exclamation oscillating between hope and fear – "*Good God!* We are going to see *Impressionist* sculptors!"[13] – he was still drifting in a definitional vacuum. Of course, various approaches to interpreting the Impressionist movement had already been circulating since 1876, but none of them referred specifically to sculpture.

The dissimilarity of the sculptures featured in the Impressionist exhibitions and the changing constellations of the group of artists participating in that very show necessitate a clarification of the terminology. Initially, Claretie and other contemporary reviewers regarded the sculptures on display in the exhibitions as Impressionist. After the turn of the century, a new definition was attempted, now with a focus on the works' modern character and the relationship between painting and sculpture. In keeping with the temporal distance, this endeavour no longer revolved solely around the works of sculpture that had been on view in the Impressionist exhibitions, but above all around two artistic figures active at the time, namely Rodin and Rosso, who contributed decisively to a renewal of the medium. In this context, a survey initiated by Edmond Claris in 1901 for the newspaper *La Nouvelle Revue* and forming the point of departure for his 1902 publication *De l'Impressionnisme en sculpture* played a major role.[14] The key question was whether modern sculpture – at the time referred to Impressionist – in particular that by Rodin and Rosso, had disproved Baudelaire's damning assessment of 1846. The respondents to the survey unanimously agreed that it had. Rodin's and Rosso's works accordingly now came to be considered prototypical proofs of the existence of Impressionist sculpture.

What the two artists had in common was their attempt to integrate the immediacy of the working process into the conception of their sculptures in the form of peaks and pits on the surfaces, along with visible traces of their fingertips. An outstanding example is Rodin's terracotta *Head of Saint John the Baptist* (figs. 4 and 5; cat. 102). Here the aim was no longer the final and inevitable polishing, cleaning or patination, but, again and again, to leave the sculpture in an unfinished state as an expression of a process in continual flux. According to this approach, the torso, the *non-finito* – that is, the practice of leaving unprocessed areas as they were – and the imperfect surface sufficed to capture the essence of a sculpture and its state as a work in progress at a certain moment in time. Let us recall here the unvarnished paintings of the Impressionists, whose lively surfaces differed resolutely from the smoothness of Salon art and likewise allowed the viewer to take part in the painting process, if after the fact. Even the flickering light on the surfaces of these sculptures was factored in.

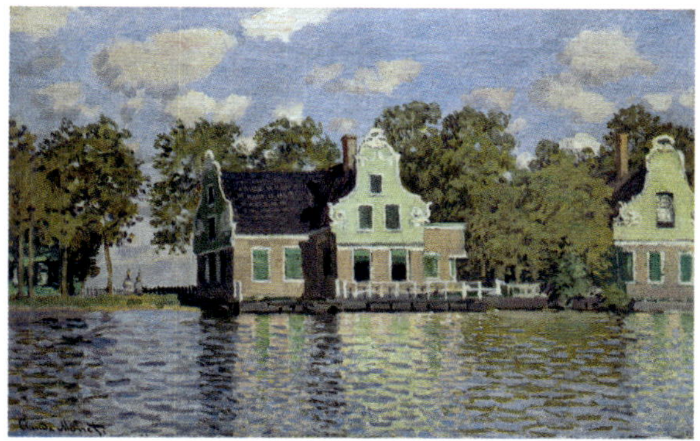

6 Claude Monet, *Houses by the Bank of the River Zaan,* 1871,
oil on canvas, 47.7 × 73.7 cm, Städel Museum, Frankfurt am Main

Twentieth-century art history placed Auguste Rodin's sculptural oeuvre in the broader context of Impressionism. While he did not participate in any of the eight Impressionist exhibitions, on at least one occasion he did present his works in direct juxtaposition with paintings by the chief exponent of the Impressionist movement, Claude Monet (fig. 6). In June 1889, the Georges Petit gallery in Paris opened the exhibition *Claude Monet – Auguste Rodin,* featuring 145 paintings by Monet and 36 sculptures by Rodin (see cat.80–84).[15] It was Monet's first retrospective, and he had not only initiated it but also done everything in his power to ensure that it would come about.[16] Rodin, for his part, had already established himself as a member of the jury of the Exposition universelle and a Knight of the Legion of Honour, and considered his name to be the poster child for the event. For the discussion of Rodin as an "Impressionist sculptor", this exhibition was of fundamental importance already on account of its unique constellation alone. Rodin and Monet took a similar approach to their motifs, for example, but also the degree of execution. In the catalogue, Rodin entitled five of his sculptures "études", and Monet (like the other artists participating in the Impressionist exhibitions) had already long cultivated an emphasis on the tentative nature of the object depicted.

Yet Rodin's and Rosso's productive phases played out at a time when resistance to the Impressionists' supposed aestheticism was beginning to stir. The Symbolists, for example, demanded that artists lend expression to the permanently valid order lying concealed behind the fleeting appearances. They produced imagery populated with religious and mythological figures and aimed at blurring the boundaries between reality and illusion. In their works, timelessness took the place of the time-bound; the vision supplanted the impression. No sooner had Rodin's oeuvre been classified as Impressionist than it was also often subsumed under the category of Symbolism. And indeed, the sculptor not only pursued much the same themes as the adherents to that style, but also shared their effect-aesthetical objectives.

Despite this terminological uncertainty, Claris and the authors who cited him treated Impressionist sculpture as an established fact. A case in point is Julius Meier-Graefe and his *Entwickelungsgeschichte der modernen Kunst,* which was published in Germany in 1904 and advanced to become a veritable bestseller. He began his chapter on "Impressionismus in der Plastik" (Impressionism in Sculpture) with a passage devoted to the relationship between sculpture and painting. The painterly, he argued, had also come to dominate sculpture in France, leading to an assimilation of visual habits and a public that learned to appreciate in sculpture precisely those qualities it was already long accustomed to in Impressionist painting.[17] Like Claris, he repudiated Baudelaire's frontal assault on sculpture by pointing out the various possibilities of relief, which satisfied Baudelaire's call for a single vantage point (see cat. 3).[18] In the further course of his deliberations, he placed sculptural Impressionism in a larger historical context. He posed the question of whether it was perhaps in fact an "extreme of the Baroque", then going on to introduce the term "Baroque Impressionism" a few sentences later.[19] His Swiss colleague Heinrich Wölfflin picked up on the idea and inverted it, concluding in his *Principles of Art History* (1915) that the painterly modelled sculpture of the Baroque "cannot be described as anything other than impressionistic".[20]

Claris's and Meier-Graefe's certainty with regard to the existence of Impressionism in sculpture was countered by authors who were uncomfortable with the concept and held the view that sculpture could, per se, not be Impressionist. In 1905, for example, Max Osborn formulated the problem of the contradiction between the idea of ephemerality as a characteristic of Impressionist painting and motionlessness as an inherent quality of the sculpture medium: "Modern sculpture – those are two words and two fierce opponents. There the flowing, nervously moved, wistfully urging, seething, festering. Here the solid, calm, reliable, self-contained,

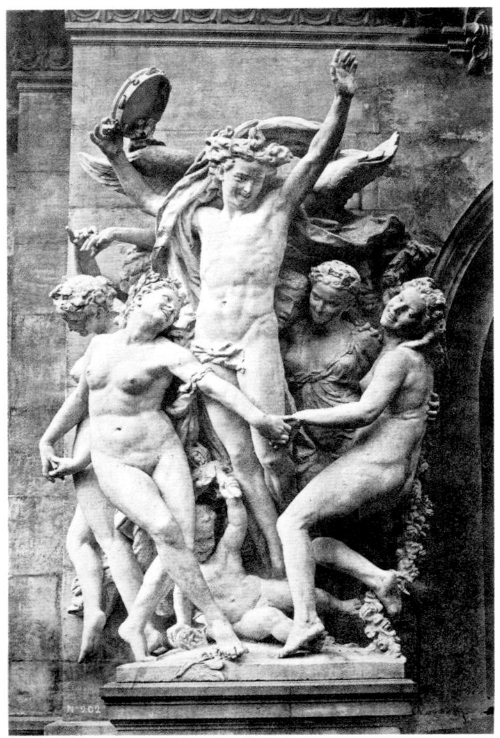

7 Jean-Baptiste Carpeaux, *The Dance*, 1865–1869,
Opéra Garnier, Paris, photography by
Louis Émile Durandelle, 1875, Musée d'Orsay, Paris

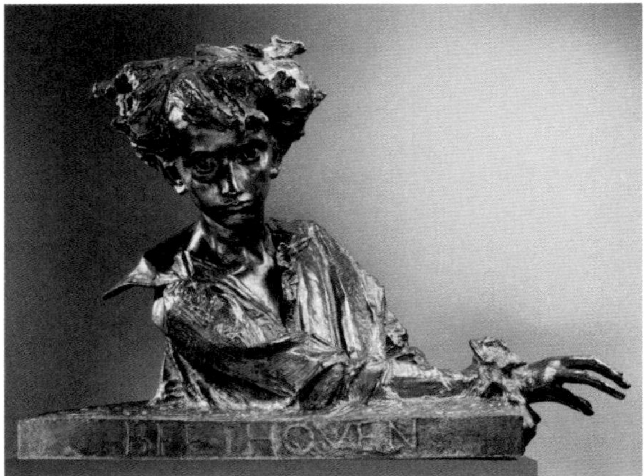

8 Giuseppe Grandi, *Beethoven*, 1874, bronze, 67.3 × 89.5 × 33.9 cm,
The Gilgore Collection, Dr. Sheldon G. Gilgore and Irma H. Gilgore,
Italian Art 1850–1925, Gilgore Museum, Naples, FL

finished [...]. A chasm gapes between these worlds. Who will build a bridge across it? How will the spirit of an age that [...] finds a likeness of its vision in Monet's surging floods of light [...] flow into stone and bronze?"[21] In a manner symptomatic of the conception of the terms in early twentieth-century Germany, Osborn thought of "modern" and "Impressionist" as synonyms.[22] As we learn from his enumeration, what he meant by Impressionist/modern was a specific perception and an adequate representation of the radical upheavals that marked his time.

These voices are mere excerpts from a debate still in progress today. On the one hand, there was talk of "Impressionist sculptors" ("sculpteurs impressionnistes") and "Impressionist sculptures" ("sculptures impressionnistes")[23] as far back as 1881, and the terms remained in use for some 40 years – presumably in part as coinages deemed capable of catering to the needs of the market.[24] On the other hand, apart from a few isolated studies,[25] there has been no critical examination of the concept in the surveys of nineteenth-century and modern sculpture – or if there has, it was treated only marginally or dismissively.[26] Research on the period under consideration (1880 to 1920) has focused on other observations and issues – for example, the search for inner coherence or the juxtaposition of consolidation and decomposition of form or of defiguration and analytical construction.

To this day, therefore, the study of Impressionist sculpture has been complicated by the fact that no clear-cut definition of the same appears possible. There is no nutshell for "Impressionist sculpture" any more than there is for "Impressionism"; indisputably, however, Impressionism *in* sculpture exists – in multifaceted form.

Before we examine these various aspects in the following on the basis of certain sculptural examples, we should undertake two definitions *ex negativo.* Not every sculpture that is distinguished by, firstly, dynamic depiction or, secondly, sketchy execution is necessarily to be classified as Impressionist. As a French representative of the former, we can cite Jean-Baptiste Carpeaux (1827–1875) – a teacher of Rodin at the Parisian Petite École for a brief period – and particularly a work he developed for the Opéra Garnier: *Dance* (fig. 7). The sculptural group undeniably depicts a wild course of movement; in its conception of the figures and careful treatment of the surfaces (a respect in which it differs greatly from its preliminary studies), however, the finished work is entirely classical. Giuseppe Grandi (1843–1894) provides an instructive example of the latter above-mentioned aspect – the partially sketchy execution – in sculptures such as his *Young Beethoven* (fig. 8). In Italian, this style is referred to as *bozzettismo,* a term aptly derived from *bozzetto,* a roughly executed preparatory model for a sculpture.[27] It plays with the idea of a loose sketch as an aesthetic end unto itself. When, in contrast, Impressionist sculptures resemble *bozzetti* in part, then it is due to a more comprehensive overall artistic conception. An Impressionist sculpture is neither a preparatory study nor is it intended to be perceived as such. To the contrary, even in its seemingly unfinished state, an Impressionist sculpture is finished. Rosso demonstrates this to an extreme in his group *Conversation in the Garden,* featuring figures disturbingly lacking in refinement (they cannot even be described as "sketchily light") in a composition that the artist thought through in detail as a tension-filled group of three figures (fig. 9).

Regardless of which qualities we single out for closer examination in the following, one fundamental problem remains: the more categorical and formulaic the attempt to create order as we grapple with the term "Impressionist sculpture", the greater the loss of ambiguity.[28] Yet precisely ambiguity is a core attribute of art. In the case of Impressionist sculpture, the misgivings with regard to such systems of order are doubly grave because it is a sub-category of Impressionism, a term similarly difficult to define clearly and demanding even greater consideration of the temporal context. However justified the scepticism, all the more important is

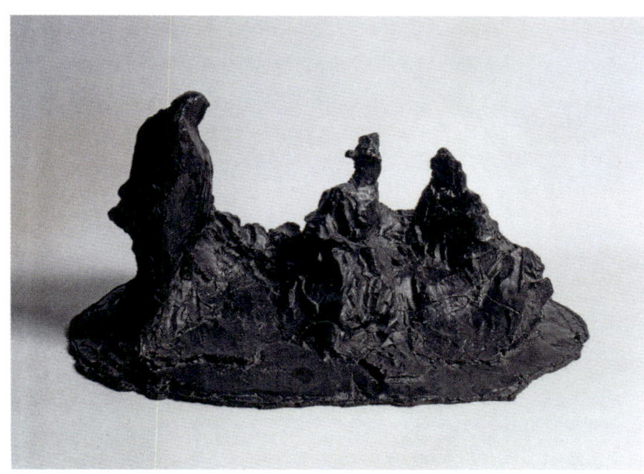

9 Medardo Rosso, *Conversation in the Garden*, 1899, bronze, 32 × 66.5 × 41.5 cm, Galleria Nazionale d'Arte Moderna, Rome

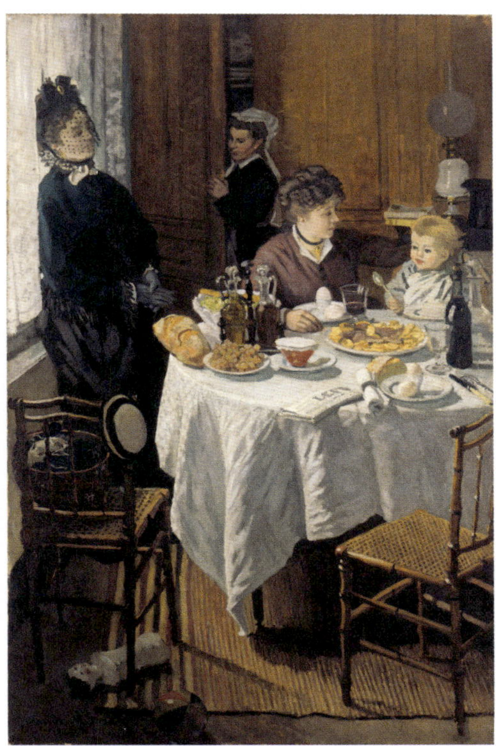

10 Claude Monet, *The Luncheon*, 1868–1869, oil on canvas, 231.5 × 151.5 cm, Städel Museum, Frankfurt am Main

it to point out that conceptual categories first and foremost serve the purpose of understanding or clarification. The introduction of the term Impressionist sculpture came about concurrently with the execution of the respective works. Today, we regard its emergence in retrospect and ask from a historical distance to what extent it can help us understand certain phenomena of the period between 1880 and 1920. The striking radicality of sculptors such as Degas, Rodin and Rosso was in many respects trend-setting, and a look at it from the unifying perspective of Impressionism in sculpture by all means proves worth our while.

Modern themes and materials

The focus on new subjects, particularly those of "modern life", was closely linked with the art of Impressionism. In 1876, on the occasion of the second Impressionist exhibition, Edmond Duranty devoted himself to this aspect and its painters in an apologia entitled *La Nouvelle Peinture:* the time had come, he proposed, for painting to represent the modern individual in their clothing and specific social milieu – whether in the private or the public sphere.[29] A selection of such paintings had already been on view in the first Impressionist exhibition, among them Claude Monet's large-scale *Luncheon* (fig. 10), showing the family in their dining room.[30] It was particularly the urban hustle and bustle on the boulevards, in the opera or in the pursuit of leisure-time activities that developed to become the motivic source par excellence. As Albert E. Elsen aptly remarked, "Parnassus had been replaced by Paris".[31] Impressionism in sculpture meant to avail itself of the inexhaustible repertoire of private, semi-public and public motifs. As in painting, a valorisation of things previously paid little or no heed also took place in sculpture. Pedestrians, *flâneurs,* dancers and even zoo animals were now declared worthy of artistic depiction.

It thus only seems logical that a three-dimensional representation of a ballet dancer – Degas's *Little Dancer Aged Fourteen* – at the sixth Impressionist exhibition should be the first sculpture ever referred to as Impressionist (cat. 4). The criticism, which was in part devastating, was essentially sparked by the fact that, with his young dancer, Degas was referring quite candidly to the prostitution rampant behind the scenes at the opera. Joris-Karl Huysmans nevertheless described it as "the only truly modern attempt at sculpture".[32] He may have taken this view because, unlike the heroic glorifications represented at the Salons, Degas had chosen a motif from modern Parisian nightlife and further emphasised its topicality by deliberately using everyday materials. The figure is made primarily of wax, which in those years had come to be regarded as an antipode to marble and bronze and associated with the promise of modernity. In 1882, for instance, in an article in the innovative periodical *Gil Blas,* Guy de Maupassant demanded the renunciation of sculpture's classical materials in favour of alternatives such as wood, clay and above all wax: "Let us smash the marbles, the moulds, the admiration for antiquity. Seek, use your imaginations, find. Explore the wood, knead the earth, model the wax! Who knows, perhaps a new museum will pave the way, reveal unknown processes, set out in a new direction."[33]

In view of the new subject matter of a society undergoing change at its very core, sculpture thus required new materials to emancipate itself from the traditions of antiquity and classicism. Artists came to consider wax – which had previously been used primarily for anatomical studies – increasingly attractive on account of its malleable consistency as well as its resemblance to human skin. The verist quality of wax comes to bear in Degas's *Little Dancer Aged Fourteen*. For sculptors like Rosso, however, this was not a decisive factor, because he applied wax to a plaster core as a semi-transparent, abstracted membrane that merely hints at the underlying structure. What is more, he took advantage of its translucency to

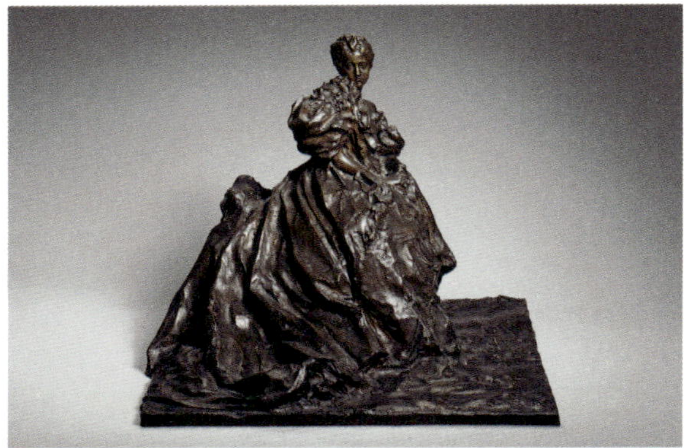

11 Paolo Troubetzkoy, *After the Ball (Adelaide Aurnheimer),* 1897, bronze, 45.5 × 52 × 53.5 cm, private collection, London (cat. 112)

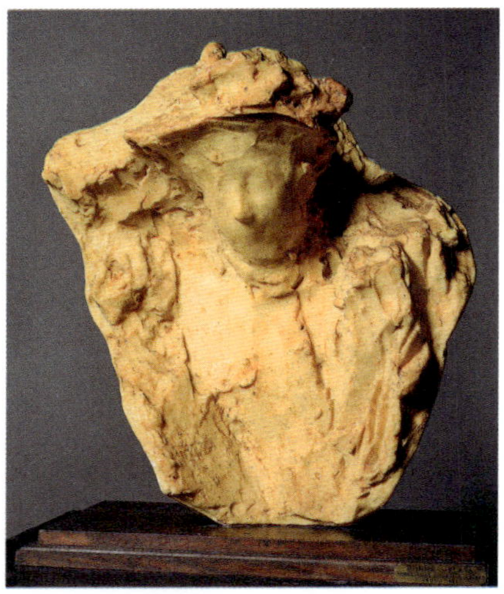

12 Francesco Rosso after Medardo Rosso, *Femme à la voilette,* 1895, cast 1950/51 after an original plaster by Medardo Rosso, wax over plaster, 63 × 63 × 33 cm, Museo Medardo Rosso, Barzio (cat. 66)

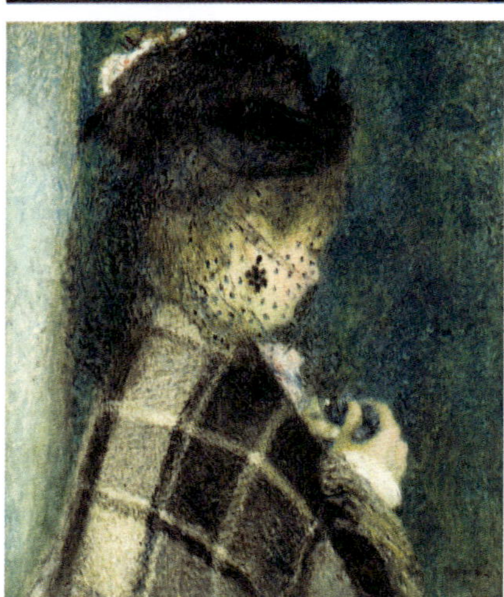

13 Pierre-Auguste Renoir, *Young Woman with a Veil,* c. 1875, oil on canvas, 61.3 × 50.8 cm, Musée d'Orsay, Paris

blur the transitions between figure and space, interior and exterior, and to create the illusion of a fleeting impression.

Yet wax was not the only means of breathing new life into sculpture. A sense of fugacity could also be achieved with traditional modelling compounds such as clay, but also with plastiline, which had only been invented around 1880. The portraits in the round by the Russian-Italian sculptor Paolo Troubetzkoy are excellent illustrations of this tendency. A wealthy artist of aristocratic origins, Troubetzkoy frequently chose his subjects from within his social milieu – for example, Adelaide Aurnheimer (fig. 11; see cat. 112) – an affluent patron of the arts whom he depicted in a dress as voluminous as splendid. Whereas he seems to have modelled her face in quite a conventional manner, he depicted her gown as an exuberant cascade of folds with numerous peaks and ridges in which his fingerprints are still visible. Even in the subsequent bronze cast of the figure, the direct handling of the material is still plain to see and constitutes a formal resemblance to the loose brushwork of Impressionist portrait painting, with which Troubetzkoy competed (see cat. 108, 111).

Figure and space

However comparable the motifs, the sculptor's formal approach differed from that of a painter with regard to the command of space. Unlike the painted depiction of motion and ephemerality, which we, as viewers, can experience ad hoc from a static vantage point in front of the work, sculpture calls upon us to move and to switch to the mode of additive seeing. To attain bold perspectives, steep views from above or below or abrupt cut-offs – all easy to achieve in painting and drawing – we must "produce" them ourselves. We must virtually adopt the role of the artist and take up ever-new positions around the work. In the case of Degas's *Little Dancer Aged Fourteen,* this means that the figure cannot be grasped in its entirety from any predefined angle but offers fresh and enlightening views from every perspective. Nor does it create the semblance of a fleeting impression. What becomes manifest in this hyperrealistic sculpture, rather, is a synthesis, a concentration of impressions of a dancer.

Rosso took an entirely different approach. In his *Femme à la voilette* (fig. 12, cat. 66). for example, he strove for a figural conception based on vagueness of focus as a means of slurring the boundaries between figure and space. At the same time, rather than intending us to circle around the work, he assigned us a specific angle from which to view it. By incorporating the atmosphere surrounding his figures, Rosso overcame the distance between sculpture and painting – his veiled lady does not separate herself from the surrounding space by way of a clearly drawn contour any more than, for instance, Pierre-Auguste Renoir's (1841–1919) *Young Woman with a Veil* (fig. 13). Rosso freed sculpture of a shortcoming Richard Hamann would characterise in 1907 with the words: "But it always remains a deficit that air cannot be modelled."[34]

The works by Ernesto Bazzaro (1859–1937) and Antoine Bourdelle (1861–1929) exhibit differences in sculptural strategy comparable to those between Degas and Rosso. Bazzaro's sculpture *Study after Nature (Three Figures Seated on a Bench)* (fig. 14; cat. 116) depicts two diagonally intertwined ladies chatting and an old man placed somewhat apart from them on a bench. From the base and the sitting surface to the individual figures, the group displays a homogeneous, vibrant style. The light in this scene taking place *en plein air* skips easily across the bronze's countless bumps and pits, refracting in all directions. With its expansive composition, the work invites the viewer to contemplate it from all sides. In his *Siesta on the Sofa* (fig. 15; cat. 119), Bourdelle takes a different route. In a manner far removed from the conventions for the depiction of a sleeping Endymion, he presents us with a wholly unprettified slumbering contemporary. Having virtually

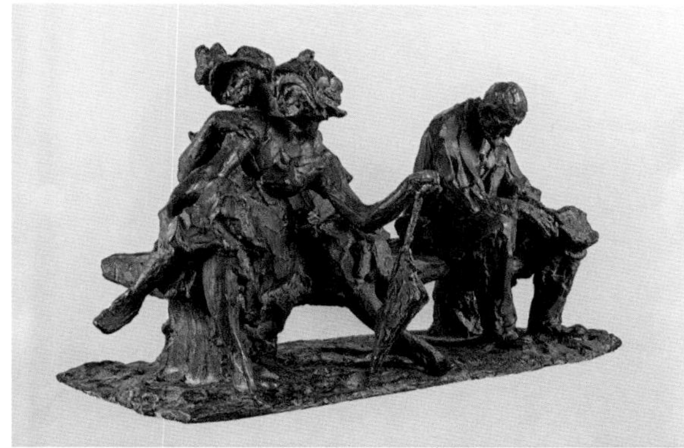

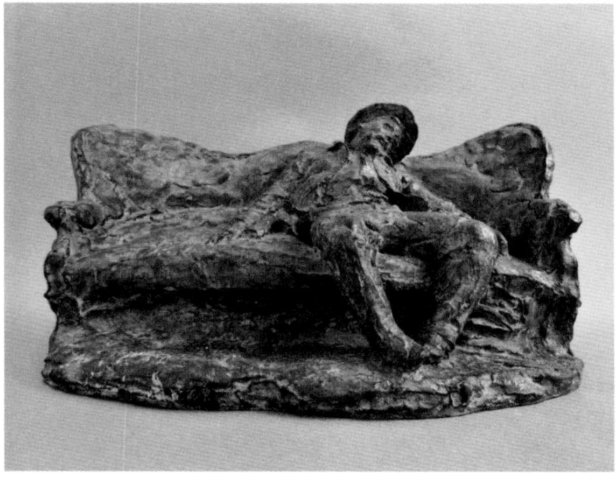

14 Ernesto Bazzaro, *Study after Nature* (*Three Figures Seated on a Bench*) c. 1900–1910, bronze, 52 × 92 × 36 cm, private collection (cat. 116)

15 Antoine Bourdelle, *The Siesta*, 1894, bronze, 20.3 × 41 × 22.8 cm, Musée Bourdelle, Paris (cat. 119)

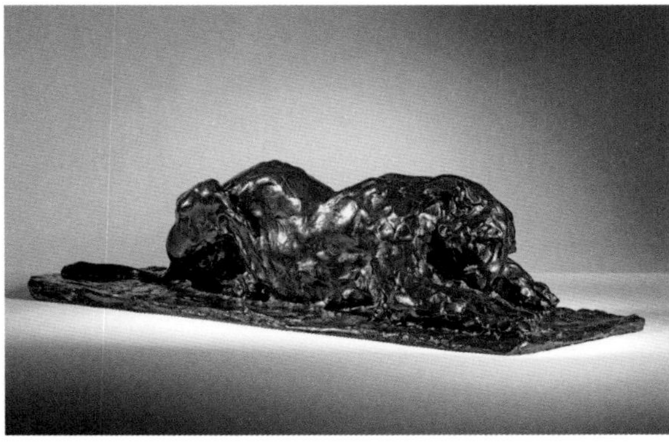

16 Rembrandt Bugatti, *Lioness Eating*, 1903, bronze, 16.5 × 70 × 22 cm, The Sladmore Gallery, London (cat. 126)

become one with the large piece of furniture by dint of the surface treatment, the sleeper clearly demands to be viewed from the front, as he is hardly higher than the sofa's ample back. The artist has thus largely precluded the experience of depth, instead adhering to pictorial solutions already long established in painting. These differing approaches to the handling of space are symptomatic of the sculptures produced in the Impressionist orbit: multiplicity of viewing angles was as much a subject of artistic experimentation as singleness of the same.

The ephemeral versus the statuesque

Citing a photographic term, the Impressionists are attributed with capturing fleeting moments in virtually 'snapshot-like' manner. In painting, however, it is far easier to halt time in the midst of movement than in sculpture, whose materiality and heaviness seem diametrically opposed to this endeavour. Sculptors seek to overcome this supposed disadvantage of their profession by depicting transitory states of the kind that became increasingly common from the 1880s onwards – consider, for example, Degas's unstable dancers or Bugatti's animals struggling to keep their balance. Yet sculptors referred to the essence of the times not only with the choice of "endangered" poses or restlessly formed surfaces that reacted strongly to every change of light, but also by leaving traces of the working process behind. Where these traces are retained, they convey a palpable sense of the artist's acting hand, in a sense even re-enacting the work's genesis. The decline of canonical iconography towards the end of the nineteenth century brought about a shift of focus on the part of artists, painters and sculptors alike; they now became increasingly interested in the production process and the role played by the material. There are even works whose motifs are almost impossible to recognise, as in the case of Bugatti's *Lioness Eating* (fig. 16; cat. 126), whose form emerges from the surging materiality of the bronze cast only upon closer inspection. Bugatti, who modelled his figures primarily in plastiline, worked with the foundry of Adrien-Aurélien Hébrard in Paris, one of the most important venues for the sculptors of the turn of the century. Hébrard's production director Albino Palazzolo (p. 50, fig. 9) mastered the art of translating finely nuanced modelling into bronze (a feat he would also accomplish later in the casts of Degas's waxes). Placement on unusually low bases seems to have been another means of countering the ennoblement of classical academic sculpture.

The sculptures' presentation forms, with regard to their bases but also their staging in exhibitions, took on increasing importance in the late nineteenth century, as Nina Schallenberg discusses in detail in her contribution to this catalogue. In this context there were regular "jump scares",[35] for instance when Rodin buried his *Eve* (1881; cat. 95) in sand at the Salon of 1898 or refrained from a base for his *Burghers of Calais* (1895–1899; cat. 80–84) – as was also the case with Rosso and his group *Impression de Boulevard* (1896/97; cat. 64). Let us also recall Degas's *Tub* (around 1889; cat. 29), a revolutionarily modern sculpture conceived for viewing from above at a steep angle (but, it must be added, viewable to only a few of the artist's friends and acquaintances during his lifetime). These new presentation forms blocked the viewers' retreat to long-established routine, instead demanding an active individual visual experience of them again and again. As Juliane Betz and Dietmar Rübel explain in their contributions to this volume, photography also permitted an unusual and novel way of looking at the sculptures. Particularly Rodin and Rosso made use of that medium to steer the perception and reception of their sculptures in a certain direction. To this end, Rodin worked with various photographers whose images oscillate between the documentary, the atmospheric and the pictorialist in style, as in the case of his *Balzac* (figs. 17, 18). Photography was by all means capable of influencing whether a sculpture was perceived as Impressionist

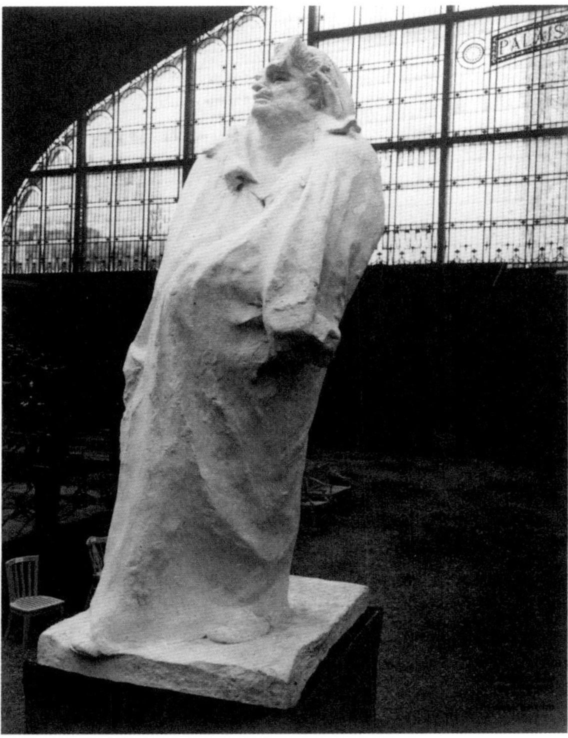

17 Eugène Druet, *The monument for Honoré de Balzac at the Palais des Machines in the Salon exhibition, Paris, 1898,* 1896–1900, photograph, gelatin silver print, 39.4 × 29.5 cm

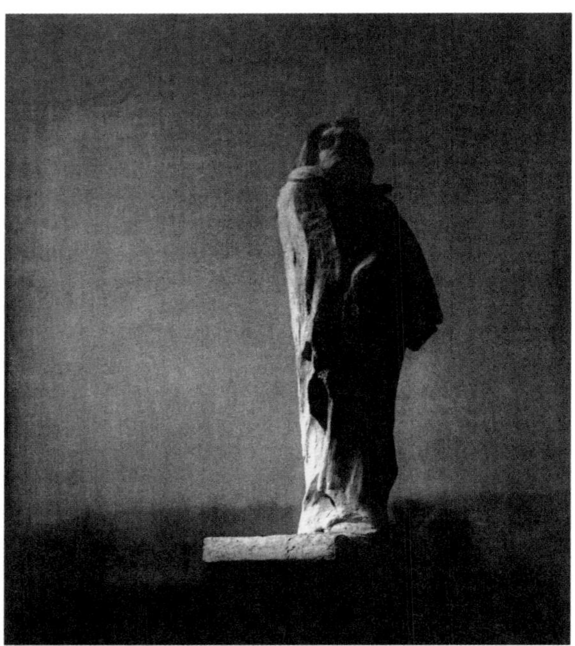

18 Edward J. Steichen, *Balzac, the Open Sky – 11 P. M.,* 1908, printed 1909, direct carbon print, 48.7 × 38.5 cm, The Metropolitan Museum of Art, New York

or not, as it played with certain light situations that could endow the work with an appearance now ponderously heavy, now immaterially light.

Colour and light

In the late nineteenth century, there was – with regard to painting – a great deal of scientifically oriented discussion about the anatomy of the eye, optics and the sensory impression as well as its pictorial reproduction. The debates over Impressionist sculpture, however, hardly considered those themes, despite the fact that the issue of how sculpture is perceived came very much into focus around 1900. One reason for this discrepancy may have been the slight temporal delay: Impressionist sculpture only became a subject of spoken and written discussion almost a decade after its counterpart in painting. What is more, the arguments pertaining to painting revolved strongly around light and colour or, more precisely, around colour harmonies. In sculpture, on the other hand, the matter of material had precedence – polychromy remained a stranger to Impressionist sculpture, the only exceptions being Degas's *Little Dancer Aged Fourteen* (cat. 4) and a small number of works in wood by Gauguin.[36] In the place of the colour scale, sculptors have a wide palette of tonal values at their disposal. Rodin's answer to the question of whether the use of colour was the domain of the painter or the sculptor is instructive. As he spoke, Rodin reportedly shone a lamp on an ancient figure to bring out the play of light on its surface: "Isn't this a prodigious symphony in black and white? [...] As paradoxical as this seems, the greatest sculptors are as much colorists as the best painters or, rather, the best printmakers. They play so skilfully all the possibilities of relief, they combine so well the boldness of light and the modesty of shadow, that their sculptures are as luscious as the most chatoyant etchings."[37] Rodin was not the only one to refer to printmaking in his argumentation, as we learn from Astrid Reuter's contribution to this catalogue, in which she devotes herself explicitly to "cross-media". With its lines incised or bitten into the surface of a copper plate, for example, the technique of etching (likewise practised by Rodin) reveals a close affinity to three-dimensional work, much like monotype, a method of which Degas made intensive use.

By using a lamp to demonstrate the effects of light and shade, Rodin was referring indirectly to an issue under quite vehement discussion at the time: the ideal illumination of sculpture. In addition to the natural light Rodin, for one, favoured, artificial light sources – for example, the electric light so highly appreciated by Degas and Rosso – were becoming increasingly available. In 1846, Baudelaire had assessed the fact that sculptors had no influence on the light as a disadvantage. The fact that everything depended on the lighting, which was a matter of chance, was a "humiliating thing"; the painter, on the other hand, imbued the painting with light himself.[38] This was an allusion to the idea that light found its way onto the canvas by way of colour. Stéphane Mallarmé specified this thought in 1876 as follows: "As no artist has on his palette a transparent and neutral colour answering to open air, the desired effect can only be obtained by lightness or heaviness of touch, or by the regulation of tone."[39] Yet these painterly options by all means have their equivalents in the handling of the surface of a sculpture. Hollows, humps, depressions, bulges and gaps in and on the surface allow great opportunities for light to come into its own on and around the sculpture – far greater than smooth surfaces stretched flat. Although they are not polychrome, the dynamically modelled areas in the works of the sculptors introduced here exhibit a richly nuanced play of light that is entirely on a par with that of impressionist paintings.

From Bugatti's, Troubetzkoy's and Rodin's expressive gestural modelling to the remarkable verism of Degas's *Little Dancer Aged Fourteen* and the space-integrating sculptures by Rosso, all five of the key artists in our exhibition countered the complaisant examples on view at the Salon with works that, around the turn of the century, freed sculpture from the fetters of convention. Their approaches differ too greatly to allow us to draw a homogeneous picture of Impressionist sculpture. Not every three-dimensional work by an artist in the Impressionist orbit can be regarded as Impressionist – no more than every sculpture shown at an Impressionist exhibition. Nevertheless, there are approaches to a 'sculpture in Impressionism' that deserve to be taken seriously, and that broaden our understanding of a stylistic current hitherto dominated by painting, printmaking and drawing. The exhibition invites its visitors to explore the various modes of sculptural expression and consider them in all their diversity.

We would like to thank Juliane Betz and Fabienne Ruppen for their valuable collaboration within the framework of our joint work on this project.

1 In keeping with the meaning of the French word *sculpture*, the term "sculpture" is used in the following as a superordinate category – independently of the execution process. In other words, it refers to works made not only by subtractive techniques such as carving, but also by additive techniques such as modelling.

2 With reference to Camille Claudel's art, Salmon observed: "Il démontre encore l'inanité de l'impressionnisme sculptural, démonstration faite, hélas!" Salmon 1919, p. 76.

3 "Car – voilà l'originalité de cette Exposition des Indépendants – ils commencent à affirmer leur indépendance sous la forme sculptée. Ce n'était pas assez de la couleur. Il leur faut la cire, ou le plâtre ou le bronze. Nous allons avoir, *bone Deus*! des sculpteurs *impressionistes* [sic]!" Claretie 1881; quoted in: Berson 1996, vol. 1, p. 335 (emphasis in original); see Elliott 2014, p. 208.

4 Baudelaire [1846] 1977.

5 On the status of sculpture in France, see Elliott 2017; in Italy, see Licht 1994.

6 Elsen 1974, pp. 4–5.

7 See Boehm 2003.

8 See, for example, the contributions to the eight Impressionist exhibitions in: exh. cat. Washington/San Francisco 1986.

9 See Clark 1985; Herbert 1988.

10 See Cugini 2006.

11 See Shiff 1984; Berson 1996, vol. 1.

12 See Brettell 2000; Callen 1982; exh. cat. London 1990; Callen 2000; exh. cat. Cologne/Florence 2008.

13 See the quotation in note 3 (Claretie 1881; quoted in: Berson 1996, vol. 1, p. 335).

14 Claris 1901; Claris 1902 (French); see Lista 1994, pp. 125 ff.; Gülicher 2011, pp. 40 ff.

15 See fundamental discussions in: Dunn 1978; exh. cat. Paris 1989. Also see the contribution by Dominik Brabant in this catalogue, pp. 174–183, here p. 180. On Rodin's exhibition practice, see Gülicher 2011, pp. 73–85; on this exhibition specifically, see pp. 74–75. We thank Fabienne Ruppen for her valuable pointers.

16 See the correspondence between the two artists pertaining to the exhibition, reprinted in: exh cat. Paris 1989, pp. 210–215.

17 Meier-Graefe 1904, vol. 1, pp. 303–312, here p. 303.

18 Ibid., p. 310.

19 Ibid., p. 305.

20 "Ja, ohne die Möglichkeiten zu besitzen, die der zweidimensionalen Malerei als der Kunst des grundsätzlichen Scheinens offenstehen, greift die Plastik doch auch ihrerseits zu Formbezeichnungen, die mit der objektiven Form nichts mehr zu tun haben und nicht anders denn als impressionistisch bezeichnet werden können." Wölfflin 1915a, p. 59.

21 Osborn 1905.

22 Müller 1990, p. 47.

23 See the contribution by Fabienne Ruppen in this catalogue, pp. 24–34, here p. 34, note 68.

24 Becker 1998, p. 125.

25 Exh. cat. Lugano 1989; Chevillot 2010; Elliott 2014; Elliott 2016. In preparation for the exhibition, a two-day symposium under the heading "Impressionistische Skulptur: Flüchtigkeit in Wachs und Bronze" took place at the Städel Museum in Frankfurt am Main on 31 January and 1 February 2019. The evening lecture by Bernhard Maaz, entitled "Was ist und zu welchem Ende studieren wir 'impressionistische' Plastik", will be published in: Maaz 2020.

26 See Giedion-Welcker [1955] 1961; Read 1966; Elsen 1974; Tucker 1974a; Janson 1985; exh. cat. Paris 1986a; Maaz 2010. Also see exh. cat. Karlsruhe 2007, p. 13; Siegmar Holsten, for his part, rejects the term "Impressionist sculptor": "Zwar standen diese Bildhauer [Rodin, Degas and Rosso, the author] in engem Kontakt mit den Malern des Impressionismus, aber am Wesen ihrer Plastik, die an die Dinglichkeit und die Ausdruckskraft von Körpern gebunden bleibt, eignet sich dieser auf Landschaft und Farblicht bezogene Stilbegriff kaum."

27 Licht 1994, p. 25.

28 Bauer 2018 offers interesting insights on this idea.

29 "[L]'individu moderne, dans son vêtement, au milieu de ses habitudes sociales, chez lui ou dans la rue." Duranty [1876] 1946, p. 42. Baudelaire had already previously demanded that the subject matter of art be brought up to date; Baudelaire [1863] 1989; see Doetsch 2007.

30 See exh. cat. Washington/San Francisco 1986, p. 121. Edmond Duranty had motifs of this kind in mind when he spoke of "painters of modern life"; Duranty [1876] 1946, p. 45. There he also describes how inhabitants and domestic furnishings are mutually dependent and complementary and concluded his enumeration of everyday occurrences with the imminent joint partaking of the "déjeuner": "Il sera en train de déjeuner avec sa famille."

31 Elsen 1974, p. 10.

32 "[L]a seule tentative vraiment moderne […] dans la sculpture"; Huysmans 1883a, p. 227.

33 "Brisons les marbres, les moules et les admirations antiques. Cherchez, imaginez, trouvez. Fouillez le bois, pétrissez la terre, modelez la cire! Qui sait, un musée nouveau ouvrira peut-être la route, révélera des procédés inconnus, lancera sur des traces nouvelles." Maufrigneuse [De Maupassant] 1882. Huysmans had likewise already referred to the modernity of the material in connection with Degas's *Little Dancer Aged Fourteen*; see Hecker 2016, p. 30.

34 Hamann [1907] 1923, p. 31.

35 Schallenberg 2017.

36 Blühm 2010, p. 34.

37 Rodin 1912, p. 76.

38 Baudelaire [1846] 1977, p. 273.

39 Mallarmé [1876] 2002, p. 195.

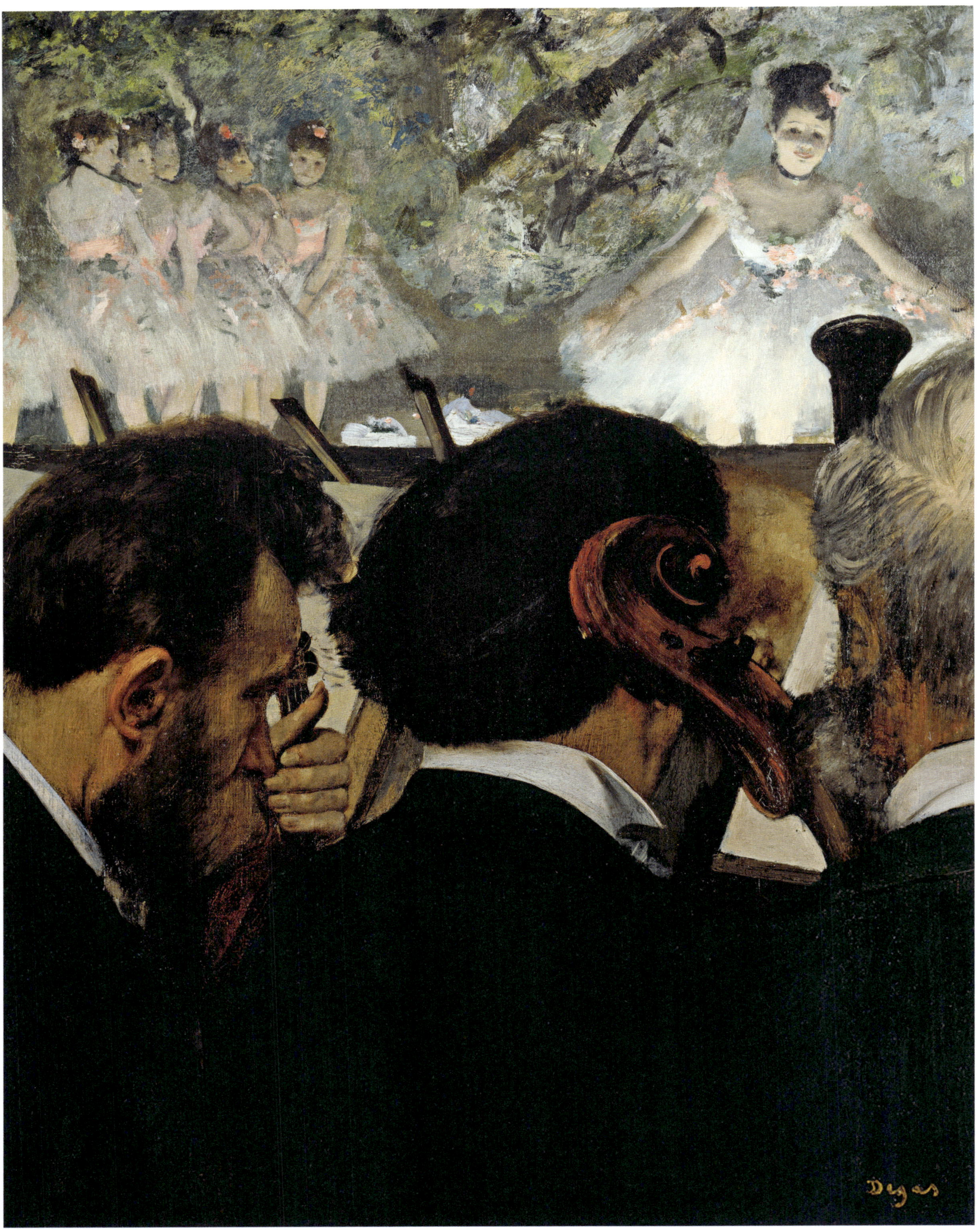
Degas

"Good God! We are going
to see *Impressionist* sculptors!"

Jules Claretie, 1881

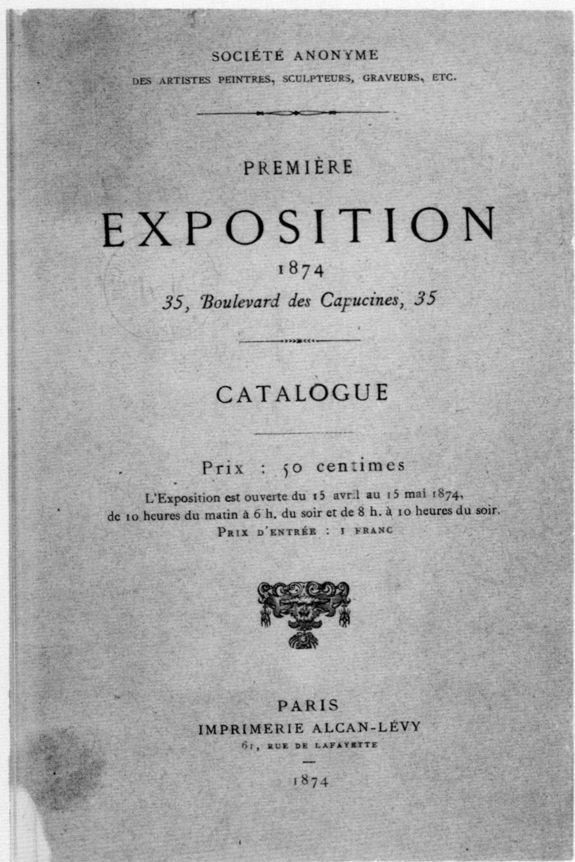

1 Cover of the catalogue accompanying the first Impressionist exhibition, 1874

Fabienne Ruppen

Flight of fancy or sculpture of the future?

On the historical term "Impressionist sculpture"

In standard references on French sculpture of the nineteenth century, the term "Impressionist sculpture" is usually sought in vain. Where it does turn up, it is generally ranked as useless on the grounds that Impressionism is primarily a painterly phenomenon that cannot be applied to other artistic media.[1] Patrick Elliott, however, has recently adopted a different perspective on the attributes associated with Impressionist painting – for example, sketchiness of execution, the concern with motifs in motion, or the effort to capture a fleeting moment. According to Elliott, these characteristics certainly do have their equivalents in sculpture, for which reason "Impressionist sculpture" can by no means be flatly denied its existence.[2]

The term is in fact a historical one, and a discussion of it can already be considered legitimate in view of the sometimes heated debates over what it means. It first appeared in connection with the so-called Impressionist exhibitions taking place in Paris between 1874 and 1886. These shows are well documented and have been the subject of extensive art historical investigation.[3] In the following, the author will undertake to evaluate the known sources – first and foremost, the exhibition catalogues and contemporary reviews – with a systematic view to the sculptures shown. In total, it was a mere 17 works of sculpture that awaited the visitors over the course of the eight exhibitions. Apart from the physical properties of those works, the focus was above all on the reactions they prompted. The reception history of the term "Impressionist sculpture" offers insights into the attributes that artists, critics and theorists associated with it in the late nineteenth century, while also showing how the connotations changed as time went on. What is more, the example of sculpture virtually shines a spotlight on the fact that the understanding of Impressionism was inconsistent from the start and remained in a constant state of flux.

Impressionisms

We have numerous studies of Impressionism in art, especially Impressionist painting, at our disposal.[4] According to Richard Shiff, this research has been guided by roughly four main issues, each of which have sparked an entire complex of discourse.[5] Firstly, the definition of Impressionism can be based on the criterion of affiliation: an Impressionist is anyone whose works were featured in at least one of the Impressionist exhibitions. However, the constellations changed from one year to the next – a circumstance that, along with the heterogeneousness of the works presented, led to ongoing discussion in the contemporary press as to which of the participants were truly "Impressionist".[6] Secondly, certain motifs are considered "impressionist" – namely, subjects of modern life and those that can be observed *en plein air* such as landscape views. Yet these two categories are not entirely suitable as disqualifiers, as portraits and depictions of interiors likewise drew on the repertoire of contemporary everyday life, which tended to play out in urban and rural environments alike. Thirdly, Impressionism is associated with a certain style and a specific technique. Characteristic elements are the palette of bright hues and the sketchy look of the brushwork. The latter conveys the impression of a moment captured rapidly and spontaneously and ran counter to the doctrine of the École des Beaux-Arts, which called for a flawless surface permitting no inferences whatsoever about the painting act. Finally, the fourth thread of the art historical research concentrates on the objectives of Impressionism. This focus is problematic in that shared artistic principles go almost unmentioned in the contemporary sources – even in texts by critics close to the Impressionists such as Jules-Antoine Castagnary, Théodore Duret and Georges Rivière.[7] In fact, the Impressionists did not follow any principles – on principle. On the theoretical level, they thus took a stance against the academy and its strict code of rules. As a common approach, we can perhaps cite a certain relationship to reality based on the conception – prevalent at the end of the nineteenth century – that an "impression" was composed of both subjective and objective elements. Castagnary had already emphasised this fundamental combination in 1874 in one of the first definitions of Impressionism, according to which the Impressionists did not reproduce a faithful portrayal of the landscape unfolding before their eyes, but their own individual perception of it.[8]

Every study of "Impressionism" should take these multifarious scholarly approaches as discussed by Shiff into account. Where sculpture is concerned, the decisive criterion, initially, was participation in the group exhibitions. In the following, the focus will therefore be on the body of works that fulfilled that condition.

The diversity of Impressionist media

Unlike the definition of "Impressionism", the term's origins are a matter about which art historians agree. It was coined in connection with an exhibition presented from 15 April to 15 May 1874 in the studio vacated not long before by the photographer Nadar in the Boulevard des Capucines near the Paris opera (see p. 290, fig. 1). By organising the show, a group of artists had initiated a platform for themselves as an alternative to the official Salon that had taken place regularly since 1697 and was reserved for works approved by a jury.[9] One of the contributions to the show was a painting by Claude Monet (1840–1926) entitled "Impression, *Soleil levant*"[10] (see p. 13, fig. 3). In an allusion to this title and the tentative character of the depiction, the critic Louis Leroy, writing in the magazine *Le Charivari,* sarcastically referred to the participating artists as "impressionnistes".[11]

Seven further exhibitions took place over the course of the following twelve years. On the occasion of the third in 1877, there was reportedly a sign above the entrance announcing the "Impressionnistes".[12] Now, if not earlier, the artists had themselves adopted the label previously used by critics. What is more, during this edition of the show they launched a short-lived magazine entitled *L'Impressionniste* featuring texts by authors sympathetic to their cause.[13] A painting had given the group its name and painting was the chief concern of the contributions to the magazine.[14] The question thus arises as to whether the term "Impressionism" was reserved for that medium.

The statutes drawn up by the organisers of the first exhibition did not call for any kind of limitation, and the founding members included not only painters but also sculptors, engravers and lithographers.[15] The group accordingly announced itself as the "Société anonyme des artistes peintres, sculpteurs, graveurs, etc." on

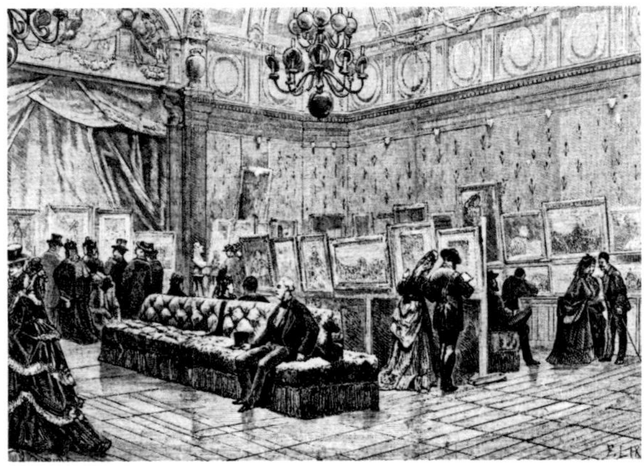

2 Anonymous artist, *Exposition de peinture au cercle de l'Union Artistique*, Paris, undated

the cover of the catalogue to its first exhibition of 1874 (fig. 1).[16] In addition, the list of works contained in that publication provides evidence that Monet, for example, showed not only paintings (five), but also pastels (four). And that was no exception: two thirds of the altogether 58 artists participating in the eight exhibitions were represented by at least two different media or techniques.[17] A statistical evaluation of the catalogues illustrates the composition of this media spectrum.[18]

Altogether, the exhibitions encompassed some 1,980 works, including approximately 1,298 paintings, 463 drawings, 161 prints, 32 fans and 17 sculptures (fig. 3). Painting was thus the clearly prevailing medium, but, at an average of over 32 per cent, works on paper also represented a significant proportion which peaked at roughly 45 per cent in 1874 and 1880.

This range of media is comparable to that of the official Salon.[19] Unlike drawings and prints, sculptures played only a minor role in both. At the Salon, they accounted for an average of 16.4 per cent of the works on view in the years 1861 to 1890.[20] In 1874, for instance, this meant 569 catalogue numbers, which had no trouble filling the imposing central hall of the Palais de l'Industrie (see p. 276, fig. 1). The first Impressionist exhibition, held the same year, featured a mere ten; the fourth and fifth one each, the sixth three and the seventh and eighth, again, only one sculpture each, amounting to a maximum share of 4.6 per cent. In the majority of the exhibitions, there was a ratio of one sculpture to approximately 200 works hanging on the walls.

Little is known about how the objects were presented in the Impressionist exhibitions.[21] At the official Salon, paintings, works on paper and sculptures were each assigned an area of their own, where they were arranged in alphabetical order by artist's last name.[22] In the Impressionist exhibitions, on the other hand, the works were grouped primarily by artist and only in a few exceptional cases by medium.[23] This practice is to be understood against the background of the artists' societies that increasingly formed in the latter decades of the nineteenth century. Like the Société des aquarellistes français, for example, they concentrated on one medium and organised exhibitions reserved specifically for that medium. In contrast, the selection and arrangement of the works in the Impressionist exhibitions mirror the desire to offer more holistic insights into individual artists' oeuvres. The participating artists were permitted to choose whatever works they liked for the area assigned to them, thus gaining new liberties in the presentation of their art – also with regard to medium.[24] Depending on the number of participants and the floor plan of the venue (which changed from one exhibition to the next), an artist sometimes even had an entire room to themselves.[25] Although we have only rudimentary sources on the furnishings of the venues, we do know that, like those of the Salon, they included (at least in part) sofas, rocking chairs and the like – that is, furniture conducive to the homeliness of the atmosphere (fig. 2).[26] Thus, even in the case of a single, free-standing sculpture in a room, among the various furnishings it will hardly have stood out as starkly as its singularity might suggest. The fact that sculptures were present in small numbers might have led them simply to be overlooked – or, just as conceivably, to attract quite a lot of attention. The visitor reactions discussed in the following suggest that the latter was the case.

The 17 sculptures in the Impressionist exhibitions

For the artists taking part in the Impressionist exhibitions, work in the medium of sculpture was nothing unusual per se. In a letter Paul Gauguin wrote to Camille Pissarro in 1882, Gauguin spoke of a spreading "mania for sculpture".[30] He went on to refer to Edgar Degas's horse sculptures and Pissarro's presumably non-extant figures of cows. In their increasingly conceptual working processes, however, both Degas and Pissarro used sculpture primarily as an aid in the

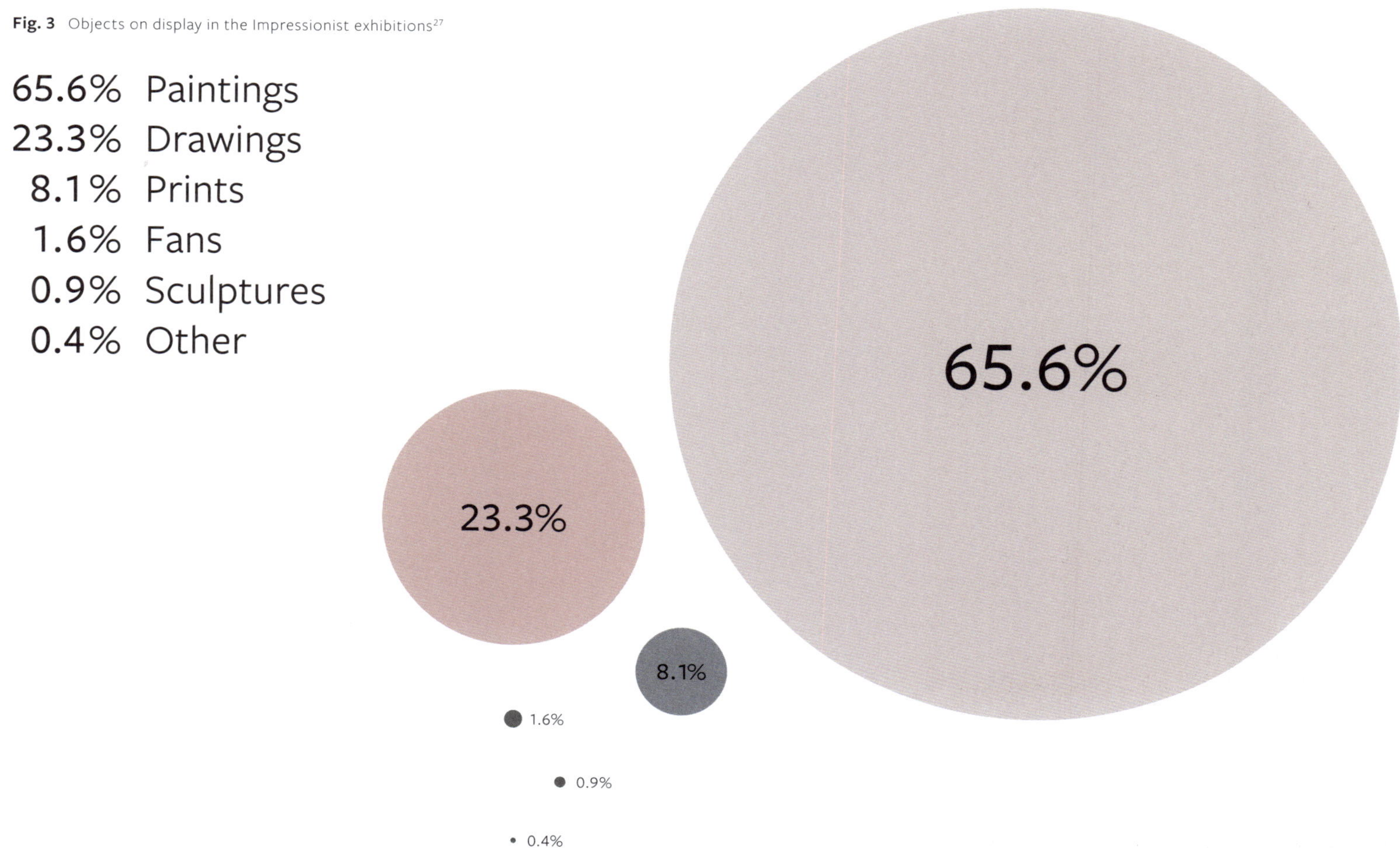

Fig. 3 Objects on display in the Impressionist exhibitions[27]

65.6% Paintings
23.3% Drawings
8.1% Prints
1.6% Fans
0.9% Sculptures
0.4% Other

Exhibition	Participants	Objects on display	Paintings	Drawings	Prints	Fans	Sculptures	Other
1874	31	216 (+x)	40 (+62)	56 (+5, +x)	38	0	10 [4.6%]	5[28]
1876	19	288 (+x)	69 (+118)	39 (+22, +x)	40	0	0	0
1877	18	245	89 (+116)	29	11	0	0	0
1879	16	263 (+x)	75 (+73)	65 (+16, +x)	6	23	1 [0.4%]	4[29]
1880	19	267 (+x)	44 (+100)	61 (+5, +x)	50 (+x)	6	1 [0.4%]	0
1881	14	178 (+x)	29 (+91, +x)	52 (+2)	1	0	3 [1.7%]	0
1882	9	212	115 (+66)	30	0	0	1 [0.5%]	0
1886	18	266 (+x)	66 (+100, +x)	81 (+x)	15	3 (+x)	1 [0.4%]	0
Total	**58**	**1,980** (+x)	**527** (+771, +x) [65.6%]	**413** (+50, +x) [23.3%]	**161** (+x) [8.1%]	**32** (+x) [1.6%]	**17** [0.9%]	**9** [0.4%]

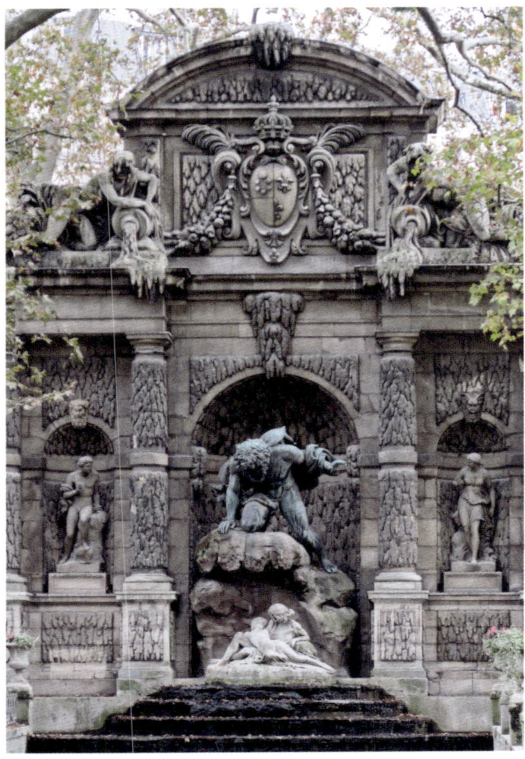

4 Auguste-Louis-Marie Ottin, *Fontaine Médicis*,
Jardin du Luxembourg, Paris

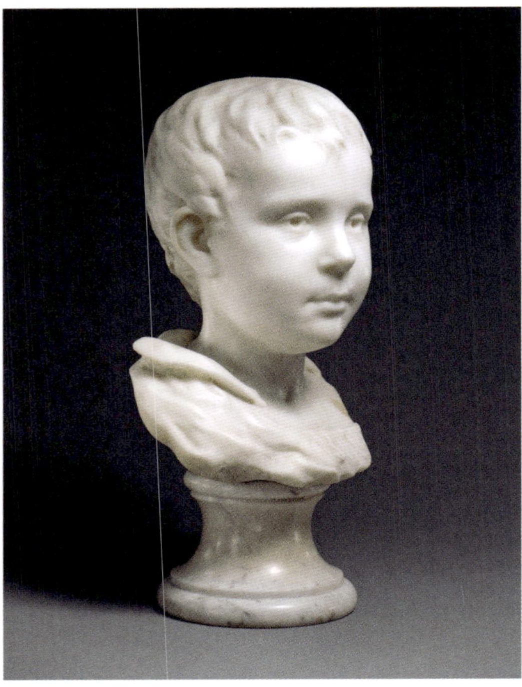

5 Paul Gauguin, *Émile Gauguin*, c. 1877/78, marble,
43 × 23.2 × 20 cm, The Metropolitan Museum of Art,
New York, Gift of the Joseph M. May
Memorial Association, Inc., 1963

execution of their drawings and paintings. In fact, Degas deliberately and emphatically kept his three-dimensional works to himself as "private" objects.[31] This may explain why only very few sculptures were on display in the eight exhibitions, despite the artists' fundamental openness to the medium.

The 17 sculptures presented in the Impressionist exhibitions were the works of three artists. Auguste-Louis-Marie Ottin (1811–1890) was the only one of them who had trained as a sculptor as well as the only artist to present sculptures at all (ten altogether) in the first show of 1874. He had completed his training at the École des Beaux-Arts, exhibited regularly in the official Salon and received numerous commissions from the French state. Notwithstanding his academic background, he was actively involved in the Société anonyme. As we know from the organisation's statutes, he was not only a founding member but also acted as treasurer and his private address served as the official place of business.[32] Yet despite his close personal connection to the venture, his sculptures did not blend in particularly well with the other works in the Impressionist exhibition. To the extent that they can be identified, three of them bore a relation to the *Fontaine Médicis* in the Jardin du Luxembourg, for which Ottin had developed a mythological figural group from 1852 onwards (fig. 4).[33] Another three were busts, of which one was dedicated to Jean-Auguste-Dominique Ingres, the representative par excellence of nineteenth-century academic French art (cat. 1).[34] A further two were versions of an antique-style "Jeune Femme portant un vase" (Young Woman Carrying a Vase; cat. 2). Already the choice of subjects alone explains why progressive critics mentioned Ottin's sculptures only in enumerations, if at all.[35] On account of their reputable standards, on the other hand, the more conservative reviewers considered them a welcome exception to works they regarded for the most part as rather bizarre.[36]

As we learn from a comparison with the sculptures Ottin submitted to the Salons of 1874 and the following years, he clearly made an effort to adapt to the respective context.[37] For the official framework, he chose works in materials such as marble and bronze and, in one case, a plaster model conceived for realisation in bronze.[38] Thus whereas these were pieces that catered to (potential) public patrons, for the more informal presentation he decided in favour of downscaled versions of sculptures he had executed up to 35 years earlier (see cat. 1–2) in four cases. They not only offered an overview of the entire breadth of his abilities but, on account of their lower prices, were attractive for private buyers. According to the catalogue of the Impressionist exhibition, Ottin also showed hitherto unidentified terracottas (see cat. 37, fig. 2). This type of ceramic clay was highly popular among artists as a working material because it was far more affordable than bronze or marble. What is more, thanks to its softness, it permitted more rapid, spontaneous handling. Terracotta sculptures are accordingly often thought of as sketch-like in character – such that, of all the works Ottin submitted, the ones he made in this material may thus have been most worthy of the term "Impressionist", although even contemporary authors did not label them as such.

In the subsequent Impressionist exhibitions, taking place in 1876 and 1877, there were no sculptures on view. The art critic Louis Edmond Duranty benevolently assessed what he called a "pleasant little sculpture" – the only one in the fourth exhibition of 1879 – adding that it had by all means succeeded in arousing public interest.[39] It was by Gauguin, who, remarkably, made his debut in the Impressionist exhibitions with his first sculptural endeavour, a white marble bust he had presumably executed around 1877/78 (fig. 5).[40] As far as the material was concerned, he thus followed in Ottin's footsteps; in terms of motif, however, he went quite his own way: in keeping with the Impressionist liking for everyday life, he portrayed his son Émile. The following year, in the fifth exhibition, he entered a portrait of his wife Mette, likewise in the form of a marble bust (fig. 6). This work met with more

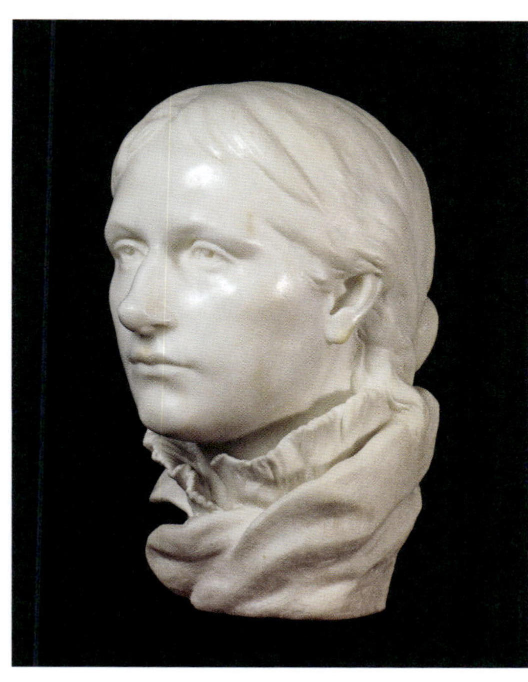

6   Paul Gauguin, *Mette Gauguin*, 1879, marble,
34 × 18.5 × 26.5 cm, Courtauld Gallery,
London, Samuel Courtauld Trust

positive response in the press than his seven paintings did. Élisée-Louis Baron de Montagnac, for instance, observed that Gauguin definitely seemed to have a feel for sculpture, but lost his head as soon as he turned his attention to painting.[41] Other conservative critics likewise received the bust favourably; in fact, it was one of the very small number of works they discussed in laudatory terms.[42]

As Anne-Birgitte Fonsmark has pointed out, Gauguin's marble sculptures of his wife and son are conventional in their execution and, unlike his painted likenesses, of an exceptionally "market-oriented" character.[43] This suggests that, like Ottin, he used the format of the Impressionist exhibition, or at least the first two in which he participated, as a means of acquiring potential clients. The same can scarcely be conjectured in the case of another sculpture, originally also designated for display in the fifth exhibition of 1880: Degas had announced a "Petite Danseuse de quatorze ans", which is listed in the catalogue as a wax statuette. The display case reserved for it in the show, however, remained empty.[44] The curiosity thus aroused with regard to the *Little Dancer Aged Fourteen* may well have fuelled the reactions the sculpture then elicited at the sixth Impressionist exhibition in 1881, where Degas finally presented it after all (see cat. 4). It was with reference to this work that, in his column for *Le Temps*, Jules Claretie first spoke explicitly of "Impressionist sculptors". This was by no means meant as a compliment. Quite to the contrary, he was aghast at the fact that the Impressionists' striving for originality had spread beyond painting and that, from now on, they would also be seeking to assert their independence in sculpture as well.[45] Paul Mantz, on the other hand, lauded the expansion of the spectrum to include sculpture as the exhibition's real novelty, greatest accomplishment and only truly memorable element.[46]

In the debates over Impressionism's uniqueness and modernity, the medium of sculpture accordingly played a key role. Within this context, Claretie was outraged above all by the artists' disparagement of traditional materials such as wax, plaster and bronze. The conservative critic Bertall[47] wrote a detailed description of the *Little Dancer Aged Fourteen* in which he likewise concentrated on the material. He assessed Degas's use of a genuine tutu as an innovation, but in the same breath called it into question by limiting its relevance to costumers and modistes.[48] The unorthodox combination of materials – also including human hair – was tantamount to an affront against the long-established sculptors' profession. At the same time, it reinforced the impression of the faithful reproduction of reality. Another critic evaluated this aspect as a novelty and it led him to rank Degas's contribution quite positively as an attempt at "realism in sculpture".[49] The writer Joris-Karl Huysmans countered with the opinion that it was precisely the figure's "terrible reality" that made a person sick, and all that was left to the undoubtedly befuddled and embarrassed public was to flee to safety as quickly as possible.[50]

Realism was in fact the virulent category that dominated the contemporary discussion of the *Little Dancer Aged Fourteen* as a whole. As Fronia Wissman has elucidated, reviewers of the sixth exhibition also discussed various paintings as "realistic". They were thus alluding to the participating artists' ideological affinity to realistic and naturalistic tendencies in literature, which many of them had themselves espoused as writers. In their critiques of art, they accordingly had no objections to the unprettified depiction of the everyday actions of simple people, either in painting or in sculpture. Instead they lamented what they considered to be the unfinished state that identified the ugly and deformed as characteristic of modern life.[51] When it came to sculpture, not only the degree of finish but also the choice of materials played a central role. Particularly the case of the *Little Dancer Aged Fourteen* – made of a material (wax) that sparked strong associations of human skin – was regarded as an unsettling tightrope act between realism and illusion.[52] Huysmans expressly emphasised the modern character of wax, ranking

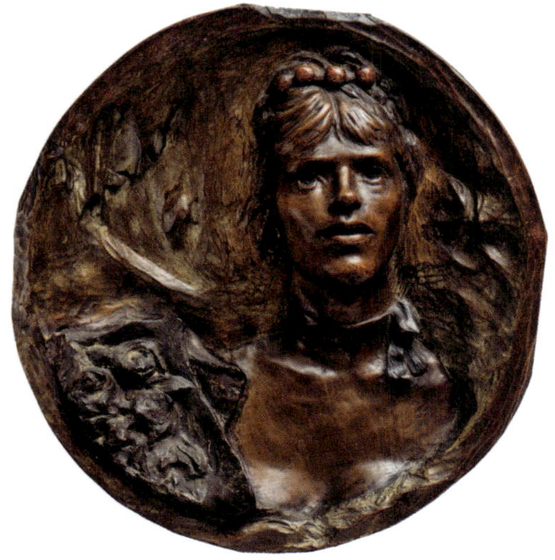

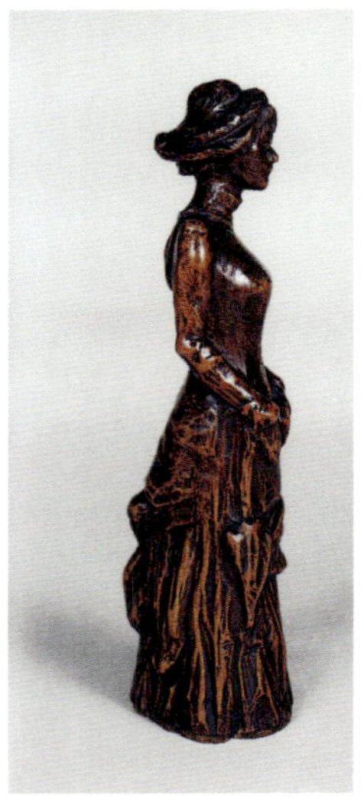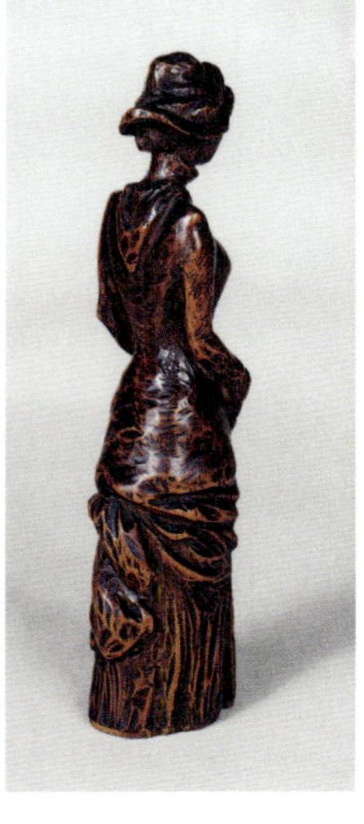

7 Paul Gauguin, *La Chanteuse*, 1880, mahogany, plaster,
partially coloured and gilded, diameter 53 cm,
depth 13 cm, Ny Carlsberg Glyptotek, Copenhagen

8 Paul Gauguin, *Dame en promenade*, c. 1880,
laurel, red and white colour, height 25 cm,
Kelton Foundation, Santa Monica

only wood as comparable in that respect. Unlike marble, stone and bronze, he reasoned, wood bore no connection to antiquity – the academy's paramount point of reference. To the contrary, it was reminiscent of the pictorial programmes of medieval churches, whose "primitive" artistic language was attracting a great deal of attention in avant-garde circles of the late nineteenth century. Huysmans moreover pointed out the material qualities of wood: it was soft, adaptable and thus predestined for the execution of suitable portraits of the modern Parisienne, whose beauty sprang from a balanced blend of naturalness and artificiality.[53] As Fonsmark has rightly pointed out, there is something almost absurd about the fact that Huysmans advocated for wood only in general terms, then going on to envision what remarkable results an artist like Degas (whom he considered a highly gifted sculptor despite his criticism of the *Little Dancer Aged Fourteen*) might achieve with it. After all, the same exhibition featured two sculptures by Gauguin in that very material.[54] Like his two marble busts, Gauguin had executed the medallion *La Chanteuse* (*The Singer;* fig. 7) and the free-standing statuette of *Dame en promenade* (*Lady Strolling;* fig. 8) naturalistically. However, he had captured the two women immediately after or in the midst of carrying out an activity: the singer – to judge from her bouquet – after her performance, and the anonymous lady out for a stroll (although, depicted as a standing figure, she derives her movement from the title only). The model for the first was Valéry Roumy, who enjoyed fame as a singer on Montmartre around 1880.[55] The anonymous walker, for her part, presumably reproduces precisely the type of modern Parisian woman Huysmans so longed to see carved in wood (by Degas).[56]

In both cases, Gauguin thus depicted modern-life themes of the kind considered Impressionist. By doing so, as well as by adopting an experimental approach to traditional materials, he was presumably reacting to Degas's *Little Dancer Aged Fourteen,* which he had already seen in the months before the exhibition.[57] For the *Chanteuse* he used a combination of wood and plaster, and what is more, both the medallion and the statuette are among the earliest known examples in which he practised polychromy. The result was a decorative effect reminiscent of craftwork.[58] By juxtaposing decorative and realistic elements, Gauguin ultimately created the tension Duranty had already identified as an attribute of Impressionism in his pamphlet *La Nouvelle Peinture* published in 1876.[59]

Progressive critics nevertheless singled out Degas as the true sculptor of the exhibition.[60] They considered Gauguin's sculptural works entirely lacking in innovation. The *Chanteuse* they thought pretentious; the simple rural folk were capable of carvings more interesting than his *Dame en promenade*.[61] Even those who had praised his marble busts could find nothing positive to say about the two works in wood. The journalist Antony Valabrègue, for instance, curtly observed that the "attempts at polychrome sculpture, with their coarse modelling" were not worth mentioning.[62] Huysmans, on the other hand, described *Dame en promenade* as "Gothic in its modernity".[63] He was thus linking Gauguin's sculpture with the contemporary tendency to rediscover medieval folk and church art. Yet with his reference to the Gothic style – over which the French generally claimed primacy – he was also characterising the work as an expression of national pride.

In the seventh exhibition, taking place in 1882, Gauguin once again associated himself with that tradition through his choice of materials. He used a found wooden torso, presumably a spolium of a sacred work made by an artist long dead.[64] On it, he mounted the head of his son Clovis modelled in wax (fig. 9).[65] The portrayal of a family member in these materials amounted to a synthesis of his earlier sculptures and was more warmly received than his earlier works in wood. Paul de Charry even went so far as to say that *Clovis* was modelled in so admirable and vibrant a manner that already this sculpture alone made a visit to the show worthwhile.[66]

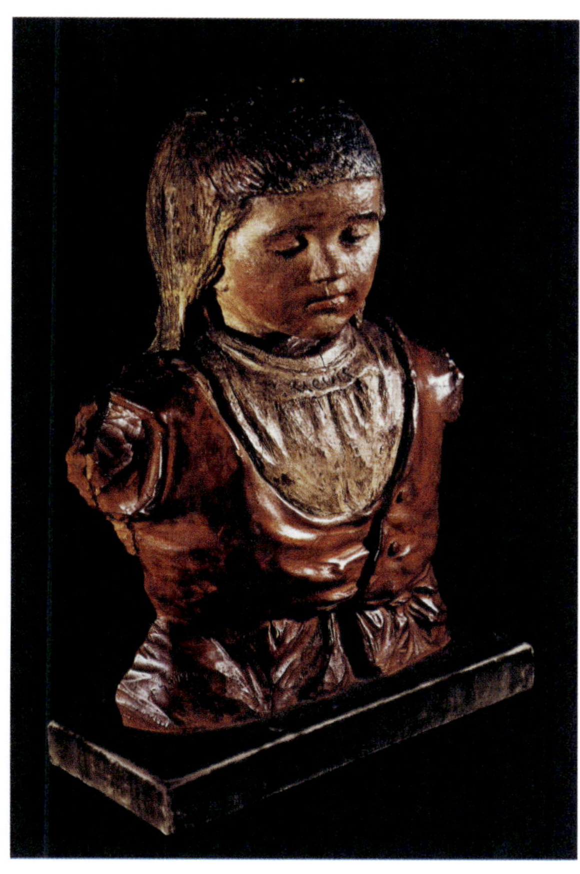

9 Paul Gauguin, *Clovis*, 1881, wax, walnut, height 40 cm, whereabouts unknown

Gauguin continued working in wood and presented his relief *La Toilette* (see cat. 3) in the last Impressionist exhibition staged in 1886.[67] At the time, the sight of an "Impressionist sculpture" was still considered as much a rarity as ever, as an exclamation by an anonymous reviewer reveals.[68] Whereas several critics dismissed the nude in profile seated under a tree and combing her hair as a bizarre attempt at wooden sculpture,[69] Félix Fénéon called the "sincere and delicate" work one of the show's "attractions". He regretted only that Gauguin had refrained from the use of colour in this latest entry and expressed the hope that future exhibitions would once again feature polychrome sculptures in materials such as wood, glass paste and wax.[70]

In two respects, Fénéon's critique is a representative example of the contemporary reception of the sculptures in the Impressionist exhibitions. For one thing, it focuses on material. Of all the reviews of the 17 sculptures that might be designated as "Impressionist" on the basis of their presentation in one of the eight shows, the majority addressed this aspect. Whereas the various authors ascribed fundamental importance to the experimental handling of the artistic media in the case of the paintings as well, in their assessments of the sculptures they paid particular attention to the choice of materials. And secondly, Fénéon recognised that the genre's true potential lay in the material. He equated "Impressionist sculpture" with modern sculpture, a "sculpture of the future", as Armand Chaulieu had already called it in connection with Degas's *Little Dancer Aged Fourteen*.[71] Material and modernity would also dominate subsequent discussions of the topic, even if the general drift of the latter now took a new direction.

Fleeting categories

Even before the last Impressionist exhibition had ended, a second phase in the reception of "Impressionist sculpture" set in. On 2 June 1886, the writer Edmond Thiaudière referred to Medardo Rosso (1858–1928) as its true founder, citing the sketchy character of two bronzes the Italian artist had on display in the Salon at that point in time.[72] The focus thus shifted from the Impressionist exhibitions to an artist uninvolved in them. After the turn of the century, Auguste Rodin (1840–1917) also served as a figurehead of the lively debate that now got underway. Here Edmond Claris, a critic and the author who had penned an essay entitled "L'Impressionnisme en sculpture", played a key role. First appearing in print in June 1901 in the magazine *La Nouvelle Revue*, the text drew on a survey the author had taken of artists, critics and collectors.[73] Against the backdrop of a *paragone* between painting and sculpture revived by Charles Baudelaire, Claris emphasised the independence of sculpture and placed it on a par with Impressionist painting. He perceived a "current of renewal" in sculpture which the German art historian Julius Meier-Graefe lost no time in integrating as an additional narrative thread in his *Entwickelungsgeschichte der modernen Kunst* (first published in 1904) that devotes an entire chapter to "Der Impressionismus in der Plastik" (Impressionism in Sculpture).[74] A discussion of Claris's and Meier-Graefe's conceptions of "Impressionist sculpture" would require an extensive study of its own. Several of the following catalogue texts examine individual aspects of their deliberations;[75] here, however, the author will limit herself to outlining the fundamental change that now came about in the meaning of the term. What is decisive in this context is that Claris and Meier-Graefe undertook an explicit comparison of sculpture and painting. Rosso and Rodin served them as ideal examples because theirs were the works that most aptly exhibited attributes of Impressionism understood as painterly – for example, sketchy execution and visible traces of the working process. In a manner comparable to the press reviews of the sculptures shown in the Impressionist exhibitions, Claris and Meier-Graefe concentrated on the artistic material. Their focus, however, was on the effects achieved with the material – for instance, ephemerality, light and shade, all of which they considered sculpture as capable of conveying as painting.

Only in the past recent decades did a third reception phase arise, which, for its part, regarded precisely those painterly criteria that Claris and Meier-Graefe had systematically shown to be manifest in the works of Rosso and Rodin to be irreconcilable with sculpture. This development went hand in hand with the increasing isolation of the media in general, as a consequence of which drawing and printmaking were likewise no longer treated as integral parts of multimedia working processes, but rather discussed independently of one another.[76] Such partitioning is compatible neither with Rosso and Rodin nor with the artists participating in the Impressionist exhibitions, whose oeuvres are distinguished, for the most part, by an interplay between media. Gauguin's polychrome sculptures are a case in point, as they almost demonstratively transcend supposed medium boundaries. Moreover, this reception phase frequently applied a narrower definition of Impressionism, associating it chiefly with landscape views – in contrast to the figural depictions mostly encountered in sculpture.[77] In other words, it is an approach that draws lines not only between media but also between genres. It may be significant that the topic of "Impressionist sculpture" has, over the past few years, come up for discussion primarily within the framework of monographic studies concerned with the more general question of the extent to which certain artists – for example, Gauguin and Degas – can be classified as Impressionists.[78] Their sculptures have been discussed, alternatively, as (hyper)realistic, primitivist and Symbolist; these terms, however, are likewise appropriate only in individual cases.

In summary, it can be said that neither a medium, a motif nor any particular artistic oeuvre can be indiscriminately defined as Impressionist. Already the heterogeneous group of the 17 sculptures presented at the Impressionist exhibitions makes it obvious how necessary it is to examine each object individually with an eye to possible points of intersection. The history of the reception of "Impressionist sculpture" thus ultimately serves to illustrate the dilemma of categorical systems in general: in terms of lifespan, they are no more enduring than Impressionism's fleeting moments.

1   See the insightful first overview of the theme by Catherine Chevillot, who nevertheless – in terms of both form and content – cites a number of "Impressionist" attributes that she identifies in paintings and sculptures alike; Chevillot 2010.

2   Elliott 2014.

3   See exh. cat. Washington/San Francisco 1986; Berson 1996.

4   Rewald 1973 [1946] is still one of the fundamental studies on Impressionism. For helpful bibliographies, see exh. cat. Washington/San Francisco 1986, pp. 497–505; Richard R. Brettell, "Bibliographical Essay", in: Brettell 2000, p. 236.

5   Shiff 1986, pp. 67–70.

6   The extent to which certain artists who did not participate in any of the Impressionist exhibitions were possibly even "more Impressionist" was likewise a topic of discussion. On the many different reasons for participating or not participating, ranging from artistic principles to the desire for affiliation with a group or even financial considerations, see exh. cat. Washington/San Francisco 1986. The only artist who took part in all eight Impressionist exhibitions was Camille Pissarro.

7   See Shiff 1986, pp. 67–70.

8   "Ils sont *impressionnistes* en ce sens qu'ils rendent non le paysage, mais la sensation produite par le paysage. [… I]ls sortent de la réalité et entrent en plein idéalisme." Castagnary 1874; quoted in: Berson 1996, vol. 1, p. 17 (emphasis in original).

9   On the Salon, see Sfeir-Semler 1992. From 1874 to 1886, the Salon took place annually, from 1882 organised by the "Société des Artistes Français"; see ibid., pp. 54–64.

10   Punctuation and emphasis as in: exh. cat. Paris 1874, p. 15, no. 98.

11   Leroy 1874.

12   "Ils ont mis à la porte de leur exposition le mot impressionniste afin de ne pas être confondus avec d'autres et parce que ce mot les désignaient d'une façon fort claire pour le public." Rivière 1877a, p. 3. A caricature by Cham appearing in

Le Charivari on 16 April 1877 shows the sign with the inscription "EXPOSITION / DES PEINTRES IMPRESSIONNISTES" over the entrance to the exhibition. For an illustration, see Berson 1996, vol. 1, p. 196. On the use of the term "impressionnistes" by the artists themselves, see Eisenman 1986, esp. p. 51.

13 The magazine came out only four times – on 6, 14, 21 and 28 April 1877. The editorial office was located at 22 bis, rue Laffitte. The Didot-Bottin of 1877, pp. 449, 1149 (category "TABLEAUX [MARCH. DE]") has "Masson, *commissionnaire en tableaux et objets d'art*" at this address.

14 This may be attributable to the fact that, along with the seventh Impressionist exhibition, the third was the one recording the least diversity of media; 84 per cent of its artworks were paintings. An article on decorative art by an anonymous painter represents an exception in that it also addresses itself to modern decorative sculpture; Anonymous [Un peintre] 1877.

15 A reprint of the statutes is found in: Anonymous 1874.

16 The catalogues of the second to the sixth as well as the eighth exhibition, however, referred only to painting; they were entitled "Catalogue de la [2ᵉ/3ᵉ/4ᵐᵉ/5ᵐᵉ/6ᵐᵉ/8ᵐᵉ] exposition de peinture". No copy of the seventh is known to have survived, but, according to an extant transcript, its title ("Catalogue de la 7ᵐᵉ exposition des artistes indépendants") mentions no medium at all. For reprints of all catalogues, see Berson 1996, vol. 1.

17 Camille Pissarro and Edgar Degas, for example, were quite extreme in this respect. Pissarro participated in all eight exhibitions. The total of 177 Pissarro catalogue numbers includes paintings (also in distemper), gouaches, pastels, etchings and fans. Degas took part in seven of the exhibitions, at which, according to the catalogue entries, he showed paintings (likewise partly in distemper, in a combination of distemper and pastel or "à l'essence"), pastels, drawings, etchings, monotypes and a sculpture.

18 For identification of the objects, see Berson 1996, vol. 2. Even if many of the works have yet to be identified and it has moreover been shown that the catalogue entries are neither complete nor always correct, the catalogues constitute the most important source on this question.

19 For a study of the presence of drawings in exhibitions taking place in Paris between 1860 and 1890 and also addressing their quantitative proportions in the Salons as well as the Impressionist exhibitions, see DeWitte 2017. On fans as a medium, see Gerstein 1982.

20 See the table "Les Salons", in: Pingeot/Le Normand-Romain/Lemaistre 1982, n. p. In comparison to the average of 7.5 per cent from 1831 to 1860, the proportion of sculptures had thus more than doubled.

21 For an instructive evaluation of the existing information, see Ward 1991. No views of the exhibitions have come down to us; the descriptions of contemporary critics serve as the primary sources.

22 Starting in 1861, the arrangement of the works according to the academic genre hierarchy gave way to a largely alphabetical arrangement; see Ward 1991, pp. 600–601. On the presentation of the objects in the Salon, also see Sfeir-Semler 1992, pp. 82–85.

23 For details, see the lengthy contributions on the eight exhibitions in: exh. cat. Washington/San Francisco 1986. The second exhibition, in which Degas's and Berthe Morisot's contributions were divided, was an exception. Their works on paper were on view with paintings by Marcellin Desboutins in the first room; Morisot's paintings followed in the second, and Degas's in the third; see Clayson 1986, p. 146. Clayson draws primarily on Philippe Burty's description of the venue (Burty 1876). On this subject, also see: Ward 1991, p. 604.

24 For a discussion of the emphasis on the individual within the framework of the exhibitions, see Ward 1991, pp. 600–601.

25 This opportunity presented itself, for example, to Degas in the sixth exhibition of 1881; see ibid., p. 611.

26 See the review by Gustave Geffroy, who describes "canapés algériens et des fauteuils-berceuses"; G. G. [Geffroy] 1881; quoted in: Berson 1996, vol. 1, p. 342. On the interior decoration of exhibitions in those years, see Ward 1991. Even potted plants were not uncommon in exhibitions of the late nineteenth century.

27 An assessment based on the exhibition catalogues and also taking into account other works whose presence in the shows Berson was able to prove within the framework of her extensive study; Berson 1996, vol. 2, p. 283. Objects with collective numbers have been counted singly as far as possible (+ x); the works not specified in any catalogue appear in parentheses.

28 Nos. 87–91: enamels.

29 No. 2: faience; nos. 23–25: "panneaux décoratifs".

30 "Décidément la manie de la sculpture se développe. Degas fait (il paraît) des chevaux en sculpture et vous faites des vaches; vous me demandez des renseignements sur les maquettes en fer mais mon pauvre ami je n'en sais pas plus long que vous." Letter from Paul Gauguin to Camille Pissarro, Paris, end of October/beginning of November 1882, quoted in: Gauguin 1984, pp. 34–35, no. 28. English quoted in: Fonsmark 2005b, p. 190.

On Pissarro's sculptures and a discussion of this letter as well as the wire figures Gauguin recommended, and which he also sketched in this letter in the form of a cow, see Thomson 1983. On the Impressionists' growing interest in the medium of sculpture, see Fonsmark 2005b, p. 190.

31 On Pissarro, see Thomson 1983. Anne-Birgitte Fonsmark moreover calls attention to a letter in which Pissarro mentions a sketch for a wooden sculpture; exh. cat. Copenhagen/Fort Worth 2005, pp. 138–140, no. 22, here p. 140. In said letter, he wrote: "J'ai dessiné aussi quelques petits motifs de sculpture en bois, du gothique pur avec des petits ornements, c'est merveilleux. C'est là que l'on s'aperçoit du réalisme de cette époque." Letter from Camille Pissarro to Lucien Pissarro, Rouen, 20 November 1883, quoted in: Pissarro 1980, vol. 1, pp. 251–254, no. 190, here p. 252. On Degas, see the contribution by Alexander Eiling in this catalogue, pp. 46–57. Apart from the artists mentioned in the following, other participants in the Impressionist exhibitions, for example Morisot, Pierre-Auguste Renoir and Jean-François Raffaëlli, presented sculptures in public in other contexts.

32 "Le siège social est fixé à Paris, provisoirement chez M. A. Ottin, trésorier, rue Vincent-Compoint, n° 9." Anonymous 1874. Michel Melot already put this fact on record; Melot 2010, p. 10. On the reasons for Ottin's active dedication to the Impressionist cause, see cat. 1–2.

33 The catalogue lists "Acis et Galathée [sic]" as no. 120, "Jeune Faune" as no. 121 and "Nymphe chasseresse" as no. 122; exh. cat. Paris 1874, p. 17; also see this catalogue, p. 37, fig. 2. According to the object file in the Louvre, the "Amour et Psyché. Groupe marbre" listed as no. 119 is an alternative title for *Acis et Galatée*; Musée du Louvre, Paris, archive of the Département des Sculptures, inv. no. RF 5.
It is unclear which sculpture the title "Le Dernier Mousse du Vengeur. Plâtre" (no. 127) refers to.

34 No. 125: "Buste. Terre cuite"; no. 126: "Buste de Ingres. Réduction en plâtre"; no. 128: "Buste de M. B***. Terre cuite". On the *Bust of Ingres*, see cat. 1.

35 See Burty 1874a; Drumont 1874; E. d'H. [d'Hervilly] 1874; Anonymous 1874a. On the reception of Ottin, see cat. 1–2.

36 For a review that emphasises Ottin's contributions in favourable terms, see De Montifaud 1874; on this subject, see cat. 1–2.

37 Other artists – such as Monet, who continued to submit works to the Salon – likewise complied with the requirements of the respective exhibition format; see Isaacson 1986, p. 385.

38 Ottin's contributions to the Salons of

these years were: 1874, no. 3079: "La Vérité; – statue marbre"; 1876, no. 3522: "Thésée précipitant Scyron à la mer; – groupe, fonte de fer"; 1882, no. 4719: "Triomphe de la République; – bas-reliefs, plâtre"; 1886, no. 4379: "Portrait de M. Cantagrel; – buste, marbre."

39 "D'excellents dessins au fusain de M. Lebourg, et une petite sculpture agréable de M. Gauguin, la seule sculpture qu'il y ait là, ont excité aussi, les premiers surtout, intérêt des visiteurs." Duranty 1879; quoted in: Berson 1996, vol. 1, p. 219. English quoted in: Brettell 2005, p. 44.

40 On Gauguin's early sculptures, see Gray 1963, pp. 1–32; Fonsmark 2005a. On *Buste d'Émile* see ibid., pp. 74–76, no. 6. Pissarro and Degas had only invited Gauguin to join the group a week before the opening, for which reason his contribution(s) are not listed in the catalogue. Ronald Pickvance assumes that, apart from the sculpture, he also presented paintings *hors catalogue* in this exhibition, which, however, have yet to be identified; Pickvance 1986, pp. 248, 260. On this subject, also see: Brettell 2005, esp. pp. 44–45.

41 "M. Gauguin qui me paraît tres sensé en sculpture, si j'en juge par son buste en marbre, perd la tête quand il se livre à la peinture." De Montagnac 1880; quoted in: Berson 1996, vol. 1, p. 302.

42 Henry Trianon, for example, praised Gauguin's skilful handling of the sculptor's tools and objected only to his summary treatment of the hair: "Il n'y a qu'un seul envoi de sculpture, et cet envoi mérite d'être cité. Il est signé: Mette. C'est une tête de jeune femme qui se termine à la naissance du cou. Il y a là un habile et sincère maniement de ciseau. Le modelé a les rondeurs fuyantes et les méplats adoucis de la jeunesse. Si la chevelure avait été traitée moins sommairement, il n'y aurait presque rien à reprendre dans ce joli morceau." Trianon 1880; quoted in: Berson 1996, vol. 1, p. 313. It may have been Gauguin's then landlord at Impasse Frémin, Jules-Ernest Bouillot, and/or his neighbour there, Jean-Paul Aubé, who deserved this praise. Both were academically trained sculptors and could well have been involved in the execution of Gauguin's marble sculptures; see exh. cat. Copenhagen/Fort Worth 2005, pp. 74–79, nos. 6, 7, here pp. 76–78 (Anne-Birgitte Fonsmark).

43 Exh. cat. Copenhagen/Fort Worth 2005, pp. 76–79, no. 7, here p. 79 (Anne-Birgitte Fonsmark).

44 On Degas's *Little Dancer Aged Fourteen*, see cat. 4.

45 "Car – voilà l'originalité de cette Exposition des Indépendants – ils commencent à affirmer leur indépendance sous la forme sculptée. Ce n'était pas assez de la couleur. Il leur faut la cire, ou le plâtre ou le bronze. Nous allons avoir,

bone Deus! des sculpteurs *impressio-nistes* [sic]!" Claretie 1881; quoted in: Berson 1996, vol. 1, p. 335 (emphasis in original).

46 "A vrai dire, l'élément nouveau de l'exposition du boulevard des Capucines, le fait dont il faudra se souvenir, c'est l'entrée, plus ou moins triomphale, des indépendants dans un art qu'ils n'avaient pas encore songé à rajeunir, la sculpture." Mantz 1881; quoted in: Berson 1996, vol. 1, p. 358.

47 Bertall was the pseudonym of Charles-Albert d'Arnoux; see Pickvance 1986, p. 243.

48 "Signalons encore un essai nouveau de sculpture, exposé en vedette au milieu d'un des salons. C'est une danseuse. Naturellement, cette danseuse est affreuse, elle est modelée en terre cuite, et vêtue d'un petit jupon en véritable mousseline blanche. Nous avons vu des groupes d'adeptes, nihilistes hommes et femmes, se pâmer d'aise devant cette danseuse et sa jupe de mousseline. C'est là du moins une innovation. Des horizons nouveaux semblent s'ouvrir pour les costumiers et les modistes." Bertall [d'Arnoux] 1881; quoted in: Berson 1996, vol. 1, p. 330. On Degas's *Little Dancer Aged Fourteen*, see cat. 4.

49 "Voilà vraiment une tentative nouvelle, un essai de réalisme en sculpture. Un artiste vulgaire eût fait de cette danseuse une poupée, M. Degas en a fait une œuvre de forte saveur, de science exacte, sous une forme vraiment originale." C. E. [Ephrussi] 1881; quoted in: Berson 1996, vol. 1, p. 337.

50 Regarding Degas: "[… L]a curiosité de son exposition […] est tout entière dans une statue de cire intitulée *Petite Danseuse de quatorze ans* devant laquelle le public, très ahuri et comme gêné, se sauve. La terrible réalité de cette statuette lui produit un évident malaise; toutes ses idées sur la sculpture, sur ces mémorables poncifs recopiés depuis les siècles, se bouleversent." Huysmans 1883a, p. 226.

51 Wissman 1986, pp. 340–341.

52 Ibid., pp. 341–342. On the use of wax since antiquity, see the contribution by Alexander Eiling in this catalogue, pp. 46–57, here p. 48.

53 "Il y a, dans ces œuvres [medieval church sculptures, the author] si réalistes, si humaines, un jeu de traits, une vie de corps qui n'ont jamais été retrouvés par la sculpture. Puis, voyez comme le bois est malléable et souple, docile et presque onctueux sous la volonté de ces maîtres; voyez comme est et légère et précise l'étoffe des costumes taillée en plein chêne, comme elle s'attache à la personne qui la porte, comme elle suit ses attitudes, comme elle aide à exprimer ses fonctions et son caractère. Eh bien, transférez ce procédé, cette matière, à Paris, maintenant mettez-les

entre les mains d'un artiste qui sente le moderne comme M. Degas, et la Parisienne dont la très spéciale beauté est faite d'un mélange pondéré de naturel et d'artifice, de la fonte en un seul tout des charmes de son corps et des grâces de sa toilette, la Parisienne avortée de M. Chatrousse viendra à terme." Huysmans 1883a, pp. 229–230.

54 Fonsmark 2005a, p. 128.

55 On this identification, see exh. cat. Copenhagen/Fort Worth 2005, pp. 134–137, no. 21, here p. 136 (Anne-Birgitte Fonsmark).

56 Theodore Reff was the first to explain that it was presumably Degas who inspired Gauguin to choose this motif; Reff 1976, pp. 262f. Also see: exh. cat. Copenhagen/Fort Worth 2005, pp. 138–140, no. 22 (Anne-Birgitte Fonsmark).

57 Fonsmark 2005a, pp. 126–128.

58 Exh. cat. Copenhagen/Fort Worth 2005, pp. 134–137, no. 21, here p. 134; pp. 138–140, no. 22, here p. 138 (Anne-Birgitte Fonsmark). In this connection, Fonsmark points out the significance of the ancient terracotta figures that had come to light in Asia Minor and Greece in 1874 and thereafter.

59 Wissman 1986, pp. 339, 350.

60 "Et quand nous parlons de sculpture, nous ne pensons pas le moins du monde à M. Paul Gauguin. Il a exposé, il est vrai, un médaillon qui, à en croire le catalogue, représenterait une Chanteuse. Ce morceau hardi semble inspiré par cette pensée que la réalité n'est qu'une chimère dont un artiste vraiment libre ne doit pas s'occuper beaucoup. […] Le véritable, le seul sculpteur de l'académie intransigeante, c'est M. Degas." Mantz 1881; quoted in: Berson 1996, vol. 1, p. 358.

61 "Quant à la sculpture; qu'est-ce que cela peut bien vouloir dire et prouver? Je ne parle pas de la *Dame en promenade*, qu'on a l'audace de montrer au public. J'ai connu dans mon pays plus d'un petit *Gardeur de bêtes* qui sculptaient, au bout de bâtons, des figurines plus intéressantes que cela; mais la *Chanteuse*, ce grand médaillon prétentieux?" De Montagnac 1881; quoted in: Berson 1996, vol. 1, p. 361.

62 "Je laisse de côté les essais de sculpture polychrome, les grossiers modelages signés Gauguin, et exposés pour le plus grand 'esbattement' de ce public qui ne vient aux expositions de ce genre que pour s'y amuser." Valabrègue 1881; quoted in: Berson 1996, vol. 1, p. 370. Henry Trianon described the *Chanteuse* as so ugly that it made the viewers want to scream: "'La Chanteuse' est un médaillon de grandeur naturelle, bois de poirier sur fond d'or. Elle est de face et presque de ronde-bosse, pas assez toutefois, d'où il résulte un effet choquant pour qui veut la regarder par un plan oblique. Ah! par exemple, elle

est d'une laideur et d'une maigreur à faire crier." Trianon 1881; quoted in: Berson 1996, vol. 1, p. 368.

63 Huysmans 1883a, p. 242: "[I]l [Gauguin, the author] a exposé aussi une statuette en bois gothiquement moderne […]." On Huysmans's conception of the Gothic style, see exh. cat. Copenhagen/Fort Worth 2005, pp. 138–140, no. 22, here p. 140 (Anne-Birgitte Fonsmark). English quoted in: Fonsmark 2005a, p. 140.

64 Fonsmark 2005a, pp. 129–131. Fonsmark explains that reusing found objects was an established element of Gauguin's artistic process.

65 The combination of the two materials that Huysmans propagated as modern will presumably have exceeded his expectations. However, his report on the 1881 exhibition did not appear in print until 1883, for which reason *Clovis* cannot be understood as a direct reaction to it.

66 "M. Gauguin a une petite tête de *Clovis* admirable de modelé et de vie. C'est charmant et vaut à lui seul toute son exposition." De Charry 1882; quoted in: Berson 1996, vol. 1, p. 384. Charles Flor, on the other hand, expressed himself in markedly negative terms: "M. Paul Gauguin a vraiment tort de faire de la sculpture." Flor 1882; quoted in: Berson 1996, vol. 1, p. 388.

67 On the making of this work, see cat. 3.

68 "Cette année, l'exposition des impression-nistes – la huitième en date – est installée 1, rue Laffitte, dans les salons du second étage. Cinq salles lui sont réservées et montrent, en tout, environ trois cents œuvres: peinture à l'huile, aquarelles, dessins au noir, pastels – ceux-ci en grand nombre; – on y remarque même un bas-relief en bois sculpté! De la sculpture impressionniste, cela ne s'est pas vu souvent!" Anonymous 1886; quoted in: Berson 1996, vol. 1, p. 471.

69 "Une sculpture sur bois, un être émacié et bizarre." Adam 1886; quoted in: Berson 1996, vol. 1, p. 428. Jean Ajalbert, for his part, referred to *La Toilette* in an enumeration as an "attempt": "[…] un essai de sculpture sur bois […]." Ajalbert 1886; quoted in: Berson 1996, vol. 1, p. 432.

70 "En 1881, M. Gauguin, en même temps, que M. Degas sa *Petite Danseuse* de cire, montrait une figurine en bois colorié (*Dame en promenade*) et un médaillon (*la Chanteuse*); cette année sur le poirier que nous avons le regret de voir mono-chrome, sa femme nue s'enlève en demi-relief, la main aux cheveux, assise rectangulairement dans un paysage: c'est d'un modelé sincère et délicat, et certainement l'un des attraits de ces salles. Espérons qu'aux expositions prochaines nous seront présentés des spécimens de sculpture polychrome en bois, en pâte de verre et en cire." Fénéon 1886; quoted in: Berson 1996, vol. 1, p. 443.

71 "Cette dernière exposition [the sixth Impressionist exhibition, 1881, the author] fit quelque bruit à cause du nombre des toiles exposées, de leur diversité comme geure et comme talent, et aussi à cause de la sculpture impressionniste – la sculpture de l'avenir – dont plusieurs spécimens, dus au ciseau de M. Degas, le chef de la nouvelle école, furent exhibés aux yeux du public ébahi." La Fare [Chaulieu] 1882; quoted in: Berson 1996, vol. 1, p. 399. For a discussion of the attributes associated with modern sculpture in the contemporary press, and the particular prominence given to the choice of materials in that context, see Scott 1998, esp. p. 107.

72 "[I]l demande au bronze de traduire en de puissantes pochades ou ébauches des impressions neuves. Il fonde ainsi, et magistralement, la sculpture impression-niste." Thiaudière 1886. Edmond Thiaudière made these remarks in his review of the official Salon, which in 1886 opened on 1 May. The eighth Impressionist exhibition took place from 15 May to 15 June 1886. Rosso adopted the term "impressions" and used it from the mid 1880s onwards in the titles of his own works – more specifically, in pieces in which he endeavoured to capture figures in a certain moment while at the same time taking the surrounding space and the light situation into account; Hecker 2017, p. 63. On Thiaudière and Rosso, see the contri-bution by Eva Mongi-Vollmer in this cata-logue, pp. 126–133, here pp. 126–127.

73 Claris 1901 (French). The following year, it came out in German and Spanish translations and, as an expanded French version, in book form; Claris 1902 (French); Claris 1902a (German); Claris 1902b (Spanish).

74 Meier-Graefe 1904, vol. 1, pp. 303–312.

75 See esp. cat. 85–88, 89–94.

76 On the negation of Impressionist printmaking, see Melot 2010; on drawing, see Brettell 2017.

77 Siegmar Holsten, for example, points out that "Impressionism" as a "stylistic term referring to landscape and colour light" is unsuitable for describing sculptural works by Rodin, Degas and Rosso; Holsten 2007, p. 13. Joel Isaacson discusses these criteria as those that constituted the conception of Impressionism formulated by Théodore Duret in his text *Les Peintres Impression-nistes*, published in 1878, and demon-strates that the latter took only certain aspects into account; Isaacson 1986, p. 375.

78 See exh. cat. Copenhagen/Fort Worth 2005; exh. cat. Roubaix 2010.

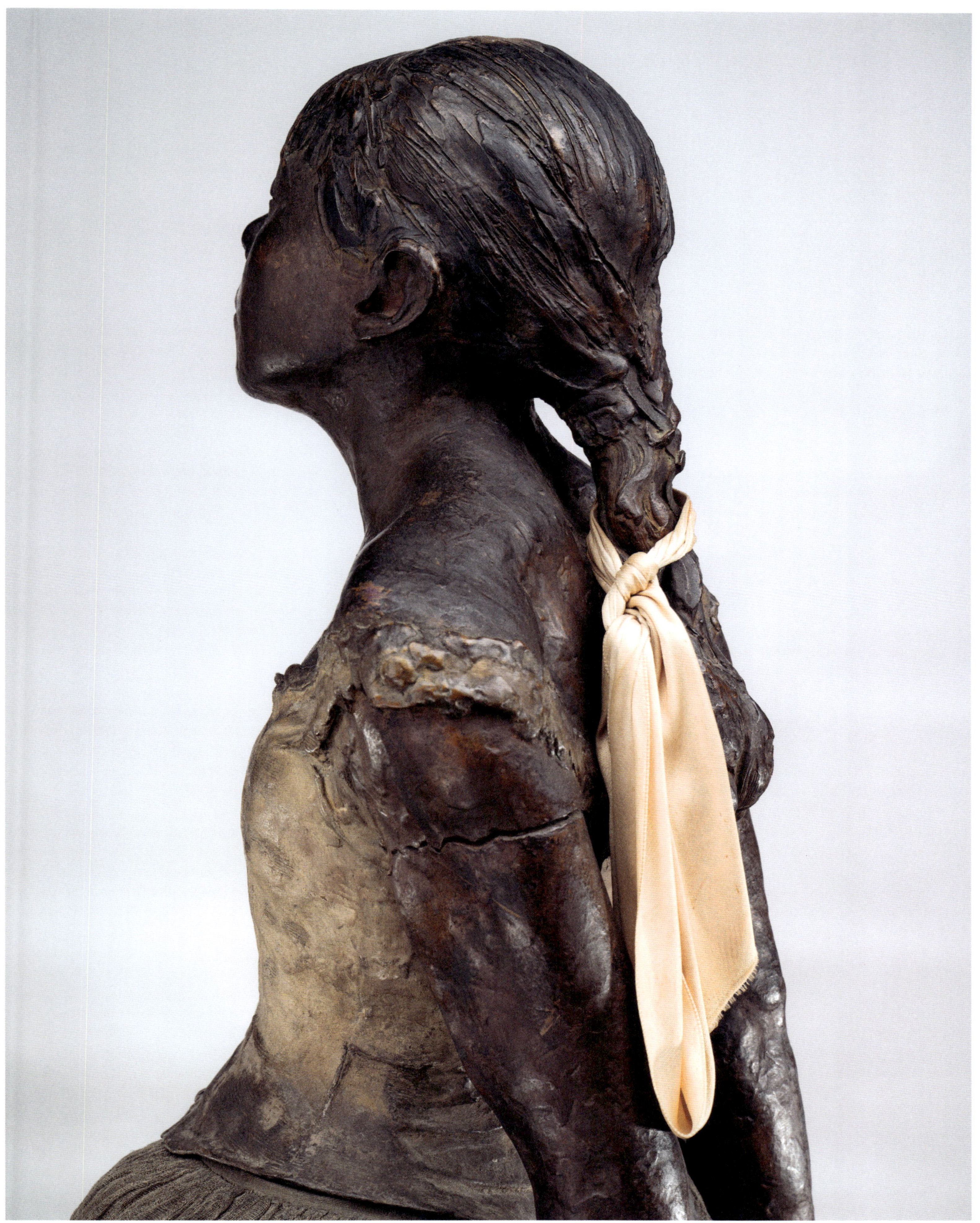

Auguste-Louis-Marie Ottin – the first Impressionist sculptor?

"Sculpture is only represented by a single name, Monsieur Auguste Ottin", wrote Marc de Montifaud in his review of the first Impressionist exhibition.[1] Auguste-Louis-Marie Ottin, born in Paris in 1811, was a student of the distinguished sculptor David d'Angers, began attending the École des Beaux-Arts in 1825, and achieved success early on (fig. 1). He was just 25 when he won the Prix de Rome in 1836, after which he spent four years as a resident scholar at the Académie de France in Rome. After his return, he gave his debut at the Salon of 1841, where he regularly presented his work until 1886 and was given multiple awards. He received further acknowledgement in the form of numerous commissions from the public sector; his sculptures adorn the opera and the Palais du Louvre in Paris, for example.[2]

Ottin presented ten works in the first Impressionist exhibition of 1874, which corresponded with more than half of the total of 17 sculptures represented in the eight exhibitions. One of the works on display, as can be read in the catalogue, was a *Buste de Ingres*. Then as now, Jean-Auguste-Dominique Ingres was regarded as the epitome of academic art in France of the nineteenth century. It may therefore come as a surprise that, of all people, his portrait was represented in an exhibition that saw itself as an alternative platform for artists whose works were not accepted to the official Salon.[3] This can be explained by personal connections that date back to Ottin's stay in Rome. At the time, Ingres was the president of the Académie de France and directly commissioned Ottin to produce his portrait.[4] Ottin completed a marble bust in 1841 that he presented on the occasion of the Exposition universelle in Paris in 1855.[5] In 1839/40, he worked on the plaster version that he showed at the Impressionist exhibition and which, as a part of Ingres's estate, entered the collection of the Musée Ingres in Montauban in 1867 (cat. 1).[6]

This preparatory version of the *Bust of Ingres* is characteristic of the works that Ottin contributed to the exhibition in the Boulevard des Capucines in several ways. For one thing, it did not provide insight into a current project but instead presented an undertaking he had successfully completed decades earlier. This temporal distance to the work's execution applied to all of Ottin's exhibits – as far as they can be identified.[7] For another thing, the catalogue identifies the *Bust of Ingres* as well as three other of his works as "réductions" (fig. 2).[8] This implies that in view of this exhibition context, Ottin made a conscious decision to present versions that were intended for a private buying public. As far as the Ingres portrait is concerned, at 61 centimetres the marble bust, which is now in the Villa Medici in Rome, is only nine centimetres taller.[9] It remains uncertain how the scale behaves relative to the three remaining reductions, which are bronzes: except for the *Bust of Ingres*, up to now none of the ten versions of Ottin's sculptures presented in the Impressionist exhibitions could

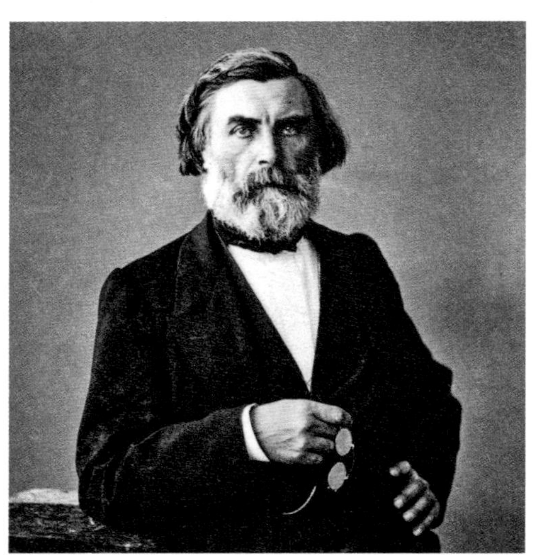

1 Studio Nadar, *Ottin, sculpteur* (detail), c. 1900 (print), photograph on albumen paper, from *Album de référence de l'Atelier Nadar*, vol. 2, Bibliothèque nationale de France, Département des Estampes et de la photographie, Paris

be identified or localised, but only some of the reference works. The evidence that the catalogue supplies with respect to their properties is all the more valuable.

Besides the *Bust of Ingres*, the unidentified work *Le Dernier Mousse du Vengeur* (The Last Sailor on the Vengeur) was also wrought out of plaster. Moreover, there were three terracotta works on display – one likewise unidentified "Buste de M. B***" (Bust of Mr B***) and two versions of a "Jeune Femme portant un vase" (Young Woman Holding a Vase). A marble version of the latter is being shown in our exhibition that Ottin had already presented at the Salon in 1861 and is known today by the slightly modified title of *Young Girl Holding a Vase* (cat. 2).[10] The fact that he showed the figure in the Impressionist exhibition twice, and both times in terracotta, suggests that they were states that (albeit in retrospect) rendered the working process visual. At least in this respect, therefore, Ottin's objects exhibited the element of the momentary and the transitory associated with Impressionism. In terms of the motif, his sculptures contradicted what was henceforth referred to as an "Impressionist" repertoire of themes, which primarily fed on everyday subjects. *Le Dernier Mousse du Vengeur* dealt with a historic event, the naval battle on 13 Prairial, that the French revolutionary fleet had fought out with the English Royal Navy on 1 June 1794.[11] Furthermore, the *Bust of Ingres* made indirect reference to the sitter's insistence on objects borrowed from antiquity.[12] Ottin complied with this appeal both with a mythological group of figures that he had developed for the *Fontaine Médicis* (p. 28, fig. 4) in the Jardin du Luxembourg in Paris as well as with the *Young Girl Holding a Vase*. The latter was the only motif the de Montifaud elaborated on with a brief laudatory description: with respect to the twist of the body, the sculptural execution and the delicate curve of the arm elegantly reaching for the amphora, the figure offered qualities to be taken seriously.[13] Furthermore, at least the version available to us refers back directly to Ingres's formal language.[14]

Thus, Ottin's figures that are elsewhere either classified as neo-classicist, Gothic, baroque or Romantic cannot be called "Impressionistic" either based on the motif or on their execution. All the more, their cohesive, smooth surface prompts us to imagine them in a dialogue with paintings by Monet, for instance, from whose open brushstroke they clearly set themselves apart. These contrasts were not mentioned in the press commentaries on the exhibition; with the exception of de Montifaud's report, Ottin's contributions were only addressed in the form of lists. His one-time participation is neither mentioned in the reception of his oeuvre, which remains sparse to this day, as opposed to his regular appearances at the Salon.[15] Instead, in more recent research on Impressionism, Ottin was brought in as striking proof of the fact that, unlike the historical and sociological phenomenon of Impressionism, an "Impressionist aesthetic" never existed.[16]

This argumentation actually makes implicit reference to Ottin's reasons for his participation, which will have been primarily of a socio-political nature. As an obituary that appeared in a December 1890 issue of *Revue Socialiste* illustrates, he was active in the education and promotion of artists all his life.[17] In 1868, he published a drawing manual that was methodically employed in numerous Parisian schools.[18] In addition, he held various education-policy offices and acted as an educational inspector for drawing. What is particularly relevant in our context is a pamphlet on exhibition and funding opportunities for the visual arts that he published in 1870, in which he defended the concept of the *Salon des Refusés* at which the works that were not admitted to the Salon were presented from 1863 onwards.[19] Going beyond this solution, Ottin recommended that independent groups of artists should organise exhibitions that were to be financially and spatially supported on the part of the government. As Paul Tucker accurately remarked, he will have championed the young Société anonyme out of utter conviction, in which he was not only a passive member but also functioned as treasurer.[20] After all, the founding statues of the Société declared that its prime objective was "the organisation of free exhibitions with no jury or honorary awards and in which every member can show their works".[21] In contrast to his sculptures, Ottin's concern was thus indeed in keeping with the other initiators of the newly founded platform. Even in his young years, he had fought against an authoritarian government during the French Revolution of 1830 and remained a staunch socialist his entire life. As such, he ultimately stood for the political dimension of Impressionism as an alliance of "independents" and "intransigents", as the artists who participated in the exhibitions used to refer to themselves.[22] — FR

— 17 —

OTTIN (Auguste-Louis-Marie).
9, rue Vincent - Compoint (18ᵉ arrondissement), Paris.

119. Amour et Psyché.
Groupe marbre.
120. Acis et Galathée.
121. Jeune Faune.
122. Nymphe chasseresse.
Réductions en bronze des sculptures décoratives de la fontaine Médicis, au Luxembourg.
123. Jeune Femme portant un vase.
Terre cuite.
124. Id. id.
Terre cuite.
125. Buste.
Terre cuite.
126. Buste de Ingres.
Réduction en plâtre.
127. Le Dernier Mousse du Vengeur.
Plâtre.
128. Buste de M. B***.
Terre cuite.

OTTIN (Léon-Auguste)
2, rue Bervic (18ᵉ arrondissement), Paris.

129. Après la messe à la campagne.
130. Au Château (Sannois).
131. La Butte Montmartre, versant sud.

2 List of Ottin's works in the catalogue accompanying the first Impressionist exhibition, 1874

1 "La statuaire n'est représentée que par un seul nom, M. Auguste Ottin, qui a donné des réductions en bronze des sculptures décoratives de la fontaine de Médicis, au Luxembourg, *Amour et Psyche*, *Acis et Galathée*, *Jeune faune*, *Nymphe chasseresse*, ainsi que deux sujets: *Jeune femme portant un vase*; ces deux copies offrent des qualités sérieuses dans la tournure, le modelé, et l'élégante arcature du bras qui vient se rattacher à l'amphore, avec une courbe délicate. A l'œuvre de M. Ottin, il faut encore ajouter: le *Buste de Ingres*, réduction plâtre [sic]; le *Dernier mousse du Vengeur*, plâtre; et le *Buste de M. B****, terre cuite." De Montifaud 1874, p. 30.

2 On Ottin and his background, see Lami 1921; Le Normand 1981, pp. 259–260; Gaudichon 1983.

3 Ingres was moreover indirectly represented in the same exhibition in the form of two etchings after his works made by Félix Bracquemond; see exh. cat. Paris 1874, nos. 24, 25.

4 See Le Normand 1981, pp. 265–266, no. 118.

5 The catalogue accompanying the Exposition universelle lists the bust under no. 4522. On the various versions of the bust, see Lami 1921; Le Normand 1981, pp. 265–266, no. 118.

6 On the genesis of the work, see Le Normand 1981, pp. 265–266, no. 118.

7 Ottin had presented the marble group "Amour et Psyché" listed in the exhibition catalogue under no. 119 at the Salon in 1847 (no. 2137); in addition, a marble group of the same name was on display at the Salon of 1861 (no. 3533). Nos. 120–122 were produced in connection with the *Fontaine Médicis*. Ottin completed a part of this group, "Acis et Galathée", in 1859; the state commissioned him to produce the figures in the lateral niches, "Jeune Faune" and "Nymphe chasseresse", in 1865. He presented nos. 123 and 124, both listed as "Jeune Femme portant un vase", in a version with two children in marble first at the Salon of 1857 (no. 3044) and in a second version, alone, in 1861 (no. 3532). See Lami 1921.

8 Nos. 120–122: "Réductions en bronze des sculptures décoratives de la fontaine Médicis, au Luxembourg"; no. 126: "Réduction en plâtre"; exh. cat. Paris 1874, p. 17.

9 The height of the other versions varies between 53 and 58 centimetres; see Le Normand 1981, pp. 265–266, no. 118.

10 See note 7. With reference to contemporary critics, Bruno Gaudichon states that Ottin already presented a figure with two children in marble at the Salon of 1857, while no mention is made of accompanying figures for the version presented in 1861, whereby the latter is probably the sculpture now in Poitiers; Gaudichon 1983, no. 69.

11 I would like to thank Gabriel Batalla for pointing this out.

12 On the Greek tradition Ingres propagated at the Académie de France, see Le Normand 1981.

13 See the quote mentioned in note 1.

14 Gaudichon makes reference to two obvious parallels with Ingres's painting *The Source* (*La Source*, 1820–1856, Musée d'Orsay, Paris); Gaudichon 1983, no. 69. This same work was also the subject of one of Bracquemond's etchings; exh. cat. Paris 1874, p. 6, no. 25 (collective number for six etchings).

15 See Lami 1921; Gaudichon 1983; Kjellberg 2005; Treydel 2017.

16 "La catégorie de l'impressionnisme, entendue au sens large (les participants aux expositions impressionnistes), a une cohérence historique et sociologique, mais une esthétique introuvable: on y trouvait jusqu'à Auguste Ottin, l'auteur de la fontaine Médicis du jardin du Luxembourg [...]." Chevillot 2010, p. 54.

See also Tucker 1986, p. 105; Fonsmark 2005a, p. 126.

17 See Malon 1890. On Ottin's political motivations, see also Gaudichon 1983.

18 Ottin 1868.

19 Ottin 1870.

20 Tucker 1986, p. 115, note 55. On Ottin's function as treasurer, see the essay by Fabienne Ruppen in this catalogue, pp. 24–34, esp. p. 28.

21 "Une société anonyme coopérative [...] ayant pour objet: 1° l'organisation d'expositions libres, sans jury ni récompenses honorifiques, où chacun des associés pourra exposer ses œuvres [...]." Anonymous 1874. It remains to be clarified whether Ottin's son, Léon-Auguste Ottin (1836–1918), made the contact. He participated in both the first as well as the second Impressionist exhibition: in 1874 with seven works, including a watercolour and a lithograph; in 1876 with 22 works. See exh cat. Paris 1874, pp. 17–18; exh. cat. Paris 1876, pp. 17–19.

22 On the Impressionists' choice of a name, see Eisenman 1986.

Auguste-Louis-Marie Ottin –
the first Impressionist sculptor?

Cat. 1

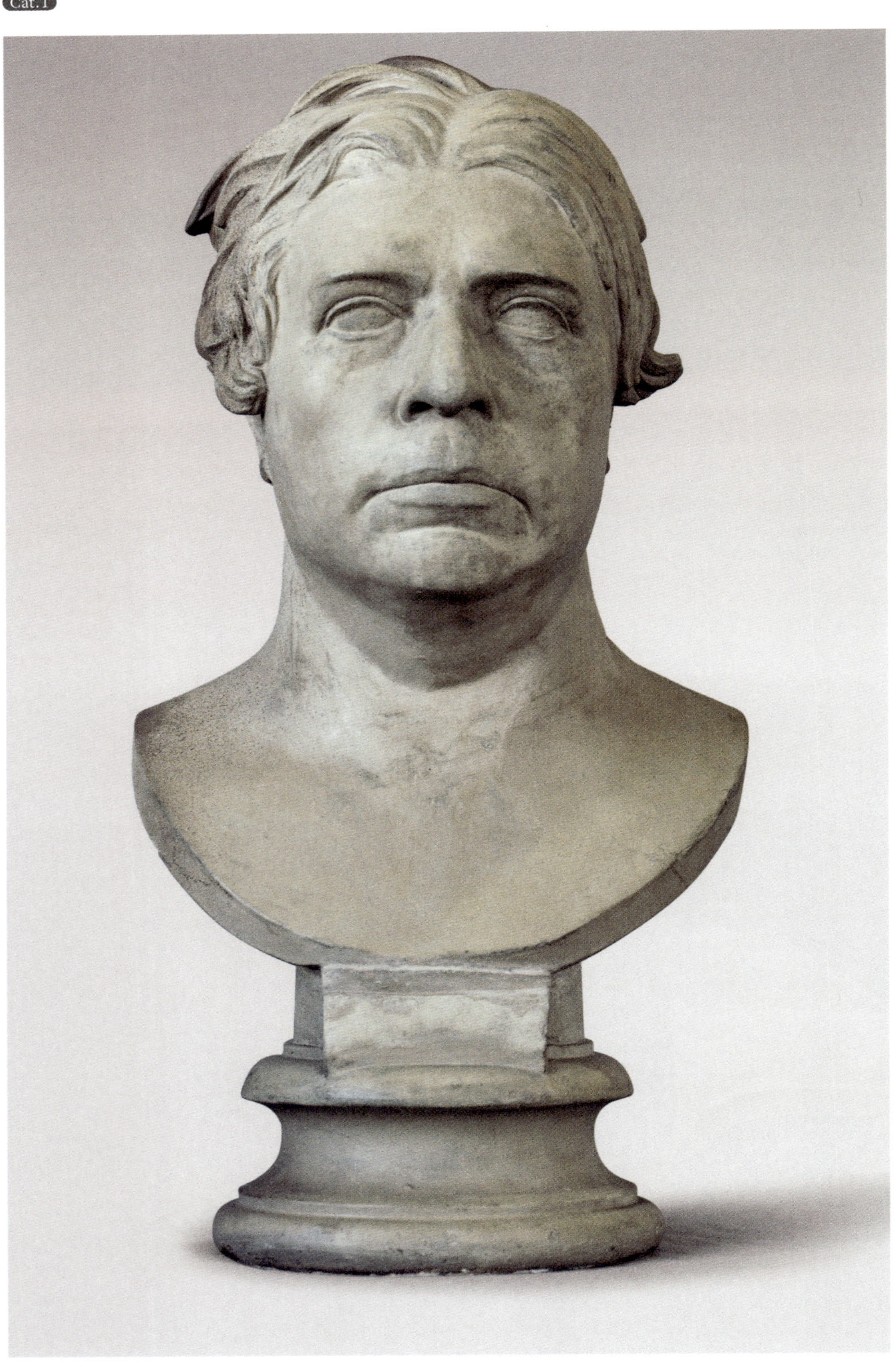

Cat. 2

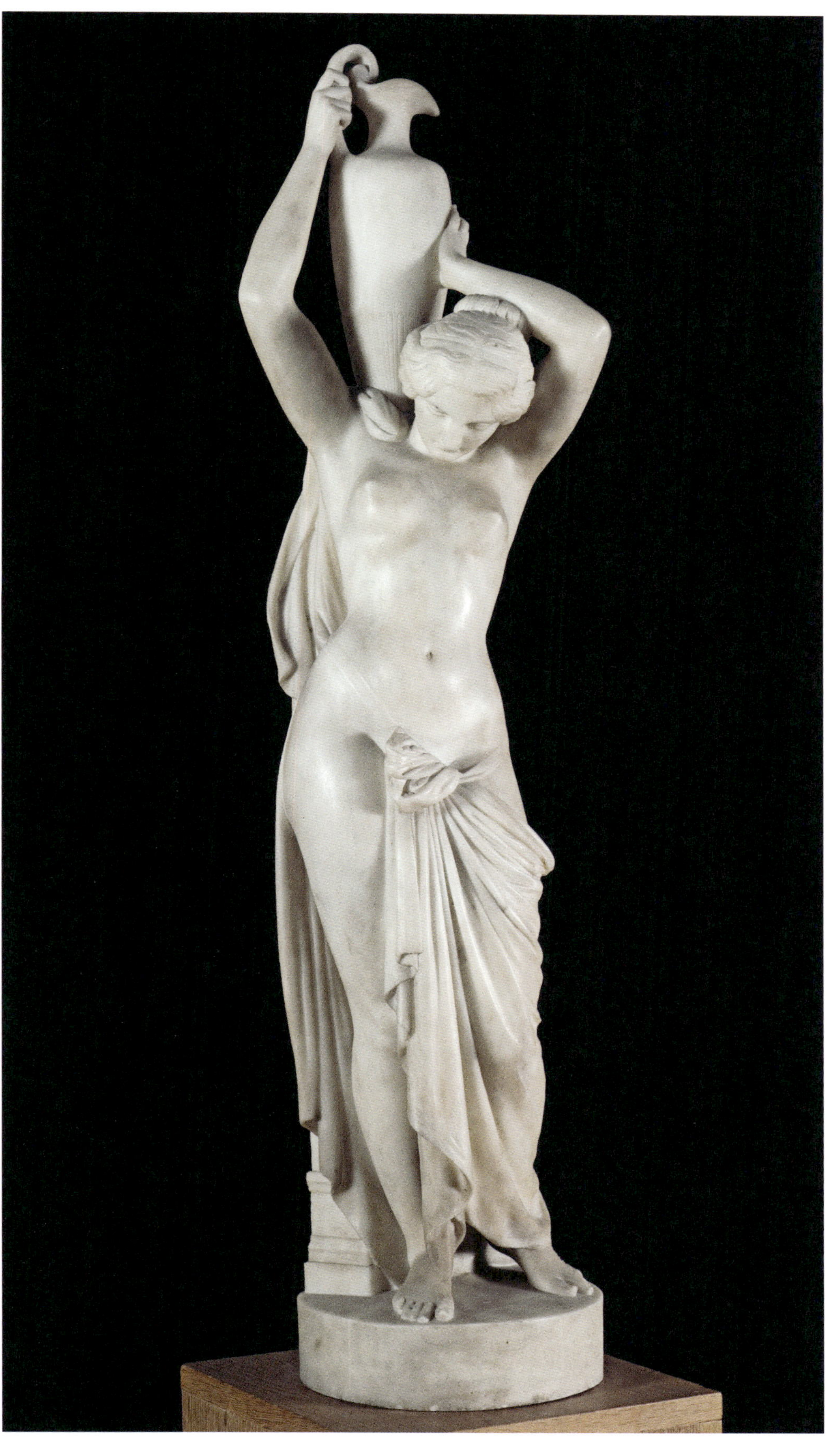

An Impressionist relief? –
Paul Gauguin's *La Toilette*

"One rarely sees Impressionist sculpture!" – This is what an astonished critic called out at the sight of Paul Gauguin's *La Toilette* in the eighth Impressionist exhibition in 1886. Although "around 300 works" were on display in five spaces, the wooden relief stood out from the wealth of paintings, watercolours, drawings and pastels.[1] The decisive factor was probably less the inconspicuous motif of an androgynous[2] nude in profile sitting under a tree and brushing their hair, but rather its implementation as a bas-relief and the circumstance that it was the only sculpture in the exhibition. Unlike the sculptures in the round shown in the previous exhibitions, the carved depiction was not free-standing but hung on the wall between the other exhibits. Yet the raised elements engendered a proximity to the viewer that was more immediate than the paintings or the works on paper. Because, similar to the latter, a relief prescribes viewing from the front, the genre served Edmond Claris, for instance, as a powerful argument against Charles Baudelaire's claim that due to sculpture's indetermination with respect to the viewer's standpoint, it was inferior to painting.[3]

Like the genre of the relief, the material that Gauguin used – wood, in this case from a pear tree – was a crucial subject of the contemporary debate on modern sculpture.[4] The critic Joris-Karl Huysmans in particular advocated its use. In one of his reviews published in 1883, he praised it as steeped in tradition and – with reference to its relatively soft consistency, which allowed its malleable handling – at the same time, as exceptionally suitable for the shaping of contemporary motifs.[5] Yet Gauguin was the only artist who exhibited works out of wood in the Impressionist exhibitions:[6] he had already developed *La Toilette* in 1882, just shortly after the sculptures *La Chanteuse* and *Dame en promenade* (p. 30, figs. 7–8), which he presented in 1881.[7] Camille Pissarro was probably responsible for the decision to integrate this work about four years after its completion into the last Impressionist exhibition. The dedication "à mon ami Pissarro [to my friend Pissarro] / 82 / P. Gauguin" at the right edge next to the figure's back refers to the first owner of the relief.[8] As becomes apparent from the correspondence between the two artists, Pissarro took great pleasure in it,[9] which likely encouraged Gauguin to request it as a loan in 1886.[10]

The fact that *La Toilette* was added to the exhibits at short notice and does not appear in the exhibition catalogue illustrates Gauguin's acute need to present the work in this specific context. He also presented 19 paintings in the same exhibition.[11] The relief fitted into his selection of primarily rural scenes, including one with female bathers, both in terms of format (with its 34.1 by 55 centimetres, it was nearly as large as some of the paintings)[12] as well as motif.[13] The paintings and the relief reflected what was regarded as an Impressionist, everyday subject, often observed *en plein air*. This applies to the majority of the total of 51 works that Gauguin showed in five of the eight exhibitions. However, the formal composition of his paintings with a rigorously structured, characteristic brush stroke and strongly contoured planes justifiably gave rise to discussions about whether his assignment to Impressionism was warranted.[14] Yet with six sculptures, besides Ottin, he was indisputably the most prominent sculptor in the Impressionist exhibitions, at least in terms of quantity.

Although prior to that Gauguin was primarily known as a painter, he debuted in the fourth Impressionist exhibition with a marble bust (p. 28, fig. 5). This would have anticipatory character for his oeuvre to the extent that sculpture was to continuously gain importance in it.[15] He frequently moved at the threshold to handicrafts and produced elaborately decorated pieces of furniture as well as ceramic vessels. *La Toilette* illustrates his approach, according to which the results achieved in different media were to be seen as a unity.[16] Hence the relief served as a reference for a copy that he – prepared by means of a squared charcoal study – applied in glazed barbotine to a stoneware jardinière following the Impressionist exhibition.[17] He transferred a depiction of a Breton shepherdess that he had previously realised as a painting to its other long side, by which he later shifted the site-independent motif from *La Toilette* in relation to a region in which he would not begin sojourning until the summer of 1886. Furthermore, it prompted a comparison with the folkloric polychromatic reliefs that he admired there.[18]

La Toilette is exemplary for the cross-genre working process of many of the artists who participated in the Impressionist exhibitions; on the material level, the sum of Gauguin's sculptural contributions reflects the pleasure in experimentation that contemporary critics rated as the characteristic feature of Impressionist sculpture. — FR

> "One rarely
> sees Impressionist
> sculpture!"
>
> Anonymous, 1886

---

1 "Cette année, l'exposition des impressionnistes – la huitième en date – est installée 1, rue Laffitte, dans les salons du second étage. Cinq salles lui sont réservées et montrent, en tout, environ trois cents œuvres: peinture à l'huile, aquarelles, dessins au noir, pastels – ceux-ci en grand nombre; – on y remarque même un bas-relief en bois sculpté! De la sculpture impressionniste, cela ne s'est pas vu souvent!" Anonymous 1886; quoted in: Berson 1996, vol. 1, p. 471.

2 Félix Fénéon recognised a woman; Fénéon 1886. Christopher Gray described the figure as a young girl; Gray 1963, p. 156, no. 44. However, the child's body could also be that of a boy.

3 Claris 1902a (German), pp. 31–32; see Albert Bartholomé, in: ibid., p. 32. Julius Meier-Graefe referred to the remark by Bartholomé quoted by Claris; Meier-Graefe 1904, vol. 1, pp. 309–310. Medardo Rosso and Auguste Rodin used other strategies for the purpose of refuting Baudelaire's argument; see cat. 64–69, 80–84.

4 See Scott 1998, esp. p. 107.

5 See Huysmans 1883a, pp. 229–230; see also the essay by Fabienne Ruppen in this catalogue, pp. 24–34, esp. p. 30.

6 On the importance of wood in Gauguin's oeuvre, see, for example, Childs 2014, esp. pp. 37–39; Hargrove 2007, esp. p. 75; Fonsmark 2005a, esp. p. 128.

7 On these two sculptures, see the essay by Fabienne Ruppen in this catalogue, pp. 24–34, esp. p. 30.

8 For a detailed photograph of the dedication, see Gray 1963, p. 119.

9 This proceeds from Gauguin's thanks for Pissarro's praise; see the letter from Paul Gauguin to Camille Pissarro, 9 November 1882, in Gauguin 1984, pp. 35–36, no. 29.

Cat.3 Paul Gauguin, *La Toilette*, 1882; pear wood, 34.1 × 55 × 7 cm;
signed: "à mon ami Pissarro / 82 / P. Gauguin";
Musée d'Art moderne et contemporain de Strasbourg, inv. no. 55.998.6.1

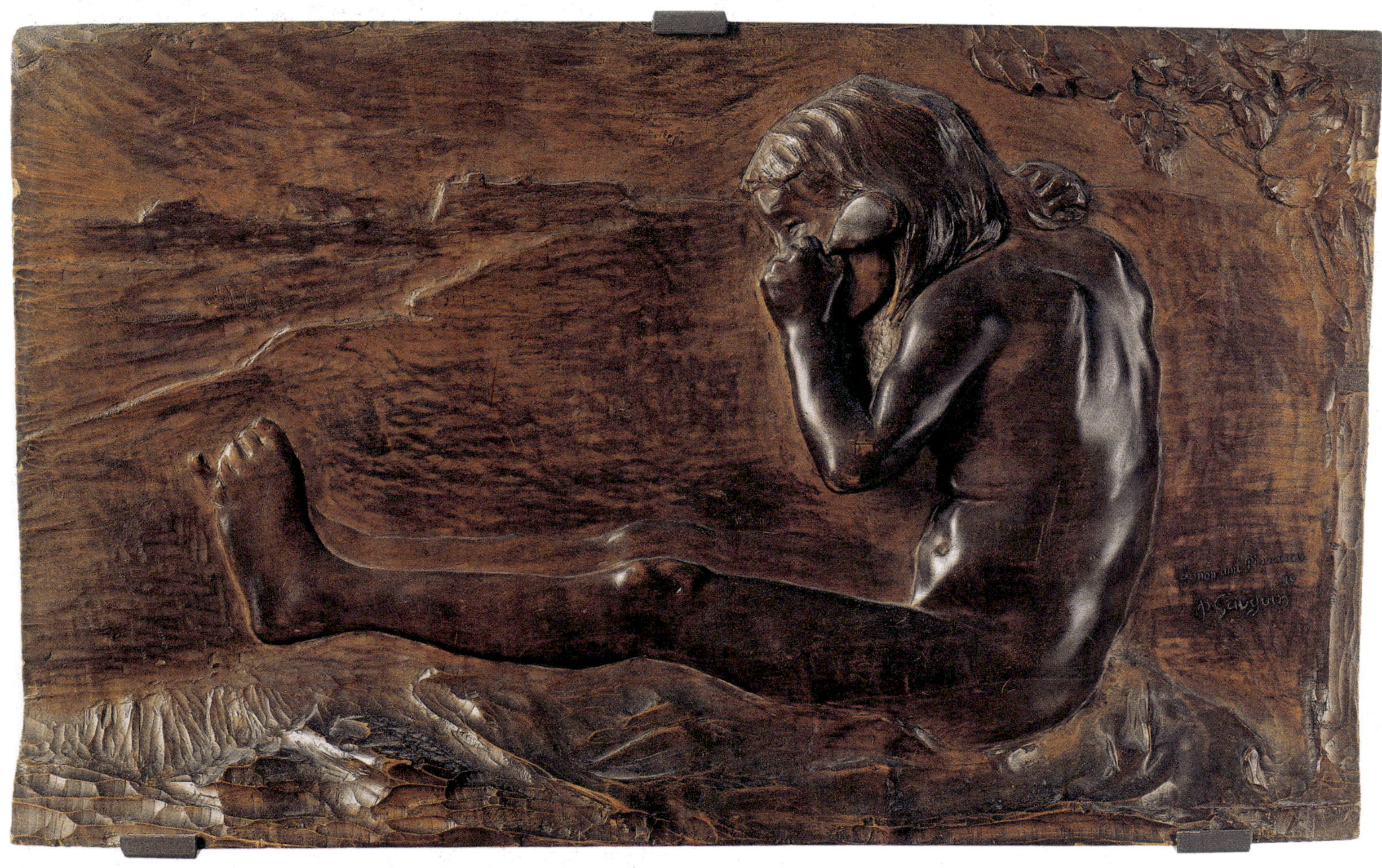

Cat.3

10 "Vous serez bien aimable quand vous enverrez vos tableaux à l'Exposition d'y ajouter le petit bas-relief en bois que vous avez de moi […]. Je désire l'exposer à moins que vous n'y trouviez inconvénient […]." Letter from Paul Gauguin to Camille Pissarro, early May 1886, in ibid., p. 124, no. 96.
11 See Berson 1996, vol. 2, pp. 242–244. For a discussion of these paintings as well as the arrangement and quality of Gauguin's choice of works, see Brettell 2005a.
12 See no. 59, "Falaises", for which Berson specifies dimensions of 38 × 56 cm; Berson 1996, vol. 2, p. 244.
13 See no. 53, "Les baigneuses".
14 For detailed information on this subject, see exh. cat. Copenhagen/Fort Worth 2005.
15 On the various phases of Gauguin's production of sculptures, see Childs 2014, esp. pp. 37–38.
16 "Examinez les [les tableaux, the author] attentivement en même temps que le bois que la céramique. Vous verrez que tout celà se tient ensemble." Letter from Paul Gauguin to Théo van Gogh, 20 or 21 January 1889; in Gauguin 1983, pp. 148–175, no. 22, esp. p. 159 (underlining in the original).
17 On this jardinière and its dating, see Gray 1963, 156–157, no. 44. On the work's genesis, see Fonsmark 2005c. For an illustration of the study, see ibid., p. 288, fig. 219. On the motifs, see exh. cat. Copenhagen/Fort Worth 2005, pp. 298–301, no. 58 (Anne-Birgitte Fonsmark).
18 See Hammacher 1973, p. 84.

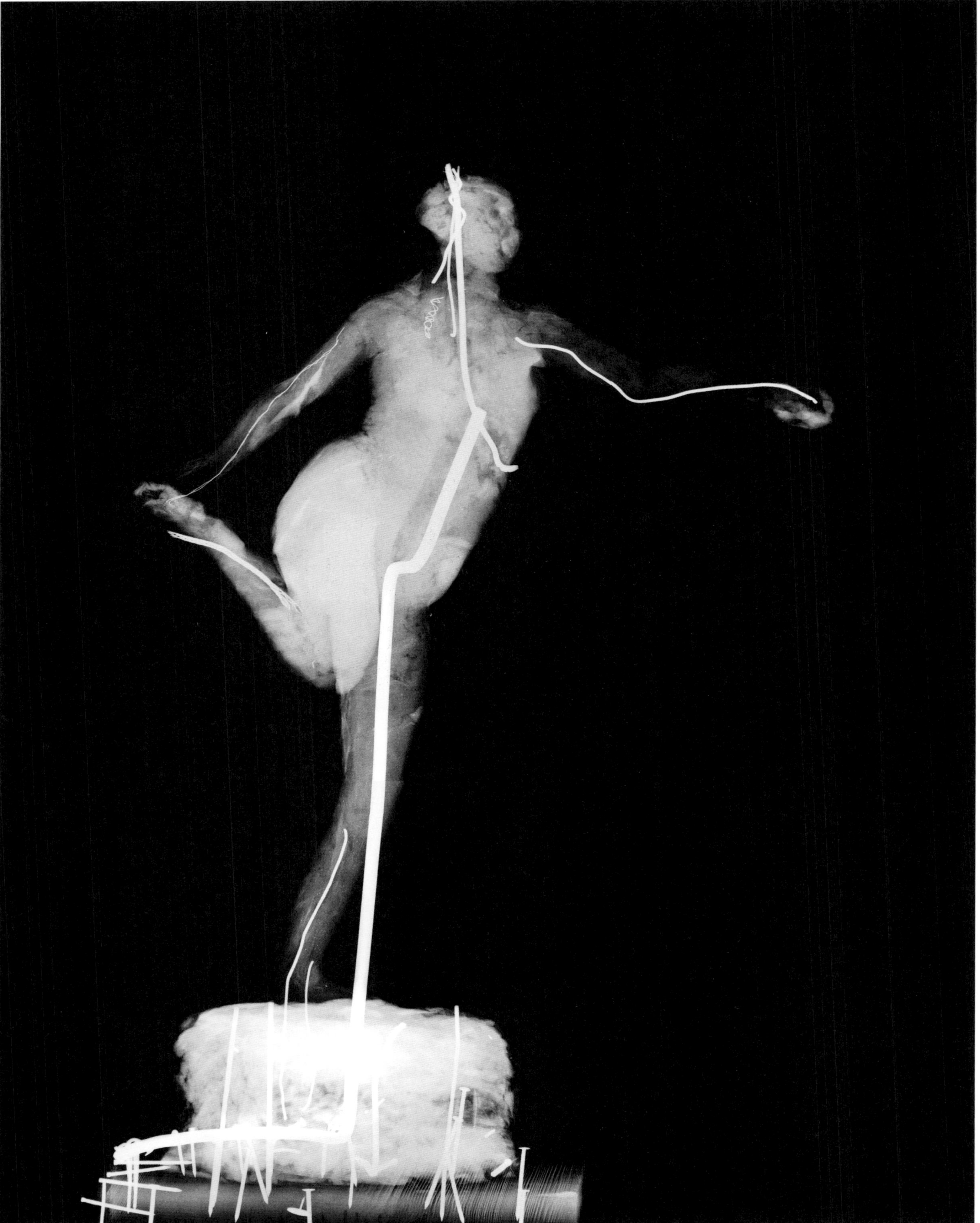

Edgar Degas

Edgar Degas

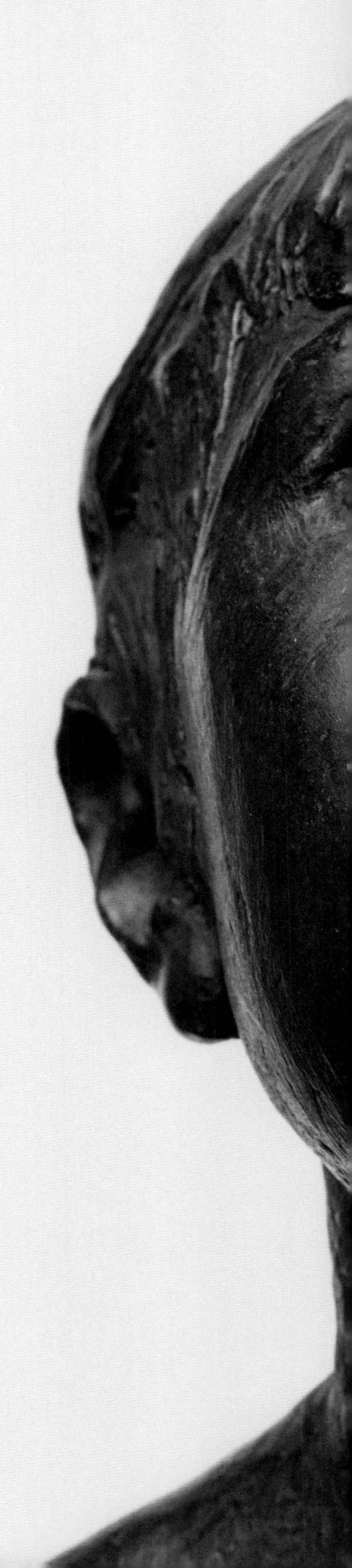

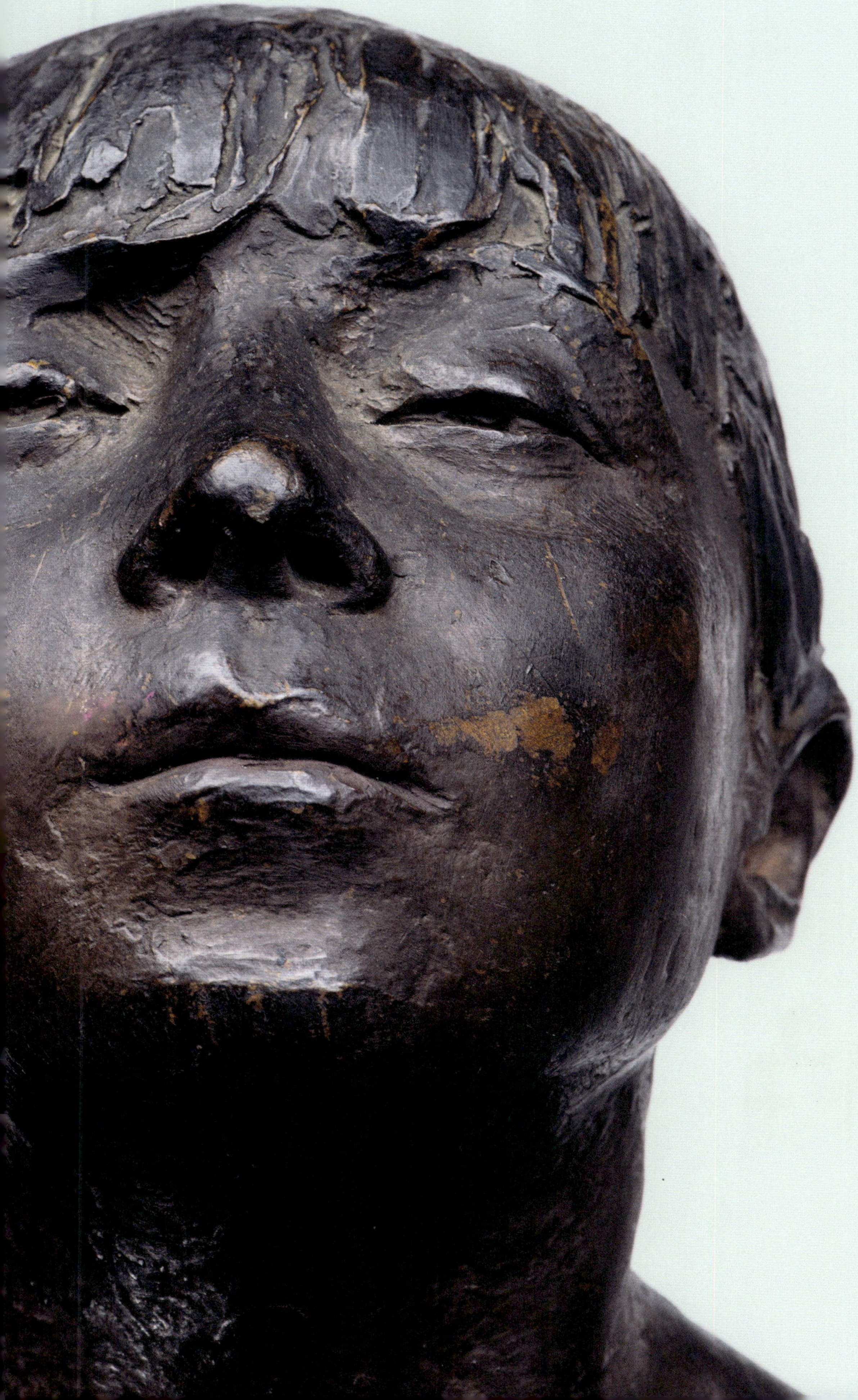

Edgar Degas

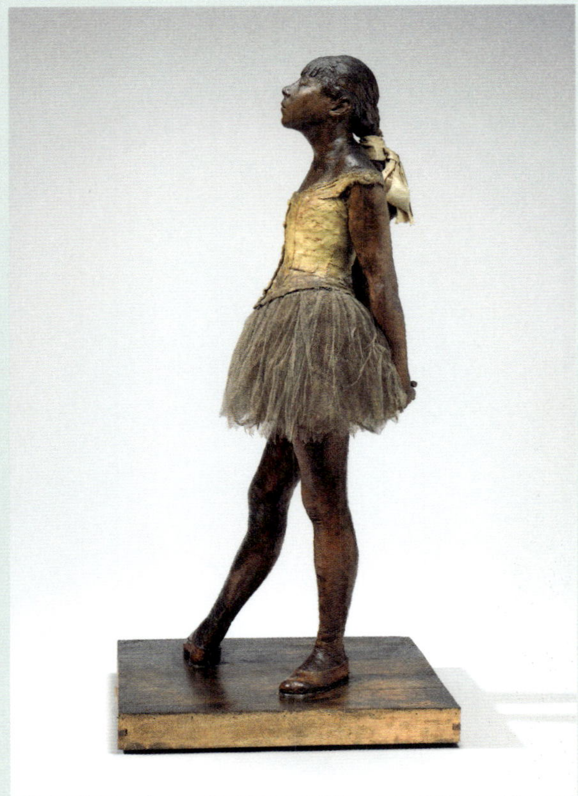

1 Edgar Degas, *Little Dancer Aged Fourteen*, 1878/1879–1881, pigmented beeswax, clay, metal armature, rope, paintbrushes, human hair, silk and linen ribbon, cotton faille bodice, cotton and silk tutu, linen slippers on wooden base, 94.4 × 35 × 35.8 cm, National Gallery of Art, Washington D.C.

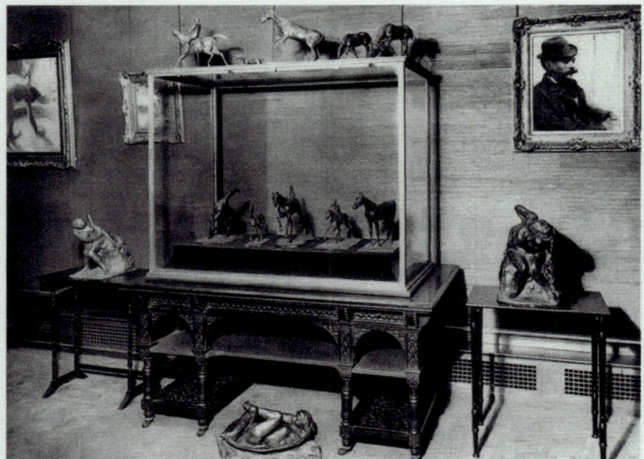

2 First exhibition of bronzes by Degas at the Durand-Ruel Gallery, New York, 6–27 December 1922

Alexander Eiling

"Now more than ever I feel the need to convey my impressions of form through sculpture"[1]

Edgar Degas's sculptures and their role in his working process

In 1931, the French journalist and critic François Thiébault-Sisson published an article in the magazine *Le Temps* describing his encounter with Edgar Degas in Clermont-Ferrand in August of 1897.[2] Blending narrative passages with interview sequences recalled from distant memory, the text – entitled "Degas sculpteur raconté par lui-même" (Degas, the Sculptor, Tells His Own Story) – focuses exclusively on the role played by sculpture in the artist's working process. This is remarkable in that, apart from the scandalous presentation of his *Little Dancer Aged Fourteen* (fig. 1; also see cat. 4) in the sixth Impressionist exhibition in 1881, Degas had never shown a sculpture in public.[3] The majority of his contemporaries regarded him as a chronicler of modern Parisian life whose oeuvre consisted primarily of oil paintings, pastels and drawings as well as the products of his experiments in printmaking.[4] Sculpture hardly figured in the perception of his work. After his death in 1917, however, his heirs found 150 small-scale sculptures in his studio, evidently executed by the artist over a period of several decades. To make them, he had worked primarily with wax but also with a wide range of other materials. The heirs selected approximately half of these objects for bronze casts, which they had produced from 1919 onwards in the foundry of Adrien-Aurélien Hébrard in Paris. Thiébault-Sisson's article was thus published at a point in time when the bronzes had already long awakened international interest in the previously unknown sculptural portion of Degas's oeuvre. A determined sales campaign, complete with exhibitions[5] (fig. 2) and articles in newspapers[6] and even fashion magazines[7] (fig. 3), had contributed substantially to this public awareness. The strategy was crowned with success: a major exhibition of Degas's bronzes opened at the Paris Musée de l'Orangerie in July 1931 after the French state had purchased an entire set of them for the Louvre.[8] Thiébault-Sisson could thus be sure of an audience for his recollections, especially considering the rapidly increasing perception of Degas as an artist of national importance, but also in view of the top prices his works were fetching on the art market.[9]

   As the bronzes made their way into a growing number of collections following their initial presentation in 1921, the role of sculpture in Degas's oeuvre became a frequent topic of discussion. What is more, in the effort to comprehend the complex interrelationships between his two- and his three-dimensional techniques, numerous exhibitions were devoted to this aspect of his art.[10] The Städel project considers Degas's sculptures from a specific point of view – the question as to the existence of "Impressionist sculpture". This appears worthy of discussion

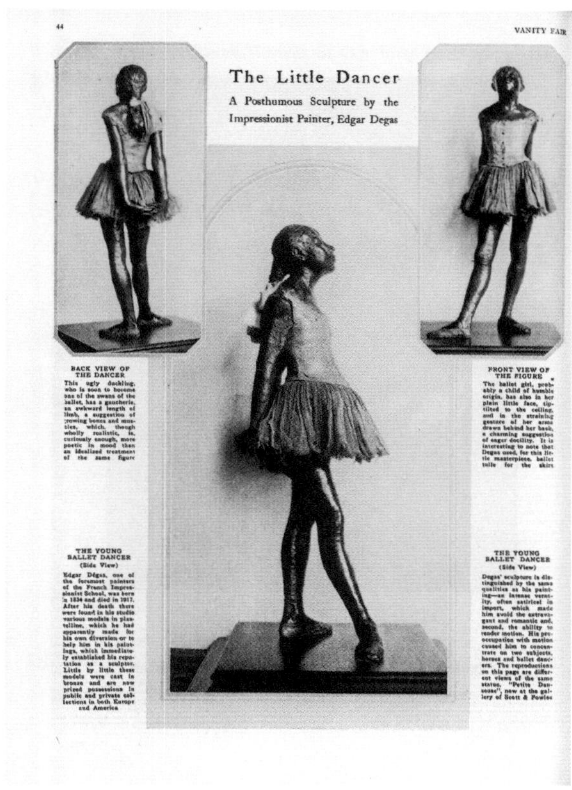

3 "The Little Dancer: A Posthumous Sculpture by the Impressionist Painter, Edgar Degas", from *Vanity Fair* (March 1925), p. 44

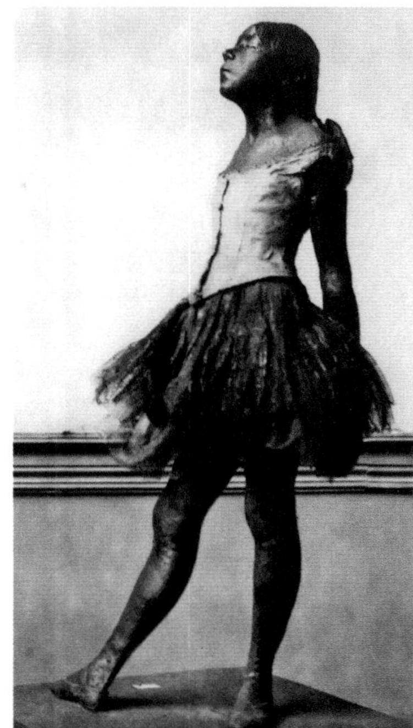

4 Edgar Degas, *Little Dancer Aged Fourteen*, photograph by Gauthier, 1917/18, Musée d'Orsay, Paris

in relation to Degas because, even if he is considered one of the Impressionist spearheads, his extremely constructive and methodical manner of working in two-dimensional mediums has little to do with the spontaneity or the attempt to capture fleeting moments generally attributed to Impressionism. Before we can draw any conclusions about Degas's classification as a potentially "Impressionist sculptor", we must therefore take a closer look at his sculptural working process, motifs and production methods.

The sculptures

Altogether 70 original Degas sculptures have come down to us, all of which bear a direct connection to the groups of motifs he favoured throughout his career: dancers, bathers and boudoir scenes, horses and jockeys. There are also three portrait busts,[11] a depiction of a schoolgirl with a hat and bag[12] and a relief scene of people picking apples.[13] With few exceptions, the figures appear as nudes without pronounced facial features, their limbs summarily conceived. The artist presumably executed them between the 1860s and 1911, and hardly one of them can be dated exactly. Their heights range from about eight centimetres[14] to just under one metre.[15] It cannot be ruled out that Degas also made sculptures of other motifs. A large proportion of the three-dimensional works found in the studio were evidently in such poor condition that only 80 of them were inventoried – the rest not being deemed worthy of preservation.[16] To document these sculptures, the heirs engaged the services of a photographer by the name of Gauthier (his first name is unknown), whose views of them provide important information on their original appearance (fig. 4).[17] The 72 photographs taken in December 1917 and January 1918 show 55 of the sculptures found in the studio from various angles. Some 30 of the inventoried works were evidently not photographically documented.

In 1956, the collector Paul Mellon purchased all of the artist's surviving sculptures en bloc and distributed them among several museums in the years that followed. The National Gallery in Washington received the lion's share of 52 works, followed by the Virginia Museum of Fine Arts, Richmond (9), the Musée d'Orsay, Paris (5), the Fitzwilliam Museum, Cambridge (3), and finally the Yale University Art Gallery, New Haven (1). The National Gallery had in-depth technical investigations of the material carried out and published the results in a comprehensive study in 2010.[18] Those findings enable us to come to reliable conclusions about Degas's sculptural oeuvre and his unconventional working manner. Every one of his works merits individual consideration, as – being an artist who loved to experiment – he did not follow any fixed procedure, and moreover took great liberties in combining different materials.

The *Little Dancer Aged Fourteen* (fig. 1) exhibits the widest range of materials. Degas had developed it over a period of several years in preliminary drawings and a sculptural study (p. 58, figs. 1–2)[19] before presenting it to the public for the first time in 1881. It consists for the most part of pigmented beeswax, which the artist formed over an armature he had constructed himself from iron, wire, wood, paintbrushes, rope and clay.[20] He took the greatest pains to create as realistic an impression as possible, using a wig made of human hair as well as a bodice, a tutu and ballet shoes. The figure's strikingly real presence sparked a tremendous wave of criticism. People considered it a downright insult because the artist had dared to portray an "ordinary dancer" from the Paris opera, in the public perception a place of vice and debauchery. His dancer was equated with a prostitute, and the critics thought of her appearance as a monument to decadence, an expression of debility or criminal tendencies and under no circumstances worthy of artistic depiction. The purpose of sculpture, as taught by the art academy and demanded by the conservative public, was to idealise and super-elevate. Degas, however, had negated that purpose.

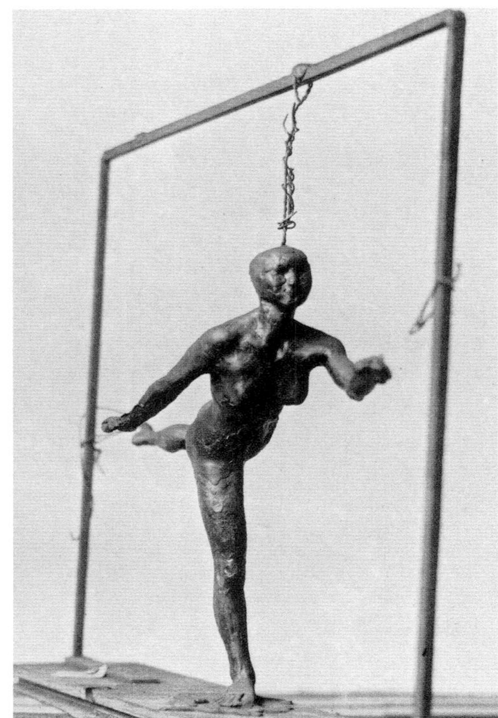

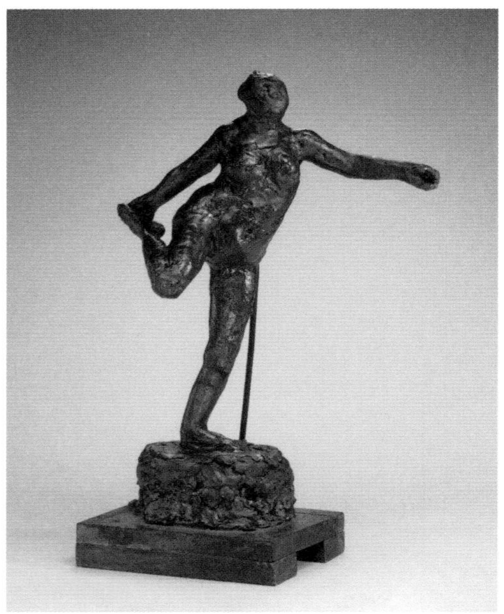

5 Edgar Degas, *Arabesque over the Right Leg, Left Arm in Front*, photograph by Gauthier, 1917/18, Musée d'Orsay, Paris

6 Edgar Degas, *Dancer Holding Her Right Foot in Her Right Hand*, possibly 1900/11, pigmented beeswax, plastiline, metal armature on wooden base, 53.1 × 14.5 × 38.5 cm, National Gallery of Art, Washington D.C.

It was in part his choice of wax that triggered this response: as the material most closely resembling human skin, wax was not by coincidence the fundamental building block of the waxworks that came into fashion in late nineteenth-century Europe (for example, Madame Tussauds in London and the Musée Grévin in Paris). Despite the long tradition of wax sculpture – ultimately going back to antiquity and culminating in the seventeenth and eighteenth centuries in portraits of absolutist rulers – the use of the material in Degas's time was considered unconventional and indecent. It was accepted in the nineteenth century for miniature works or models for anatomical study, but not for the production of an autonomous sculpture in the artistic context.[21] Wax evokes a sense of vitality somehow tinged with mortality, and in those days had therefore come to be associated more strongly with the negative aspects of corporality, being denied any and all aesthetic value in the process.[22] In an article entitled "Grammaire des arts du dessin" published in 1865, for example, Charles Blanc had described polychrome wax sculptures as "false cadavers".[23] The rejection of wax in the academic context may be one reason why several avant-gardists (among them Gustave Moreau and Medardo Rosso) and their circles increasingly favoured its use.[24] And whereas it appealed to artists working in the realist mode on account of its mimetic qualities, those seeking to capture movement and convey immediacy appreciated it for its easy workability and manipulatable consistency.[25]

The surface of the *Little Dancer Aged Fourteen* is for the most part very smooth and exhibits hardly any traces of the production process. In this respect, it is difficult to reconcile with our present-day conception of "Impressionism", whose defining characteristics are sketchiness and ephemerality. What we have here, quite to the contrary, is a hyperrealistic sculpture frozen in posed statuesqueness.[26] Nevertheless, it was with reference to this figure that the writer and theatre critic Jules Claretie first fielded the term "Impressionist sculptor" – a species of artist whose emergence, however, he feared more than welcomed: "Here is the originality of this Exposition des Indépendants – they are starting to affirm their independence in the form of sculpture. Colour was not enough. They must have wax or plaster or bronze. *Good God*! We are going to see *Impressionist* sculptors!"[27]

Degas's small-scale sculptures, on the other hand – which were reserved for the privacy of his studio and known only to a few friends and colleagues – are distinctly more "Impressionist" in character than the *Little Dancer Aged Fourteen*. In most cases, a wooden board (usually waste wood such as pieces of plank flooring) served as the base on which an armature was mounted. Radiographic examinations have shown that the artist far preferred constructions he made himself out of wire over the prefabricated ones available in artists' supply shops, which he used only rarely.[28] His dancers' fragile poses, with their raised or outstretched legs and arms, sometimes required an external structure for stability, likewise mounted on the wooden base (fig. 5). These were wires or rods and in some cases frame-like constructions from which the figures were literally suspended.

Once the artist had fashioned the armature, he proceeded by forming the sculpture around it. As in the case of his *Little Dancer Aged Fourteen*, he used a wide range of different materials for this purpose: in addition to beeswax and clay, we also encounter wood, plaster, textiles, ropes, corks from wine bottles, porcelain and modelling compounds that were new at the time, for example plastiline, whose high fat and sulphur content protected it from drying out and kept it soft longer, giving the artist more time to process it. Waxes and modelling compounds could be purchased ready to use and already dyed in different colours from artists' supply shops (such as Sennelier or Maison Hutant). Nevertheless, Degas evidently often coloured his materials himself. In correspondence with the pigments he used to that end, his sculptures range from shades of black and brown to reds and even

7   Edgar Degas, *Dancer Holding Her Right Foot in Her Right Hand*, photograph by Gauthier, 1917/18, Musée d'Orsay, Paris

8   Radiograph of Edgar Degas's wax sculpture *Dancer Holding Her Right Foot in Her Right Hand*, National Gallery of Art, Washington D.C.

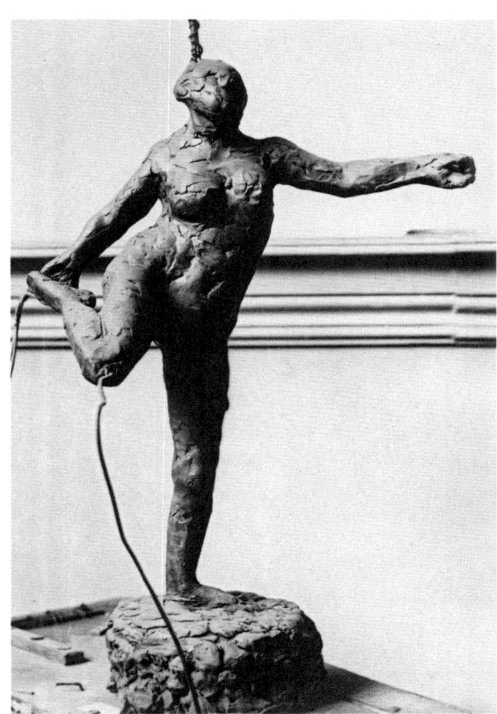

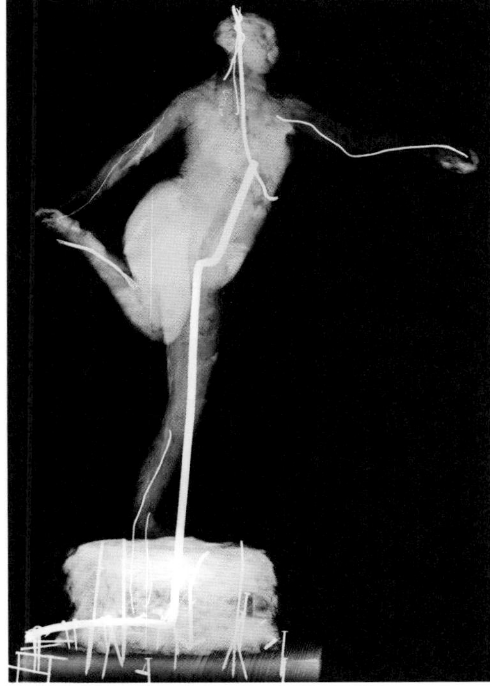

greens. In some cases, he applied paint to the surface. He moreover added *objets trouvés* (found objects) – for example, strips of metal[29] or a ceramic basin[30] – to his compositions. When in the literature and the following deliberations there is talk of "the waxes", it is to be understood as a generic term referring to figures made of a complex composite of materials, as in fact not one of Degas's surviving sculptures consists solely of wax.

From wax to bronze

In the case of the *Dancer Holding Her Right Foot in Her Right Hand* (fig. 6), of which there is a bronze cast in the Städel collection (cat. 16), examinations have shown that the artist fashioned the original figure from pigmented beeswax, which he formed over a brownish-green plastiline core.[31] He made the oval base purely of wax, in which, again, numerous traces of pigment were detected. The variations in the materials' content brought about different surface consistencies. The figure possesses a shiny, sticky texture that we can presumably attribute to the plastiline, whose fatty components eventually seeped through to the outside. The base made entirely of beeswax nevertheless has a matt appearance. The dancer exhibits clear traces of the production process. Little balls of the modelling compound are discernible: these the artist added step by step to the surface, flattening and pressing them into the desired form as he worked. He had made them malleable beforehand with the warmth of his hand or, where necessary, over a flame. The more detailed areas contrast with those he shaped only fragmentarily. There are finished and unfinished sections, smooth ones and rough ones. And we constantly encounter the imprints of Degas's fingers, which provide the viewer insights into the creative process. From the purely formal point of view, his sketchy modelling style follows the tradition of the *bozzetti* (*bozzetto* being Italian for sketch or design): three-dimensional sketches executed by artists from the Renaissance onward as smaller-scale preliminary studies for later sculptures. With regard to function, however, Degas's small figures differed from the *bozzetti* in that, with very few exceptions, he evidently had no intention of subsequently developing larger sculptures from them.

The photographs taken in Degas's studio in 1917/18 provide evidence that in order to stabilise the figure, the artist used wire rods fixed to its right knee and foot and, by means of a mounting on the head, moreover suspended it from a structure not visible in the photograph (fig. 7). Apart from a few vestiges, the wires are no longer visible in the sculpture's current state. Today a massive supporting rod, inserted parallel to the standing leg and anchored in the interior of the left hip (fig. 8) (as the X-ray image shows), lends the figure stability. The discrepancy between the historical photographs and the sculpture's present-day appearance reveals that it was thoroughly revised after Degas's death. The sculptor Albert Bartholomé, a close friend of the artist's, may have been responsible for the changes. He had been called in by some of the heirs to inspect the studio estate. While it is true that, in a letter to Degas's brother René, Bartholomé had insisted on the inalterability of the sculptures,[32] his involvement appears certain, particularly in view of the fact that the artist's dealer Paul Durand-Ruel entrusted him with the objects' care.[33] On the one hand, the heirs and the art dealers concerned with the marketing of the casts were well aware that interventions of too strong a nature might decrease the value of Degas's works. On the other hand, the state of the sculptures made conservation and stabilisation measures indispensable. In February 1918, for example, Paul Durand-Ruel's son Joseph wrote to his brother Georges: "The waxes are in a very bad condition and are crumbling into dust; I fear that if they are left in the studio again during the summer, there will be nothing remaining."[34] Among the descriptions of this deplorable situation there is also one referring to

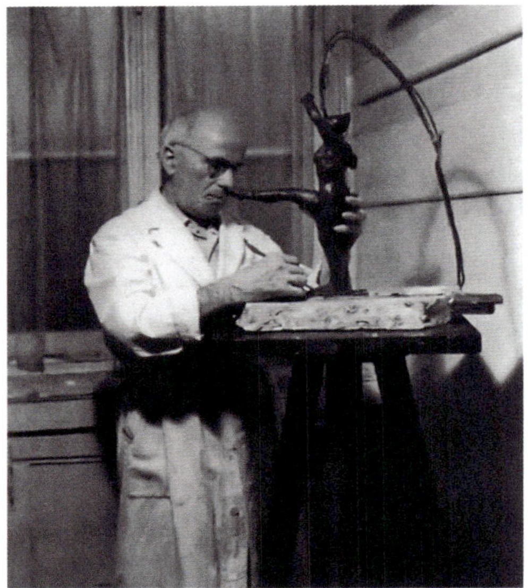

9 Albino Palazzolo with the original wax sculpture *Dancer, Fourth Position Front, on the Left Leg*, photograph, 1950s, from *Dancer Magazine* (January 1956)

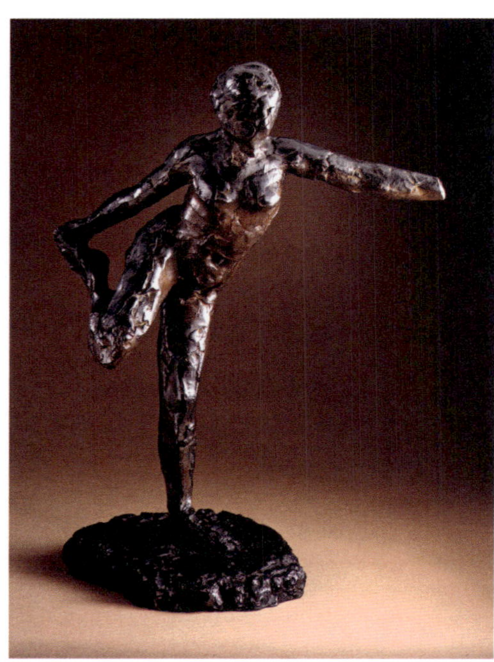

10 Edgar Degas, *Dancer Holding Her Right Foot in Her Right Hand*, possibly 1900/11, cast 1919–1921 (modèle cast), bronze, 52.1 × 36 × 21.6 cm, Norton Simon Art Foundation, Pasadena

Degas's *Little Dancer Aged Fourteen,* which was reportedly in severely damaged condition when it was discovered after the artist's death. In his monograph on Degas published in 1918/19, Paul Lafond recalls that the sculpture's arms had come off the body and were lying at its feet.[35] It is more likely, however, that the figure was broken between the upper body and the upper arms: the break line is visible in the photographs taken by Gauthier (fig. 4) and also left its mark on the later bronze cast.

Other changes indisputably came about in preparation for casting the figures in bronze, a task the heirs had entrusted to the experienced Hébrard foundry and its production director Albino Palazzolo.[36] It was long thought that the small-scale sculptures had been destroyed when the bronze casts were produced. Actually, however, they were kept in the foundry storage room and "rediscovered" in the 1950s. Before their sale to the M. Knoedler & Co. Gallery in New York in 1955, they underwent yet another round of interventions. A photo shows Palazzolo – who had already been responsible for the first casts – at work on the *Dancer, Fourth Position Front, on the Left Leg,*[37] which still exhibits parts of the exterior armature (fig. 9). At the time, Palazzolo not only smoothed the sculpture's surfaces and patched cracks, but also replaced the extensive exterior constructions with less conspicuous supports.

The multiple revisions of the sculptures in the decades following Degas's death led to an odd situation: with regard to the surfaces, the figures' early bronze casts provide clearer information about their original appearance than the 'originals' in their present-day state. The so-called "*modèle* casts" – the only ones to have been cast directly from the moulds taken of the waxes (fig. 10) – come the closest to the original state. To protect Degas's sculptures from damage, it was necessary to begin by taking negative forms of them.[38] To this end, they were coated with shellac and a thin layer of clay before being encased in plaster. After the plaster had dried, the mould could be cut into two halves and the clay removed. Then the original sculpture was returned to the plaster mould and gelatine poured in to fill the space initially taken up by the clay. After drying, the layer of gelatine was carefully removed from the figure and returned to the plaster cast. Now the caster poured molten beeswax into the gelatine mould, thus producing a wax "copy" of the original sculpture which served as the basis for making a metal cast – the *modèle* cast – by the so-called lost-wax method. Each wax model could be used for one cast only, because it got "lost" in the production process. Hence the French term for the technique, *cire perdue,* of which the English is a literal translation.[39]

In order to avoid having to revert to the Degas original and make a new wax copy for every bronze cast, the founders produced the sculpture editions from the *modèle* casts now in the collection of the Norton Simon Museum in Pasadena.[40] These are the versions most closely resembling Degas's sculptures; all other casts, including the one in the Städel Museum collection (cat. 16), were made in moulds taken from these *modèle* casts.[41] The bronzes of the editions were patinated using different compounds to create different hues. In this respect, the figures vary from one to the next and, in some cases, an effort was made to reproduce the nuanced colouration of the wax originals.[42]

The contract between the heirs and Hébrard was set out in relatively general terms and contains no information about the total number of waxes that passed into the possession of the foundry.[43] It limits the edition of each figure to 20, plus one complete set each for the heirs and the Hébrard company. Whereas the edition for the heirs was to be stamped with the number 1, the special mark to be applied to the set for the foundry was not precisely defined. In any case, all of the bronzes were to bear the "Degas" signature stamp.

"When he asked Degas the rather provocative question 'in fact, you are as much a sculptor as a painter, more so perhaps [?]', the answer was a vehement 'never!'"

After François Thiébault-Sisson, 1931

The marks ultimately appearing on the casts adhere to the contract specifications to an extent, but in many respects also depart from them. Hébrard assigned each of the figures except the *Little Dancer Aged Fourteen* and the *Schoolgirl* a motif number (1–72), which was stamped on the casts. Moreover, each of the 20 sets intended for sale received a letter serving as a series number (A–T). Contrary to the contract agreements, the edition for the heirs was stamped "HER.D" (= héritiers Degas) and the set for the foundry "HER". In addition to the motif and series number, all of the bronzes bear the "Degas" signature stamp and the foundry seal ("CIRE / PERDUE / A. A. HEBRARD") set in a rectangle (see cat. 46).[44] The casts were produced approximately between 1919 and 1937 when the Hébrard foundry went bankrupt.

As Hébrard began by casting the small-scale works, it was only in the year 1922 that the production of the *Little Dancer Aged Fourteen* got underway. Here the figure of the *Schoolgirl* represents an exception: it was not cast in bronze until the mid 1950s after the rediscovery of the original waxes.[45] Four of the original sculptures were probably destroyed in the course of producing the *modèle* casts, so that there are more motifs in bronze than in wax today. In many cases, the number of casts on the market differs from that recorded in the Hébrard archives. What is more, markings are frequently encountered that correspond neither to the contract provisions nor to the nomenclature used by Hébrard.[46]

Degas and sculpture: personal testimonials and witnesses to the times

It is more than likely that Degas would not have been happy with the posthumous sale of his figures in the form of bronze casts. According to the recollections of his art dealer Ambroise Vollard, he always opposed the casting of his sculptures in bronze because the latter was a material intended for eternity and such a legacy would have burdened him with too much responsibility.[47] This brings us to the question of what importance Degas attached to his sculptural oeuvre. The above-cited article by Thiébault-Sisson suggests that the artist expressed himself at length on the subject, providing pointers for the classification and assessment of this portion of his work.[48] According to the information given there, Degas began working in the medium of sculpture as far back as the 1860s. For decades, it accompanied his artistic work as a means of better understanding certain mechanisms of movement and ultimately of lending his paintings and drawings more expression and dynamism. The author claims that the artist spoke explicitly of "modelling attempts" ("des essais de modelage") not intended for the public. When he asked Degas the rather provocative question "In fact, you are as much a sculptor as a painter, more so perhaps[?]", the answer was a vehement "Never!" On grounds that they did not attain the degree of completion necessary for the sculptor's profession, the artist had never wanted to sell a single one of the human or animal figures he had modelled in wax. Fortunately for his reputation, he had added, these works would disintegrate over the course of time anyway.[49] It is tempting to believe these remarks, especially because they are so specific. Most of them, however – and this is a fundamental problem of the source material – are based on the memories of third parties and, what is more, were not published until after the artist's death.

The Irish author George Moore wrote one of the few articles about Degas's working manner that was published during the artist's lifetime. It is a report of Moore's visit to the Degas studio in 1890: "There is much decaying sculpture – dancing-girls modelled in red wax, some dressed in muslin skirts, strange dolls – dolls if you will, but dolls modelled by a man of genius."[50] Regarding the description indiscreet, the artist was furious with Moore and never spoke to him again.[51] In fact, his private sphere was so sacred to him that his friends and acquaintances

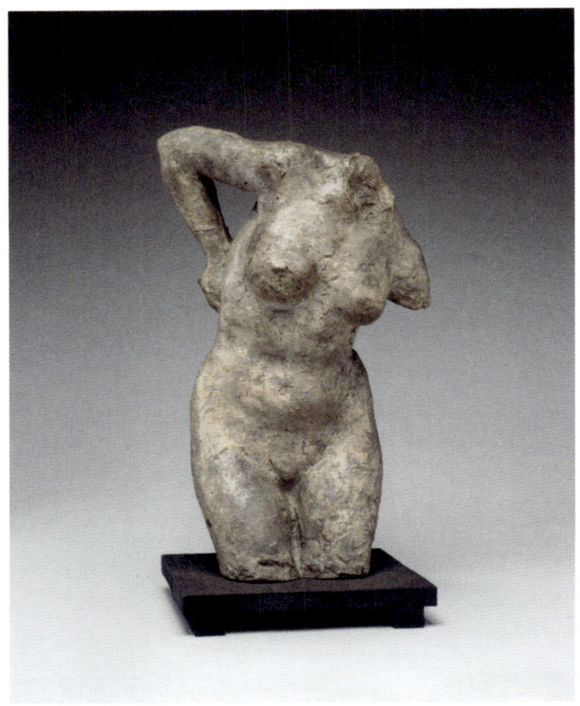

11 Edgar Degas, *Woman Rubbing Her Back with a Sponge (Torso)*,
original modelled 1880s/1890s, plaster cast by 1917,
plaster of Paris, pigments, on wooden base, 44.3 × 27.7 × 17 cm,
National Gallery of Art, Washington D.C.

did not dare make their impressions of it public as long as he was still alive. For example, it was only in 1919 – posthumously, in other words, and in concurrence with the marketing of the bronze casts – that Degas's gallerist Paul Durand-Ruel published his memoirs, which include an account of his client's lifelong concern with sculpture: "Degas has spent a good deal of time, not only in the late years of his life, but for the past fifty years, in modelling in clay [… W]henever I called on Degas, I was almost as sure to find him modelling in clay as painting."[52] According to Durand-Ruel, however, only a fraction of these works survived, as the artist took no measures to preserve them.[53]

Degas's second gallerist, Ambroise Vollard, devoted only a brief chapter to the artist's sculptural ambitions. If we are to believe that description, Degas modelled his sculptures more out of an interest in the working process as such than with the aim of carrying them to completion. Shortly before finishing a sculpture, he had destroyed it right before Vollard's eyes, which must have unsettled the gallerist to such a degree that Degas felt compelled to declare: "You think above all of what it [a work of art] was worth, Vollard, but if you had given me a hatful of diamonds my happiness would not have equalled that which I derived from demolishing [the figure] for the pleasure of starting over."[54] Degas presented a number of his sculptural endeavours in display cases in his studio, but was evidently interested in neither their longevity nor their saleability. He regarded the small objects as a private, perishable medium and firmly insisted that they were not to influence the public perception of his art.

There is evidence, however, that he was interested in the preservation of his sculptures in the medium term, so that they could serve him as study material. As Paul-André Lemoisne recalled in 1919, the artist had formed certain figures first in clay, then in plastiline, and finally in wax, because the two first-named materials had not proven durable enough.[55] He moreover engaged the help of a professional to have at least three of his works cast in plaster (fig. 11) and put the results on display in his dining room.[56] As already mentioned, Degas seems to have shied away from having his sculptures cast in bronze because this would have created a permanently unchangeable form and the impression of a "finished product". To an artist who was constantly in doubt about – and dissatisfied with – the execution of his works, the thought of a motif in an inalterable state must have been downright unbearable.[57]

Even if Degas never exhibited his sculptures in public again after 1881, their innovative force will not have been lost on artist circles. Their semi-public visibility in his studios seems to have sufficed to impress his friends and fellow artists.[58] Vollard, for example, tells of a conversation with Pierre-Auguste Renoir that – if it really happened – sheds remarkable light on the perception of Degas as a sculptor. As the report has it, Renoir praised the work of a contemporary sculptor who could compete with the old masters. Vollard assumed he was talking about Auguste Rodin, but Renoir vehemently repudiated: "Who said anything about Rodin? Why, Degas is the greatest living sculptor!"[59]

There is something decidedly ambiguous about Degas's relationship to sculpture, particularly in his communication with the outside world on the subject. In an allusion to his rapidly diminishing eyesight, he is said to have referred to his sculptural work contemptuously as "a blindman's craft" ("métier d'aveugle").[60] He thus laid a false trail by suggesting that his sculptural activities were a phenomenon of his late phase, a kind of stopgap solution.[61] In fact, he seems to have made a habit of belittling his sculptural ambitions. One reason may have been that there were quite a number of academic sculptors (including Joseph Cuvelier, Henri Chapu, Aimé-Jules Dalou and not least of all the aforementioned Albert Bartholomé) among his friends, whereas he himself had not enjoyed classical training in this medium.[62] Degas the perfectionist presumably did not want to show these friends

"This devil of a fellow wants to do sculpture, but he doesn't want to submit to the laws of that medium."

Albert Bartholomé, undated

any weakness, so he played down his sculptural oeuvre. At the same time, as an artist guided strongly by the sense of touch and obsessed with surfaces throughout his career, he obviously took great pleasure in modelling, not only towards the end of his life but over the course of many decades. Here his autodidactic approach even worked to his advantage, because he could go about forming his figures in unconventional materials and unburdened by academic norms – modernising the medium of sculpture in the process. Clearly exasperated, Bartholomé summed up Degas's single-mindedness with regard to his maverick techniques and methods as follows: "This devil of a fellow wants to do sculpture, but he doesn't want to submit to the laws of that medium."[63]

The role of sculpture in Degas's working process

Degas's three-dimensional figures served him as aids in gaining a better understanding of movement processes. Such reassurance proved particularly useful in his study of the complex gaits of horses (cat. 43–47) as well as the frequently recurring poses of ballet dancers (cat. 8–13, 14–17, 19–20, 24) which, to his mind, represented the human equivalent to his capricious depictions of animals. The unconventional poses of his bathers, with their conspicuously awkward twists and turns (cat. 25, 27–30, 35, 37), also have their counterparts in his sculptures.

Nevertheless, the question arises as to when in the course of the working process he made the figures. Did they precede his two-dimensional paintings, pastels and prints, were they a response to those works, or do they occupy an entirely independent position in his oeuvre? In her deliberations on Degas as a painter/sculptor, Ann Dumas quite rightly points out that there is hardly an artist who proceeded with as little regard for regular, linear progress.[64] His incessant scruples about his works led to constant changes, reversions and, frequently, repetitions of a form conceived long before.[65] It was not unusual for Degas to cease work on a certain motif and resume it years later, a circumstance that continues to pose a challenge to the dating of his art. Scholars have therefore only rarely succeeded in assigning one of Degas's sculptures to a specific stage in the development of a pictorial idea.[66]

It is nonetheless possible to draw a number of fundamental conclusions about Degas's working methods and the purpose his sculptures served. Throughout his career, he was interested in old-masterly techniques, which he studied in depth and transformed creatively.[67] It was not least of all through his investigation of the work of Nicolas Poussin that he was familiar with the method of developing compositions for paintings with the aid of modelled figures.[68] Contemporaries of Degas's such as Ernest Meissonier[69] and Gustave Moreau likewise made use of it. The practice of making sculptures was compatible with Degas's special predilection for out-of-the-ordinary viewing angles and framings. He could contemplate his sculptures from different perspectives, turn them, arrange them next to and in front of one another. This also enabled him to study a complicated pose over an extended period, which would hardly have been possible with a live model.[70] Not one of his sculptured figures possesses a defined or dominant display side.[71] Quite on the contrary, the poses of his dancers and bathers lure us to view them from changing vantage points. Yet we are rewarded for our efforts with ever new, different and suspenseful perspectives and impressions that make the motif fully perceivable only in their entirety.

Degas's almost manically thorough examinations of all the different possible poses of a dancer moreover coincided with a keen interest in the detailed comprehension of sequences of movement that had been sparked – also in artist circles – by the chronophotographs of Eadweard Muybridge (fig. 12), Étienne-Jules Marey and others.[72] In 1881, in the studio of the painter Charles Meissonier,

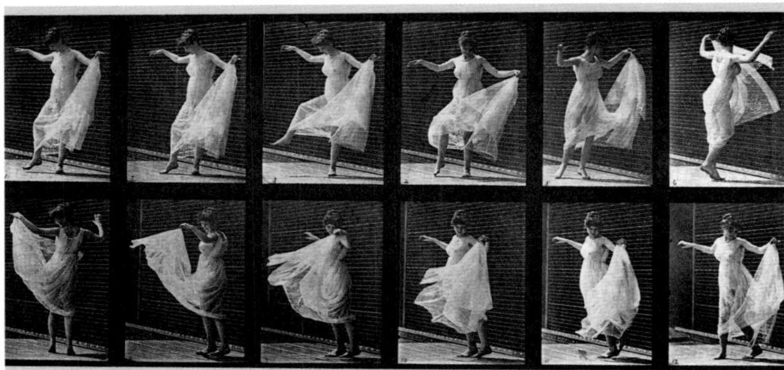

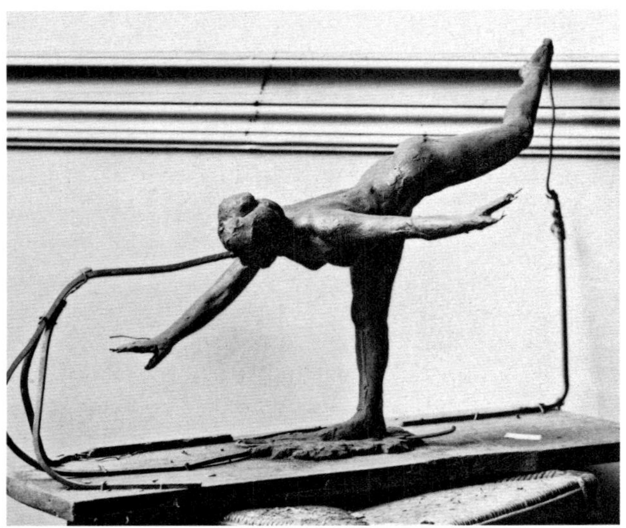

12 Eadweard Muybridge, *Dancing Fancy*, 1887, from *Animal Locomotion* (Muybridge 1887), pl. 187, Sprengel Museum, Hanover

13 Edgar Degas, *Grande Arabesque, Third Time*, photograph by Gauthier, 1917/18, Musée d'Orsay, Paris

Muybridge gave a slide lecture that made him the talk of the town in Paris. Six years later, he brought his photographic studies together in a major publication entitled *Animal Locomotion,* intended to serve as a reference work and aid to painters and sculptors. Degas was fascinated with Muybridge's photos, which he verifiably also used as inspiration for his three-dimensional works (see cat. 48).

In keeping with his penchant for experimentation, Degas made the figures in such a way as to be movable and changeable. Among other things, this explains the exterior support structures from which some of his dancers were suspended in marionette-like manner. The artist evidently changed the poses again and again, a circumstance to which numerous breaks in the armatures testify.[73] Several of the daring, gravity-defying poses would not have been possible without supporting wires – for example, the arabesques (fig. 13; see cat. 12, 13), which appear almost disconcertingly stable in the later bronze casts. The malleable wax, and above all the plastiline, which remained soft enough to form for a longer period, were particularly suitable to satisfying his demand for transformability and moreover lent his sculptures a sketchy, improvised character.

In a further step, Degas also experimented with the shadows cast by the figures, as his friend Walter Sickert recalled: "I remember the last time I was in the studio upstairs in Rue Victor Massé, he showed me a little statuette of a dancer he had on the stocks, and – it was night – he held a candle up, and turned the statuette to show me the succession of shadows cast by its silhouettes on the white sheet."[74] The translation of three-dimensional sculpture into the planarity of the shadow corresponded to Degas's lifelong search for the perfect flow of the line, the perfect contour.[75] In the foreword to an exhibition catalogue on Degas's sculptures, Sickert put this function of the figures in a nutshell: "What is sculpture but a theoretically infinite series of silhouettes?"[76]

Here it becomes evident how closely Degas's sculptural oeuvre was linked to his work in the medium of drawing. All his life, drawing was his great passion, and it forms the nucleus of his multifaceted oeuvre. In addition, sculpture was the logical continuation of drawing with other means, a way of circling around a pictorial idea three-dimensionally (fig. 14) as its form etched itself into his subconscious via the tactile shaping of the modelling compound. Degas explicitly assigned the function of thought to both techniques: "Drawing is a way of thinking, so is modelling."[77] He thus elevated sculpture to the highest level of his artistic hierarchy, side by side with drawing. Both methods mirror a working manner that is based on constant repetition and variation, and that forms one motif while already containing the seed of the next. He executed neither his drawings nor his sculptures spontaneously; neither were subject solely to the fleeting instant. Even if his process of artistic creation was characterised strongly by the great joy he took in experimentation, it was always extremely controlled and highly constructed. His affiliation with the Impressionists was questioned again and again, particularly in view of the fact that the artist himself opposed the term "Impressionist" as a label for his art.[78] As a co-organiser of the exhibitions presented by the loose association of Impressionist artists from 1874 onwards, he was personally close to the group, but in his artistic aspirations and working manner he largely remained alien to it.

The question thus inevitably arises: to what degree – if at all – can we subsume Degas's sculptures under the term "Impressionist" if this term already hardly appears suitable for his two-dimensional work?[79] The answer must take into account that our understanding of Degas's sculptural oeuvre is based on a limited selection: the works his estate administrators deemed worth keeping.[80] The subsequent revisions, the smoothing of the surfaces and, above all, the replacements of

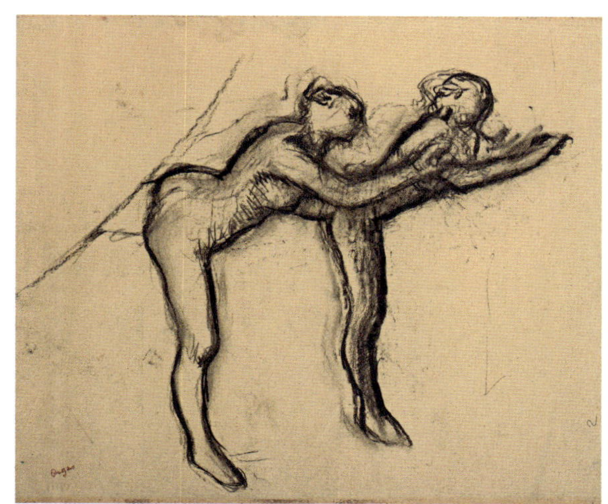

14 Edgar Degas, *Two Nude Dancers*, c. 1885–1890, charcoal
on paper, 45 × 54 cm, Paris, Galerie Chunhui & Bernard Lecomte

"What is sculpture
but a theoretically infinite
series of silhouettes?"

Walter Sickert, 1923

the exterior armatures not only decisively changed the visual appearance of most of these figures – as well as their relationship to the surrounding space – but also erased indications of their function in the artistic process.[81] As something changeable, flexible and unfinished, Degas's sculptural "snapshots" were an element of an experimental approach that corresponds much more strongly to the idea of Impressionism than many other aspects of his oeuvre. His qualities as an "Impressionist sculptor" are manifest in the openness of the forms, the visible imprints of the fingers and unsmoothed surfaces of the bases, both of which create an impression of movement and shift our attention from the object to the process of perceiving and giving form. The motif reveals itself as a pretext for the artistic process in and of itself, which in a kind of unending cycle seeks to fathom the same forms over and over again without ever arriving at a definitive conclusion.

The bronze casts of the sculptures are the result of an additional translation process in which the artist had no part, and they take the works yet another step away from the figures' original appearance. It was only with substantial losses that the casting process reproduced Degas's sketchy modelling method and polychrome elaborations of his waxes. His sculptural method was geared to transformability and transformation; frozen in a metal corset, it has come to a standstill. The transitoriness of his sculptures – their constant state of work in progress – has given way to a degree of completion the artist never intended. The bronzes evoke the misleading impression of "finished" sculptures that Degas sought to avoid all his life.[82] Yet despite their many reworkings and losses in translation, his artistic conception is apparent in the sculptures again and again. The unorthodox combinations of materials, the boldness of the positions, the liveliness of the surfaces and the richly nuanced play of light underscore Degas's innovative position as a painter/sculptor in the Impressionist circle.

1 "J'éprouve plus que jamais le besoin de traduire mes impressions de la forme en sculpture." Edgar Degas, quoted in: Thiébault-Sisson 1931; English quoted in: Francois Thiebault-Sisson, "Degas, the Sculptor, Tells His Own Story", in: Czestochowski/Pingeot 2002, p. 278.

2 Ibid., pp. 277–278.

3 On the outrage over the *Little Dancer Aged Fourteen*, see Arroyo Arce 2009; Kendall 1998.

4 On Degas's printmaking oeuvre, see the contribution by Astrid Reuter in this catalogue, pp. 296–301..

5 See Czestochowski 2002, p. 17.

6 Gsell 1918; Lemoisne 1919; Thiébault-Sisson 1921; Hausenstein 1922.

7 Anonymous 1919; Anonymous 1925.

8 *Degas: Portraitiste, Sculpteur, Musée de l'Orangerie*, Paris, 19 July–1 October 1931; see Czestochowski 2002, p. 18.

9 Degas's painting *Dancers Practicing at the Barre* (The Metropolitan Museum of Art, New York; Lemoisne 408) was sold at auction for 478,000 francs in 1912. The *Singing Rehearsal* (Dumbarton Oaks, House Collection, Washington D.C.; Lemoisne 331) fetched 100,000 francs at an estate auction in Paris in 1918. See exh. cat. Paris et al. 1988, pp. 189–190, no. 117, pp. 277–278, no. 165.

10 On the more recent projects, see exh. cat. Roubaix 2010; exh. cat. Copenhagen 2013; exh. cat. Wuppertal 2016; exh. cat. Cambridge/Denver 2017; exh. cat. Paris 2017a.

11 *Head, Study of a Portrait of Mme Salle* (large); *Head, Study of a Portrait of Madame Salle* (small); *Head Resting on One Hand, Bust*. All three sculptures are in the collection of the National Gallery of Art, Washington D.C.; see inv. cat. Washington 2010, nos. 60, 61, 63.

12 *The Schoolgirl*, National Gallery of Art, Washington D.C.; see ibid., no. 57.

13 *Picking Apples*, National Gallery of Art, Washington D.C.; see ibid., no. 59.

14 *Horse with Head Lowered*, National Gallery of Art, Washington D.C.; see ibid., no. 12.

15 *Little Dancer Aged Fourteen*, 1878/79, National Gallery of Art, Washington D.C.; see ibid., no. 15.

16 The inventory is printed in: Czestochowski/Pingeot 2002, p. 270.

17 The photographs are reproduced in: Pingeot 1991.

18 Inv. cat. Washington 2010.

19 Ibid., no. 18.

20 For a precise analysis of the materials, see the entry in: inv. cat. Washington 2010, no. 15.

21 See Waldmann 1990, pp. 6–9.

22 See Schopenhauer 1888, §213, p. 454: "Hier liegt nun eigentlich der Grund, warum Wachsfiguren keinen ästhetischen Eindruck machen und daher keine Kunstwerke (im ästhetischen Sinn) sind. […] Sie scheinen nämlich nicht die bloße Form, sondern, mit ihr, auch die Materie zu geben; daher sie die Täuschung, daß man die Sache selbst vor sich habe, zu Wege bringen. […] Darum erregt das Wachsbild Grausen, indem es wirkt wie ein starrer Leichnam." ("Here lies the true reason why wax figures do not make an aesthetic impression and are therefore not works of art (in the aesthetic sense). […] Namely, they appear not to convey the mere form, but, with it, also the material, thus bringing about the illusion that one has the thing itself before one. […] That is why the wax image arouses a sense of horror by having the appearance of a rigid corpse.")

23 "Nous en avons un exemple frappant dans les figures de cire: plus elles ressemblent à la nature, plus elles sont hideuses. […] Ils ne sont, avec leurs vrais habits et leurs vraies couleurs, que ce qu'il y a de plus horrible à voir et à dire, de faux cadavres." Blanc 1865, chap. XIV, pp. 43–44.

24 In general, see Pingeot 2010; also see the contribution by Eva Mongi-Vollmer in this catalogue, pp. 126–133, here p. 131.

25 See Papet 2018, pp. 25–26.

26 On the discussion of the extent to which the *Little Dancer Aged Fourteen* is to be assessed as realistic or impressionistic, see Schuon 2016, pp. 188–208.

27 "Car – voilà l'originalité de cette Exposition des Indépendants – ils commencent à affirmer leur indépendance sous la forme sculptée. Ce n'était pas assez de la couleur. Il leur faut la cire, ou le plâtre ou le bronze. Nous allons avoir, *bone Deus!* des sculpteurs *impressionistes* [sic]!" Claretie 1881; reprinted in: Berson 1996, vol. 1, pp. 335–336; English quoted in: exh. cat. Copenhagen/Fort Worth 2005, p. 126. Also see the contribution by Fabienne Ruppen in this catalogue, pp. 24–34, here p. 29.

28 Barbour/Sturman 2010a, p. 39.

29 *The Tub*; see inv. cat. Washington 2010, no. 42.

30 *Woman Washing Her Left Leg*; see inv. cat. Washington 2010, no. 47.

31 For a detailed description, see inv. cat. Washington 2010, pp. 242–245, no. 40.

32 "Mon opinion très nette est que personne, en fût-il propriétaire, n'a le droit d'y toucher pour y modifier quoi que ce soit." Letter from Albert Bartholomé to René De Gas, 26 December 1917, quoted in: Pingeot 1991, p. 26. "My decided opinion is that nobody, [not] even the owner, has the right to touch or modify anything whatsoever." English quoted in: Anne Pingeot, "Degas and His Castings", in: Czestochowski/Pingeot 2002, pp. 27–37, here p. 29.

33 For example, Paul Durand-Ruel wrote to Royal Cortissoz, the art critic of the *New York Herald*: "They [the sculptures] have all been entrusted to the care of the sculptor, Bartholomé, who was an intimate friend of Degas, and in the near future, work will be started by the founder, Hébrard, who will reproduce them in *cire perdue*." Quoted in: Cortissoz 1919.

34 "Les cires sont en très mauvais état et tombent en poussière; j'ai bien peur qu'il n'en reste rien si on les laisse encore passer l'été dans l'atelier." Letter from Joseph Durand-Ruel to Georges Durand-Ruel, 12 February 1918, English quoted in: Anne Pingeot, "Degas and His Castings", in: Czestochowski/Pingeot 2002, pp. 27–37, here p. 30.

35 Lafond 1918/19, vol. 2, p. 66.

36 Millard 1976, pp. 30–31.

37 Musée d'Orsay, Paris, inv. no. RF 2770.

38 On Albino Palazzolo's production process, see Adhémar 1955.

39 For a more exact description of the casting technique, see Barbour/Sturman 2010.

40 See Barbour/Sturman 2006.

41 Even if today the casts are generally referred to as bronzes, the thin-walled figures consist of an alloy of copper (approx. 80%), zinc (8–12%) and pewter (4–6%); see Barbour/Sturman 2010, p. 26.

42 This applies above all to the set of *modèle* casts, for which the greatest efforts were made to enhance them beyond the pure reproduction of the form, while the editions received more summary treatment; see inv. cat. Pasadena 2006, pp. 60–61.

43 A transcript of the contract is found in: Pingeot 1991, p. 194.

44 On the deviations and special stamp forms, see Lindsay 2010, p. 18.

45 See Czestochowski/Pingeot 2002, p. 268.

46 See Czestochowski 2002, p. 16. The inventory of the Hébrard foundry passed into the possession of the Valsuani company, which likewise engaged Albino Palazzolo. Valsuani continued the production of bronze casts of Degas's sculptures.

47 "It's a tremendous responsibility to leave anything behind in bronze – this medium is for eternity." Quoted in: Vollard 1924, pp. 112–113.

48 Thiébault-Sisson 1931.

49 "En réalité, vous êtes sculpteur autant que peintre, plus peut-être?" Edgar Degas, quoted in: ibid.

50 Moore 1890, p. 416.

51 See Gruetzner Robins 2011, p. 13.

52 Paul Durand-Ruel, in: Cortissoz 1919. In his memoirs, Durand-Ruel refers merely to "clay" as a working material and does not go into the other materials that Degas favoured – wax and plastiline.

53 "Degas must have made an enormous number of clay or wax figures, but as he never took care of them – he never had them put in bronze – they always fell to pieces after a few years […]."Letter from Paul Durand-Ruel to Royal Cortissoz, 7 June 1919, in: Cortissoz 1919.

54 "Vous pensez surtout, Vollard, à ce
que ça valait, mais m'auriez-vous donné
un chapeau plein de diamants que je
n'aurais pas eu un bonheur égal à celui
que j'ai pris à démolir ça pour le plaisir
de recommencer." Vollard 1924, pp. 112–113;
English quoted in: Millard 1976, p. 36.

55 "Celle-ci semble bien avoir été le premier
exemplaire de ce sujet qu'il reprit fréquem-
ment par la suite en glaise, puis en plastiline et en cire, à mesure que les précédents
s'effondraient." Lemoisne 1919, p. 115.

56 The works in question are *Spanish Dance*
(location unknown); *Dancer Looking
at the Sole of Her Right Foot* (private
collection); *Woman Rubbing Her Back
with a Sponge, Torso* (National Gallery of
Art, Washington D.C.). Also see exh. cat.
Cambridge/Denver 2017, pp. 198–199.

57 Degas was known for his urge to revise
already finished works again and again,
frequently leading to their destruction.
His schoolmate Henri Rouart reportedly
chained the Degas paintings in his
collection to the wall so that the artist
would not be able to take them away
with him; see Burroughs 1932, p. 144.

58 On the visibility of Degas's sculptures in
his studio and living quarters, see
Kendall 1995, p. 76: "[…] their presence
in his studio and apartment was
evidently a commonplace, known both
to the sculptural fraternity and some
of the rising generation of younger
Montmartre artists." Also see idem, in:
exh. cat. London/Chicago 1996, chap. 2:
"Degas and the Market-Place: The
Accessibility of the Late Work", pp. 31–55.

59 Ambroise Vollard, Auguste Renoir,
Paris 1920, p. 95; English translation
quoted in: Alastair Macaulay: "Workers
Wearing Toeshoes", *New York Times*, 2
September 2011, https://www.nytimes.
com/2011/09/04/arts/dance/degass-
ballet-at-the-phillips-collection-
and-royal-academy.html (accessed
24 November 2019).

60 "Avec ma vue qui s'en va, disait-il au
marchand Vollard, il faut maintenant que
je prenne un métier d'aveugle." Edgar
Degas, quoted in: Bouret 1965, p. 261.

61 The idea that Degas's sculptures were
a product of his advanced age was
extremely long-lived in the literature. In
1942, for example, Hans Graber wrote:
"Die meisten Skulpturen aber entstanden
in seiner späten Zeit, zu Anfang dieses
Jahrhunderts, als seine Sehkraft stark im
Schwinden war und er das Modellieren
sein ‚Blindenhandwerk' nannte. […] Ein
geborener Plastiker ist Degas nicht
gewesen. Hätte er in seiner späten Zeit
noch genügend gesehen, um regelmäßig
Pastelle und Zeichnungen zu schaffen,
so würde er wohl seltener modelliert
haben." Graber 1942, p. 26. ("However, he
produced most of his sculptures in
his late phase, at the beginning of this
century, as his eyesight was rapidly
decreasing and he called modelling his
'blindman's craft'. […] A born sculptor
Degas was not. If he had still been able
to see well enough to make pastels and
drawings regularly in his late phase,
he would presumably not have modelled
as often.")

62 See Avery 2017, p. 194.

63 "Ce diable d'homme veut sculpter, mais
ne veut pas se plier aux nécessités de la
sculpture." Albert Bartholomé, quoted
in: Jeanniot 1933, p. 300; English quoted
in: Rewald 1956, p. 12.

64 Dumas 2002, p. 39.

65 For a general discussion of this subject,
see: Berger 2014.

66 There is a particularly close connection
between the sculpture *Horse at the
Trough (Cheval à l'abreuvoir)* and the
painting *Mlle E[ugénie] F[iocre]; à
propos du ballet de "La Source"*, 1867/68
(Brooklyn Museum, New York; Lemoisne
146); see Berger 2014, pp. 18–21.

67 See Eiling 2014, pp. 17–18.

68 See Marques 2002, pp. 110–111.

69 See exh. cat. Karlsruhe 2007, pp.
203–206.

70 See Kendall 1996, pp. 254–256.

71 See Growe 1981, p. 147.

72 See exh. cat. London 2011, chap. 3: "The
Human Animal", pp. 130–183; Mannoni
2017, p. 69.

73 See exh. cat. Chicago 1984, p. 152.

74 Sickert 1917, p. 185.

75 See Clausen Pedersen 2013, p. 51.

76 Sickert 1923, reprint in: Sickert 2000,
pp. 455–457, here p. 456

77 Quoted in: John Rewald, *Degas: Works in
Sculpture: A Complete Catalogue*, New
York 1944, p. 2.

78 Brettell 2000, p. 203; Rey 2015.

79 See Chevillot 2010; Elliott 2014.

80 In this context, Durand-Ruel's
assessment of the sculptures found in
Degas's studio is highly instructive:
"Out of these, 30 were about valueless;
30 badly broken up and very sketchy;
the remaining 30 quite fine." Quoted in:
exh. cat. Cambridge/Denver 2017, p. 200.

81 See Armstrong 2012, p. 25.

82 "Jamais mes sculptures ne donneront
cette impression d'achevé qui est le fin
du fin dans le métier de statuaire, et,
comme, après tout, on ne verra jamais
ces essais, nul ne s'avisera d'en parler
[…]." Edgar Degas, quoted in:
Thiébault-Sisson 1931; "My sculptures will
never have the feel of being finished
which is the ultimate end in a sculptor's
workmanship, and after all, since no
one will ever see these rough sketches,
nobody will dare to talk about them […].",
English quoted in: Czestochowski/
Pingeot 2002, p. 278.

Edgar Degas's *Little Dancer Aged Fourteen* – the first Impressionist sculpture?

The fifth exhibition of the Impressionists in 1880 promised a sensation: in the catalogue, Edgar Degas – known for his motifs of modern Parisian life in the form of paintings, drawings and prints – had announced that he wanted to present the sculpture of a young dancer: "Petite Danseuse de quatorze ans (statuette en cire)".[1] In the context of this loose combination of highly diverse representatives of the avant-garde, in which sculptures had hitherto played only a very minor role, this certainly garnered attention.[2] When the show opened its doors on 1 April, the disappointment was all the greater, because the work was not among the exhibits. The artist had merely set up a glass display case in the exhibition space, whose ostensible emptiness made the lack of the dancer even more blatant. At this point in time, the critics could not have guessed that the figure would no longer take its intended place. Gustave Goetschy's article, published five days later, can therefore be understood as a hopeful commentary in anticipation of still getting to see Degas's dancer. He had heard wonderful things about a fourteen-year-old ballerina modelled after life that the artist had outfitted with a real tutu and ballet slippers.[3]

Degas did not deliver it later, but rather re-announced it for the sixth Impressionist exhibition a year later.[4] Yet his ambitions at first seemed to be ill-fated this time as well. The figure was once again not on display at the opening, but instead the same large glass vitrine that Degas had had made especially for it. The renewed absence of his key contribution to the exhibition exposed the artist to the derision of the critics, so that he must have felt nothing less than compelled to deliver his exhibit as quickly as possible. Several days after the opening, the *Little Dancer Aged Fourteen* (p. 46, fig. 1) took its place in the display case provided for it and unleashed fierce reactions that for today's viewers are probably only difficult to comprehend.[5]

Degas presented a figure out of reddish wax that was just shy of one metre in height and wearing a wig out of human hair, a bodice, a tutu and ballet slippers as well as a hair ribbon. Its head pertly raised, it is standing on a pedestal in the fourth position with feet turned outwards. Degas had fine-tuned his figure starting around 1878 and meticulously developed it with the aid of numerous drawings (fig. 1) and a preliminary sculpture (fig. 2). According to academic convention, he first studied his dancer undressed (*en deshabillée*) for the purpose of precisely determining the pose, before devoting himself to her outfit (fig. 3). However, disagreement pre-

dominates in research to this day concerning the individual working steps and their chronology – for example, regarding whether some of the very detailed drawings were produced after the model or possibly not until the sculpture's completion.[6] It is generally accepted that the model for Degas's dancer was a young ballet student at the Paris opera whose name has been passed down as Marie van Goethem. Born in 1865, the daughter of a laundress and a tailor from Belgium had moved with her family to Paris and lived in extremely modest circumstances not far from Degas's studio. She acted as a model for the sculpture between 1878 and 1881.[7]

The precision of the finished sculpture and its nearly academic genesis seem to diametrically oppose the remark made by Jules Claretie in which he, when he first saw the work, introduced the notion of the "Impressionist sculptor".[8] Towards the close of the nineteenth century, when hardly any distinction was made between movements such as Realism, Naturalism or Impressionism, Claretie appears to have used the concept as a collective term for sculptors with an unconventional approach and what for him was startling modernity. Yet his statement made a mark on art history that would find expression scarcely 20 years later in the debate over the existence of Impressionist sculpture.[9]

When *Little Dancer Aged Fourteen* was presented, most of the critics worried less about the potential presence of Impressionist sculptors and more about the ostensible decline of art. At the time, what we now consider to be the charming incarnation of a young ballerina at the Paris opera was linked with the issue of prostitution.[10] The back stage and rehearsal rooms of the opera house were a well-known erotic marketplace for the subscribers from the upper class, who went hunting there for their underaged victims. This circumstance explains those voices among the approximately 30 contemporary sources that vehemently targeted the moral decay of those being portrayed and hypocritically warned them of their fate. "I pray to heaven that my daughter does not turn into this figure, into a fallen woman."[11] Indeed, Degas had suggested this interpretation himself by presenting a pastel entitled "Physionomie de criminel" in the same room, which featured portraits of the murderers Émile Abadie and Michel Knobloch, who had been convicted in a sensational trial in Paris not long before that (fig. 4).[12] The similarities of the criminals' profile with that of the dancer were so obvious that associating the two works with one another immediately suggested itself, even though numerous

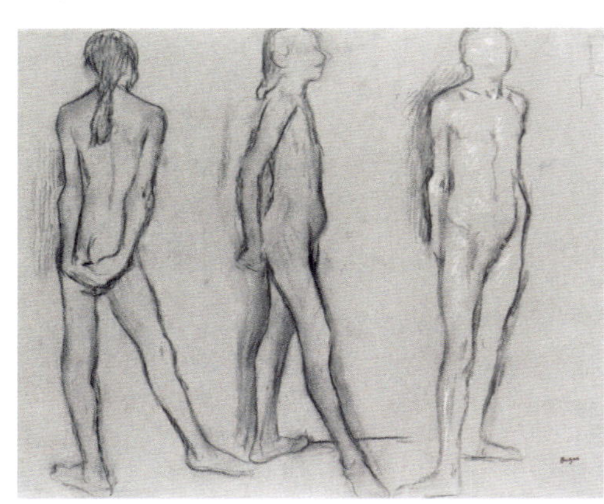

1   Edgar Degas, *Three Studies of a Nude Dancer*, c. 1878/79, charcoal, heightened with white, 47.7 × 62.3 cm, private collection

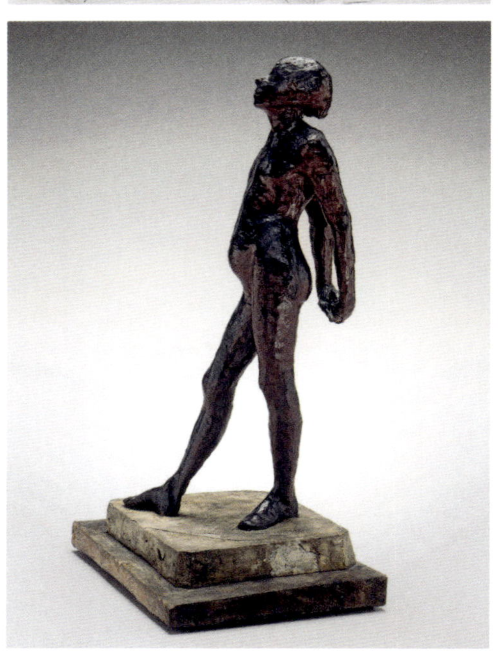

2   Edgar Degas, *Study in the Nude of Little Dancer Aged Fourteen (Nude Little Dancer)*, c. 1878–1881, pigmented beeswax, plaster core, metal and wood armatures, on plaster and wood bases, 69.5 × 29.3 × 30.3 cm (without base), National Gallery of Art, Washington D.C.

other works by the artist were exhibited in the same room.[13] In this way, the public was made to believe that deprivation had to inevitably lead to criminality, while one did not waste much thought on the blatant abuse of the underaged students of dance by upper-class gentlemen.[14] Hence all the critic Paul Mantz saw in the face of the young dancer was "the instinctive ugliness of a face on which all the vices imprint their detestable promises."[15]

This interpretation may not have been far away from Degas's own attitude. For many years, the artist showed an interest in the science of the physiognomy, in the treatises by Charles Le Brun, the studies by Johann Caspar Lavater, the theories on criminal physiognomics by Cesare Lombroso, and not lastly in the article by his friend Edmond Duranty with the title "Sur la physionomie" (1867).[16] The latter can be regarded as the later offshoot of an intense discussion on the connection between appearance and character that had been ongoing since the middle of the century.[17] Degas's sculpture thus brought social abysses into the exhibition space, and that in a remarkably naturalistic way.

The choice of the material – namely, wax – underscored this mimetic intention. In the nineteenth century, wax was reserved for reproductions of anatomic models in public collections or wax museums, where in an artistic context (to the extent that it was not a question of preliminary sculptural studies) it was more likely to cause disconcertment.[18] The perceived artlessness of the material, the base subject and the presentation in a glass display case, in the style of medical collections or the Egyptian and Etruscan departments of the Louvre, provided plenty of starting points for the criticism of Degas's wax sculpture.[19] This was occasionally very harsh: Henry Trianon called the dancer a "monster" more suited to being shown in a museum of zoology or anthropology than in an art museum. In addition, the author used terms such as "horror" or "bestiality", which emphasised the vehemence with which he reacted to the presentation.[20] Even though there were also several positive comments among the reviews – for example, by Joris-Karl Huysmans, who, despite several reservations, all the same described the *Little Dancer Aged Fourteen* as the "only really modern attempt [...] in sculpture"[21] – Degas ended his public ambitions with respect to sculpture from this point onward. As a result, his sculptural works remained reserved for the privacy of his studio, where only few colleagues and friends set eyes on them.[22]

The history of its dissemination began with the discovery of the *Little Dancer Aged Fourteen* in the artist's studio estate, as the heirs decided to have it as well as the 72 statuettes cast in bronze.[23] Whereas work on the latter commenced as early as 1919, production

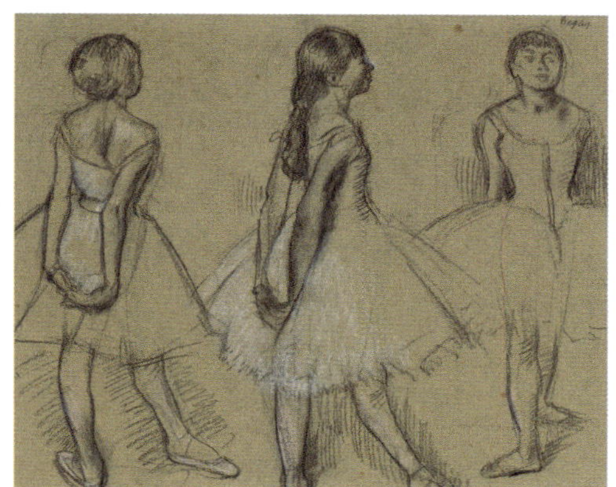

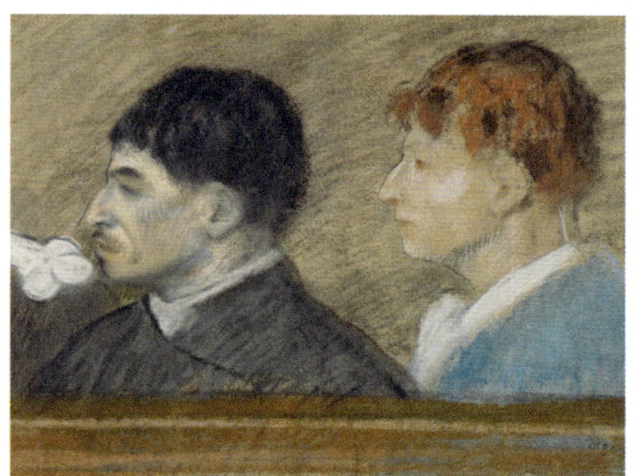

3   Edgar Degas, *Little Dancer Aged Fourteen*, three studies, c. 1878–1880, black chalk, pastel, heightened with white, 47.5 × 62.8 cm, The Morgan Library and Museum, New York

4   Edgar Degas, *Criminal Physiognomies (Émile Abadie and Michel Knobloch)*, c. 1880/81, pastel, 48 × 63 cm, private collection

of the *Little Dancer Aged Fourteen* probably did not begin until 1922. The delay can be accounted for by negotiations over the sale of the original sculpture to the American collector Louisine Havemeyer, which, however, failed due to the heirs' asking price.[24] While the casts were being planned, it was necessary to carefully consider how the Hébrard company, which was commissioned with their execution, could reproduce the accessories made of fabric and human hair in bronze. The production manager, Albino Palazzolo, decided to cast the dancer's hair as well as the bodice and ballet slippers, while the hair ribbon and the tutu were added in the form of real fabrics. The casts that one comes across today in numerous museums and private collections worldwide therefore exhibit marked differences particularly with respect to the design of the tutu, which was subjected to numerous temporary fashions and changes over the decades.[25]

Unlike the small sculptures, the bronze cast of the *Little Dancer Aged Fourteen* was not assigned a motif number, but instead the series letters "A" to "T" or "HER.D" (for the artist's heirs) and "HER" (for the foundry). In addition, there is one specimen with the letter identifier "AP" (Albino Palazzolo) as well as a number of casts without letters that were produced in the late 1930s. The question concerning the total number of bronze casts has been a subject in the research for decades: different than specified in the contract between Degas's heirs and the Hébrard foundry, one evidently did not adhere to a total of 22. The catalogue raisonné of the Degas bronzes lists 29 casts whose whereabouts have been localised.[26] Moreover, there are two plasters, of which one was used for the manufacture of the moulds, while the other one served as a colour reference for the patination of the figures.[27] It was to come as close as possible to the appearance of the original sculpture, yet recreating the delicate tones of the wax figure in the patina, which alternated between red and brown, could not always be uniformly achieved. Some casts feature a dark, opaque surface, while others are more nuanced and exhibit lighter areas, and in this way come much closer to the original. Hence the casts possess the character of unique items, although when viewing the bronzes, it must always be taken into account that it has to do with a translating process that only partly reflects the effect that Degas intended.

The prolonged genesis of the *Little Dancer Aged Fourteen* illustrates the fact that this sculpture is far remote from the embodiment of a fugitive moment observed in the life of a young ballet student at the Paris opera. Although in the last century it – due to its frequent presence in exhibitions – became a symbol of the Impressionist movement as such, it essentially symbolises its antithesis. Degas's creative process, which consistently aimed at repetition and concretion, turned his model into a representative for all of the dancers that he had hitherto created in various techniques, a synthesis of his devotion to the world of the Paris opera, which he would continue to pursue in subsequent years.[28] The combination of modern theme and exaggerated realism demonstrates Degas's ambivalent position in the circle of the Impressionists. The *Little Dancer Aged Fourteen* is therefore not an Impressionist sculpture, but a sculpture by an artist at the centre of Impressionism, however, and who constantly challenged and questioned this new movement with his works. Huysmans got to the heart of the continuous shifting of the genre boundaries in Degas's work with the words: "Monsieur Degas has revolutionised the traditions of sculpture as he has long since shaken the conventions of painting."[29] — AE

"[...] the instinctive ugliness of a face on which all the vices imprint their detestable promises."

Paul Mantz, 1881

1 Berson 1996, vol. 1, p. 261.
2 On the number of sculptures in the eight Impressionist exhibitions, see the essay by Fabienne Ruppen in this catalogue, pp. 24–34, esp. pp. 26–27.
3 "[...] une statuette en cire dont on m'avait dit merveille et qui figure une ballerine de quatorze ans modelée sur le vif, vêtue d'une vraie jupe bouffante, et chaussée de vrais souliers de danse." Goetschy 1880; quoted in: Berson 1996, vol. 1, p. 283.
4 Berson 1996, vol. 1, p. 326.
5 For a compilation of the reviews of the sixth Impressionist exhibition in 1881, see Berson 1996, vol. 1, pp. 329–374.
6 Inv. cat. Washington 2010, p. 132; see exh. cat. Washington 1984, pp. 69–83.
7 On Marie van Goethem, see inv. cat. Washington 2010, p. 127.
8 "Nous allons avoir, *bone Deus*! des sculpteurs *impressionistes* [sic]!" [*Good God! We are going to see Impressionist sculptors!*]. Claretie 1881; quoted in: Berson 1996, vol. 1, p. 335 (italics in the original). See also the essay by Fabienne Ruppen in this catalogue, pp. 24–34, esp. p. 29.
9 See Claris 1902 (French); see also the essay by Alexander Eiling and Eva Mongi-Vollmer in this catalogue, pp. 12–21, esp. p. 14.
10 See exh. cat. Omaha et al. 1998, pp. 86–88. For general information on the criticism of the sculpture, see also Jarbouai 2019, pp. 255–258.
11 "Fasse le ciel que ma fille ne devienne pas une sauteuse!" Mantz 1881; quoted in: Berson 1996, vol. 1, p. 358.
12 Druick 1989 and Druick 1998, pp. 78–88.
13 Degas presented a total of twelve works (four of them *hors catalogue*) at the sixth Impressionist exhibition in 1881; see Berson 1996, vol. 1, p. 354; vol. 1, p. 283.
14 Callen 1989, p. 14; Druick 1989, p. 239.
15 "[...] l'instructive laideur d'un visage où tous les vices impriment leurs détestables promesses." Mantz 1881; quoted in: Berson 1996, vol. 1, p. 358. For general information on the criticism of the figure, see Arroyo Arce 2009, pp. 59–63.
16 Duranty 1867.
17 Armstrong 1991, pp. 86, note 39.
18 Signs of a vindication of the material were the neo-medieval wax reliefs that Henri Cros by all means successfully presented at the Paris Salons in the 1870s. Ernest Meissonnier and Gustave Moreau also dealt with the material intensively, albeit primarily for the purpose of testing figural compositions that they later transferred to their paintings. See inv. cat. Washington 2010, pp. 129–130; exh. cat. Paris 2018, p. 68.
19 Callen 1995, pp. 21–22.
20 "Veut-il nous présenter une statuette de danse, il la choisit parmi les plus odieusement laides; il en fait le type de l'horreur et de la bestialité. Eh! oui, certes, dans le bas-fonds des écoles de danse, il est de pauvres filles qui ressemblent à ce jeune monstre [...]." Trianon 1881; quoted in: Berson 1996, vol. 1, p. 368.
21 "Tout à la fois raffinée et barbare avec son industrieux costume, et ses chairs colorées qui palpitent, sillonnées par le travail des muscles, cette statuette est la seule tentative vraiment moderne que je connaisse, dans la sculpture." Huysmans 1883a, p. 227.
22 See the essay by Alexander Eiling in this catalogue, pp. 46–57, esp. pp. 48, 52.
23 On the bronze casts, see ibid., pp. 49–51.
24 For the time being, the original sculpture remained in the archive of the Hébrard foundry. The American collector Paul Mellon acquired it in 1955. It is now in the collection of the National Gallery of Art in Washington D.C.
25 Campbell 1998; Gloor 2016.
26 Czestochowski/Pingeot 2002, pp. 265–267, no. 73; see inv. cat. Pasadena 2009, pp. 555–556.
27 See inv. cat. Pasadena 2009, p. 281.
28 See exh. cat. Copenhagen 2013, pp. 36–37.
29 "M. Degas a culbuté les traditions de la sculpture comme il a depuis longtemps secoué les conventions de la peinture." Huysmans 1883a, p. 226.

Cat. 4 Edgar Degas, Little Dancer Aged Fourteen (Petite danseuse de quatorze ans), original: wax sculpture, 1878/79–1881; metal cast, c. 1922/23; bronze (copper alloy), partially painted, cotton tutu and silk ribbon, wooden base, 98 × 35.2 × 24.5 cm (without base); stamped on the right thigh: "CIRE / PERDUE / A. A. HEBRARD", "I"; on the wooden base: "CIRE / PERDUE / A. A. HEBRARD", "I", engraved beside it to the left: "Degas"; private collection, Europe

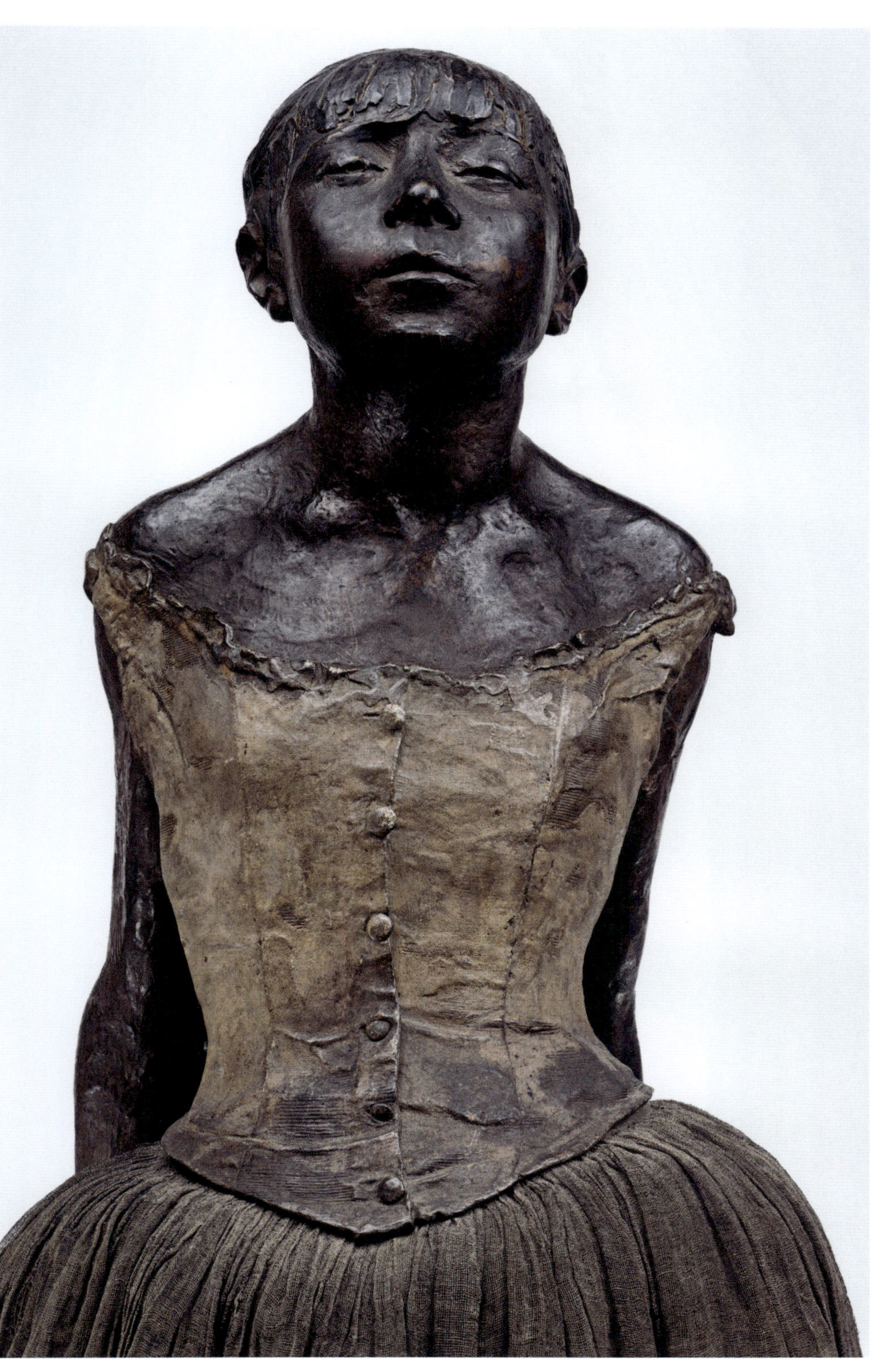

Cat.4

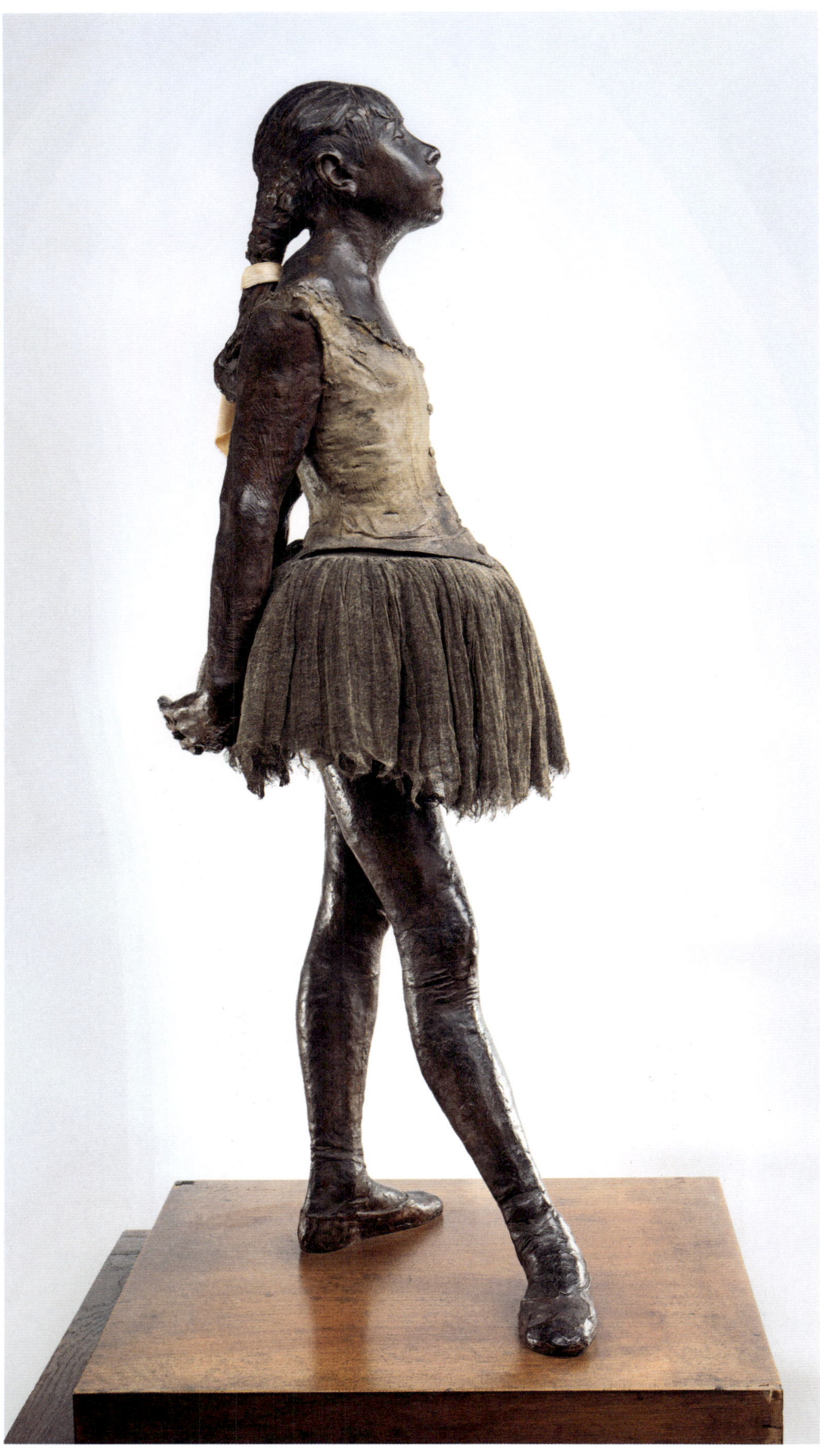

Cat. 4

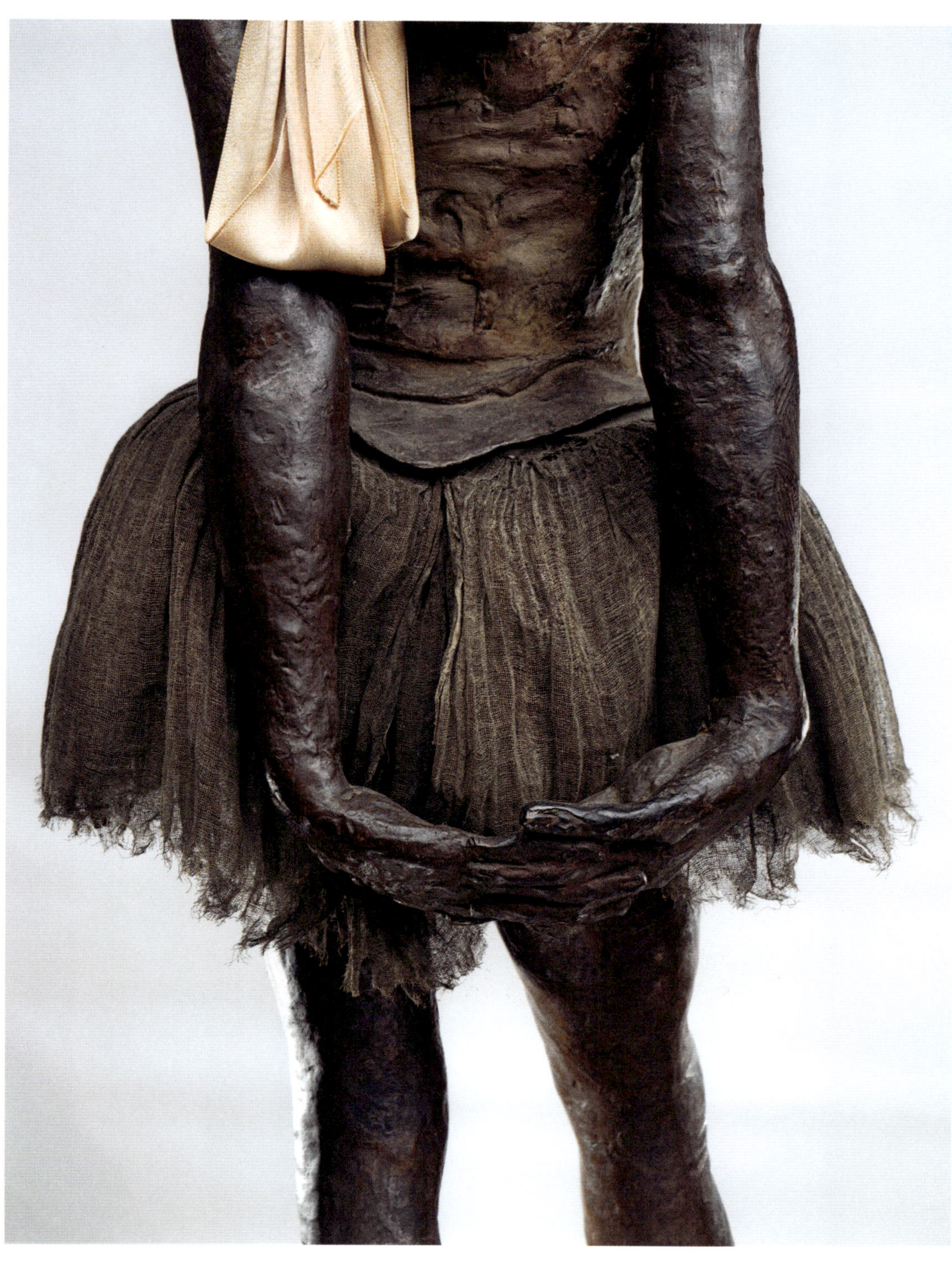

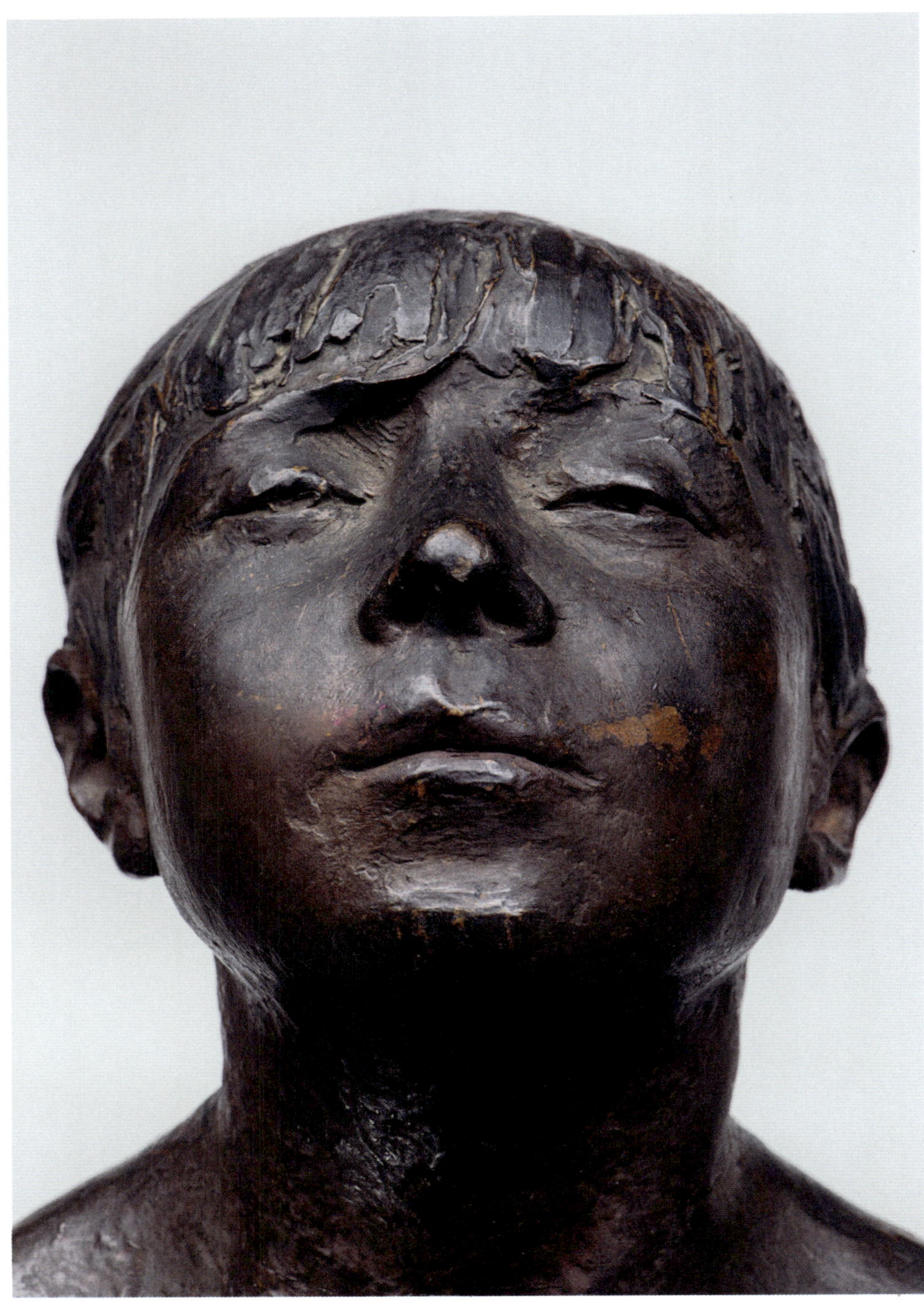

Cat. 4

Cat. 4

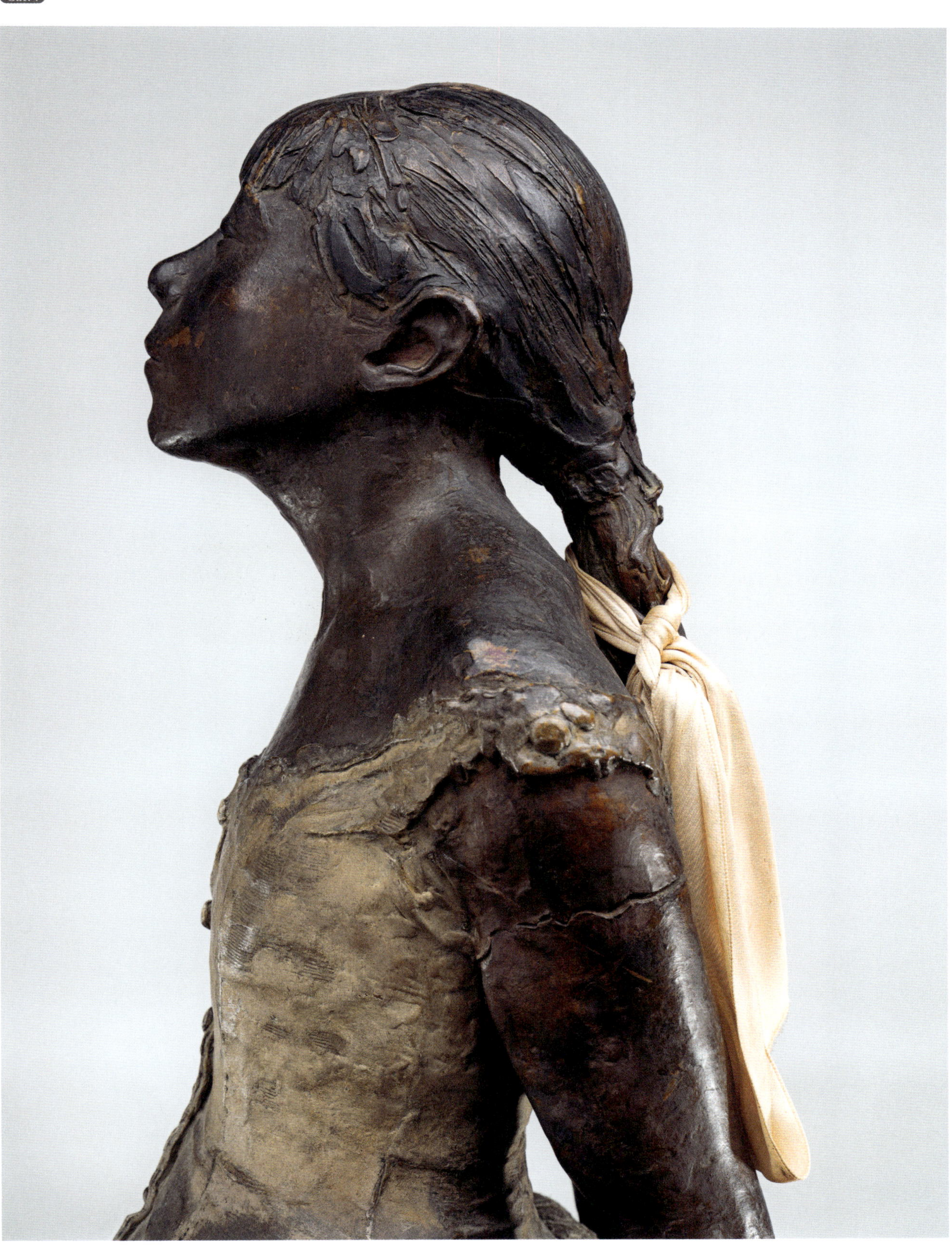

Classical poses – dancers on the stage

Degas had not only created a sensation with the presentation of his *Little Dancer Aged Fourteen* (cat. 4), but had aroused the interest of the critics even earlier with a number of unusually composed paintings. One of these is *Orchestra Musicians* (cat. 5), begun in 1872 – one of the first pictures in which Degas turned to the world of the Parisian opera and dance. He chose the uncommon perspective through the eyes of the musicians in the orchestra pit, whose heads take up the foreground in the lower half of the painting, while the upper half is devoted to the brightly lit stage and the dancers. By doing so, the middle ground is blocked out, so that the viewer's gaze jumps back and forth between a view from close up and from a distance. The sensational composition was not initially planned to be like this, but is the result of a gradual reworking process that took place at an interval of several years. Between 1874 and 1876, Degas changed the format of the painting by cutting down and adding a piece of fabric to the canvas.[1] The artist made a vertical format out of what was originally a horizontal format. Whereas the focus had previously been on the heads of the musicians, he now extended the scene by the occurrences on the stage, and in doing so gave them equal presence.

The painting's composition combines Degas's fascination with stage and theatre performances by Honoré Daumier (fig. 1)[2] and Adolph Menzel[3] with the bold perspectives of the Japanese colour woodcuts that had taken Paris by storm beginning in the 1860s.[4] With this picture, Degas permanently left his ambitions as a history painter behind and moved his body of motifs from the world of ancient Greece and Babylon to the contemporary stages of opera and ballet in Paris.[5] This paradigm shift seems to have been influenced by Daumier's dictum "Il faut être de son temps", demanding that art should be in pace with the times and not draw on bygone worlds.[6] Degas's fame is largely based on these scenes from Parisian night life, which he presented at the Impressionist exhibitions and which animated artist colleagues such as Jean-Louis Forain (cat. 22) and Walter Sickert (1860–1942; cat. 6) to develop similar compositions.

Although Degas's painting seems like a scene observed *en passant*, his composition is worked out as precisely as and ultimately just as fictitiously as the complex depictions in his history paintings. Degas may have changed his world of subjects, but he did not depart from his highly constructed and virtually old-masterly method, which was for the most part based on individual figures that he subsequently combined to develop an overall composition in his studio. In the late 1860s, in the course of his orientation to the world of ballet, he created a large number of drawings of dancers in which he repeatedly traced specific poses and movements. Executed in charcoal, chalk, gouache or thinned oil paint (essence), the ballerinas formed the two-dimen-

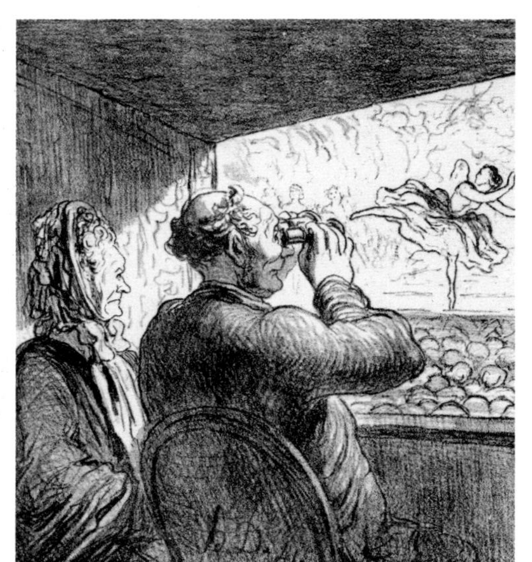

1 Honoré Daumier, *Monsieur Colimard si vous continuez à lorgner les danseuses d'une façon aussi inconvenante je vous ramène à la maison avant la fin du spectacle*, lithograph, from the series *Croquis pris au théâtre*, published in *Le Charivari* (4 May 1864), Bibliothèque nationale de France, Paris

sional ensemble for the productions on his artificially created stage, from which he continually recruited and reassembled his pictorial characters right up until into his late oeuvre.

The drawing of a *Young Dancer against the Light* (cat. 7), for example, echoes a pose as anticipated in similar form in the *Orchestra Musicians*. However, whereas Degas captured the final moment in the performance in the painting in which the prima ballerina bows before the audience, the young ballet student in his drawing seems to be taking a scrutinising look at the position of her feet.[7] The latter is presumably the English dancer Nelly Franklin, whose name and address are noted in a sketchbook that Degas had begun using in 1877.[8] As artificial as the arrangements of the dancers in his paintings are, Degas realistically captured the appearance of the model in the drawing. In this case, at the upper edge of the paper he even annotated a detail of her costume, on whose shoulder area there were apparently small pink bows ("petits nœuds roses aux épaules").

Moreover, the drawing and the painting are outstanding examples of Degas's interest in special light situations and artificial lighting.[9] He countered the *plein-air* painting of the Impressionists with the artificialness of the limelight fuelled by gas or burnt lime on the opera stage. In the drawing, the silhouette of the dancer executed in black chalk is framed by white hatching, suggesting that the figure is being lit from behind. In contrast, in the painting the dancer shines from the front, lit by the bright light beams of the spotlights, whose radiance emphasises her all the most pointedly compared with the darkness of the foreground.

Light and movement are the two factors in Degas's creative output that animated him to keep on experimenting and ultimately also represent an important catalyst for his sculptural oeuvre. The key role of these two aspects in his three-dimensional works also explains why these are referred to as "Impressionist". Whereas the presentation of the *Little Dancer Aged Fourteen* (cat. 4) at the sixth Impressionist exhibition in 1881 marked at once the beginning and the end of Degas's public ambitions in this métier, it in no way meant that he renounced this medium in private life. He had probably already begun creating numerous sculptures of dancers in wax and plastiline on improvised wire frames in the 1870s, and continued to do so until shortly before his death; however, they were posthumously cast in bronze.[10] They did not achieve the greatness and perfection of the workmanship of his *Little Dancer Aged Fourteen* and primarily constitute studies based on which Degas could better reproduce specific sequences of movement and poses. Among these small sculptures of 38 works, dancers constitute the lion's share and far outnumber bathing women (cat. 25, 27–30, 35, 38) as well as horses and equestrians (cat. 43–47).[11]

Degas's dancers can be roughly divided into portrayals of formalised ballet poses that reflect the classic arm and foot positions (cat. 10–13), but also exhibit mixed elements from ballet and folk dance (cat. 9). A second group consists of compositions that reproduce ballerinas in apparently less eventful moments – for instance, during breaks and while stretching (cat. 15, 16) as well as adjusting their clothes or putting on tights (cat. 14, 17). Although isolated gestures make reference to the dancers' costumes, save for one exception (cat. 20) the figures are fashioned as nudes with summarily captured limbs and without individual facial features. The titles do not stem from the artist himself, but were specified on the occasion of the production of the bronze casts by the Hébrard foundry, often without accurately adhering to the correct ballet terminology.[12]

These inaccuracies in their names are also reflected in a group of figures that feature the dancers in various stages of the arabesque. These are the most challenging poses of classic ballet, to which Degas devoted eight sculptures alone. The artist probably created this body of works in the years between 1885 and 1890 under the influence of Eadweard Muybridge's chronophotographs (cat. 48).[13] Based on four bronzes represented in the present exhibition (cat. 10–13), a sequence of movement can be traced that ranges from the upright figure (*première temps* or *arabesque à terre*) and a position in which the body rests almost horizontally over the right leg (*deuxième temps*) to a diagonal inflexion (*troisième temps*). It is precisely in the last position that Degas lends vividness to a fragile and tension-filled abeyance between movement and stiffness, between balance and collapsing, in which the body reaches into the surrounding space to a maximum extent. Whereas two-dimensional depictions of the arabesque in the first and second position frequently occur in the various media in Degas's overall oeuvre, the difficult third position is largely reserved for sculpture.[14]

The latter also applies to the configuration of the *Spanish Dancer* (cat. 9), for which there are only few equivalents in the drawings by Degas.[15] The presumed inspiration for the work is Jean-Auguste Barre's sculpture of the famous ballerina Fanny Elssler (fig. 2), which reaped storms of enthusiasm in 1836 with the performance of the Spanish cachucha dance in Jean Coralli's ballet *Le Diable Boiteux* (The Lame Devil).[16] The difference between Barre's richly adorned figure and Degas's sculpture freed of any embellishment could hardly be greater. While Barre fashioned a portrait of a dancer in which he, besides the reproduction of her physiognomy, directed particular attention to the embroidered dress and the floral decorations, Degas reduced the nude portrayal of his *Spanish Dancer* to her characteristic pose. In this way, Degas's sculptures penetrate to the core of movement and seek the essence of the expression without losing themselves in details. The open form of the modelling alludes to the transformational quality of these sculptural snapshots in time of a figure that came to a standstill for only an instant. — AE

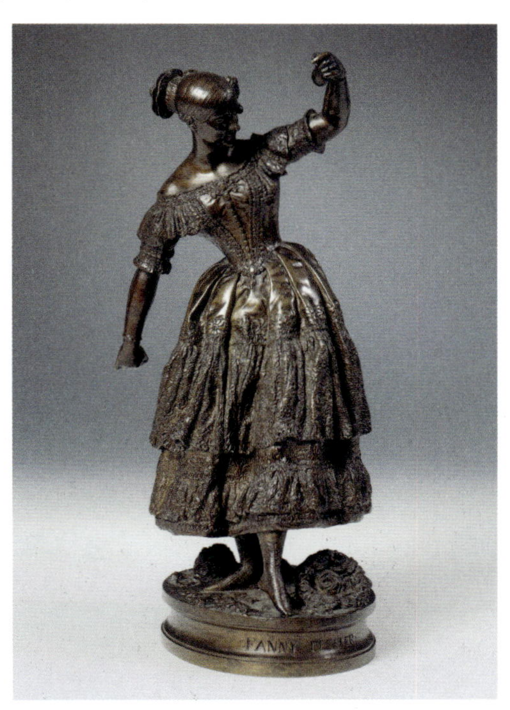

2 Jean-Auguste Barre, *Fanny Elssler*, 1837, bronze, height 43.5 cm, Victoria and Albert Museum, London

Each of the dates of Degas's small sculptures make reference to the creation of the wax originals. The casts were produced beginning around 1919 until the 1930s. Besides the motif number (1–72) and the letter of the series (A–T), all of the small sculptures also bear the signature stamp "Degas" as well as the manufacturer's mark "CIRE / PERDUE / A. A. HEBRARD". In the following, only the motif number and the letters of the series are cited.

1 See the X-ray of the painting in Loyrette 1999, p. 63.

2 See also Honoré Daumier, *The Drama*, c. 1860, oil on canvas, 97.5 × 90.4 cm, Neue Pinakothek, Munich.

3 See, for example, Adolph Menzel, *The Thêatre du Gymnase*, 1856, oil on canvas, 46 × 62 cm, Staatliche Museen zu Berlin, Nationalgalerie.

4 For general information on this, see Göthe 2014.

5 See Eiling 2014.

6 The quotation traces back to the literary historian Émile Deschamps and was not adopted as the battle cry of the avant-garde until later; Deschamps 1828; Boras 1941, p. 52.

7 See exh. cat. Karlsruhe 2014, pp. 182–186, no. 67; exh. cat. Karlsruhe 2018, p. 172 (Dorit Schäfer).

8 Exh. cat. Washington 1984, p. 88, note 5.

9 On artificial light on the opera and theatre stage, see Kisiel 2019, pp. 143–144.

10 See also the essay by Alexander Eiling in this catalogue, pp. 46–57, esp. p. 52.

11 Inv. cat. Washington 2010, p. 112.

12 Lindsay 2010a, p. 114.

13 See exh. cat. Chicago 1984, pp. 155–156, no. 74.

14 Inv. cat. Washington 2010, p. 197.

15 See Edgar Degas, *Study of a Dancer in Tights*, c. 1900, black chalk, 60 × 45.5 cm, National Museum of Serbia, Belgrade; see exh. cat. London 2011, pp. 213–215.

16 See exh. cat. Chicago 1984, pp. 153–143, no. 73.

Cat.5 Edgar Degas, Orchestra Musicians (Musiciens à l'orchestre), 1872, reworked c. 1874–1876; oil on canvas, 63.6 × 49 cm; Städel Museum, Frankfurt am Main, inv. no. SG 237 **Cat.6** Walter Richard Sickert, The Music Hall or The P.S. Wings in the O.P. Mirror, 1888/89; oil on canvas, 61 × 51 cm; Musée des Beaux-Arts, Rouen, inv. no. 1922.1.32

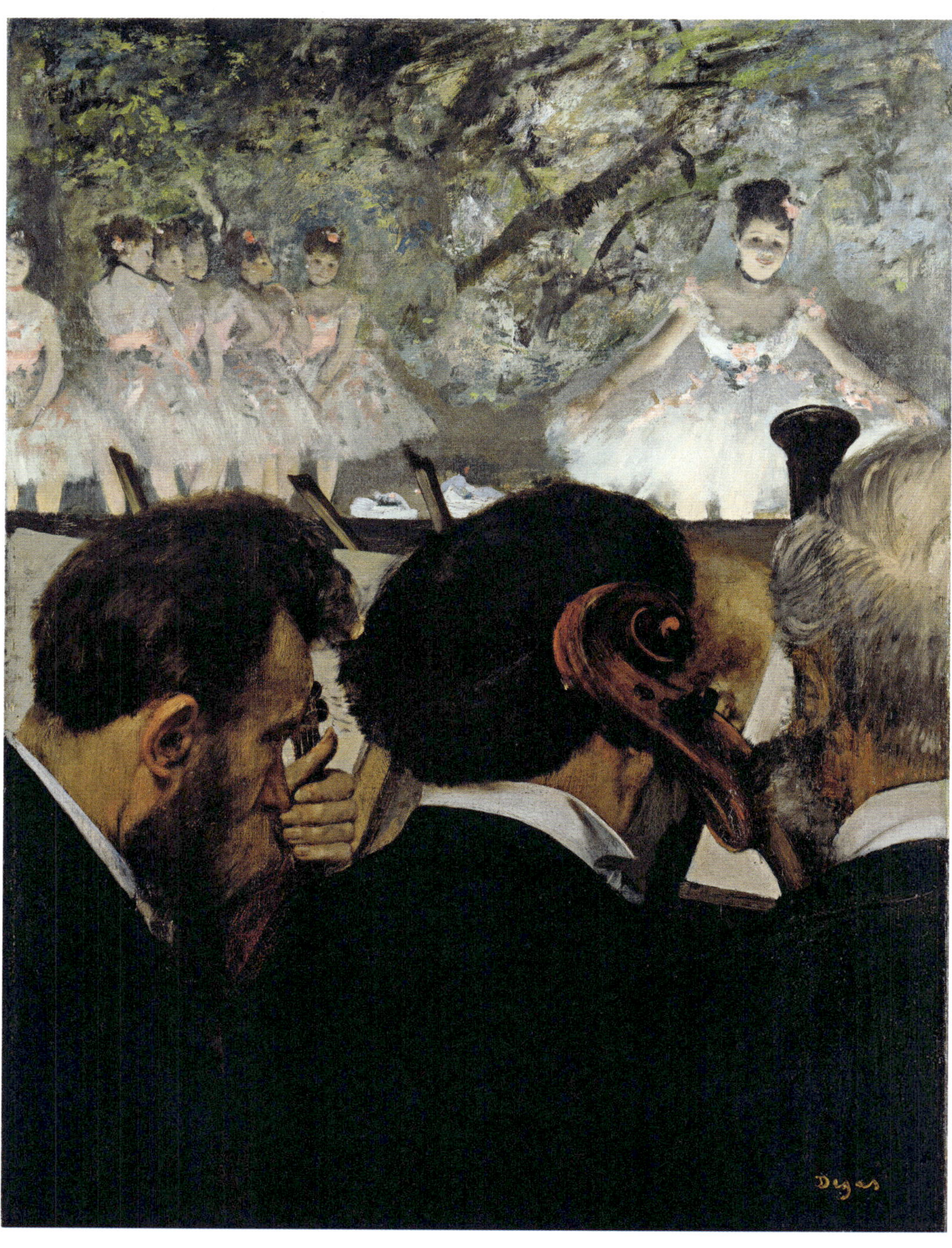

Cat.5

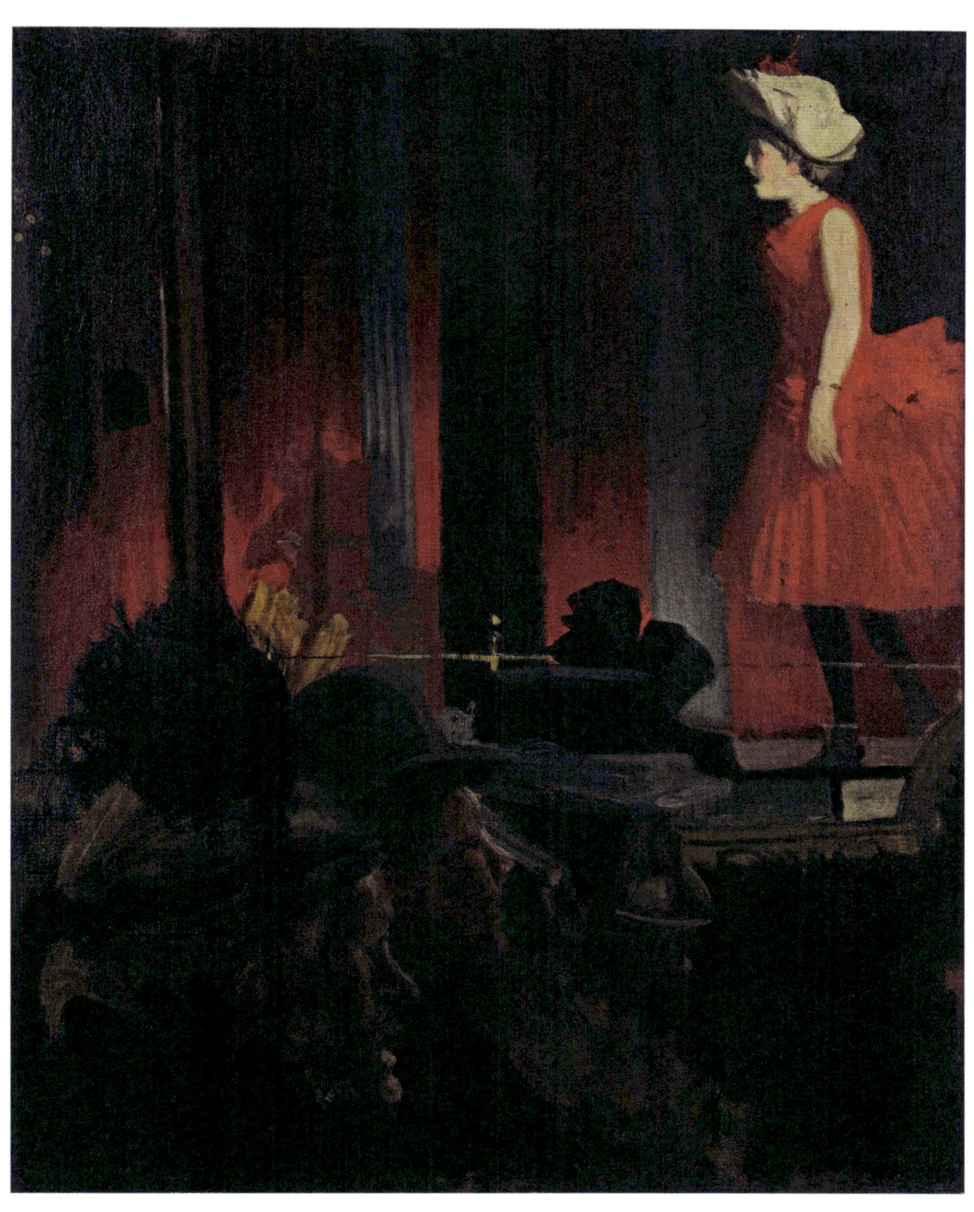

Cat.6

Cat.7 Edgar Degas, Young Dancer against the Light (Jeune danseuse à contre-jour), c. 1878; black and white chalk on grey paper, 48.8 × 30.6 cm; Staatliche Kunsthalle Karlsruhe, Kupferstichkabinett, inv. no. 1980-12 **Cat.8** Edgar Degas, Dancer, Fourth Position Front, on the Left Leg (Danseuse, position de quatrième sur la jambe, première étude), 1883–1888; bronze, 43.4 × 23 × 28 cm; stamped on the plinth: "6/O"; Städel Museum, Frankfurt am Main, inv. no. SGP 61 **Cat.9** Edgar Degas, Spanish Dancer (Danseuse espagnole), 1880s; bronze, 43.5 × 16.2 × 22 cm; stamped on the plinth: "45/R"; Ny Carlsberg Glyptotek, Copenhagen, inv. no. MIN 2678

Cat.7

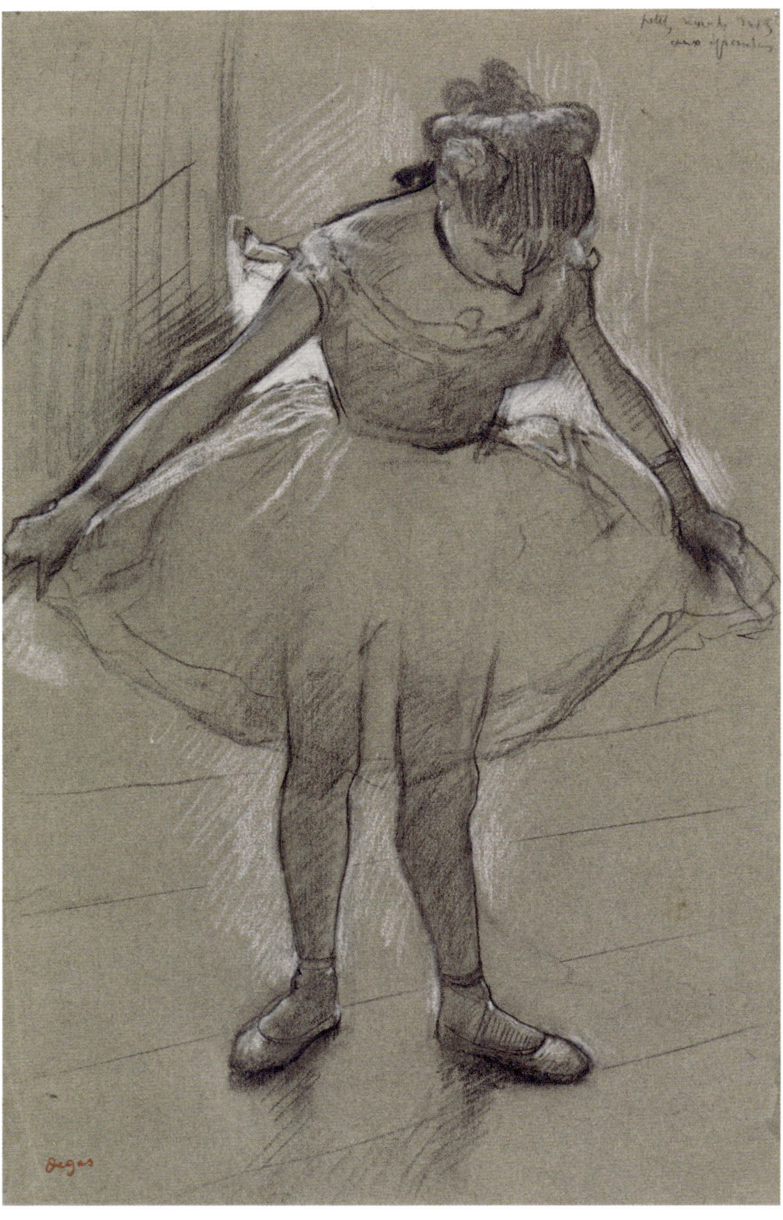

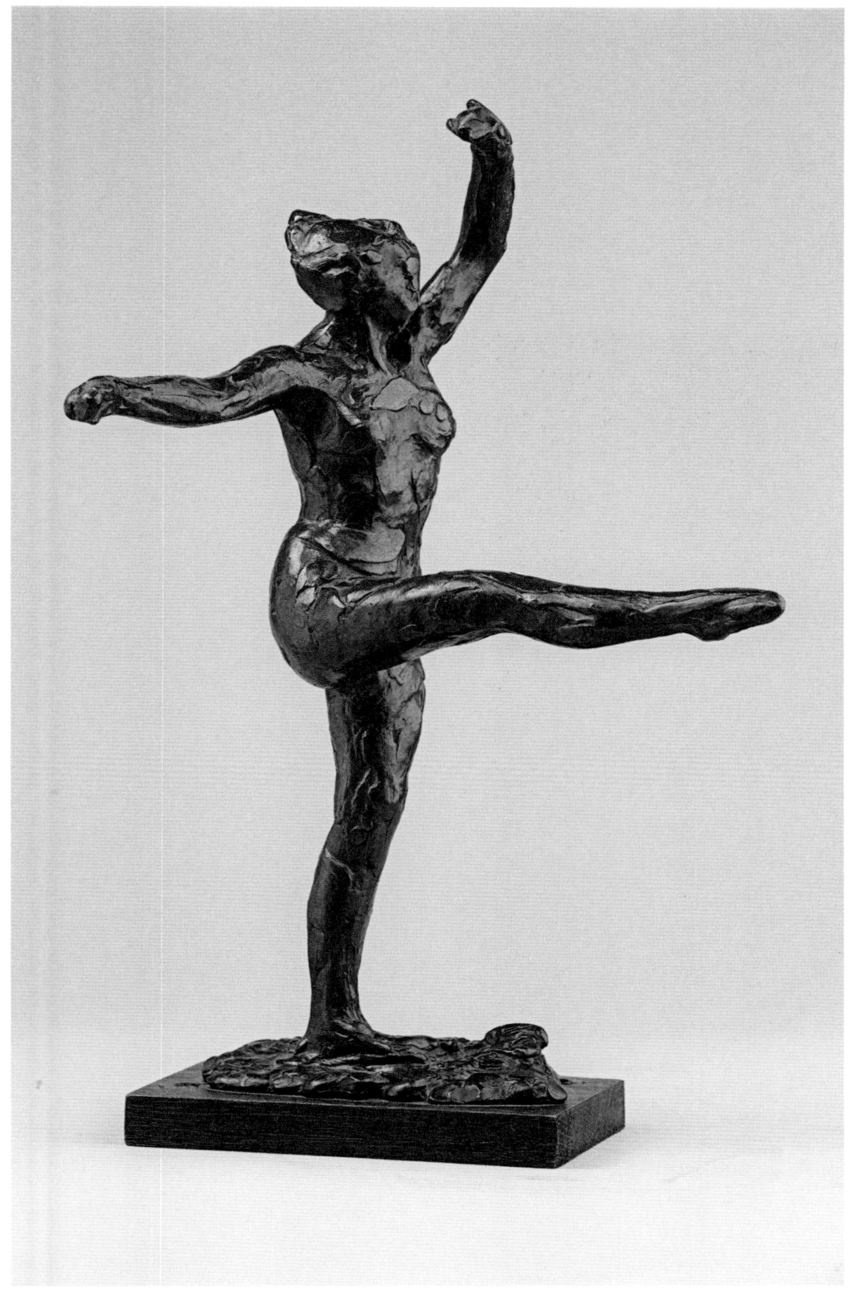
Cat.8

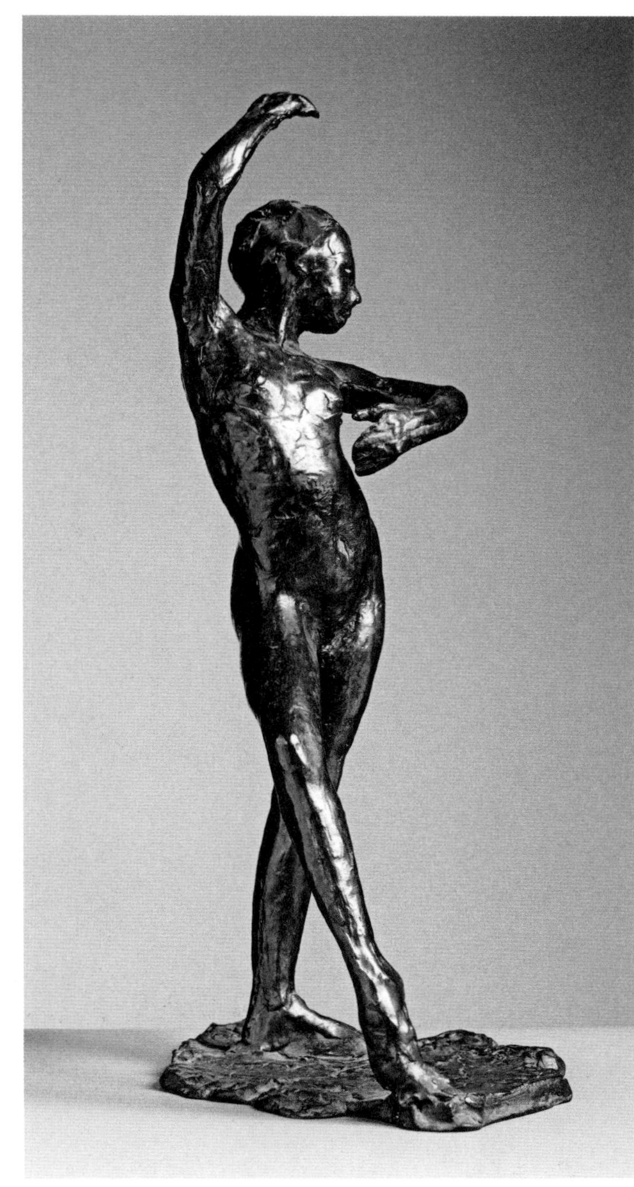
Cat.9

Cat.10 Edgar Degas, *Grand Arabesque, First Time* (Danseuse, grande arabesque, premier temps), c. 1885–1890; bronze, 48.9 × 38.5 × 26 cm; stamped on the plinth: "18/HER.D"; The Sladmore Gallery, London Cat.11 Edgar Degas, *Grand Arabesque, Second Time* (Danseuse, grande arabesque, deuxième temps), c. 1885–1890; bronze, 43 × 28 × 61 cm; stamped on the plinth: "15/O"; Hamburger Kunsthalle, Hamburg, inv. no. S-1952-20

Cat.10

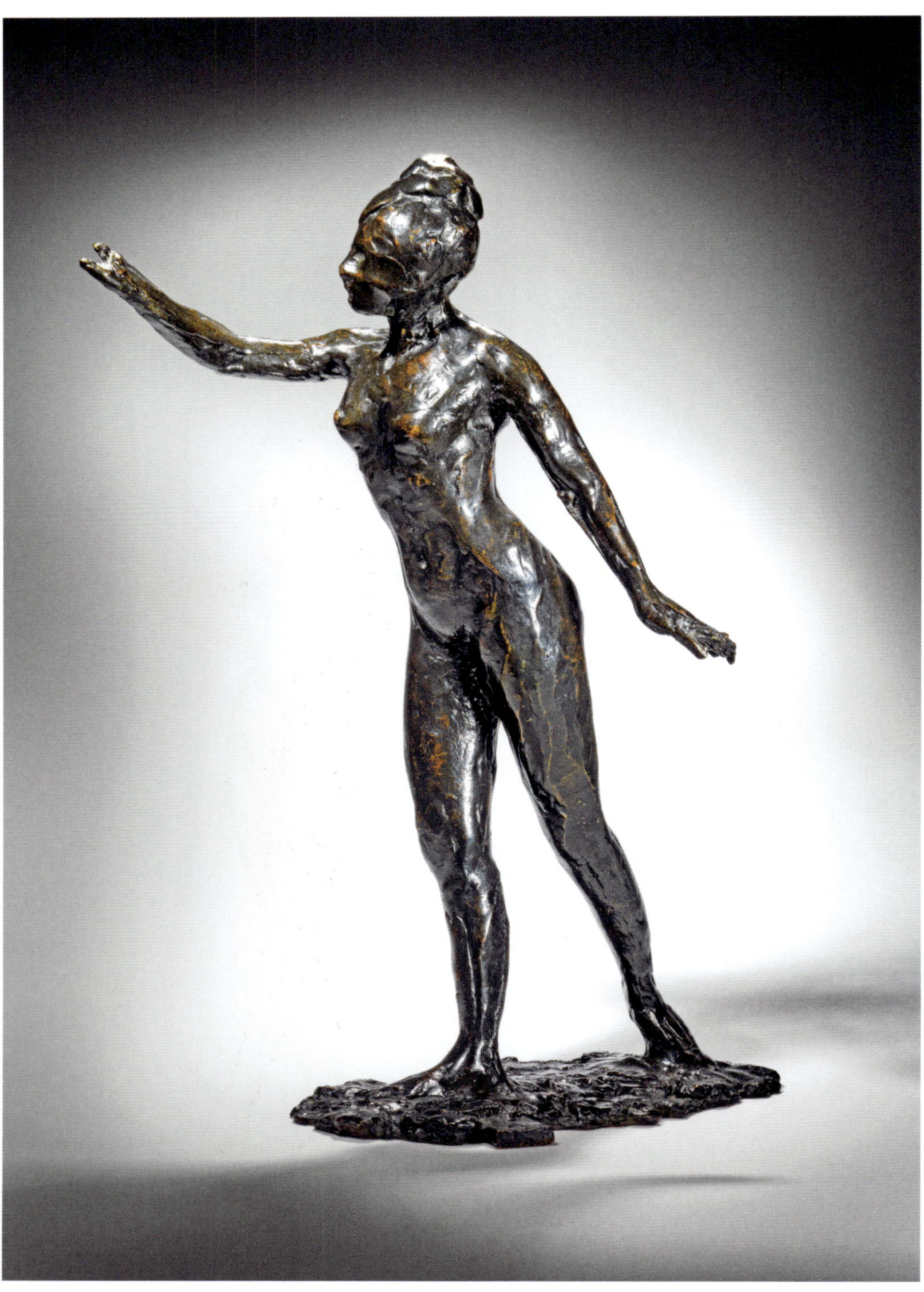

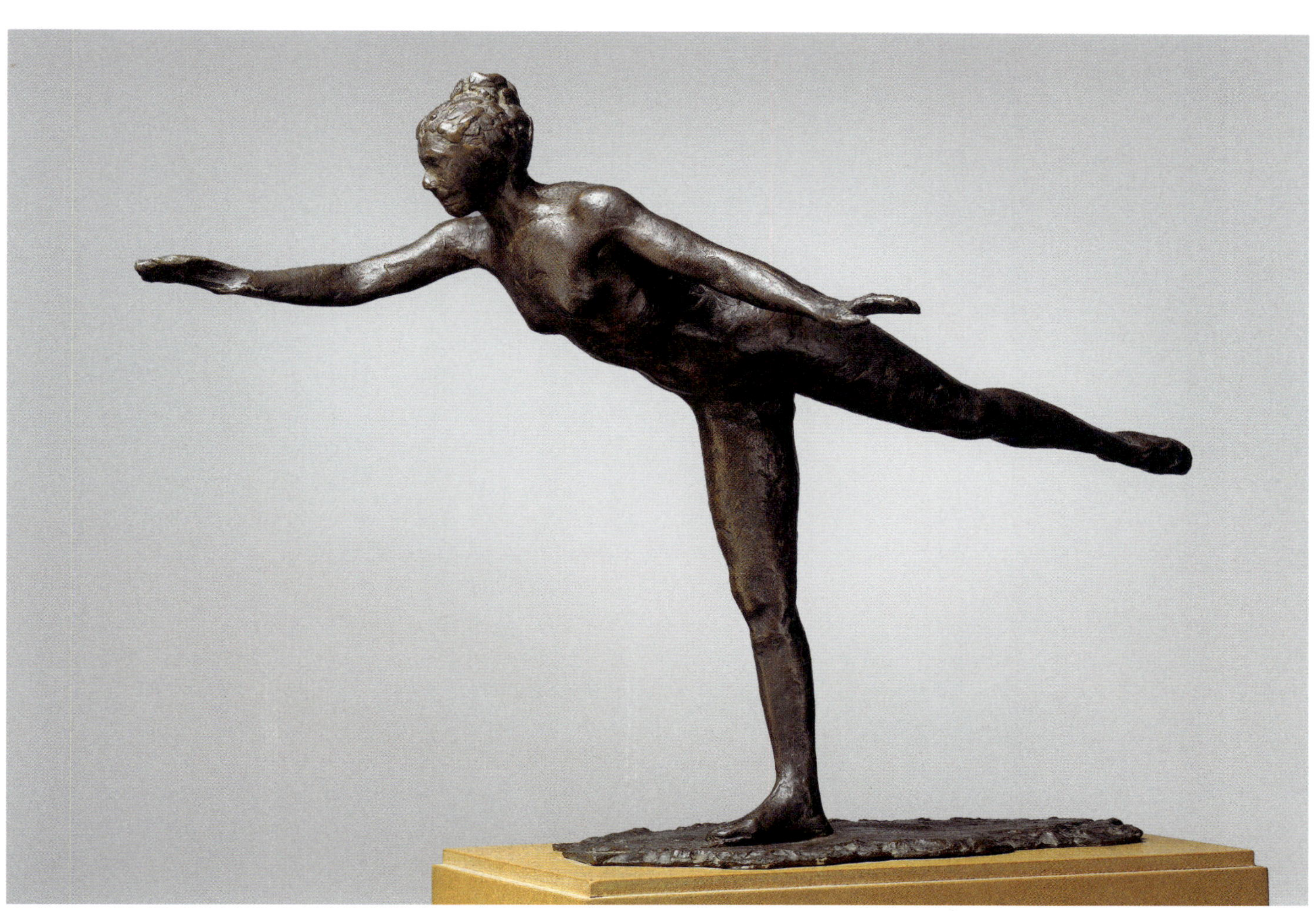

Cat. 11

Cat.12 Edgar Degas, *Grand Arabesque, Third Time (Second Version)* (Danseuse, grande arabesque, troisième temps; deuxième étude), c. 1885–1890; bronze, 40 × 50.8 × 34.3 cm; stamped on the plinth: "16/H"; Tate Gallery, London, inv. no. NO 5917 **Cat.13** Edgar Degas, *Grand Arabesque, Third Time (First Version)* (Danseuse, grande arabesque, troisième temps; première étude), c. 1885–1890; bronze, 44 × 63 × 26.5 cm; stamped on the plinth: "60/L"; private collection, London

Cat.12

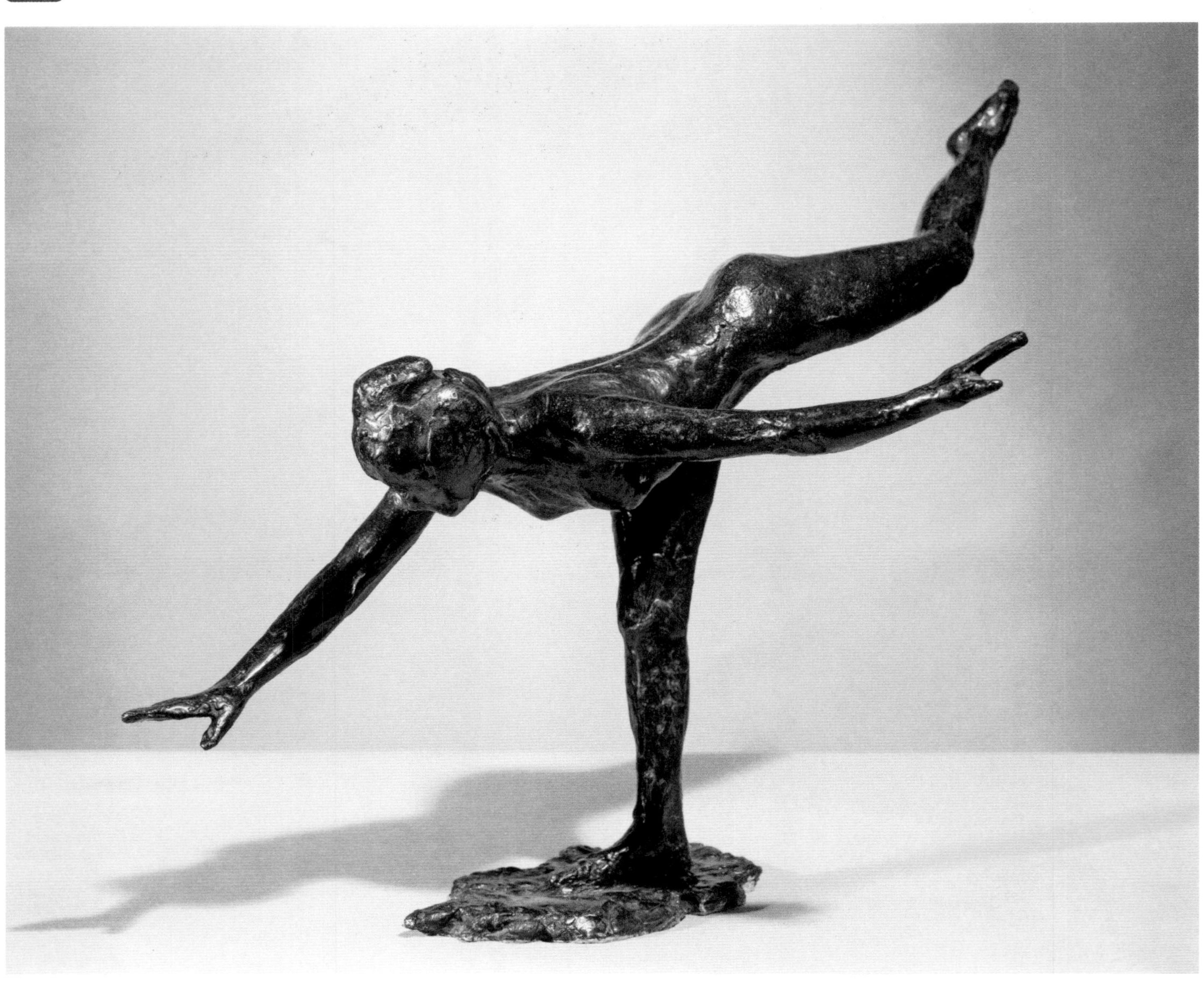

Cat. 13

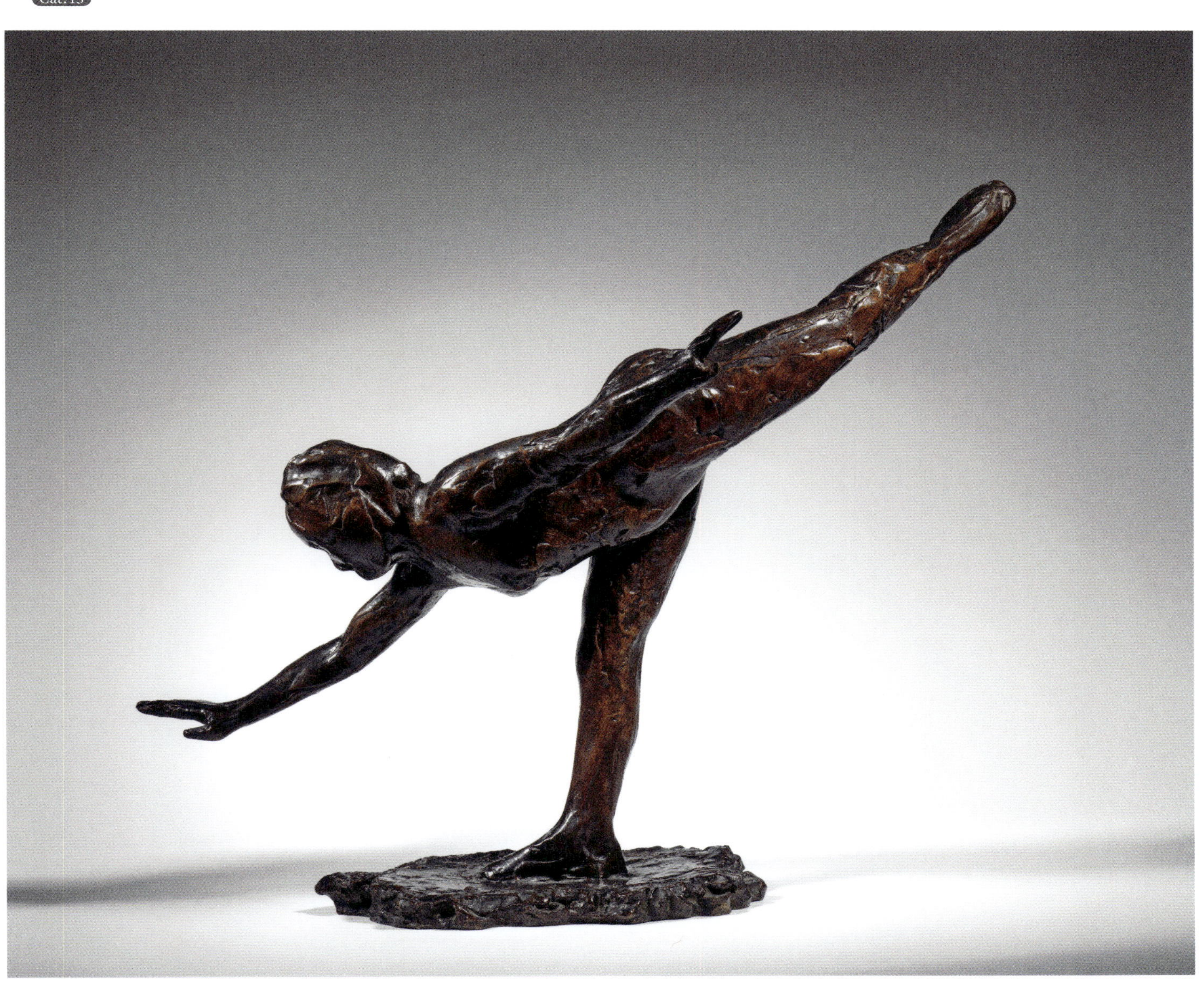

Unobserved moments – dancers offstage

When Degas began addressing the ballet, besides his interest in elegant poses he was also interested in the less glamorous moments of the métier. Among his sculptures, there are therefore numerous motifs that feature dancers stretching and warming up (cat. 16) as well as adjusting their costumes (cat. 14, 17). These less representative sequences of movements constitute an antithesis to the depictions of the human body sanctioned by the academy. Degas's dancers come across as awkward, occasionally ungraceful, but on the other hand present unusual views whose composition had no equivalent in the sculpture of the time. In these works, Degas experimented with the distribution of volumes, with weight and counter-weights as well as an arrangement of the limbs that was as multifarious as possible, whereby the viewer's gaze is guided along the figures in a constant up and down from the elbows to the ankles (cat. 24). Even cast in bronze, they still convey a vivid impression of Degas's summary modelling technique, with which he sought to work out the characteristic quality of each movement, dispensing with a detailed elaboration of the figures.

In their entirety, the sculptures reflect the thematic repertoire of his drawings and paintings, in which both sides of the everyday life of a dancer can face one another in one and the same composition. An outstanding example of this juxtaposition of rehearsal room impressions and ballet performance is the painting *Dancers on the Stage* (cat. 18). It features dancers who are about to go on stage to perform before the audience as well as dancers who are preparing to do so or are sitting on a bench waiting for their cue. Degas had a special preference for these kinds of threshold moments, for the "avant" (before) and "après" (after), terms that are included in the titles of numerous works.[1] The composition, probably initially designed in the form of drawings (fig. 1), shows the ballerinas in side or rear views with sketchily rendered facial features, with the result that none of the young women are identifiable as individuals.

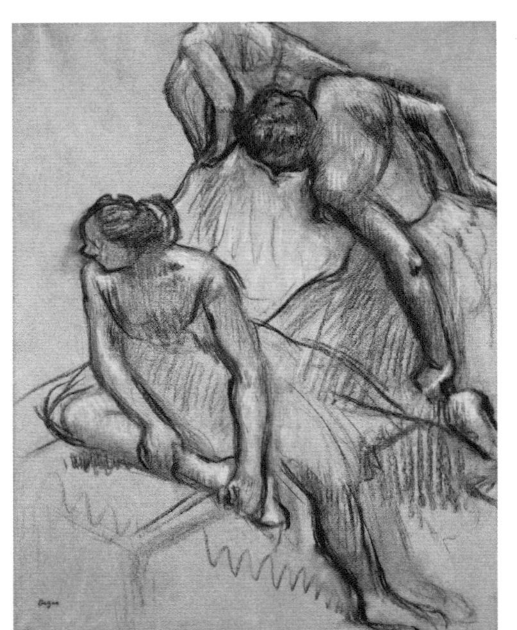

1 Edgar Degas, *Three Dancers*, c. 1889, charcoal and pastel, 59 × 45 cm, Museum of Fine Arts, Boston

The most noticeable agreement between the painting and the sculptures can be found in the figure in the middle of the group with her hands on her hips and lifting her face. This image alone features in four different sculptural versions entitled *Dancer at Rest* – two of them are unclothed (cat. 19),[2] one is outfitted with a tutu and signs of a bodice (cat. 20).[3] The latter represents an exception in the area of small-format sculptures of dancers, which Degas otherwise designed as nudes. Modelling the voluminous tutu in wax presented the artist with challenges, both with respect to the appearance of the surface as well as the stability of his construction. He stabilised it with corks that he pressed into the wax.[4] At the same time, he was aware of the fact that this unorthodox material mix was definitely problematic, as the corks could find their way to the surface and ruin the work.[5] However, he continued to make use of a wealth of materials he found in his studio – an expression of his unbroken love of experimentation. Degas fashioned the vibrant structure of the tutu by means of an open modelling technique, applying small wax globules that he spread with his fingers. For the purpose of animating the texture, he notched small indentations into the mass so that in the end, open-pored areas stood alongside smooth ones. By doing so, the sculpture reflects the light in different intensities, creating the impression of movement in the viewer's eye and evoking the illusion of lightness.

Surfaces fashioned in this way develop a productive interaction with Degas's late pastels (cat. 21), which Richard Thomson aptly described as "multicoloured high reliefs".[6] Around 1900 and due to his failing eyesight, Degas favoured pastel painting, as pastel chalk allowed him to work on the support more directly than was possible when painting with oil. In an almost sculptural manner, Degas applied the pigments one over the other in several layers and layers of lines without smearing or homogenising them, as is actually characteristic of the technique. To this end, he had to repeatedly fix the pastels in between in order to be able to apply another layer.[7] This resulted in compositions of extraordinary vibrancy and colour density whose roughly hatched surfaces correspond with the surface feel of his sculptures.

In Degas's late oeuvre, the creative processes for his two- and three-dimensional works became more and more aligned with one another. This also included the search for an ideal form, which he strove to find in a cross-genre contest. He concentrated on a few subjects and motifs, whose usability was put to the test in a permanent work in progress. The sheet with three nude dancers adjusting their invisible costumes (cat. 23), produced between 1895 and 1905, is an outstanding example of the graphic moving around a figure from three different angles.[8] By means of the turning of the heads and the bent arms, Degas conveys a continuous movement momentum that is reminiscent of the ancient sculptural group of the *Three Graces* (fig. 2).[9] The positions of the feet alone, which make reference to classic ballet positions, identify the dancers as such. Through his drawing, therefore, Degas guides viewers around his model without forcing them to change their own standpoint.

As in these large-format drawings, Degas repeated the different poses multiple times in his sculptures, in each case with minor changes regarding size, materiality or surface character. One motif that he addressed particularly intensely was the rendering of a dancer looking at the sole of her foot (cat. 15, 24). Only four versions have survived of which one Degas had cast in plaster in his lifetime in order to preserve the pose in a more durable material (fig. 3). Degas seems to have found particular pleasure in this rather profane sequence of movements – movements that required an unusual twist of the body and repeatedly opened up new, delightful views from various angles. He therefore sought to explore the rhythm of the movement in ever new attempts.[10] On the one hand, these figures constitute the antithesis of the classic dancers in arabesque (cat. 10–13); on the other, they also blur the boundaries to the range of motifs of bathing women (cat. 35) that are occasionally seen stepping out of the tub in similar poses.[11] — AE

"Must I be such a fool as to have put corks in this figure! […] Look at the back completely ruined!"

Edgar Degas, quoted in: Alice Michel, 1919

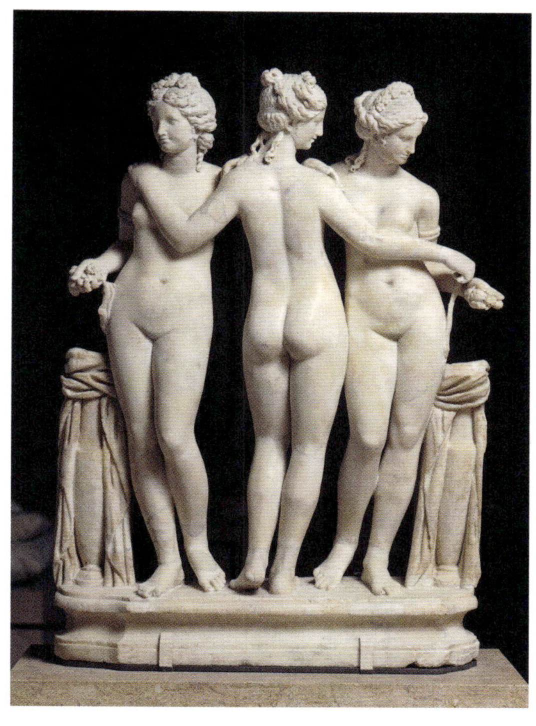

2 *The Three Graces*, Roman copy of a Greek original, second century CE, marble, height 119 cm, Musée du Louvre, Paris

1   In the area of ballet motifs, see, among others, *Danseuses roses: Avant le ballet*, 1884, Ny Carlsberg Glyptotek, Copenhagen, as well as the numerous portrayals of jockeys before the start of the race, such as *Course de gentlemen: Avant le départ*, 1862–1882, Musée d'Orsay, Paris. "Après" is generally reserved for figures of bathing women; see, among others, *Après le bain*, c. 1900, Kunstmuseum Solothurn.

2   Inv. cat. Washington 2010, nos. 19, 26; Virginia Museum of Fine Arts, Richmond, inv. no. 1993.61.

3   Virginia Museum of Fine Arts, Richmond, inv. no. 1993.63; see inv. cat. Washington 2010, p. 370.

4   Millard 1976, p. 37.

5   Degas's model Pauline quotes the artist as having said the following: "Must I be such a fool as to have put corks in this figure! Imbecile that I am, with my mania for wanting to save a few pennies! Look at the back completely ruined!" Edgar Degas, quoted in: ibid., p. 37.

6   Thomson 2009, p. 75.

7   On Degas's pastel technique, see Maheux 1992, p. 32. See also Vollard 1925b, esp. p. 66.

8   See exh. cat. Karlsruhe 2014, pp. 195–197, no. 78.

9   Exh. cat. New York/Edinburgh 2009, pp. 252–255, no. 112, esp. pp. 254–255. Legend has it that when asked by his collector Louisine Havemeyer why he depicted so many dancers, he replied: "Because, Madame, it is all that is left to us of the combined movements of the Greeks." Thomson 1995, p. 28.

10 Curt Glaser described this process as the transformation of a body into a sculptural ornament; Glaser 1922a, p. 127.

11 See Armstrong 2012, p. 26.

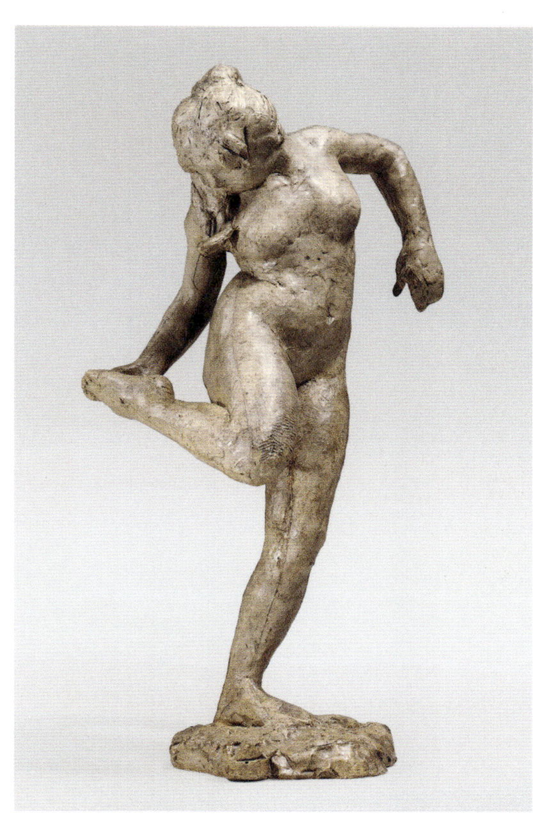

3 Edgar Degas, *Dancer Looking at the Sole of Her Right Foot*, c. 1900–1903, plaster, height 48 cm, private collection

Cat. 14

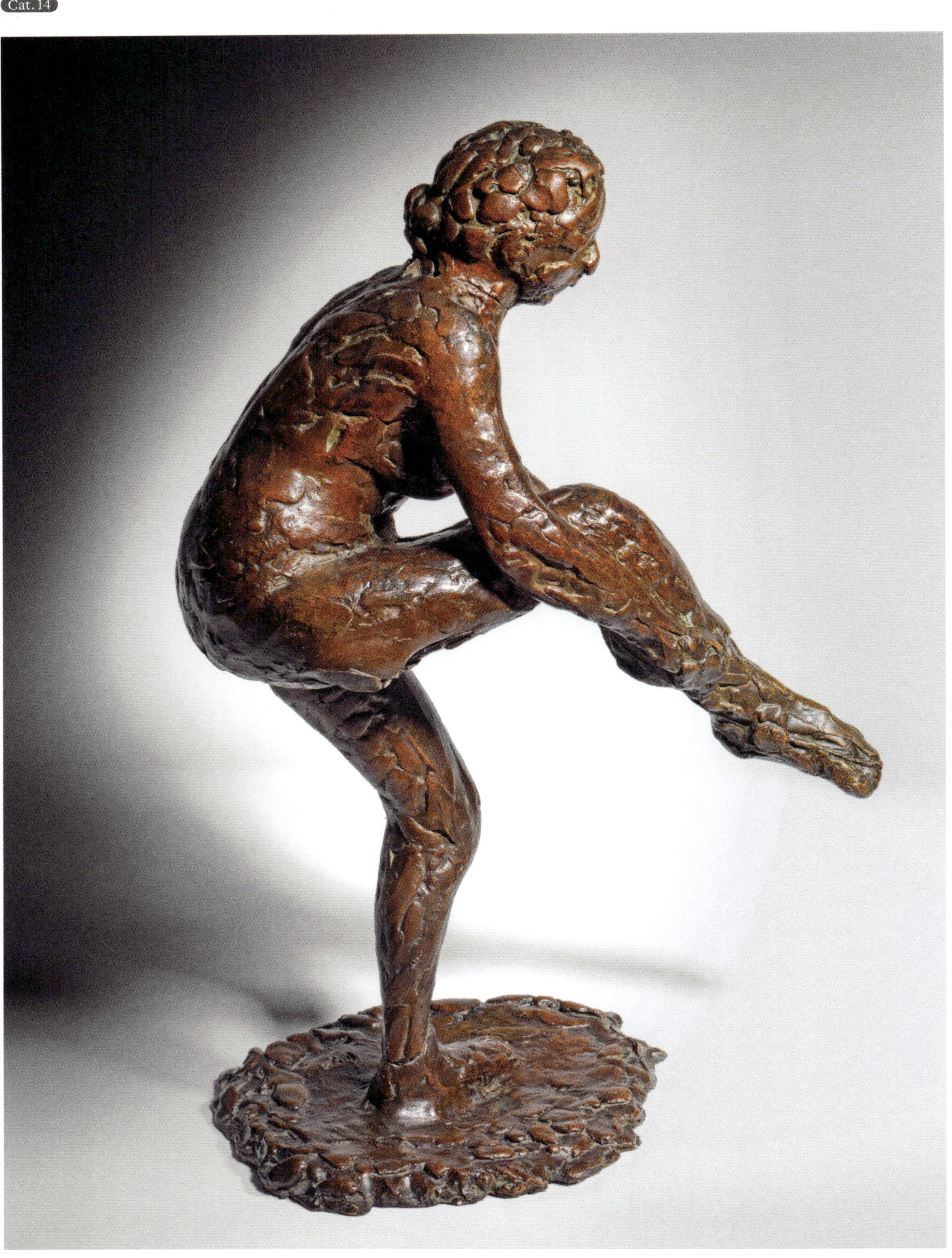

Cat. 15

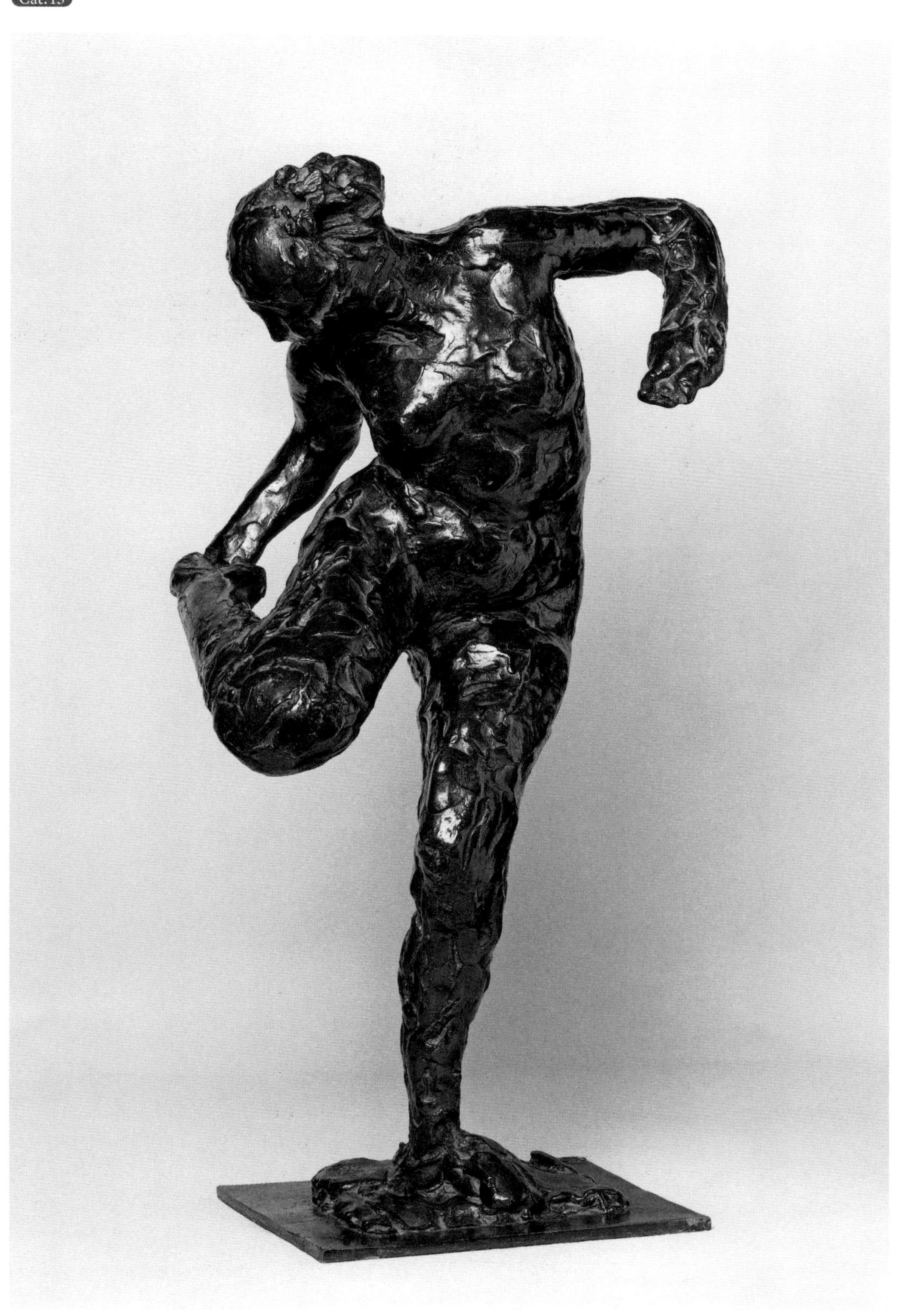

Cat.16 Edgar Degas, *Dancer Holding Her Right Foot in Her Right Hand (Danseuse tenant son pied droit dans sa main droite)*, c. 1900–1911; bronze, 53.2 × 38 × 20 cm; stamped on the plinth: "23/O"; Städel Museum, Frankfurt am Main, inv. no. SGP 63

Cat.17 Edgar Degas, *Dancer Fastening the String of Her Tights (Danseuse attachant le cordon de son maillot)*, c. 1885–1890; bronze, 43 × 21.6 × 15.3 cm; stamped on the plinth: "33/R"; Ny Carlsberg Glyptotek, Copenhagen, inv. no. MIN 2659

Cat.16

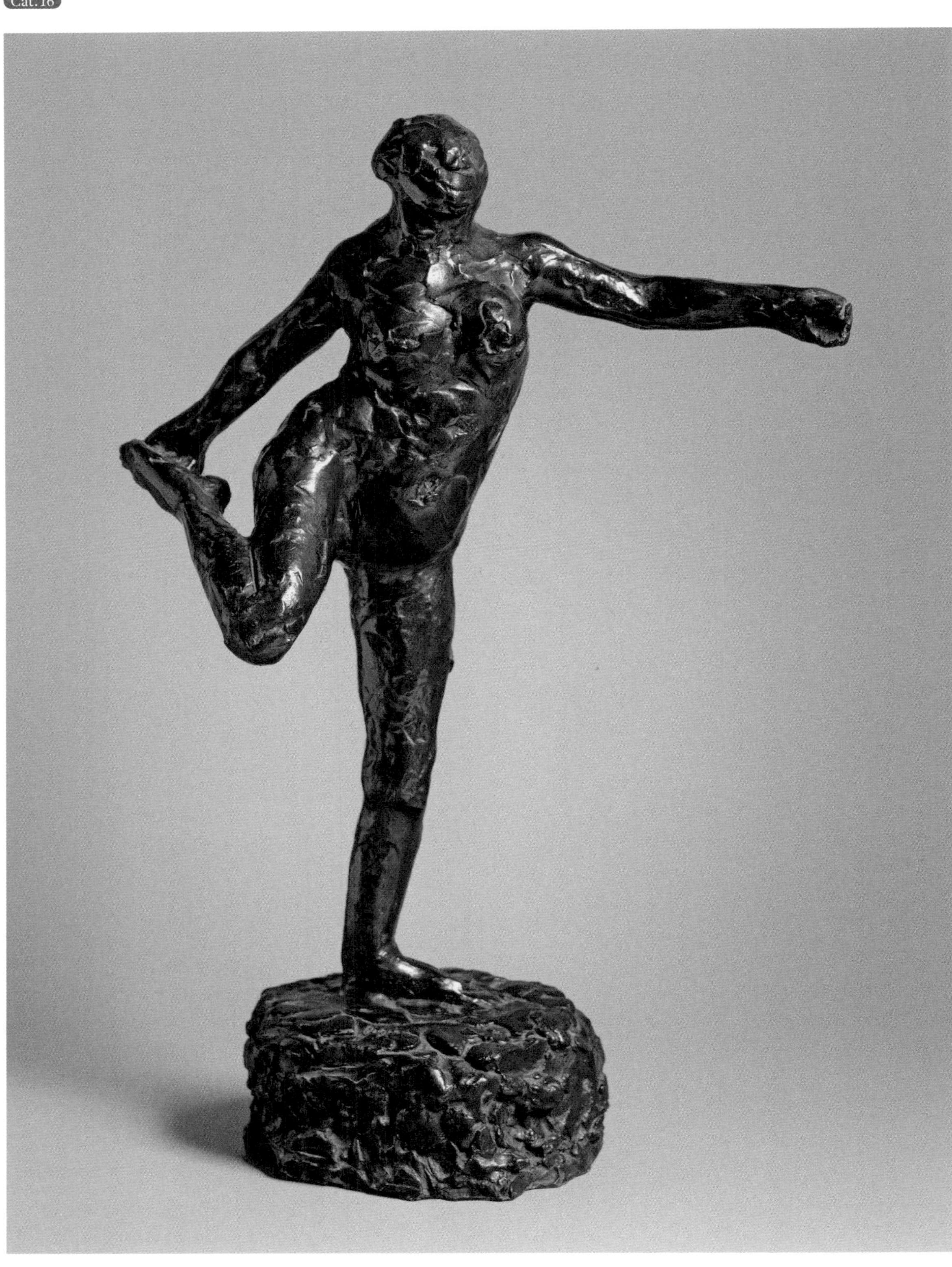

Cat. 17

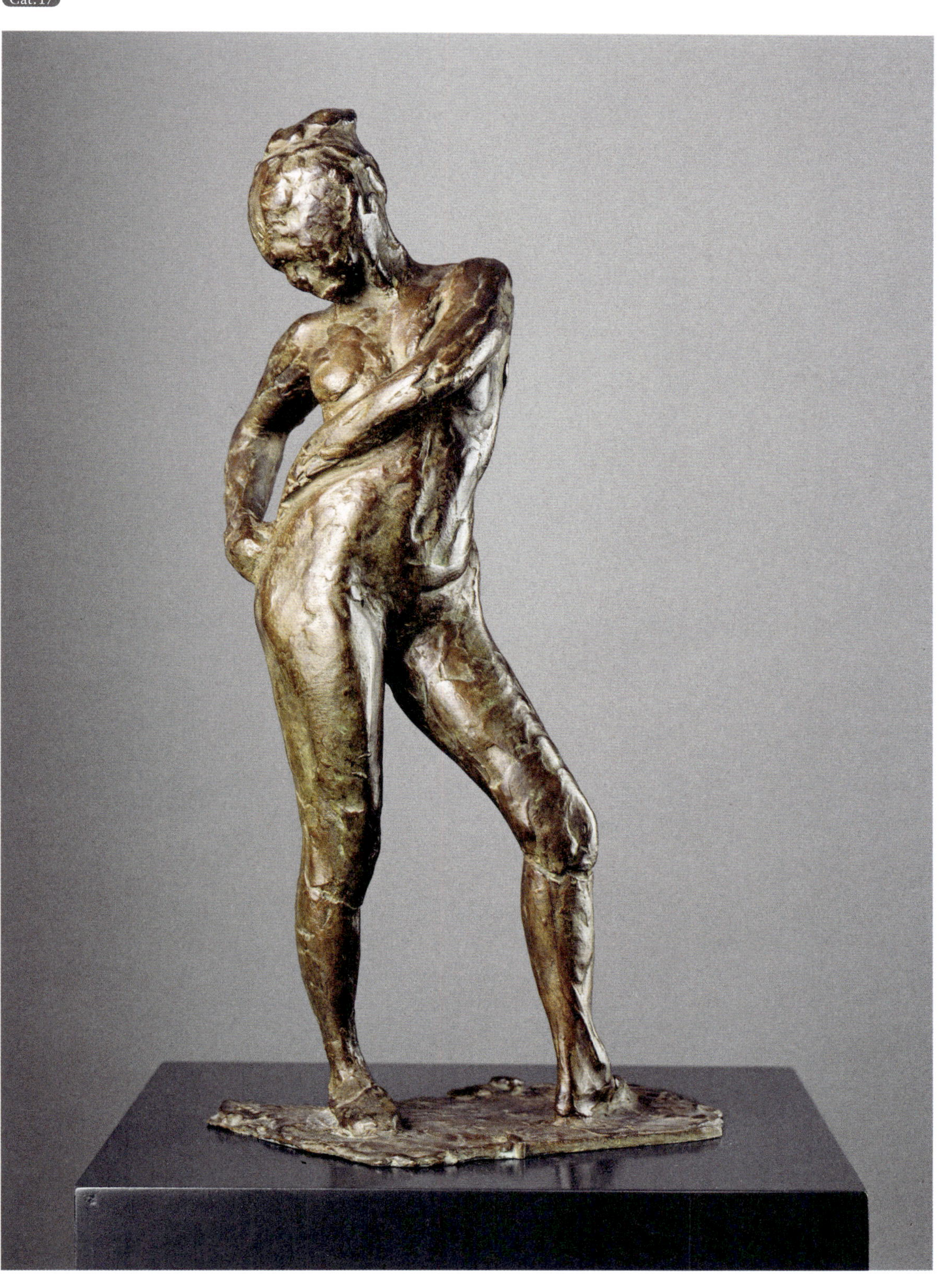

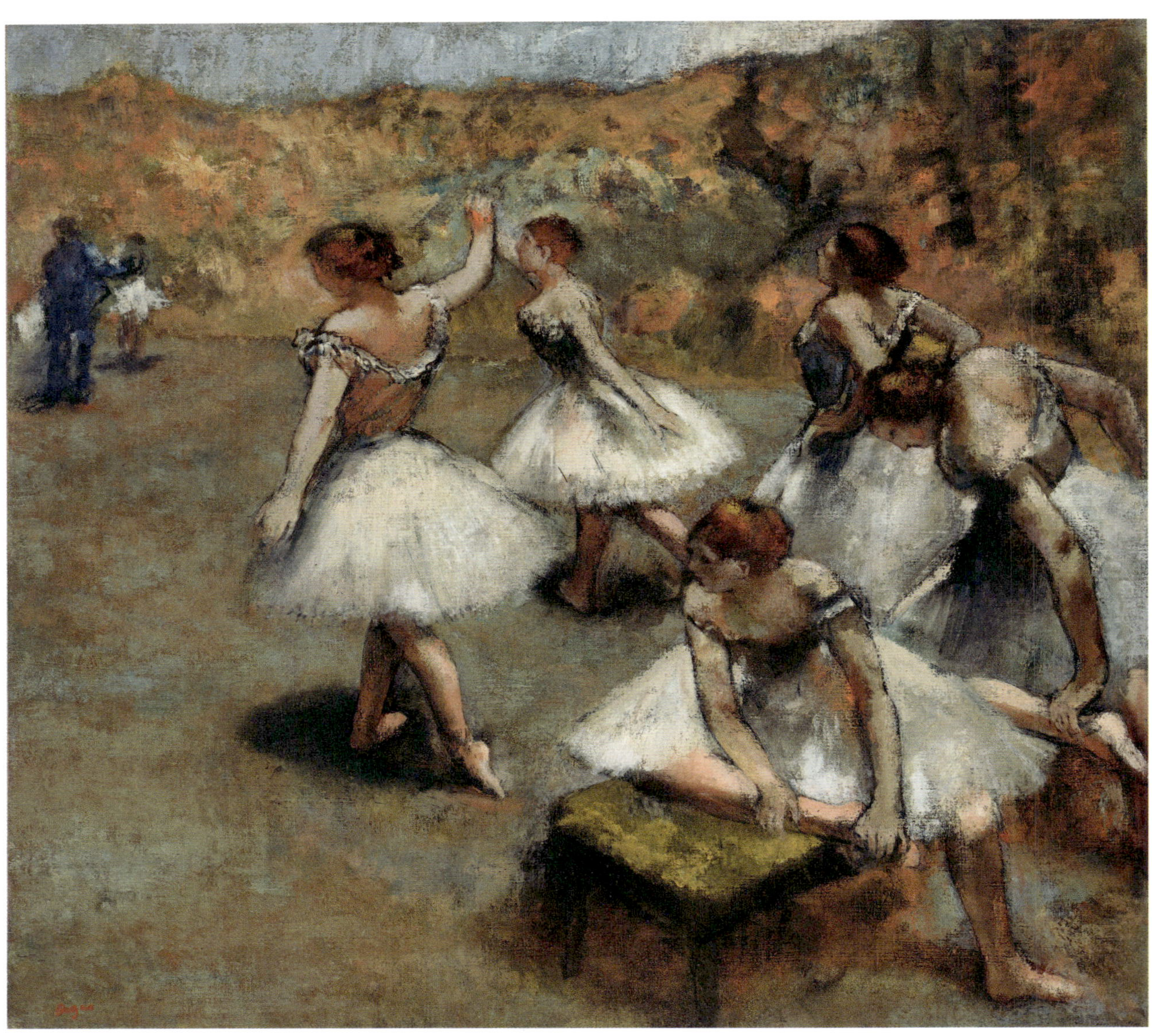

Cat.18 Edgar Degas, Dancers on the Stage (Danseuses sur la scène), c. 1889; oil on canvas, 76 × 82 cm; Musée des Beaux-Arts, Lyon, Legs Jacqueline Delubac, 1997, inv. no. 1997-29 **Cat.19** Edgar Degas, Dancer at Rest, Hands behind Her Back, Right Leg Forward (Danseuse au repos, les mains sur les hanches, jambe droite en avant, première étude), 1885–1890; bronze, 45.5 × 14.7 × 23.5 cm; stamped on the plinth: "41/HER"; private collection

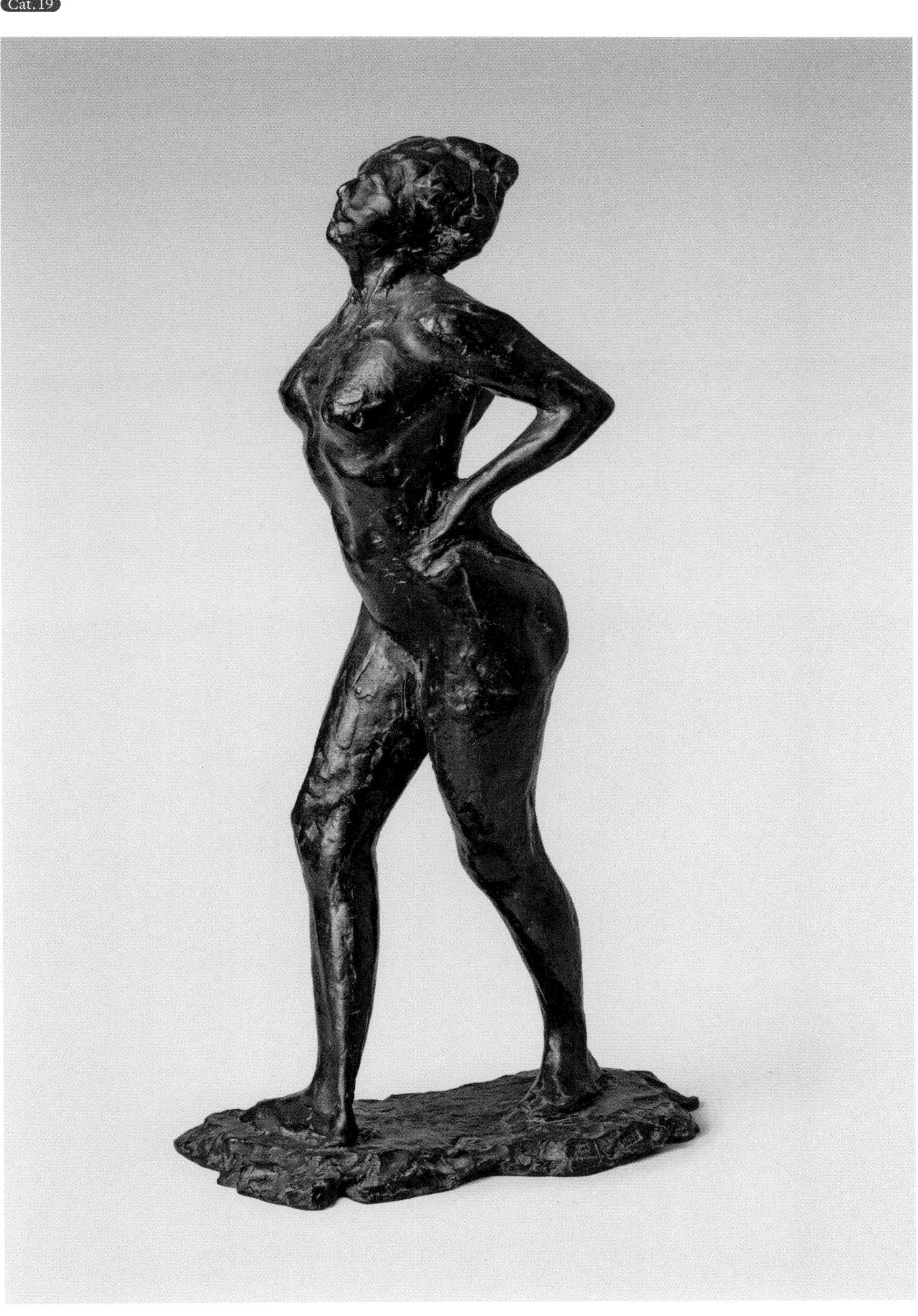
Cat. 19

Cat.20

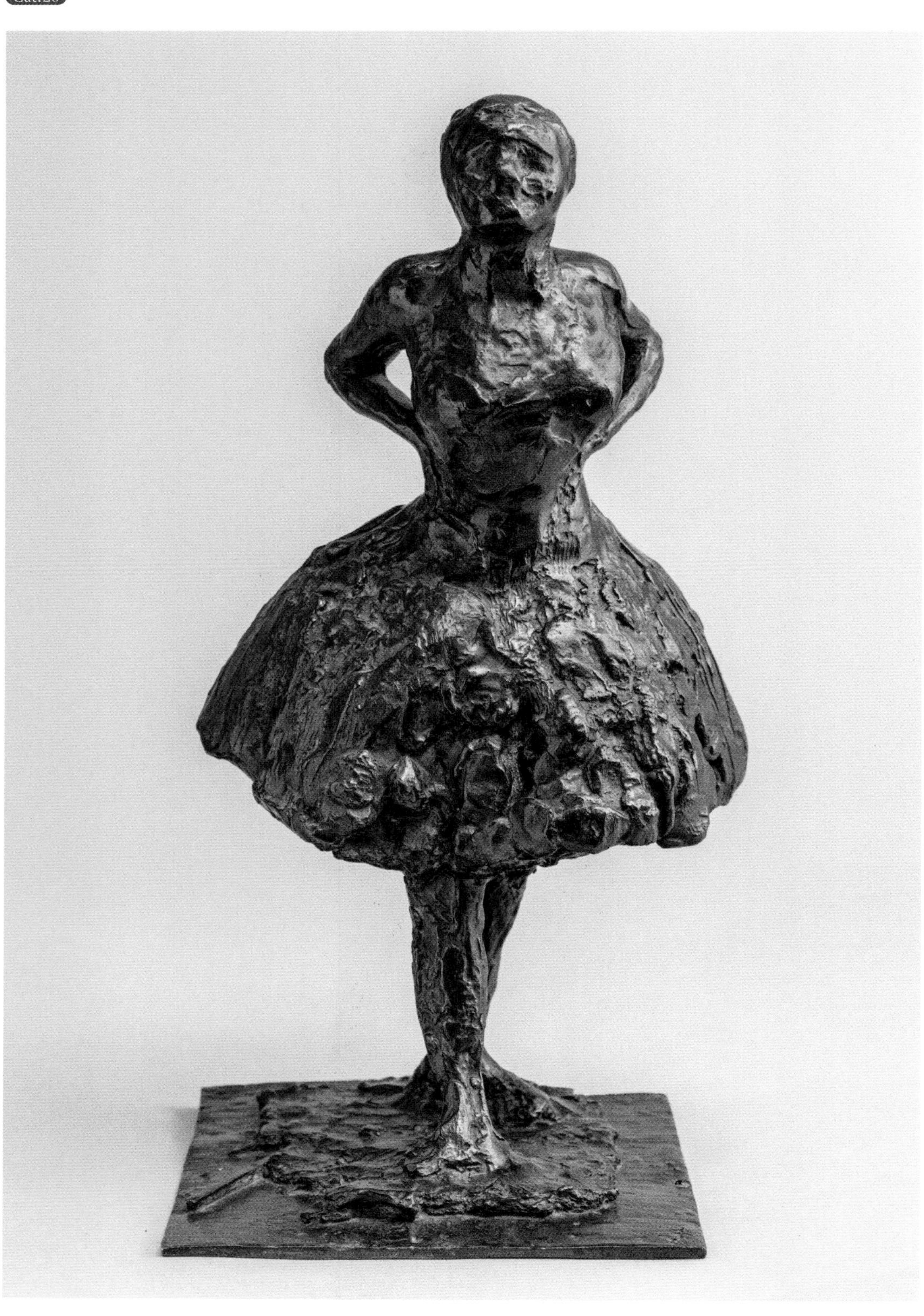

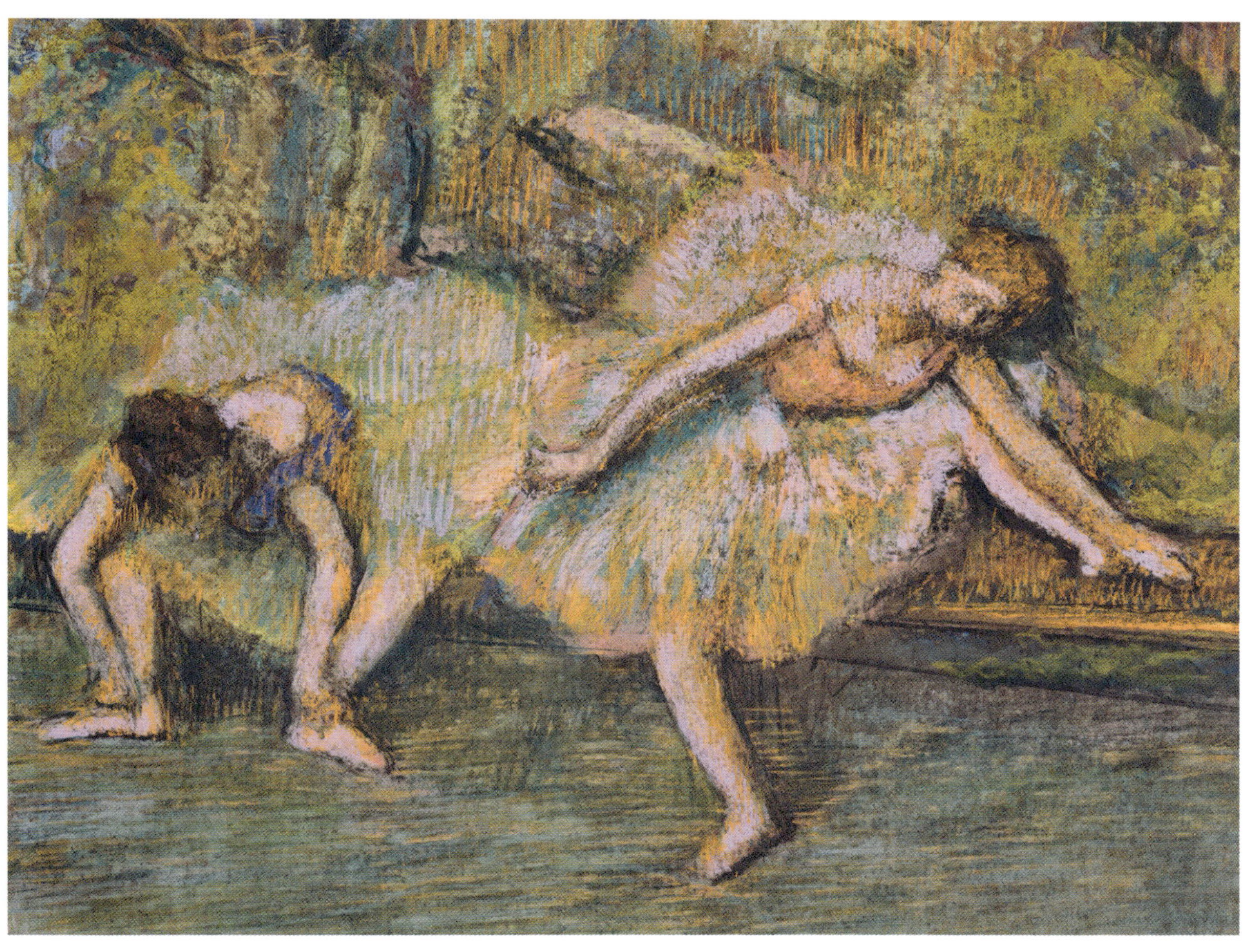

Cat. 21

Cat.22 Jean-Louis Forain, **Dancers in Pink** (Danseuses en rose), c. 1905; oil on canvas, 60.3 × 73.6 cm; Carmen Thyssen-Bornemisza Collection, Madrid, on loan at the Museo Thyssen-Bornemisza, inv. no. CTB. 1998.58 Cat.23 Edgar Degas, **Three Dancers** (Trois danseuses), 1895–1905; charcoal on tracing paper, 47.7 × 38.5 cm; Collection Jean Bonna, Geneva

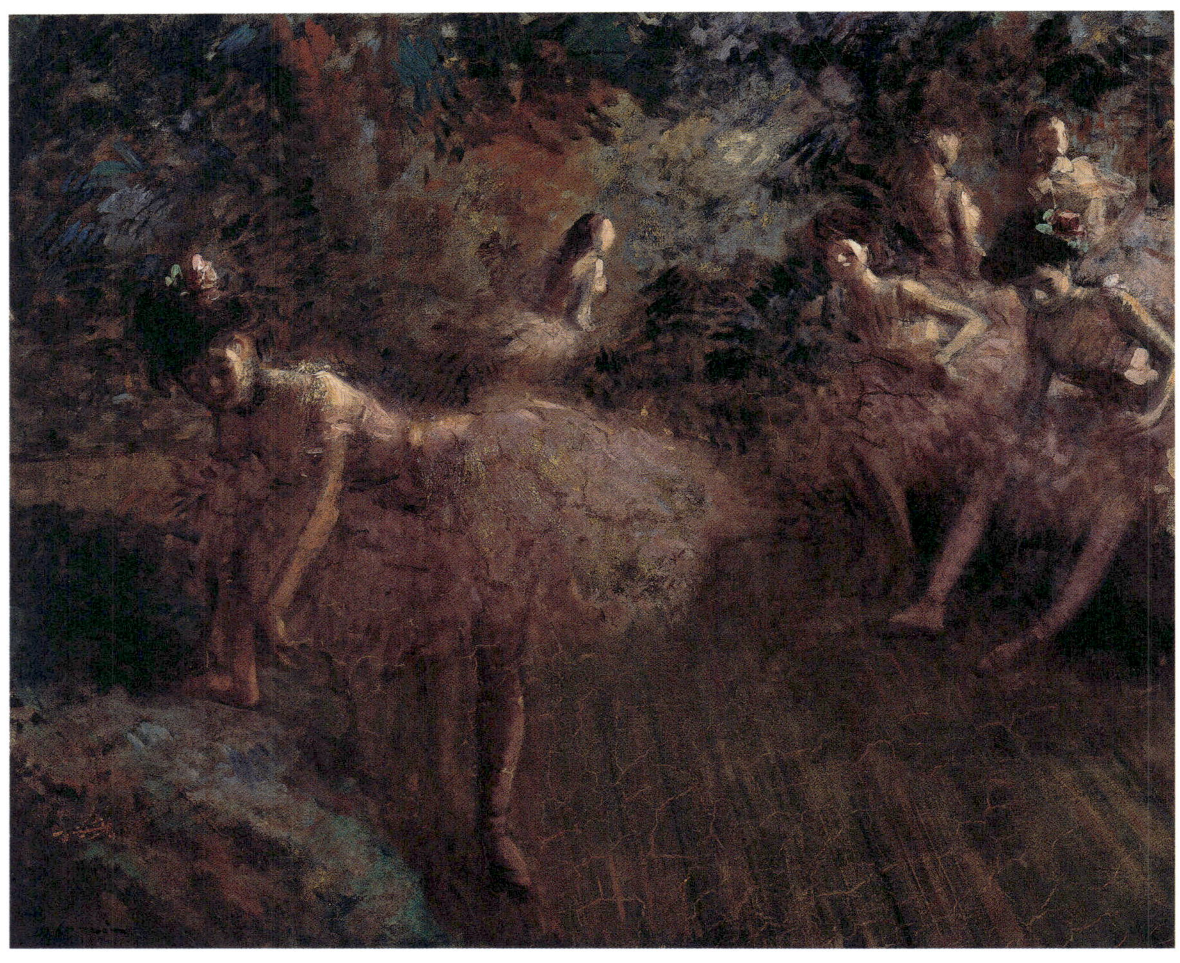

Cat.22

Cat.23

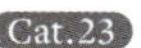

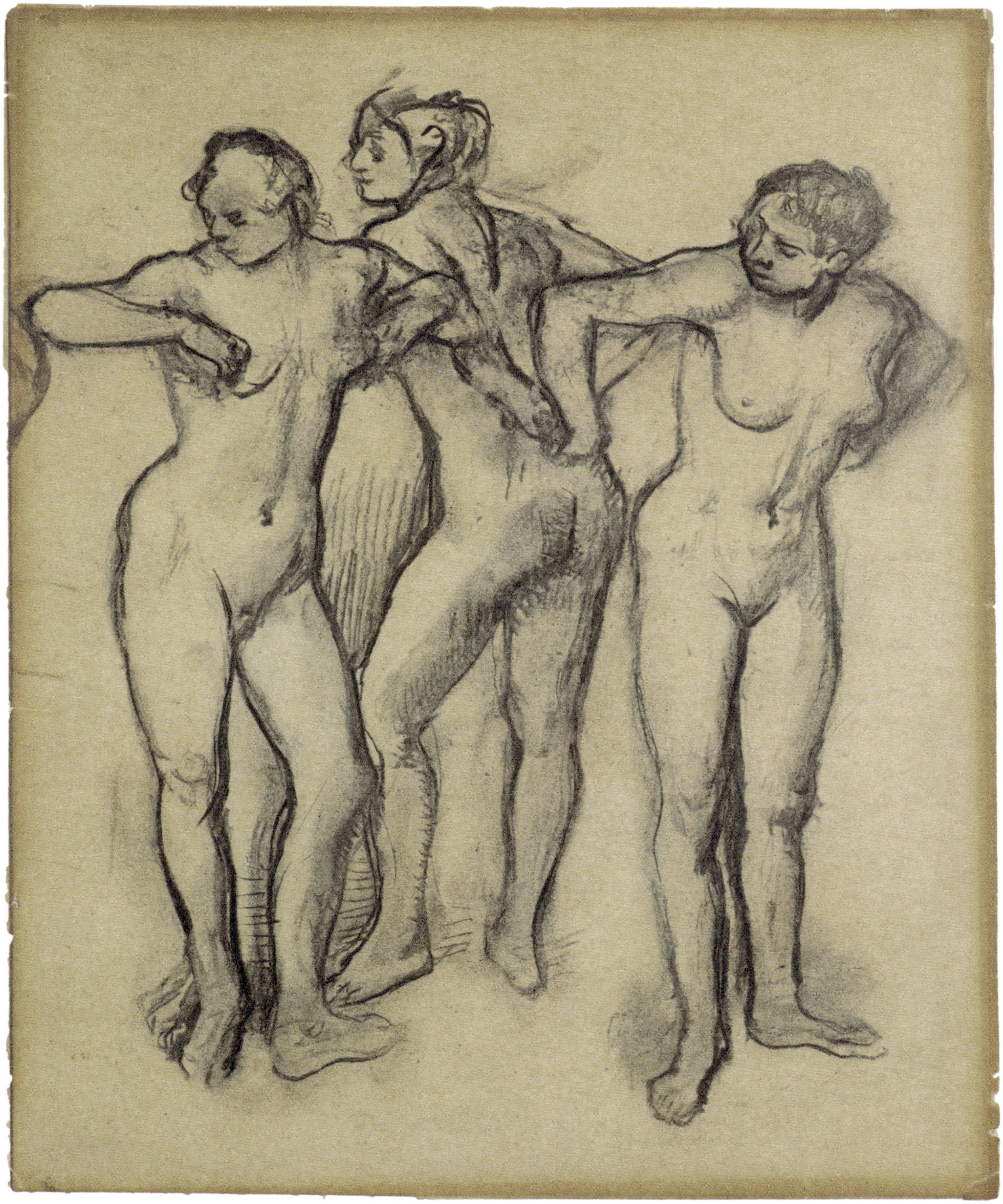

Cat.24

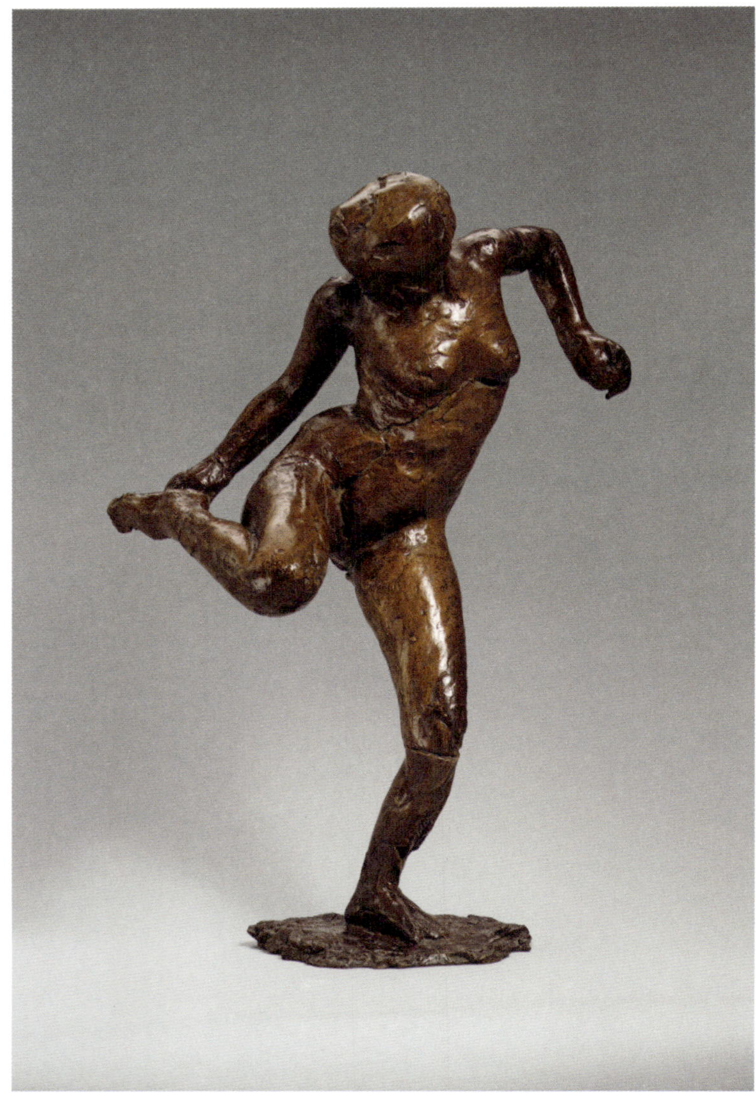
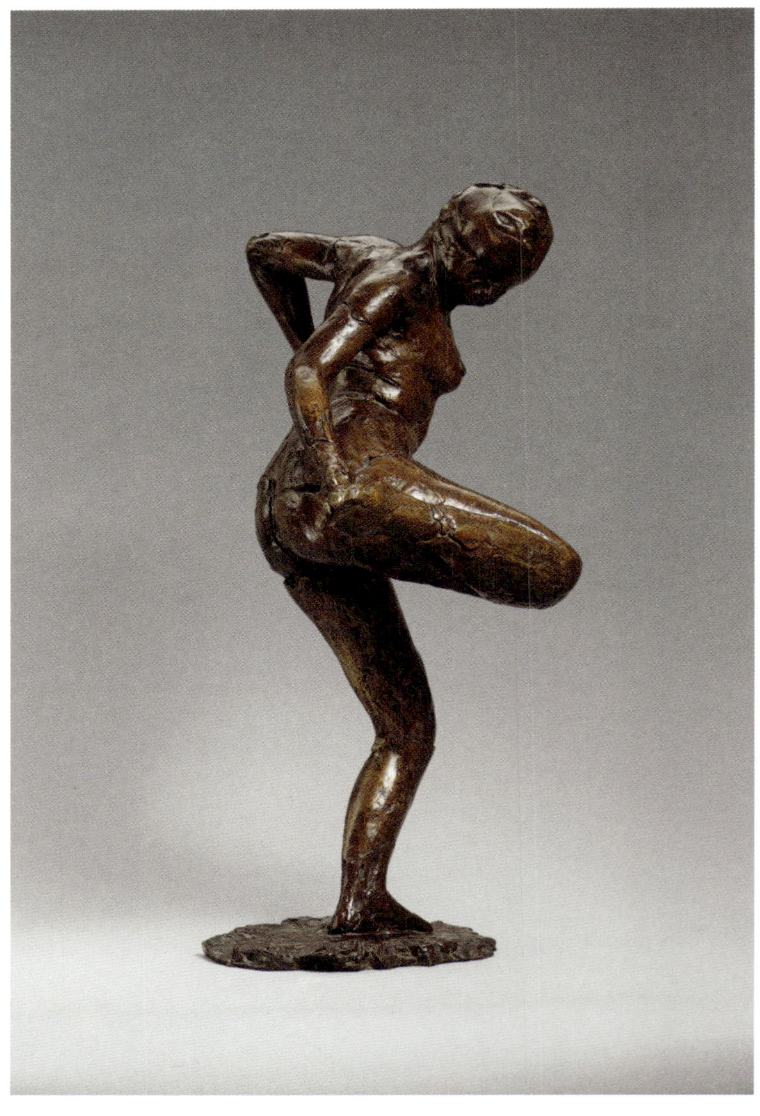

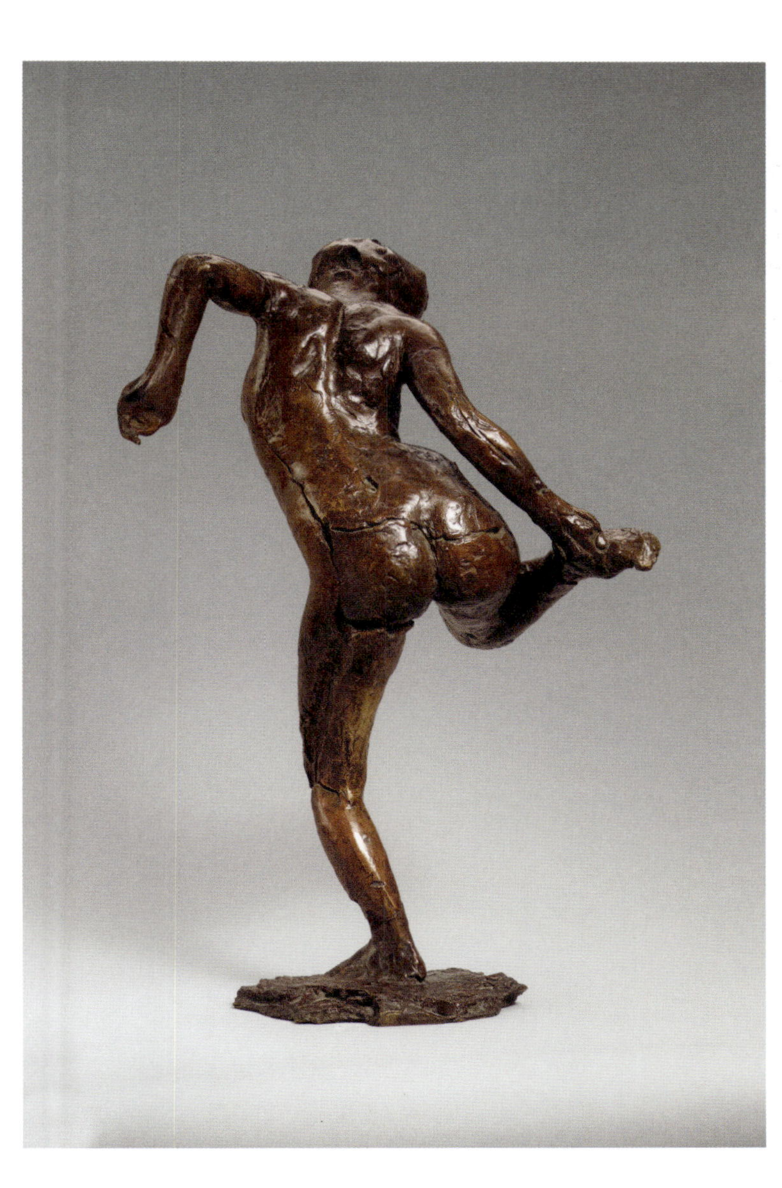
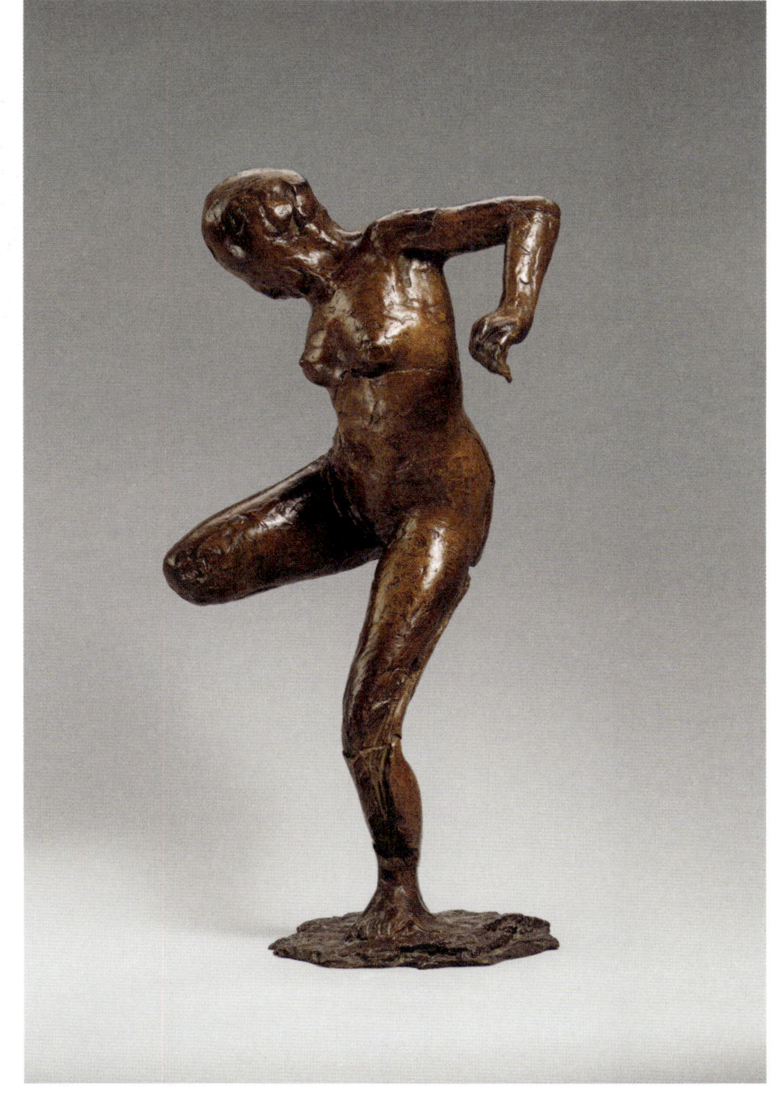

Edgar Degas's nude figures

Nude figures run like a golden thread through the work of Edgar Degas. From the beginning of his artistic career to his late oeuvre, hardly any other motif engaged him so intensely and took shape in such a wealth of technical variants than the female nude.[1] Degas initially approached the human anatomy by copying works by old masters, as prescribed by classic academic training. The young artist found references in Paris in the sheer inexhaustible collections of the Louvre, in the gallery of prints at the Bibliothèque nationale, as well as on his study tour through Italy from 1856 to 1859, during which he assembled an extensive repertoire of copies of poses and postures from Renaissance works of art. One could discern from that moment on that, whereas Degas schooled himself in the famous masters, he showed little interest in idealised nude figures oriented directly to the viewer. Instead, he copied numerous unusual details from paintings and cycles of frescoes. He concentrated on marginal figures, far from the actual image narrative, that caught his eye thanks to particular physical turns and twists.[2]

During the 1870s and 1880s, Degas brought his nude motifs up to date by integrating them into a modern context. For this purpose, he chose boudoir scenes from everyday life that show women bathing, washing, combing their hair (cat. 26) or getting ready for bed (cat. 36, 37). Their activities are neither legitimised by embedding them in a biblical or mythological narrative framework, neither do they seem to address a specific viewer. As if observed through a keyhole, Degas generally presents his models in anonymous rear views, in awkward poses concentrating on their personal hygiene, occasionally flanked by figures that assist them with getting out of the tub or with drying. At the same time, the postures and vantage points he selects are in no way captured spontaneously: they are the result of a carefully thought-out pictorial composition process that, besides orienting itself to copies after classic art history and studies after a model, was also inspired by the informal poses found in Japanese colour woodcuts (fig. 1), which became style-defining for Degas's work.[3]

Degas translated the nude figures realised in the form of pastels and monotypes, of which he presented ten in the eighth Impressionist exhibition in 1886,[4] into sculptures in the years that followed. The works assembled in this entry are five narrative objects fashioned in great detail that he produced from the 1880s to 1911 (cat. 25, 27–30). They feature women bathing, washing, drying themselves, combing their hair or being massaged. For this panorama of very different scenes from the area of personal hygiene, Degas chose not only subjects that, by academic standards, hardly seem to be worthy of being depicted in a sculpture; he also used materials such as wax and plastiline that were even more alien to art. In addition, his

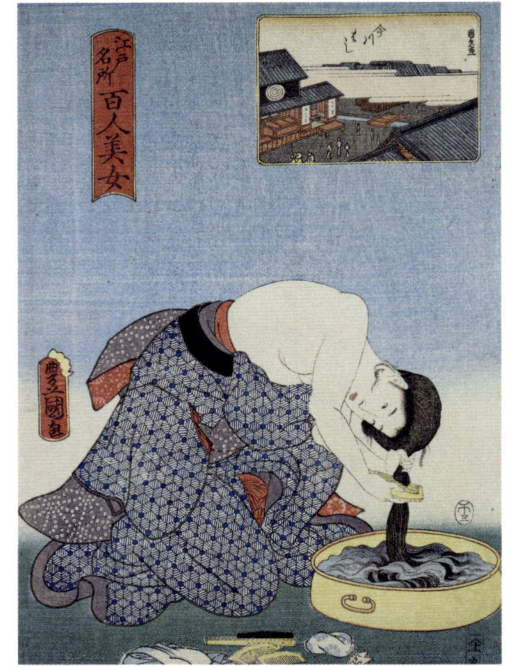

1   Toyokuni III (Utagawa Kunisada),
Young Woman Washing Her Hair, c. 1858,
colour woodcut, 36.2 × 24.5 cm,
Museum für Kunst und Gewerbe, Hamburg

unconventional approach to the craft of the sculptor reveals itself in his use of cork, plaster, wood, paper and crown cork, which he used as filling material or for stabilising purposes. He also added ceramic bowls (cat. 27), metal strips and textile fabrics stiffened with plaster in order to lend his figures as realistic an impression as possible as well as a varied structure. Attempts were made in the posthumously created bronze casts to do justice to this variety in material through the patination, which was only rudimentarily effective. The translation of the artist's sketchy modelling style appears to be clearly more successful, as traces of work and fingerprints are visible in the metal cast.

Whereas Degas could construct bold perspectives, steep top views or views from below, as well as details at his own discretion, the "pictorial mastery" of his sculptures required the viewer's intense involvement. An outstanding example of this is *The Tub* (cat. 29), probably produced in 1889, which ties in thematically with his renderings in pastel (fig. 2). Because of the edge of the tub, the unusual composition of a woman lying in a washtub can only be completely understood in an abrupt oblique view of it. This is due to Degas's aspiration to create compositions from unaccustomed visual axes in order to activate the viewer's gaze.[5] However, Degas did not assign his sculpture a defined front side, but rather offered surprising and attractive views from any perspective, thus animating viewers to continue walking around it.

Created as personal study material, these works were not initially made for an external viewer but primarily served the artist's own purposes. Hence Degas did not exhibit his sculptures during his lifetime, and he only showed this share of his oeuvre to a few friends and colleagues in the protected atmosphere of his studio. To a certain extent, these works took the place of studying after a model, and he could focus his attention on the creative process. Yet to a much greater extent, the sculpture was a part of his reinsurance strategy for the purpose of clarifying specific poses and contours and of examining them with respect to their relevance for his work. The obvious parallels between individual sculptures such as *Seated Woman Wiping Her Left Leg* (cat. 30) and portrayals as a photograph (fig. 3) and as a painting (fig. 4), produced about the same time, bespeak the close interplay of the techniques, which enriched one another and inspired the artist to undertake ever-new attempts. Dealing with a motif in a variety of different media reflects the core of the "Degas method", which opened up scope for his eagerness to experiment artistically through constant repetition and variation of a composition.

Degas's bathing women and his boudoir scenes left a lasting impression on his contemporaries. In the context of the exhibition, representative of this are two pastels by Federico Zandomeneghi

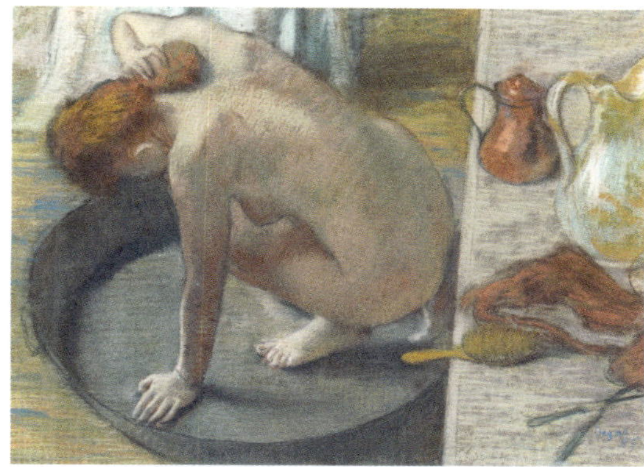

2 Edgar Degas, *The Tub*, 1886, pastel on card, 60 × 83 cm, Musée d'Orsay, Paris

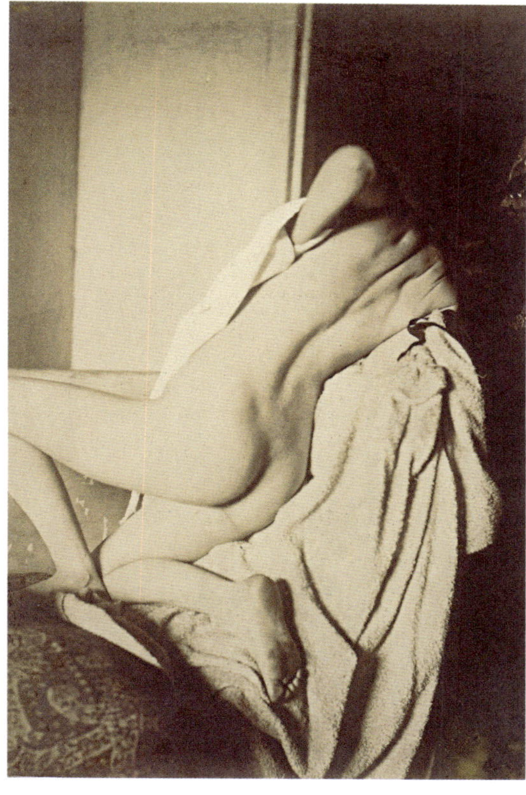

3 Edgar Degas, *After the Bath, Woman Drying Her Back*, 1896, photograph, 16.5 × 12 cm, The J. Paul Getty Museum, Los Angeles

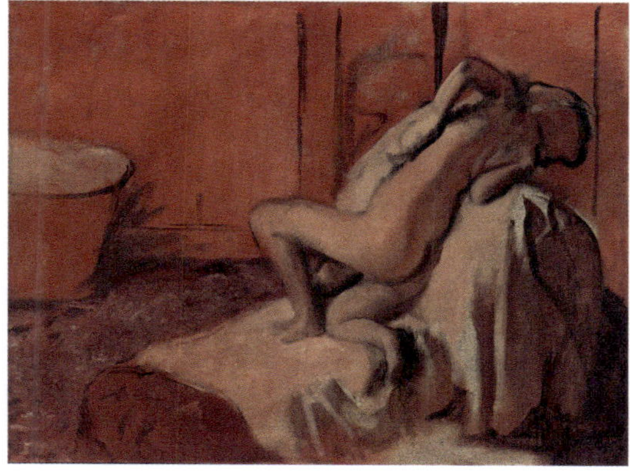

4 Edgar Degas, *After the Bath* (*Woman Drying Herself*), c. 1896, oil on canvas, 89 × 116.8 cm, Philadelphia Museum of Art

(1841–1917; cat. 31, 32). The Venetian, who resided in Paris from 1874, maintained a particularly intense relationship with Degas, whose Neapolitan family background made him the centre of the group of young Italian artists who gathered around him.[6] Zandomeneghi's work *Nude Drying Herself* (cat. 31), which can be dated to about 1887, is the faithful copy of a pastel that Degas had presented the year before in the eighth Impressionist exhibition.[7] The scene *The Awakening* (cat. 32), created approximately a decade later, also underscores the sustained model character of Degas's motifs and painting technique for Zandomeneghi's oeuvre.

Rodin's sculpture of a woman combing her hair (cat. 33), whose informal character and subject matter suggest an examination of Degas's sculpture *Woman Combing Her Hair* (cat. 25), presents itself remote from an epigonic approach to the latter's works. Degas and Rodin had a high opinion of one another, even though an intense contact or a lively artistic change remains speculative and is sparsely documented in source materials.[8] Both works exemplify the departure from a subject seemingly worthy of being depicted in a sculpture in favour of everyday scenes. In this way, Degas and Rodin made subjects accessible to a medium that painting had already tapped into two decades prior to that. The development of sculpture at the outset of the twentieth century is not conceivable without Degas and Rodin. With his reduced form of sculptural creations, it was especially Degas who opened the door to the further abstraction and deformation of bodily forms as they would become palpable some years later, in particular, in the female nudes by Henri Matisse (1869–1951; cat. 34).[9] — AE

1 For general information on this, see Thomson 1988; exh. cat. Boston/Paris 2012.

2 See Eiling 2016, pp. 122–123.

3 For general information on this, see Göthe 2014.

4 Exh. cat. Paris 1886, nos. 19–28, captioned with: "Suite de nuds [sic] de femmes se baignant, se lavant, se séchant, s'essuyant, se peignant ou se faisant peigner (Pastels)"; quoted in: Berson 1996, vol. 1, p. 422.

5 In order to be able to draw motifs from different heights, the artist considered setting up ladders or pedestals in his studio, as he noted in his sketchbooks: "Projets d'atelier [sic] / établier des gradins tout autour de la salle / pour habituer à dessiner de bas et de haut les choses." Degas 1985, sketchbook no. 30 (1877–1883), pp. 133–135, esp. p. 134, sheet 210.

6 For general information on this, see exh. cat. Edinburgh 2003.

7 Edgar Degas, *Woman Drying Her Foot*, c. 1885/86, pastel, 50.2 × 54 cm, The Metropolitan Museum of Art, New York.

8 For general information on this, see exh. cat. Wuppertal 2016.

9 See König 1997.

Cat.25 Edgar Degas, Woman Arranging Her Hair (Femme se coiffant), 1880–1900; bronze, 47 × 25.7 × 17.5 cm; stamped on the plinth: "50/R"; Ny Carlsberg Glyptotek, Copenhagen, inv. no. MIN 2681 Cat.26 Edgar Degas, Combing the Hair (La Coiffure), 1886–90; charcoal and pastel on paper, 58.9 × 47 cm; private collection

Cat.25

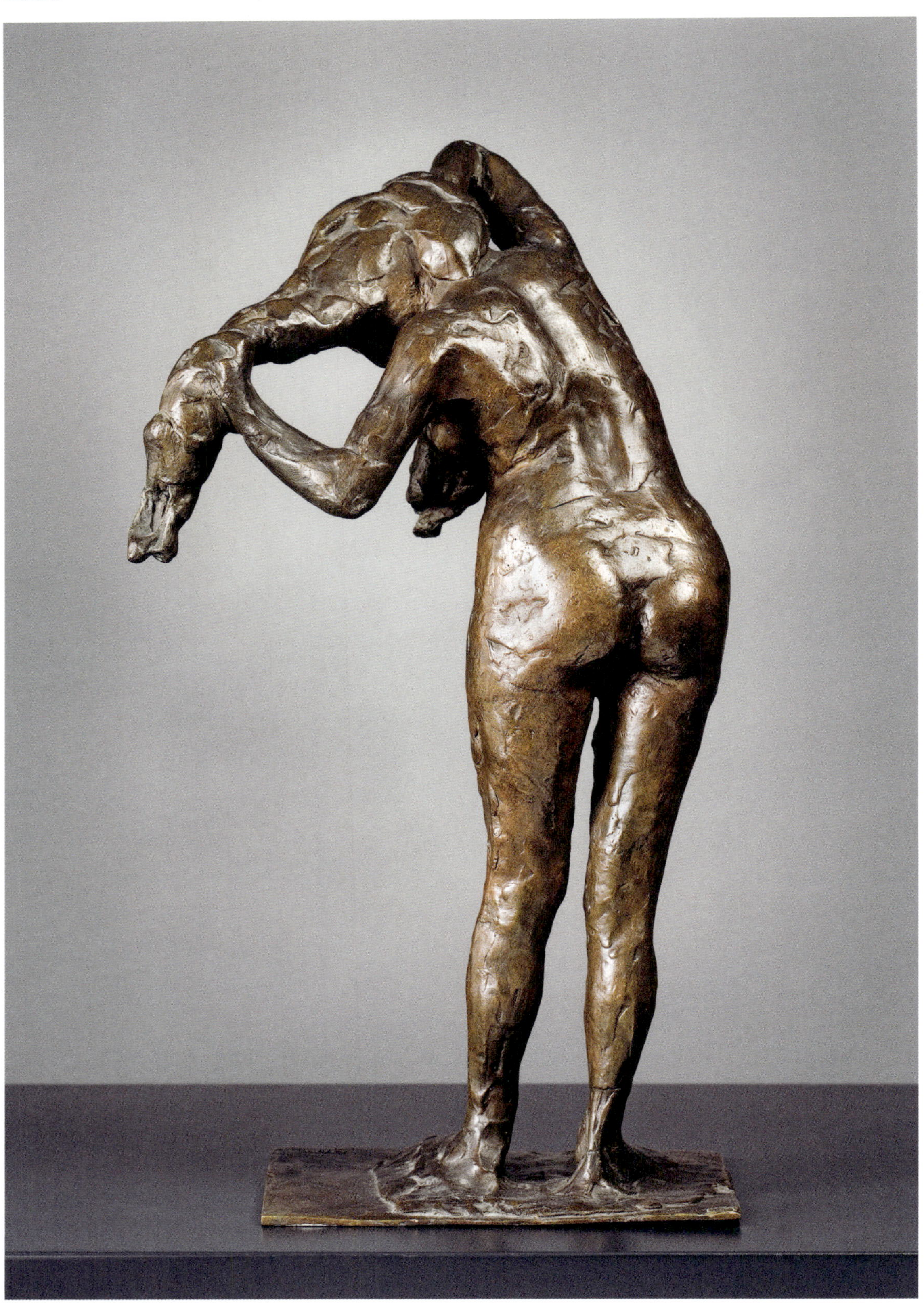

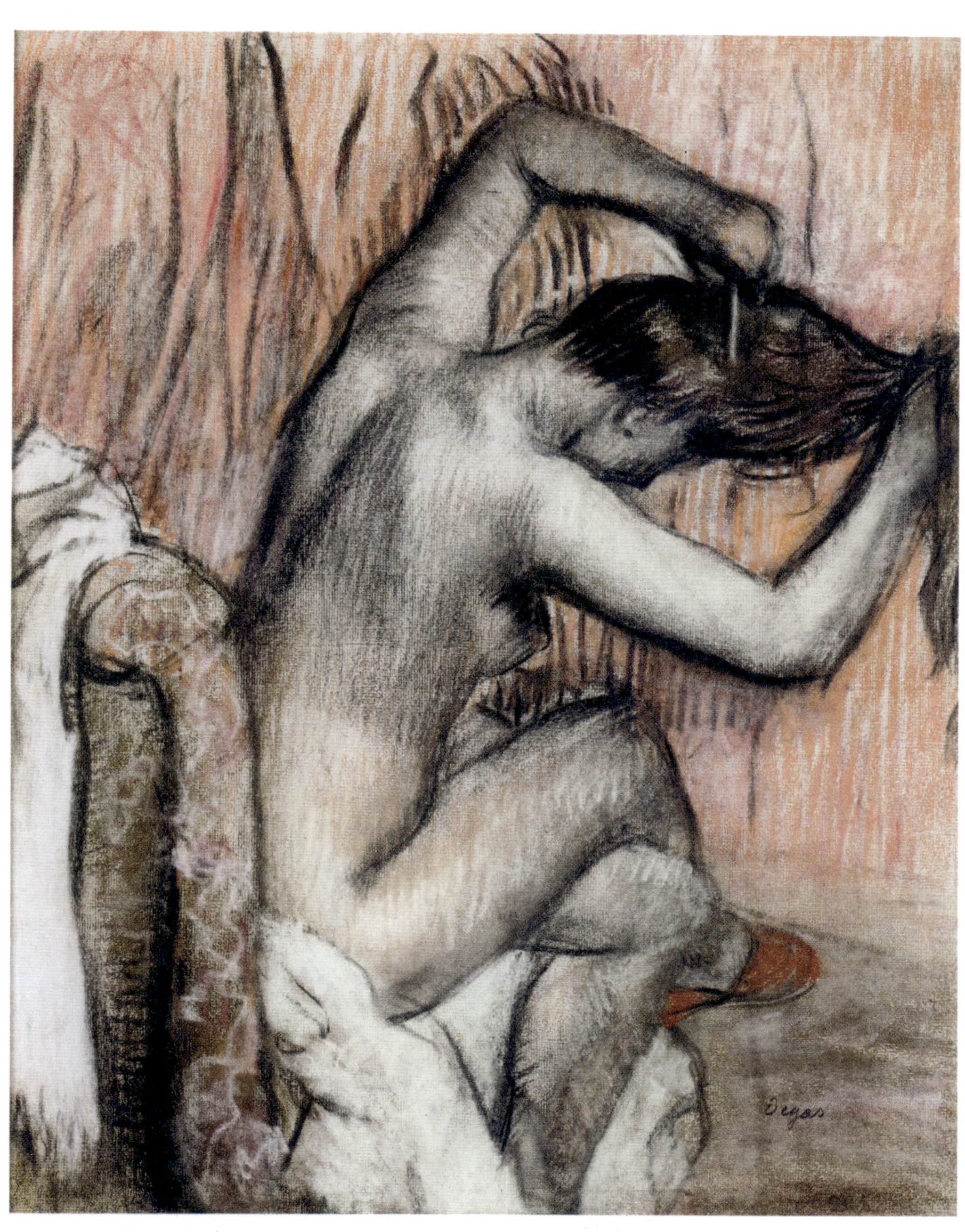

Cat. 26

Cat.27 Edgar Degas, Woman Washing Her Left Leg (Second State) (Femme se lavant la jambe gauche, deuxième étude), 1890s; bronze, 20.5 × 21.6 × 16.5 cm; stamped on the plinth: "61/R"; Ny Carlsberg Glyptotek, Copenhagen, inv. no. MIN 2699 Cat.28 Edgar Degas, The Masseuse (La Masseuse), mid 1890s; bronze, 42 × 36.4 × 41.5 cm; stamped on the plinth: "55/R"; Ny Carlsberg Glyptotek, Copenhagen, inv. no. MIN 2704

Cat.27

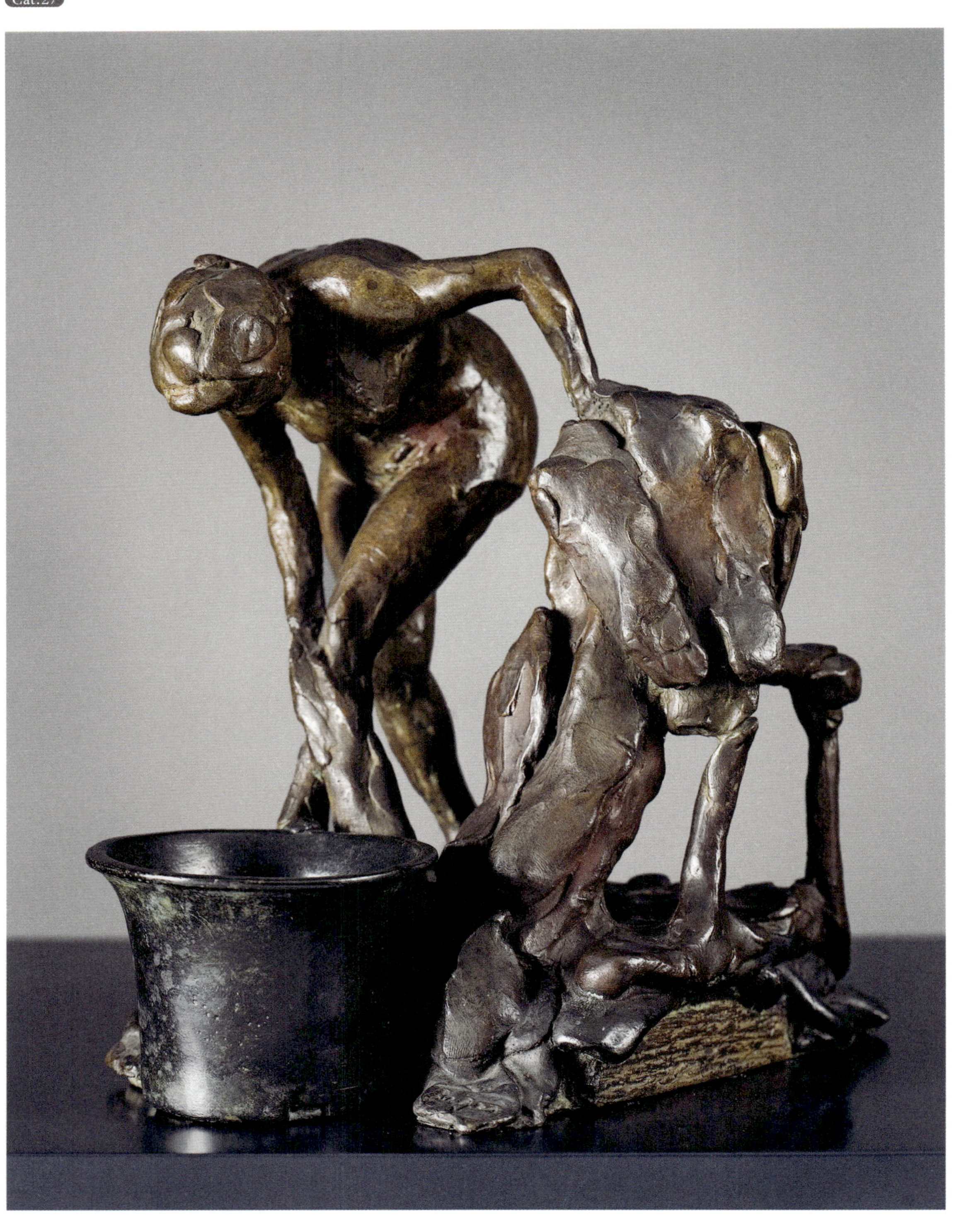

Cat. 28

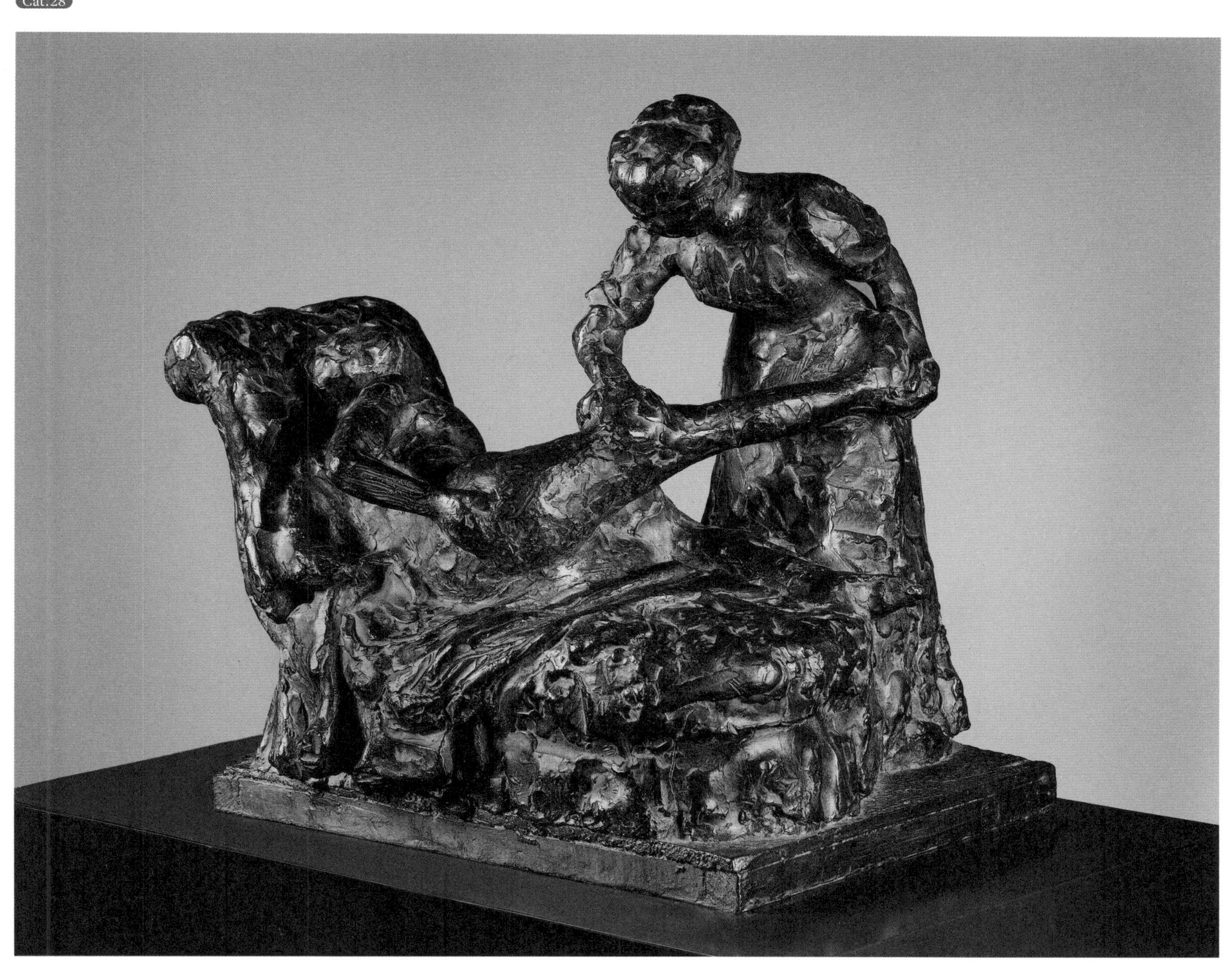

Cat.29 Edgar Degas, The Tub (Le Tub), c. 1889; bronze, 22.5 × 43.8 × 45.8 cm; stamped on the plinth: "26/P"; Musée d'Orsay, Paris, inv. no. RF 2120 Cat.30 Edgar Degas, Seated Woman Wiping Her Left Hip (Femme assise dans un fauteuil, s'essuyant la hanche gauche), 1896–1911; bronze, 45.4 × 51 × 30 cm; stamped on the plinth: "54/G"; private collection, London

Cat.29

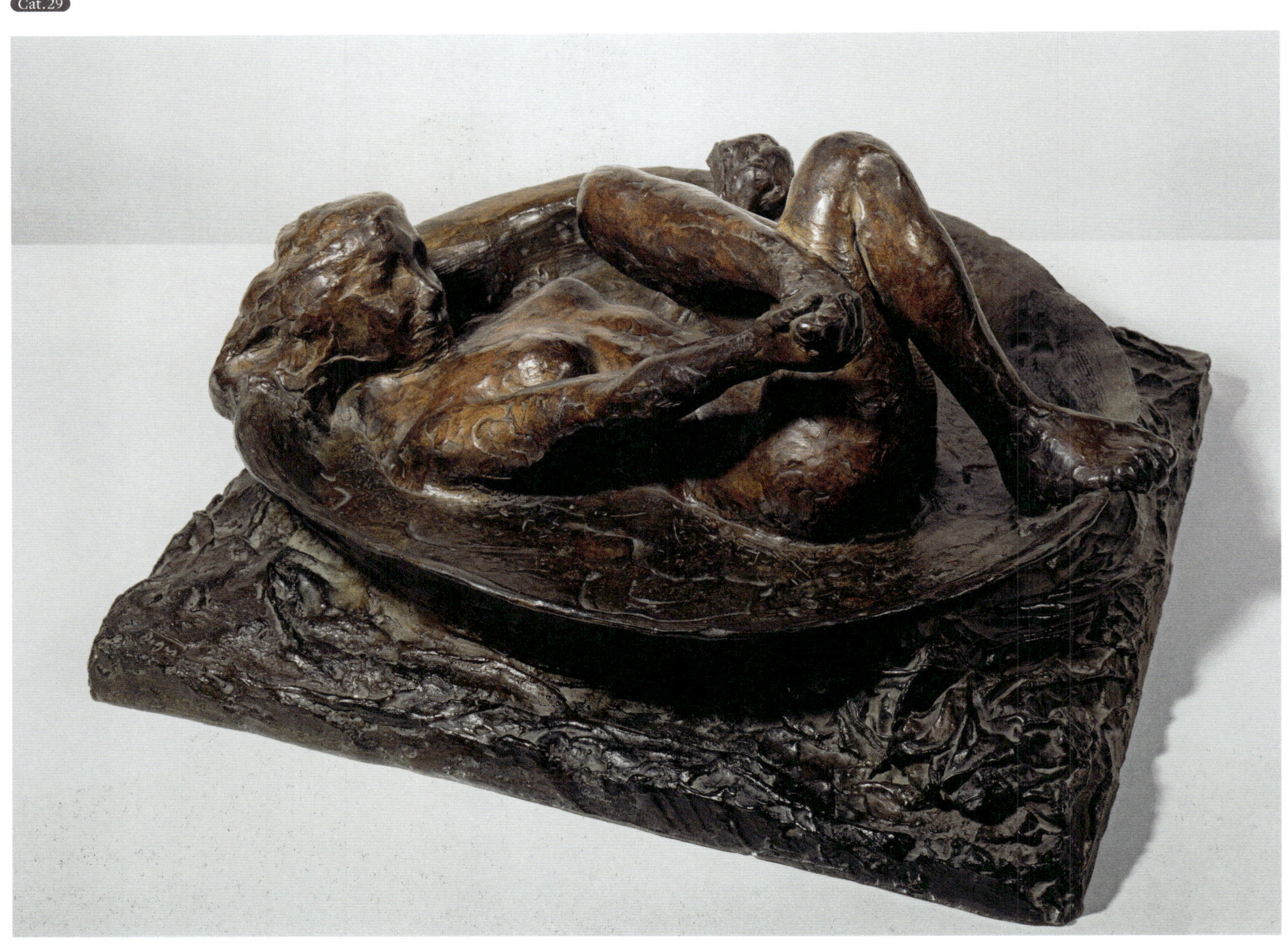

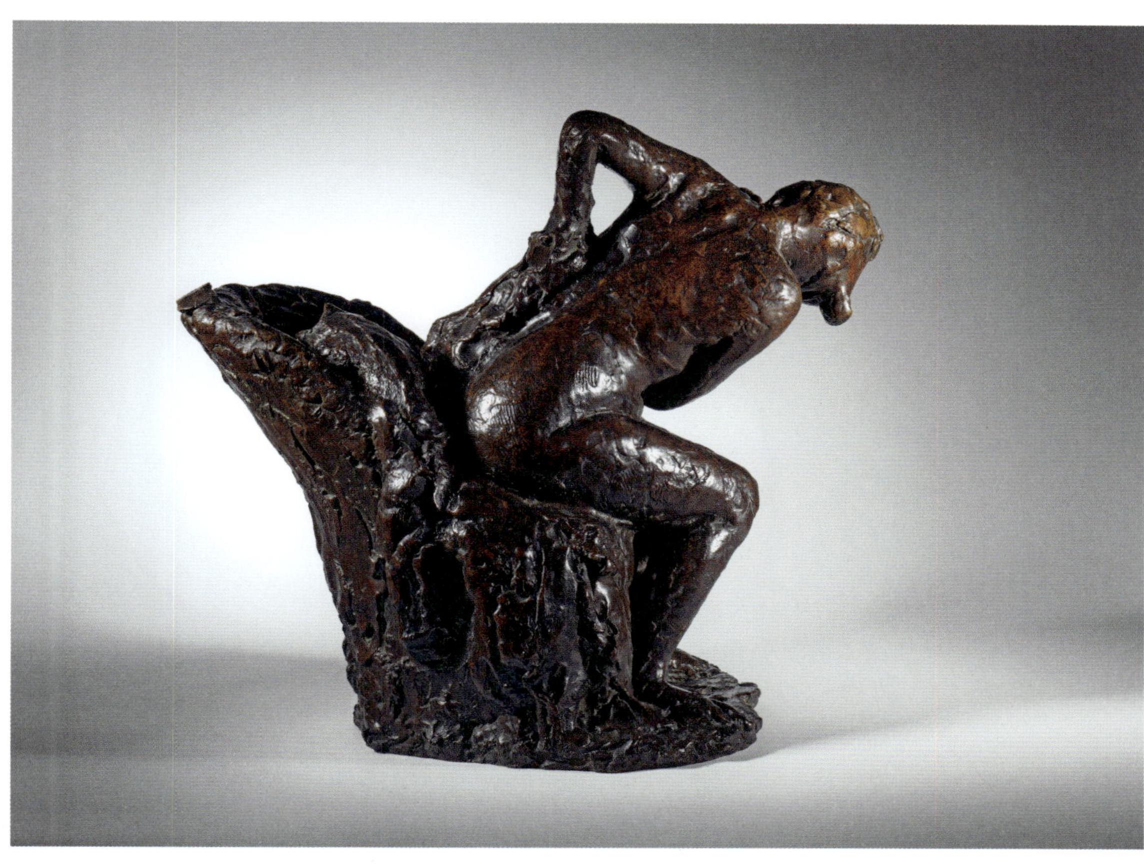

Cat.30

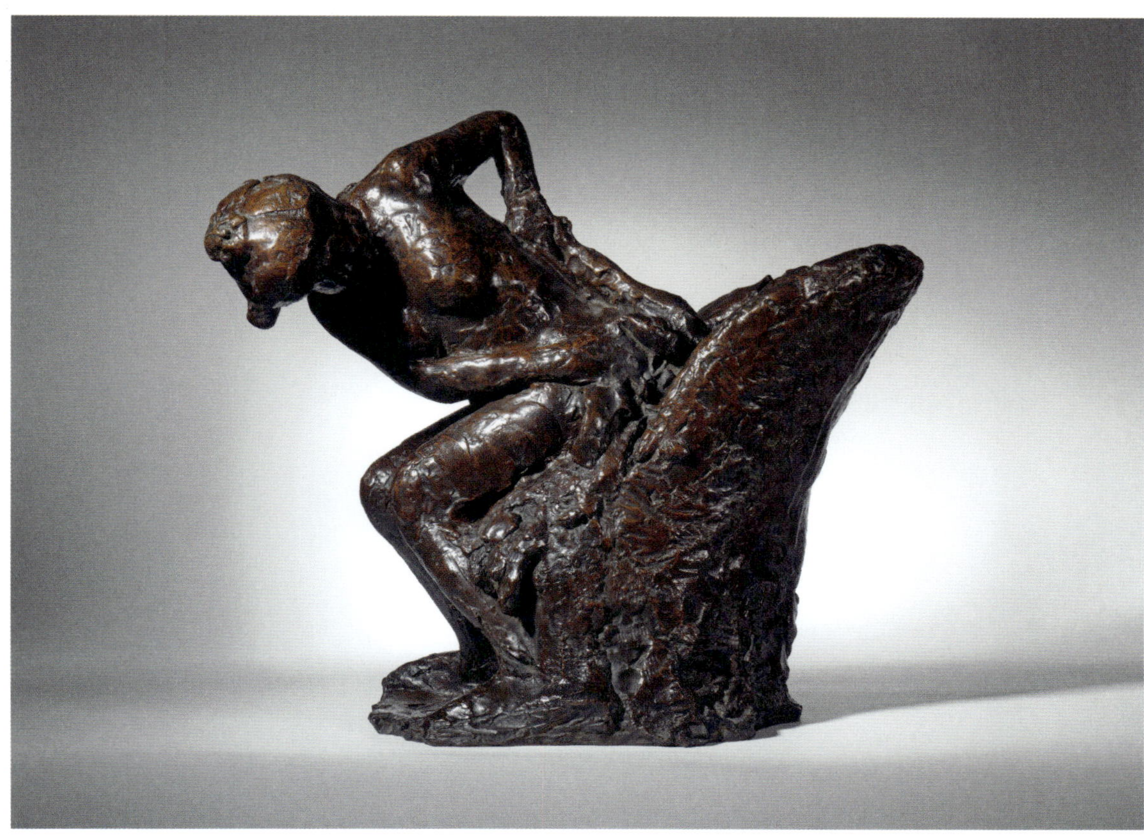

Cat.31 Federico Zandomeneghi, **Nude Drying Herself** (Femme nue s'essuyant), c. 1887; pastel on canvas, 49 × 52 cm; private collection, Courtesy Galleria Bottegantica, Milan Cat.32 Federico Zandomeneghi, **The Awakening** (Le Reveil), 1895; pastel on paper, on card mounted on plywood, 60 × 72 cm; Museo Civico di Palazzo Te, Mantua

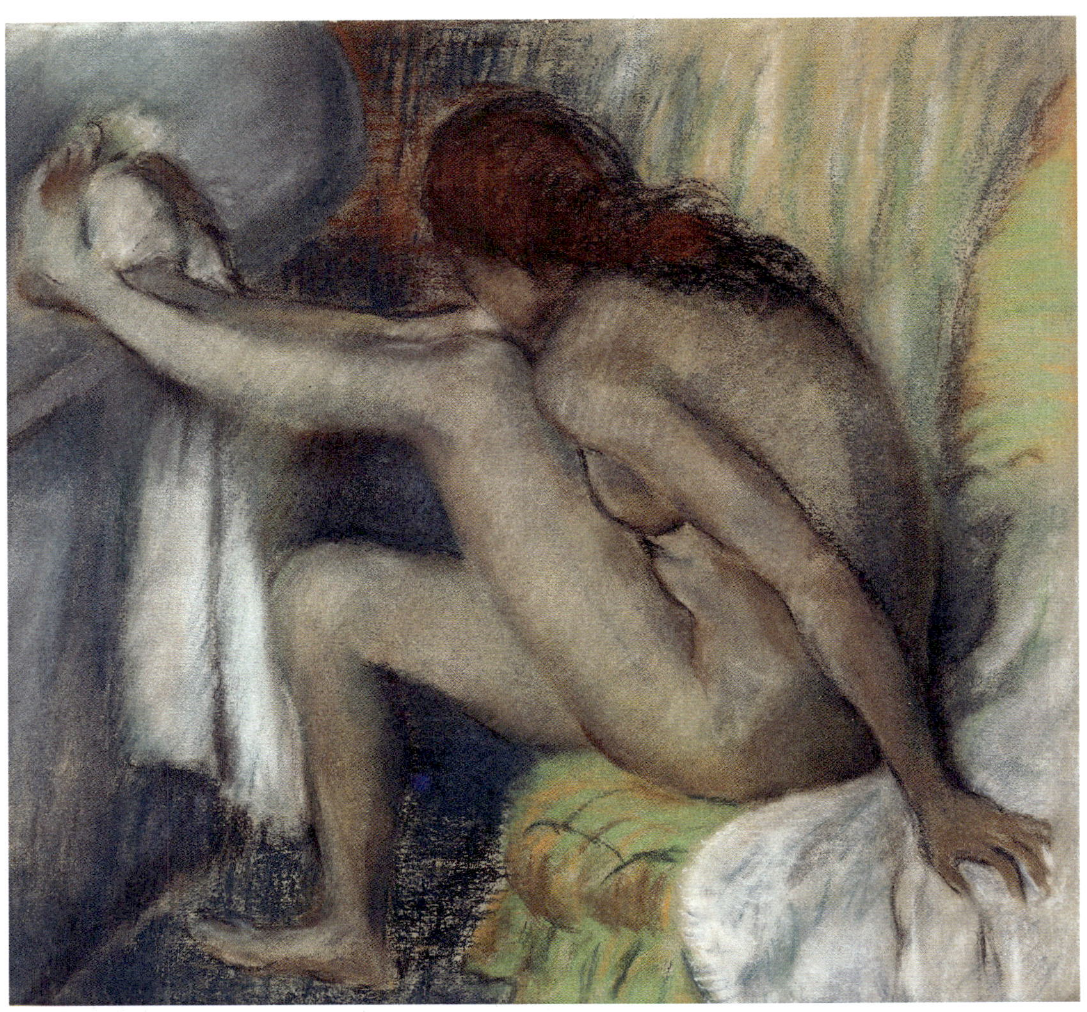

Cat.31

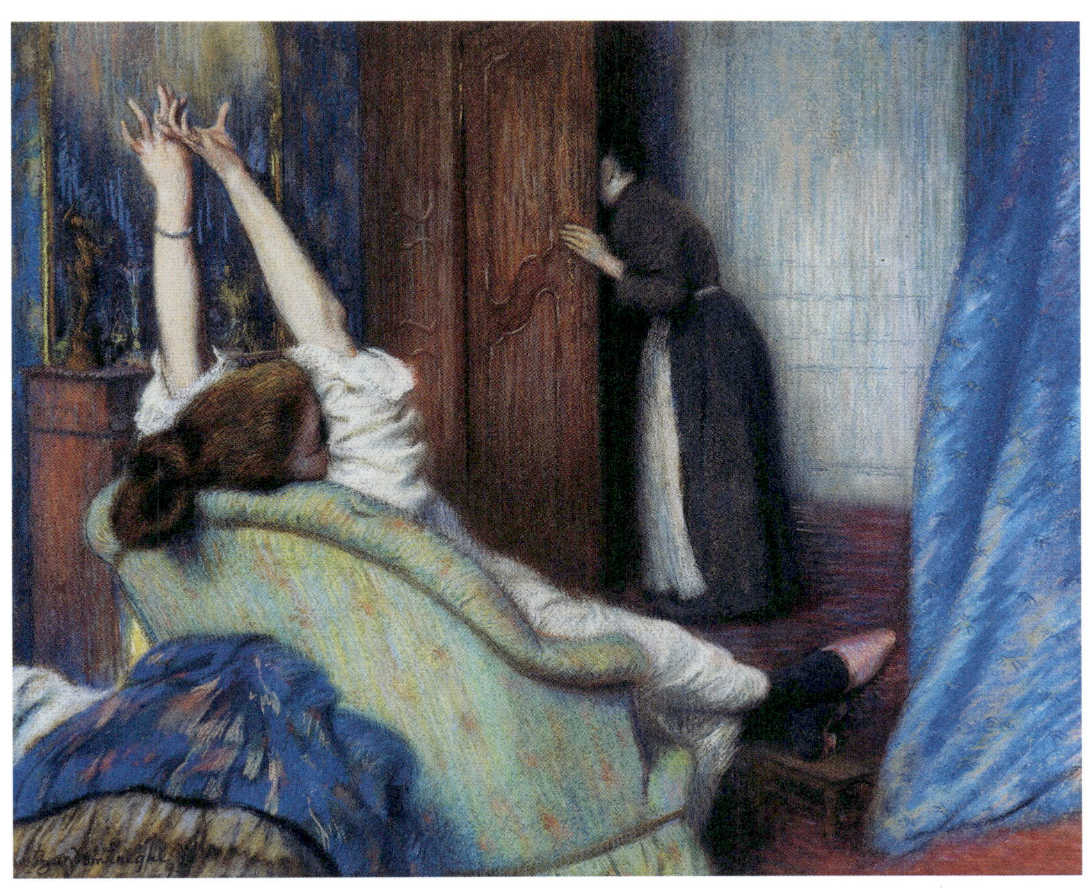

Cat. 32

Cat. 33

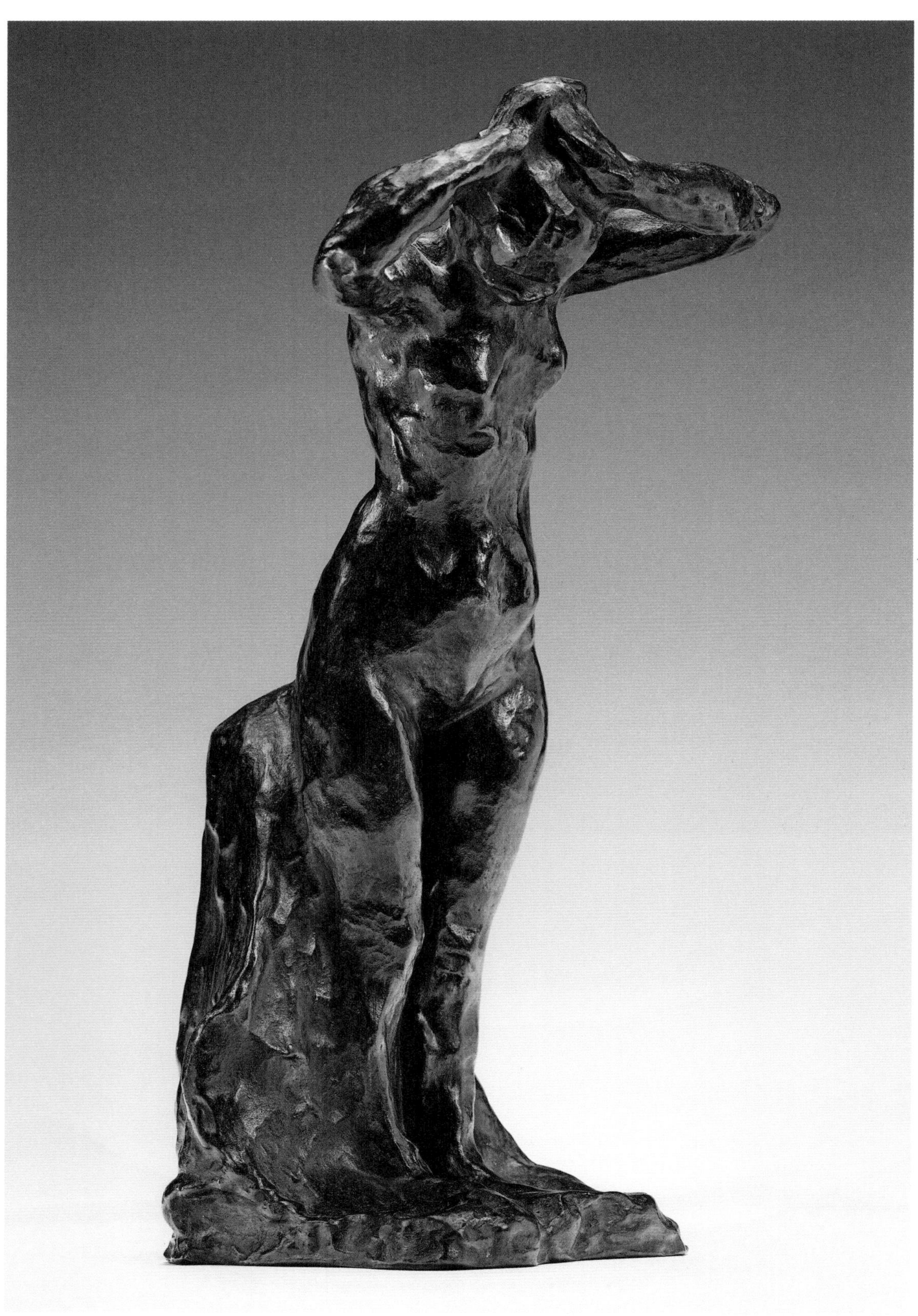

Cat. 34

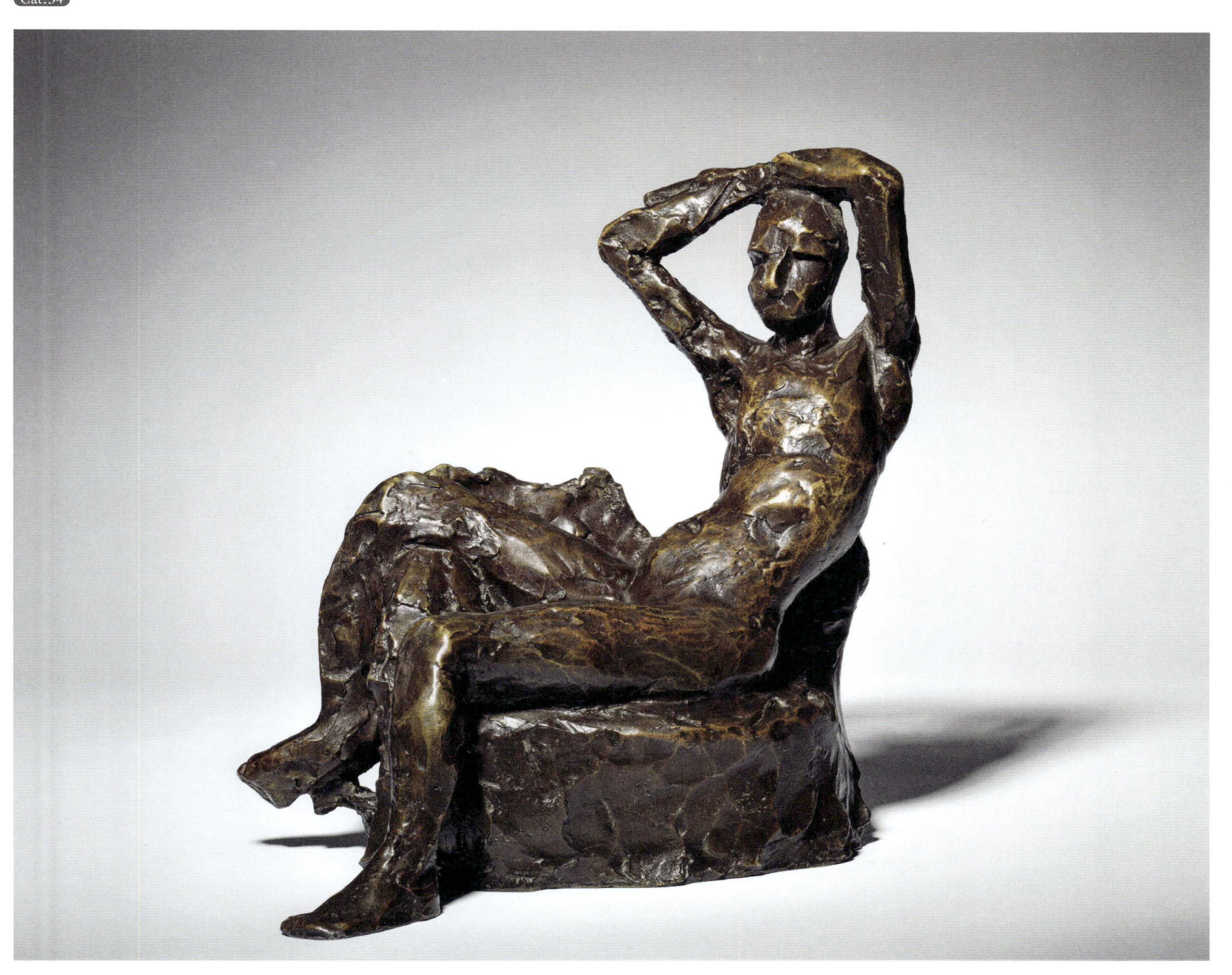

Fragments and details

In Degas's sculptural oeuvre, there are works of very different character and strongly varying degrees of completion in the area of bath and boudoir scenes. Detailed figures (cat. 27–29) can be seen alongside summarily rendered sections of the body. As contemporary witnesses report, Degas did not seem to place much value on the longevity of the figures, which for him were first and foremost study material for the production of his paintings and pastels. This circumstance also explains why of the 150 sculptures found after the artist's death, only about half of them lent themselves to be cast in bronze, while the remainder was considered to be too badly damaged.[1]

Woman Getting out of the Bath (cat. 35) belongs to the group of those works which – although preserved only in fragments – could nevertheless be cast in bronze. Smoothed zones form an exciting contrast to the crudely and openly fashioned ones in the breast area. The missing arms and feet as well as the cracks on the thighs give an impression of the highly damaged state of the wax sculpture, which was completely destroyed during the casting process.[2] The figure adopts a pose that the artist had previously developed in numerous monotypes, paintings and pastels. Their origins lie in designs for the history painting *The Wife of Candaules* (fig. 1), which the artist had worked on beginning in the mid 1850s. For this picture, Degas used a posture that he had taken from the reproduction print *Bed Time* after a painting by Jacob van Loo.[3] The pose passed over into Degas's repertoire of figures, which he constantly improved and mixed with other influences. Thus, the sequence of movements experienced a re-contextualisation in the form of his bathing women (fig. 2) and boudoir scenes (cat. 36). With this motif, Degas captured the moment of a fragile and tense balance, which, while it was borrowed from a classical source, he interpreted in a modern and non-idealised manner.

In view of the aesthetic fascination with the fragmentary and unfinished at the outset of the twentieth century, the fact that the woman getting out of the bath had only been preserved in fragments may have been the principal motivation for preserving it in bronze. While the state of the figure was due to the storage conditions in the artist's studio, there is, however, one example in Degas's sculptural body of work for which he had made a conscious decision to produce a torso. *Woman Rubbing Her Back with a Sponge (Torso)* (cat. 38) not only features the headless torso of a female nude, which is furthermore lacking an arm. The forward-inclined body as well as the elbow bent backwards to form an acute triangle acquiesce to produce a harmonious overall form without it being upset by the lack of an arm or the head. Degas's sculpture is entirely concentrated on this one particular movement, which occurs in numerous variations in his paintings and pastels (fig. 3). The central role of the pose in his oeuvre may also explain why he had the sculpture cast in plaster, as only one of four figures during his lifetime, in order to preserve the form (p. 52, fig. 11).[4] He had not originally produced it out of one piece; instead, it is an assemblage of two different parts joined at the abdomen.[5] The upper body and the arm

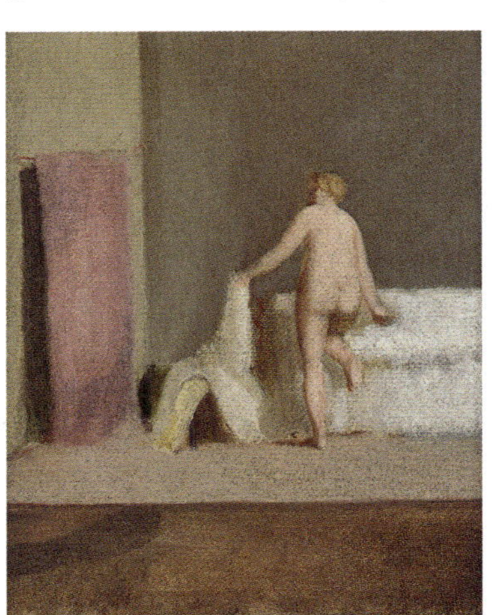

1 Edgar Degas, *The Wife of Candaules*, c. 1856, oil on canvas, 29 × 22.1 cm, private collection, Scotland

are therefore too small in relation to the lower section. Moreover, as a result of their assembly in this way, the navel is slightly off-centre. In this respect, the figure shows similarities with Auguste Rodin's famous sculpture of *The Walking Man* (cat. 104), which is one of the principle pieces of evidence for the recognition of the torso as an independent artistic form in the modern era.[6]

The form found in *Woman Rubbing Her Back with a Sponge (Torso)* reflects Degas's proclivity for unorthodox, essentially awkward poses with which he worked in the "declassification" of his art without entirely leaving the path of the classical.[7] Its shape is furthermore the logical consequence of his graphic oeuvre, in which he operated with strong cuts, focuses and fragmentations all of his life. The unconventional poses of the woman bent over a basin (cat. 39) or the female nude with her arm over her head (cat. 40) are the result of an attempt to find a self-contained and concentrated form without becoming lost in the elaboration of the hands or faces. Degas developed an almost abstract portrayal of a torso as early as the late 1870s in the print *Actresses in Their Dressing Rooms* (cat. 41), whose centre is taken up by a silhouette free of any trivial details, which anticipated his later experiments with the shadows cast by his sculptures.[8]

Degas's nude figures worked out in a combination of drawing, painting, prints and sculpture were sometimes subsequently used in unusual compositions, as in the case of the landscape pastel *Steep Coast* (cat. 42), in which the artist merged a reclining female body with an undulating coastal landscape. The horizontally canted legs and the body take up the forms of the torso, while the posture of the head as well as the hair falling vertically downwards feature similarities with the portrayal of a women whose hair is being coiffed that was produced around the mid 1880s.[9] In this way, Degas, who harboured major reservations towards the *plein-air* painting of the Impressionists, made an innovative contribution, developed out of the figure, to the landscape art of his time.

The many cross connections between the works presented here show just how closely all of the artistic techniques he used were interrelated and how mutually productive they were. The form found in one medium could be further developed and worked out more incisively in another. The medium of sculpture proved to be a catalyst in this interplay. It served reassurance purposes and, at the same time, animated Degas to continue on with further experiments. — AE

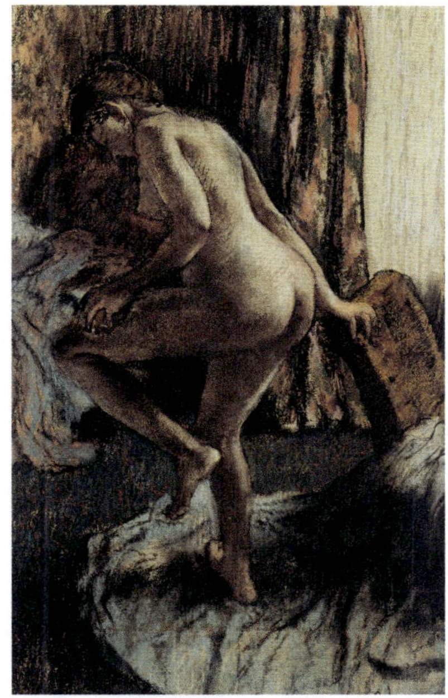

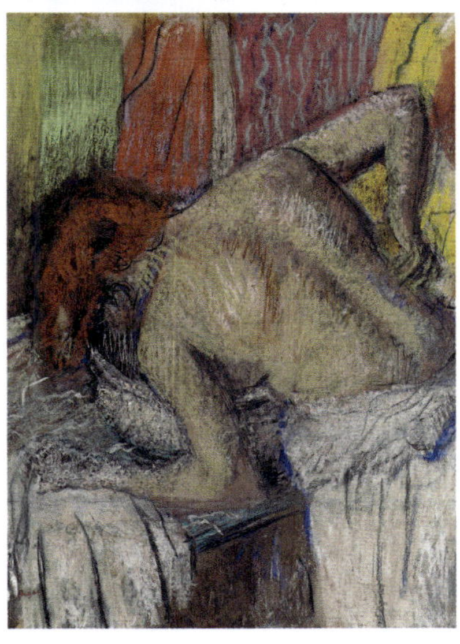

2 Edgar Degas, *After the Bath*, 1883/84, pastel, 52 × 32 cm, private collection

3 Edgar Degas, *Woman Rubbing Her Back with a Sponge*, c. 1895, pastel, 70 × 60 cm, private collection

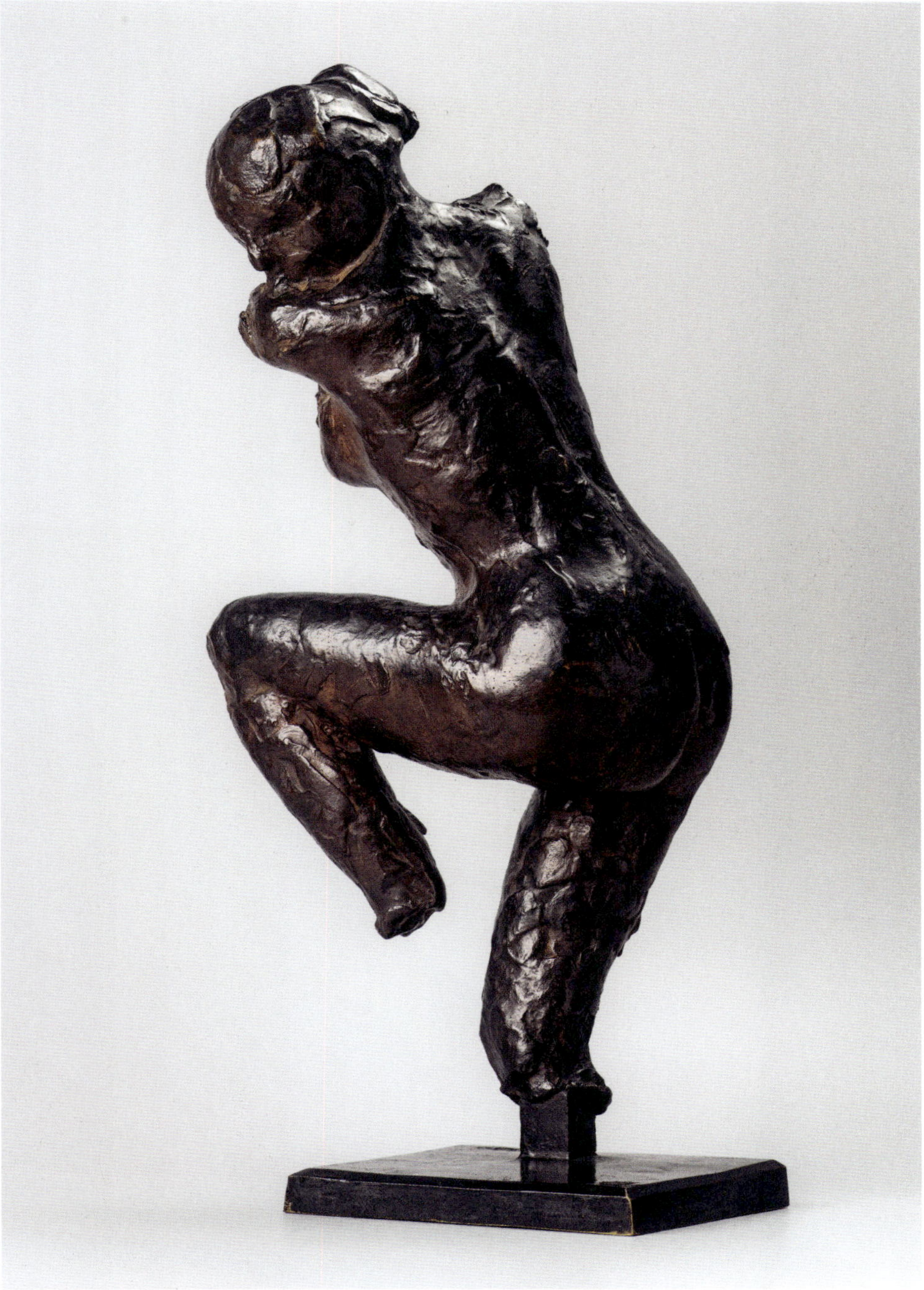

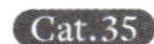

1   See the essay by Alexander Eiling in this catalogue, pp. 46–57, esp. p. 47.

2   See inv. cat. Pasadena 2009, pp. 471–472, no. 97.

3   Carlo Antonio Porporati (after Jacob van Loo), *Le Coucher*, c. 1770/80, copperplate; see Thomson 1988, pp. 32, 34. The author suspects that Degas may have seen a copy of the print in Ingres's studio. He furthermore points out the fluency of the pose, which was also re-enacted in contemporary photographs as a *tableau vivant*. See also exh. cat. 2014, pp. 248–251, nos. 115–117.

4   The other three works are *Spanish Dancer, Dancer Looking at the Sole of Her Right Foot* and *Head Resting on One Hand, Bust* (*Portrait of a Woman* [*Madame Bartholome?*]); see inv. cat. Washington 2010, pp. 367, 370.

5   See ibid., pp. 266–271, no. 45, esp. p. 266.

6   On the role of the torso in modern art in general, see exh. cat. Stuttgart 2001.

7   Thomson draws a connecting line between the torso and Titian's painting *Adam and Eve*, which Degas had studied at the Prado in Madrid during his journey to Spain; Thomson 1981; Thomson 2009, pp. 65–66.

8   See the essay by Alexander Eiling in this catalogue, pp. 46–57, esp. p. 54.

9   Exh. cat. Karlsruhe 2014, pp. 240–241, no. 110 (Dorit Schäfer).

Cat.36 Edgar Degas, **Bed Time (Le Coucher)**, 1880–1885; monotype on paper, 38 × 27.6 cm; private collection Cat.37 Edgar Degas, **Resting on the Bed (Repos sur le lit)**, 1876/77; monotype on wove paper, 16 × 12 cm; Städel Museum, Frankfurt am Main, property of Städelscher Museums-Verein e.V., inv. no. 67043 Cat.38 Edgar Degas, **Woman Rubbing Her Back with a Sponge (Torso) (Femme se frottant le dos avec une éponge, torse)**, 1880–1890, bronze, 43.7 × 29.5 × 17.6 cm; stamped on the right thigh at the back: "28/F"; Collection Museum de Fundatie, Zwolle and Heino/Wijhe, the Netherlands, inv. no. 573

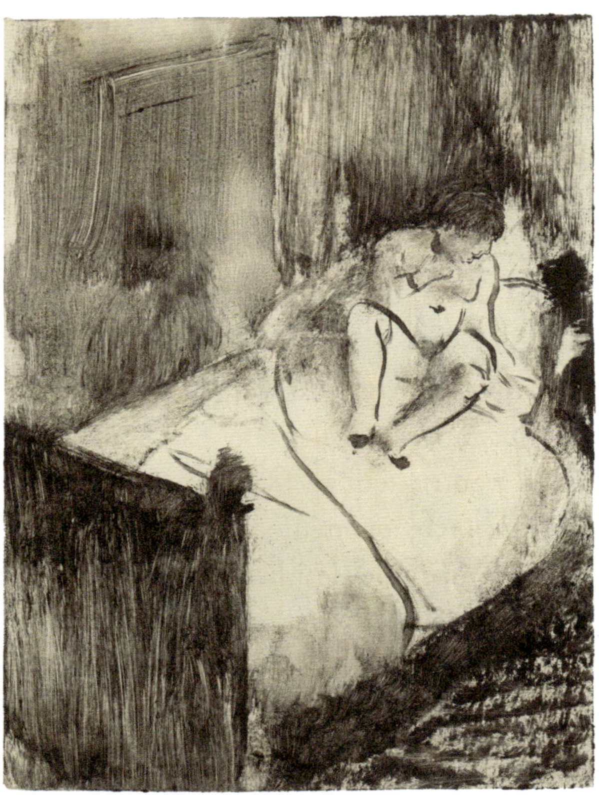

Cat.37

Cat.36

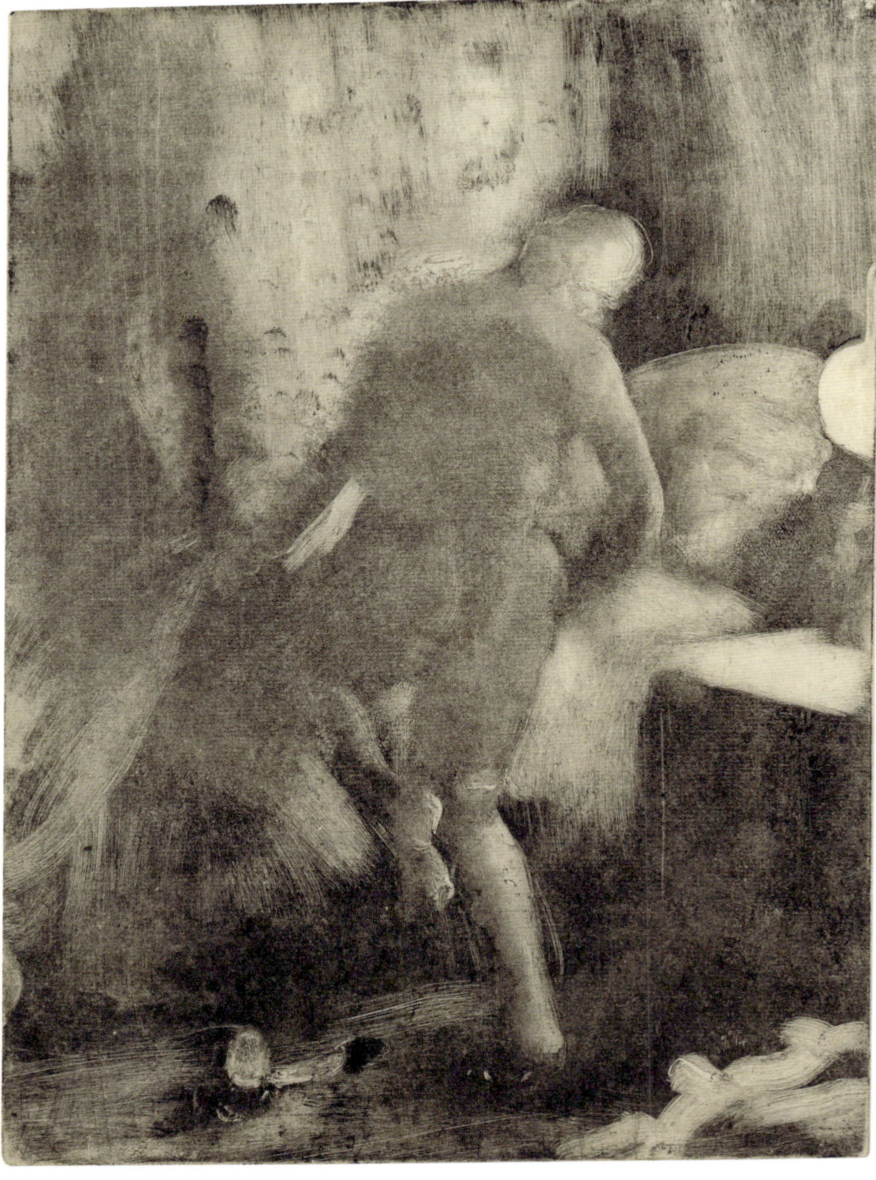

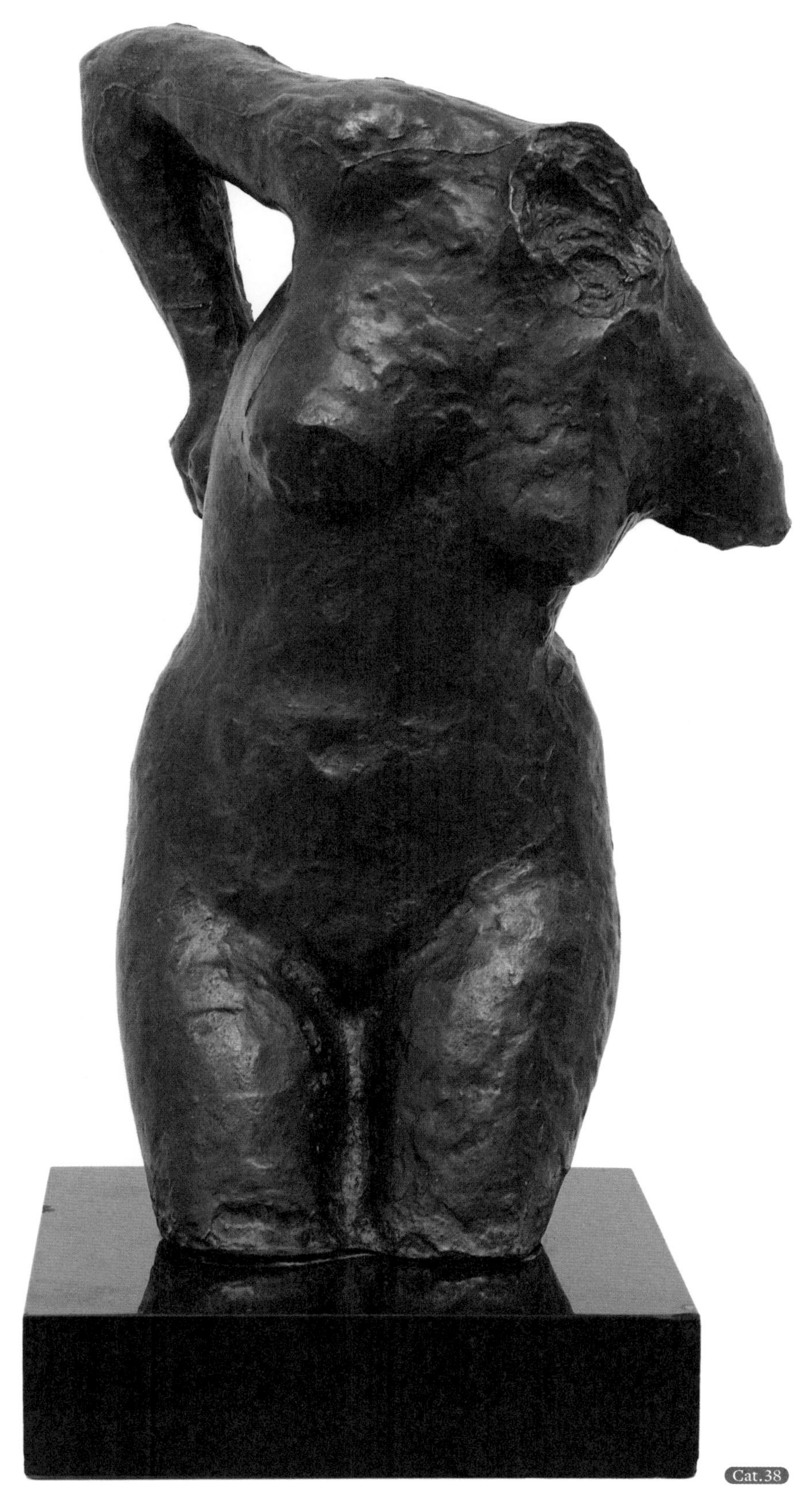

Cat. 38

Cat.39 Edgar Degas, A Woman Bent over a Basin, Washing Her Neck (Femme se lavant la nuque), 1887–1890; black chalk over charcoal, heightened with white, on laid paper, 61,4 × 47 cm; Collection Jean Bonna, Geneva Cat.40 Edgar Degas, Nude Study (Étude de nu), c. 1888–1892; charcoal and pastel on brownish paper, 56 × 37 cm; Städel Museum, Frankfurt am Main, property of Städelscher Museums-Verein e.V., inv. no. 17175

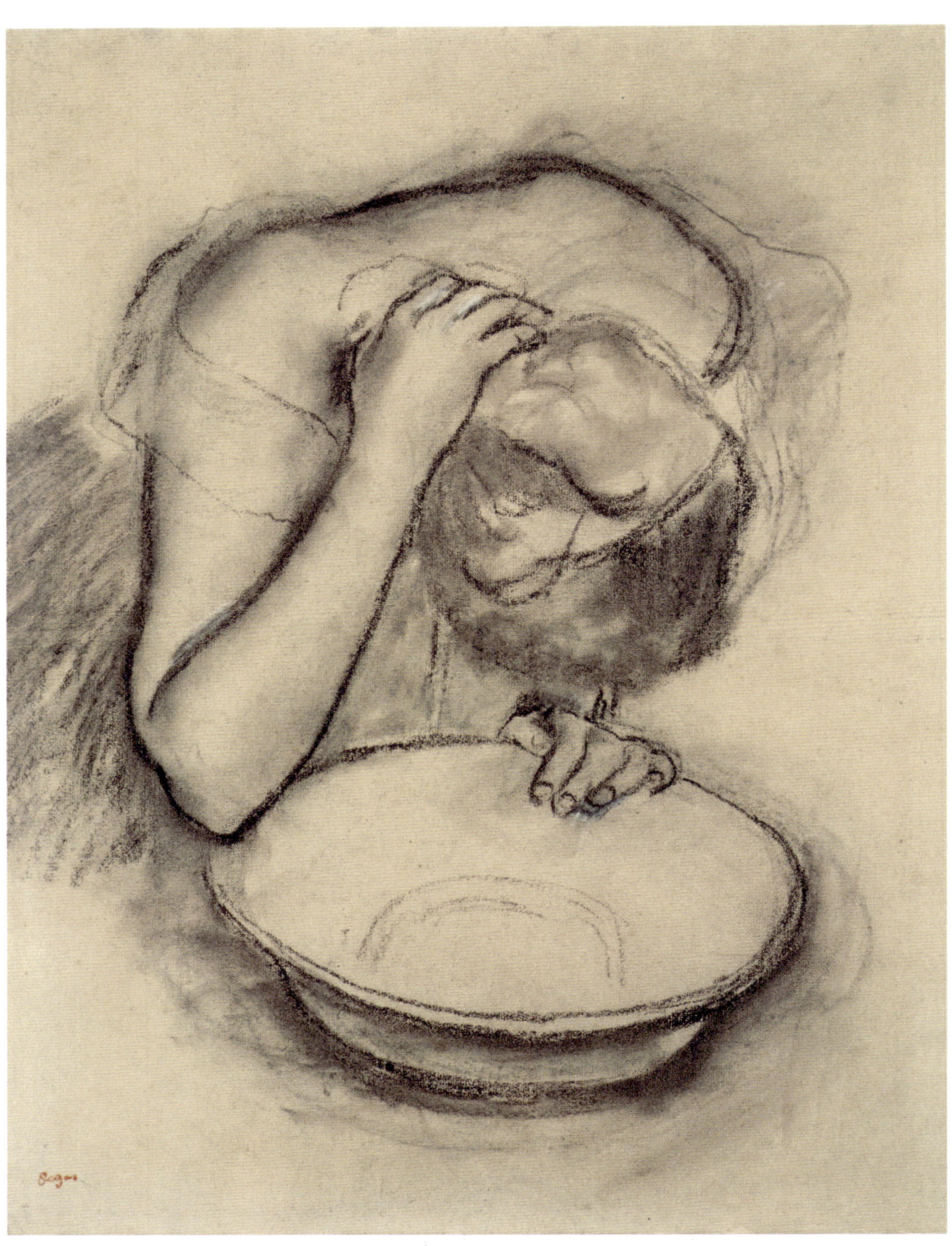

Cat. 39

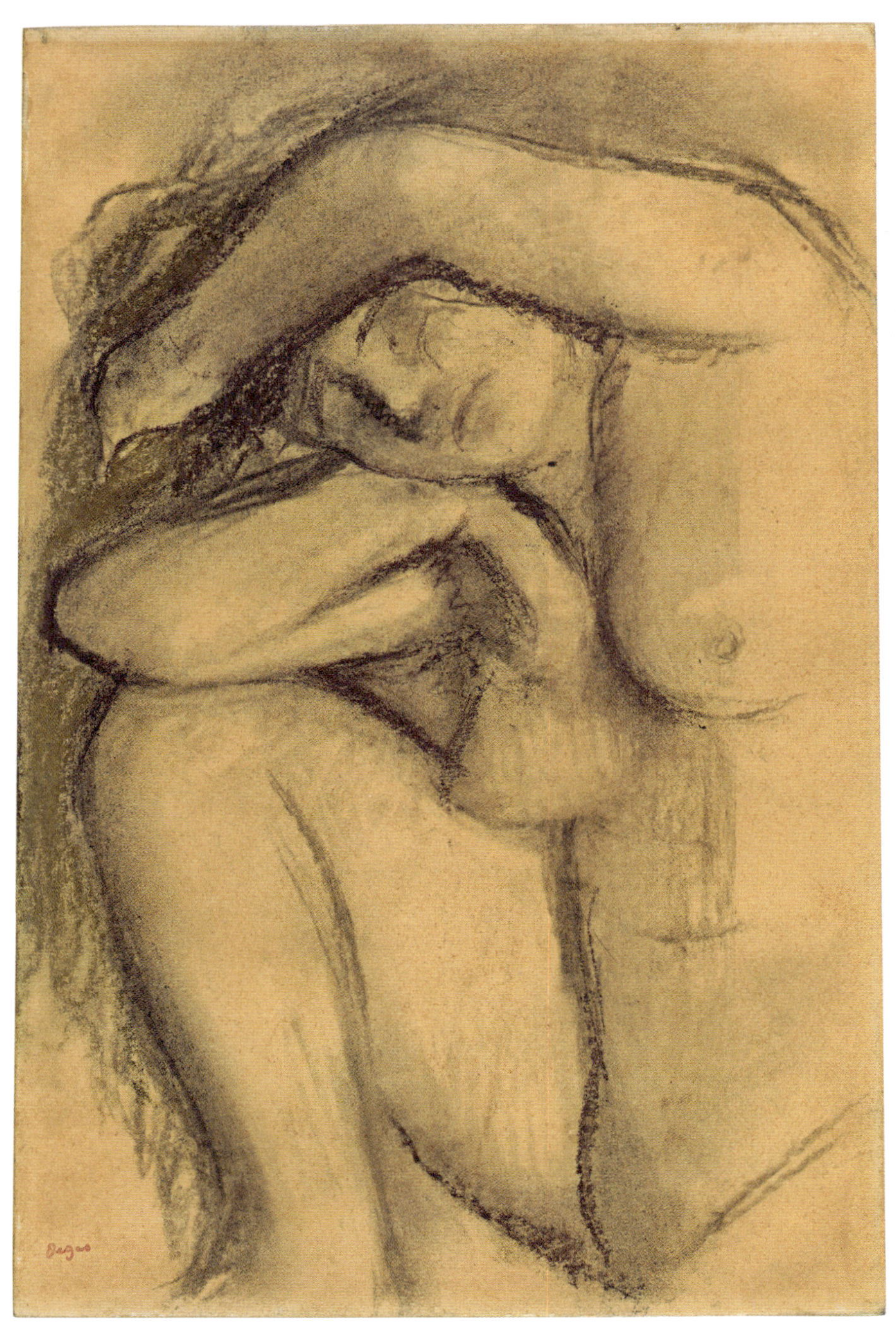

Cat. 40

Cat.41 Edgar Degas, Actresses in Their Dressing Rooms (Loges d'actrices), 1879/80; etching and aquatint on wove paper, state: IV/V, 16.1 × 21.3 cm (plate), 21.5 × 30.5 cm (sheet); Albertina, Vienna, inv. no. DG 1923/453 Cat.42 Edgar Degas, Landscape (Steep Coast) (Paysage [La falaise]), c. 1892; pastel on paper, 42 × 55 cm; private collection

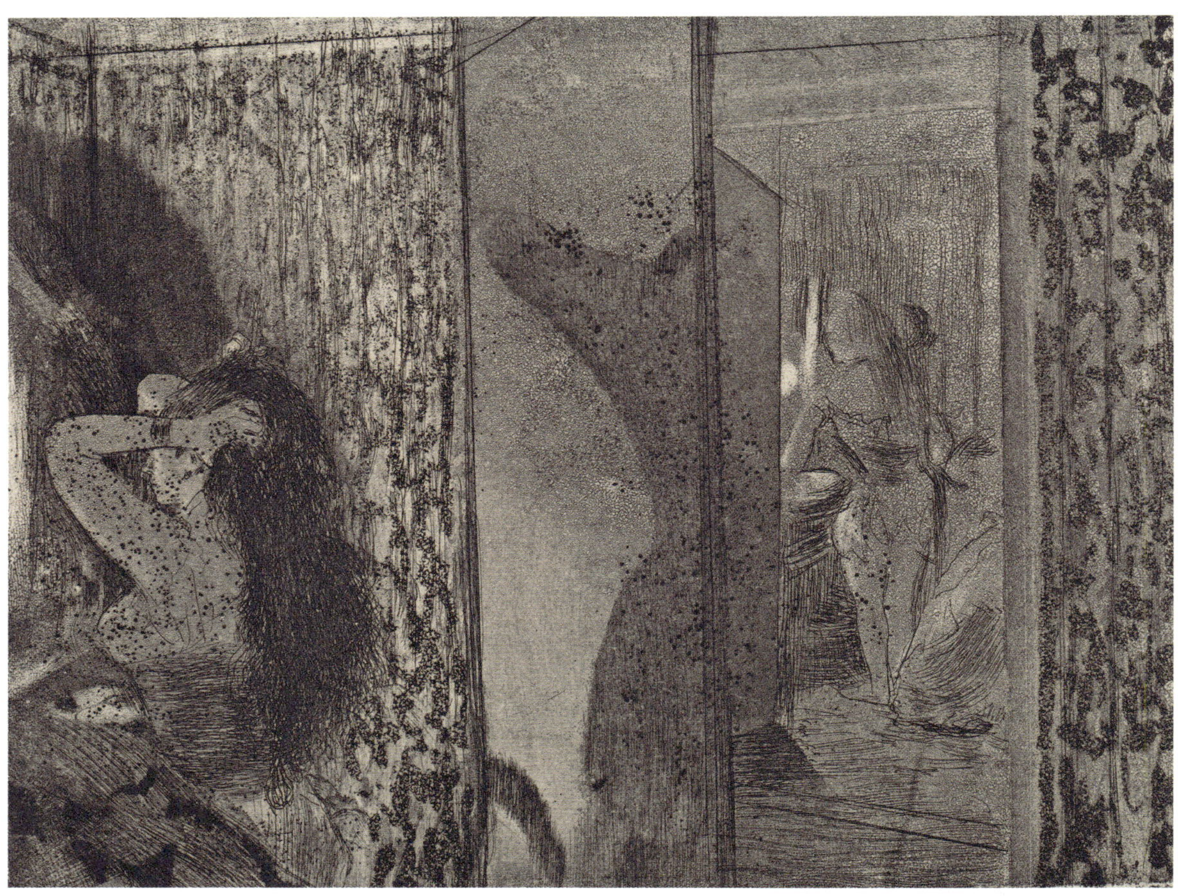

Cat. 41

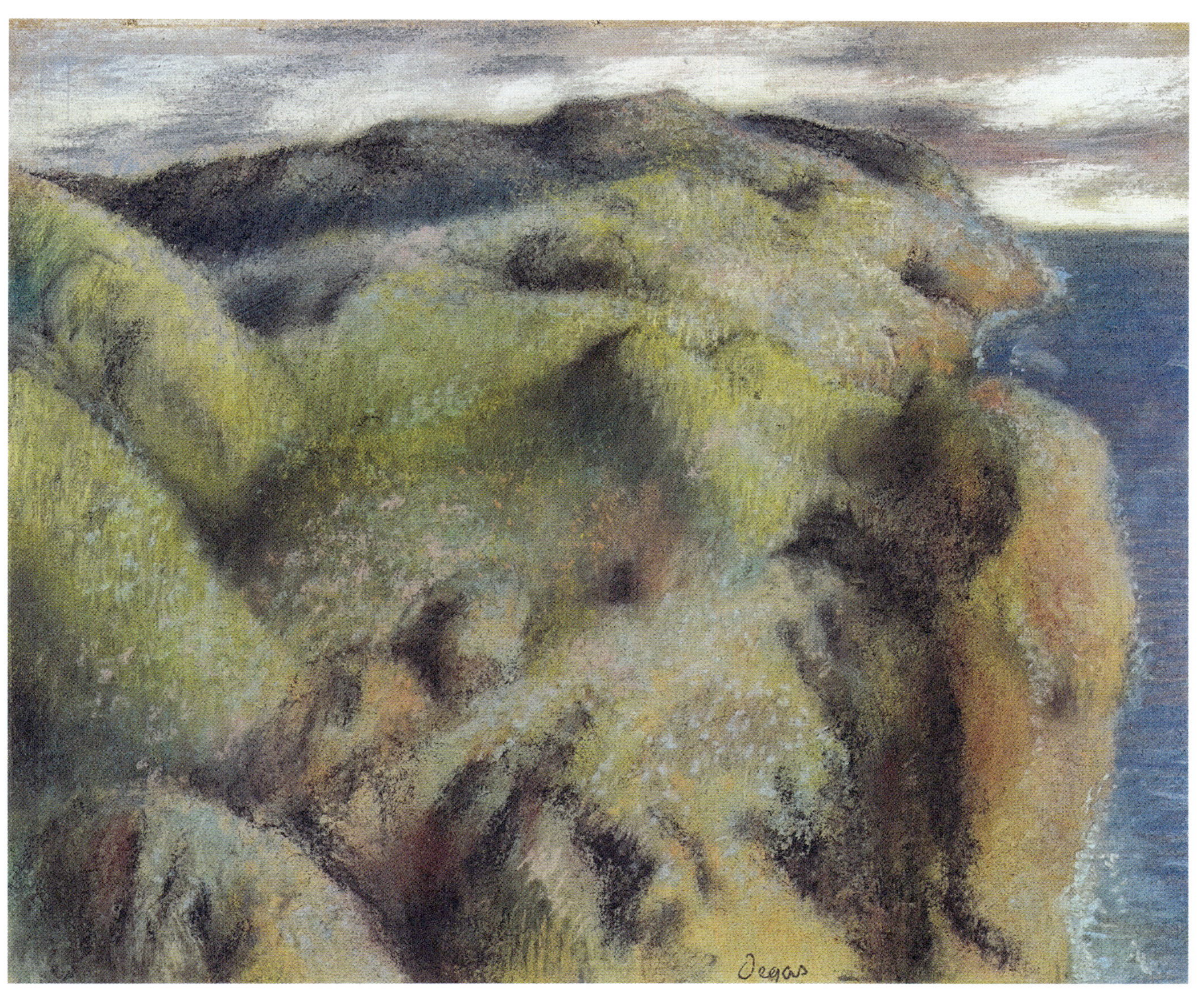

Cat. 42

"But I haven't made enough horses yet"[1] – images of horses and jockeys

Besides dancing and bathing women, horses constituted a further core complex of works in Degas's sculptural oeuvre. They mark the beginning of his creative attempts in the third dimension and flanked his efforts to capture the movements of the animals as realistically as possible in drawings and oil paintings. *Horse at a Trough* (fig. 1), produced between 1866 and 1868, is regarded as Degas's first sculpture. It is closely related to the painting *Portrait of Mlle Fiocre in the Ballet "La Source"* (fig. 2), which the artist created for the Salon in 1868.[2] It is highly probably that he began the large-format painting during his work on modelling the horse's posture in wax in order to obtain an orientation aid for the arrangement of this complex composition.[3]

Degas had already dealt intensely with the portrayal of horses prior to that. They began appearing in the early 1860s in his history paintings as well as in the compositions with scenes from the racetrack that he produced at the same time.[4] As he told the journalist François Thiebault-Sisson in 1897, he simultaneously began sculpting them for the purpose of being able to accurately reproduce the motor activity of the animals, which caused him huge difficulties.[5] The close observation of the animals, which Degas could study at the French national stud farm Haras du Pin located near the country estate of his friend Paul Valpinçon in Normandy, provided the artist with the first foundations for his horse sculptures. He also visited the racetracks in Argentan or the hippodrome of Longchamp in the Bois de Boulogne in Paris to make sketches (cat. 49). For Degas, this was the modern continuation of his interest in classic figures of equestrians and horses, which had already set in during his student days. Inspired by scenes on the metope reliefs of the Parthenon frieze, the fresco cycles of the Italian Renaissance, as well as in contemporary paintings, among others by Ernest Meissonier, of which he produced copies, Degas accumulated a body of references of equestrian motifs that he mixed with current impressions from the racetrack.[6] Hence compositions such as *Racehorses at Longchamp* (cat. 50) do not refer back to occurrences he actually observed directly but feed on copies and sketches that the artist assembled into a coherent overall picture in his studio. Degas overpainted and corrected many of his works even at an interval of several years. Thus, in the case of the painting in Boston, he reduced the number of equestrians for the purpose of emphasising the view into the distance and dynamising the pictorial space.[7]

In the mid 1860s, Degas first began to model horses that were presented in comparatively static positions.[8] One initial inspiration may have been his examination of the rather conventional sculp-

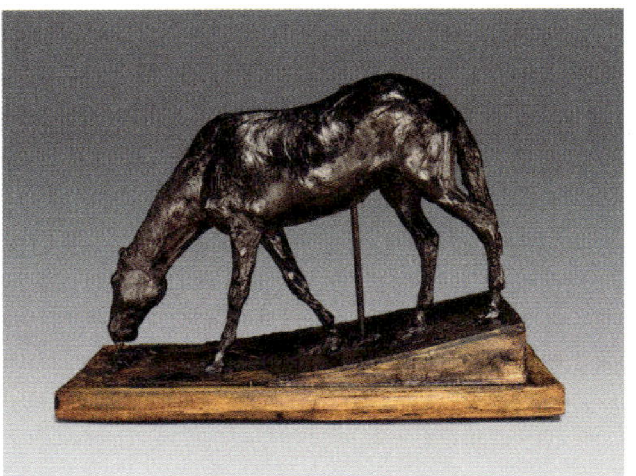

1 Edgar Degas, *Horse at a Trough*, c. 1866–1868, pigmented beeswax, 20 × 10.5 × 24 cm, Virginia Museum of Fine Arts, Richmond

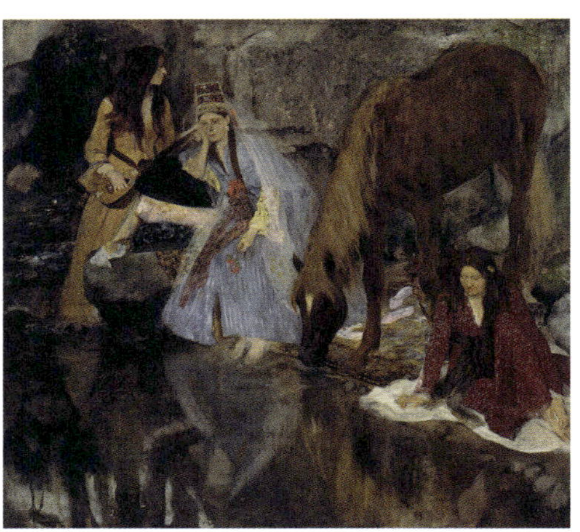

2 Edgar Degas, *Portrait of Mlle Fiocre in the Ballet "La Source"*, c. 1867/68, oil on canvas, 130 × 145 cm, Brooklyn Museum, New York

tures by the French sculptor Joseph Cuvelier, with whom he was on cordial terms.[9] Beginning in the 1870s, when capturing the anatomy of the animals in wax, Degas increasingly experimented with dynamic postures as well and attempted to reproduce specific gaits. The sculptures assembled here convey an impression of the variety and spiritedness of his sculptures, which feature horses rearing (cat. 44), trotting (cat. 46) or galloping (cat. 45). Degas structured them in an open and sketchy modelling technique yet all the time keeping their detailed elaboration. Examinations of the wax original of the galloping horse with jockey (cat. 47) revealed that Degas fit the equestrian out with a jacket and cap made of silk fabric, which he later covered with wax.[10]

When creating his horses, he advanced further and further to the origin of movement by repeating individual motifs. An important driving force for this were the chronophotographs taken by Étienne-Jules Marey and above all by Eadweard Muybridge (1830–1904), who in 1878 succeeded in producing serial photographs of various gaits of horses (cat. 48). Sequences of movements difficult for the human eye to comprehend could be made visible for the first time, thus aiding artists in their pictorial reproduction of horses. Several works by Degas – including *Horse Trotting, the Feet Not Touching the Ground* (cat. 46) – make reference to movement studies that Muybridge had published in French magazines.[11] Degas's sculptural renderings often proved to be more dynamic and animated than the forms one finds in his paintings and pastels, for which he first and foremost strove to work out the contours. In this respect, one might describe his horse sculptures as the more Impressionist share of this complex of motifs.

The enthusiasm for the modern subject of the racetrack, for movement and for speed also animated a large number of Degas's contemporaries and successors to deal with similar scenes. Besides *The Jockey* (cat. 51) by Henri de Toulouse-Lautrec (1864–1901), a particularly outstanding example is the lithograph *The Races at Longchamp* (cat. 52) by Édouard Manet (1832–1883), the bold perspective of which situated the viewer in the middle of the racetrack. The field of the jockeys can only be discerned as a dynamic knot in the distance. Even the numerous spectators lining the racetrack are nothing more than an amorphous mass of chalk marks. The shift of the visual axis in the form of a perspectival counterstroke is also characteristic of the modernity of Manet, who did not aim for the accurate reproduction of the horses and the jockeys, but rather for the dynamisation of the occurrences by means of a sophisticated shift of the viewer's standpoint. — AE

Cat.43 Edgar Degas, Horse with Head Lowered (Cheval faisant une descente de main), 1880s/early 1890s; bronze, 18.6 × 9.5 × 28.1 cm; stamped on the plinth: "22/Q"; private collection, Geneva

Cat.43

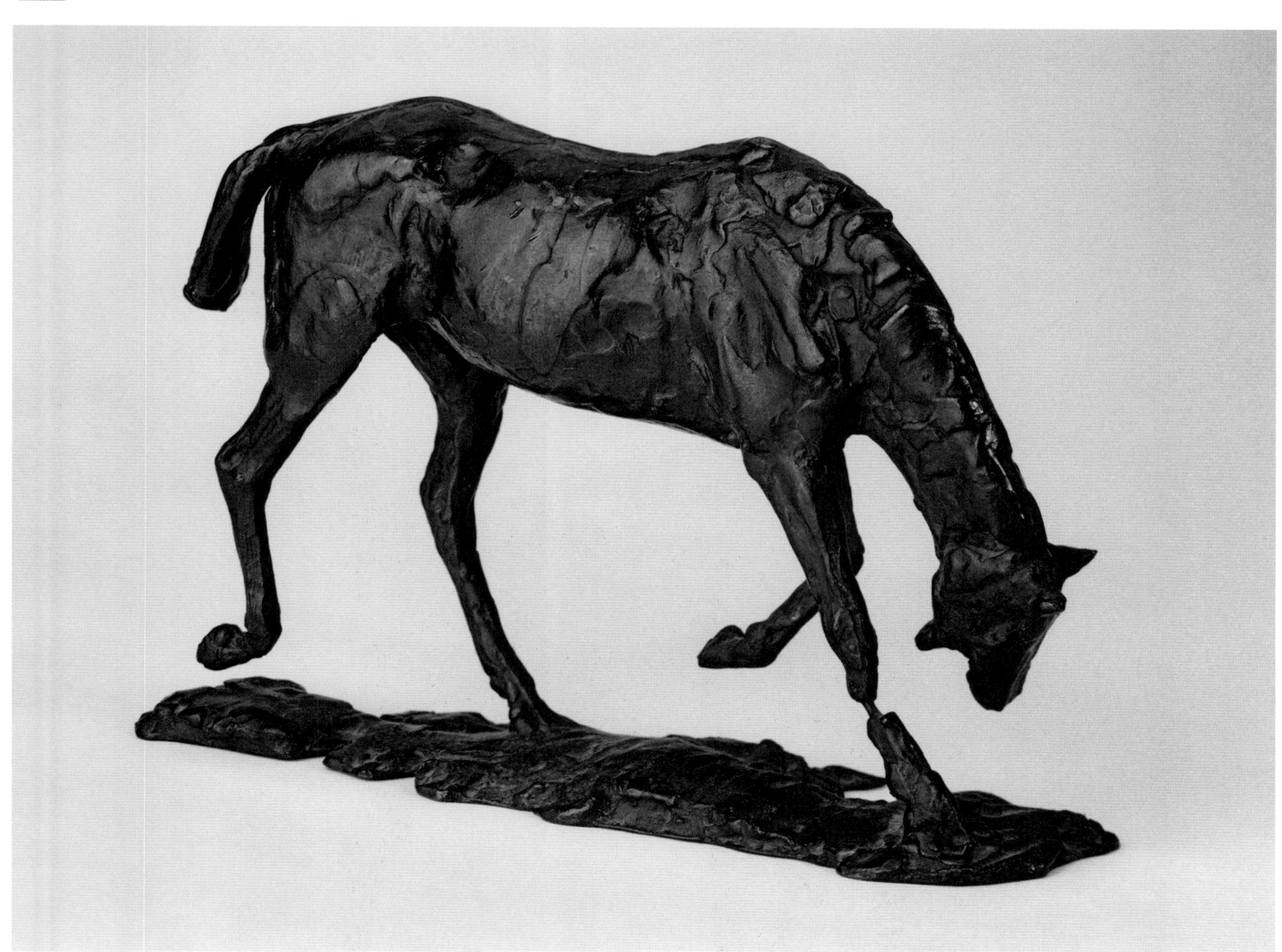

1　"[M]ais je n'ai pas encore fait assez de chevaux." Letter from Edgar Degas to Albert Bartholomé, 1888, in Degas 1931, p. 116.

2　See exh. cat. Paris et al. 1988, pp. 133–140; Berger 2014, pp. 18–21.

3　There are also discussions in the research concerning whether the sculpture was not created until after the completion of the canvas; see Boggs 1998, p. 35; Gaudichon 2010, p. 17.

4　See Eiling 2016, p. 125.

5　Thiébault-Sisson 1931.

6　See the chapter "Vom Parthenon-Fries auf die Rennbahn", in exh. cat. Karlsruhe 2014, pp. 201–225 (catalogue entries by Alexander Eiling, Sonja-Maria Krämer and Nina Trauth).

7　See the X-ray of the panting in the archive of the Museum of Fine Arts, Boston. I thank Katie Hanson and Julia Welch for their support.

8　See *Cheval à l'arrêt*; Czestochowski/Pingeot 2002, no. 38.

9　Reff 1995, p. 64.

10　Inv. cat. Washington 2010, p. 107.

11　See exh. cat. Karlsruhe 2014, pp. 219–220. nos. 95–97 (Nina Trauth); see exh. cat. Manchester/Cambridge 1987, p. 102.

Cat. 44 Edgar Degas, Horse Rearing (Cheval caracolant), c. 1890; bronze, 25.5 × 27.5 × 13 cm; stamped on the plinth: "65/O"; Staatliche Museen zu Berlin, Nationalgalerie, inv. no. B I 459 **Cat. 45** Edgar Degas, Horse Galloping on the Right Foot (Cheval au galop sur le pied droit), late 1880s; bronze, 31.6 × 20.5 × 48.2 cm; stamped on the plinth: "47/P"; Musee d'Orsay, Paris, inv. no. RF 2105

Cat. 44

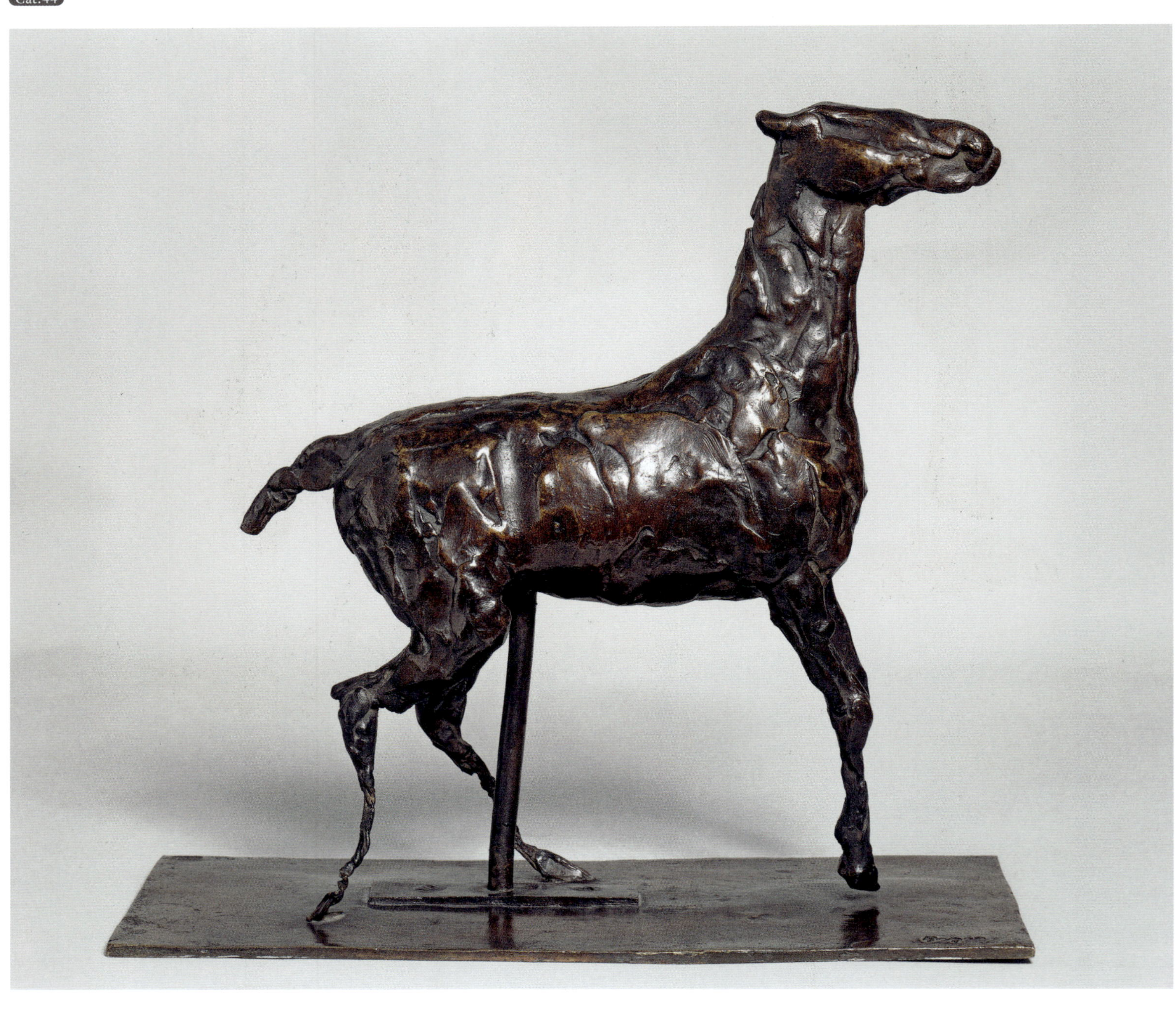

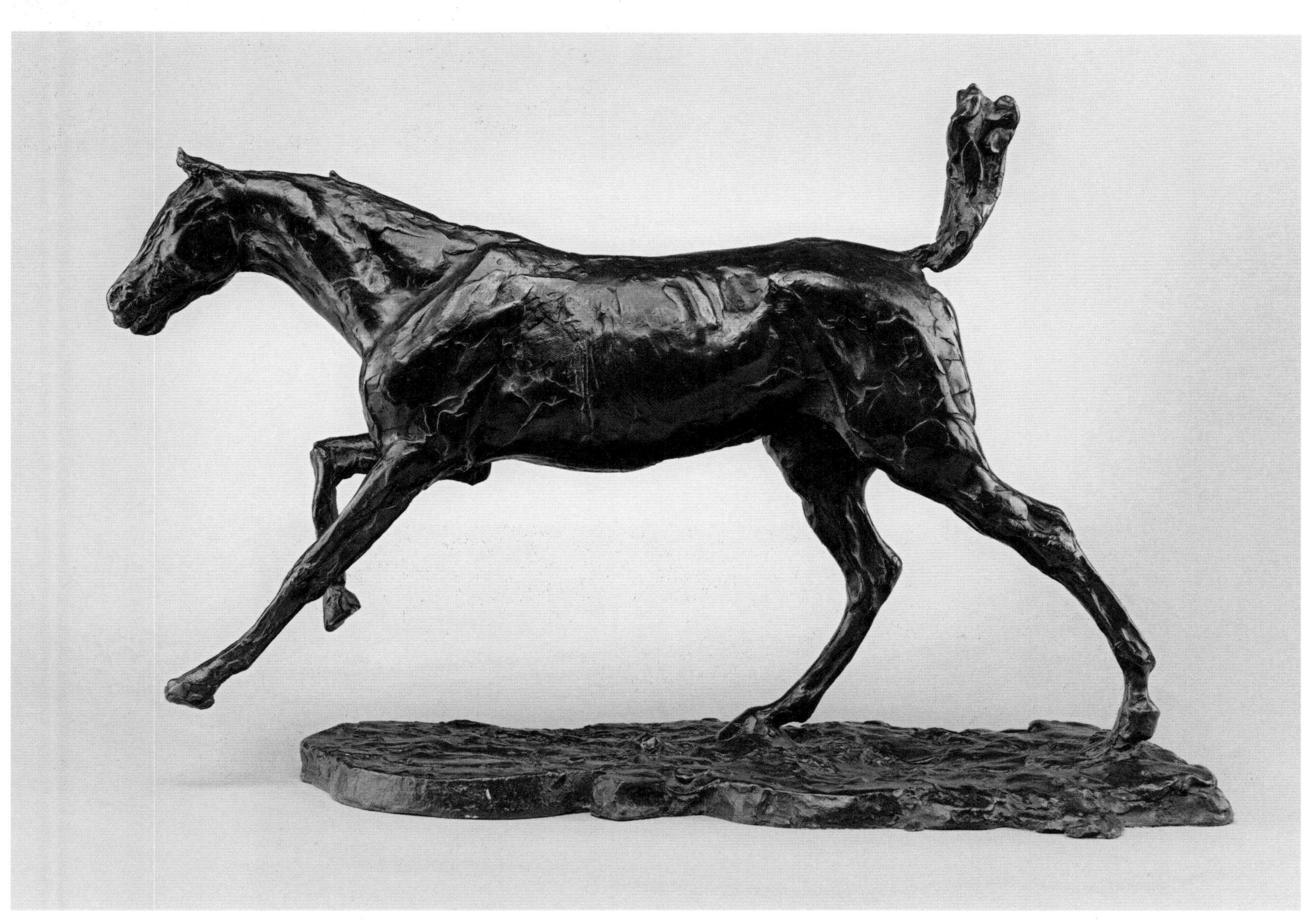

Cat. 45

 Edgar Degas, Horse Trotting, the Feet Not Touching the Ground (Cheval au trot, les pieds ne touchant pas le sol), 1870s; bronze, 22.5 × 27 × 12.7 cm; stamped on the plinth: "49/O"; Städel Museum, Frankfurt am Main, inv. no. SGP 62

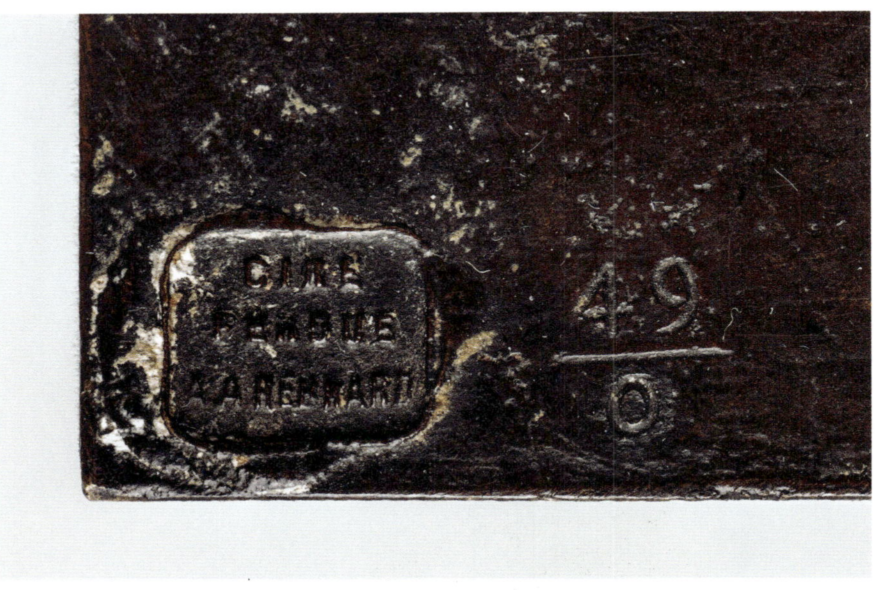

Cat.46

Cat.46

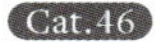

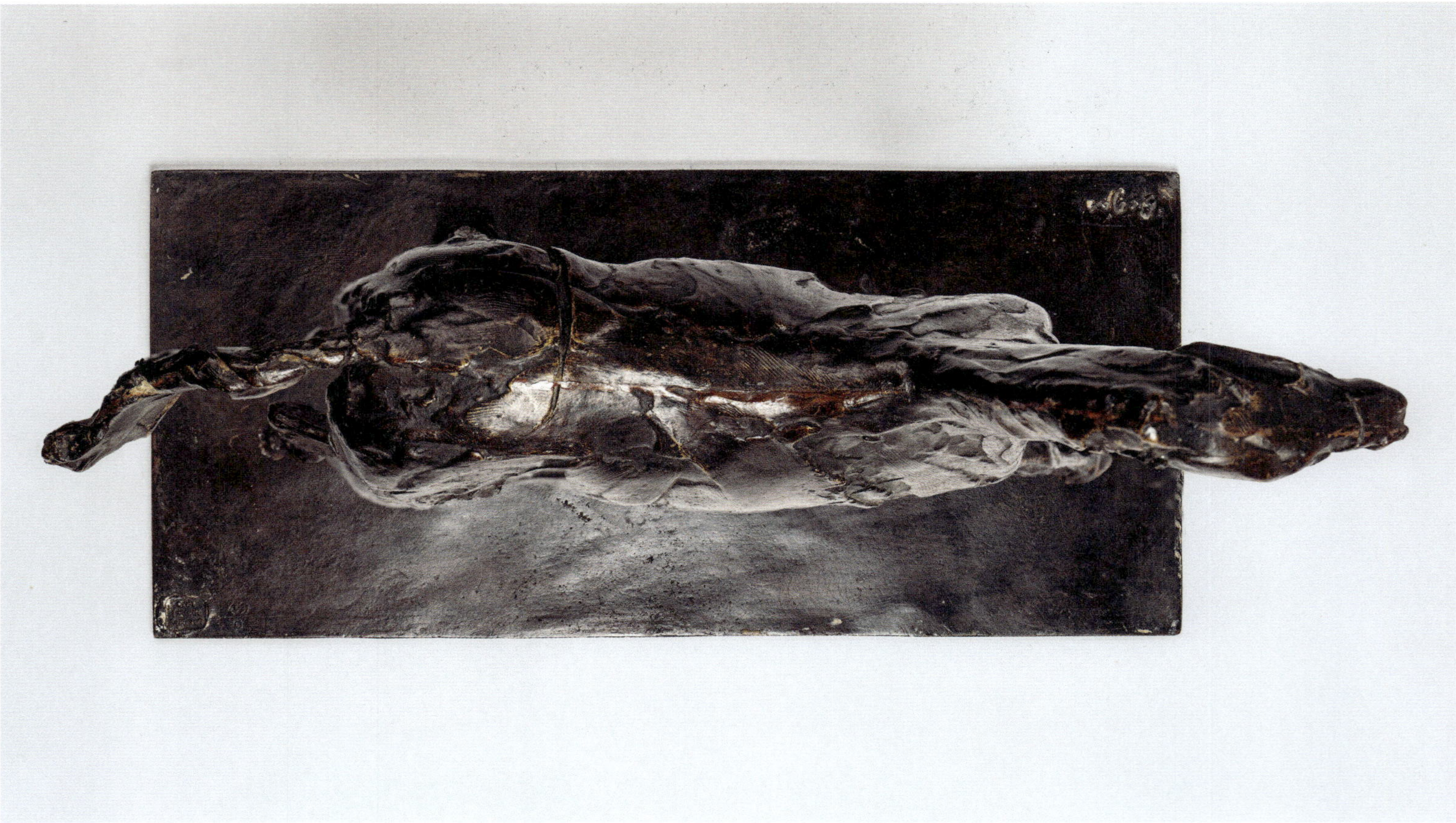

Cat.46

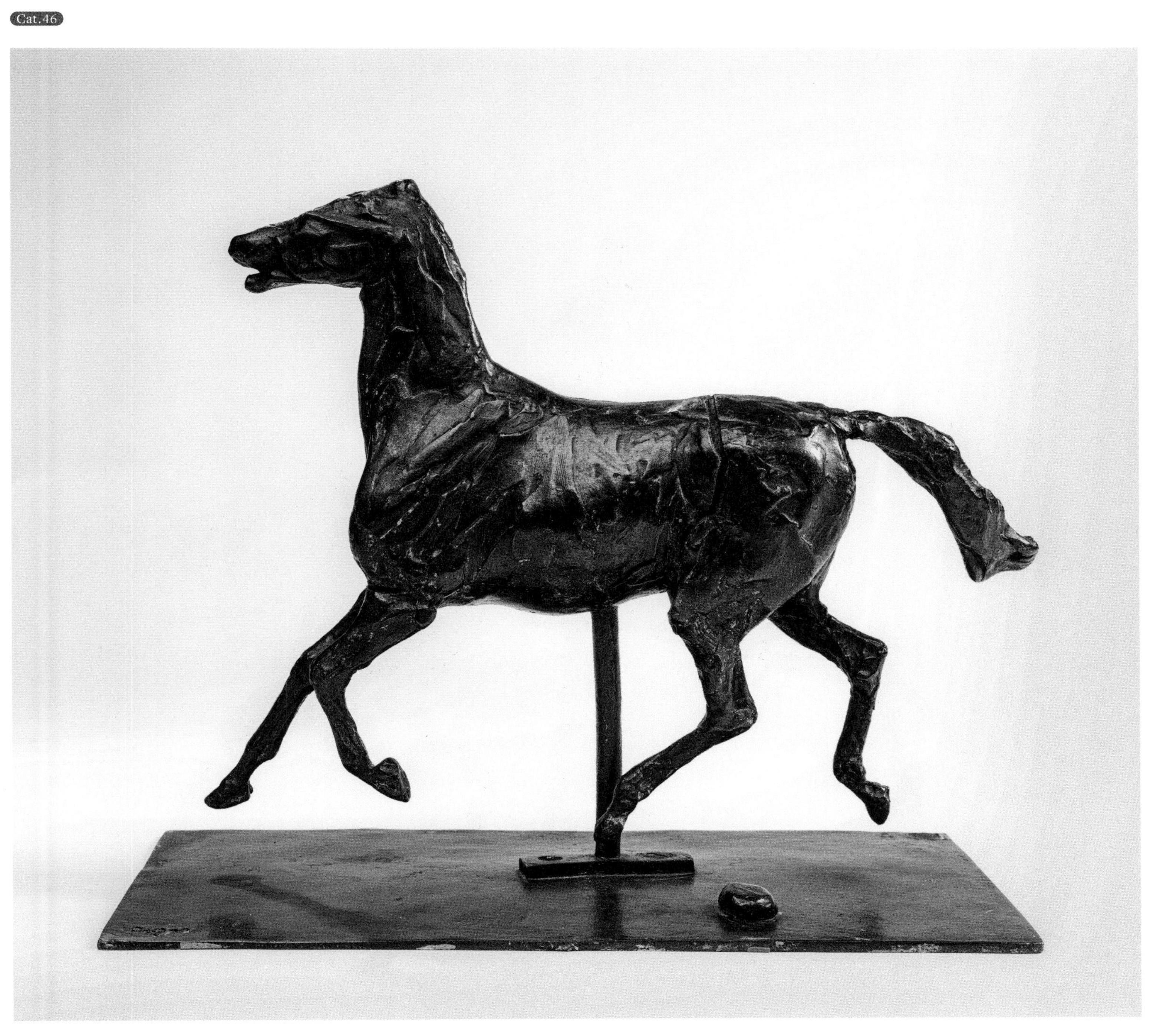

Cat.47 Edgar Degas, Horse Galloping on the Right Foot, the Back Left Foot Only Touching the Ground / Jockey with Cap (Cheval au galop sur le pied droit, le pied gauche arrière seul touchant terre / Jockey avec casquette), probably 1890s; bronze, c. 20 × 18.3 × 33.5 cm (horse), 14 × 7.5 × 6 cm (jockey); stamped on the plinth: "25/M" (horse), engraved under the right foot: "35/M" (jockey); private collection Cat.48 Eadweard Muybridge, Pandora Galloping, Saddled, c. 1885; from *Animal Locomotion* (Muybridge 1887), pl. 630; collotype, 47.6 × 60.2 cm; private collection, Frankfurt am Main

Cat. 47

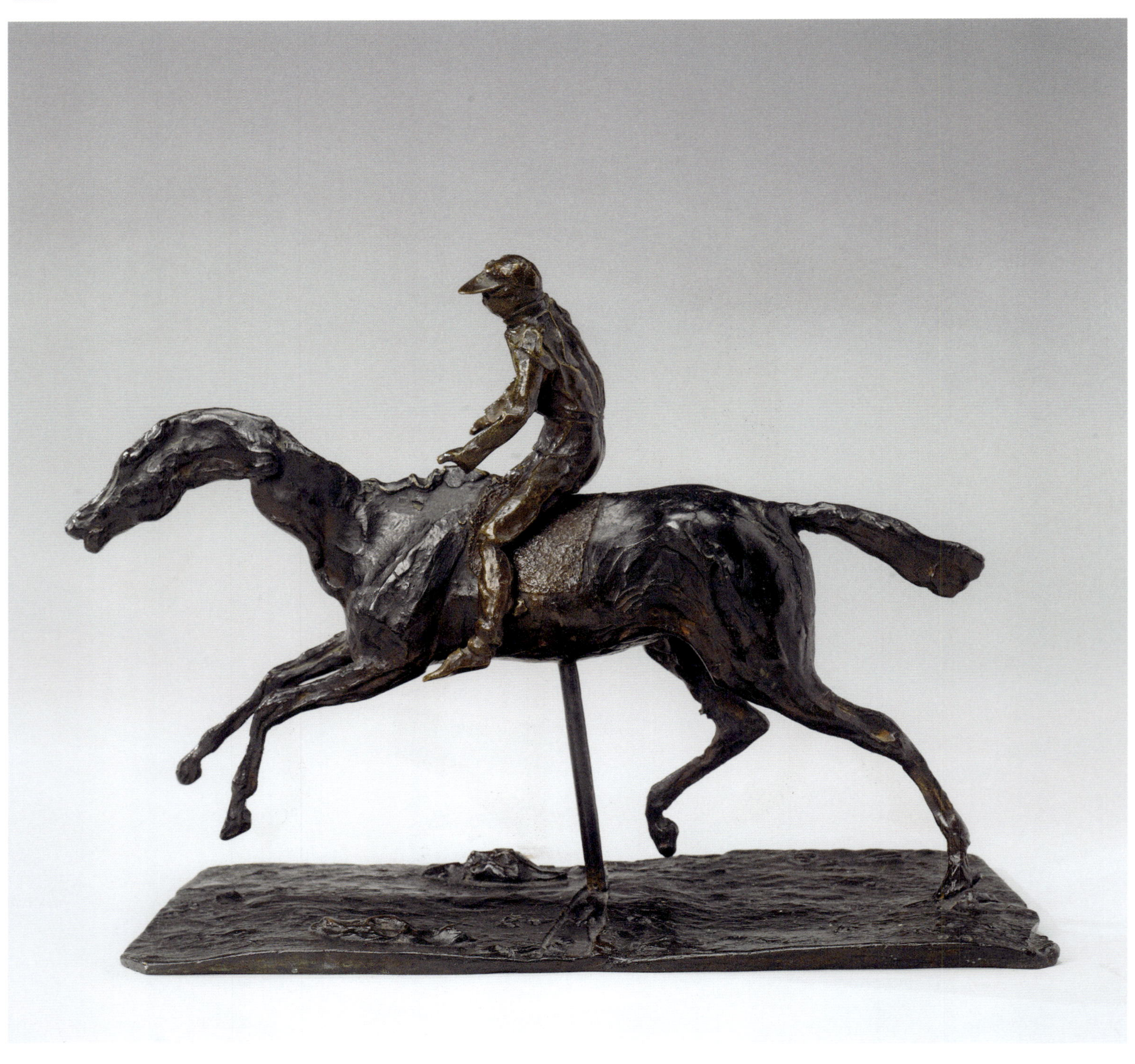

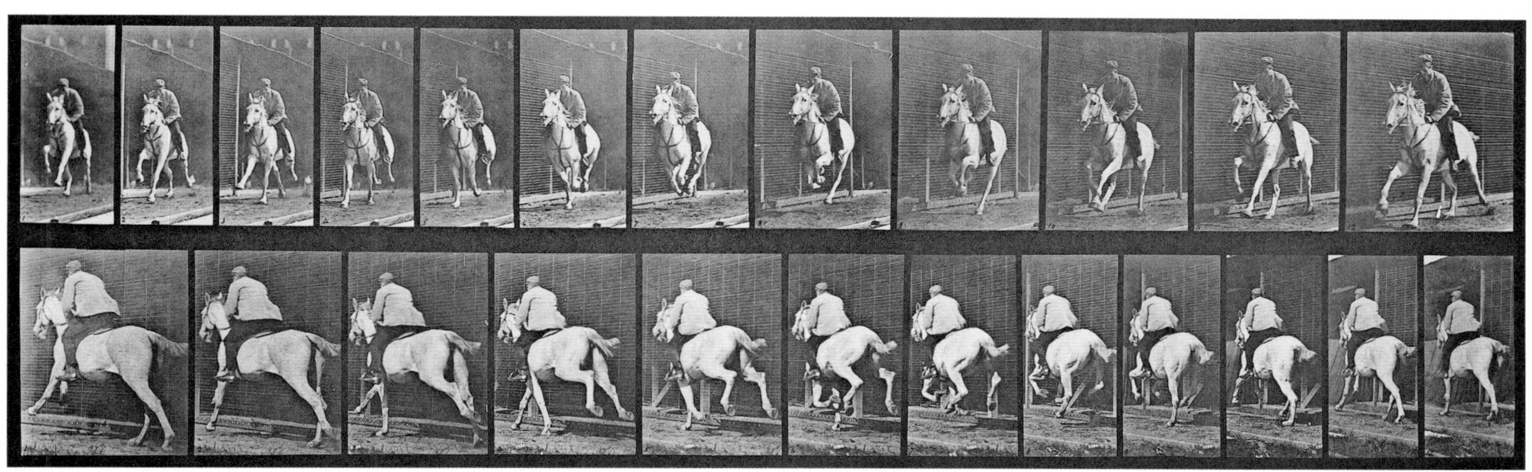

Cat. 48

Cat.49 Edgar Degas, Two Jockeys (Deux jockeys), 1866–1868; thinned oil paint, sepia and opaque white on brown paper, 30.5 × 43.3 cm; private collection
Cat.50 Edgar Degas, Racehorses at Longchamp (Chevaux de courses à Longchamp), 1871, possibly reworked in 1874; oil on canvas, 34 × 41.9 cm; Museum of Fine Arts, Boston, inv. no. 03.1034

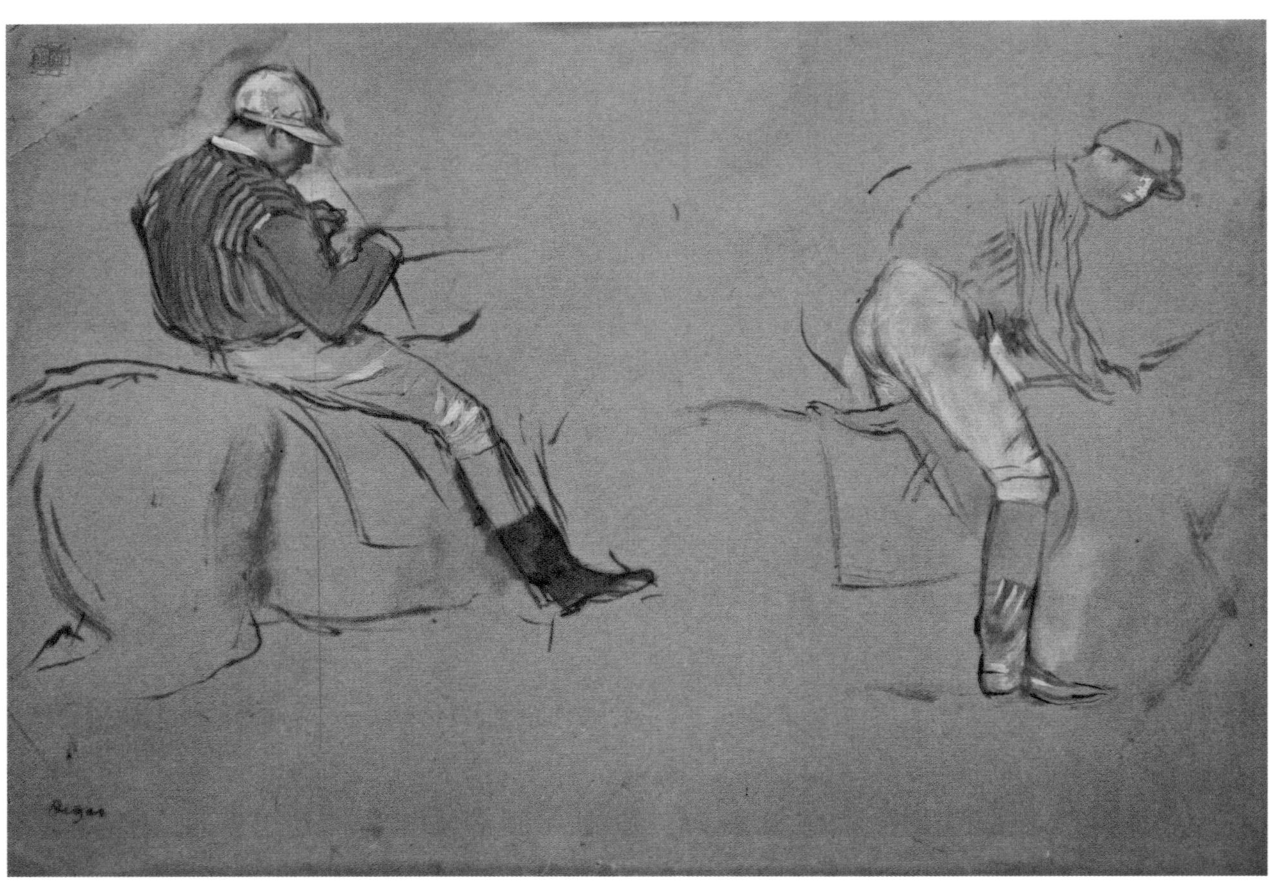

Cat.49

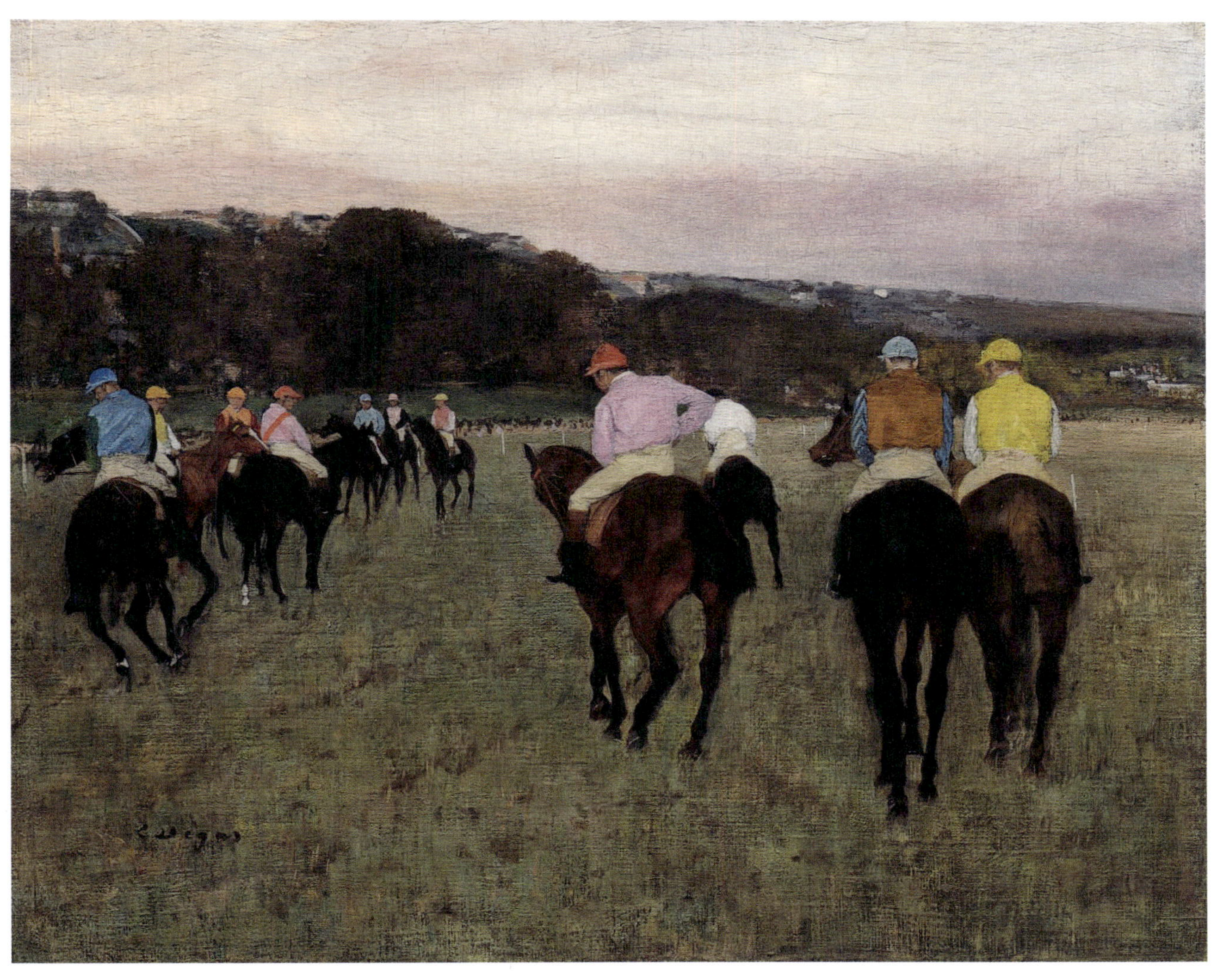

Cat. 50

Cat.51 Henri de Toulouse-Lautrec, **The Jockey**, 1899; colour lithograph, 51.8 × 36.2 cm; Städel Museum, Frankfurt am Main, inv. no. SG 64373 **Cat.52** Édouard Manet, **The Races at Longchamp (Les Courses à Longchamp)**, 1865–72; lithograph on China paper, 36 × 51 cm; Städel Museum, Frankfurt am Main, inv. no. 65232

Cat.51

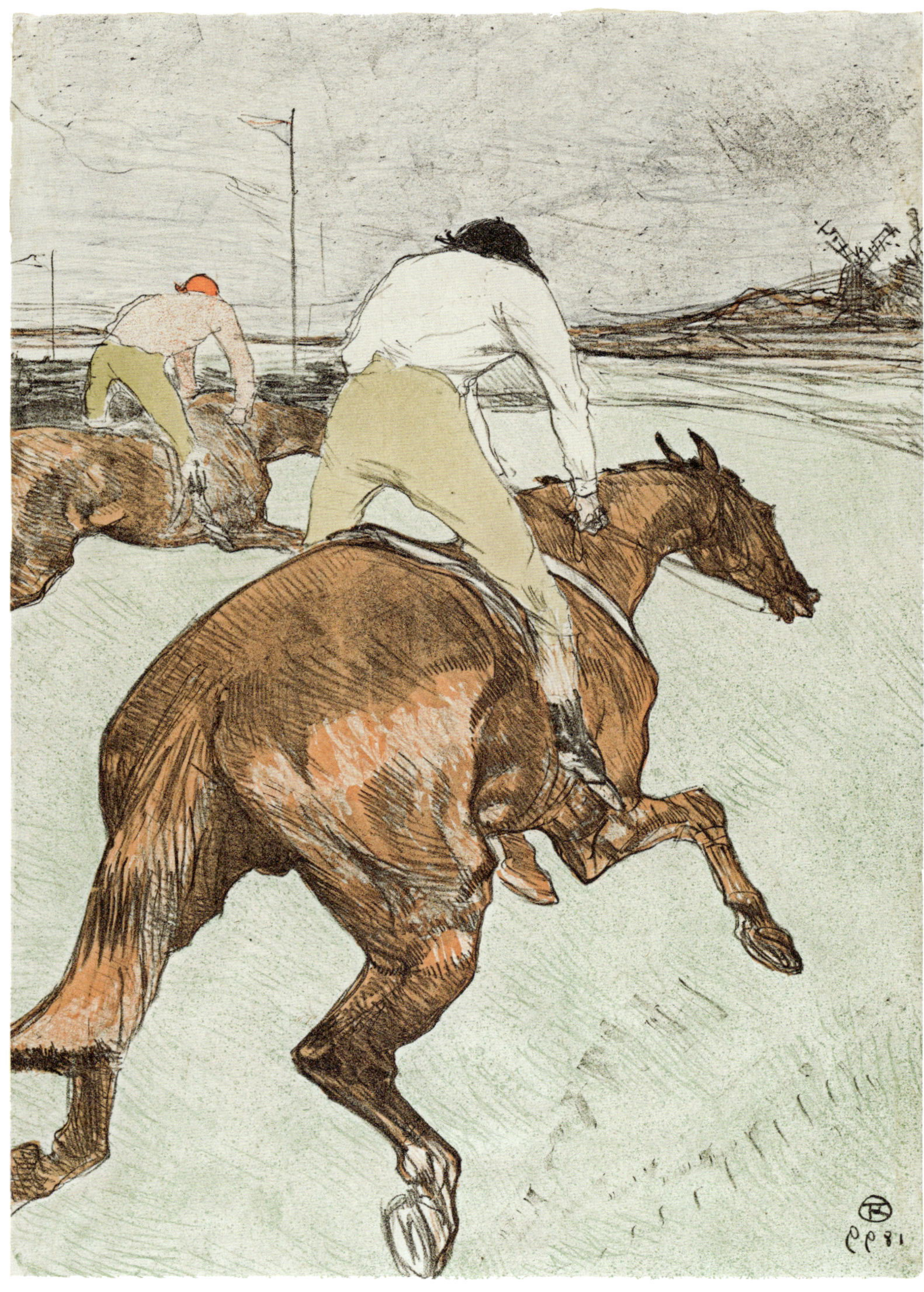

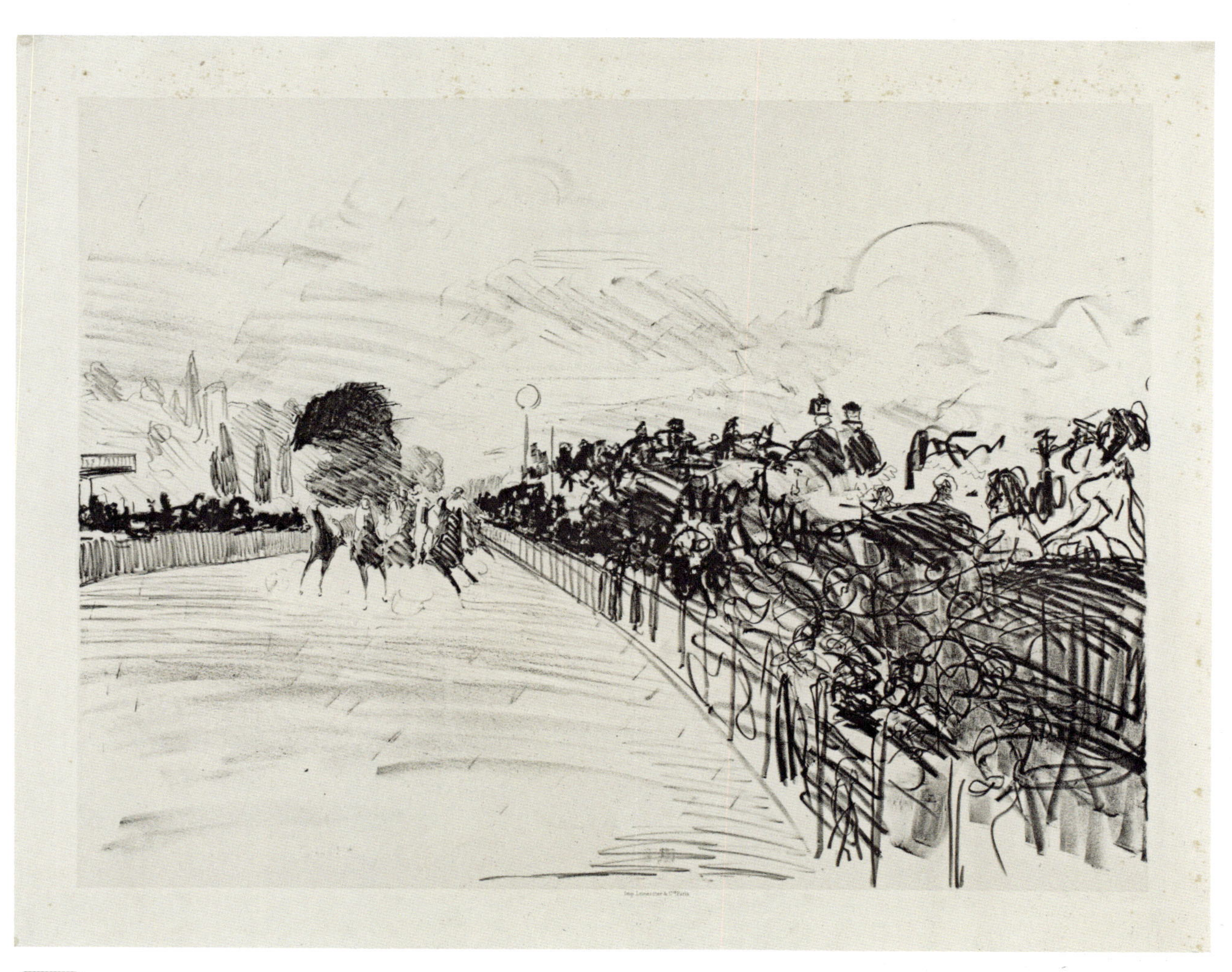

Cat.52

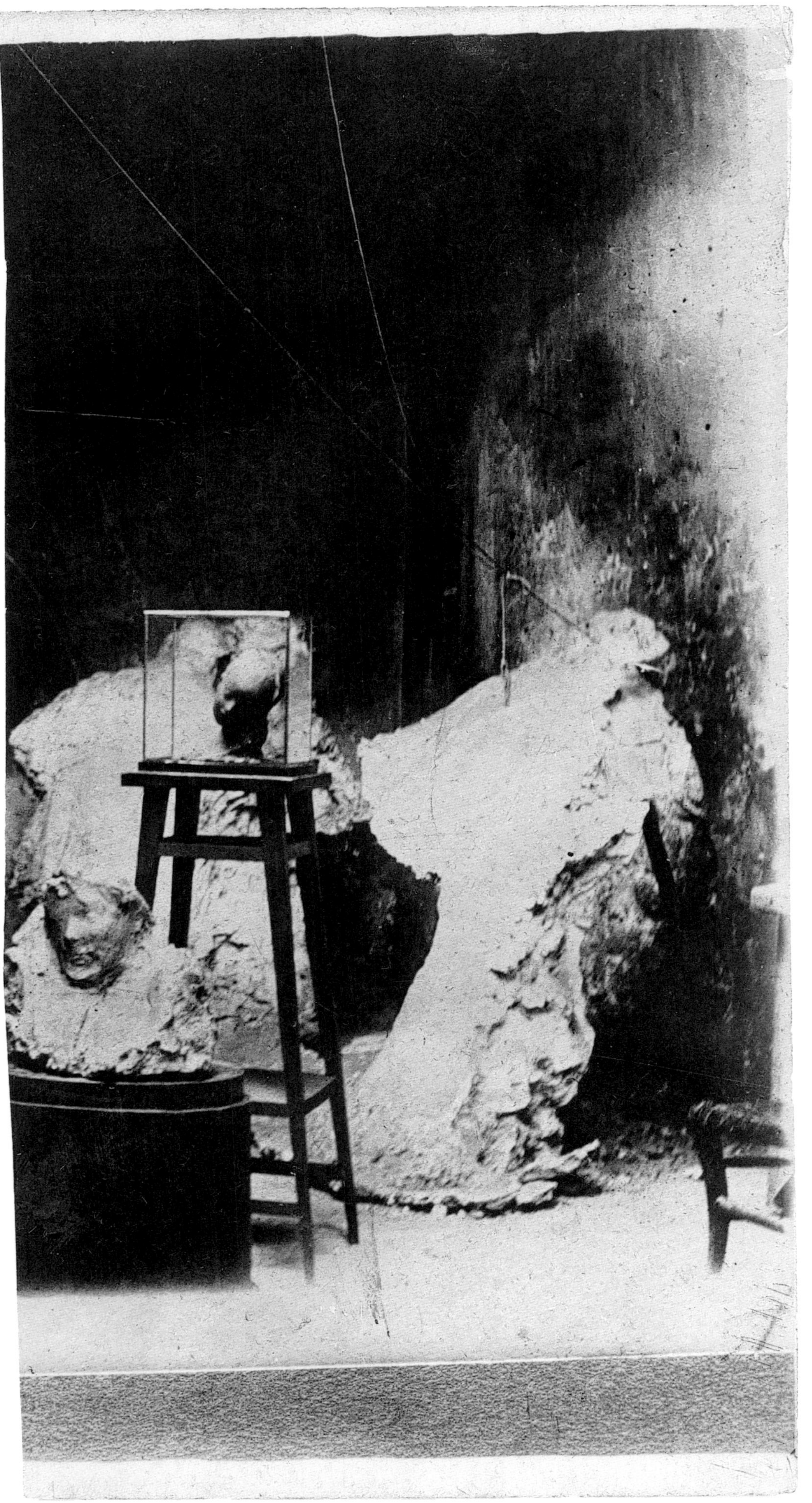

Medardo Rosso

Medardo Rosso

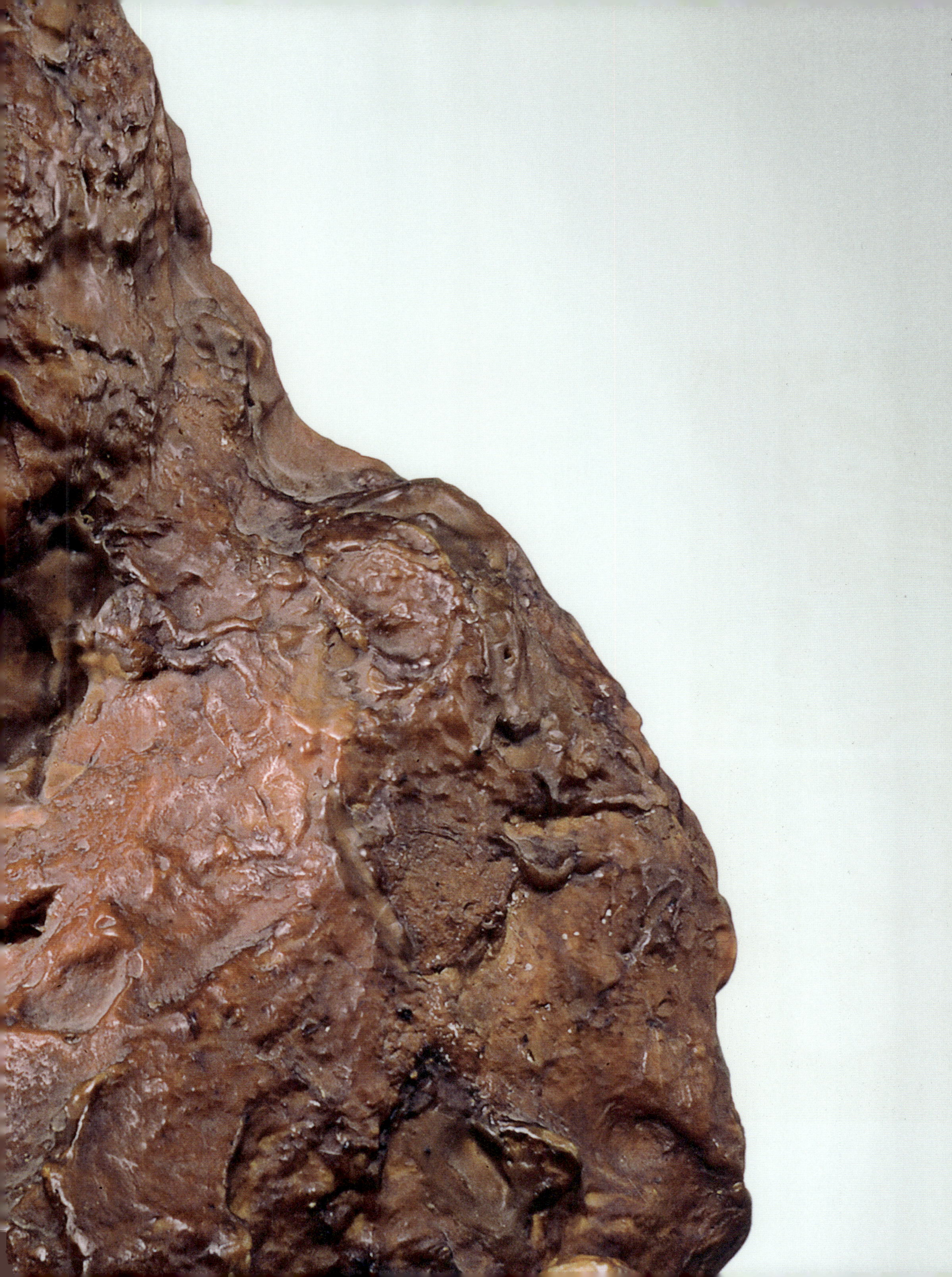

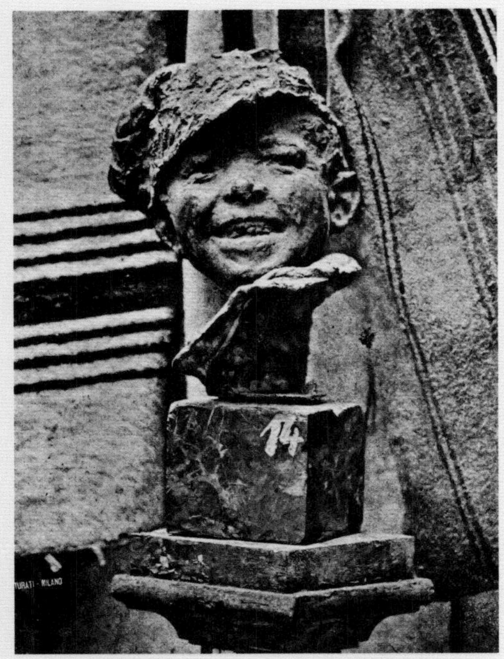

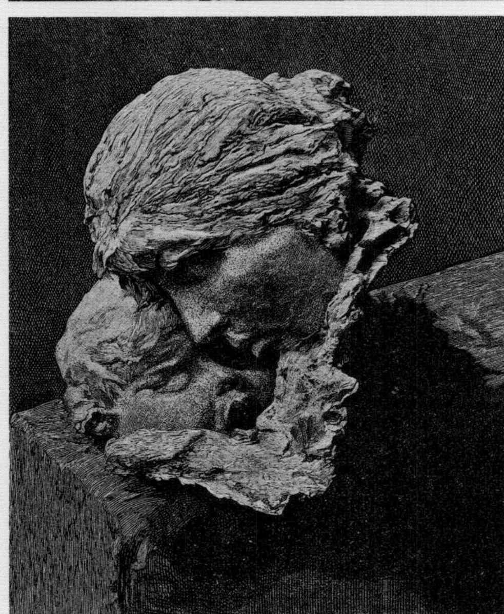

1 Medardo Rosso, *Gavroche/Il Birichino,*
c. 1882, photograph, c. 1887/88

2 Medardo Rosso, *Mère et son enfant endormis*
(*Amor materno*), 1883, reproduction
from *Illustrazione italiana,* 1886, frontispiece

Eva Mongi-Vollmer

"He is masterfully founding Impressionist sculpture" – Medardo Rosso

When pressed to reveal his roots, Medardo Rosso (1858–1928) claimed he had been born on a train. More than 30 years after his death, his friend Mario Vianello-Chiodo explained that the artist had preferred not to answer questions about his origins on principle; he had regarded such classifications as too confining.[1]

On the one hand, this anecdote testifies to Rosso's (charming) waywardness; on the other hand, it can be taken as a warning: he is not an easy artist to classify. Perhaps he would even have been happy to know that, to this day, his oeuvre has remained difficult to grasp – already with regard to quantity alone – and thus to "categorise". Scholars know little about his beginnings as a painter. Some drawings have come down to us (cat. 74–79), as well as photographs (cat. 55–57, 64), whose authorship, however, has yet to be definitively clarified.[2] Of all the media Rosso worked in, we know most about his sculptures. Even there, however, our overview of the actual objects remains sketchy, despite the several catalogues raisonnés we have at our disposal.[3] In some, entire groups of works are missing: for example, the early grave markers, the works no longer in existence or the so-called *pezzi di paragone* – a group of about 20 plaster casts of ancient and Renaissance sculptures (fig. 9) which Rosso actively incorporated into his exhibition arrangements. What is more, the various cast versions of his respective motifs have not yet undergone conclusive research. On the basis of present knowledge, it can be assumed that Rosso executed about 50 motifs between the early 1880s and 1906. For lack of object markings and sources, it is difficult to determine when exactly he developed those works. Only on occasion do his – initially cautious – exhibition activities aid us in establishing *termini ante quem,* and the constantly changing titles aggravate the research situation even further.[4] During the last 20 years of his life, Rosso did not create any new motifs, but he did frequently produce new editions of his existing works in variations and different materials such as plaster, wax and bronze (cat. 53, 54, 60, 61).[5]

Despite these unfortunate circumstances, Medardo Rosso has to this day been considered *the* representative of Impressionist sculpture.[6] "He is masterfully founding Impressionist sculpture", the art critic Edmond Thiaudière wrote in his report on the Paris *Salon* as far back as June 1886.[7] Many voices chimed in with this assessment. On the occasion of an exhibition at the La Bodinière theatre in Paris in 1893, for example, the art critic Alphonse Germain celebrated Rosso as "a veritable impressionist of sculpture".[8] And Edmond Claris not only paid explicit tribute to him as an Impressionist sculptor in his authoritative text of 1902, but even elevated him above Auguste Rodin: "Where Rodin stopped, that was Medardo Rosso's starting point."[9] Julius Meier-Graefe concurred with this estimation in 1904 in *Modern Art:* in the chapter on "Impressionism in Sculpture", he repeatedly compared Rosso to Rodin – to the disadvantage of the latter.[10]

But what had prompted Thiaudière to refer to the Milanese artist – an almost complete unknown in France at the time – as an Impressionist sculptor back in 1886? The Italian had never even visited any of the eight Impressionist exhibitions taking place in Paris between 1874 and 1886, to say nothing of participating in them.[11] In fact we have no answer as to why the enthusiastic Thiaudière labelled Rosso an Impressionist; we do, however, know which of the artist's works the critic had in mind in that context: the two bronzes *Gavroche/Il Birichino* and *Mère et son enfant endormis* (*Amor materno*), both executed in 1882/83 (figs. 1 and 2).[12] Still in existence today in several casts, the *Gavroche* can be considered an example of the socially oriented Realism that Rosso initially cultivated. The cube-shaped stone serving the head as a base, however, was a novelty with its unfinished surface. The surface of the *Amor materno* group, for its part, depicting a popular mother-and-child motif, exhibits a conventional approach in its high degree of detail and finish.[13] At the same time, the ensemble of two closely joined heads is abruptly cut off in an unusual manner – it looks as if it had been torn out of a larger context. What is more, neither the emphatic view from above nor the mounting of the work at the end of a wooden board – as seen in the photo of 1886 – corresponded to visual habits of the time.[14] In the case of both busts, Rosso decided in favour of a tentative and spontaneous-looking presentation form rather than a classically stable one. In the conception of his contemporaries, this reference to a handling of the motif that might change at any moment evidently sufficed to admit Rosso's work to the Impressionist orbit.

Who was Medardo Rosso? He was born in 1858, not on a train but in Turin; the family moved to Milan in 1877. In May 1882 – he had completed his military service and was now 24 – he enrolled at the Accademia di Brera in Milan.[15] In March of the following year, the school expelled him after he and fellow students such as Giovanni Segantini advocated for improvements in life-drawing instruction, albeit resorting to violent means to advance their cause (see cat. 74–79).[16] Rosso's further artistic development continued in association with a movement called "La Scapigliatura" (the dishevelled ones).[17] Initially literary in orientation and later active in the visual arts as well, this group of bohemians aspired towards a unity of poetry, music and painting. Whereas in terms of subject matter, the painters Tranquillo Cremona (cat. 115) and Daniele Ranzoni were rather conservative, their loose application of the paint and emphasis on painterly substance – as opposed to the linear apprehension of the object – were attributes they shared with their (pre-)Impressionist contemporaries in Paris. This is not to claim that the French possessed model character for the Italians; they were far too little known in Italy for such a role.[18] Serving to loosen up the painting surface, the restless style of brushwork practised by the Scapigliati painters had an impact on the Milanese sculptor Giuseppe Grandi, whose famous 1875 statuette of *Marschall Ney* was on display at the Accademia di Brera in the form of a plaster cast (fig. 3).[19] Rosso's work of the early 1880s exhibits a similar approach. As seen in the subjects of his loosely modelled busts and statuettes of hoodlums and guttersnipes, however, he devoted his work more to the social issues of his time than the Scapigliati (fig. 4).

In May 1889, Rosso moved to Paris, in part for financial reasons. Living in precarious circumstances, he soon rented a studio for himself in the Boulevard de Clichy in Montmartre.[20] He had already carried out important works by this time such as *La Portinaia* (1883/84; cat. 53, 54), the monumental multi-figured group *Impressione d'omnibus* (1883/84; cat. 57) and *Aetas Aurea* (1886; cat. 58). The journalist

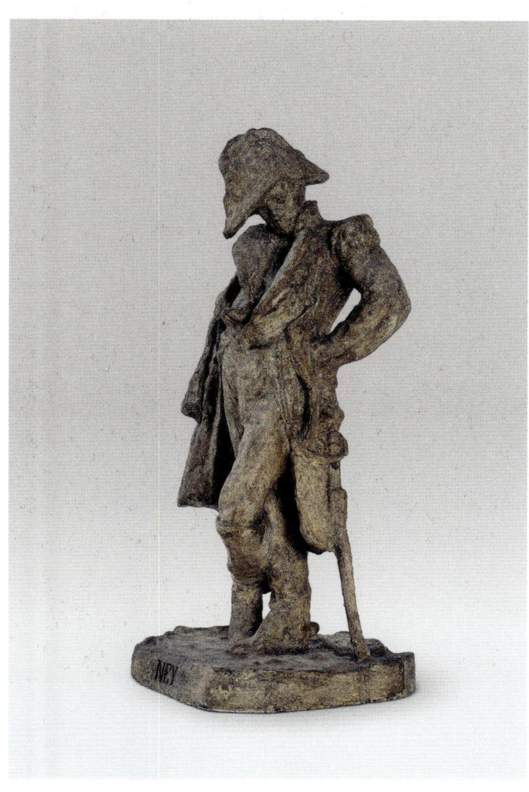

3   Giuseppe Grandi, *Marshal Ney*, 1875, plaster, 32.5 × 16.5 × 13.5 cm, Galleria d'Arte Moderna, Milan

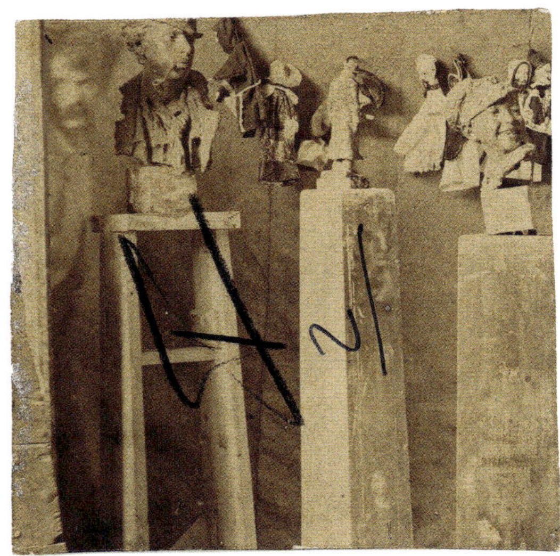

4   Medardo Rosso's studio in Milan, 1883, photograph on albumen paper, 7.6 × 7.7 cm, private collection

Medardo Rosso

"Sculpture is not only equal to painting in every way [...], but is perhaps called upon to surpass the latter."

Medardo Rosso, quoted in: Claris 1902

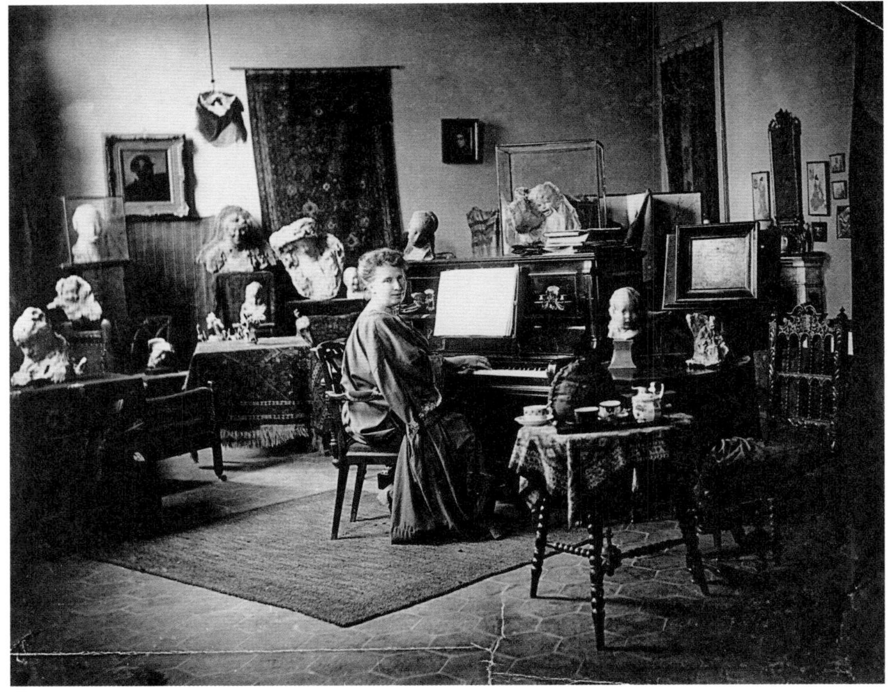

5 Etha Fles in her apartment in Rome, c. 1913, photograph, RKD – Netherlands institute for art history, The Hague

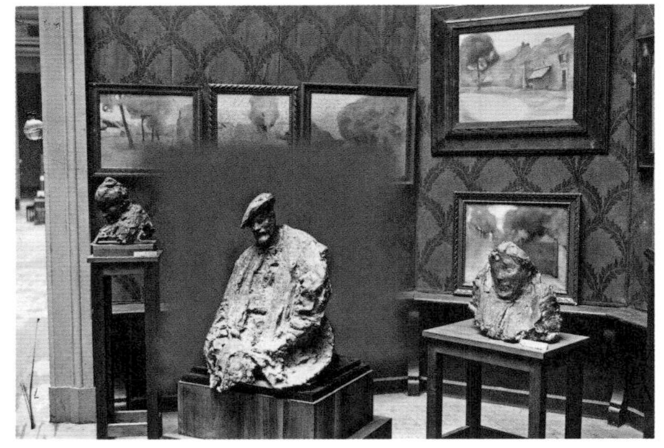

6 Salon d'Automne, Paris, 1904, with Medardo Rosso's *La Portinaia*, 1883/84, *Henri Rouart*, 1890, and *Madame Noblet*, 1897, photograph, 16.2 × 23.2 cm, private collection

Felice Cameroni accompanied Rosso to the French capital, where he reported for Italy on the world's fair of 1889 as well as on the exhibition *Claude Monet – Auguste Rodin* at Galerie Georges Petit. With Cameroni's help, Émile Zola was persuaded to pose as the owner of *Gavroche/Il Birichino*, Rosso's bust of a street urchin, at the Exposition universelle, although the work did not actually belong to him.[21] The same year, Rosso made the acquaintance of the collector Henri Rouart, a supporter of Impressionism (see cat. 70), and, presumably through that connection, Edgar Degas.[22] All in all, however, we know very little about Rosso's life in Paris – what he saw, what moved and inspired him. Unlike many of his compatriots, he rarely described the Parisian attractions in his letters to Italy – neither the newly erected Eiffel Tower nor the museums or exhibitions or even the nightlife.[23] We do know that he did not succeed in familiarising a broad Parisian public with his works. In the 1890s, he took part in only two exhibitions: at La Bodinière theatre in 1893 and the *Salon des Champs-Élysées* in 1895.[24] Notably, the presentation in the foyer of La Bodinière theatre made such a strong impression on Auguste Rodin that he invited Rosso to an exchange of sculptures.[25] Over the years, however, Rodin's initial appreciation gave way to rivalry, fuelled not least of all by the press (see cat. 63).[26]

In this first decade in Paris, Rosso gradually turned his artistic attention from the proletarian milieu to the bourgeoisie. This is evident in the statuettes of *Man Reading a Newspaper* and *The Bookmaker* (cat. 62, 63), the striking bust of the *Femme à la voilette* (cat. 66) and, of course, the large-scale sculptural group *Paris la nuit* (64; p. 280, fig. 8), which did not survive the times. With this shift of interest, Rosso aligned himself closely with the painting of Impressionists such as Camille Pissarro, Claude Monet and Gustave Caillebotte, who determinedly devoted themselves to the everyday affairs taking place on Baron Haussmann's boulevards.

It was not until the turn of the century that Rosso began to enjoy international recognition for his art.[27] At the Paris world's fair of 1900, in which he participated as a sculptor and caster, he caught the attention of the Dutchwoman Etha Fles.[28] She immediately became his most important collector and patron, and it was with her help that Rosso now made a name for himself in Holland (fig. 5).

In 1902, Edmond Claris published *De l'Impressionnisme en sculpture,* which gave Rosso yet another boost; here as well, Etha Fles was involved, as she had translated Claris's essay of the same title into German the previous year.[29] By way of these writings, Rosso came to be stylised as the originator of Impressionist sculpture, which at the start of the twentieth century was conceived of as a "struggle for liberation, a true revolution".[30]

It was also in 1902 that Rosso, meanwhile 44 years of age, had his first solo exhibitions: at Kunstsalon Keller und Reiner in Berlin and Museum für Kunsthandwerk in Leipzig. In the titles of his works, he began to make increasing use of the word "impression". The tendency culminated in the Paris Salon d'automne of 1904, which featured 17 works with this addition to their titles (fig. 6).[31] In 1906, just one year after a further important solo presentation at the *Kunstsalon Artaria* in Vienna, Rosso carried out his last sculpture, the bust *Ecce Puer* (fig. 7).[32] The following year, he again received public recognition in his adopted homeland when the French state purchased two of his works,[33] but in general the Parisian public no longer paid him much attention. In 1910, in his native Italy, on the other hand, after 21 years of absence, an exhibition entitled *Prima esposizione italiana dell'Impressionismo francese e delle sculture di Medardo Rosso* at the Lyceum in Florence celebrated him as an Impressionist.[34] Not long thereafter, Etha Fles reappeared on the scene with another form of support: starting in 1913, she donated altogether 17 of the artist's works to several public Italian collections.[35] Already in 1912, the *Futurist Manifesto* had paid him express homage – as a key innovator on the road to overcoming Impressionism![36] Compelled in part by the circumstances of the First World War, Rosso returned to Milan, where he died in 1928.

As an inventor of motifs, Rosso was active for about 25 years, until about 1906 – a phase that does not correspond to his art-theoretical endeavours. On the contrary, it was not until around 1900, when his fame had begun to spread, that he took to recording his thoughts in writing and publishing them – albeit in linguistically unconventional manner.[37] What is more, his increased participation in exhibitions went hand in hand with growing interest in him as a person and as an artist on the part of art scholarship and newspaper arts sections: ever more authors addressed themselves to the loner Rosso. As is still the case today, those writers liked to quote things he had said about himself – for example, his description of something that had come to pass in 1883: the shadow of a passing couple had made a stronger impression on him than the persons themselves. He could not have grasped the shadow he so admired with his hands; the figures he certainly could have. This story was first published in the magazine *La Stampa* in 1923 – that is, 40 years after the occurrence.[38]

In 1883, the year of the said "Brera experience", the artist was working on the sculpture of his concierge, the *Portinaia.* Scholars consider this profile bust of an old woman a key work because it is the first to exhibit the deliberate haziness that, from today's point of view, has become emblematic of Rosso. As he had observed his subject in passing, a "standing second" had had to suffice to capture the essentials.[39] This brief instant had inscribed itself in the object itself in the form of a blurred contour (cat. 53, 54) – and that was the actual novelty. Whereas the work bears within it the attribute of the "observation en passant", Rosso wished for stasis on the part of the beholder: the portrait subject is recognisable only from a certain vantage point. Seen from the wrong position, she virtually dissolves into an enigma. By adopting this complex approach, Rosso was subscribing to the development of Impressionism in painting, which, since the 1860s, had been discussed primarily in terms of the physiology of perception.[40] The focus was no longer on the supposed objectiveness of an object's representation, but on the reproduction of a subjective impression.

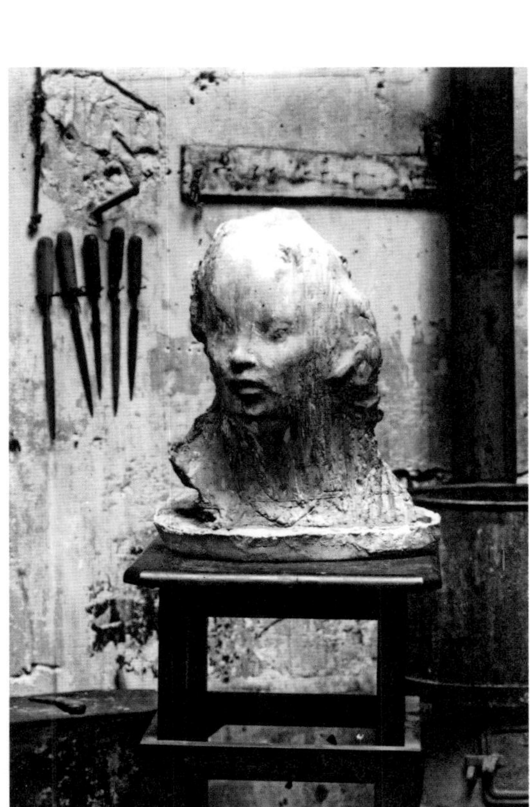

7 Medardo Rosso's studio on the Boulevard des Batignolles in Paris, 1906, with *Ecce Puer,* photograph, private collection

Medardo Rosso

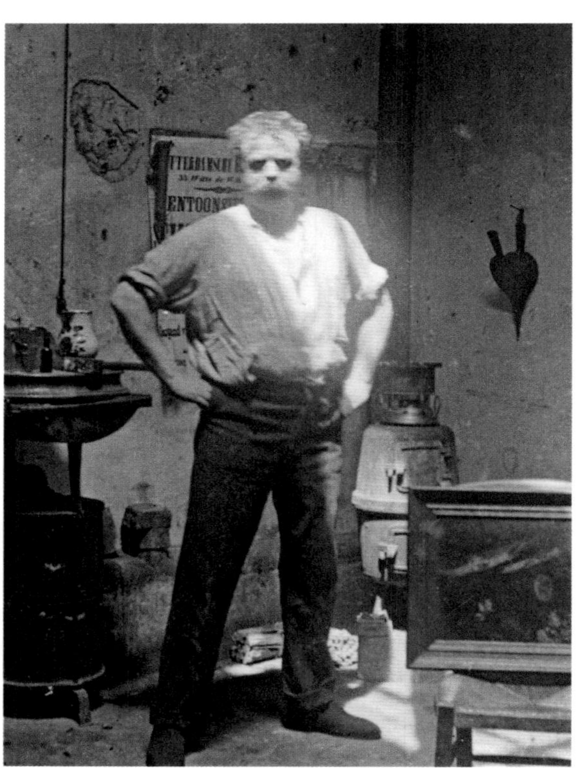

8   Medardo Rosso in his studio on Boulevard des Batignolles in Paris, after 1901, photograph, private collection

Yet Rosso's *Portinaia* is difficult to decipher even from the correct viewing angle, because the artist captured not only the concierge herself, but also the surrounding space.[41] In other words, rather than giving the figure a self-contained form, he opened her form to space.[42] He sought to capture the atmosphere enveloping a person as much as the person themselves. In 1886, it was precisely this emphatic incorporation of the surrounding space that, in the work *Aetas Aurea,* led not only to a blurring of the contours of mother and child, but also to a virtually indissoluble oneness of figure and space. At the same time, the artist was explicitly not concerned with emphasising the mass, but, on the contrary, with visualising the immateriality of figure and space to equal degrees. "Nothing is material in space", Claris quoted him as saying in 1902.[43] In 1905, Rosso even had the sentence "Rien n'est matériel dans l'espace" printed on the cover of the exhibition catalogue for the *Kunstsalon Artaria* in Vienna (see cat. 58).[44] In his *Aetas Aurea,* a sculpture flatter than it is round, he refrained from clear indications of the setting, thus also departing from the classical means of indicating space in a relief with the aid of a vanishing point.[45]

With his conception of sculpture, Rosso thus pursued goals similar to those of the Impressionist painters. It was no longer the colour of the object that determined the logic of their works, but successions of colour and streaming light. And not least importantly, the detailed brushwork of the paintings had its counterpart in the dynamic surfaces of the sculptures. Rosso himself repeatedly pointed out the affinity between the two media. What is more, he took pains to exhibit his works side by side with paintings – for example, by Paul Cézanne, Pierre-Auguste Renoir, Eugène Carrière and Giovanni Segantini.[46] In 1896, Camille de Sainte-Croix quoted another one of Rosso's statements: "Painting? Sculpture? There is only one art."[47] Edmond Claris repeated this observation in his text of 1902: "Nothing is material in space. Thus understood, art is indivisible. There is not painting on the one hand and sculpture on the other."[48] If anything, Rosso thought sculpture had a slight advantage over painting, because with reference to colour he wrote: "Sculpture is not only equal to painting in every way [...], but is perhaps called upon to surpass the latter. Does it lack colour, for example? Does it not have at its disposal the science of tonal values instead? Does it not have in its black and white everything it needs to represent movement, light and shade?"[49]

In connection with his 1906 exhibition at Eugene Cremetti Gallery in London, Rosso made a comment on Impressionist sculpture that appeared in *The Daily Mail* the following year. In it, he explained at greater length how he conceived of the equality of space and matter. Space, he observed, was defined by light, matter and perception. It took light to enable relationships and values between matter and its surroundings – and of key importance here was tonality, which could be perceived at first sight. Without light, an artwork had no *raison d'être*. He repeatedly stressed that his sculptures were to be grasped visually, not by touch. The first impression of the perception was the most important.[50] In other words, it was not the corporality of an object but its visual appearance in atmospheric fusion with the surrounding space that formed the foundation of Rosso's aesthetic.[51] He thus rejected the traditional conception of sculpture aimed at tactile perception.[52] And in fact his figures no more appear to be made of an inner (bone) frame than of flesh, blood and skin (see cat. 73). Julius Meier-Graefe put the lack of corporeality of Rosso's sculptures in a nutshell in 1904 when he wrote: "This brain art no longer has a body."[53] Here we have yet another aspect that places Rosso's work in the vicinity of Impressionist painting, in which bodies have more of a flat than a round appearance.

With his emphatic 1907 invocation of light, Rosso meant several things. On the one hand, he was referring to the light in which he observed his subject and, on the other hand, to the light shining on the finished artwork for the pur-

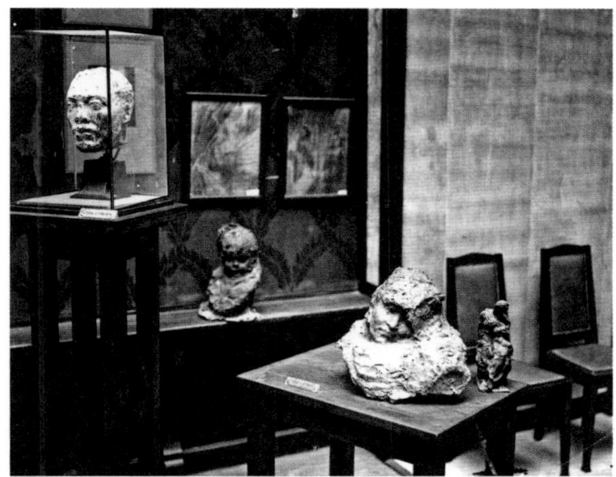

9 Salon d'Automne, Paris, 1904, with Medardo Rosso's *Memnon after a Classical Model*, 1902–1904, *Bambino al sole*, 1892, *Carne altrui*, 1883/84, *Madonna Medici after Michelangelo*, before 1904, photograph

pose of viewing it. He carefully controlled the light sources in exhibition situations and, like Edgar Degas, favoured electric light.[54] He moreover attached paramount importance to the material in which he executed his sculptures. Whereas the light appears to glide or leap across the surface of his bronzes, it virtually suffuses the figures in wax (see cat. 54, 61–63). Here it is important to point out that Rosso cast both his waxes and his bronzes in the lost-wax technique (*cire perdue*) using a gelatine mould. In both media, the starting point was a figure formed in a soft material (clay) and then cast in plaster; the plaster cast then served as the basis for the casts in bronze and wax.[55] Until well into the 1990s, the majority of scholars assumed that Rosso had formed his wax works with his fingers rather than casting them.[56] Whereas his bronzes were cast in Milanese foundries as far back as the 1880s, he did not produce works cast in wax (around a plaster core) until his Paris period, from 1895 at the latest. From that moment on, not only Rosso set great store by the wax medium, but also art critics, especially those partial to Symbolism.[57]

As casting took on ever greater importance for Rosso, he became increasingly involved in the process. He had learned the basics in Milan from Albino Palazzolo – the very founder who would later be responsible for the casts of waxes from the estate of Edgar Degas. Rosso set up a foundry in Paris in the courtyard of the house at Impasse Marie-Blanche 5 in 1892, and four years later moved it to his studio and enlarged it when he himself moved to the Boulevard des Batignolles (fig. 8). In February of 1890, he had written to Felice Cameroni that he wanted to take sole responsibility for the casts: "I do not want others to make creations on my stuff. Good or bad I want my own stuff."[58] By 1902, if not before, he was virtually staging his casting activities as events.[59] The visitors experienced Rosso as the artist-creator, on the one hand, and the vigorous and adept craftsman, on the other.[60] The creation process became visible and – in keeping with his intent – remained perceivable on the object. The lost-wax technique lent itself particularly well to this strategy. The artist left casting channels in place on the finished work just as he did cracks and dents caused by the mould. He smoothed these traces away only in part, and in general it can be said that the classical finish was as absent from the surfaces of his sculptures as the coat of varnish from the Impressionist painters' canvases.[61] Rosso championed a holistic creation process – a cause that remained an innovative exception in sculpture. Edgar Degas, an artist extremely well versed in numerous techniques, was very close to Rosso in this respect.[62] The latter mastered and practised a range of media, which enabled him to cross the boundaries between them with ease. What is more, his technical expertise made it possible for him to vary his subjects with every new cast: with regard to the casting material, the colouration (which could be changed by using different pigments), the chromatic effects of the surface and the visibility/invisibility of the seams.[63] With this interest in variation, Rosso departed – much like the painter Claude Monet – from the conception of the *one* conclusive work. This approach would prove to take on key significance in the twentieth century.

Rosso revolutionised sculpture on various levels, in several cases taking his cue from concepts of the Impressionist painters. Like them, he became receptive to subject matter from his private surroundings and vibrant modern-day life. And in his handling of these subjects, he took a radical step – particularly in his large-scale sculptural groups *Impressione d'omnibus* (1883/84; cat. 57) and *Paris la nuit* (1896/97; cat. 64) – in that, with his life-size figures, he created a modern counterbalance to the historical monument without resorting to any pathos, or even narrative elements, whatsoever.[64] Yet it was not only with his subjects that he entered uncharted territory. He also strongly sharpened the focus on the object's appearance. Like the Impressionist painters, for example, he introduced the element of time to the motif by representing it with "precise imprecision"[65] – that is, as it would be perceived with a sweeping gaze. He was equally concerned with the beholder's perception. He dealt with the latter just as "despotically" (in the meaning of Charles Baudelaire[66]) as a painter by presenting his sculptures as works graspable from only *one* vantage point and a predetermined height, on unconventional bases and, in part, disconcertingly truncated. What is more, he frequently put his small-scale figures in so-called "gabbies" (cages), yet another means of narrowing the scope of the viewer's visual relationship to the work (fig. 9).[67] By controlling the incidence of the light, he made the surface modulation and the material the key vehicles of his aesthetic, in which context they did not necessarily bear a meaningful connection to the subject.

Rosso suspended the previously clear boundaries between the media of sculpture and painting whilst also incorporating drawing and photography, including photographs of photographs.[68] The fluidity of the boundaries corresponded to that of the working steps. Everything remained under his control – was his "own stuff". This approach ultimately led to a liberation from the compulsion to carry a work to the utmost completion. As in painting, variation offered a truly viable alternative. A comprehensive view of Rosso's actions and artistic production reveals that his chief interest was in the transitions and margins. This applied not only to his figures and their relationship to space, but also to various media and techniques. The artist who had supposedly been born on a train attached paramount importance to continuous, unobstructed progression.

No other sculptor came as close to the (constantly changing) conception of Impressionism in sculpture as Rosso. Using biological terms that are rather disconcerting for the present-day reader, Curt Seidel observed in 1913: "The virility of the purely Impressionist instinct is not as pronounced in any other contemporary as in Rosso."[69] Yet this should not mislead us to reduce his oeuvre to the Impressionist aspect. International research on his work proves how fundamentally important it was for modern sculpture.[70]

1   "Non amava dire in che città era nato; non gli piacevano tali precisazioni, sempre per il suo concetto nemico delle classificazioni; a chi insisteva in proposito, preferira rispondere che era nato in treno, dato che suo padre era funzionario delle ferrovie." Letter from Mario Vianello-Chiodo to Margaret Scolari Barr, 27 November 1959, Archives of Marco Vianello-Chiodo, London, quoted in: Hecker 2018, p. 111.

2   On the discussion of the photographs' authorship, see Stix-Marget 1998; Becker 1999; Bertelli 2004; Gülicher 2011, p. 190; Taylor 2019, p. 60.

3   Borghi 1950; exh. cat. Milan 1979; De Sanna 1985; Fagioli/Minnuno 1993; Mola/Vittucci 2009. On the problematic issue of the catalogues raisonnés, see Brunk 2012, pp. 93 ff. Thanks to Birgit Brunk for generously and collegially granting me access to her hitherto unpublished dissertation.

4   Brunk 2012, pp. 103 ff.

5   Ibid., p. 91. Brunk devoted her dissertation specifically to this aspect; also see Moure 1996, pp. 36 ff.

6   Chevillot 2010, p. 54; Elliott 2014, p. 209; Taylor 2019, p. 60.

7   "Il fonde magistralement la sculpture impressionniste." Thiaudière 1886.

8   "Un véritable impressionniste de la sculpture"; Eremite 1893, p. 373.

9   Claris 1902 (French), p 19; Claris 1902a (German), p. 11; also see note 28 below.

10   Meier-Graefe 1904, vol. 1, pp. 291 ff. An English translation was published in 1908.

11   On the Impressionist exhibitions, see the contribution by Fabienne Ruppen in this catalogue, pp. 24–34.

12   Thiaudière 1886 refers to Rosso as "vraiment originale" in terms of execution and conception.

13   This bronze may have survived in a private collection in Paris; see exh. cat. Rovereto/Turin 2004, p. 88.

14 Gülicher 2011, p. 110; also see the contribution by Nina Schallenberg in this catalogue, pp. 276–282.

15 For a fundamental discussion of the state of research on the partially contradictory biography, see: Hecker 2017.

16 No legal action was taken against Rosso for his involvement until he used violent means to force fellow students to sign an accompanying petition; see Hecker 2017, p. 42.

17 On the Scapigliati, see Caramel 1984, p. 11; Licht 2003, p. 13; Lista 2003; Quinsac 2009.

18 In scholarship on the subject, it is generally assumed that the two developments took place more or less independently of one another. Only a few figures such as the Florentine art critic Diego Martelli, the Milanese journalist Felice Cameroni and the painter and critic Vittore Grubicy made an effort to enlighten the Italian public about the current tendencies in Paris; otherwise interest in Impressionism long remained negligible in Italy; see Stix-Marget 1998, p. 32; Hecker 2017, p. 20.

19 Exh. cat. Milan 2017, p. 198.

20 Hecker 2017, p. 110.

21 Ibid., p. 114.

22 Brunk 2003, p. 22.

23 Hecker 2015; Hecker 2018, p. 110.

24 Hecker 2017, pp. 124 ff.

25 Claris 1902 (French), p. 62; Claris 1902a (German), p. 31.

26 On what is presumed to be the two artists' first encounter, see Lista 1994, p. 77; on the disagreement between them, see Lista 1994, pp. 84 ff. The articles by Morice 1895 and Mauclair 1895 played a decisive role. Pingeot 2000, however, puts the conflict into perspective based on further detailed reading of the sources.

27 Hecker 2018, p. 112.

28 As is so often the case with Rosso's participation in exhibitions, it is unfortunately not possible to reconstruct exactly which works represented Rosso in the Italian pavilion of the world's fair. The presentation was changed partway through the fair, and five of his works were integrated into the retrospective on Giovanni Segantini; see Hecker 2017, pp. 181 ff. On Rosso's participation as a sculptor and caster, see Mola 2009, p. 12.

29 Claris 1902 (French). Fles (Claris 1902a [German]) translated Edmond Claris's essay.

30 Claris 1902a (German), p. 39; paraphrase of Claris 1902 (French), p. 61.

31 Brunk 2003, p. 29.

32 On the discussion of the last work, see Brunk 2012, p. 34. Whether or not *Madame X* was executed even later, around 1910–1913, has yet to be clarified.

33 At the behest of the French prime minister Georges Clemenceau, the French state purchased *Femme à la voilette* in wax and *Ecce Puer* in plaster; see Zimmermann 1998, p. 517; Brunk 2003, p. 32.

34 Zimmermann 1998.

35 Brunk 2003, p. 26.

36 "The work of Medardo Rosso [...] is revolutionary, modern [...]. In sculpture as in painting, renewal is impossible without looking for the STYLE OF MOVEMENT, that is, making a systematic and definitive synthesis of the fragmentary, accidental and hence analytical approach of the Impressionists." Umberto Boccioni: "Technical Manifesto of Futurist Sculpture", 11 April 1912, quoted in: Caws 2001, p. 175. On Rosso and the Futurists, Schwarz 2003a; exh. cat. Rovereto/Turin 2004.

37 Schenkenberg 2018, p. 37. Rosso communicated in a combination of Italian, French and dialect forms with arbitrary observance of the rules of grammar and syntax: on this topic, also see Moure 1996, p. 36.

38 "Just then, I saw a couple passing by. [...] At that moment, the colour tone of the shadow was more eloquent than the people. [...] if I attempt to capture that shadow on the ground, it will be impossible; yet it is a tone that exists like any other, guided by my emotion, which is what gives me all these colours; and I cannot hold them in my hand either, therefore I touch it and yet I do not touch it." Ambrosini 1923; English translation quoted in: Taylor, 2015, p. 74. The English passage can also be found in Hecker 2017, p. 42. However, the passage of these recollections in which he states that he did not need Albert Einstein's findings on space and time for his observations is less often quoted in the secondary literature – even though it provides evidence that Rosso cannot have committed his memories to writing until a long time after the actual experience.

39 Boehm [1977] 2017, p. 141.

40 Gülicher 2011, p. 41.

41 Ullrich 2002, p. 32.

42 Lista 1994, p. 7.

43 Claris 1902 (French), p. 55; not in Claris 1902a (German).

44 Schallenberg 2017, pp. 34 ff., with illustration of the catalogue cover.

45 For a fundamental discussion of Rosso's conception of space, see De Sanna 1985.

46 Stix-Marget 1998, p. 54.

47 Sainte-Croix 1896, p. 379; quoted in: Becker 1998, p. 1, with a fundamental analysis of Rosso's relationship to painting.

48 Claris 1902 (French), p. 55; not in Claris 1902a (German).

49 Claris 1902 (French), p. 58; Claris 1902a (German), p. 27.

50 Rosso 1907; reprint of the English text in exh. cat. Frankfurt 1984, pp. 56–58.

51 Schnell 1987, p. 291.

52 In 1778, Johann Gottfried Herder came to the conclusion that haptic perception was the most reliable of all the senses; for more information, see Rübel 2012, pp. 10 ff.

53 Meier-Graefe 1904, vol. 1, p. 293. In the second edition, Meier-Graefe expressed himself in more dramatic terms: "It is sculpture for the ethereal ones who withdraw from the coarse interests of the noisy world to quiet alcoves, for the sensitive ones in whom the sound of the harp reverberates, whom a clear word injures, for the longing ones who thirst for rare flowers; the sculpture for the readers of the Huysmans and Mallarmé." Meier-Graefe 1915, vol. 3, p. 470.

54 Foa 2019, p. 21. In 1879, Edgar Degas had advocated for electric light in the Impressionist exhibition.

55 For more in-depth discussions of this topic, see Pullen 1994; Hecker 2010; also see the introduction by Alexander Eiling and Eva Mongi-Vollmer in this catalogue, pp. 12–21.

56 It was Derek Pullen who finally clarified this matter in 1994; Pullen 1994. Also see Cooper 2003; Hecker 2010; Bushart 2016, p. 211.

57 De Sanna 1985, p. 24; Hecker 2016; also see the contribution by Alexander Eiling in this catalogue, pp. 46–57.

58 Letter from Medardo Rosso to Felice Cameroni, 14 February 1890, quoted in: Bushart 2016, p. 209. English translation quoted in: Hecker 2017. Also see the contribution by Dietmar Rübel in this catalogue, pp. 290–295.

59 Mola 2009, p. 12. A detailed account of a Rosso casting event is found in: Ettore Cozzani, in: *Vita d'Arte. Rivista mensile illustrata d'arte antica e moderna*, 3, 5, March 1910, pp. 103–117: "[...] in the dark you see his beautiful, muscular figure lit from below by purple, sulphur-yellow and red flames, stooped and hunched with strain. Acrid smoke fills the room. Not a word is spoken. [...] And then, in the silence and darkness, the trail of liquid fire flows off, and by mysterious ways and means a new, palpable miracle of beauty emerges."

60 "As if he were opening a shrine, the artist removes a piece of sculpture from a receptacle in the corner, slowly raises it up and presents it to the audience. [...] He puts on leather spats and armours himself entirely in leather, sprinkles himself with water and grasps a large pair of iron tongs." Cozzani 1910 (see note 58).

61 On the discussion of varnish in Impressionist painting, see exh. cat. Cologne/Florence 2008, pp. 166 ff.

62 Also see the contributions by Alexander Eiling, pp. 46–57, and Astrid Reuter, pp. 296–302, in this catalogue.

63 Hecker 2017a, pp. 10 ff.

64 Elsen 1974, p. 30.

65 Boehm 2003, p. 111, on Impressionist painting.

66 Baudelaire [1846] 1977; on this aspect, also see the introduction by Alexander Eiling and Eva Mongi-Vollmer in this catalogue, pp. 12–21.

67 Also see the contribution by Nina Schallenberg in this catalogue, pp. 276–282.

68 Taylor 2019.

69 Seidel 1913.

70 Whereas in Italy the interest in Rosso has never ceased, he still rarely receives notice in France. The international study of Rosso began in 1963 with Margaret Scolari Barr at the Museum of Modern Art (exh. cat. New York 1963). In the US and England, research on Rosso has been pursued actively and continually to the very present; see exh. cat. London 2017 and exh. cat. St. Louis 2018. In the German-speaking world, the exhibitions at the Frankfurter Kunstverein in 1984 (exh. cat. Frankfurt 1984) and at Kunstmuseum Winterthur and Stiftung Wilhelm Lehmbruck Museum, Duisburg, in 2003/04 (exh. cat. Winterthur/ Duisburg 2003) have been of major importance. Unfortunately, no catalogue of the compelling 2017 exhibition of Rosso's work in Ghent, curated by Gloria Moure, has been published. For discussions of how Rosso is classified in important surveys of twentieth-century sculpture, see Calvo Serraller 1996, pp. 59 ff.; Lista 1994, pp. 8 ff.

In the laboratory – *La Portinaia*

In 1883, Medardo Rosso created an artistic memorial in honour of the concierge of his residential building in Milan. In doing so, he devoted as little attention to her individual features as he did to the iconographic attributes of a *portinaia* – for instance, the typical concierge cap. Instead, in his rendering of this figure he concentrated on her occupational singularity: he observed her in passing at the threshold between outside and inside. It was imperative to capture this wraithlike impression of her head in profile and sunken between her shoulders. After 1900, Rosso extended the title *La Concierge* or *La Portinaia*[1] to become *Impression d'une concierge*, which since 1904 can also be read on the pedestal of the bronze that is now in Budapest (cat. 53).[2] The concierge was a popular literary figure, among other things since the publication of Émile Zola's novel *Pot-Bouille* in 1882 – translated into Italian by Rosso's friend Felice Cameroni. However, in the visual arts Honoré Daumier had dealt with it as early as from 1847 in the lithographic series *Locataires et propriétaires*. In Italy, on the other hand, Rosso was the first one to portray the figure.[3] In retrospect, he lent the subject from "modern life" a further psychological dimension. In an interview with Luigi Ambrosini in 1923, he said that whereas he had quickly produced his *Portinaia in situ*, hence capturing a "lively moment", the result was that of prolonged, even burdensome mutual observation. This was why he felt "cured" after its completion. "I had gotten the concierge out of my system."[4] According to Rosso, the inner image, which intensified over a prolonged period of time, merged with the outer one achieved through direct visual perception.

One intuitively believes to recognise the most sensitive and pure, original version of the *Portinaia* in the one in wax – hence, in that soft and malleable material in which many sculptors, such as Edgar Degas, modelled their works. Rosso, however, cast his wax busts after a clay model with the aid of gelatine moulds and employing the lost wax casting method (*cire perdue*).[5] His waxes over a plaster core are therefore also casts like his plasters and bronzes and, accordingly, the result not of the first step in the creative process but of the last one. There were many advantages to the wax cast. It required less effort, was more economical and was possible without the support of third parties. Yet Rosso did not begin with the wax casts until long after his bronze casts. We are familiar with the first version of his *Portinaia* as the bronze from 1883 at the Toyota Municipal Museum of Art; another version in bronze was also on display at the world's fair of 1889.[6] The first wax version originated more than 20 years later, namely in 1905.[7] The wax cast being presented here (cat. 54) was shown in 1910 at the major exhibition *Prima esposizione italiana dell'Impressionismo francese e delle sculture di Medardo Rosso* in Florence and was subsequently acquired by the exhibition organiser Giuseppe Prezzolini.[8]

Independent of their chosen material, the casts are characterised by polymorphous surfaces; craters, air bubbles and impurities were retained. Rosso also dispensed with the subsequent removal of ridges as they develop when joining two abutting moulds. This causes the surfaces to seem like hardened liquids in which the flowing and bubbling of the cast is inscribed. Rosso dyed the wax, which varied in terms of its consistency, with various pigments, such as with vermillion or verdigris.[9] The reason for the appeal of the waxes is also undoubtedly that fact that they allow light to penetrate the surface of the work and as a result underscore Rosso's notion of the parity of space and matter. The soft, partially translucent surface was highly interesting for those critics and theorists that propagated Symbolism in the 1890s. Charles Morice, for example, praised Rosso's use of wax for this very reason. In an issue of *Le Soir* from September 1895, Morice wrote that "Wax [is] his preferred material and the only one, undoubtedly, that lends itself to the needs of this conception of art."[10]

Over the course of his life, Rosso developed around 20 versions of the *Portinaia*, none of which resembles any of the others.[11] He varied the material, the colouring, the section and the pedestals.[12] By doing so, he opened up independent alternatives of action that cannot be understood as stages on the path towards a goal.[13] Yet neither are the different versions meant to be a self-contained series; they are not numbered, let alone signed and dated.[14] Rosso's versions did not originate – as, for example, the series of haystacks and poplar-lined roads that Claude Monet began painting in the 1880s (in the nineteenth century, the term "series" meant more or less what we call a group of works today) – "before the motif" or en bloc.[15] Rather, he created them over a period of up to 20 years after a model developed once. It was not the change of light or atmosphere that animated Rosso; rather, purely aesthetic decisions gave rise to the numerous unique pieces.

A figure related to the *Portinaia* found its way into Rosso's innovative *In tranvai* (1883/84) ensemble of sculptures, known as *Impressione d'omnibus* since the 1890s at the latest. Never rendered in durable material, the five-part group of figures was destroyed in 1887 on route to the *Esposizione artistica nazionale illustrata* in Venice.[16] All that has survived is a photograph of the work taken prior to 1887, or rather a photograph of the original one (cat. 57). Rosso lined up five clay busts alongside each other on a table – the one on the outer right displays features of the *Portinaia*. He connected the individual figures, both physically and visually, from the hips down with a cloth that served to keep the clay moist. The white surface that forms the background for the group cut out of the first photograph corresponds with this planar cloth. Whereas the ensemble was clearly geared towards providing a frontal view, its two-dimensionality was further highlighted in the later processing of the photograph. The overall silhouette and the distribution of the figures seems more important than the space.[17] It is precisely this photograph,[18] which Rosso showed many times in Paris from 1889 onwards, that is the source of the unconfirmed legend that Degas thought it was the photograph of a painting.[19]

However, Rosso did not only present photographs of his works to friends, colleagues and collectors, but in exhibitions as well – for example, in 1889 at the world's fair.[20] Yet it was not until 1920, during preparations for the *Mostra d'Arte Sacra* in Venice, that Rosso asked the exhibition organiser to place his *Portinaia* (called *Saint Ursula* in the context of the presentation) near photographs of the same.[21] The *Portinaia* motif appears 20 times in the body of photographs, totalling approximately 500, of Rosso's sculptures. The questions concerning the authorship of the photographs, the prints, the photographs of photographs or reproductions as well as the cropped images and montages has not been completely clarified, but it is generally agreed that Rosso had a large share in their origin.[22] Unlike photographs of works by Auguste Rodin, those of Rosso's sculptures are of each of them in their completed state.[23] The picture did not serve to document the working process or accompany it experimentally, but rather to examine or channel the perception of the final figures. Rosso repeatedly varied the viewer perspective by sometimes capturing the figure more from the side, and other times more strongly from the top and thus from a foreshortening perspective (cat. 55, 56). He also changed the incidence of light, whereby, unlike many of his colleagues, he preferred electric light.[24] Rosso often subsequently cut the coarse-grain photographic paper or a finished reproduction into irregular shapes, which in several cases he mounted on card or paper, again taking a picture of it.[25] The outlines of the paper gave rise to a new silhouette and the versions of the sculpture found their natural continuation in the photograph.[26] Time and again, the close cropping deleted the surrounding space, causing the three-dimensionality of the figure to recede in favour of planarity. Rosso's photographs of sculpture therefore conceal more than they reveal,[27] and yet they are firmly embedded in his working method with all of their singularities. — EM-V

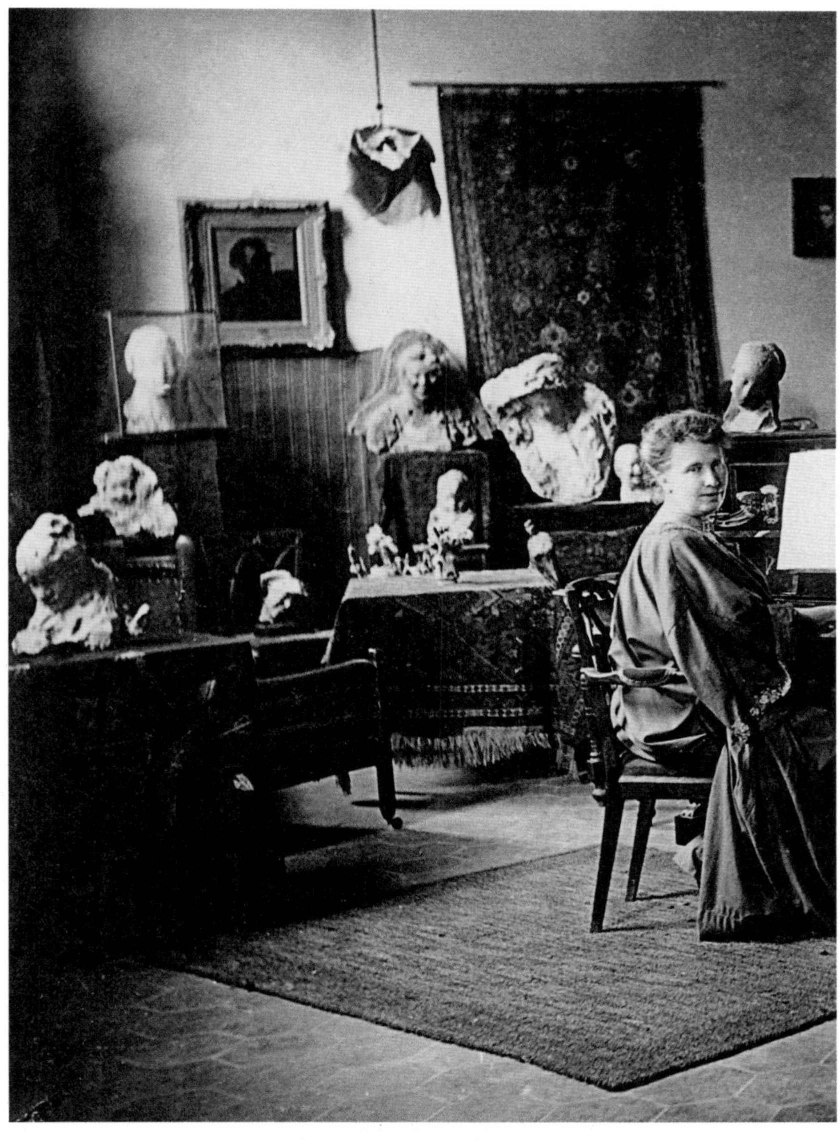

1 Etha Fles in her apartment in Rome, c. 1913, photograph, RKD – Netherlands Institute for Art History, The Hague (detail)

1   Hecker 2017, p. 76, note 73: the title *La Portinaia* has been commonly used since 1887, and since 1892 *La Concierge*.

2   The plaque was affixed on the occasion of the Parisian Salon d'automne in 1904; see also exh. cat. Milan 2015, p. 47.

3   Hecker 2017, p. 76; Hecker 2018a, p. 97.

4   Ambrosini 1923. Complete quote in: Witkovsky in Hecker 2018a, p. 58.

5   Detailed descriptions of the individual working steps in Pullen 1994; Hecker 2010.

6   Hecker 2015, p. 144.

7   Galleria Nazionale d'Arte Moderna, Rome; see exh. cat. Milan 2015, p. 47.

8   Mola/Vittucci 2009, p. 250, no. 11e; see also Droth 2017.

9   Pullen 1994, p. 62; Hecker 2017a, pp. 9 ff.

10 Charles Morice, quoted in: Hecker 2017, p. 149; see also the introduction by Alexander Eiling and Eva Mongi-Vollmer in this catalogue, pp. 12–21.

11 Brockhaus 2003, p. 54.

12 Birgit Brunk deals with the subject of the variations in her dissertation; Brunk 2012, esp. pp. 177 ff.; see also Hecker 2016.

13 Boehm [1988] 2017, p. 138.

14 Rosso only signed and dated his works on rare occasions; see Hecker 2010, p. 728; Hecker 2017a, p. 12.

15 On terminology in general, see Heinrich 2017, esp. p. 75.

16 Hecker 2017, pp. 80 ff.

17 De Sanna 1985, p. 17.

18 Mola/Vittucci 2009, p. 92.

19 Claris 1902 (French), p. 21; Claris 1902a (German), p. 13; Hecker 2017, p. 85.

20 Rosso always carried photographs of his works with him; Stix-Marget 1998, p. 37.

21 The prints, on the other hand, were available for purchase; see Gülicher 2011, p. 190.

22 Becker 1999, p. 159; Brockhaus 2003, p. 55; Gülicher 2011, p. 190. Time and again, the artist undeniably appears as a protagonist in his photographs (cat. 57).

23 See also the essay by Juliane Betz in this catalogue, pp. 284–289.

24 Witkovsky 2018, p. 63.

25 Ibid., p. 61.

26 Taylor 2019, pp. 57 ff.

27 Rübel 2014, p. 114.

Cat.53 Medardo Rosso, Impression d'une concierge (La Portinaia), 1883/84, cast in 1887; bronze, 45 × 37 × 21 cm; Museum of Fine Arts, Budapest, inv. no. 52.139.U
Cat.54 Medardo Rosso, La Portinaia, 1883/8; cast in 1910, wax over plaster, 38.5 × 31 × 17.5 cm; Collection PCC, Switzerland

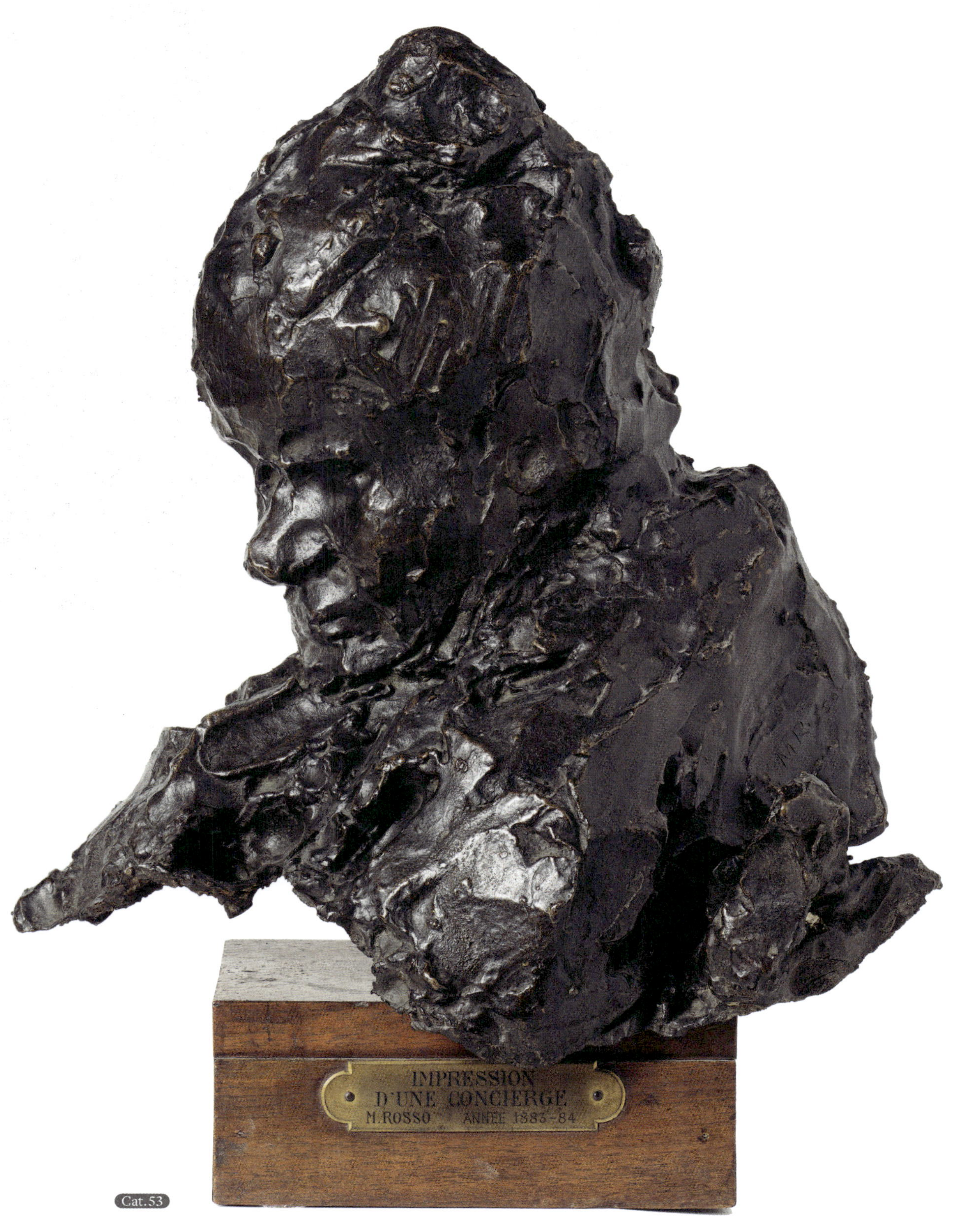

IMPRESSION
D'UNE CONCIERGE
M.ROSSO   ANNÉE 1883–84

Cat.53

Cat. 54

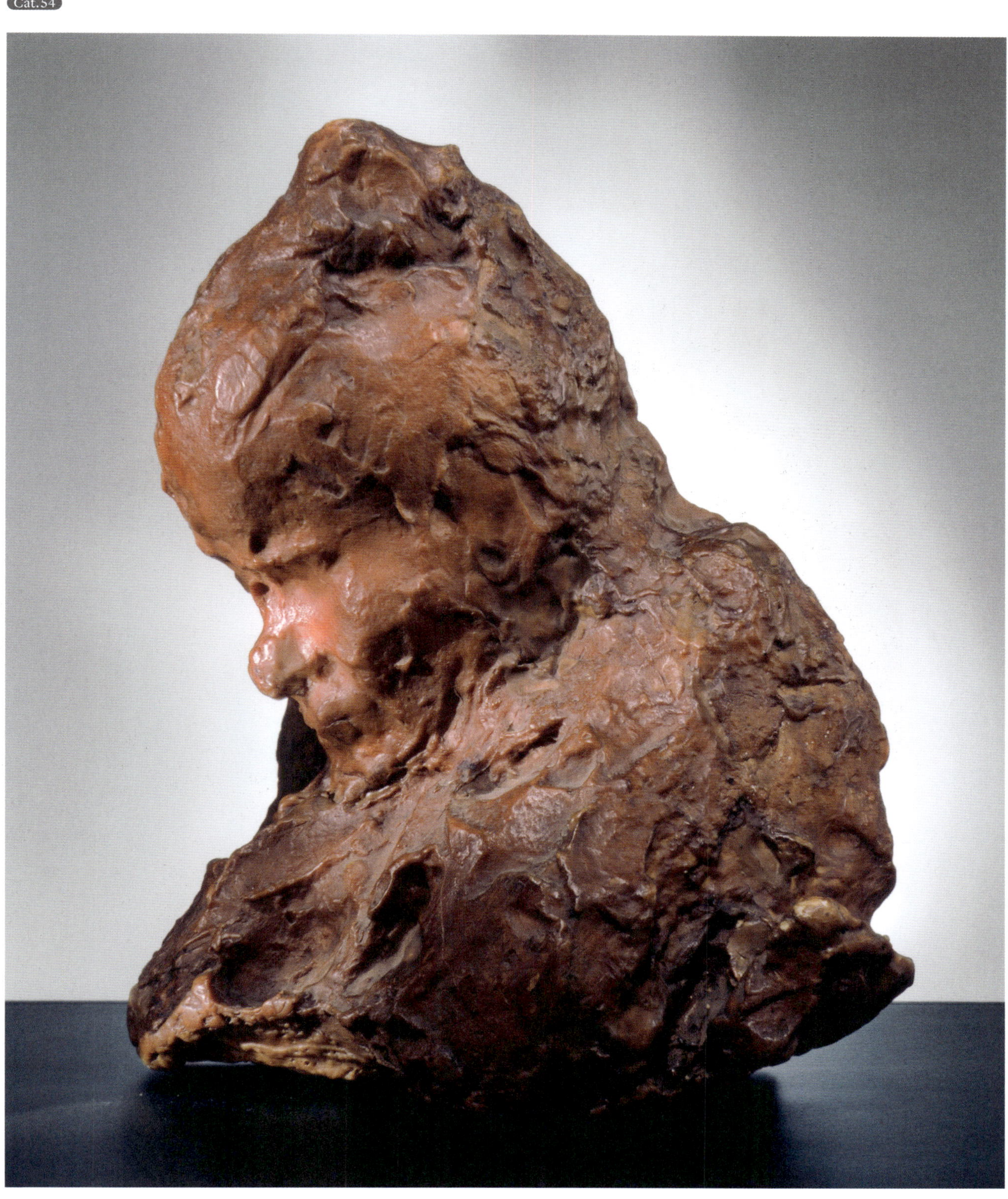

Cat.55 Medardo Rosso, Photograph of a photograph of *La Portinaia*, 1910–1914; platinum print, 14 × 7 cm; private collection **Cat.56** Medardo Rosso, Photograph of a photographic reproduction of *La Portinaia*, 1920–1925; aristotype, cropped, 14.3 × 8.5 cm; signed in his own hand: "a concierge 1882"; underneath: "1883"; private collection **Cat.57** Medardo Rosso, Photograph taken of a damaged photograph of *Impressione d'omnibus* (1883/84), before 1889; albumen paper, cropped asymmetrically, heightened with white at the centre, mounted on card, red edging, 13.9 × 21.6 cm (photograph), 18.8 × 24.8 cm (card); signed in different handwriting, top centre: "L'inquadrato tutto"; bottom: "il doppio dell'altezza"; private collection

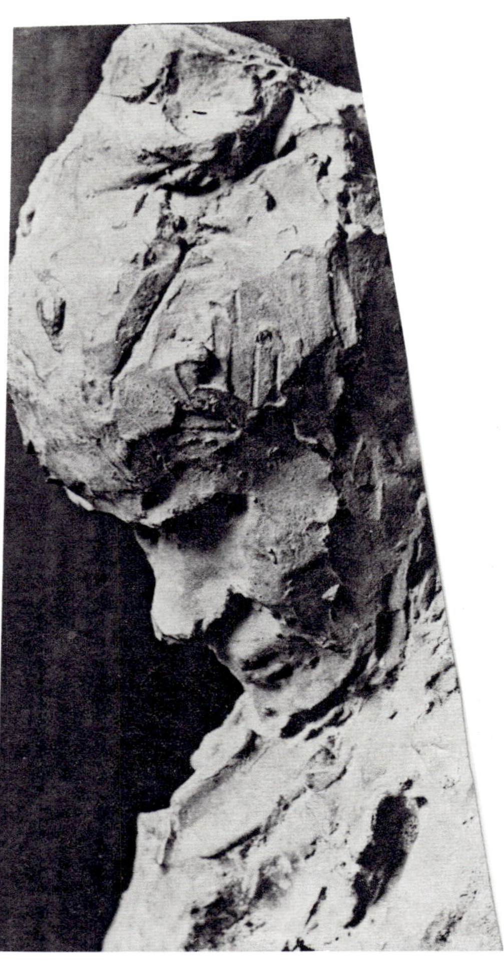

Cat.55

Cat.56

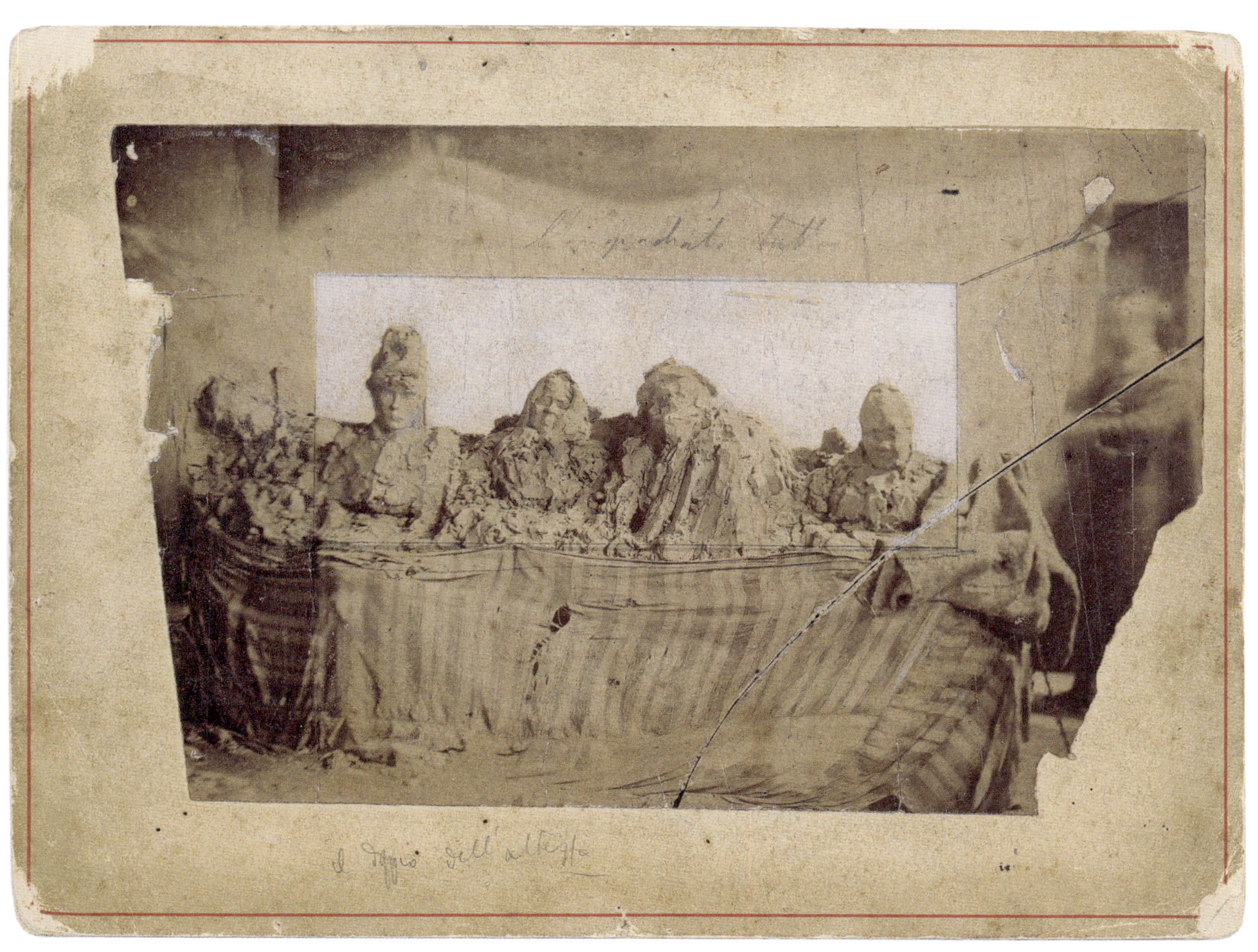

Cat. 57

Medardo Rosso's son Francesco was born in Milan in November 1885. Rosso devoted his intimate work *Aetas Aurea* (cat. 58) to him and his wife, Giuditta Pozzi.[1] The mother closely embraces the child's small body, pressing her mouth to his cheek. On the occasion of the exhibition of the work in the *Esposizione artistica nazionale illustrata* in Venice, on 14 August 1887 Rosso stated: "I try to excite human passions through the impression."[2]

The motif of a mother with her infant enjoyed enormous popularity at the close of the nineteenth century.[3] With *Amor materno*, Rosso had himself developed a more naturalistic version as early as 1883 (p. 126, fig 2). The contrast to *Aetas Aurea* could hardly be greater. In the latter bronze, mother and child seem to dissolve to the limits of readability in the diffuse, planar surroundings. Because the flat sculpture is plainly designed to be viewed exclusively from the front, it bears the features of a relief.[4] However, a clearly recognisable, level relief background, to which the portrayal would make reference in terms of perspective, is missing.[5] In Rosso's oeuvre, area in itself was not a criterion of any essential importance, as for him space was the superior reference. In his words, the sculptural figure contributed its spatial effect per se to the artwork, even to the advantage of the sculptor over the painter: "Painters have to first simulate perspective, whereas it is by nature innate in the plastic material, namely as a succession of foreground, middle ground and background inherently localised in it."[6]

If one takes a closer look at the bronze *Aetas Aurea*, cast around 1905,[7] what stands out is its pronounced choppiness, not only in terms of the lines but the partially porous surface as well. The highly nuanced patination ranging from gold to green as well as the light chamotte particles left behind by the casting process produce the differentiated colour effect. The surface of the sculpture became increasingly important in the second half of the nineteenth century, not only for Rosso but in general.[8] Rosso's (mostly) single-handed casting and patinating gained him utmost respect. In 1905, Ludwig Hevesi lauded him when he wrote: "What a craftsman he is, what a caster. He casts everything himself, of course. And what a master of patination. Each casting of his models is unique, for its painterly-sculptural features are singular."[9] Indeed, Rosso attached a great deal of value to the chromaticity of the sculpture – however, not in the sense of the polychromatic experiments and coloured versions by his contemporaries. For his summarily employed colour did not follow the logic of the object, but solely the aesthetic logic of the surface. And as was already the case with reference to the rendering of spatiality, in sculpture Rosso recognised a slight advantage over painting for this very same reason. The "science of the tonal values" made up for the "lack" of colours.[10] One could get the impression that Rosso saw painting as essentially competing with sculpture.[11] However, drawing this conclusion would mean missing an even more important aspect of Rosso's basic understanding – namely, that of the unity of the arts. In Paris, Rosso closely communicated with the painter Eugène Carrière (1849–1906), who was known to engage in a lively dialogue with Auguste Rodin

(cat. 93).[12] Carrière presumably even once owned the bronze version of *Aetas Aurea* now at the Musée d'Orsay in Paris.[13] It is uncertain when exactly Rosso got to know the trained lithographer. In any case, in 1890 – soon after Rosso's arrival in Paris – the two were studio neighbours. It was precisely during this period that Carrière's new style of painting began to crystallise; his motifs were deliberately blurred and done in an almost monochromatic, mostly dark palette. As a result, he directed his painterly interest increasingly towards the chromatic nuances of a tonal value between light and dark – therefore, towards its variation under the influence of light. Carrière's painting *Sleep* from 1890 (cat. 59) not only shares the subject of Rosso's *Aetas Aurea*. Like Rosso, Carrière also confronted the viewer with a portrayal that was difficult to decipher. Neither space nor figures can be clearly recognised and diffuse into one another. This similarly holds true for the relation between the in part thinly and drily applied paint and the canvas that frequently shows through.

These artistic approaches bear witness less to competition between the genres and more to exploring the possibilities of which aspects of the respective media can be made productive for others, and which cannot. It was no accident that Rosso repeatedly aspired to present his sculptures in conjunction with paintings – which was also the case in 1906 in the Carrière hall of the Petit Palais.[14] For artists like Rodin, Carrière and Rosso, the highest precept was to more strongly underscore the unity of the arts. Camille de Sainte-Croix passed on Rosso's words as early as in 1896: "Painting? Sculpture? There is only one art."[15] Thus, they stood in the best tradition of the multimedia-based approach that was also represented in the exhibitions of the Impressionists.[16]

It is therefore no wonder that contemporaries also referred to the inspiring comparison. Critical voices, like that of Camille Mauclair, remained the exception: in an issue of *Mercure de France* from 1895, he disparagingly ranked Rosso's works in wax as "bad parodies".[17] In 1896, Edmond de Goncourt described Carrière's paintings positively as "in the fashion of a sculptor".[18] And in 1904, Louis Vauxcelles noted the following about Rosso: "He is the Carrière of sculpture."[19] It was in this spirit that Julius Meier-Graefe also connected the two artists: "[...] he [Rosso] is already quite the painter here [...]; at the time, he could be ranked in close proximity to Carrière [...]."[20] — EM-V

"He is the Carrière
of sculpture."

Louis Vauxcelles, undated

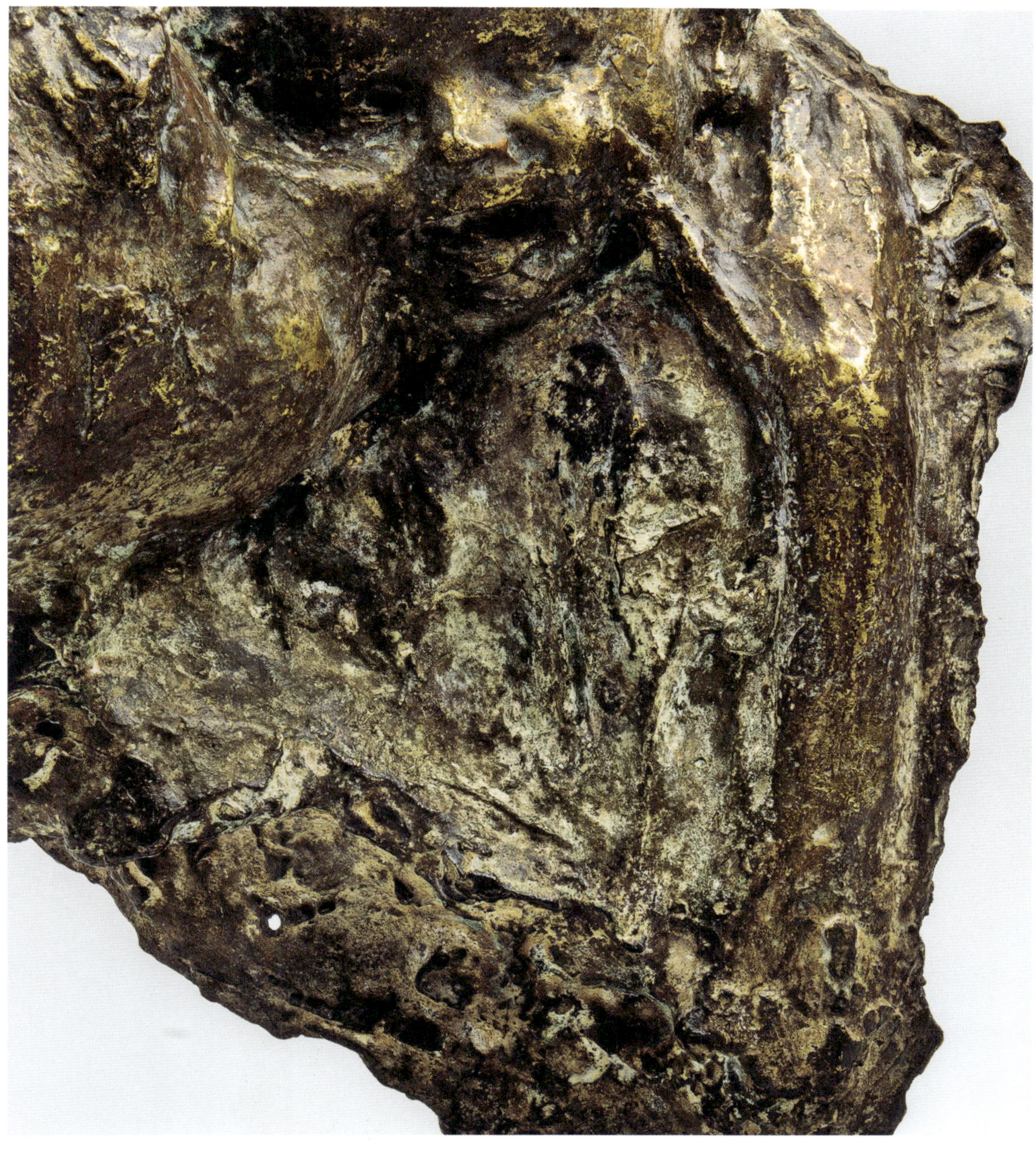

Cat.58 Detail

1 Mola/Vittucci 2009, p. 98.
2 Hecker 2017, p. 94.
3 Becker 1998, p. 2.
4 Braunfels-Esche 1980.
5 Schenkenberg 2018, p. 41, summarises the discussion of this aspect since Krauss 1977 and Cooper 2003.
6 Hevesi 1905, p. 174; quoted in: Stix-Marget 1998, p. 116.
7 Caruso/Schallmeiner 2014, pp. 108 ff.
8 In the nineteenth century, technological developments resulted in an even more multifaceted patination, even turning it into an individual form of artistic expression; see Blühm 2010, p. 48.
9 Hevesi 1905; quoted in: Bushart 2016, p. 217.
10 Claris 1902a (German), p. 27; Claris 1902 (French), p. 58.
11 For more detail, see Becker 1998.
12 Exh. cat. Tokyo/Paris 2006.
13 Mola/Vittucci 2009, p. 256.
14 "[…] his 'âge d'or', which […] at his request was placed not only in the Eugène Carrière hall at the Petit Palais, but expressly between two visionary paintings by the master." Fles 1922, p. 17; see Stix-Marget 1998, p. 54.
15 Sainte-Croix 1896, p. 379; quoted in: Becker 1998, p. 1.
16 See also the essay by Fabienne Ruppen in this catalogue, pp. 24–34.
17 Mauclair 1895; quoted in: exh. cat. Winterthur/Duisburg 2003, p. 24: "Monsieur Rosso astonishes the bourgeoisie by mysteriously selling them waxes that can only withstand a single light, that are bad parodies, falsified and tinted, lithographs by Eugene Carrière, and that have no durable plastic." Mauclair fundamentally opposes Rosso's understanding of sculpture while propagating Rodin's pre-eminence.
18 De Goncourt 1892, p. IX; quoted in: 1998, p. 139.
19 "È il Carrière della scultura." Louis Vauxcelles, quoted in: exh. cat. Milan 2015, p. 51.
20 Meier-Graefe 1904, vol. 1, p. 296; on this, see also Chevillot 2010, p. 57.

Cat.58 Medardo Rosso, **Aetas Aurea** (**The Golden Age**), 1886, cast c. 1905; bronze, 53 × 39 × 25 cm; Städel Museum, Frankfurt am Main, inv. no. St.P 670
Cat.59 Eugène Carrière, **Sleep**, 1890; oil on canvas, 66.2 × 82.3 cm; Städel Museum, Frankfurt am Main, inv. no. 2414

Cat.58

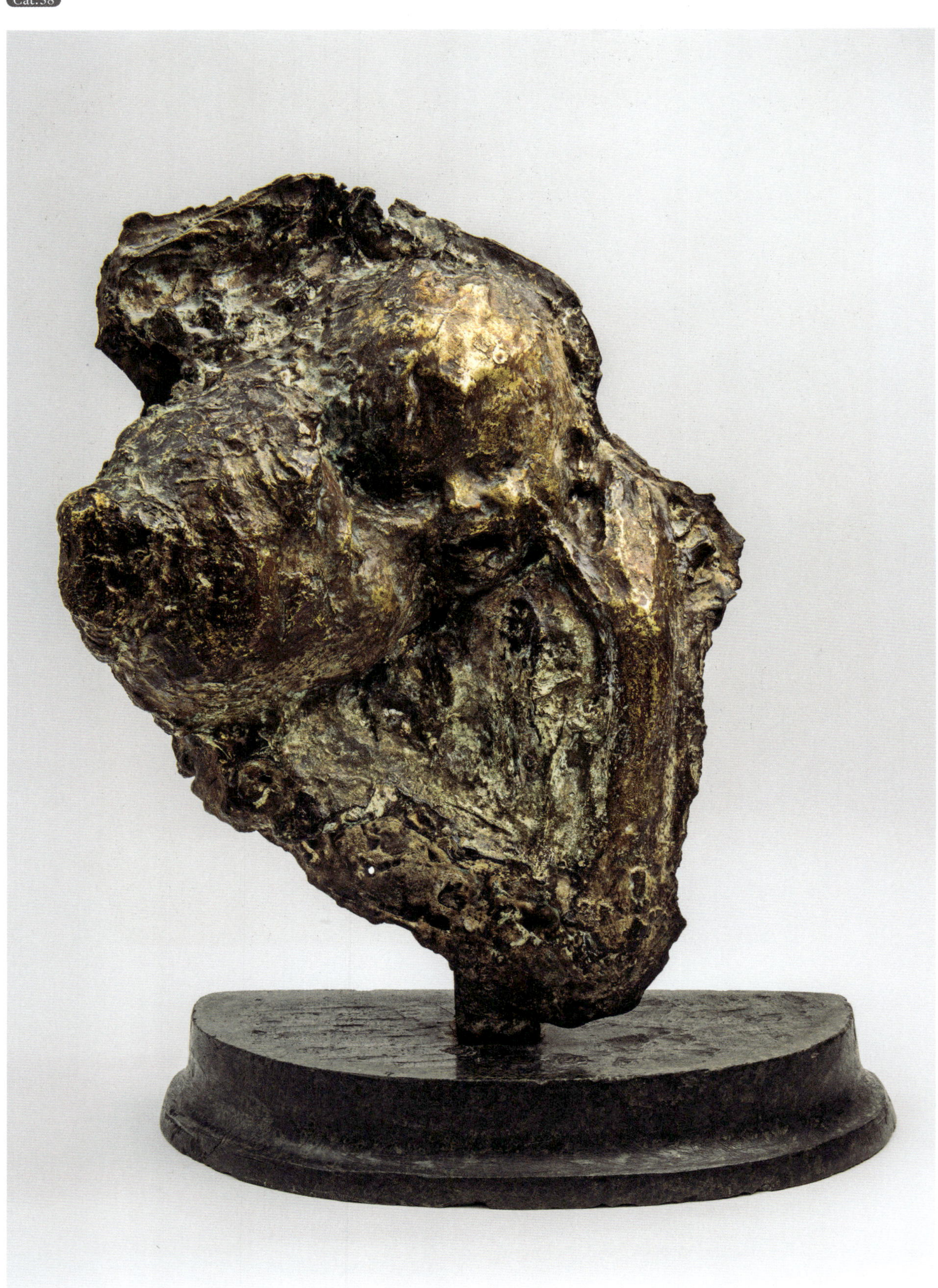

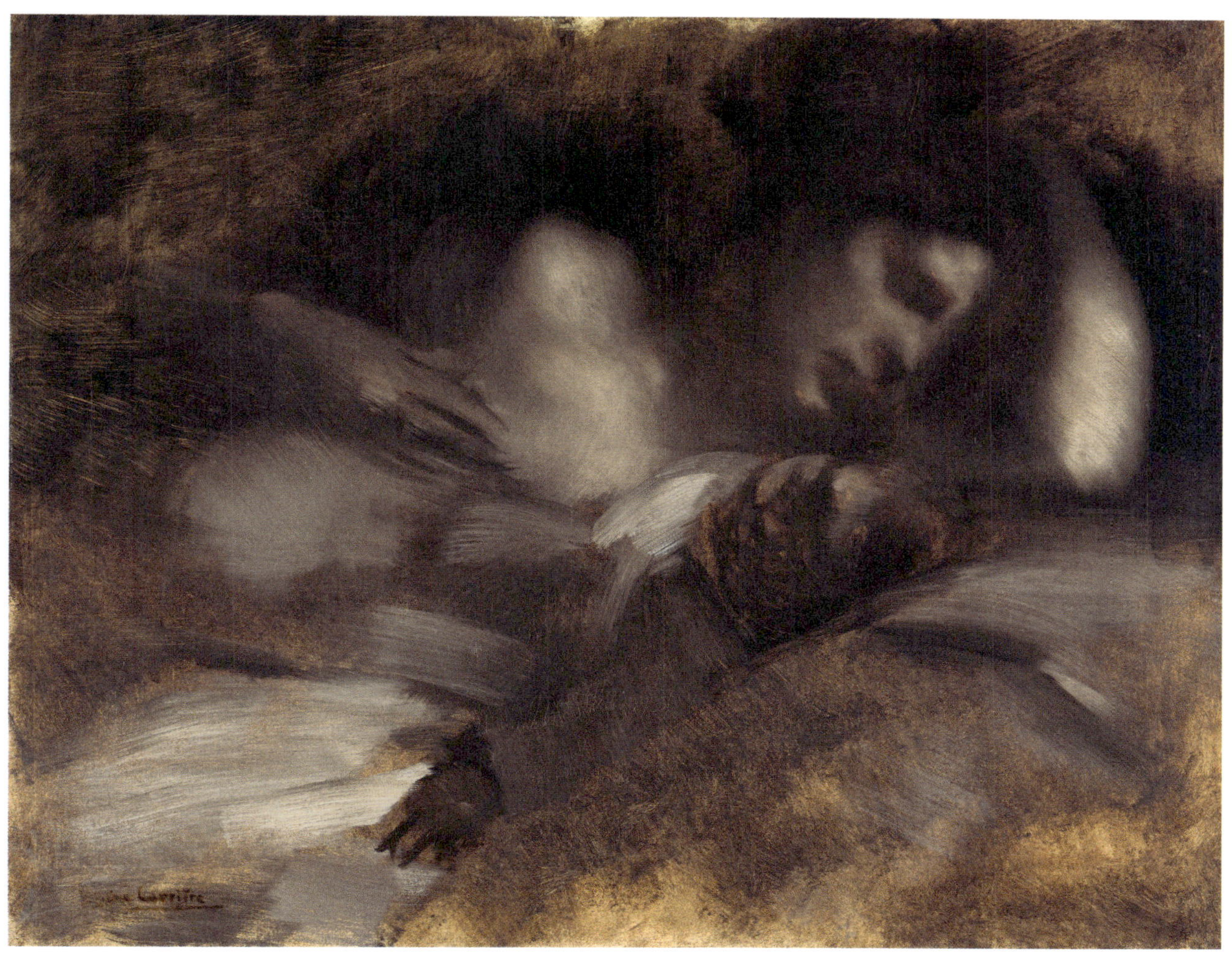

Cat.59

Parisian impressions *en miniature*

Shortly after his arrival in Paris in 1889, Medardo Rosso became so seriously ill that he had to be admitted to Lariboisière hospital for one month. He created several small sculptures soon after his release, hoping to be able to settle his debts through their sale.[1] These included the figure of a sick man wrapped in a coat and wearily bending forward in a high-backed armchair.[2] The surface of the work also appears to be "afflicted" due to the marked working – it is as futile to look for elaborate details as it is for smoothed areas. When Rosso presented his work – presumably a bronze version[3] – in 1893 under the title *Après la visite* in the group exhibition at the Théâtre La Bodinière, the press compared his rough working method to "the ease of a sketch"[4] and hence made reference to a central feature of what was being discussed at the same time with an eye toward Impressionist painting.[5]

Rosso presented the patinated plaster version (cat. 60) shown here for the first time at the 1889 world's fair in Paris. The plaster cast served as a reference for later castings in bronze or wax and exhibits the corresponding wear marks.[6] The first wax version of the *Sick Man in Hospital* is documented by a photograph from Dresden taken before 1902.[7] The wax version in Berlin (cat. 61), on the other hand, stems from the collection of Umberto Giordano, a composer who was friends with Rosso and to whom this cast is dedicated.[8]

In 1894, five years after the *Sick Man in Hospital*, Rosso produced the statuette of a *Man Reading* (cat. 62). Equipped with hat and newspaper, it is probably an anonymous stroller resembling those on the boulevards and in the parks of Paris.[9] Like *Sick Man in Hospital*, *Reading Man* is also to be regarded from the side, whereby one's point of view should ideally be somewhat elevated.[10] This signed wax cast was presented at the XVI Biennale di Venezia shortly after Rosso's death in 1928, in remembrance of the deceased with a bouquet of red roses before the pedestal.[11] Although it was produced in 1894, for unknown reasons the *Man Reading* was not shown in public for the first time until 1910, in Florence.[12] The statuette is particularly striking due to two features. Like the back of the armchair in the *Sick Man in Hospital*, the entire figure extends diagonally into the space. However, unlike the *Sick Man in Hospital*, the body is not embedded in a horizontal plane. For in the case of the *Man Reading*, the space achieves a physical presence by means of the mass rising up from the side of and behind the figure – one looks in vain for a perpendicular orientation system.[13]

With its title, Rosso also left *The Bookmaker* (cat. 63) in anonymity. However, we know from sources that this stately figure shows Eugène Marin, the son-in-law of the collector Henri Rouart, who had sat for Rosso as early as 1890 (cat. 70). *The Bookmaker*, also known as *Homme aux courses* and *Sportsman*, was produced around 1894 in the context of outings to the horse races in Auteuil that Rosso, Rouart, Marin and Edgar Degas undertook together.[14] Rosso exhibited the figure for the first time after the turn of the century, almost simultaneously in wax (in Berlin and Leipzig in 1902) and in bronze (in Vienna in 1903).[15] It is highly probable that the wax figure now in Rovereto is the one that was on display in 1914 at the XI Biennale di Venezia.[16] The light glides undisturbed along the smooth, tense sur-face areas, causing the unusual dark, green pigmentation of the wax to take full effect. The summarily constituted, massive body of the man in coat and top hat almost braces itself against the space even more markedly that the man reading a newspaper. Like the *Man Reading*, *The Bookmaker* is not embedded in a horizontal ground surface but tilts in the bulging setting. In view of these creations, it was not by chance that Jole De Sanna spoke of inverted spatial perspective – the head of the figure tilted forward actually seems proportionally smaller than his body thrusting backward.[17]

The dispute over the competition between Auguste Rodin and Rosso ignited itself on these small sculptures, which prompted Edmond Claris to make an attempt at clarification in 1902.[18] For when Rodin presented his *Balzac* (cat. 85–88) to the public in 1898, Rosso and his advocates believed to recognise fundamental elements from his oeuvre – in particular of these statuettes.[19] It is quite possible that Rodin was familiar with Rosso's sculptures, even though they were not shown in exhibitions until later. The artists' initial estimation of one another is proven not lastly by their exchange of works in 1893: Rodin gave a *Torso* (cat. 106) to Rosso, who in turn received a *Rieuse*.[20] In 1922, Etha Fles still argued in the interests of Rosso when she described his *Sick Man in Hospital* as inspiration for *Balzac*, as in both cases it was only the head that was elaborated whilst the rest of the body was wrapped in a coat.[21]

This particular dispute was a question of the marked tilt of the individual figure and hence its unconventional relation to space.[22] If one takes a closer look at this aspect, then it should first be noted that the tilting of a figure was by all means widespread in artistic practice, as was already the case in Honoré Daumier's *Ratapoil* from 1851 (cat. 122), but also in Edgar Degas's portrayals of *Mary Cassatt at the Louvre* created around 1880 (cat. 123).[23] Yet the difference between the respective relation of figure and space is more important than the diagonal. While in its three-dimensional massiveness and monumental size *Balzac* clearly dominates the surrounding space, Rosso's statuettes – only to be viewed from an ideal standpoint – lose themselves in that very space. The distinctive feature of these figures is precisely that they do not enter into a disruptive relationship with their surrounding space, which is definitely the case for *Balzac*.[24] In this respect, with their works Rodin and Rosso stand for opposing positions, not for adaptations.[25] — EM-V

> "[...] the ease of a sketch."
>
> Alphonse Germain, 1893

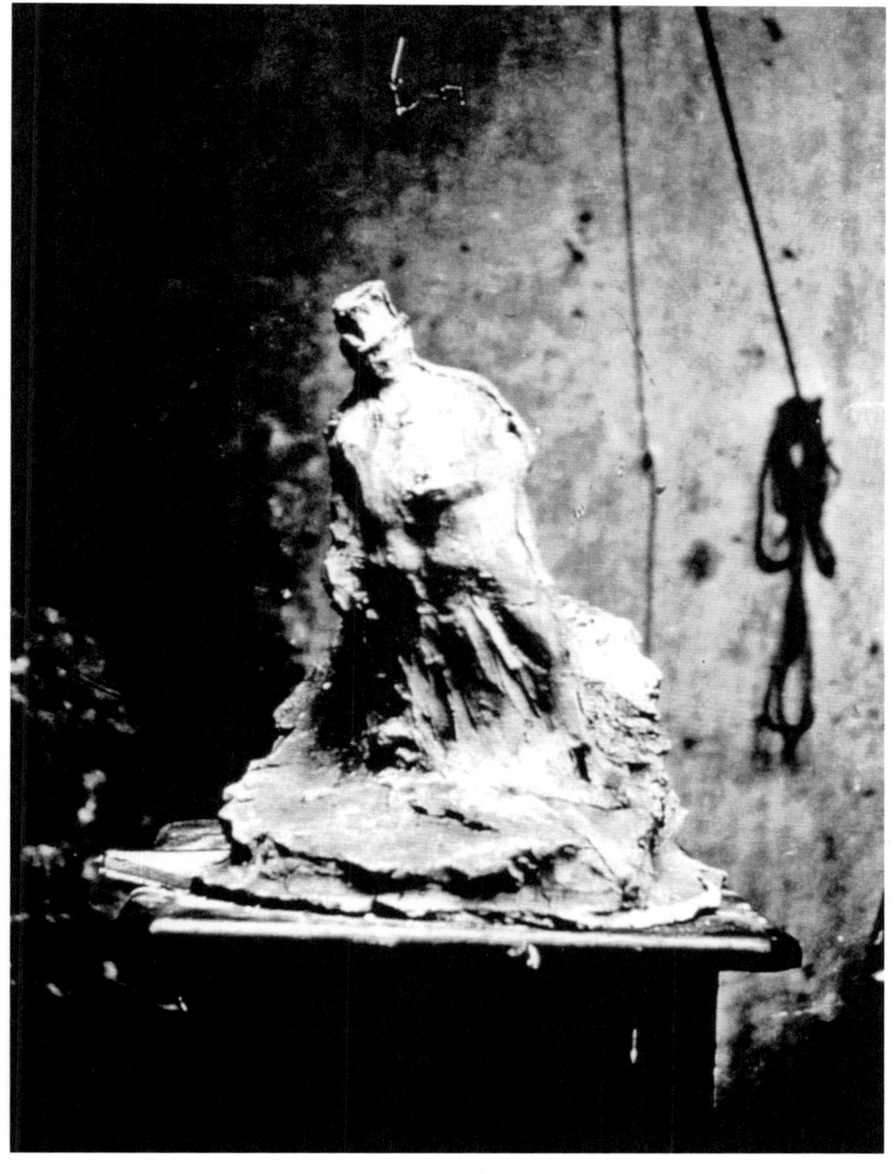

1   Medardo Rosso, *Il Bookmaker* (1894), c. 1910–1920, photograph, 7.7 × 4.7 cm, private collection

1 "Ho finito all'ospedale un' impressione d'un convalescente. È una piccola figura che quando la vedrai ti piacerà. Vedi che anche qui potendo ho cavato profitto. È una cosa nuova. È piaciuta molto, ora l'ho data a formare." Letter from Medardo Rosso to Felice Cameroni, 3 January 1890, Civica Biblioteca d'Arte del Caste lo Sforzesco, Milan; quoted in: exh. cat. Milan 1998, p. 130; also quoted in a slightly different form in Mola/Vittucci 2009, p. 104; on this, see also Hecker 2010, p. 731.

2 This figure may also symbolically represent the modern artist, as Hecker 2017, pp. 125 ff., suspects.

3 The first bronze version is verified for 1890; Mola/Vittucci 2009, p. 104.

4 Eremite 1893, p. 373: "avec une dés involture de croquis"; quoted in: Hecker 2017, p. 127; on this, see also Hecker 2010, p. 731.

5 See the essay by Fabienne Ruppen in this catalogue, pp. 24–34.

6 Mola/Vittucci 2009, p. 265, no. 20a. The plaster bust *Madame Noblet* (1897/98) is one example of the fact that Rosso exhibited such model plaster casts as works in their own right and even sold them, in this particular case to the important collector Louis-Sylvain Noblet (cat. 65); see Hecker 2016, p. 30.

7 Mola/Vittucci 2009, p. 104.

8 Förschl 2006, p. 633.

9 As examples for modern everyday subjects, Duranty [1876] 1946, p. 45, cites crossing the street or checking to see what time it is at a public square.

10 Stix-Marget 1998, p. 60.

11 Mola/Vittucci 2009, p. 306, nos. 29–30.

12 *Prima esposizione italiana dell'Impressionismo francese e delle sculture di Medardo Rosso*, Lyceum Club, Florence; see Brunk 2003, pp. 33 ff. It was the same bronze version that is now at the der Galleria d'Arte Moderna in Florence.

13 Mola 2007, p. 70.

14 Exh. cat. Rovereto/Turin 2004, p. 160; exh. cat. Milan 2015, p. 81.

15 Mola/Vittucci 2009, pp. 308–309.

16 Ibid., p. 310, no. 30e.

17 De Sanna 1985, p. 21.

18 Hecker 2017, pp. 161 ff.

19 According to Sainte-Croix 1898; on this, see Lista 1994, p. 106.

20 Claris 1902 (French), p. 62; Claris 1902a (German), p. 31.

21 Fles 1922, p. 21.

22 Kolberg 1990; Hecker 2017, pp. 161 ff.

23 See the essay by Astrid Reuter in this catalogue, pp. 296–302.

24 Licht 1994, p. 28; on this, see also Boehm [1977] 2017, p. 46, who explores how Rodin caused "space to become something to disappear into" with his *Balzac*.

25 Lista 1994, p. 11.

Cat.60 Medardo Rosso, Malato all'ospedale (Sick Man in Hospital), 1889; plaster, patinated, 23.5 × 30.5 × 28 cm; Museo Medardo Rosso, Barzio Cat.61 Medardo Rosso, Malato all'ospedale (Sick Man in Hospital), 1889, lifetime cast; wax over plaster, 23 × 21.5 × 22.5 cm; signed at the front on the plinth: "M. Rosso / à Giordano"; Staatliche Museen zu Berlin, Nationalgalerie, inv. no. NG 43/72

Cat.60

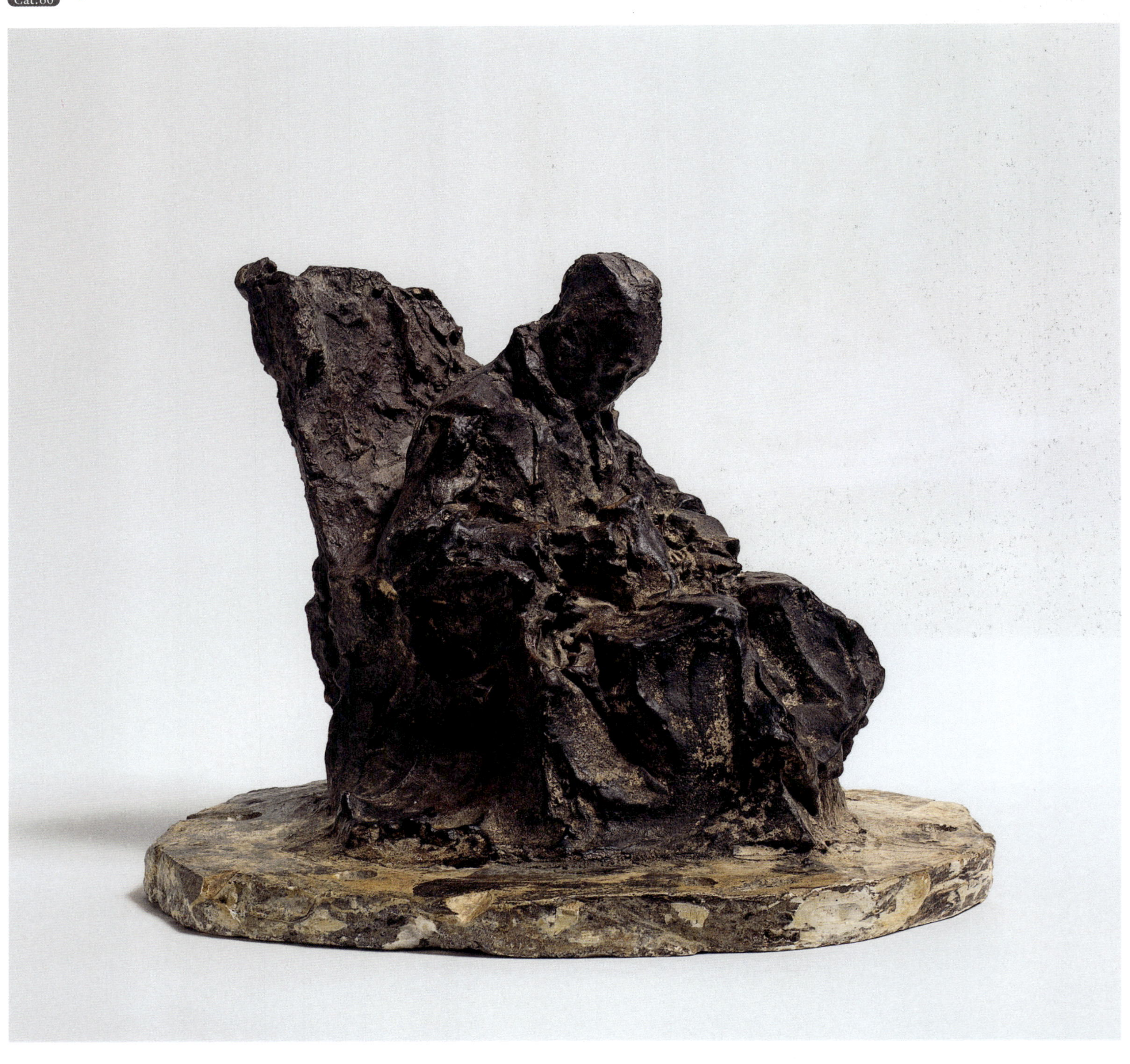

Cat.61

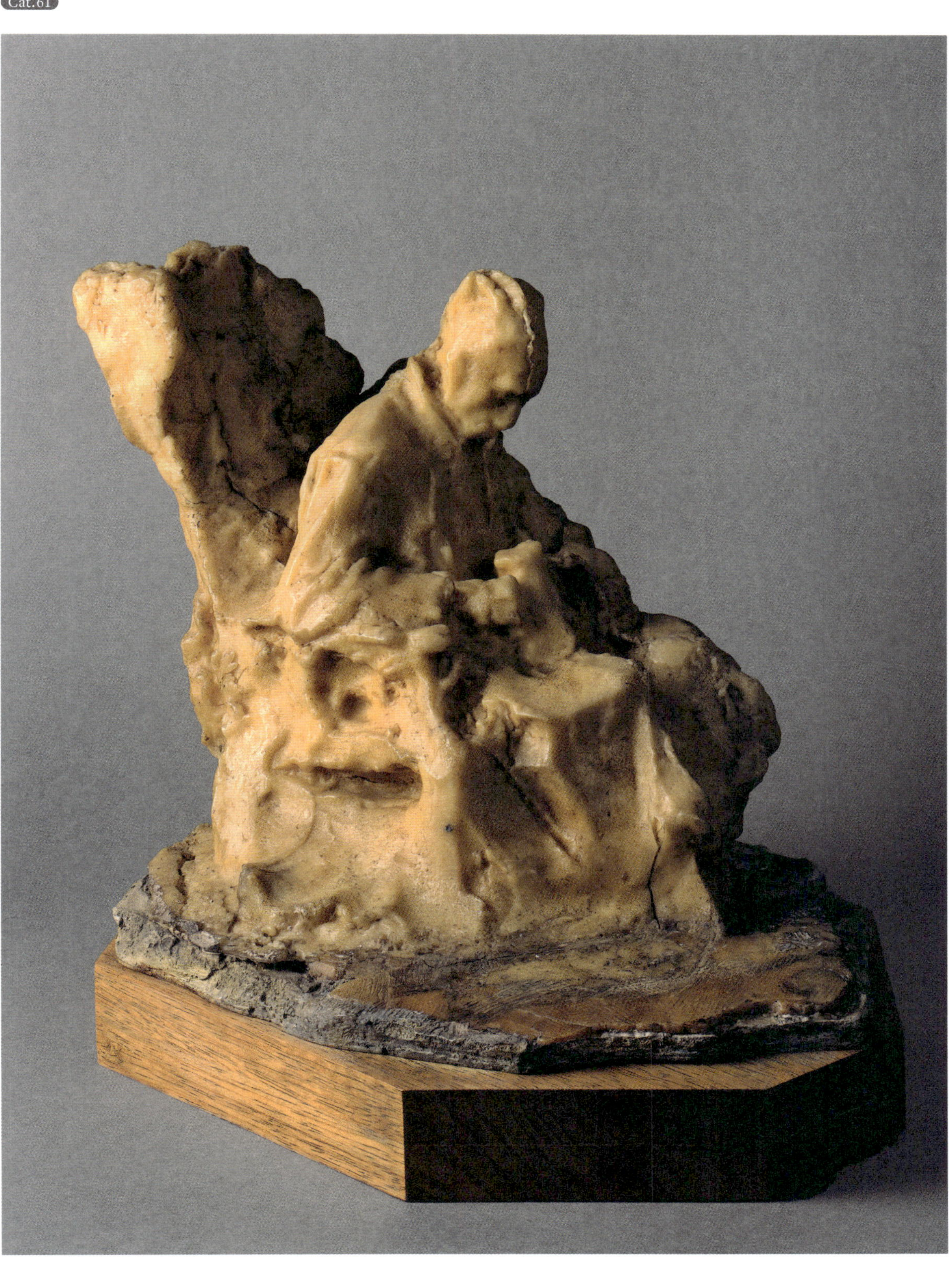

Cat.62 Medardo Rosso, L'uomo che legge (**Man Reading**), c. 1894, cast in 1926; wax over plaster, 29.5 × 30.5 × 29.5 cm; signed: "M. Rosso"; Museo Medardo Rosso, Barzio Cat.63 Medardo Rosso, Il **bookmaker**, 1894, cast before 1914; wax over plaster, 48 × 43 × 46 cm; Mart – Museo di arte moderna e contemporanea di Trento e Rovereto/Collezione VAF-Stiftung, inv. no. VAF 668

Cat.62

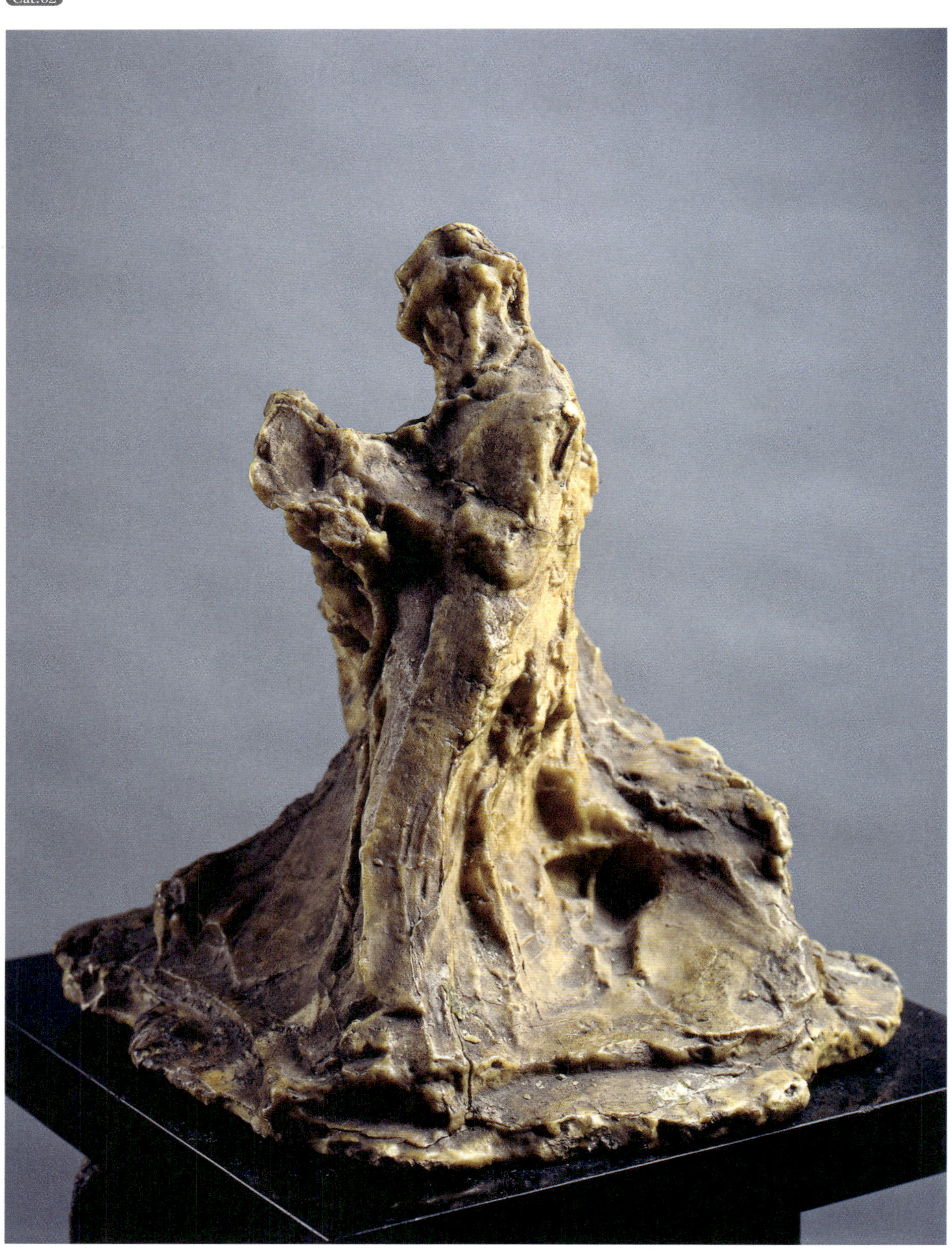

Cat.63

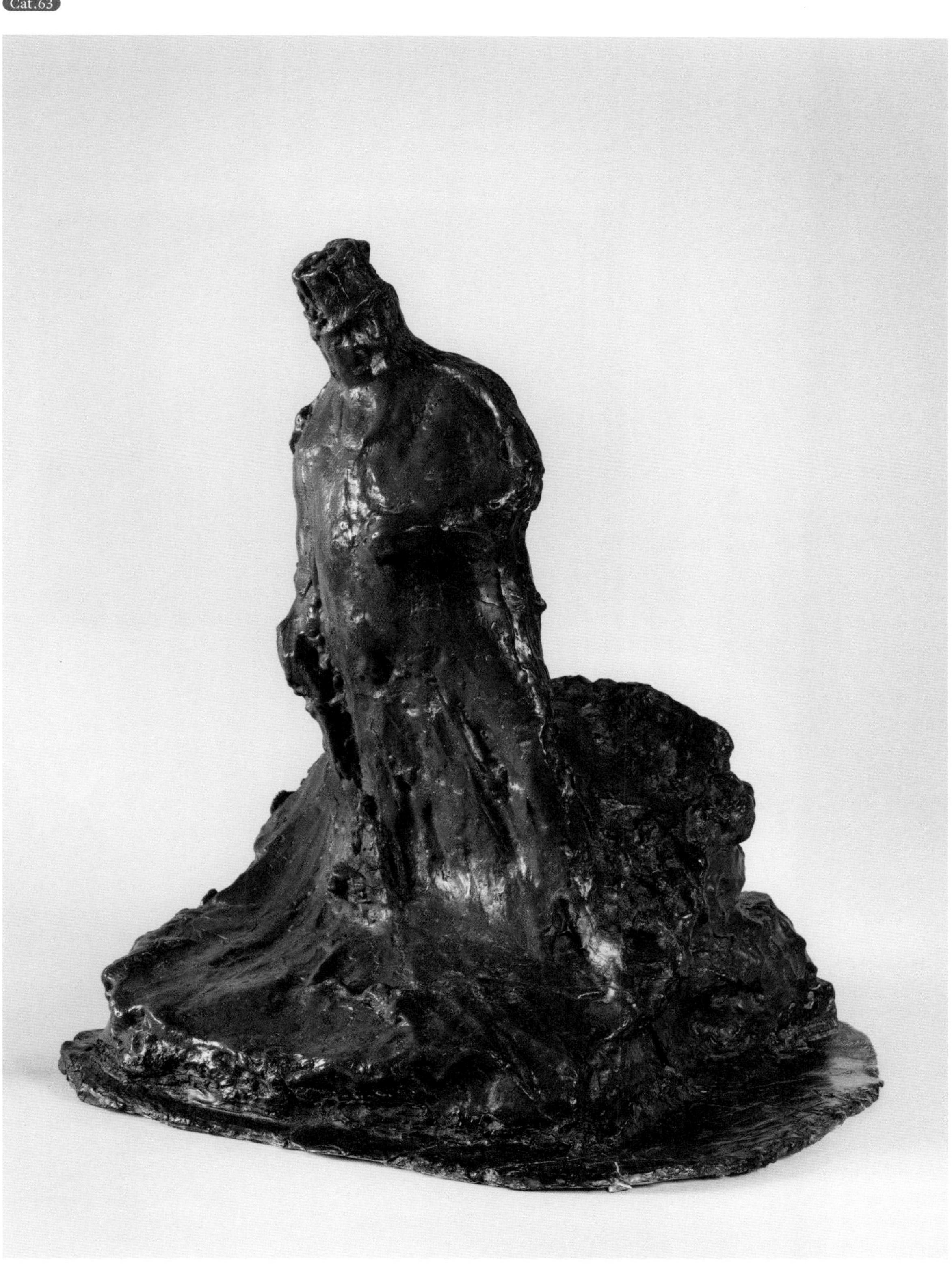

A moment's monument

Cat.64 Medardo Rosso, Reproduction of a photograph of *Impression de boulevard, le soir (Paris la nuit)* (1896/97), 1898; on card, 17.7 × 24.3 cm (photograph), 18.2 × 24.7 cm (card), scratched in the middle; signed: "M. Rosso / Paris la nuit / Impression de Boulevard esterieur"; private collection

In his volume of poetry *Les Fleurs du mal* from 1857, Charles Baudelaire dedicated the following lines to a woman passing by: "The street about me roared with a deafening sound. Tall, slender, in heavy mourning, majestic grief, a woman passed, with a glittering hand raising, swinging the hem and flounces of her skirt; agile and graceful, her leg was like a statue's."[1] While observing the passing figure, the distinct shape of a leg abruptly caught the poet's eye. It was not a leg but the bust of a veiled woman passing by that Medardo Rosso moulded in his *Femme à la voilette* (cat. 66). In 1906, he appropriately described this work as "a moment's monument".[2] With his *Femme à la voilette*, Rosso adopted a typical aspect of modern urban life in Paris – namely, the streams of masses of people strolling on the wide boulevards in which individuals were in a position to disappear or, as Baudelaire worded it in his essay "The Painter of Modern Life", it was possible for individuals "to set up house in the heart of the multitude, amid the ebb and flow of movement, in the midst of the fugitive and the infinite."[3] Rosso used a veil as a layer separating the female passer-by and the viewer.[4] The area framing the bust underscores the brevity and singularity of the moment, as a rear view of the passer-by is impossible. Precisely when Rosso dealt with this subject in the 1890s is still being discussed.[5] However, it is undoubtedly one of those motifs that were cast in wax early on.[6] In an article from 1895, Charles Morice praised a wax version due to the indefinite, fleeting consistency of the material.[7]

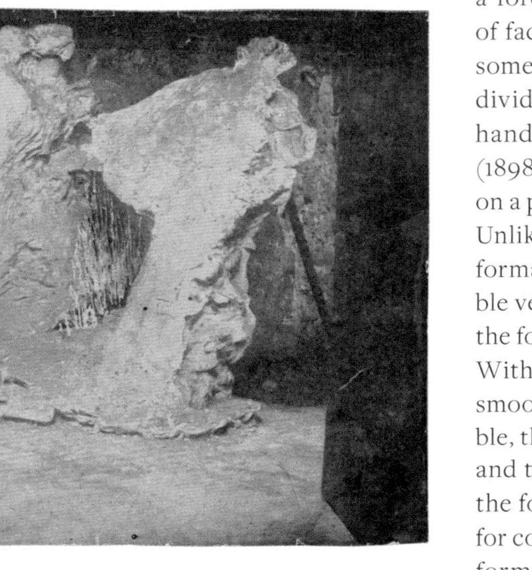

Cat.64

At first glance, based on the summary treatment of her slightly tilted head in the diffuse setting and its proportions, the figure resembles the anonymous female passer-by depicted in *Madame Noblet* (cat. 65). It is all the more surprising that the plastic bust is an express portrait. Anne Loustau, the wife of Rosso's collector friend Louis-Sylvain Noblet, was one of the few personages that Rosso portrayed.[8] He cast the plaster shown here in 1926 after a model that he created in 1897 for the collector Giuseppe Ricci Oddi (Galleria Nazionale d'Arte Moderna, Rome).[9] The traces of the palette knife and the fingers on the rough surface were more pronounced than the physiognomic details. In his portraits, Rosso was also interested in the concentrated moment of perception and not in objective representation.

The graphic artist and painter Eugène Carrière created a similar effect in his lithograph *Bust of a Young Girl* (cat. 67), in which the face shines out hazily as if behind layers of gauze. However, unlike Rosso's figures, Carrière's young girl seems isolated from life and simultaneously placeless. The two female busts by Edgar Degas and Auguste Rodin are also introverted. Degas's small bronze *Woman Resting Head on One Hand* (cat. 69) is characterised by the melancholic gesture of the hand supporting the face, that hand that markedly protrudes from the head and shoulder silhouette en bloc.[10] The individual elements become a unit again through the horizontal base of the work, which lacks plinth and pedestal and seems like a section from what was originally a larger whole and thus bears the character of a fragment. Rodin's marble version of *Madame Fenaille* (cat. 68) is closely related to Degas's bust in terms of form, as it also presents the shoulder and head area of a woman whose tilted face is partially covered by her prominent left hand.[11] This very same hand is missing in all of the earlier versions of the portrait bust; Rodin first added it in the plaster model he produced in 1898[12] for the marble that originated as from 1905. Due to its more male-seeming nature, in the plaster from 1898 it seems like a foreign set piece. As a matter of fact, Rodin repeatedly created something new from different individual parts. He also used this hand in his assemblage *L'Adieu* (1898), which he produced based on a portrait of Camille Claudel.[13] Unlike the plaster cast, the hand is formally integrated into the marble version of *Madame Fenaille*, as the focus is now placed elsewhere. With the gentle emergence of the smooth body from the rough marble, the elegant tilting of the neck, and the fingers placed loosely on the forehead, the stone bust aims for continuously flowing lines and forms. The slightly translucent *non-finito* marble underscores this harmonious basic tenor[14] – particularly as distinguished from the deliberately unfinished nature of the base block.[15] These works, produced since 1885 but more and more frequently from 1900 onwards, in which part of the stone was only roughly hewed or remained entirely unworked, were seen in parallel to the method of the Impressionists, as here it was a question of exposing the artistic methods and shifting interest from the object to perception.[16] In different materials, Rosso, Carrière, Degas and Rodin succeeded in integrating the portrayal of a woman's face or bust into the discourse on "fugitive" modernity and its reception by deliberately obscuring, fragmenting or emphasising the finished in the unfinished.

In terms of content, Rosso's striking bust *Femme à la voilette* is connected with his larger-than-life three-part group *Paris la nuit* from 1896/97. Like the monumental group *In tranvai* (1883/84; cf. cat. 57) from the Milan period, it has only been passed down in photographs. Rosso sold the only version of it before 1902 to Noblet, who besides the portrait of his wife also owned a wax cast of *Femme à la voilette*.[17] The plaster group was subject to destruction due to its improper placement in his garden. The importance that Rosso attached to this work became apparent in his attempt in 1900 to have it placed in Rodin's exhibition hall at the Place de l'Alma: "My dear friend, I have a piece three meters by two[,] would you be willing to exhibit it for me in your

Pavilion[?]." This endeavour was in no way compatible with Rodin's interests and failed accordingly.[18] However, the idea of being able to view *Paris la nuit* within sight of Rodin's *Burghers of Calais* (as of 1884; p. 185, fig. 1) is definitely appealing. They embodied the opposite poles of what a "modern history painting"[19] could be: on the one hand, with *The Burghers of Calais*, the visualisation of an historical event in a contemporary sculptural version, and, on the other hand, the rendering of a contemporary occurrence without a historical dimension in the form of the "burghers of the Parisian boulevard". With his motif, however, Rosso closely tied in with the painting of Camille Pissarro, Claude Monet or Gustave Caillebotte, who all decidedly examined the activities on Baron Haussmann's boulevards.

If one considers the photograph of the group *Paris la nuit (Impression de boulevard)* – published in 1902 in Claris's book on Impressionist sculpture[20] – as well as the mounted reproduction exhibited here (cat. 64), it becomes apparent that unlike *Femme à la voilette*, it does not seem to have been designed *en face*, but to the contrary: in all of the surviving photographs, the group of hurrying, in part obliquely placed people is always portrayed from the back. Thus, the group clearly distances itself from the viewer. Its hustling stride or the viewer's remaining behind – or even the isolated artist's, as Hecker suspects[21]

– becomes the central theme. Another photograph indicates that the right-hand figure was designed to stand so obliquely that it had to be held by a rope (p. 280, fig. 8). In this context, we may once more call to mind the disagreement between Rosso and Rodin, among other things caused by the question of who it was that originally introduced such tilted, out-of-balance figures into sculpture (cf. cat. 63).[22] In addition, like Rodin in the case of his *Balzac* and *The Burghers of Calais*, Rosso also apparently designed the group without a base, thus standing directly on the floor. In the photograph, it is situated on a deep point in the room with a large empty area between it and the photographer or viewer. Although there is no conclusive certainty with respect to the authorship of the photographs, the shading on this reproduced photograph in all probability stems from Rosso himself as does the inscription with his name and the title of the work. Like a painter, Rosso intervened in the distribution of the mass on the support by closing the gap between the figures, in doing so condensing them to produce a dark, impermeable area.[23] At this moment, he no longer viewed the work as a sculpture but as a picture. All that is left to us is inevitably "just" the photographic image. Even though this group of figures did not survive, it can nevertheless undoubtedly be regarded as one of the most innovative contributions to modern sculpture ever. — EM-V

1   Baudelaire [1857] 1954, p. 311.
2   Exh. cat. London 1906, p. 13; quoted in: Mola/Vittucci 2009, p. 162.
3   Baudelaire [1863] 1964, p. 9.
4   Based on this example, Jole De Sanna therefore speaks of a dispersion in space, hence of two different substances that separate and do not dissolve into one another, in contrast to the fusion of figure and space that is often the case in Rosso's works; De Sanna 1985, p. 24.
5   On the various dates and titles, see Mola 2007, p. 82; Hecker 2017, p. 125.
6   Mola 2009a, p. 26. The work shown here is a cast produced by Rosso's son Francesco around 1950/51; see Mola/Vittucci 2009, p. 363, no. 11a. Cf. also Hecker 2017a, p. 17.
7   Morice 1895; quoted in: De Sanna 1985, p. 24. The version that entered the collection of the Palais du Luxembourg in Paris in 1907 was also out of wax.
8   Exh. cat. Rovereto/Turin 2004, p. 170; exh. cat. Milan 2015, pp. 95 ff.
9   Mola/Vittucci 2009, p. 323, nos. 33a, 33e.
10 Degas also employed this melancholic gesture in portraits of his sister Thérèse: see exh. cat. Karlsruhe 2014, pp. 100 ff. On the bust, see Czestochowski/Pingeot 2002, pp. 242–243.
11 Barbier 1987, no. 11; on Maurice Fenaille, Rodin's friend and collector, see exh. cat. Rodez 2000.
12 *Madame Fenaille*, bust, around 1898, plaster, Musée Rodin, Paris, inv. no. S. 1775.
13 Le Normand-Romain 1998, p. 29. For more detail on the prolonged origination process of the portraits of Madame Fenaille, from which four marble, three terracotta and 13 plaster versions were made between 1898 and 1917, see Le Normand-Romain 1998, on the present marble bust esp. p. 69; Le Normand-Romain 2000.
14 Becker 1998, p. 66, relates Rosso's growing propensity towards wax with Rodin's increasing use of marble. Wohlrab 2016, p. 70, points out that when working with marble, Rodin always had an assistant, in this case Louis-Dominique Mathet; on this, see also the essay by Dominik Brabant in this catalogue, pp. 174–183.
15 For more details on this, see Wohlrab 2016.
16 Ibid., p. 136.
17 Mola/Vittucci 2009, p. 313, no. 31b.
18 Hecker 2017, p. 157, where the quote from the letter from Rosso to Rodin can be found (the original is in the Fonds historique, Musée Rodin, Paris, shelf mark Ros-5410).
19 Rivière 1877, p. 309. On the occasion of the Impressionist exhibition of 1887, Georges Rivière speaks of "modern histories" in reference to several large-format paintings by Pierre-Auguste Renoir – including *Le Bal du moulin de la Galette* (1876, Musée d'Orsay, Paris).
20 Claris 1902 (French), p. 103; not in Claris 1902a (German), on this, see also Taylor 2019.
21 Hecker 2017, p. 172.
22 Ibid., pp. 161 ff.
23 Stix-Marget 1998, p. 232.

Cat.65 Medardo Rosso, **Madame Noblet**, 1897, cast in 1926; plaster, 66 × 43 × 25 cm;
Galleria d'Arte Moderna Ricci Oddi, Piacenza, inv. no. 169 Cat.66 Francesco Rosso after
Medardo Rosso, **Femme à la voilette**, 1895, cast in 1950/51 after an original plaster
by Medardo Rosso; wax over plaster, 63 × 65 × 33 cm; Museo Medardo Rosso, Barzio

Cat.65

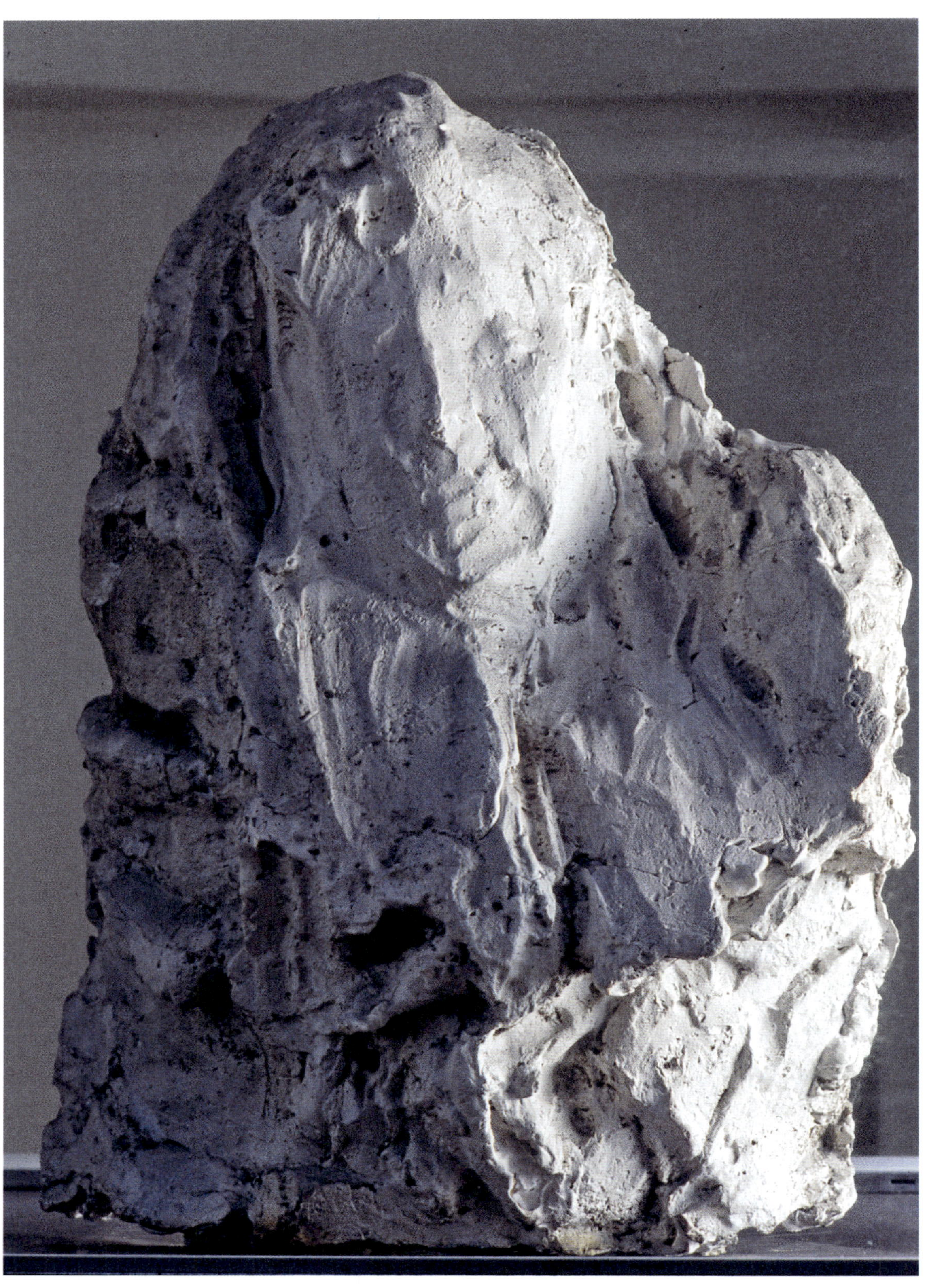

Cat. 66

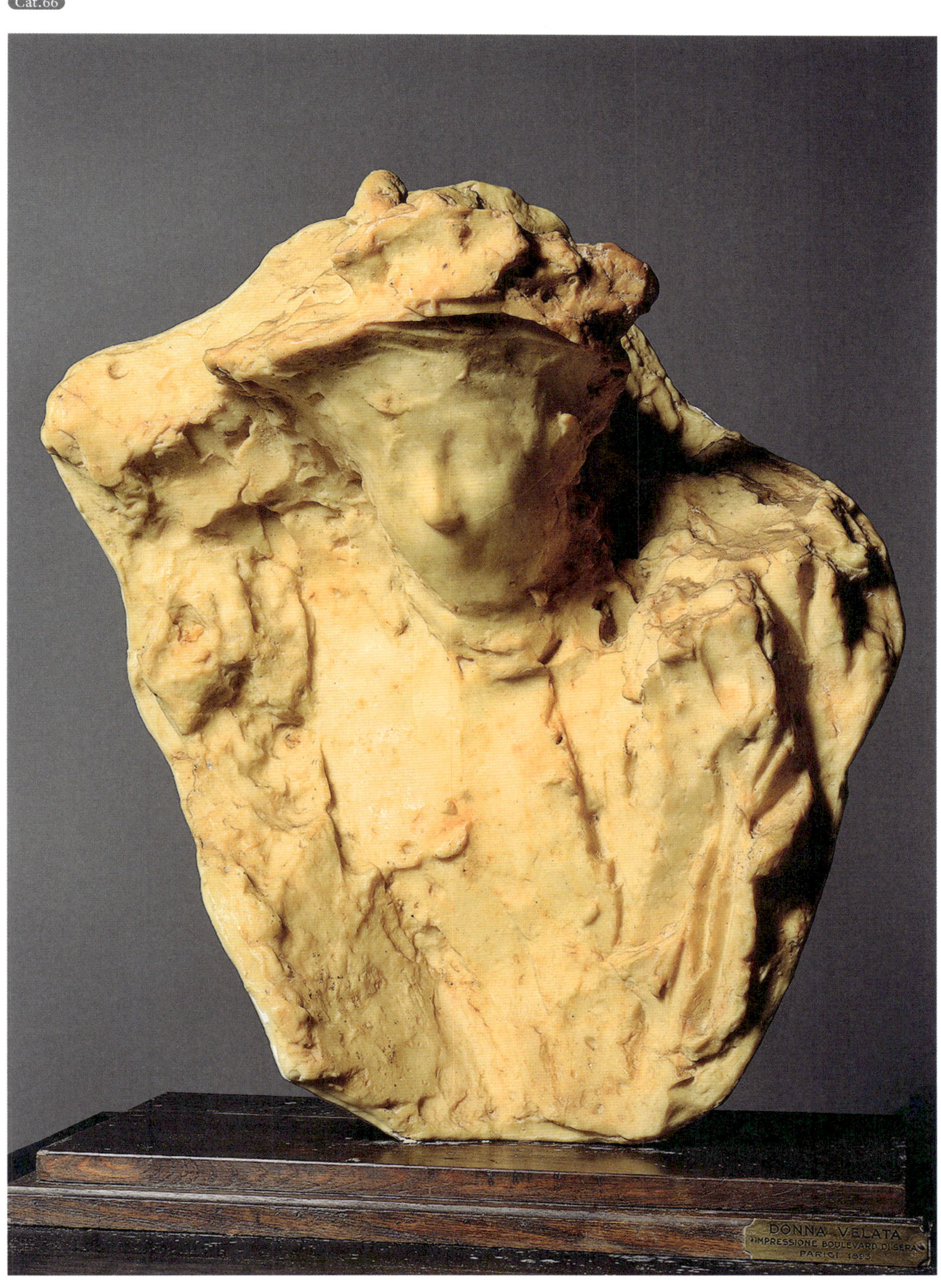

Cat.67 Eugène Carrière, **Bust of a Young Girl**, 1890; lithograph, partially scratched, on white wove paper, 49.3 × 35.6 cm (sheet); Staatsgalerie Stuttgart, Graphische Sammlung, inv. no. A 1986/6277 **Cat.68** Auguste Rodin, with the assistance of Louis-Dominique Mathet, **Madame Fenaille**, 1905–1908; marble, 58.5 × 81 × 64 cm; Musée Rodin, Paris, inv. no. S.01199 **Cat.69** Edgar Degas, **Woman Resting Head on One Hand, Bust (62)**, 1892; bronze, 12.3 × 17.5 × 16.2 cm; Collection Museum de Fundatie, Zwolle and Heino/Wijhe, inv. no. 574

Cat.67

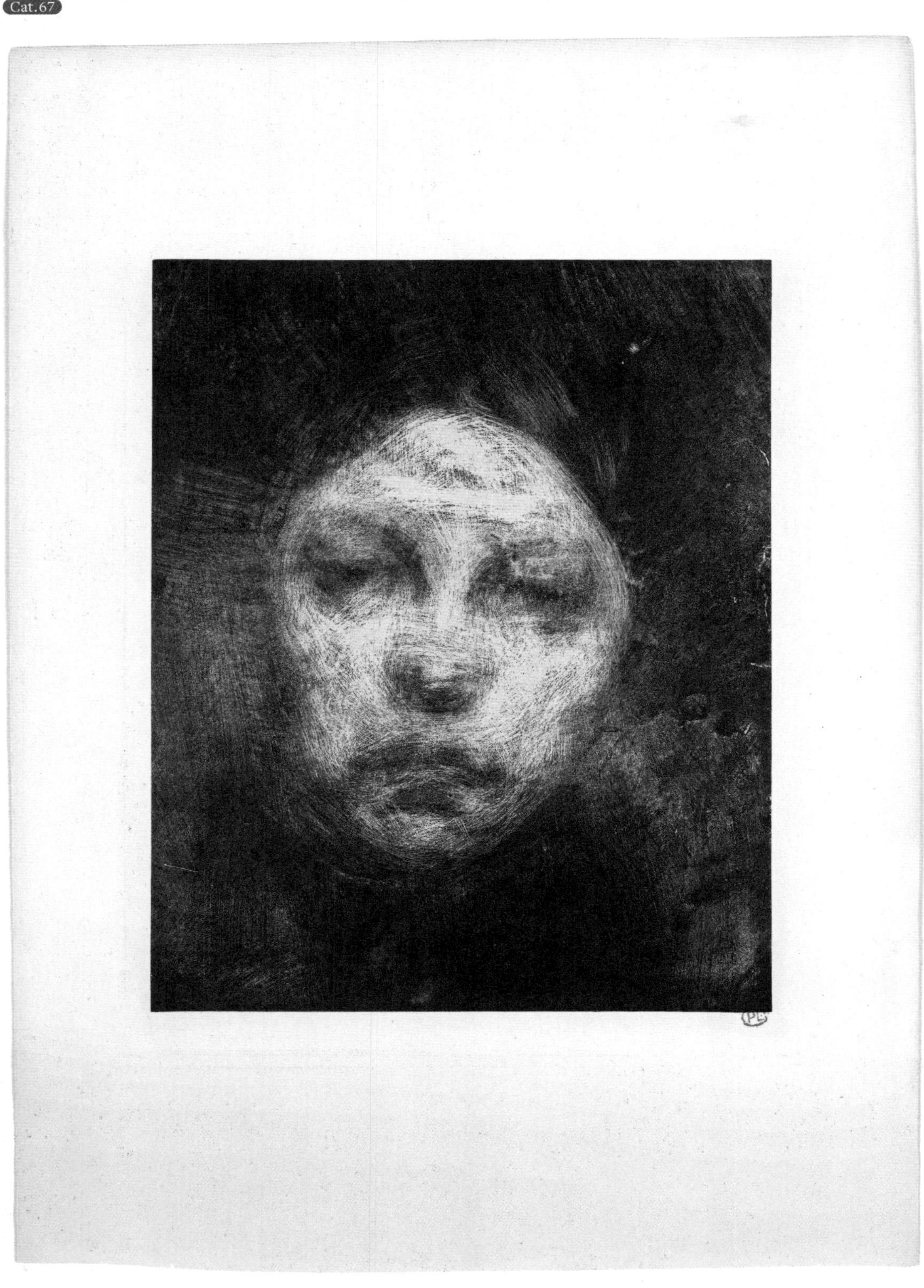

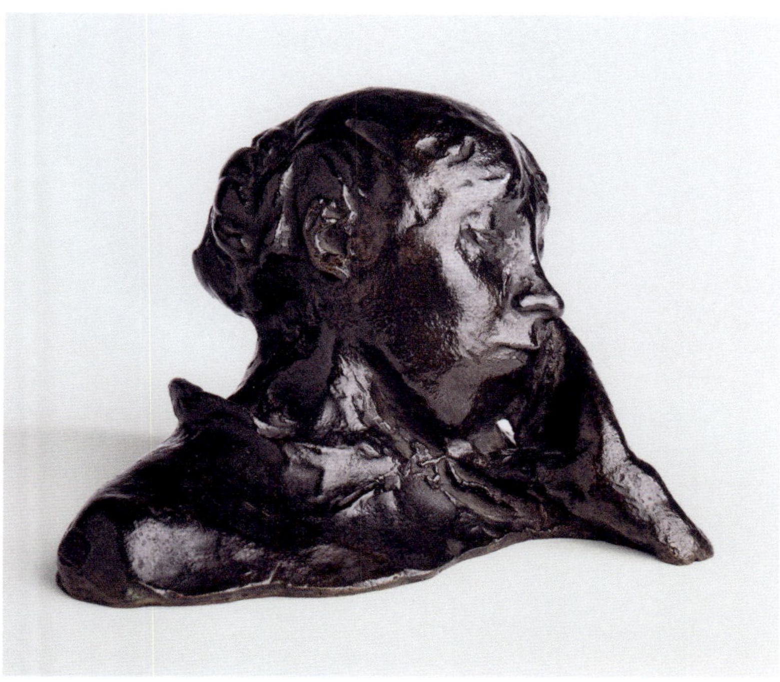

Cat.69

Cat.68

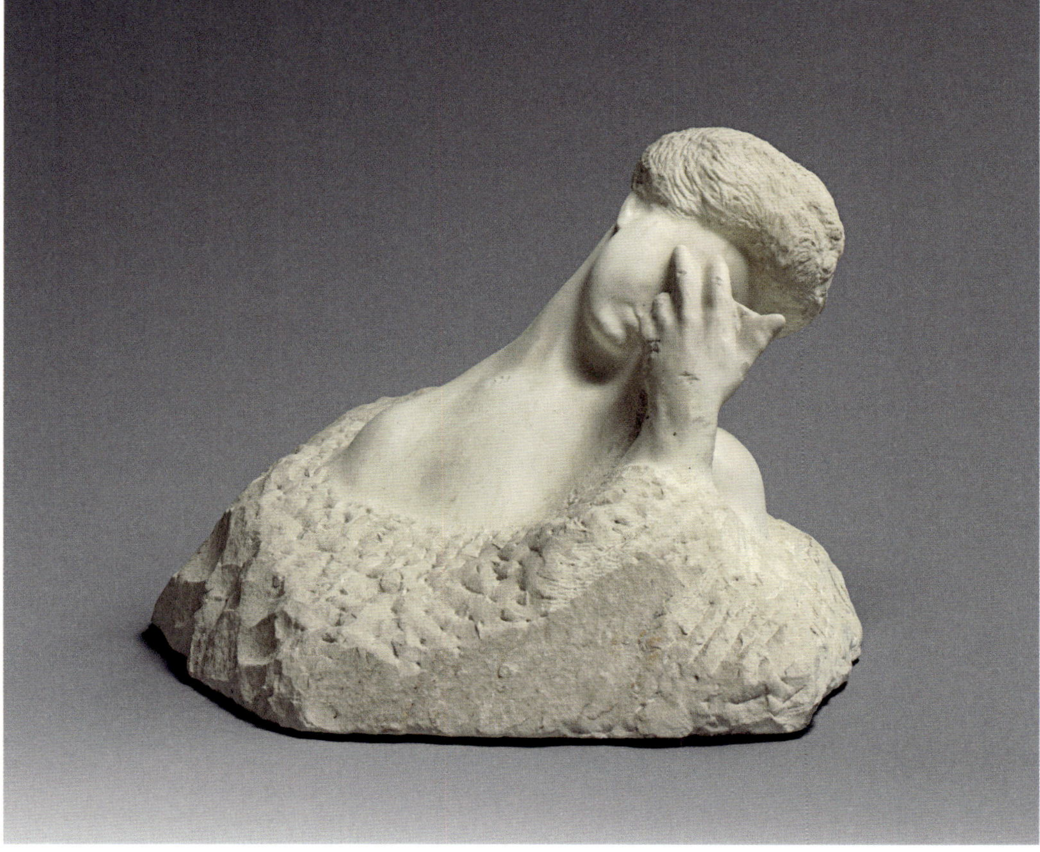

The portrait of Henri Rouart

The portrait of Henri Rouart is the largest surviving figure in Medardo Rosso's oeuvre, since the life-sized groups *Impressione d'omnibus* (1883/84; cat. 57) and *Paris la nuit* (1896/97; cat. 64) were unintentionally destroyed not long after each of them were created. Unlike Rosso's numerous anonymous figures, it is an explicit portrait: it depicts the influential engineer, inventor, painter, collector and committed patron of the arts Henri Rouart (1833–1912). He had co-initiated and participated in the Impressionist exhibitions and owned works by Edgar Degas, Claude Monet, Pierre-Auguste Renoir, Paul Cézanne and many others. Rosso presumably met him shortly after arriving in Paris in 1889.[1] It was probably in his endeavour to financially support and promote Rosso, who at this point in time was ill and impoverished, that Rouart – who had already acquired a *Gavroche* bronze – consented to sitting for a portrait.[2]

In 1930, Henri Rouart's son Eugène committed his memories of the origin of the work to paper, whose reliability, however, can be called into doubt, not least due to chronological inconsistencies. Eugène reported that his father had sat while in a state of poor health. Rosso created a clay figure in close proximity to Rouart and cast it by means of a gelatine mould directly in the courtyard of the parental home.[3] However the events may have progressed, this first cast presented here possesses an irregular surface that seems to give an account of its creation in the form of chamotte particles left behind in the recesses, open holes and nails remaining in the metal.[4]

The sculpture presents Rouart slightly larger than life-size as a frontal seated figure wearing a beret and a painter's smock. The oval silhouette of the convexly curved form is nearly devoid of any volume. Rather, the furrowed surface seems to open up into the space before it. If one looks at it from the side, one detects light protrusions and recesses, but no apertures or hollow spaces. Looked at from the front, this surface area, which is difficult to deduce as a figurative portrait, transforms into a coherent portrait that is animated by the lightly protruding parts of the head and the left arm. Rosso later explained: "When, from the beginning, the tonality seems to move back and forth between background and foreground, the viewer believes to perceive a movement of life."[5] In 1900, he made an effort to buy back the work, which was also on display that same year at the Paris world's fair in the context of the Giovanni Segantini exhibition – as, incidentally, was also Paolo Troubetzkoy's similarly large but extremely expansive half-figure portrait of Segantini (cat. 109). Rouart refused to sell it; in turn, Rosso noted on the back of the written refusal: "Rouart loves his portrait – admittedly, rather late, but still."[6]

In 1902, Rosso explained the importance of the surroundings that influenced the creation of the portrait to Edmond Claris: "The impression you make on me is not the same one if I see you in a garden or in the midst of other people in a salon or on the street."[7] Rosso's understanding of the portrait once more manifests itself in this work: it is not the psychological dimension of the person, but solely the materialisation of his impression on the artist that constituted the motive and the goal. — EM-V

1 Salon d'Automne, Paris, 1904, with Medardo Rosso's *La Portinaia*, 1883/84, *Henri Rouart*, 1890, and *Madame Noblet*, 1897, photograph, 16.2 × 23.2 cm, private collection

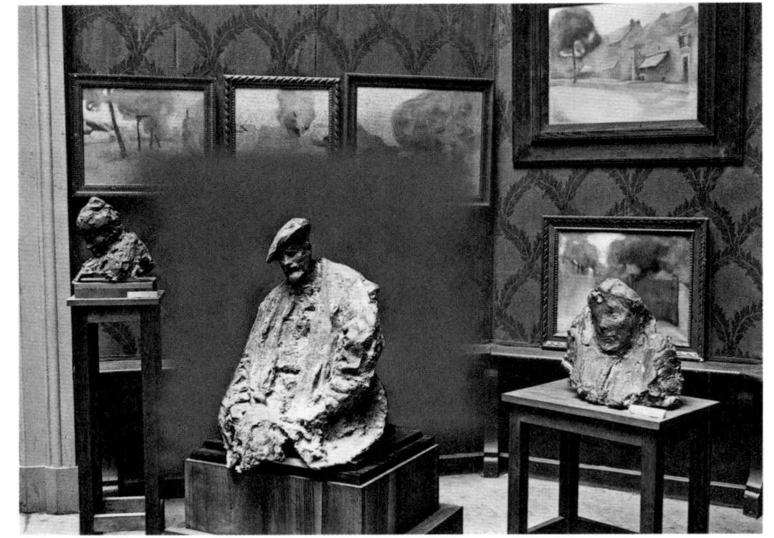

1 For further information on Henri Rouart, see Schwarz 2003, pp. 156 ff.; Foa 2019, pp. 13 ff.

2 Rouart's son-in-law later served as the model for *The Bookmaker* (cat. 63). On the portraits created by Rosso, see Merkel 1995, pp. 137 ff.

3 Rouart 1930, quoted in: Schwarz 2003, p. 168; see also Mola/Vittucci 2009, p. 274, no. 23b.

4 On the production marks on the casts made by Rosso himself, see Hecker 2017a, p. 13. On provenance, see Mola/Vittucci 2009, p. 274, no. 23b.

5 Claris 1902 (French), p. 52; not in Claris 1902a (German).

6 "Rouart aime son portrait – un peu tard mais enfin."; letter from Henri Rouart to Medardo Rosso, 26 August 1900, Museo Medardo Rosso, Barzio, archive; quoted in: Schwarz 2003, p. 172.

7 Claris 1902 (French), p. 52; not in Claris 1902a (German),

Cat.70 Medardo Rosso, **Henri Rouart**, 1890; bronze, 93 × 71 × 50 cm;
Kunst Museum Winterthur, gift of the gallery association, 1964, inv. no. 978

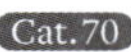

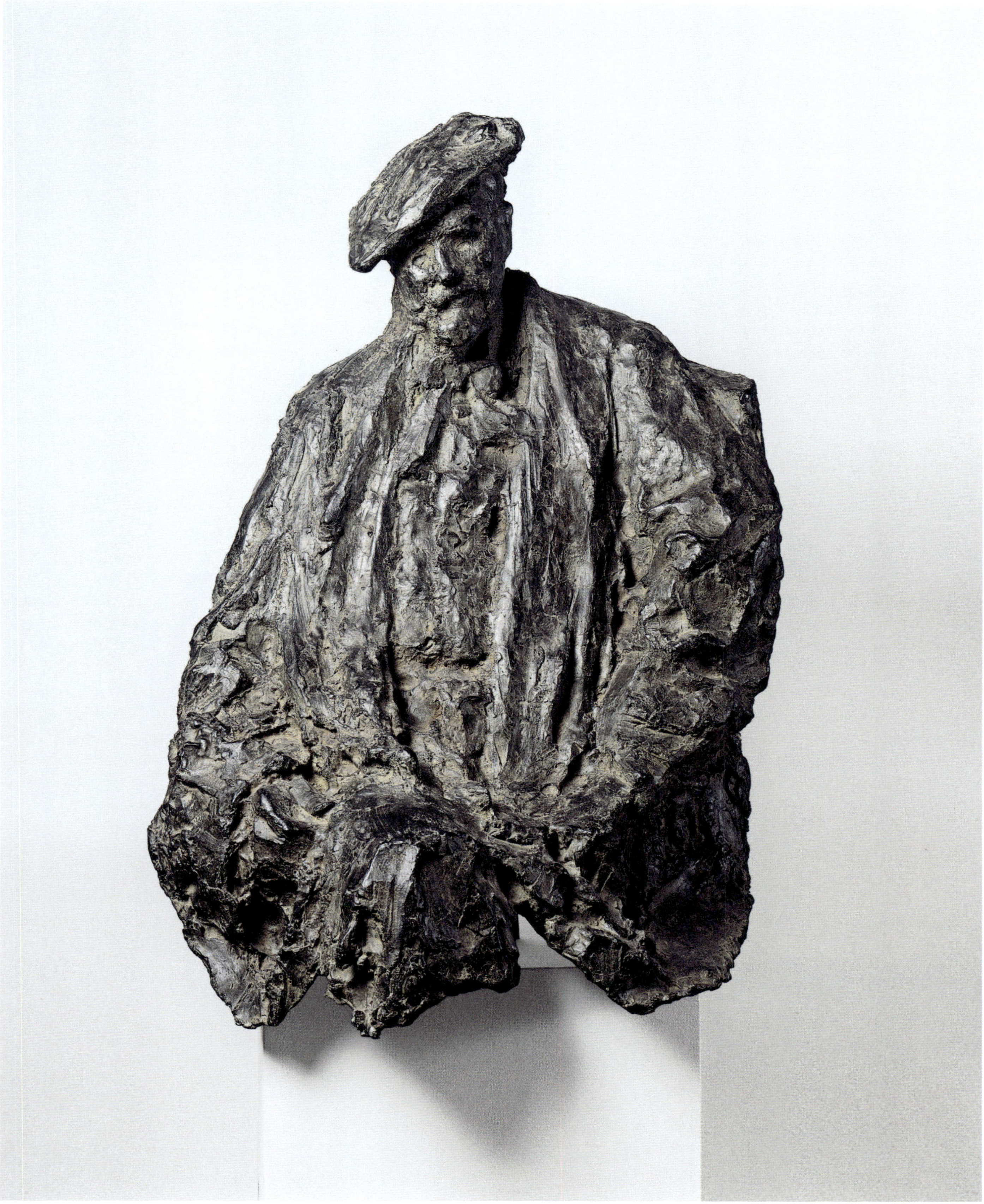

Cat.70

Children's heads

Medardo Rosso celebrated his greatest successes with portraits of children. The artist did not cast, sell, exchange or give away any other figure more often than he did *Jewish Child*, created in 1862.[1] In private depictions of an intact, sheltered life, children were also a central motif in painting by the Impressionists, such as in works by Berthe Morisot or Claude Monet (p. 17, fig. 10). Rosso's work *Aetas Aurea* (1886; cat. 58) is also to be mentioned in this respect. Yet his sculptures from the 1890s are different, as they do not address experienced protection but rather the need for protection.

In Rosso's *Bambino al sole* of 1892 (cat. 73), the delicate features of the small child are carved, slightly contorted, out of an only roughly modelled upper body. The title of the work not only incorporates the viewing condition in natural and changeable light,[2] but its sensuously perceptual warmth as well. As a result, it is precisely this palpable sharing in the moment that becomes profoundly accessible. In view of a child's head by Rosso, Julius Meier-Graefe spoke about art "of our time, when one escapes from the noise of the world into discrete spaces and in the evening, by mild light, in the presence of such delicate things recovers from the endlessly less refined interests that take up the day."[3] The art critic's enthusiasm secured Rosso's participation in the pioneering exhibition *Entwicklung des Impressionismus in Malerei und Plastik* (The Development of Impressionism in Painting and Sculpture) mounted by the Vienna Secession in 1903. A version of *Bambino al sole* was also shown there, yet Rosso evidently did not win over every visitor: "In Rosso's work, Impressionism finishes off the viewer. It is unacceptable to wrap features in veils to the point that all that one sees are intimations."[4]

The bronze version of the motif in Essen exhibits the characteristic traces of the production process. The porous surface covers the cast from the scraggy, irregularly ascending plinth to the facial area, although greater smoothness was achieved in the cheeks and the nose. This version was evidently on display in important international exhibitions since the world's fair in 1900 in Paris.[5] The encyclopedic collector Karl Ernst Osthaus acquired the work in 1904 for his Folkwang Museum in Hagen.[6]

Rosso created another child subject entitled *Enfant à la Bouchée de pain* around 1897 (cat. 71). The dark rust-brown cast stands out due to its overall dimensional massiveness, which seems to be almost disproportionate to the child's small face. In her memoirs, the collector Etha Fles gives an account of the nighttime presentation of this work in Rosso's studio in Paris: "'Stay in that corner,' he motioned, "and lit a match that illuminated his *Bouchée de pain*, the face of a child he had seen in the arms of its mother as it was being fed. It's mouth full of bread, nose and eyes almost lost between the round forehead and chubby cheeks. [... S]o he let the flame flicker with delicate affection over this subtle vision or burgeoning life [...]."[7]

A picture taken by an anonymous photographer[8] has survived that shows the plaster cast on exhibit here in a narrow vitrine, developed by Rosso, in the Salon d'automne of 1904 – in the excellently furnished Salle Cézanne (fig. 1). Rosso cast a bronze version of this subject around 1902 that displays fragments of the front only as a very thin matrix (figs. 2 and 3).[9] A comparison of the version in the round and the flat one reveals that Rosso did not lose sight of the importance of the levels behind the main display side, despite his decided view that an artwork should be looked at from a specific standpoint. Tamara Schenkenberg pointed out the examples in which the reverse sides are substantially rougher, nearly unworked, and do not seem to bear a relationship to the front, at least in terms of form. She fittingly describes their effect as "defiant and deeply vibrant".[10] In fact, in the case of *Enfant à la Bouchée de pain*, the unformed mass that expands downwards is an essential part of its overall appearance. This example also proves Rosso's basic premise that "nothing is divisible"[11] and is therefore a unity: the visible quality and its underlying invisible one cannot be separated.

A look at *La Maternité* (cat. 72), a bronze that Antoine Bourdelle (1861–1929) created in 1893, is interesting in this connection. Bourdelle began working as an assistant in Auguste Rodin's studio that same year. His influence can be detected in the almost separate existence of the tactile working of the hair and clothing as well as the marked interest in clearly distinguishable volumes – child, breast and bust constitute separate units.[12] Unlike Rosso's busts of children, in its arrangement the group reaches far into the space diagonally. What is surprising is the reverse side. Making no attempt at realistic depiction, Bourdelle piled up the unsmoothed clay, even creating a concave interior space without any content-related purpose in this unformed mountain. Like Rosso's *Enfant à la Bouchée de pain*, in terms of aesthetics the rear side bears no compelling relationship to the front view. The essential difference to Rosso lies in the fact that Bourdelle invites the viewer to look at the bronze from all sides by means of the dynamic basic disposition of the figure, thus emphasising his working method. In the presentation of 1904, Rosso, on the other hand, limits the viewer's gaze to the front and calls for perceiving the overall mass from this perspective. — EM-V

1 Hecker 2017, pp. 130, 133.

2 Schnell 1987, p. 292.

3 Meier-Graefe 1904, vol. 1, p. 292.

4 S.G., "Zur Ausstellung in der Wiener Sezession", *Das Vaterland*, 26 January 1903; quoted in: Stix-Marget 1998, p. 84.

5 See the essay by Eva Mongi-Vollmer in this catalogue, pp. 126–133, here p. 128.

6 Mola/Vittucci 2009, p. 286, no. 26b; Hecker 2017, p. 192. Osthaus bought the figure along with a version of the *Jewish Child*. That same year, the collector bought Auguste Rodin's *Eva* and *The Golden Age*. On French art in the Osthaus collection, see Fleckner 2010.

7 Etha Fles [1919], quoted in: *Medardo Rosso: Ten Bronzes*, exh. cat. Peter Freeman, Inc., New York (New York/Paris, 2016), p. 71; originally published *in Elsevier's Geïllustreed Maandschrift,* no. 11 (July/December 1919). https://issuu.com/blulaboratori/docs/medardo_rosso_ten_bronzes_2016 (accessed 31 October 2019).

8 There was talk as early as 1905 of "friends of the artist" having produced installation views after the conclusion of the presentation; see Hecker 2017, p. 206.

9 Mola/Vittucci 2009, p. 321, no. 35a (plaster), p. 322, no. 35c (bronze); Schenkenberg 2018, p. 42.

10 Schenkenberg 2018, p. 51.

11 Claris 1902 (French), p. 55; not in Claris 1902a (German).

12 On Bourdelle, see Merkel 1995, pp. 159 ff.; Le Normand-Romain 2009, esp. p. 238; Chevillot 2017.

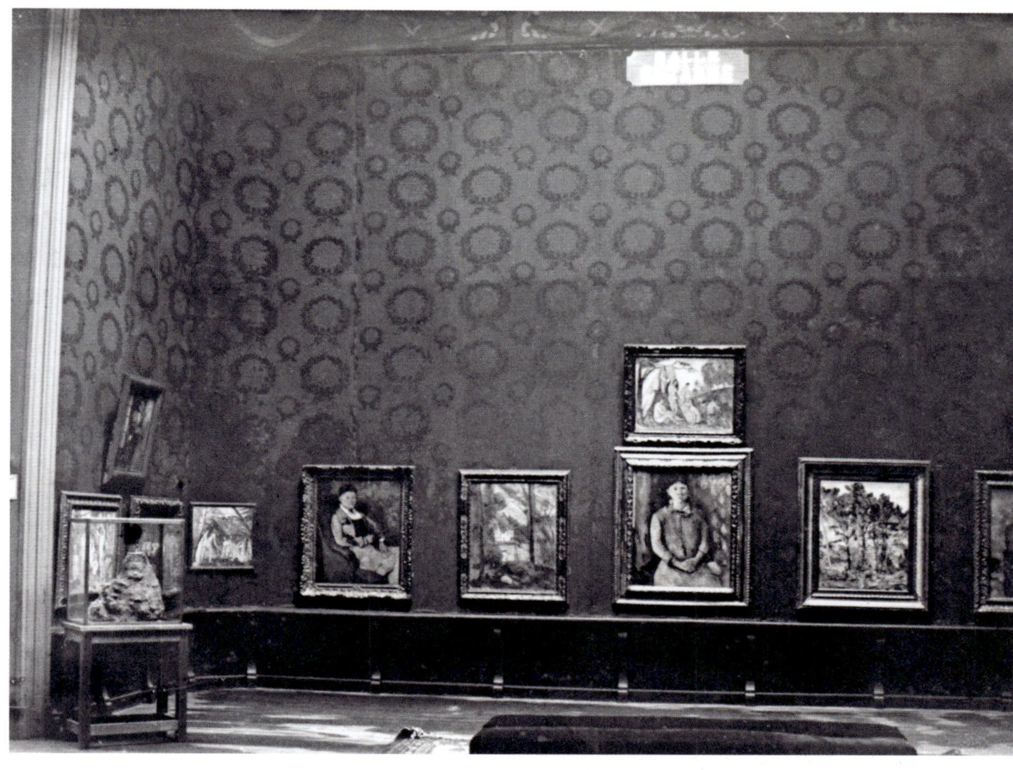

1 Salon d'Automne, Paris, 1904, view into the Cézanne Hall with Medardo Rosso's
Enfant à la Bouchée de pain, c. 1897, photograph

2 Medardo Rosso, *Enfant à la Bouchée de pain,* c. 1897, bronze, 33 × 38 × 9 cm,
Gallerie degli Uffizi, Galleria d'arte moderna di Palazzo Pitti, Florence

3 Installation photograph from the exhibition *Medardo Rosso: Experiments
in Light and Form,* Pulitzer Arts Foundation, St. Louis, Missouri, 2016/17

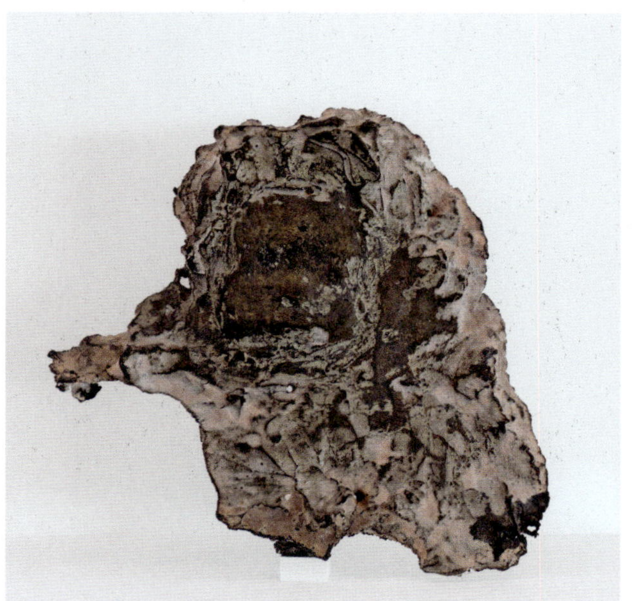

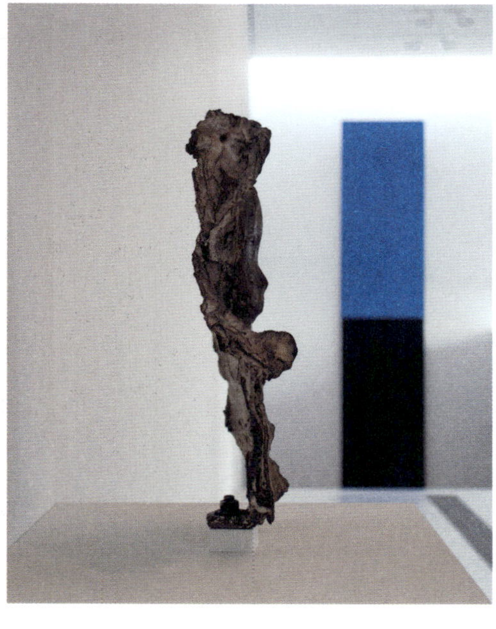

Cat.71 Medardo Rosso, *Enfant à la Bouchée de pain* (Child in the Soup Kitchen), c. 1897; plaster, patinated, 48.5 × 48 × 39 cm; private collection **Cat.72** Antoine Bourdelle, *La Maternité* (Maternity), c. 1893; bronze, 51 × 43 × 36 cm; The Sladmore Gallery, London

Cat.71

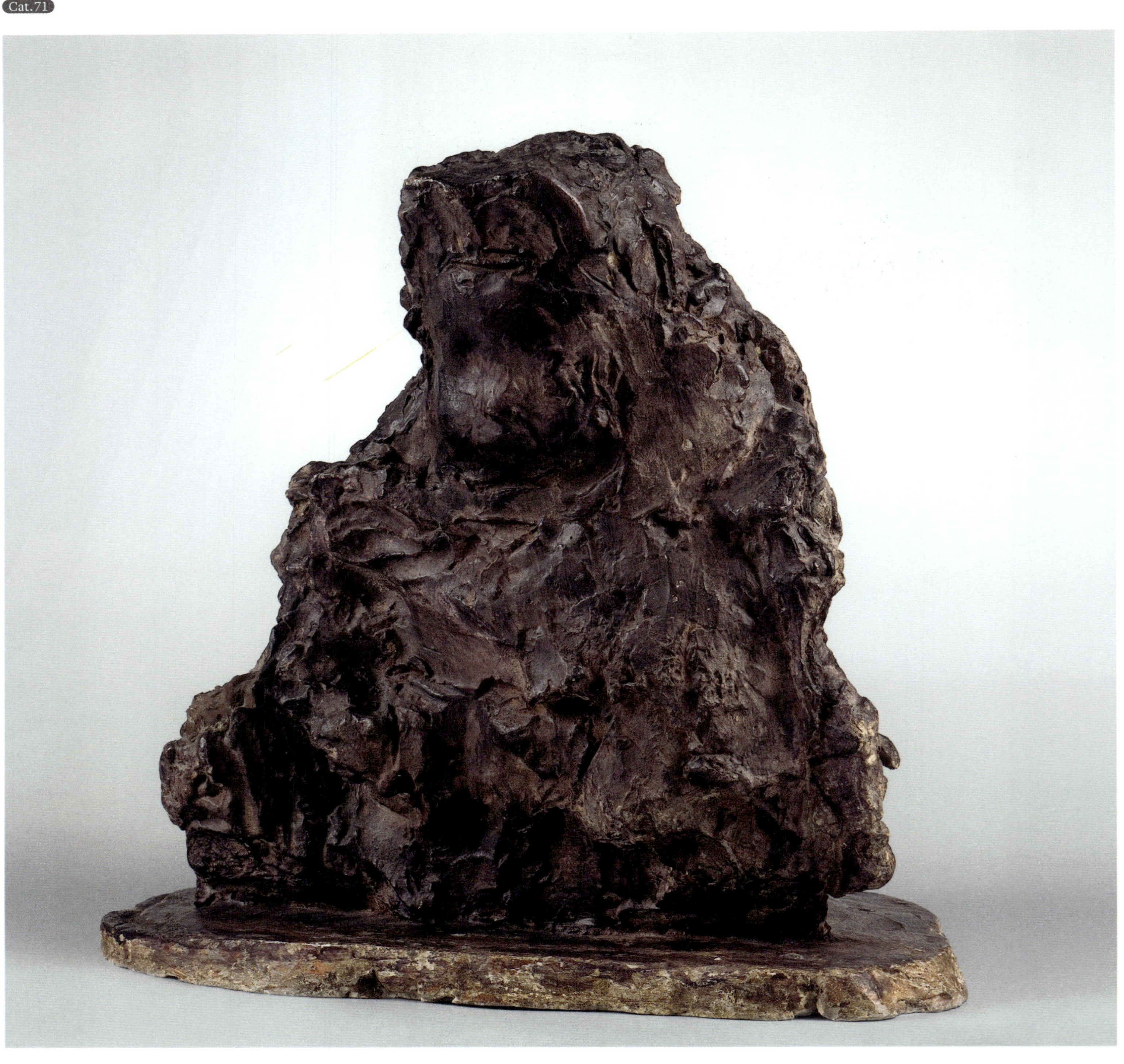

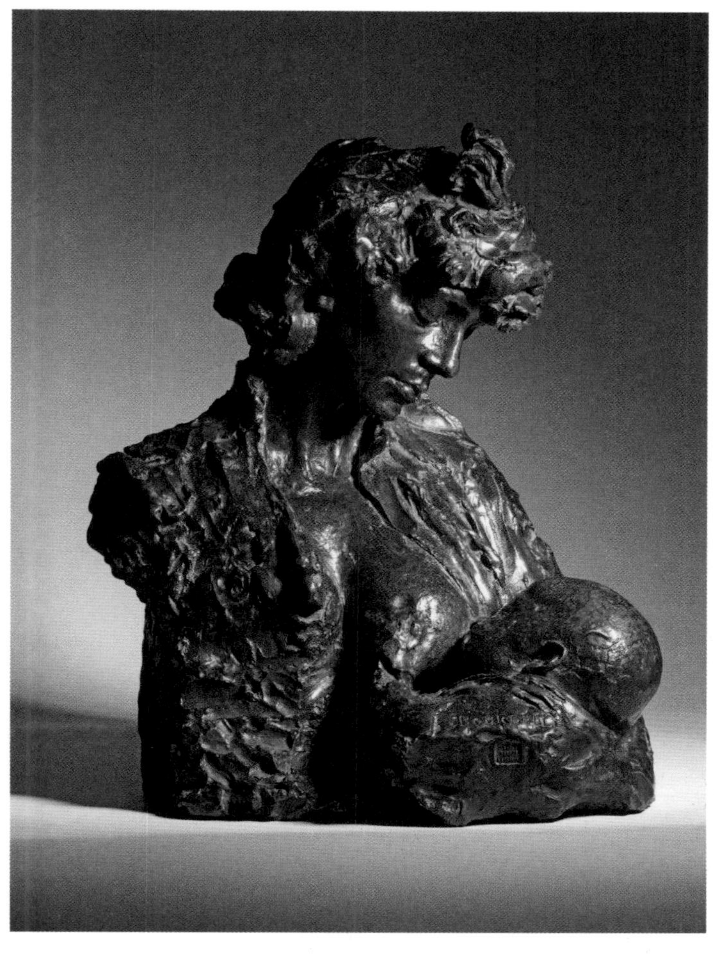

Cat.72

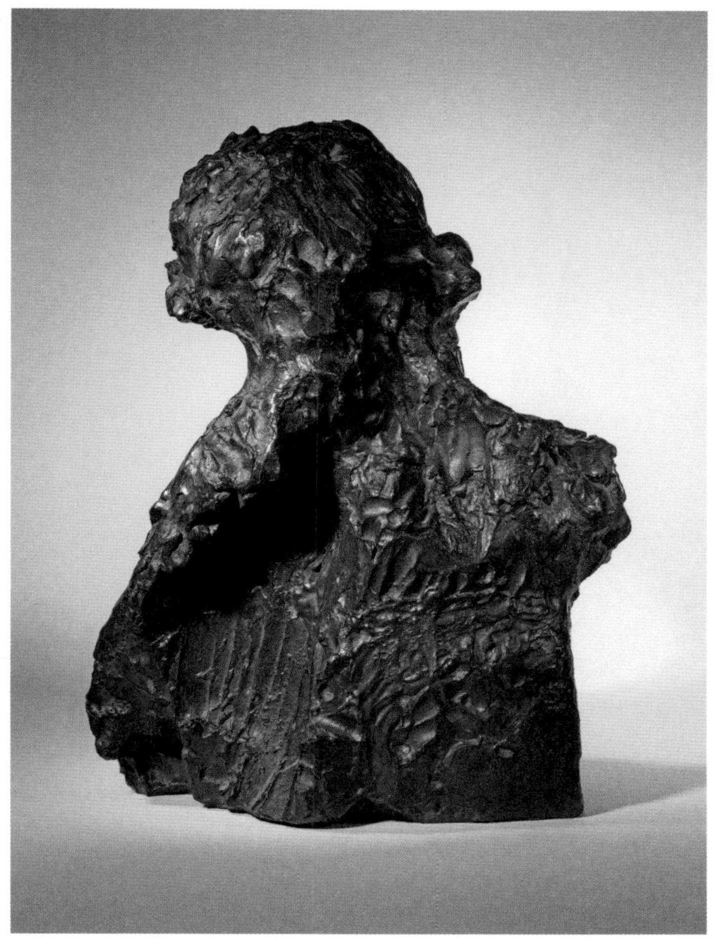

Cat.73 Medardo Rosso, **Bambino al sole**, 1892, cast before 1900; bronze, 35.5 × 27 × 25.5 cm; signed: "MRosso"; Museum Folkwang, Essen, inv. no. P 66

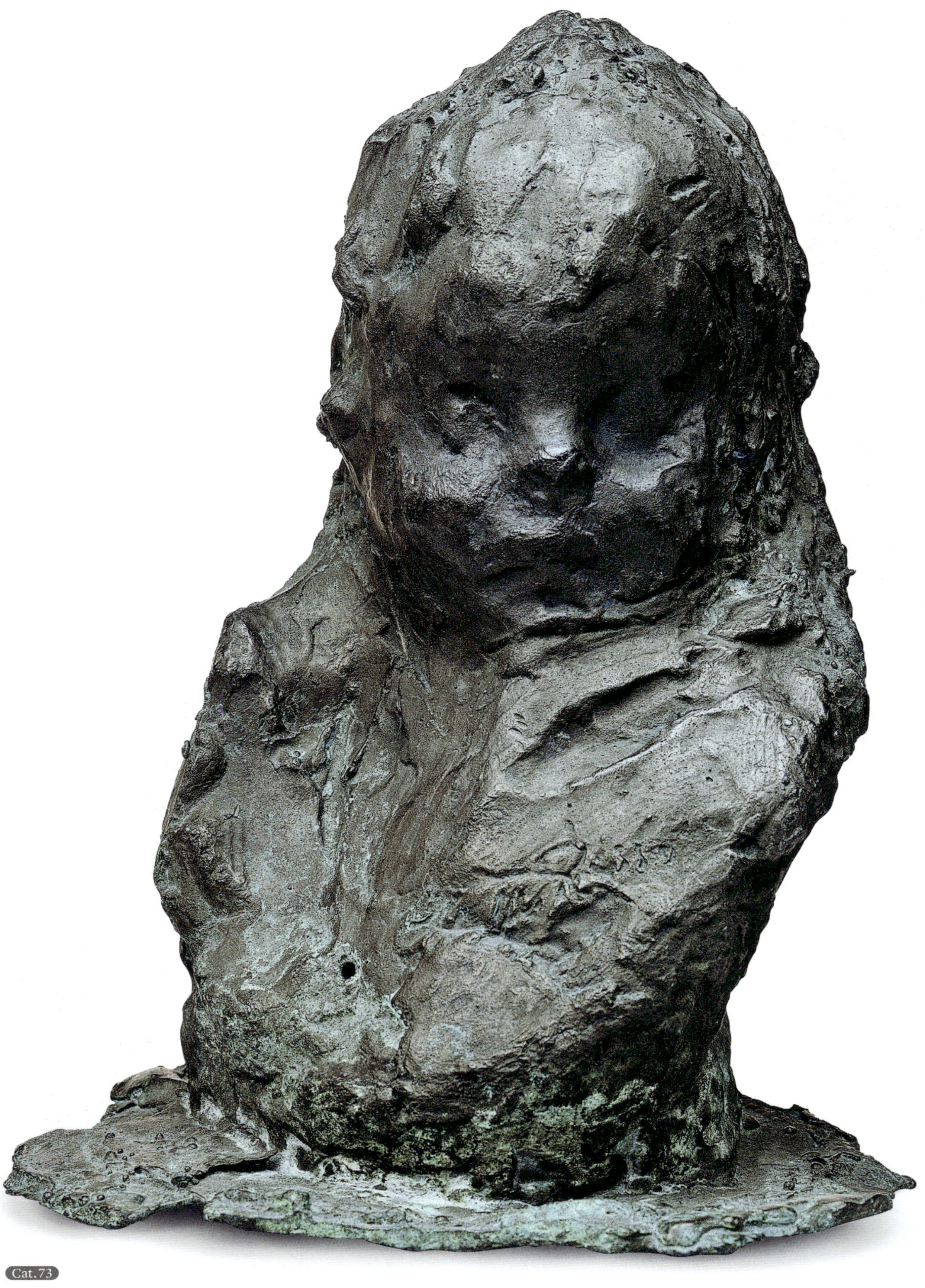

Cat. 73

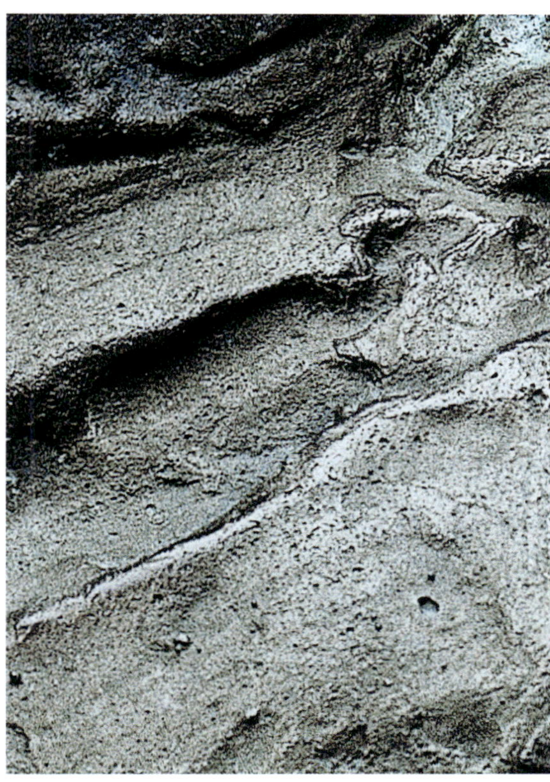

Cat.73 Detail

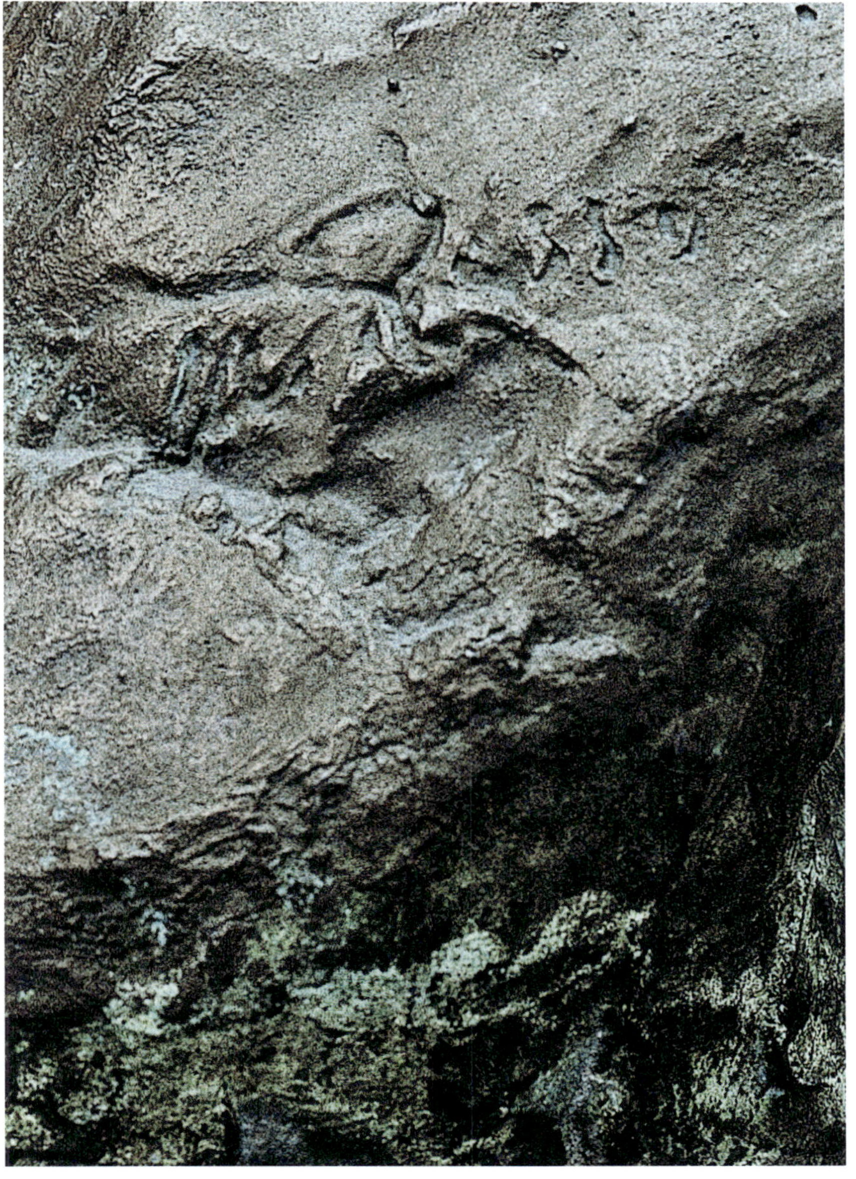

Spaces on paper

Drawing was of almost fateful importance to Medardo Rosso. Due to his overbold efforts allowing the use of live models (and dead animals) in drawing classes, his artistic training at the Accademia di Brera in Milan came to an abrupt end in 1883: he was expelled from the art school. Yet Rosso remained loyal to drawing all his life. In her description of his overall oeuvre, his biographer, Etha Fles, mentioned a "selection of very sensitive black-and-white drawings".[1] For many of the approximately 100 drawings that have survived, the context and date of their origin are vague, not least because the drawings are rarely directly related to the sculptures, which can often also not be precisely dated. They therefore continue to be exhibited or published without any details concerning their date of origin. However, there are indications for the dating of some groups of works – for instance, when the artist drew on the reverse sides of printed invitations or on envelopes, or when he used letterhead from a hotel in London, which can be linked with a stay there in 1896.[2] He also exhibited a few drawings in London in 1906.[3] In 1990, Luciano Caramel made the convenient attempt to carefully group the drawings according to motif and time-related aspects – a classification to which research continues to make reference to this day.[4] As casually as the drawings were probably executed, most of them are carefully monogrammed with "MR". And Rosso presumably took pictures of several of the drawings himself.

If one excludes his early body of works, several characteristics can be read out of Rosso's graphic oeuvre that in turn generally relate to the sculptural works. In drawing as well as sculpture, one central concern was the diffusion of figure and space combined with the dissolution of clearly recognisable, since clearly delimited, bodies.[5] This can be achieved through dispensing with the outline, which is the case for the pencil drawing *Figure on a Road* (cat. 75) as well as for the untitled work executed in the same technique (cat. 76). The figures originate solely by means of the respective extent of hatched areas without having been clearly delimited by an outline either beforehand or afterwards. Whereas Rosso at least specifies perspective through a steeply ascending diagonal line in the case of *Figure on a Road*, he limits its construction in the untitled drawing without any additional structure to the diagonal staggering and successive decrease in size of the figures. Inherent in both drawings is an exciting interplay between the concreteness of the object and that of the line and the paper.[6] At the same time, neither can the subject be separated from the surrounding space, nor can its depiction be detached from the material used. It is assumed that these street scenes originated in the Paris years around 1895 – hence the period during which Rosso worked on his sculptural group *Paris la nuit* and on *Femme à la voilette* (cat. 64, 66).[7]

The four landscapes shown here originated in a completely different context. Rosso's longstanding close confidante and patron Etha Fles had settled near Lake Geneva at the beginning of the First World War. The artist visited her multiple times there in 1916 and in

1917.[8] It was presumably during these sojourns that he devoted himself to drawing the landscape in the region. If one contemplates the two works *Country Road with Two Figures in the Foreground* (cat. 77) and *Mountain Landscape with Two Figures* (cat. 78), it becomes apparent that Rosso initially created the perspectival space by using a diagonal line that leads downwards to a supposed vanishing point. However, in both drawings he evidently pursues different interests in the further treatment of the space. Due to the hard cutting of the dyad at the front edge of the drawing and the steep sense of depth in *Country Road with Two Figures in the Foreground*, the space of the landscape extends far beyond the limits of the sheet into the sphere of the viewer. By contrast, in the drawing *Mountain Landscape with Two Figures*, Rosso integrates the full-figured couple rhythmically into the vegetation along a horizontal, merely varying the direction of the lines in the respective areas. The sequence parallel to the edge of the sheet offsets the arc ascending vigorously from the bottom left to the right again – the central-perspective space that was opened up gently concluding in the middle ground.

In the washed India ink drawing *Landscape with Bodies of Water* (cat. 79), Rosso keenly and loosely combines the geometric, horizontal–vertical structure with the layers that lie one on top of the other. Like a stage box, a dark border applied with a wide brush frames this impactful, mysterious spatial vision that radiates from the sheet's ground. Far apart from the concrete object, the materials used mostly seem to remain what they are: paper remains light, lines remain lines, areas remain areas.[9] Drawing with pen and brush is apparently the actual subject matter – the surface of the water merely the occasion for it. This reflection is reminiscent of Rosso's observations of a shadow that he experienced as physically as he did the individual casting it.[10] It is precisely these indirect aspects of figures and space that would become increasingly important in sculpture of the twentieth century.[11]

The pencil drawing *Landscape with Two Large Trees at the Right* (cat. 74) is no less enigmatic. There is a loose arrangement of more or less concentrated, hatched areas on the sheet's ground, much of which is left in its original state. The hand holding the brush repeatedly moved from the bottom left to the top right, creating the impression of hillsides – the work is thus referred to as a landscape. However, a concrete composition cannot be discerned. Analogous to Edgar Degas's pastel *Landscape (Falaise)* (cat. 42), this depiction can also be interpreted as a reclining female nude seen from behind if one compares it with the singular India ink drawing *Reclining Female Nude* (fig. 1).[12] The progression of the lines of the thighs, back and head bear a striking resemblance to the "progression of the landscape" in *Landscape with Two Large Trees at the Right*, although the ink version formulates the body more distinctly in its dramatic light-and-dark configuration. It is ultimately the tonal values that transform the depiction into a likeness – a likeness whose model is up for discussion.

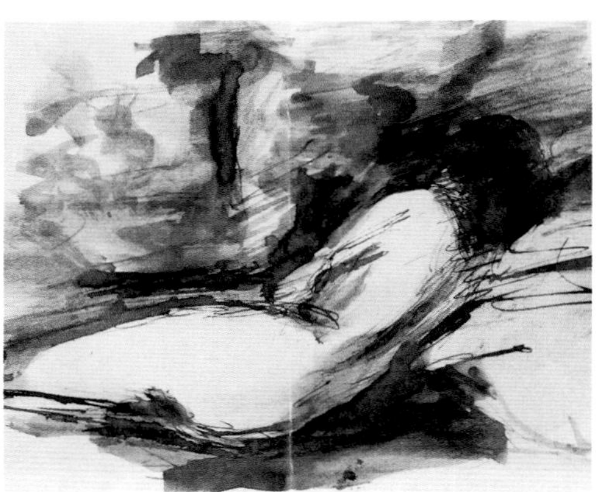

1 Medardo Rosso, *Reclining Female Nude*, after 1900, ink on paper, 53 × 58 cm, private collection

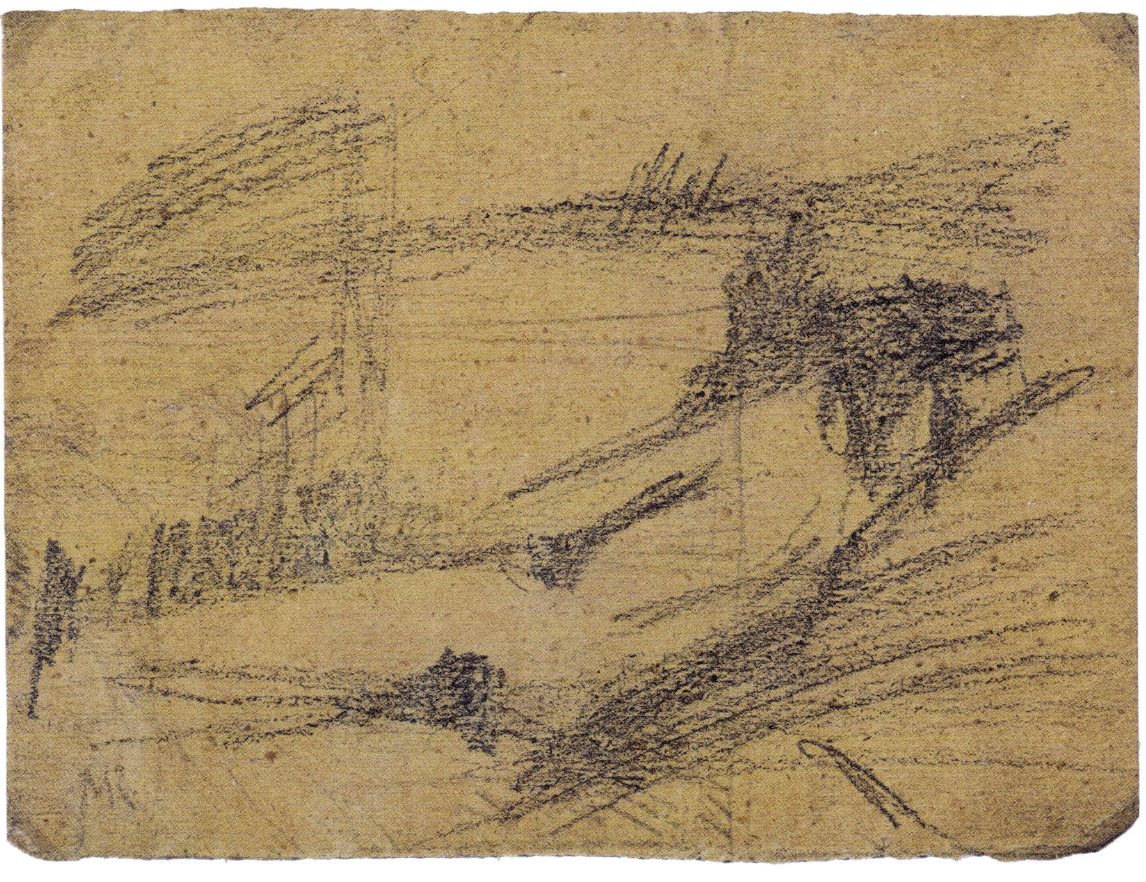

Cat. 74

Rosso's drawings also testify to his conception that nothing in space is material.[13] Perception cannot distinguish between a figure and its shadow. Yet Rosso not only perceived the object as radically transformed, but the space as well. He broke away from Euclidian geometry and instead worked with unmeasurable values, which also included voids and volumes in space.[14] The drawings, which frequently varied in terms of technique, served as a broad field of experimentation for his specific adaptation of the world. — EM-V

1   Fles 1922, p. 35.
2   Hauptman 2018, p. 73.
3   Exh. cat. London 2017, p. 69.
4   Exh. cat. Madrid 1990.
5   Nicolson 1994, p. 46.
6   Franz 2003, p. 180.
7   Exh. cat. Madrid 1990, p. 12.
8   Ibid., p. 16.
9   Franz 2003, p. 180.
10 See the essay by Eva Mongi-Vollmer in this catalogue, pp. 126–133, esp. p. 129.
11 On this, see, for example, the exhibition Negative Space: Trajectories of Sculpture, ZKM | Center for Art and Media Karlsruhe, 2019, (still) without a catalogue.
12 Exh. cat. Madrid 1990, p. 87, grapples with the date and sees it as having originated after the end of the First World War. Rosso had presented the drawing to Carlo Carrà, with whom the artist maintained close contact, particularly during his final years in Milan.
13 Claris 1902 (French), p. 55; not in Claris 1902a (German).
14 For more details on this, see De Sanna 1985; Boehm [1977] 2017.

Cat.75 Medardo Rosso, **Figure on a Road** (**Figura su strada**), undated; pencil on paper, 20 × 16 cm; signed bottom right: "MR"; Collection PCC, Switzerland

Cat.76 Medardo Rosso, Untitled, undated; pencil on paper, 17.5 × 13.5 cm; signed bottom right: "MR"; private collection

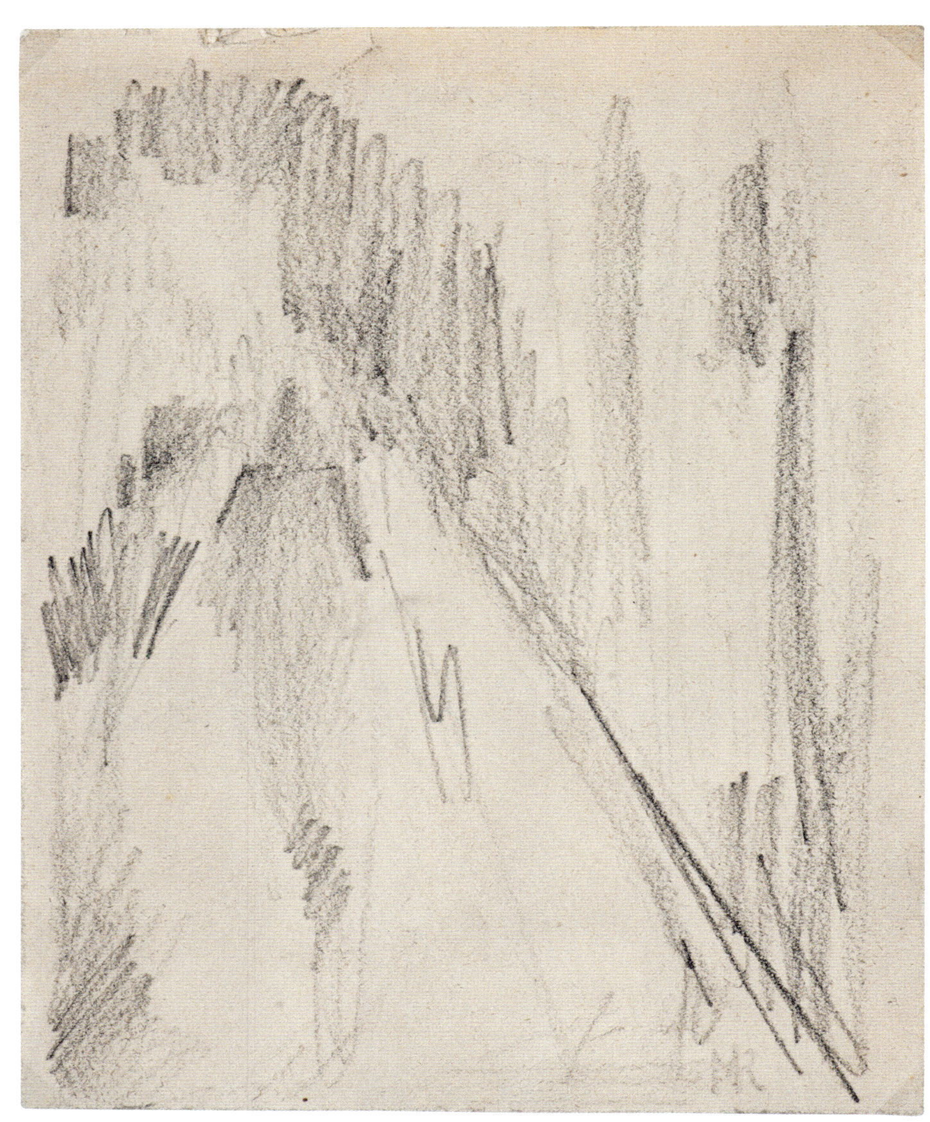

Cat.75

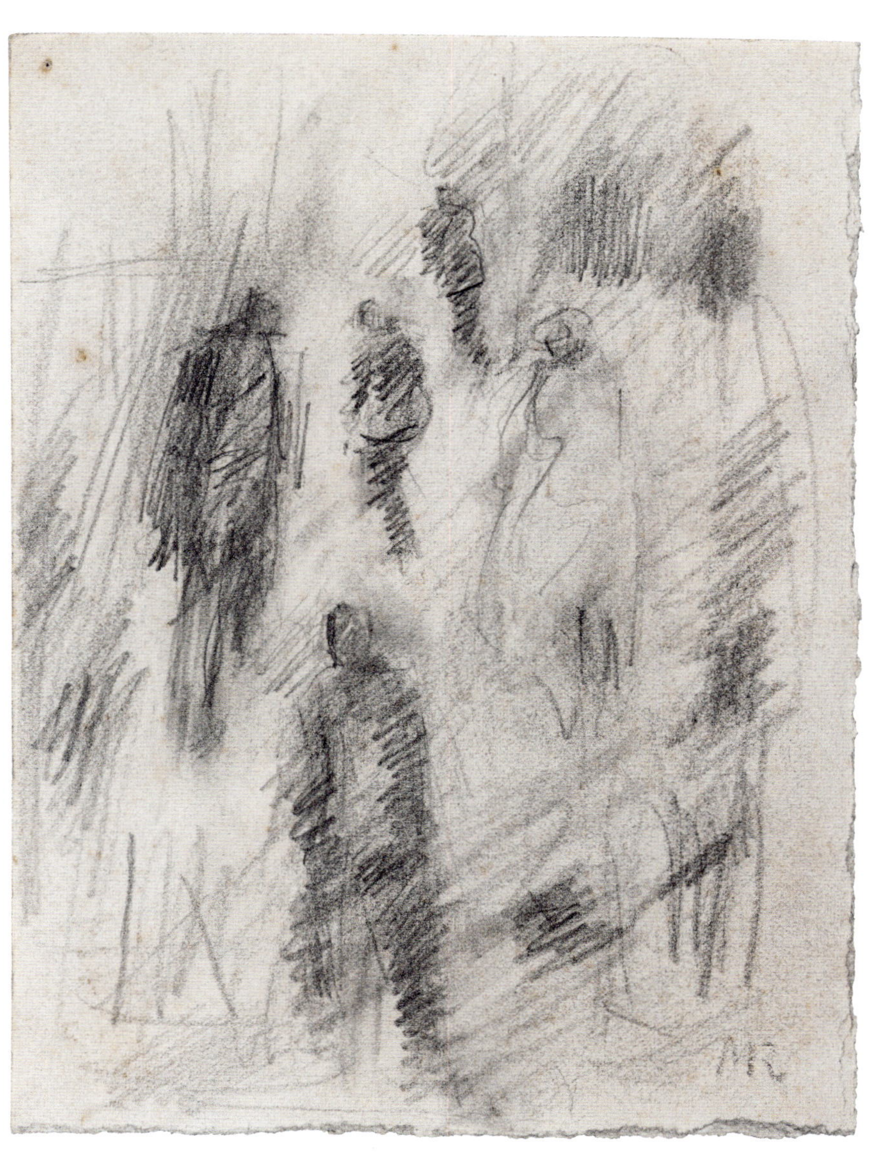

Cat. 76

Cat. 77 Medardo Rosso, Country Road with Two Figures in the Foreground (Strada di campagna con due figure in primo piano), c. 1916–1918; pencil on paper, 23 × 31 cm; signed bottom left: "MR"; Collection PCC, Switzerland Cat. 78 Medardo Rosso, Mountain Landscape with Two Figures (Paesaggio di montagna con due figure), c. 1916–1918; pencil on paper, 20.6 × 20.8 cm; signed bottom right: "MR"; Collection PCC, Switzerland Cat. 79 Medardo Rosso, Landscape with Bodies of Water (Paesaggio con specchio d'acqua), c. 1916–1918; washed India ink on paper, 18.9 × 27 cm; signed bottom right: "MR"; Collection PCC, Switzerland

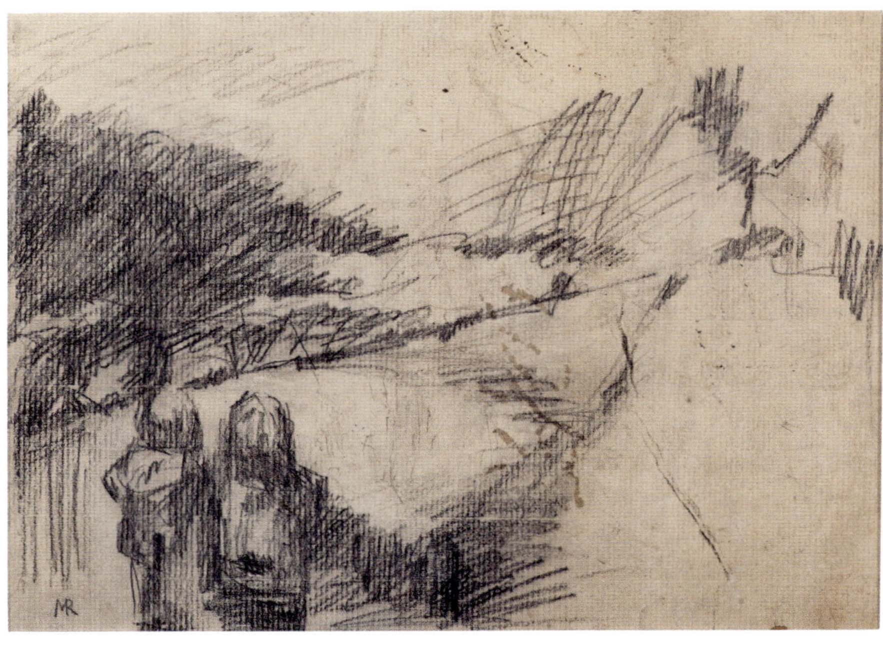

Cat. 77

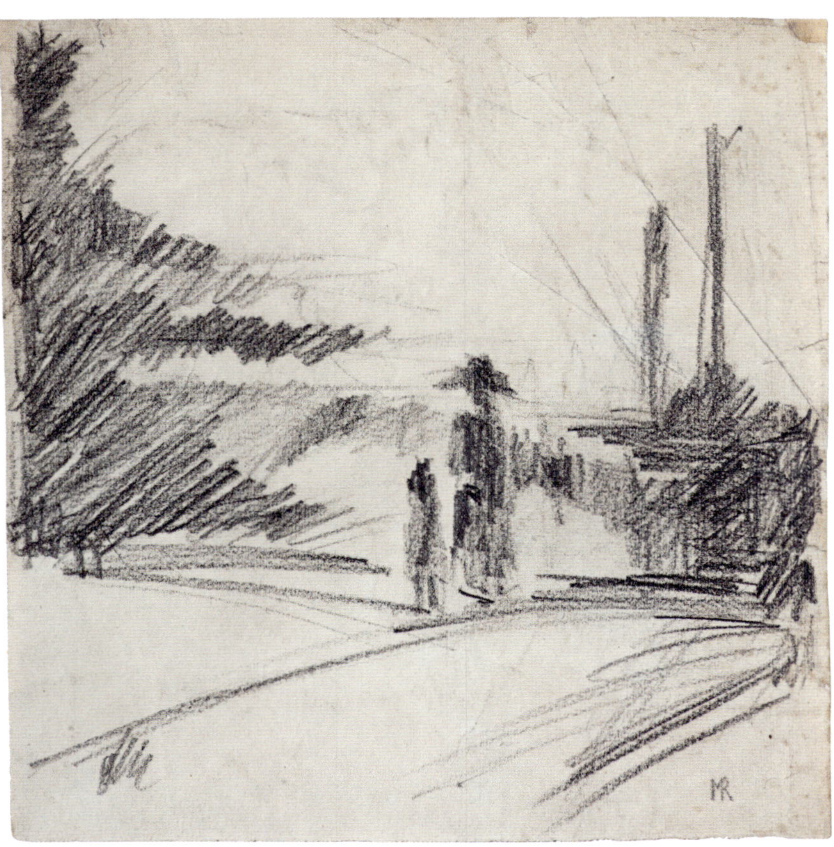

Cat. 78

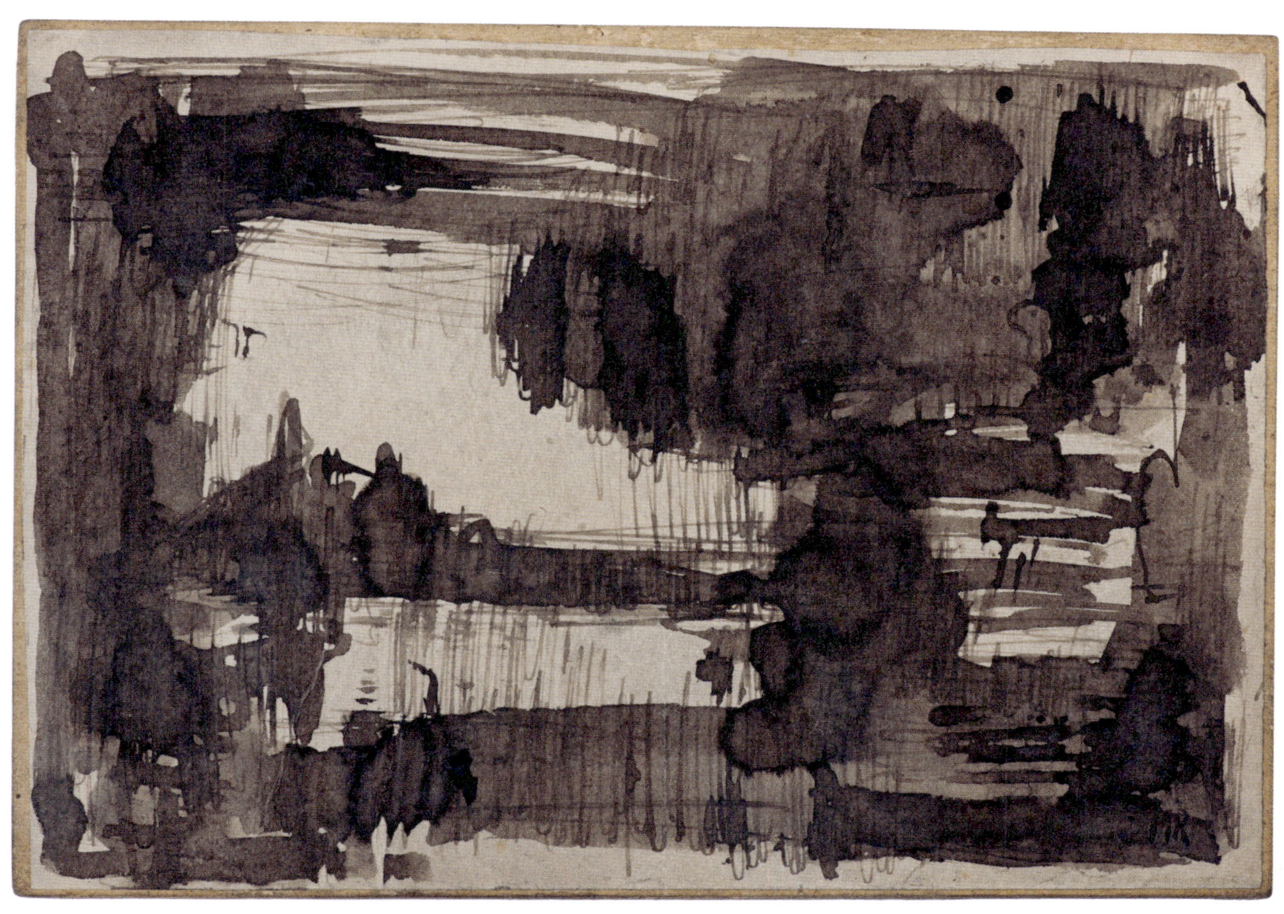

Cat. 79

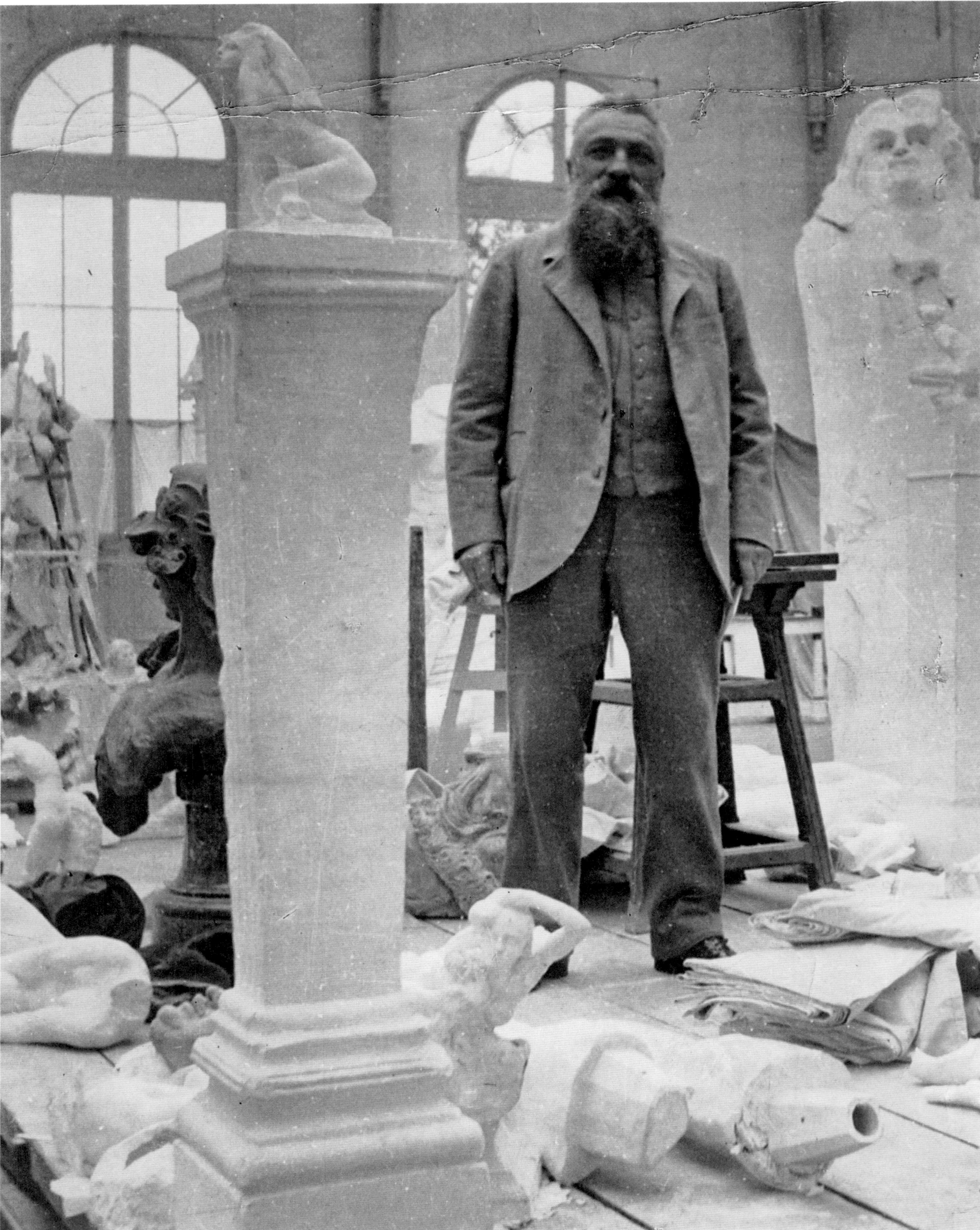

Auguste Rodin

Auguste Rodin

Auguste Rodin

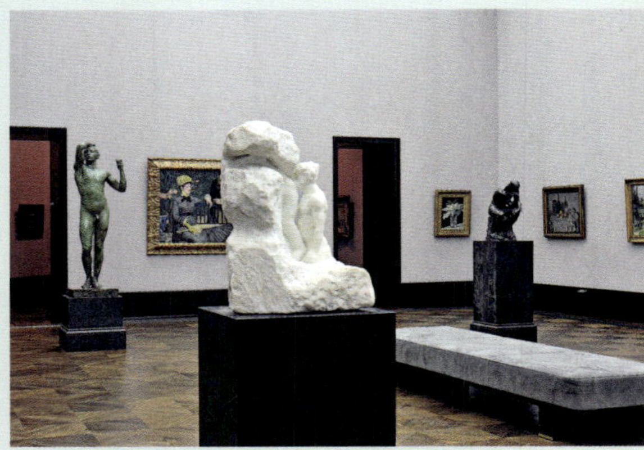

1 Auguste Rodin's *The Age of Bronze* (left) in the Alte Nationalgalerie, Berlin

Dominik Brabant

Auguste Rodin and Impressionism

Convergence and expressions of distance
in sculpture and painting

Auguste Rodin (1840–1917) and Impressionism: this is not a relationship that can be easily understood by drawing on common art historical concepts such as that of artistic influence.[1] On the basis of this premise, the question of the chronology, scope and legitimacy of classifying Rodin as an Impressionist artist will be posed in the following – namely, in view of three important stages in his artistic career in which the perception of his oeuvre was more or less expressly characterised by this artistic movement. In order to trace Rodin's connections to Impressionism, it makes sense to not only inquire into his concrete ties to the circle of Impressionists as well as into his motifs, but above all to focus on the materials he used and the aesthetic effects associated with them. For contemporary art criticism – as well as for later generations of art historians – these were key criteria for their assessments. Beforehand, however, some light shall be shed on the multifaceted and surely ambivalent connections between the sculptor and Impressionism, whereby both artistic-aesthetic as well as historical-biographical aspects will be taken into account.

Rodin in the circle of the Impressionists?
Convergence, distinction and ambivalent (self-)assessments

In some museums that focus on art of the nineteenth century, such as the Musée d'Orsay in Paris or the Alte Nationalgalerie in Berlin, the public encounters Rodin's bronze sculpture *The Age of Bronze* (1875–77) in rooms that are devoted to Impressionism (fig. 1). This curatorial setting is by all means consistent: just as Rodin demanded processual perception from his viewers with his often precariously positioned figures and, in most cases, their restless surface, it is generally known that the Impressionists were likewise concerned with the presentation of a new type of vision and expression that simultaneously aimed at momentariness and animation.[2] In fact, Rodin worked on rendering an image of the world and of man that was characterised by transitoriness not only in this early sculpture, but in his entire artistic corpus – from his main works such as *The Burghers of Calais* (of 1884; cat. 80–84) to his nude drawings done with rapid lines and small quantities of colour glazes, from the little-known landscape paintings in the style of the Barbizon painters of the 1870s to his statuettes of male and female dancers, with which the artist sought to capture their artistic figures of movement.[3]

Besides such fundamental aesthetic parallels between Rodin's works and Impressionist painting, there are further connections: when, for instance, Émile Zola – as one of the most prominent advocates of Impressionist painting –

understood the impasto applied to the canvas with a brush as nothing less than the material trace of the artistic temperament,[4] one can definitely compare such a conception of the creative artistic process with that of Rodin, who neither smoothed away nor otherwise hid the traces of his own work on the surface of his clay, plaster and bronze sculptures. This allowed those who viewed Rodin's finished works to also share in the sculptor's subjective appropriation of reality, which took place in the dialogue between eye and hand, between the perception of a model and its shaping in the artistic material. This also holds true for the bronze casts, although in this case the tool marks in the material were shifted into the distance due to the process of translating the sculptures from model into finished cast (cat. 89–94).[5] As an art history that is more critical towards modernist myths has reiterated since the 1980s, the emphasis on originality and single-handedness so characteristic of Rodin thus came into conflict with the fundamental reproducibility of bronze sculptures.[6] Yet it is precisely these casts whose assignment to Impressionism seems most promising. This is due not least to the specific quality of the material, which lends itself to the creation of an exciting play of shimmering light reflexes and dark shadow areas. In terms of its aesthetic effect, this in turn corresponds with the Impressionist preference for the painterly depiction of foliage suffused with light and colourfully animated crowds as found in numerous landscapes and cityscapes.[7] It is therefore no wonder that Rodin's bronze sculptures in particular have been assigned to a broadly defined concept of Impressionism in some overviews on the history of modern statuary. In a chapter on "Impressionism and Sculpture" in Jean Selz's study *Modern Sculpture: Origins and Evolution* (1963), for example, 12 of a total of 18 black-and-white illustrations feature bronzes.[8]

The impression that Rodin's bronze sculptures are akin to Impressionism is further confirmed by a comparison with his marble sculptures, no less famous. As is commonly known, the artist had most of these executed by assistants. The translucent effect of the white marble was intended to evoke a dreamy, transfigured atmosphere. These works consequently radiate little of the animation or even nervousness so characteristic of the bronze sculptures; rather, they are used to stage, in an often even Symbolist pictorial language, metamorphoses from stone to flesh, from unenlivened to seemingly enlivened matter, from stages of solidness to fluidness, and finally from material weight to their transcendence into an emotional spirituality (fig. 2).[9]

Distinctions also appear to make sense in another respect, especially in comparison with the sculptural works by Edgar Degas and Medardo Rosso. Unlike Degas, whose works were regularly represented at the Impressionist exhibitions mounted since 1874 and who in this context presented his notorious sculpture of a *Little Dancer Aged Fourteen* (cat. 4) in 1881,[10] Rodin did not associate at the time with the circle of ever-changing artists who participated in the exhibitions.[11] In fact, Rodin probably would not meet the sculptor Claude Monet, the one of whom he was nearest to, until around 1885.[12] The reason for the late initiation of this contact is first of all of a biographical nature: whereas Rodin belonged to the same generation as some of the most prominent Impressionists, during the heyday of their group exhibitions in the 1870s he spent most of his time in Brussels and not in Paris. For a young sculptor who depended on official commissions for his costly works, the working situation was far from easy, not least in the wake of the Franco-German War. In order to be able to support his family, Rodin took on employment with, among others, Albert-Ernest Carrier-Belleuse and subsequently performed decorative sculptural work on buildings in Belgium.[13]

However, what is more important than such biographical constellations is the fact that even in later years, when he was already regarded as a successful artist, Rodin evidently placed a great deal of value on not being publicly perceived as an

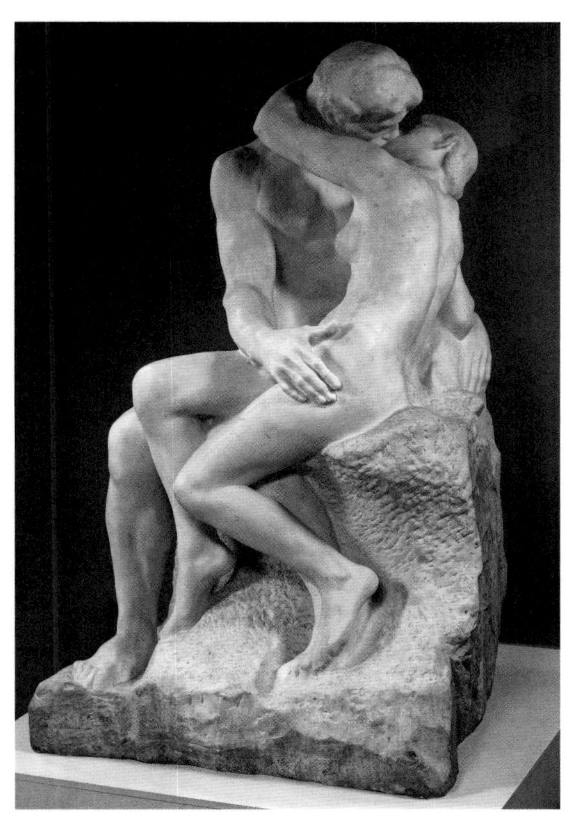

2 Auguste Rodin, *The Kiss*, c. 1882, marble version from 1888/89, 181.5 × 112.5 × 117 cm, Musée Rodin, Paris

Impressionist sculptor. This becomes particularly apparent in Edmond Claris's book entitled *De l'Impressionnisme en sculpture,* published in 1902, which had already been preceded by an essay for the *Nouvelle Revue* the year before.[14] In the essay, Claris took up the discussion about the rival "Impressionist" sculptors Rodin and Rosso[15] that had been smouldering since 1898 and assembled columns by the most important sculptors, Impressionist artists and art-critic elite at the time. In both Claris's introductory essay as well as in Rodin's own commentary, it is not Manet, Monet or Degas who are mentioned as references for Rodin's sculptural approach, but rather the art of antiquity from the Egyptians and Greeks to the Romans, on the one hand, and, on the other hand, long-gone masters who belong to the art historical canon, such as Michelangelo and Rembrandt (in Rodin's commentary), Jean-Baptiste Carpeaux, François Rude and Jean-Antoine Houdon (in Claris).

Although Rodin does not provide any information about possible connections in this publication, even so, his statement on the artistic maxims that were important to him gives us a sense of a certain elective affinity to these – namely, in that he expressly claims the method of appropriating reality artistically for himself that the Impressionists had already established earlier, and which, as mentioned above, was introduced into the debate of art criticism, most forcibly by Zola. Thus, Rodin emphasises the subjective perception of nature necessary for his sculptural practice, for which only the artist's own temperament, specific sensitivity and current state of mind are to be regarded as gauges of artistic interpretation.[16] The ambitious art critic Gustave Geffroy, whose commentary follows Rodin's, confirms this line of interpretation by, on the one hand, describing Rodin as a revolutionary who courageously broke with academic sculpture; on the other hand, however, he also called him a classic sculptor of his times and placed him in a direct line of tradition with ancestors that reached back far into the past, such as Michel Colombe, Jean Goujon or Germain Pilon, who were active in the fifteenth and sixteenth centuries. In more modern times, only few sculptors carry on this line – Jean-Baptiste Carpeaux, for instance. Yet Geffroy also suggested parallels between Rodin and the Impressionists, at least when he mentions Claude Monet, Pierre-Auguste Renoir, Camille Pissarro and other artists and describes Rodin's drawings as the results of an artistic search for truth comparable to their aspirations. Similar to the Impressionists, for Rodin it was also a question of the adequate portrayal of a reality that was vibrant and animated all along and, at the same time, invariably fugitive.[17]

A look at the conversation with Rodin that Paul Gsell published in 1911 under the title of *L'Art* also confirms the impression that Rodin deliberately remained silent about his relationship with Impressionism. Once again, one does not find any direct reference to Impressionism or to Impressionist painters or sculptors, whereas there is indeed mention of a realist like Gustave Courbet or a sculptor like Aimé-Jules Dalou, who today is generally regarded as a realist or naturalist.[18] This decidedly distant stance, however, markedly distinguishes Rodin from Rosso, who art critics explicitly assigned to sculptural Impressionism as early as 1886 and who also shared this classification. Research therefore deliberated whether Rodin did not perhaps so vehemently repudiate being classified as such in order to elude the competitive situation with the Italian sculptor that escalated in the years around 1900.[19]

Beyond these aspects of artistic self-fashioning, objective reasons also speak for characterising Rodin's references to the Impressionist movement as a relationship between both proximity and distance, as the cosmos of motifs he created is certainly more protean, perhaps even more heterogeneous than that of the Impressionist painters.[20] A brief glance at *The Gates of Hell* (fig. 3) suffices to illustrate this aspect.[21] Admittedly, it is correct that the composition of the surface of this monumental sculpture can initially be perceived as a flickering, restless texture in the posthumously rendered bronze version and that the work's tendency

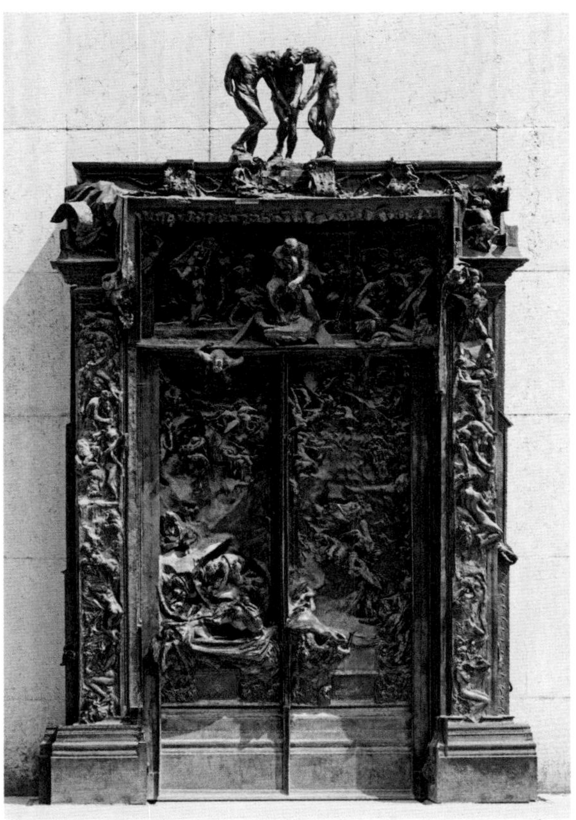

3 Auguste Rodin, *The Gates of Hell,* after 1880, cast 1928, bronze, 635 × 400 × 85 cm, Musée Rodin, Paris

towards the dissolution of form corresponds with an Impressionist concept of painting. However, unlike the Impressionists, Rodin did not exactly consider himself to be bound to a depiction of modern everyday reality and to the social types in nineteenth-century Paris, which becomes particularly apparent based on this work.[22] With his predominately unclothed figures, he rather aimed at lending his personal perspective a vividness that came across as a timeless *conditio humana*. Allusions to the contemporary or even to *la vie moderne,* as Charles Baudelaire developed in 1863 using the example of Constantin Guys, would have more likely hindered the achievement of such an aim.[23] It was in *The Gates of Hell* in particular that Rodin pursued a rather "un-Impressionist" desire to revisit traditional motifs and iconographic sources – in this case, Dante's *Divina Commedia*.[24] As early as 1900, Anatole France recognised that with this work, Rodin had begun a radically pessimistic meditation on the timeless destiny of humankind that was remote from the belief in progress espoused by numerous Impressionists. For the writer, the figures in *The Gates to Hell* were embodiments of a human race thrown back on its insatiable erotic appetite as well as its physical conditionality.[25]

After all, Rodin was remarkably critical of the new media of the time – in particular, of so-called chronophotography. Owing to inventions by Étienne-Jules Marey and Eadweard Muybridge, from the 1870s it was possible to depict complex sequences of movement in their individual elements for the first time. Rodin told Gsell that employing this technique only enabled observing the movement of humans or animals in its respective intervals. Yet as a consequence, the photographed individual appears to be frozen in a particular pose, indeed, veritably petrified. Thus, it was the task of the traditional genre of sculpture to illustrate the duration of a sequence of movements – and not just a moment frozen in time – within a single representation.[26]

If one takes a look at art historical reception from Rodin's explicit or implicit distance markings with respect to Impressionism, it becomes apparent that his self-confident aspiration of being perceived as a sculptor beyond the various "isms" was subsequently taken up by numerous art historians in the twentieth century. Authors such as Albert E. Elsen, Rosalind Krauss, Penelope Curtis or Alex Potts successfully stylised Rodin into the "father of modern sculpture", whereby his connections to Impressionism appear to be irrelevant.[27]

By contrast, in her study of sculpture in Paris between 1905 and 1914, published in 2017, Catherine Chevillot also explicitly addresses the question of the sustainability of the concept of Impressionist sculpture and statuary – and in the process arrived at a rather unequivocal assessment: Whereas, in her opinion, assigning Rosso to Impressionism is definitely accurate, since he (like Monet and Pissarro) was primarily concerned with rendering ephemeral phenomena visible as well as staging a fluid sense of perception, Rodin does not fall into this category. She justifies this not only with the publicly effective expression of his distance vis-à-vis this style, but first and foremost with the various opinions of each one of the artists regarding the role of light for the overall sculptural effect: Rosso caused his works to appear to be thoroughly dematerialised with the aid of the incidence of light and its reflection or absorption by the material, whereas Rodin preferred to use light effects to achieve heightened expressivity.[28] This distinction is as appropriate as it is understandable. Yet such a broad exclusion of Rodin from the extensive field of Impressionist art can cause all of those aspects of his creative work that bear a relation to this movement, however remote or indirect, to be all to quickly overlooked.

For this reason, in view of art history's rather inconsistent evaluation of Rodin, three pivotal moments from his career shall be highlighted in which something like the sculptor's convergence towards an Impressionist conception of art appears to become apparent, or where art criticism suggests such convergence.

Auguste Rodin

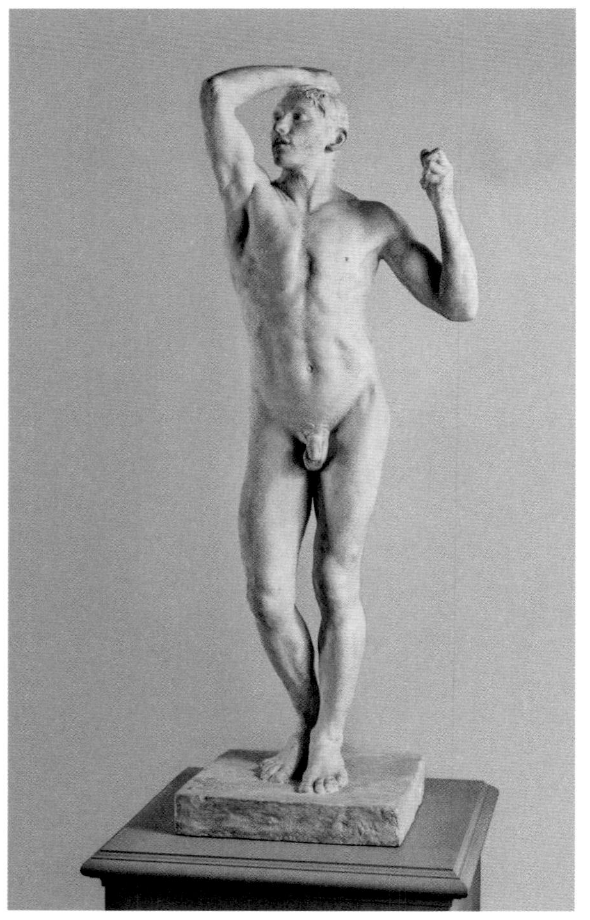

4 Auguste Rodin, *The Age of Bronze*, 1875–77, plaster from 1898, 180 × 71.1 × 58.4 cm, National Gallery of Art, Washington D.C., Gift of Iris and B. Gerald Cantor, In Honour of the 50th Anniversary of the National Gallery of Art

Impressionism as the withdrawal of meaning?
The Age of Bronze in the mirror of contemporary art criticism (1877)

Rodin's breakthrough as a successful sculptor came relatively late. The artist, born in 1840, did not receive his first commission for a major government-initiated project, namely *The Gates of Hell,* until 1880.[29] Prior to that, his career as an artist had been marked by many a bitter setback; failing three times to be accepted into the École des Beaux-Arts to study art was particularly painful.[30] In addition, in 1877, he had to endure an art scandal created by wary critics on the occasion of the exhibition of his first nearly life-size sculpture, *The Age of Bronze* (fig. 4). In light of the plaster version shown at the Cercle artistique et littéraire in Brussels, an anonymous reviewer for the *Étoile belge* insinuated that the artist had possibly used the method of casting the work directly from a living model.[31] That same year, Rodin presented the sculpture at the Salon in Paris. Similar suspicions concerning its production were again voiced on the part of art critics. Charles Tardieu, for instance, wrote in *L'Art* that whereas the rumours about Rodin were baseless, in view of the almost slavishly mimetic reproduction of the natural model they were definitely understandable to a certain extent.[32] Rodin subsequently made an effort to get the state to acquire the work and in 1880 organised a commission of experts to convince themselves of the impeccable production of the sculpture. In a letter to the undersecretary of state Edmond Turquet, sculptors such as Henri Chapu, Alexandre Falguière and Carrier-Belleuse supported Rodin's cause, since in their opinion a casting process did not come into use.[33]

As the comments made by art critics on the occasion of the first exhibition in 1877 show, for the somewhat confounded public, those aspects of the sculpture that one might in hindsight understand as typically "Impressionist" – for example, the highly differentiated non-classic shaping of the work's surface without discernible distinctions between the individual body areas or the precarious ponderation of the stationary motif – did not predominate at first. Their reactions were initially determined by the motif-related vagueness of the figure, which on its first presentation was still called *The Vanquished* and later bore, among others, the titles *The Awakening Man* and *The Man of the First Ages*. In an early stage of the production process, before it was presented publicly, the figure, for whom a Belgian soldier named Auguste Neyt had acted as a model, still held a spear in its left hand. With this attribute, one could have seen the nude motif less problematically as a slightly melancholy allegory of France's loss of the war.[34] Thus, the informed Salon public might have interpreted it as an antipode to Antonin Mercié's triumphant *David* (fig. 5) with his foot on Goliath's head, a sculpture that enjoyed major success when it was exhibited in 1872.[35]

For the critics, the disturbing impression of vibrancy that seemed to radiate from the plaster figure was no less problematical than the motif-related ambiguity. This was not only the starting point for the accusation that it was cast from a living model, but also confronted the viewer with a new type of sculptural physicality and immediacy. In this case, entrenched interpretations of art that inquired into established motifs or anecdotal elements did not contribute to understanding it.[36] On behalf of their public, so to speak, art critics attempted to gain access to this new form of sculptural expression in various ways – for instance, by reducing the sculpture to a mere preparatory study[37] or declaring it to be a demonstration of realism inspired by antiquity.[38]

To put it bluntly, during these years Rodin's artistic strategy therefore consisted in the art of omission, or more precisely, in dispensing with traditional attributes as well as academic body images. From today's point of view, these aspects of his work may only to a limited extent appear to be elements of a genuinely Impressionist art. Yet they lead to the heart of the discussion about Rodin as an Impressionist sculptor *avant la lettre* as it took place in the years after 1900. Claris, whose above-mentioned publication already shifted Rodin and Rosso into the spotlight, defined Impressionist painting not only based on the fact that artists understood how to commit the atmospheric light conditions to the canvas with the use of a new colour palette and an apparently spontaneous brushstroke; rather, for him the artistic revolution of this movement consisted primarily in the fact that the Impressionist painters had departed from traditional aesthetic conventions in order to break with the coldness and rigidity of academic art with its fixed tradition-oriented repertoire of motifs.[39] Similarly, with Rodin and Rosso one was also entering a "period of pure creation" to the extent that those artists drew their inspiration exclusively from nature and from themselves.[40] Rodin's twofold strategy of a motif-related, iconographic obscuration of his figures while simultaneously emphasising the lifelike singularity of the body being portrayed could, by analogy, therefore be understood together with the compositional methods of Impressionist art.

From Realism and Naturalism to Impressionism: Rodin between the Salon and the exhibition scene

With an approach comparable to his first scandalous work, Rodin presented his energetically striding but now slightly larger-than-life *Saint John the Baptist* (cat. 103) in a plaster version (National Gallery of Art, Washington D.C.) in 1880. The sculptor once more dispensed with traditional attributes such as the lamb, the cross-staff or the banderol that reads "Ecce agnus dei". Rodin again positioned himself in trenchant contrast to older and more conventional notions, including that of a young Saint John by Paul Dubois (fig. 6), which had been exhibited at the Salon of 1864.[41]

However, beginning in 1882 a significant shift in the reception of Rodin's sculptures became apparent that was set in motion by open-minded critics. This journalistic advocacy of the sculptor paved the way for the assignment of his work to Impressionism, even though this term was not mentioned itself. Moreover, critics such as Philippe Burty or Louis de Fourcaud wrote mostly positive reviews of the work that had been produced since 1878, but also of the portrait bust of the artist *Jean-Paul Laurens* (fig. 7), exhibited for the first time in Paris in 1882. Yet now one was increasingly interested in Rodin's innovative accentuation of the arousal that became apparent in the figures' facial features and muscle fibres, which suggested heightened awareness or concentration. At the same time, they emphasised the bold individuality of Rodin's sculptures – in particular, his achievement of having uncompromisingly represented Saint John the Baptist's physical tension and nervous energy, contrary to academic rules.[42] Burty deliberately distinguished Rodin from academic eclecticism.[43] Louis de Fourcaud, however, also explicitly characterised Rodin's sculptural pursuit of the truth as "modern".[44] At the same time, Rodin's works were now increasingly being interpreted on the horizon of a realist and naturalist concept of art. Burty, for example, attempted to identify an artistic filiation for Rodin's novel imagery and placed what the artist referred to as his naturalistic work in the tradition of the likes of François Rude, David d'Angers or Antoine-Augustin Préault, whom one would today certainly assign to the different varieties of Romanticism.[45]

In the course of the 1880s, critics such as Octave Mirbeau[46] and Gustave Geffroy,[47] who are now regarded as prominent champions of Impressionism, advanced to become emphatic proponents of Rodin's art. At this time, the nascent sculpture *The Gates of Hell,* which still largely escaped public view, was increasingly becoming an object of fascination in the press. The art critics disclosed the first details about it in 1881.[48] After Rodin had presented individual figures from the range of motifs for *The Gates of Hell* in exhibitions (e.g. in *Exposition des arts libéraux*

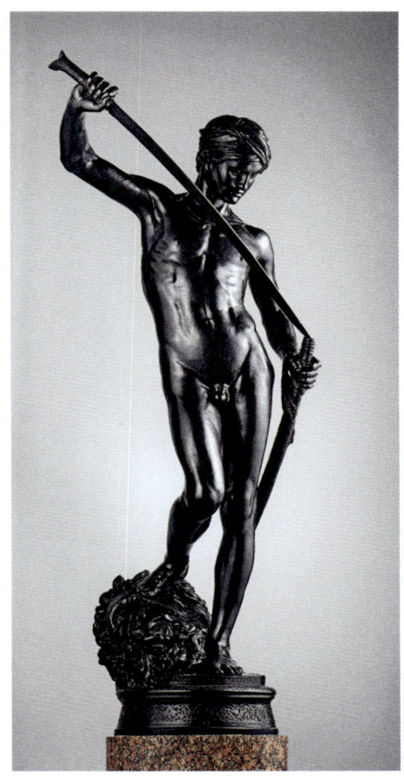

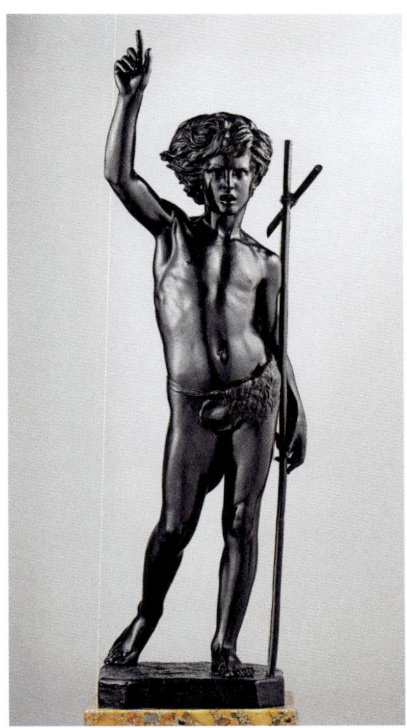

5 Antonin Mercié, *David,* c. 1872, bronze, 84.1 × 76.8 × 83.2 cm, Musée d'Orsay, Paris

6 Paul Dubois, *Saint John the Baptist as a Child,* 1861, bronze, 163 × 58 × 64 cm, Musée d'Orsay, Paris

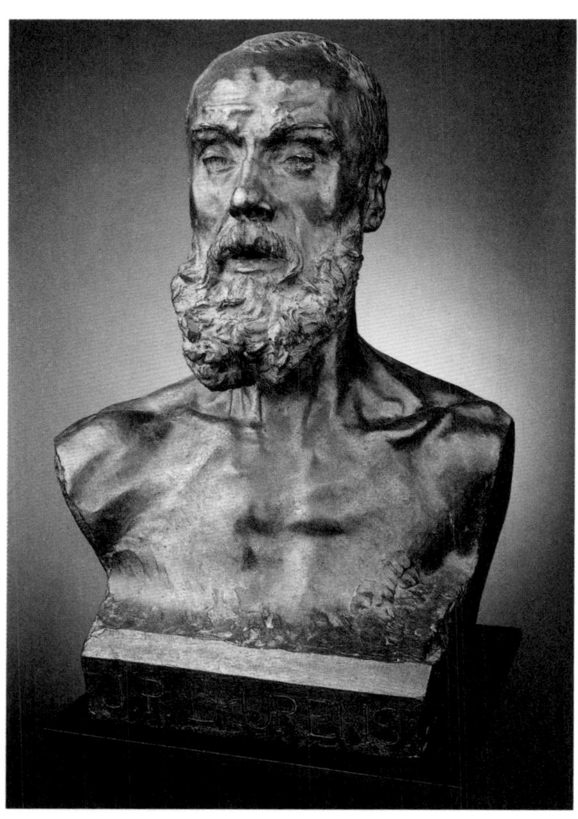

7 Auguste Rodin, *Jean-Paul Laurens*, 1882, bronze, 37 × 58 × 33 cm, Musée des Augustins, Musée des Beaux-Arts, Toulouse

in Rue Vivienne in Paris in 1883), a first description of it, written by Mirbeau for the journal *La France,* was published in 1885.[49] By contrast, a direct comparison of Rodin's works with Impressionist painting became possible in 1889 – namely, on the occasion of the exhibition organised to take place concurrent with the 1889 Exposition universelle with 36 works by the sculptor in plaster, bronze and marble in conjunction with 145 paintings by Monet at Georges Petit's gallery. Mirbeau wrote the opening essay on Monet,[50] while Geffroy penned the one on Rodin: he connected the artist's works with the art doctrine of naturalism and the compositional methods of Impressionism – but did not mention the term.[51]

In his essay, Geffroy introduced, among other things, a new way of looking at *The Gates of Hell,* which was not presented in the exhibition in its entirety but for which individual figures, such as what is now the famous *Thinker,* stood in its place, so to speak.[52] At this point in time, one could also already view the still unfinished *The Gates of Hell* in Rodin's studio, as documented in a photograph taken by William Elborne.[53] For example, there is an entry in Edmond de Goncourt's *Journal* in 1886 in which he gives an account of a visit to Rodin's studio and describes the aesthetic impression of amorphous animation that the work had left on him.[54] In any case, in his line of argumentation Geffroy placed particular emphasis on Rodin's unacademic approach.[55] For the sculptor, Dante's text simply provided the requisite framework within which Rodin's "tragic and complex representation of nature and life"[56] could be given complete expression in a universal validity that outlasted the ages. The sculptor succeeded in liberating the literary original from its historical context and in doing so render it all-embracing. This is followed by the observation that Rodin's *The Thinker* was not, as Mirbeau had stressed in an earlier article,[57] to be understood first and foremost as a portrait of Dante. Rather, he was an unclothed poet who "wore none of the signs that would allow recognising an epoch or a nationality".[58] Moreover, with the numerous individual figures in *The Gates of Hell* Rodin sought to bring home a "physiological humanity in its various actions" to his public.[59] When Geffroy then explicitly compares the sculptor to a scientist, for whose activity observational accuracy and an objective representation of what one has seen are imperative, he hardly conceals his sympathy for the ideal image of the naturalistic and subsequently even Impressionist artist as Émile Zola had conceptualised him in his work *Le Roman Expérimental* of 1880.[60]

Impressionism as an epochal phenomenon: stages of Rodin's historicisation after 1900

Even after the turn of the century and following the retrospective at the Place de l'Alma in 1900 that Rodin himself organised, his work was associated with Impressionism – and above all in German-language criticism. Rodin opened his exhibition in a pavilion (which he had built for this purpose and later had reconstructed at his estate in Meudon) barely six weeks after the beginning of the world's fair. He could therefore reckon with an international public that could acquire an extensive overview of his work on this occasion.[61]

At the same time, Rainer Maria Rilke's monograph on Rodin, begun in 1902 and published in 1903, would soon set the tone for an image of the sculptor oriented around a philosophy of life.[62] Whereas Rilke warned his readership against prematurely assigning Rodin's sculptures to Impressionism, just several lines later he rated his portrait drawings as a "wealth of material", namely insofar as they offered the attentive viewer's eye an "abundance of impressions [...] collected with [...] precision and boldness".[63] Similarly, in view of Rodin's innovative aesthetic of the fragmentary, the poet noted the originally hostile reactions by the public, most notably those to the armless statue *The Inner Voice (Meditation)*, and related this scepticism with the public's initial lack of understanding with which they responded

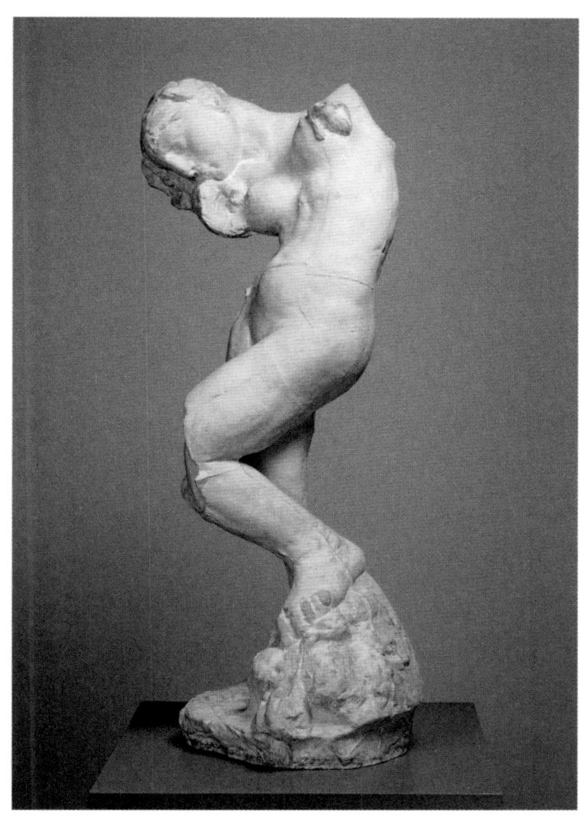

8   Auguste Rodin, *The Inner Voice (Meditation)*, 1886,
plaster, 149.5 × 70 × 60 cm, Staatliche Kunstsammlungen
Dresden, Albertinum

to "the way the Impressionists cut trees off at the edges of paintings" in the 1870s and 1880s. Similarly, today it is merely a sign of "petty pedantry" if one assumes "that a body without arms can never be whole" (fig. 8).[64]

With respect to such references to Impressionism, in other passages Rilke sought to approximate Rodin's art to Impressionism without explicitly labelling him as a proponent of this movement. One leitmotif in his line of argumentation is Rodin's solitude early in his career: like the Impressionists, albeit without the support of a sworn group of artists, he had to find his way to an artistic language of his own, beyond the reliable structures of an official art system, as an "unknown, his hands searching blindly for bread".[65]

In order to substantiate Rodin's heroic battle against academic norms, Rilke also went into the mask of *Man with a Broken Nose* of 1863/64 (cat. 89), Rodin's earliest submission to the Salon, which also exhibits the facial features of a proletarian by the name of Bibi as well as those of Michelangelo, and which was promptly rejected by the Salon jury.[66] Rilke invoked the sculpture's impact on the viewer by pointing out the numerous irregularities on the work's surface, hence the famous *modelé*, and the light reflexes it elicited: "The fullness of life is gathered in these features, and there are absolutely no symmetrical planes on the face. Nothing is repeated, no spot remains empty, mute, or neutral." Rilke continued: "Holding this mask and turning it slowly, one can't help but be astonished by the constantly changing profiles, none of which are in any way uncertain, incidental, or indefinite."[67] Nearly 40 years in retrospect, the poet inscribed the work into the history of that anti-academic portraiture as emphatically as it was, however with a different accentuation, also pursued by the Impressionists.[68]

One such understanding of Rodin's contribution to the artistic mentality and work of Impressionism then found expression in the exhibition *Entwicklung des Impressionismus in Malerei und Plastik* (The Development of Impressionism in Painting and Sculpture) mounted by the Vienna Secession in 1903 (fig. 9). The introductory essay of the catalogue almost laconically notes that Impressionism could meanwhile be considered to be "something axiomatic – historical".[69] From the standpoint of the curators, no attempt had yet been made to retrospectively reconstruct Impressionist pictorial conception up to painting of the early modern period. Accordingly, the path through the exhibition began, among other things, with works by Tintoretto, Rubens, Velázquez and Delacroix as well as with sculptures by Houdon and Rude before the undisputed "figureheads" of Impressionism were presented: Manet, Monet, Degas and others. Two works by Rodin, namely *The Hand of God* and the *Portrait of the Sculptor Alexandre Falguière,* stood alongside sculptures and statues by Constantin Meunier, Rosso and others as examples for the "Ausbau des Impressionismus" ("Development of Impressionism", the title of a section of the catalogue) in the space devoted to sculptural art.[70] Even though he is not explicitly mentioned in the official catalogue, it is not difficult to discover the signature of the enterprising art writer Julius Meier-Graefe behind the narrative of a search for forerunners of an Impressionist pictorial concept, which constituted the basis for this exhibition.[71] In the first edition of his enormously popular *Entwicklungsgeschichte der modernen Kunst* (History of the Development of Modern Art, 1904), whose role in making French Impressionism known in Germany can scarcely be overestimated, Rodin – along with Rosso – was to be even more resolutely stylised as the initiator of Impressionist sculpture. In contrast, its representatives – according to Meier-Graefe artists such as Bernhard Hoetger, Gustav Vigeland and others – were rated as mere epigones.[72]

Rodin's connections to Impressionism, as the present contribution was intended to elucidate, were always intimately linked with the multilayered debates on the subject of his oeuvre. These originated, as it were, in a dialogue between

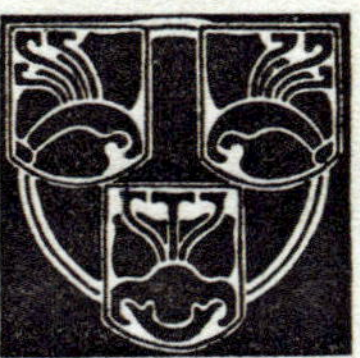

art and art criticism or art history, between sculptural works and those interpretive publications that sought to give the public an understanding of Rodin's work or classified it in terms of the history of style. Hence Rodin's Impressionism is characterised by that mutability, animation and unrest that he, as well as the Impressionist painters, strove for in their art.

9 Title page of the catalogue accompanying the exhibition *Entwicklung des Impressionismus in Malerei und Plastik*, Secession, Vienna, 1903

1 On the criticism of such and comparable art historical models, see Pfisterer/Tauber 2018.
2 Jarrassé 1993, pp. 40–44; see Cugini 2006; Zimmermann 2016.
3 See Bierwirth 2018; exh. cat. Paris 2018.
4 See Le Men 2010, pp. 139–209.
5 See inv. cat. Paris 2007.
6 See Krauss 1981; Getsy 2010.
7 See exh. cat. Potsdam 2017.
8 Jean Selz 1963, pp. 89–150; see Tucker 1974, pp. 15–40.
9 See exh. cat. Paris 2012; Wohlrab 2016.
10 See the essay by Alexander Eiling in this catalogue, pp. 46–57, esp. p. 54.
11 See Finckh 2016.
12 Exh. cat. Paris 1989, p. 23.
13 Butler 1993, pp. 69–90.
14 Claris 1902 (French).
15 See Bellonzi 1970, pp. 13–20.
16 Claris 1902 (French), pp. 12–13, 32–34.
17 Ibid., pp. 40–45.
18 On Courbet, see Rodin 1911, pp. 308f.; on Dalou, see ibid., pp. 178, 181–83.
19 Elliott 2014, pp. 209–214.
20 See the essay by Fabienne Ruppen in this catalogue, pp. 24–34, esp. pp. 24–25.
21 See Schmoll genannt Eisenwerth 1983b.

22 On the motifs in Impressionist painting, see Clark 1999; exh. cat. Aarhus 2015.
23 Baudelaire [1863] 1994.
24 See Elsen 1985; Audeh 2002.
25 France 1900.
26 Rodin 1911, pp. 84–89.
27 Elsen 1974; Krauss 1977; Curtis 1999; Potts 2000.
28 Chevillot 2017, pp. 89–95.
29 See Bothner 1993.
30 Butler 1993, p. 11.
31 Anonymous 1877.
32 Tardieu 1877.
33 Butler 1980, p. 3.
34 Le Normand-Romain 2013, pp. 34–36.
35 Janson 1985, pp. 190, 199–200.
36 See Brabant 2017, pp. 19–45; Hatt 2004.
37 Tardieu 1877; Timbal 1877.
38 Rousseau 1877.
39 Claris 1902 (French), pp. 2–7.
40 Ibid., pp. 1–28, quote: p. 10: "période de création pure".
41 See Jarrassé 1993, pp. 46–48.
42 De Fourcaud 1882; Leroi 1882.
43 Burty 1882.
44 De Fourcaud 1882.
45 Burty 1882.

46 See Black McCoy 2006; exh. cat. Paris 2010.
47 See Salbert 1963; Paradise 1985.
48 Butler 1980, p. 5.
49 See ibid.; Mirbeau 1885.
50 Mirbeau 1989.
51 Geffroy 1889. The dealer–critic system that emerged in those years, in which artists, critics and art dealers created platforms for artists to present their work to the public that served as alternatives to the traditional Salon exhibitions, can be observed here in virtually paradigmatic way; see White/White 1965.
52 See exh. cat. Paris 1989, p. 104, no. 27.
53 See Le Normand-Romain 2013, p. 74.
54 De Goncourt 1959, pp. 562–563.
55 Yet it can be deduced from the numerous reviews of the exhibition that Rodin was not perceived as a member of this group despite the juxtaposition with the most prominent Impressionist; see exh. cat. Paris 1989, pp. 217–238.
56 "[R]eprésentation tragique et complexe de la nature et de la vie"; Geffroy 1889, p. 61.

57 Mirbeau 1885.
58 "[N]'ayant aucun des signes qui font reconnaître une époque ou une nationalité"; Geffroy 1889; quoted in: exh. cat. Paris 1989, p. 62.
59 "[H]umanité physiologique dans ses actions diverses"; ibid., p. 65.
60 Zola 1880; see Brabant 2017, pp. 84–95.
61 See exh. cat. Paris 2001.
62 Rainer Maria Rilke, *Auguste Rodin* [1902], 2011); see Kopp 1999. In this connection, not forgetting Georg Simmel's first essay on Rodin from 1902, which was no less crucial for his German-language reception; Simmel [1902] 1995. See Schmoll genannt Eisenwerth 1976; Brabant 2009.
63 Rilke [1902] 2011, p. 76.
64 Ibid., p. 18.
65 Ibid.
66 See Schmoll genannt Eisenwerth 1983a.
67 Rilke [1902] 2011, p. 32.
68 See exh. cat. Louviers 2016.
69 "Vorwort" (Foreword), in exh. cat. Vienna 1903, pp. 14–19, esp. p. 14.
70 Ibid., pp. 23–35.
71 See Kramer 2001.
72 Meier-Graefe 1904, vol. 1, pp. 263–312.

"The fullness of life is gathered
in these features, and there are absolutely
no symmetrical planes on the face.
Nothing is repeated, no spot remains
empty, mute, or neutral."

Rainer Maria Rilke, 1902

The Burghers of Calais –
a monument with Impressionist features

Art history of the twentieth century dealt with the sculptural oeuvre of Auguste Rodin in the wider context of Impression. The sculptor was not assigned to this context until around 1900 – among other things because of a lack of overlapping biographical aspects with the Impressionists.[1] Hence Rodin did not participate in any of the eight Impressionist exhibitions, for instance; instead, the jury admitted him to the Salon for the first time in 1875. Only once in his lifetime did a comprehensive juxtaposition of his sculptures with Impressionist paintings take place: in 1889, Georges Petit mounted the exhibition *Claude Monet – Auguste Rodin*.[2] Its presentation is documented solely by a photograph of the large-figured "Groupe de bourgeois de Calais" in which paintings or their frames are faintly apparent behind the sculpture (fig. 1).[3] Listed as number 1 in the catalogue and unanimously judged by the press to be the main work in the exhibition, the public saw the group of figures for the first time at Petit's exhibition.

The six burghers became famous in 1347 when, in an act of selflessness, they surrendered themselves to the English king, Edward III, and brought him the key to the city gate of Calais in order to end the siege and avert the pillage and destruction of their city. In 1884, Rodin applied to the City of Calais for the commission of a monument, which he was awarded in 1885. He subsequently worked on numerous studies of individual limbs, heads and figures before presenting a plaster of the complete group in 1889.[4] Scaled-down copies of five of the six figures are on display in our exhibition. Rodin had commissioned them himself in 1895, the year of the monument's inauguration. With the aid of a mechanical reduction technique perfected in his workshop, that very same year his assistant Henri Lebossé produced the bronzes of Jean d'Aire (cat. 80), carrying the key, and of Pierre de Wissant (cat. 81), captured as he was turning and holding an arm at a right angle before his face. The youngest burgher, Jean de Fiennes, who with both arms seeks to fend off the harm that threatens him (cat. 82), followed in 1898; in 1900 Andrieu d'Andres, bent with his head buried in his hands (cat. 84); and finally, in 1902/03, the oldest, Eustache de Saint-Pierre (cat. 83), around whom the others cluster in the final group.[5]

Thematically, the *Burghers of Calais* clearly set themselves apart from the motifs of contemporary life to which the Impressionists had devoted themselves. However, Rodin's rendering of the historical material was judged as comparably unconventional and modern. Press reviews declared him a revolutionary who radically broke with the traditions of sculpture and reformed the genre in the same way as Monet did painting.[6] This was first of all due to the "new approach to enhancing public spaces" to which Gustave Geffroy referred in his introductory text for the catalogue that accompanied Petit's exhibition.[7] Contrary to the requirements placed on monuments that prevailed in the nineteenth century, Rodin designed a loose juxtaposition of his *Burghers of Calais* on a single level – instead of a pyramidal arrangement.[8] The content-related message cannot be completely understood until one walks around the group, as a sequence of actions takes place between the figures.[9] In this way, Rodin called for the viewer to move, assigned him an active role, and at the same time warned against Charles Baudelaire's criticism, according to which sculpture is subordinate to painting based on its multifaceted aspect (which Baudelaire considered to be vagueness).[10] In contrast, with his *Burghers of Calais*, Rodin proved that a good sculptor knows how to employ precisely this fact as potential and is capable of inscribing an element of decisiveness in any and all possible views.[11]

In this respect, the mode of presentation played a crucial role, because, as otherwise customary for monuments, the group was intended to stand on the ground (fig. 1; see p. 13, fig. 2).[12] By dispensing with a base, Rodin permitted encountering the sculpture at eye level and shifted the focus from the collective heroic deed to the individual drama suffered by those being portrayed.[13] As the contemporary reviews of Petit's exhibition demonstrate, this presentation lent the historical actors an immediacy that situated them in the here and now. One felt taken back to the fourteenth century as a veritable witness of the occurrence.[14] The illusionistic design of the arrangement of the folds as well as the facial features heightened this impression, whereby the individualisation had its limitations to the extent that for Andrieu d'Andres, Rodin once again made use of the face he developed for Jean d'Aire.

Even though none of the exhibition reviews referred to Rodin as an Impressionist, they did attest to the same orientation to nature, power of observation and realistic reproduction by means of a novel manner of expression as they had established for Monet.[15] While his paintings transported viewers to the depicted landscape, making them come alive at a specific time of day and under specific weather conditions, viewers of Rodin's sculptures saw themselves confronted with such strong human emotions that they were left speechless: "They are not Apollo, but men whose flesh cries out, whose eyes are charged with the explosion of a soul, whose faces reflect the anguish of the last hour of life. They are frustrated, and real."[16]

The expressiveness of the figures, which can be traced back to Rodin's skill and his sensitivity, was of central importance in the contemporary reviews.[17] As Geffroy stated more precisely, it was his ability in particular to lend a timeless dimension to the deceptively realistic figures.[18] This balance between the moment and eternity will have reinforced Paul Cézanne in his esteem for the sculptor.[19] After all, Rodin succeeded in that very transfer of Impressionism into something lasting that Cézanne himself strove for in his paintings.[20] Ironically, due to this aspiration, Cézanne was regarded as a special case amongst the Impressionists as early as in the 1870s and 1880s, inasmuch as one even assigned him to this movement in the first place. Conversely, with respect to Rodin, it was precisely the consummated synthesis of spontaneous emotion and symbolic radiance that would prove to be among the decisive factors for his categorisation as an "Impressionist sculptor" after the turn of the century, as demonstrated by the discussion surrounding his *Balzac* (see cat. 85–88). — FR

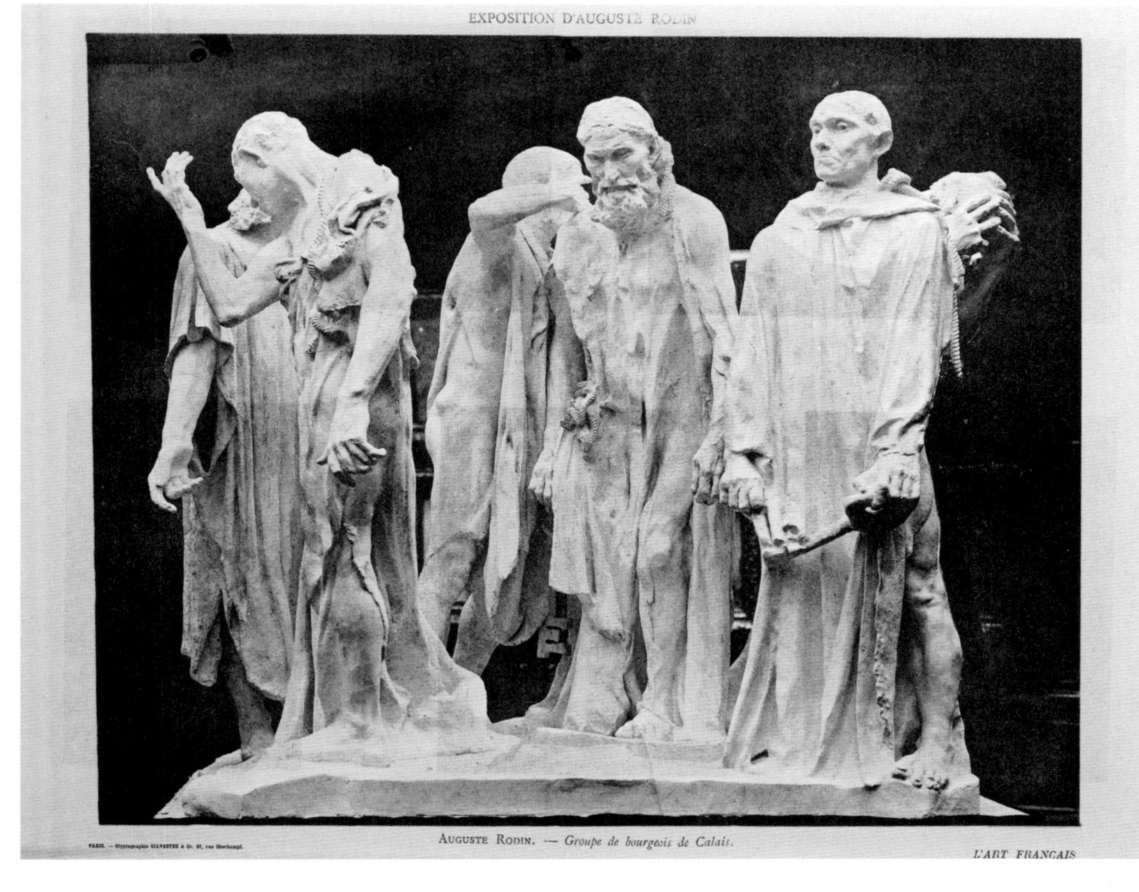

1 *Auguste Rodin. – Groupe de bourgeois de Calais*, from *L'Art français* 3, no. 115 (6 July 1889)

1 See the essay by Dominik Brabant in this catalogue, pp. 174–183, esp. p. 175.
2 Exh. cat. Paris 1889. On this subject in general, see Dunn 1978; exh. cat. Paris 1989. See also the essay by Dominik Brabant in this catalogue, pp. 174–183, esp. p. 180. On Rodin's exhibition practice, see Gülicher 2011, pp. 73–85; especially on this exhibition, pp. 74–75.
3 See Beausire 1989, p. 45.
4 See Geffroy 1889, p. 77. There is extensive literature available on Rodin's *Burghers of Calais*; on this subject in general, see exh. cat. Calais/Paris 1977; Le Normand-Romain/Haudiquet 2001.
5 On these reductions, see Antoinette Le Normand-Romain, "Les Bourgeois de Calais", in inv. cat. Paris 2007a, vol. 1, pp. 211–241, esp. pp. 215–216. The figure of Jacques de Wissant was not executed in miniature.
6 See, for example, Jean Le Fustec, "Avec Rodin, c'est une révolution. Violemment, cet artiste rompt avec la sculpture classique." Le Fustec 1889; quoted in: exh. cat. Paris 1989, p. 229. See also Octave Mirbeau, "Ce sont eux qui, dans ce siècle, incarnent le plus glorieusement, le plus définitivement, ces deux arts: la peinture et la sculpture." Mirbeau 1889a; quoted in: exh. cat. Paris 1989, p. 225.
7 "C'est le défilé de ces bourgeois que Rodin a été chargé d'installer sur une place de Calais. […] [A]ffirmant à la fois une vision nette de l'humanité et une conception nouvelle de la décoration des places publiques." Geffroy 1889, p. 79.
8 Rodin took a decided stance against a pyramidal composition, which he linked with Jacques-Louis David and the École des Beaux-Arts; see exh. cat. Paris 1989, pp. 168–169.
9 See Rodin [1912] 1983, pp. 32–36. In this regard, Paul Gsell, editor of the conversations with Rodin, spoke of a "scenic value of art"; ibid., p. 36.
10 On Baudelaire's theory of a "unité de point de vue", see the Introduction by Alexander Eiling and Eva Mongi-Vollmer in this catalogue, pp. 12–21, esp. pp. 12–13, 15.
11 See Auguste Rodin, in Claris 1902 (French), pp. 31–33. Thus, Rodin distinguishes himself decidedly from Rosso; see the essay by Eva Mongi-Vollmer in this catalogue, pp. 126–133, esp. 132.
12 Rodin's concept for the base for the *Burghers of Calais* changed multiple times; for details on this, see Gülicher 2011, pp. 85–88.
13 "[…] [J]'avais pensé que placé très bas le groupe devenait plus familier et faisait entrer le public mieux dans l'aspect de la misère et du sacrifice, du drame dis-je." Letter from Auguste Rodin to Omer Dewavrin, 8 December 1893, quoted in: exh. cat. Calais/Paris 1977, p. 76, no. 91.
14 "Désormais les six hommes qui sont partis de la halle de Calais, […] à la foule des vivants d'aujourd'hui, comme ils ont été mêlés à la foule du quatorzième siècle." Geffroy 1889a; quoted in: exh. cat. Paris 1989, p. 220. "Je ne parlais point, pris aux entrailles comme si j'avais été vraiment un témoin de ce sacrifice." Anonymous 1889; quoted in: ibid.
15 See the essay by Dominik Brabant in this catalogue, pp. 174–183, esp. pp. 179–180. Regarding this, see also the introductory catalogue texts by Geffroy on Rodin and Octave Mirbeau on Monet. Geffroy traced the novel character of Rodin's sculptures, as did Mirbeau that of Monet's paintings, to the technique; Geffroy 1889, esp. p. 61; Mirbeau 1889.
16 "Ce ne sont pas des Apollons, mais des hommes dont la chair crie, dont le regard est chargé de l'explosion d'une âme, dont le visage reflète l'angoisse de la dernière heure de vie. Ils sont frustes, et réels." Le Fustec 1889; quoted in: exh. cat. Paris 1989, p. 229. See also Mirbeau 1889a.
17 See, for example, Edmond Jacques's assessment: "Rodin, lui, c'est la passion, la puissance, la vie. Il pénètre l'âme de ses sujets, et ses portraits, depuis longtemps célèbres, ne sont pas seulement des représentations de la forme extérieure; il a deviné les pensées maîtresses de cerveaux qu'il modèle, et il les imprime sur les fronts, dans les yeux, sur les lèvres, qui s'animent sous son ébauchoir." Jacques 1889; quoted in: exh. cat. Paris 1989, p. 237.
18 "[I]l a mis sous ces voiles des charpentes, des systèmes nerveux, tous les organes de la vie, des êtres de chair et de sang. […] Mais, ceci fait, il est allé, comme toujours, vers l'expression durable, vers le symbole, vers la synthèse." Geffroy 1889, p. 82.
19 Geffroy, for example, tells of Cézanne's respect for Rodin; after an encounter with the sculptor, Cézanne is said to have exclaimed to Geffroy: "Il n'est pas fier, monsieur Rodin, il m'a serré la main! Un homme décoré!!!" Geffroy 1922, p. 196.
20 According to Maurice Denis, Cézanne is said to have expressed himself as follows: "J'ai voulu faire de l'impressionnisme quelque chose de solide et de durable comme l'art des Musées." Denis 1920, p. 251.

Cat.80 Auguste Rodin, **Jean d'Aire**, 1895, cast 1915–1917 (Alexis Rudier Fondeur); bronze, 47 × 15.5 × 11.5 cm; private collection Cat.81 Auguste Rodin, **Pierre de Wissant**, 1895 or 1899, cast 1935–1945 (Alexis Rudier Fondeur); bronze, 45 × 17 × 16 cm; private collection

Cat.80

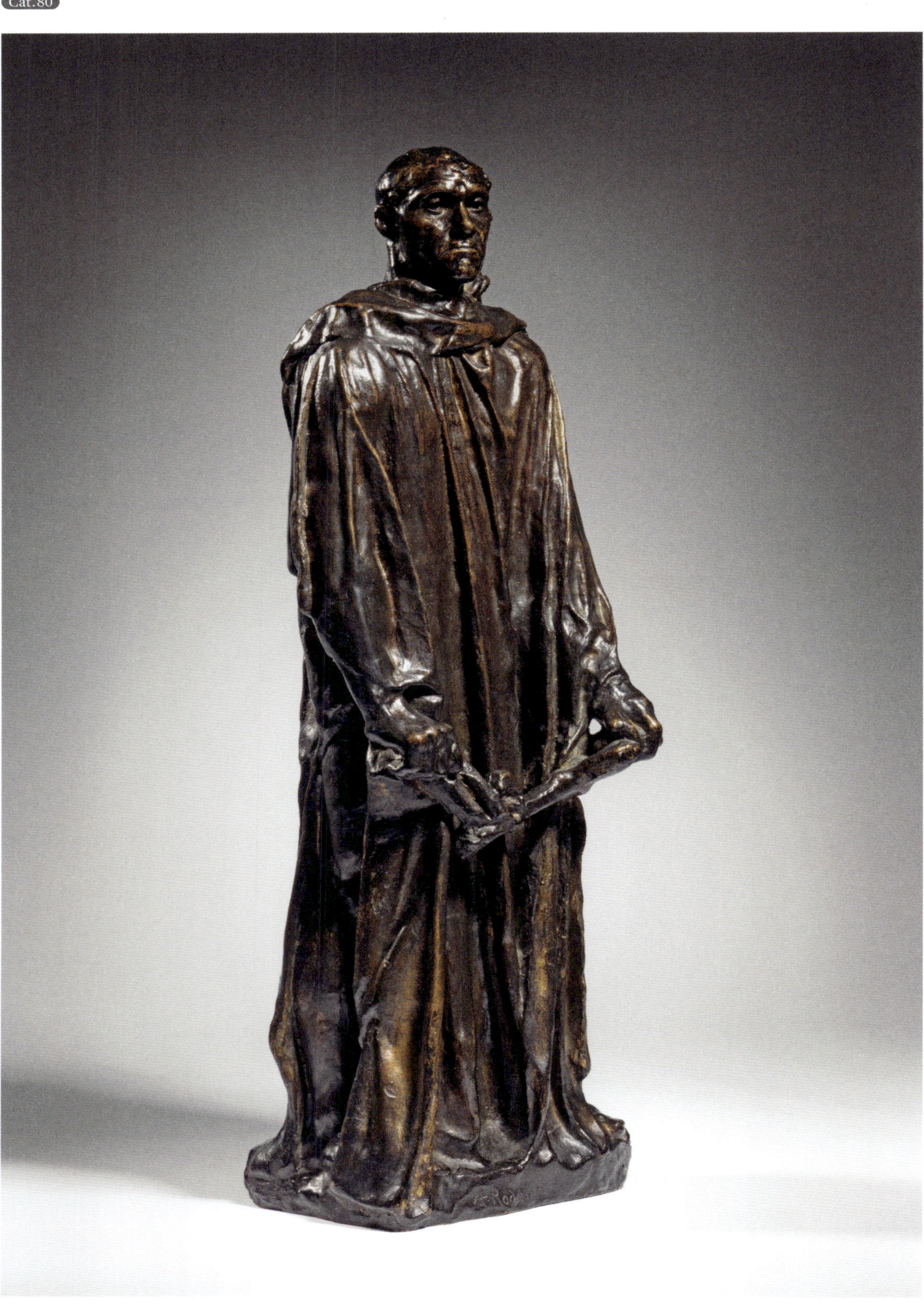

Cat.81

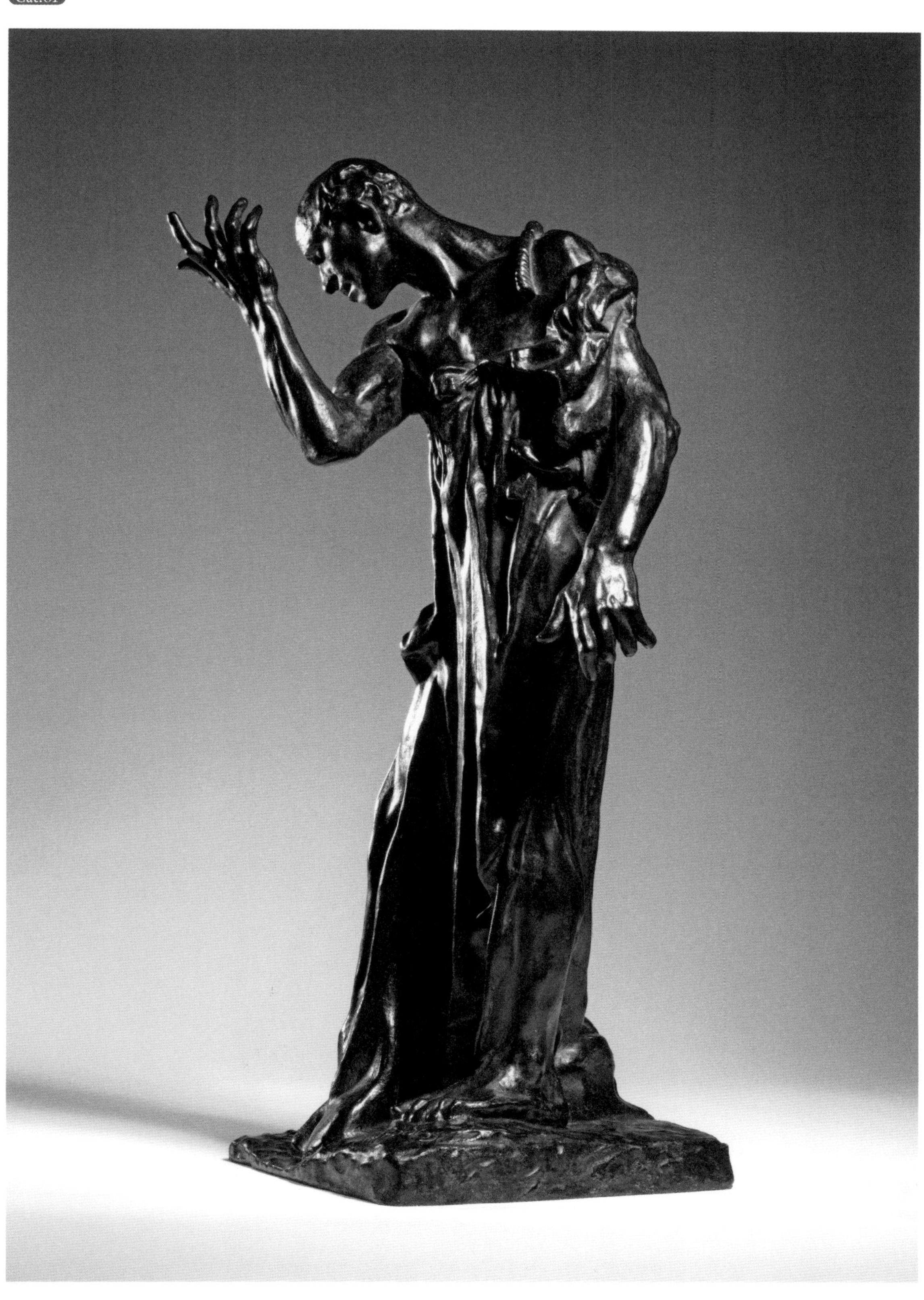

Cat.82 Auguste Rodin, **Jean de Fiennes**, 1895 or 1899, cast 1920–1925 (Alexis Rudier Fondeur); bronze, 45 × 17 × 16 cm; private collection Cat.83 Auguste Rodin, **Eustache de Saint-Pierre**, 1902/03, cast 1930–1950 (Alexis Rudier Fondeur); bronze, 47 × 24.5 × 17 cm; private collection Cat.84 Auguste Rodin, **Andrieu d'Andres**, 1900, cast 1945 (Alexis Rudier Fondeur); bronze, 43 × 21 × 21 cm; private collection

Cat.82

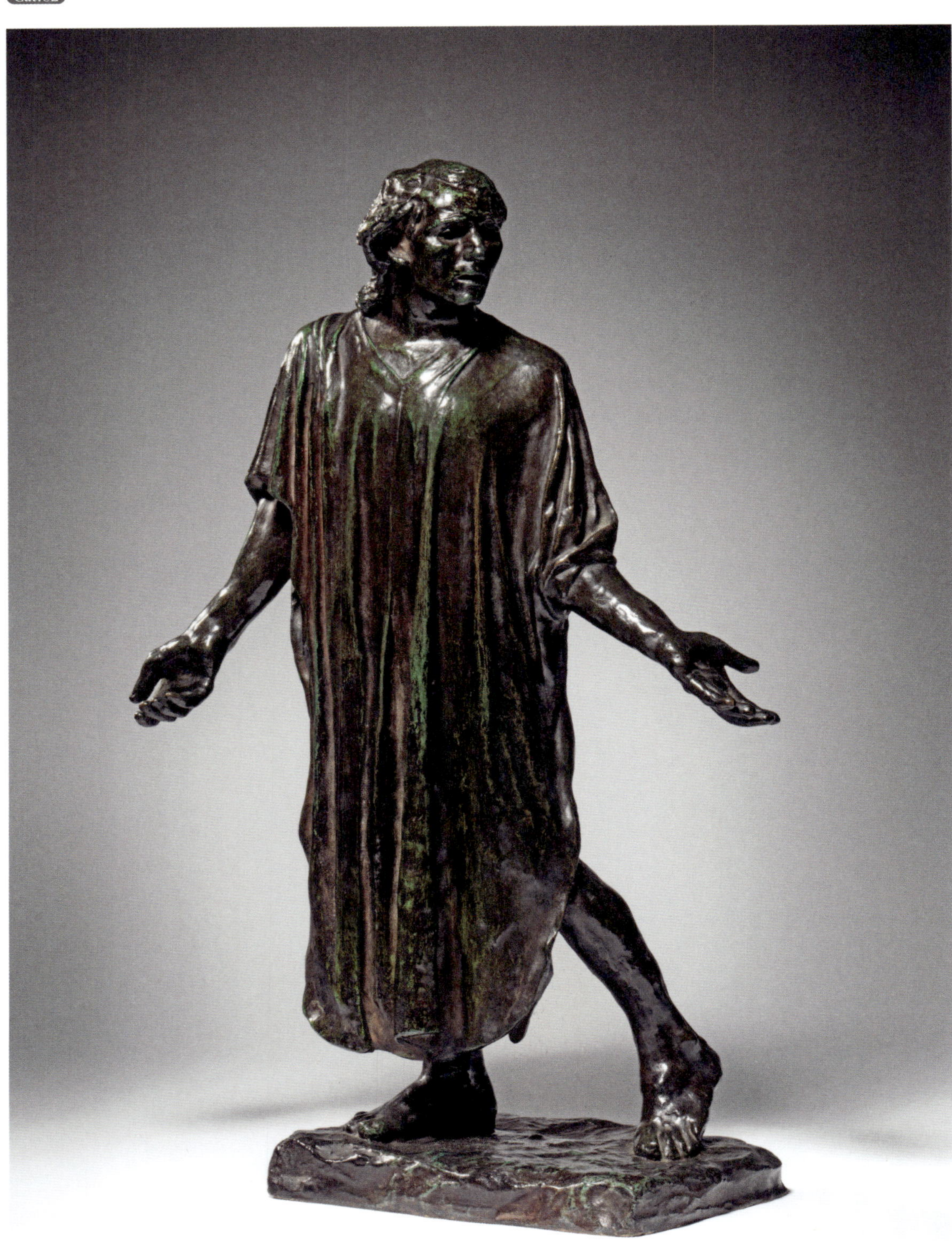

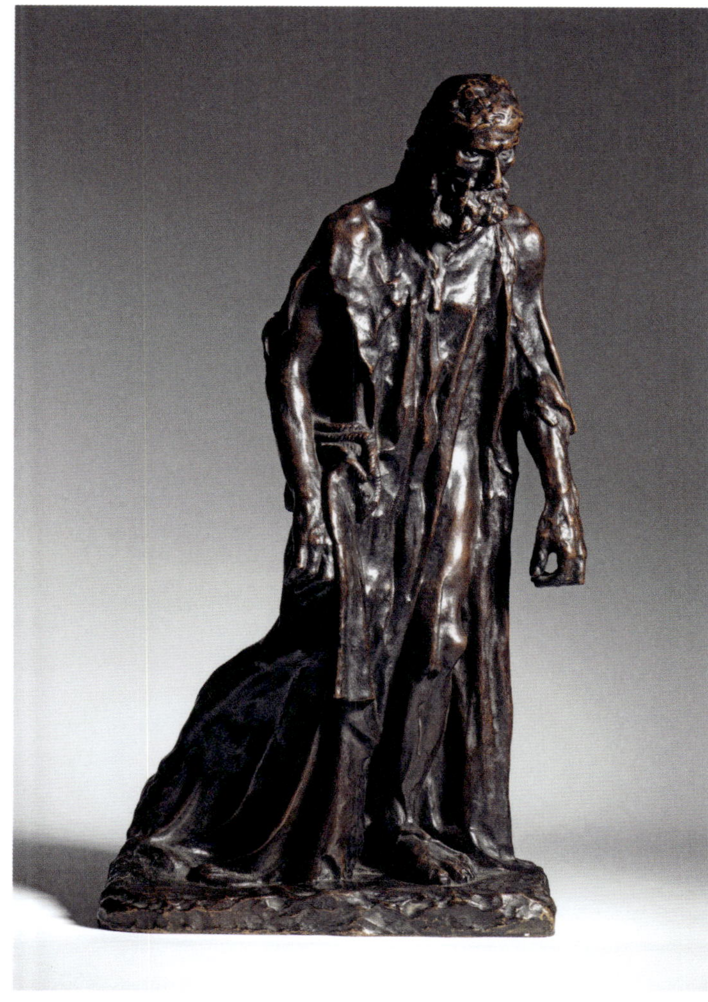

Cat.83

Cat.84

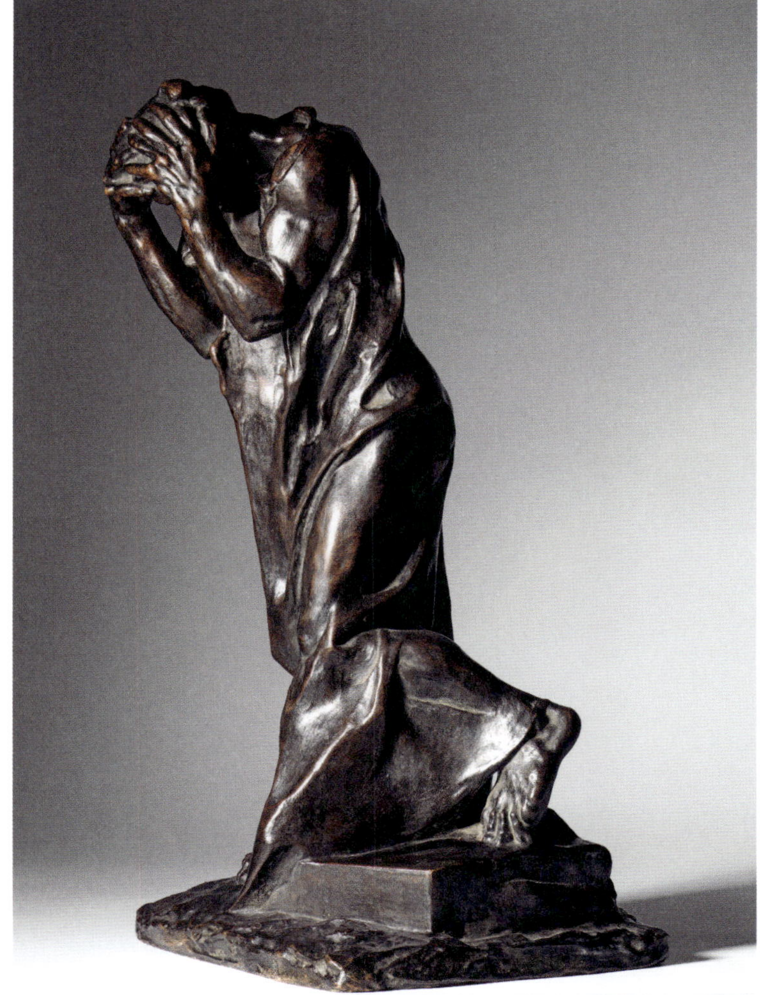

Auguste Rodin's *Balzac* – the embodiment of Impressionist sculpture?

Auguste Rodin was not explicitly referred to as an "Impressionist sculptor" until after the turn of the century – based on his sculpture *Balzac*.[1] Commissioned in 1891 by the Société des Gens de Lettres, the creation of the figure took seven years and involved, among other things, excursions to Tours, the home town of Honoré de Balzac (1799–1850), which were conceived as study trips. In 1892, after Rodin decided to portray the poet in the monk's cowl he normally wore when he worked, he initially set to work on nude studies.[2] As the poet Rainer Maria Rilke, who temporarily worked as Rodin's secretary, recorded, for this purpose he used "live models of similar physical proportions [...]. The men he employed for this task were heavy, sturdy types, with thick legs and short arms."[3] These model studies resulted in a bust with crossed arms (cat. 85) as well as a standing nude with splayed legs, his left hand on the hollow of his back and his right extended outward with a raised thumb (cat. 86). Rodin ultimately clothed the poet in a simple robe that almost seems to coalesce with the body and devour it, so to speak (cat. 87).

Rodin presented his *Balzac* for the first time in a plaster version at the Salon in 1898. Medardo Rosso saw the figure there and recognised such striking parallels with his own sculpture *The Bookmaker* from 1894 that he accused Rodin of having used it as a model (see cat. 63). The undeniable similarities between the two works led to a personal rift between the two friendly sculptors; however, the parallels contributed in no small measure to Rodin and Rosso being referred to as the two main representatives of "Impressionist sculpture" from then on.[4] Both sculptors played a crucial role in Edmond Claris's enthusiastic endorsement of this "renewal movement" as well as in a chapter on "Impressionism in Sculpture" based on it in Julius Meier-Graefe's *Entwickelungsgeschichte der modernen Kunst* (Modern Art. Being a Contribution to a New System of Aesthetics) both published shortly after the turn of the century; they chose Rodin's *Balzac* as the embodiment of "Impressionist sculpture".[5] In their opinion, this sculpture epitomised the orientation to nature that was essential for Impressionist sculptors and painters alike. Rodin himself even expressed the necessity to turn away from arbitrary conventions and towards nature.[6] Claris took this up and stated that, in the case of *Balzac*, Rodin reproduced the impression received directly from nature in the same way as an Impressionist painter;[7] in it was found "no arrangement, nature itself was the main speaker".[8] This assessment was rooted primarily in his impression of facing not a sculpture, but the true Balzac, which is understandable in view of Eugène Druet's photograph, in which the sculpture dramatically delivers itself from darkness (cat. 88).

Claris furthermore stressed that Rodin "*saw*" the writer "draped in the folds of a cloak, walking back and forth in his room, his head thrown backwards".[9] This seeing is to be understood as penetrating the motif, which other critics had already established more than ten years previously regarding the *Burghers of Calais* (see cat. 80–84). By capturing the character traits of the author, the sculptor called attention to the man behind the celebrity and enabled the viewer to have a quasi-real encounter with the deceased.[10] Rodin knew how to create this closeness in other sculptures as well – in particular by placing emphasis on the expressive qualities of those being portrayed, hence by means of facial expressions and gestures (see cat. 89–92).[11] Whereas those who commissioned the *Balzac* rejected it as unrecognisable, others regarded the few clearly fashioned physiognomic features as the essence of the writer's personality: "Balzac's face sparkles with life, a piece of breathing flesh."[12] This description by Meier-Graefe is reminiscent of the reactions to Edgar Degas's presentation of the *Little Dancer Aged Fourteen* in 1881 (see cat. 4), whose "terrible reality" had been horrifying at the time.[13] As early as 1889, reviewers of the joint exhibition of Rodin and Claude Monet considered such realistic features to be a positive attribute connecting the sculptor and the painter (see cat. 80–84), and they still aroused enthusiasm 15 years later. The closeness to reality observed by Claris and Meier-Graefe made reference to an impressionistically interpreted immediacy.[14] This is due to a markedly non-illusionist execution in which traces of work, such as fingerprints and casting seams, were not smoothed but, comparable to the brushstrokes in Impressionist paintings, remained visible (see cat. 90–91).[15]

Despite such indisputable formal parallels between Impressionist painting and Rodin's sculpture, the analogies made by Claris and Meier-Graefe are problematic, as they applied criteria that were developed scarcely 30 years earlier with respect to painting but made no mention at all about the sculptures displayed in the Impressionist exhibitions. Instead of the fact of their participation in the exhibitions, the artistic technique comparable with painting served them as grounds for assigning Rodin and Rosso to Impressionism. Around two decades after Claretie,[16] they announced a second birth of Impressionist sculpture, according to which it began considerably later than the style of painting provided with the same label. Although the sculpture was evaluated as equally progressive, in this way they placed it in the succession of painting. Given this implicit vanguard role of the latter, it is hardly surprising that Rodin rejected the label of "Impressionist sculptor", emphasising that "[s]culpture is either strong or weak" but "not 'impressionist'".[17] — FR

> "[...] no arrangement,
> nature itself
> was the main speaker."
>
> Edmond Claris, 1902

Cat.85 Auguste Rodin, *Balzac, Bust of Nude Study C*, c. 1892/93, cast 1918–1927; bronze, 44.5 × 37 × 33.5 cm; private collection, London **Cat.86** Auguste Rodin, *Balzac Study (Nude Study A)*, 1893–1895; bronze, 40.7 × 29.8 × 18.8 cm; stamped on the inside: "A. Rodin", on the plinth: "© Musée Rodin", "Rudier / Fondeur PARiS", signed on the plinth: "A. Rodin"; Städel Museum, Frankfurt am Main, inv. no. St.P 469

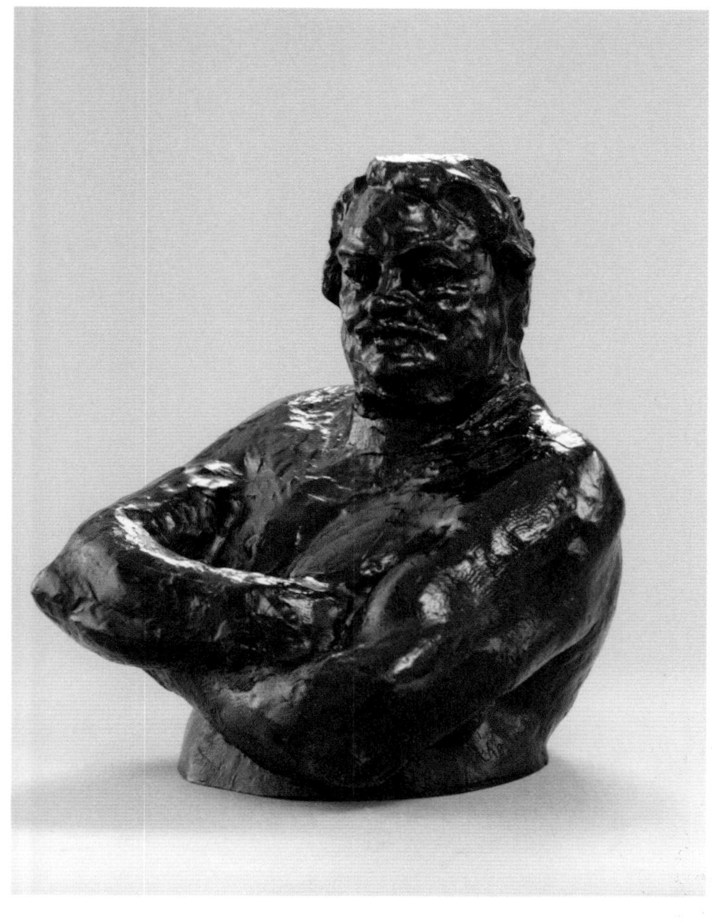

Cat.85

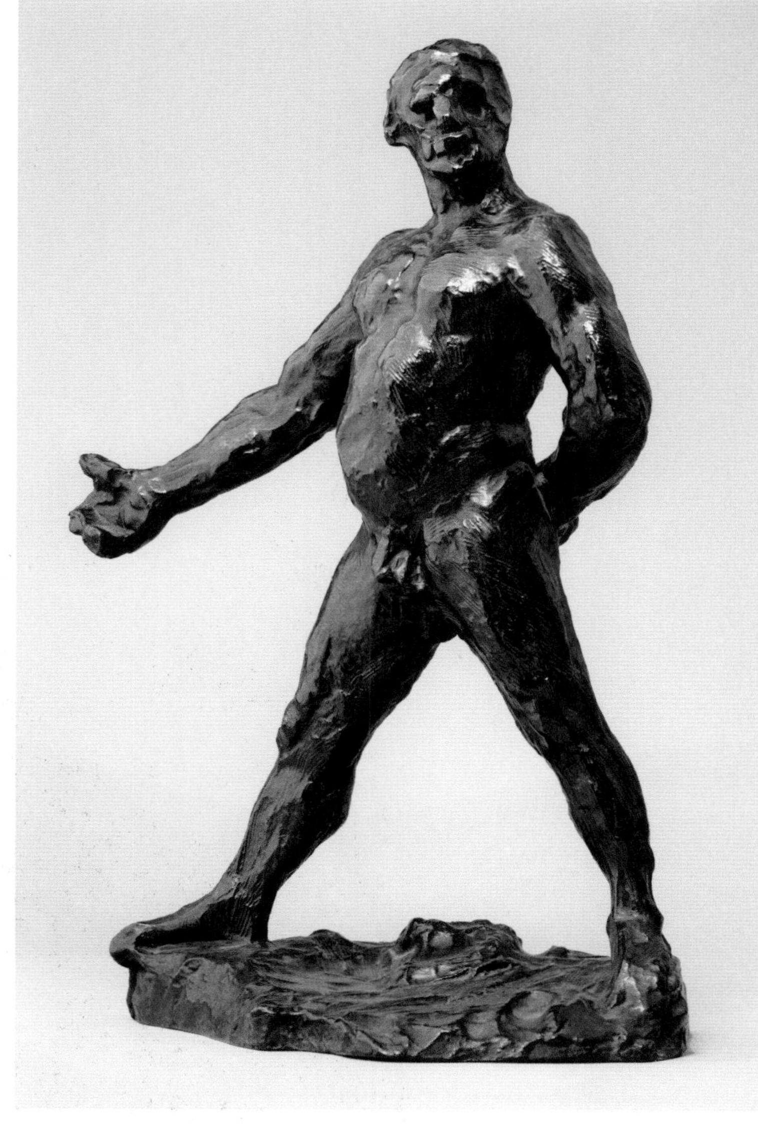

Cat.86

1 Elliott 2014, p. 210.
2 On the genesis of the work, see inv. cat. Paris 2007a, vol. 1, pp. 164–190.
3 Rilke [1902] 2011, p. 64.
4 Thus with Camille de Sainte-Croix, it was initially an advocate of Rosso who mentioned Rodin in this connection within the scope of a comparison of the two artists; see Elliott 2014, p. 213. On Rodin and Rosso, see the contribution by Eva Mongi-Vollmer in this catalogue, pp. 126–133, esp. pp. 126–127.
5 Claris 1902 (French), pp. 1, 10, 13; Meier-Graefe 1904, vol. 1, pp. 303–312. De Sainte-Croix also acknowledged *Balzac* as the initial spark for the discussion; however, he pointed out that Rosso had already achieved something similar 15 to 20 years prior to that; Camille de Sainte-Croix, in Claris 1902 (French), pp. 58, 61. Claris initially named *Balzac* as

Rosso's point of departure, while he changed sides in his 1929 article and stated that Rodin drew inspiration from Rosso for his *Balzac*; Claris 1929, p. 134. Claris was not the first one to understand Rodin as part of a "renewal movement": Jean Le Fustec spoke of a "mouvement artistique actuel" with reference to Monet and Rodin; Le Fustec 1889; quoted in: exh. cat. Paris 1989, p. 229.
6 See Auguste Rodin, in Claris 1902 (French), pp. 31–38.
7 Claris 1902 (French), p. 5.
8 "Dans *le Balzac* pas d'arrangement. La nature se compose elle-même."; ibid., p. 13.
9 "Il [Rodin] l'a [Balzac] VU, drapé dans son large manteau, se promenant à travers sa chambre, la tête en arrière [...]"; ibid., p. 14 (small caps in the original).

10 "Dans cette silhouette qui nous est apparue sous le jeu des lumières, n'avons-nous pas, en effet, été frappés par la grâce et la souplesse de ces formes en mouvement, n'avons-nous pas eu la sensation nette de la vie, du génie de Balzac?" Ibid., p. 15.
11 See the essay by Dominik Brabant in this catalogue, pp. 174–183, esp. p. 178. Nina Schallenberg discussed this aspect under the heading of "caractère"; Gülicher 2011, p. 26.
12 "[D]as Gesicht Balzacs von Leben sprüht, ein Stück atmenden Fleisches." Meier-Graefe 1915, vol. 3, p. 470.
13 Huysmans 1883a, p. 226. See the essay by Fabienne Ruppen in this catalogue, pp. 24–34, esp. p. 29, as well as p. 34, note 50.
14 The realistic, animated quality, which had also established itself in the late 1860s as

a feature of modern sculpture, can be classed as being in the tradition of the Pygmal on topos; see Scott 1998, p. 111.
15 See, for example, Meier-Graefe 1904, vol. 1, p. 304. The same author wrote in a later edition: "Man verbot dem Gießer jeder Retusche an der Impression und ehrte die Gussnaht wie ein Jungfernhäutchen." Meier-Graefe 1915, vol. 3, p. 474.
16 See Claretie 1881. See the essay by Fabienne Ruppen in this catalogue, pp. 24–34, esp. pp. 31–32.
17 "'Sculpture is either strong or weak', [Rodin] said; 'it is not "impressionist" as a sketch might be. If you use marble and bronze, your work must be well studied and continuous in its development.'" Anonymous 1907. See the essay by Dominik Brabant in this catalogue, pp. 174–183, esp. pp. 175–176.

Auguste Rodin's *Balzac* –
the embodiment of Impressionist sculpture?

 Auguste Rodin, Balzac, Second to Last Study, 1897, cast 1955 (Georges Rudier); bronze, 109.1 × 46.2 × 43 cm; private collection, London Eugène Druet, The Monument for Honoré de Balzac in the studio in the Dépôt des marbres (half-figure), 1896–1900; gelatin silver paper, 39.5 × 29.5 cm; Staatliche Museen zu Berlin, Kunstbibliothek, inv. no. 2009,80/111

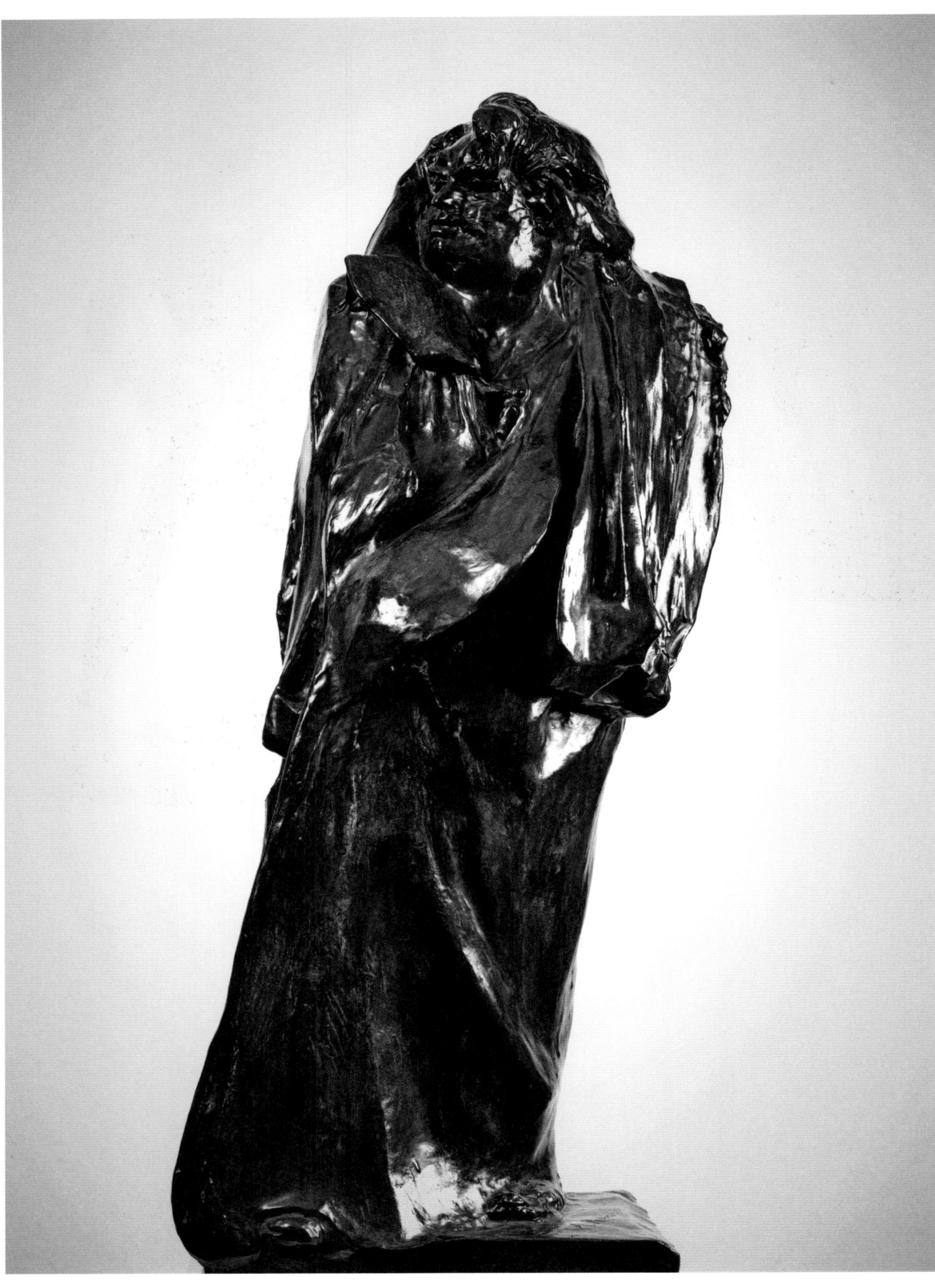

Cat.87

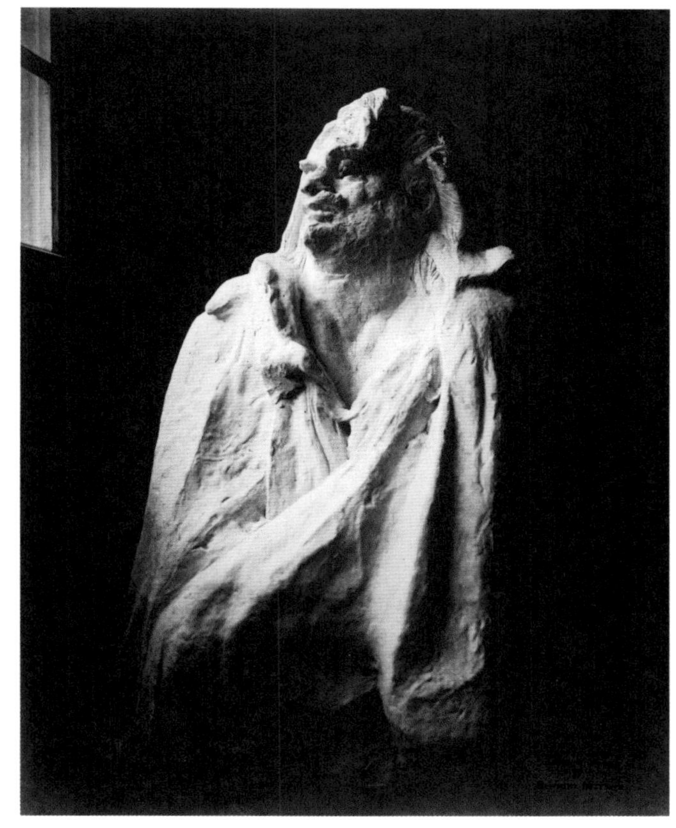

Cat.88

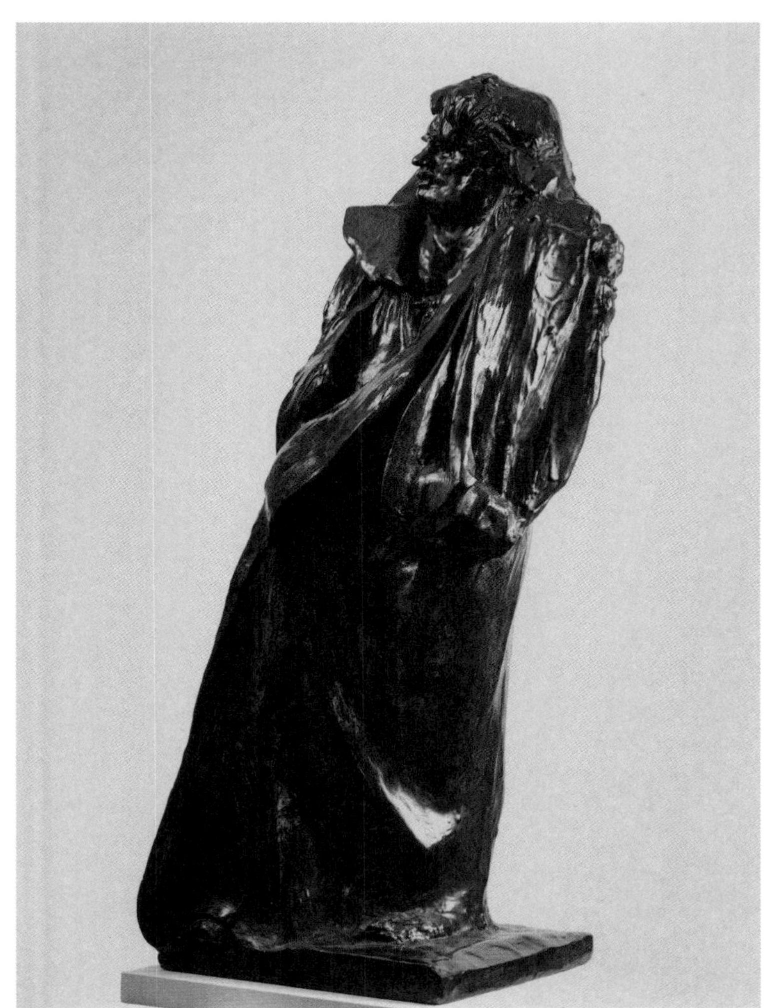

Cat.87

 # Impressionist surfaces – Auguste Rodin's busts

If one seeks concrete correlations between Rodin's sculptures and Impressionist paintings, it is worth taking a closer look at their surface character. The mask *Man with the Broken Nose*, for instance, presumably already produced in 1863, exhibits an equally as animated texture as the landscapes by Claude Monet painted in brushwork with a schematic allure (cat. 89; see p. 13, fig. 2). Furrows on the forehead extending to between the eyes form wrinkles that resemble valleys; eyebrows and beard sit in prominent nodules on the undulating face, which the curls draw near in wave-like bulges. Rodin referred to the diverse "topography" as the first example of a successful "modelé", which is why, in retrospect, he attached primal importance to this portrait of a casual labourer from the Paris horse market for his subsequent works.[1]

He adhered to this way of handling the artistic material all his life, to which the busts of the politicians Victor-Henri, Marquis de Rochefort-Luçay and Georges Clemenceau, which were produced much later, exemplarily testify. In the first one, the kneaded, flattened and smoothed-out material is combined with the "Latin classic type" that Rochefort embodied for Rodin (cat. 90).[2] By primarily fleshing out the facial features, the sculptor placed emphasis on the preliminary design character that dominates the overall impression, as neck and chest area are only structured schematically. He nonetheless considered the figure finished in this state. Nor can the fact that the version presented here was executed in plaster be understood as an indication of an intermediate state. Rodin deemed his plasters autonomous works that he not only exhibited, but also gave away and sold.[3]

Rodin's busts resulted from an intense study of the models, whose physiognomies as well as their character and their constitution he sought to capture during numerous sessions.[4] The undertaking was particularly tedious in the case of the *Bust of Georges Clemenceau*, of which Rodin ultimately had two versions cast in bronze that differ most notably in the shaping of the neck and the base of the shoulders (cat. 91).[5] The surface of the second version being shown here is smoother, which is why Anne-Birgitte Fonsmark classified it as less "Impressionist".[6] Nevertheless, even this toned-down relief is of an animatedness that understandably reminded Julius Meier-Graefe of viscous dough.[7] Responsible for this are the many varied instruments with which Rodin worked the surface. Round indentations trace back to his fingers and conspicuous parallel grooves stem from a modelling tool. Camille Claudel's (1864–1943) *Bust of Auguste Rodin* (cat. 92) demonstrates just how characteristic this approach was for Rodin. As an intermittent student and workshop assistant, she was very well familiar with his practice. By modelling his portrait in an equally differentiated way, she not only demonstrated her abilities, but, by skilfully taking up Rodin's signature style, she simultaneously produced a homage that made the portrait seem like a self-portrait.[8]

The freely modelled clay studies by sculptors of older generations, such as Honoré Daumier (1808–1879) or Jean-Baptiste Carpeaux (1827–1875), can be regarded as precursors to Rodin's *modelé*, though their schematic features were smoothed when they were rendered in bronze. However, Rodin defied this convention and left the broken-up textures in this medium, thus taking a conscious aesthetic decision. Meier-Graefe already recognised basic parallels with the characteristic sweeping brushwork of Impressionist painting in the emphasis of the individual signature readable herein.[9] This approach can be understood as an expression of the desire for individuality and as a demonstration of artistic authenticity in both genres, as photography – which had long since well established itself in the late nineteenth century – had taken the place of painting and sculpture in the production of faithful likenesses.[10]

Moreover, the irregular surface of Rodin's sculptures fulfilled a principle function in the reproduction of the subject with respect to the portrayal's verisimilitude – namely, by facilitating the shimmering plays of light and shadow that Impressionist paintings also sought to capture. Contemporary sources and art historical research likewise cite the deliberate inclusion of light as a characteristic of each "Impressionist sculpture".[11] With its either dull, lustrous or reflecting quality, bronze is therefore particularly suitable. Hence it is hardly surprising that it was particularly Rodin's bronzes that were regarded as Impressionist.[12] In fact, unlike paintings, the sculptures worked out of this material were not only capable of reproducing the effect of fluid light, but also generating it – under changing lighting conditions or by the viewer's movement around the object. At least in this sense, sculpture can be considered more impressionistic than painting.

Owing to a narrow detail compared with full-figure depictions, Rodin knew how to stage light and shadow in his busts in an exceedingly trenchant way. Surface irregularities, edges and fractures transform hair, skin and clothing into flickering light or dark areas. In his portrait of the sculptor, this characteristic served Eugène Carrière as the actual motif, which he transferred into the tonal value of the black-and-white spectrum in a lithograph (cat. 93). Rodin and Carrière were good friends from the 1880s until the latter's death. The two artists thought highly of and supported one another, and they both collected each other's works. Rodin owned eight paintings by his friend alone. Carrière, on the other hand, portrayed the sculptor multiple times, such as in the present lithograph from 1897. The face exhibits a markedly sculptural effect, which recalls softly modelled clay sculptures. At the same time, it can be considered exemplary of both Carrière's painterly as well as his printed oeuvre, which is characterised by blurring, dispensing with the elaboration of details and monochromy.[13]

As early as 1902, Camille Mauclair described the closeness of the two artists and their creative work as follows: "Rodin paints in marble, and Carrière sculpts with shadow."[14] This characterisation becomes especially vivid in the second lithograph (cat. 94). It was produced at the behest of Rodin as a poster motif for his exhibition at the Pavillon de l'Alma, which took place at the same time as the

> **"There is also a bit of Impressionism in any sculpture."**
>
> Julius Meier-Graefe, 1915

Cat.89 Auguste Rodin, **Man with the Broken Nose** (L'Homme au nez cassé), 1863/64; mask, type 1, 3rd model, cast before 1885; bronze, 31.5 × 19.5 × 15.5 cm; signed on front below hairline: "Rodin"; Albertinum/Skulpturensammlung, Dresden, inv. no. ZV 1288

world's fair in 1900. It features Rodin as the creator of *The Awakening*, out of whose hands the figure seems to ascend like a shadow. As an "ombre flottante"[15] (fluid shadow), it becomes apparent as a black area before a source of light. Carrière's lithographs illustrate why Meier-Graefe saw in Rodin a "hybrid of painting and sculpture".[16] He deemed the difference between the media a "grossly material matter"[17] and announced: "There is also a bit of Impressionism in any sculpture."[18] — FR

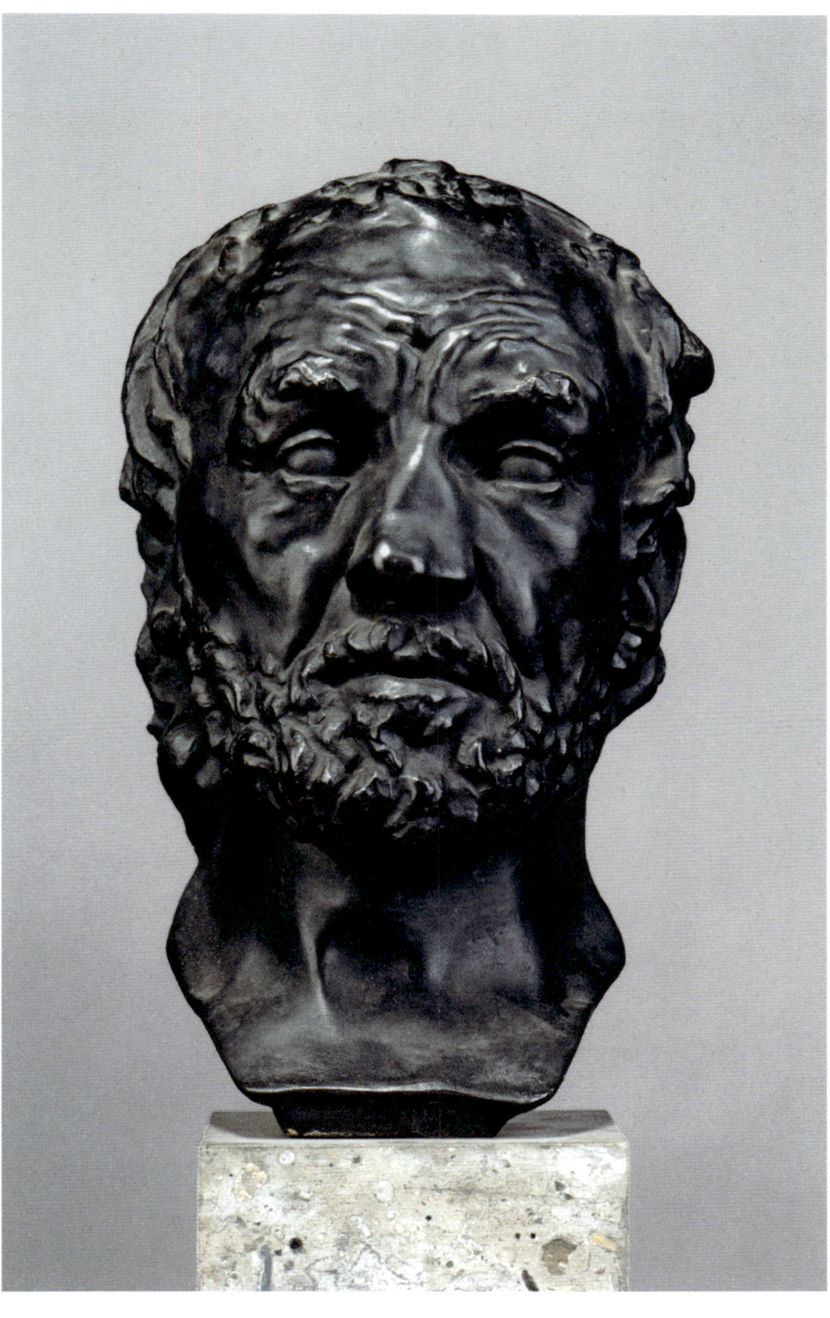

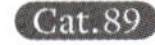
Cat.89

1 "That mask determined all my future work. It is the first good piece of modeling I ever did." Auguste Rodin, in Bartlett 1889; quoted in: Elsen 1965, p. 21. See also the essay by Dominik Brabant in this catalogue pp. 174–183, esp. p. 181. On the genesis of the work, see inv. cat. Paris 2007a, vol. 2, pp. 413–419.
2 "I have never found the Latin classic type as pure as in Rochefort." Rodin [1912] 1983, p. 57.
3 On Rodin's plasters, see Höcherl 2003.

4 See, for example, Geffroy's description of Rodin's Rochefort bust; Geffroy 1889, pp. 73–74.
5 On the genesis of the bust of Clemenceau, see inv. cat. Paris 2007a, vol. 1, pp. 267–270.
6 Exh. cat. Copenhagen 1988, p. 146, no. 33.
7 Meier-Graefe 1904, vol. 1, p. 306.
8 Exh. cat. Paris/Poitiers 1984, pp. 37–40, no. 11, esp. p. 40 (Bruno Gaudichon). On Claudel's work on the bust, see Schmoll genannt Eisenwerth 1994, pp. 52–57.

9 Meier-Graefe 1904, vol. 1, p. 304.
10 Elliott 2014, pp. 209–211.
11 Meier-Graefe 1915, vol. 3, p. 472; Chevillot 2010, p. 58; Elliott 2014, pp. 209, 216–217.
12 See the essay by Dominik Brabant in this catalogue pp. 174–183, esp. p. 175. For an extensive study of the different effect of Rodin's bronzes and marbles, see Schnell 2016.
13 On Carrière and Rodin, see exh. cat. Tokyo/Paris 2006. See also the essay by Astrid Reuter in this catalogue, pp. 296–302, esp. pp. 296–297.

14 "Rodin peint en marbre et Carrière sculpte en ombre [...]." Mauclair 1902, p. 70.
15 Meier-Graefe 1915, vol. 3, p. 472.
16 Ibid., p. 469 ("Mischling von Malerei und Skulptur"). Meier-Graefe also spoke of "sculptors' painting" ("Malerei der Bildhauer"); ibid., p. 474.
17 Ibid., p. 472 ("grob materielle Angelegenheit").
18 Ibid., p. 469.

Cat.90 Auguste Rodin, **Bust of Victor-Henri, Marquis de Rochefort-Luçay**, before 1897; plaster, height 75 cm; Belvedere, Vienna, inv. no. 342a Cat.91 Auguste Rodin, **Bust of Georges Clemenceau**, 1911, sand cast 1912; bronze, 48.4 × 32.3 × 30.5 cm; signed below left shoulder: "A. Rodin", stamped on interior: "A. Rodin", on the base: "Alexis Rudier / Fondeur PARIS"; Musée Rodin, Paris, inv. no. S.00480

Cat.90

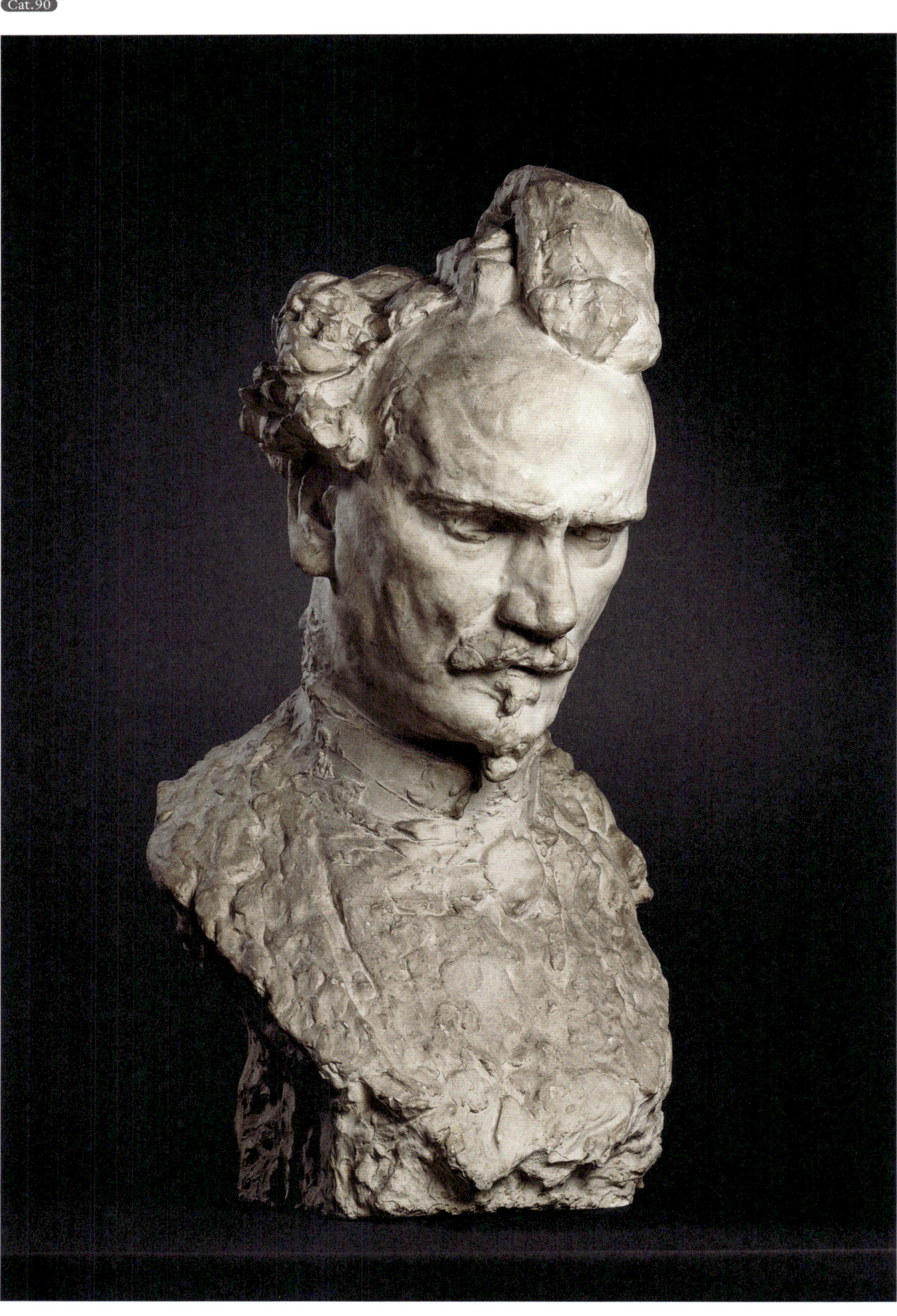

Cat. 91

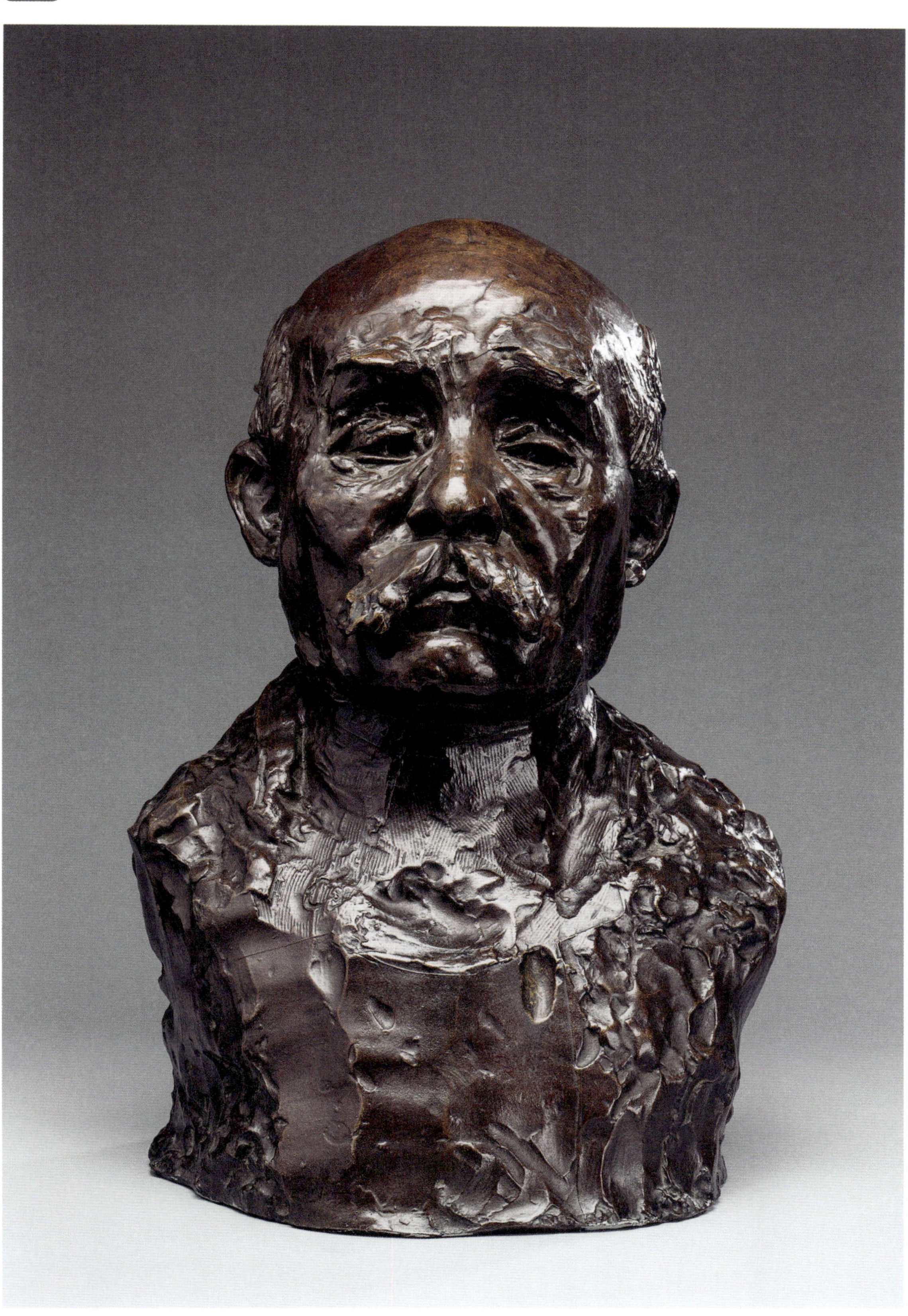

Cat.92 Camille Claudel, **Bust of Auguste Rodin**, c. 1892; bronze, 39.5 × 25 × 27 cm; Centre national des arts plastiques, France, inv. no. FNAC 7817, on permanent loan to the Musée d'art et d'industrie, Roubaix, inv. no. D 995-2-67 **Cat.93** Eugène Carrière, **Auguste Rodin**, 1897; lithograph on Asian paper, 61.4 × 44.9 cm (sheet), 53.1 × 35.1 cm (plate); Staatliche Museen zu Berlin, Kupferstichkabinett, inv. no. 415-1907 **Cat.94** Eugène Carrière, **Rodin Sculptant**, 1900; lithograph on Japanese simili paper (?), 63.7 × 49.2 cm; Staatliche Museen zu Berlin, Kupferstichkabinett, inv. no. 163-1963

Cat.92

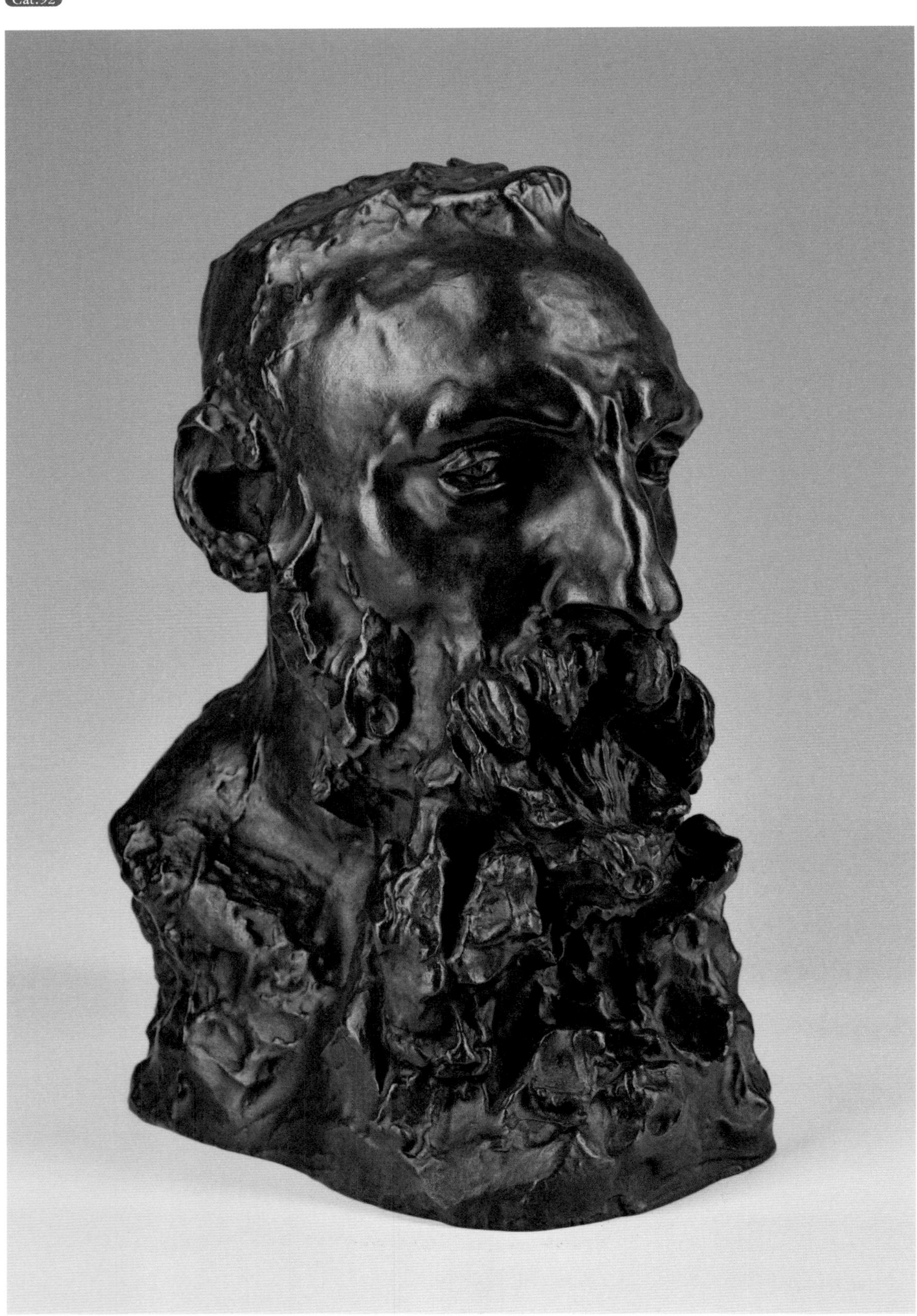

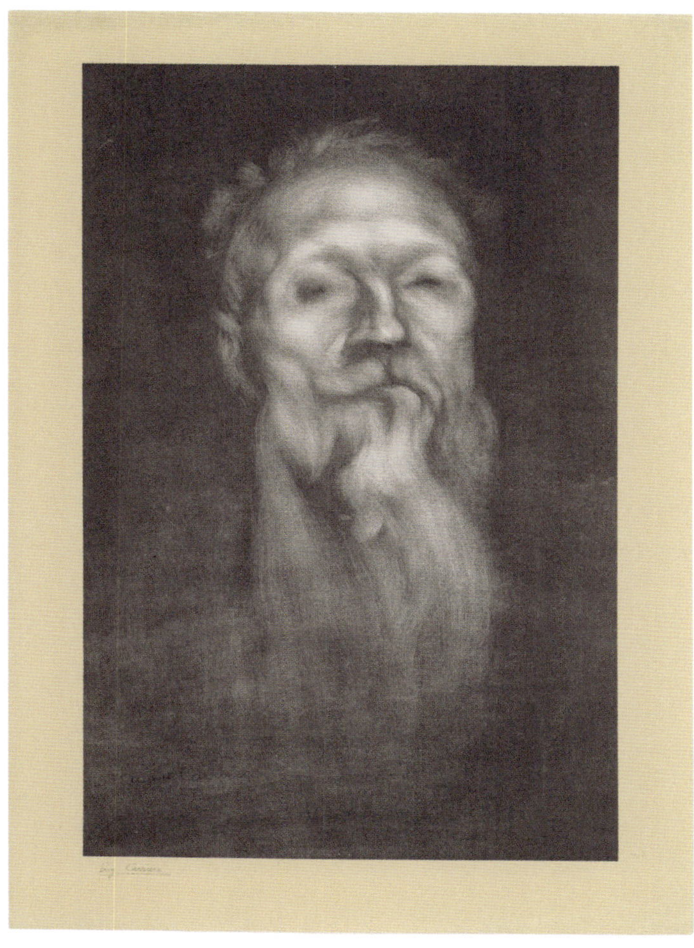

Cat. 93

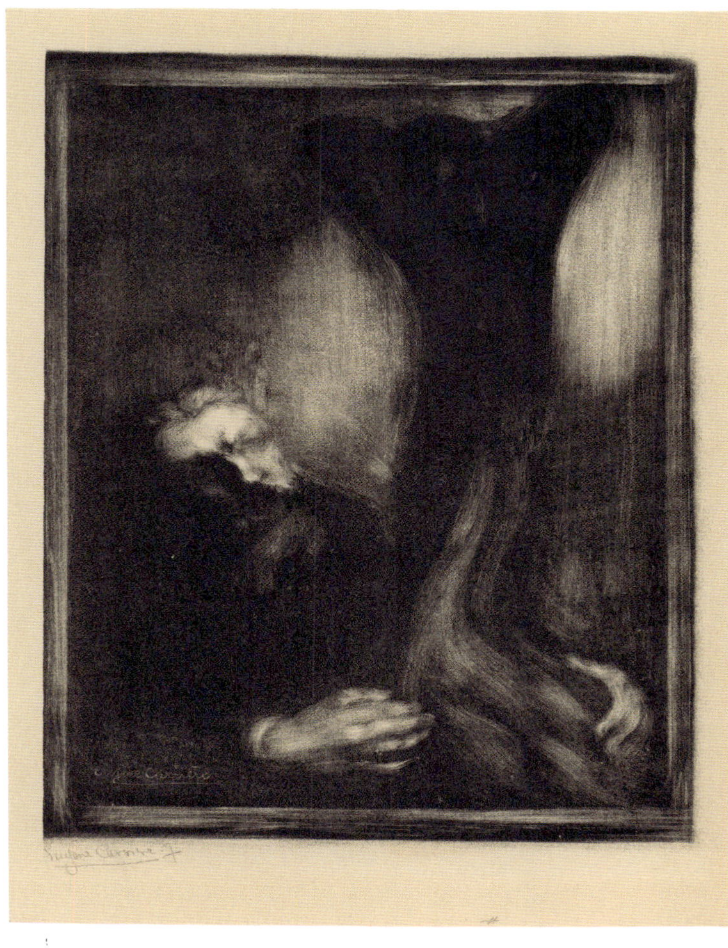

Cat. 94

Unfinished yet complete – Auguste Rodin's *Eve*

The state commission for *The Gates of Hell* that Rodin had received in August 1880 brought him the recognition and financial security he long wished for.[1] Moreover, the commission was associated with a studio at the Dépôt des Marbres, which Rodin used until his death and which can therefore be seen in numerous photographs of his sculptural works. He created a copious number of studies for *The Gates of Hell*, which was supposed to depict scenes from Dante's *Divina Commedia*. In October 1880, he requested an additional sum for "two colossal figures" that he wanted to place at the side of the gates.[2] These were the first sculptures produced for *The Gates of Hell*, namely *Adam/The Creation of Man* (1881)[3] and *Eve* (cat. 95) – both of them reflect Rodin's encounter with the art of Michelangelo during his trip to Italy in 1876.[4] *Eve* stands in the classic contrapposto – her weight on one leg, the other one bent and her foot put down somewhat higher – on an uneven plinth that is reminiscent of natural ground. She is naked, embraces her upper body, and bends her head so far downward that her face is hardly recognisable. This gesture is meant to be understood as a sign of shame, as the expression of her cognisance of the Fall. Rodin's *Eve* therefore clearly distinguishes itself from portrayals of her, more common at the time, of the "first woman" as a naked beauty *before* the Fall.[5]

The artist probably began work on *Eve* in early 1881, developing the figure's pose with his model, as had been his practice since the late 1870s.[6] The young woman, presumably Maria Abbruzzesi,[7] can be assigned particular significance for the figure to the extent that she was pregnant at the time, which is why her body changed from one sitting to the next. Rodin did not notice this at first, as he explained towards the end of his life; although he wondered about having to repeatedly adapt the plaster to his model, he did not understand why until she no longer wanted to come. Rodin stressed that he did not deliberately choose a pregnant model, but that this circumstance proved to be "an accident – fortunate for me" and that it "singularly helped with the character of the figure".[8] He ends his account with the statement: "That is why my Eve is unfinished."[9]

It is surprising that he would still say this in 1913, since, after abandoning his work on *Eve* (which occurred in early 1882 at the latest[10]), the plaster figure stood untouched in his studio for nearly 20 years. Because it clearly distinguishes itself from the other, more smoothly modelled works from the early 1880s, it must have seemed "unfinished" to Rodin in the truest sense of the word at the time.[11] In 1899, however, when the sculptor presented it to the public for the first time, he assessed the same sculpture completely differently. Thus, Rodin staged the first bronze cast of *Eve*, produced in 1897, in a spectacular way at the Salon de la Société nationale des Beaux-Arts. The artist placed the approximately life-sized figure in the rotunda of the Galerie des machines used by the sculpture department (see p. 278, fig. 2) – without a pedestal and apparently also without a plinth as this was buried in the sandy ground.[12] Exhibition visitors therefore encountered it directly and at eye level, which caused a great deal of irritation at the time (see cat. 80–84). Yet not only was the form of

presentation commented on, but also the design of the figure itself. Louis de Fourcaud considered *Eve*'s pose to be particularly expressive; however, he rejected the "unpolished" and "unfinished" surface treatment.[13] Despite his criticism of the modelling, he praised the figure's highly eloquent pose or her silhouette as "one of the most magnificently invented statues that I know [...]".[14] Measured against the number of casts recognised to date as well as the partly scaled-down and smoothed versions of the sculpture,[15] this assessment was generally accepted throughout the twentieth century.[16]

In 1907, Rodin himself referred to the version of *Eve* produced 26 years prior to that as "an interesting work, certain parts of which have remained sketchy" and pointed out that the first bronze casts based on the first plaster model were much more expressive than the casts of the "completely" worked marble version executed by his assistant Antoine Bourdelle between 1901 and 1906.[17]

Over the years, the "unfinishedness" that had accidentally resulted in 1881 or 1882 proved to be an important step for Rodin in his creative work. However, he did not present *Eve* in public until his sculptural concept had become markedly more developed.[18] By means of the repeated prominent positioning of the figure in the years 1899 and 1900,[19] he succeeded in demonstrating what he intended and was capable of doing with his *modelé*: he could cause the sculptures to appear animated as a result of the varying surface, and the play of light this produced, thus also indirectly illustrating ideas or – in the case of *Eve* – feelings in a very powerful way.[20] This was aided by dispensing with the elaboration of those details that Rodin saw as "worthless" and obstructive for capturing the "principle thoughts" of his works.[21] The photographs that Eugène Druet (1867–1916) took, under the guidance of Rodin, of the bronze cast of *Eve* also illustrate the conscious use of these creative means (cat. 96; p. 285, fig. 3).[22] The one on display in the exhibition shows the dark bronze figure in a three-quarter view in front of the plaster *Gates of Hell*. The incident light from the side highlights the uneven modelled front of the body as well the shameful pose averting the world. *Eve* appears in an entirely different light in the photograph by Jacques-Ernest Bulloz (1858–1942): in his image (cat. 97), the bronze becomes apparent as a light figure against the neutral black background, and it comes across as much more withdrawn due to the frontal view. Any indication of the concrete surroundings in which the photograph was taken is missing, and therefore of the dimensions of the work. All that becomes blatantly visible in this image as well is the seemingly unusual modelling of 1899 that was so important for Rodin. — JB

> "[...] one of the most magnificently invented statues that I know [...]"
>
> Louis de Fourcaud, 1899

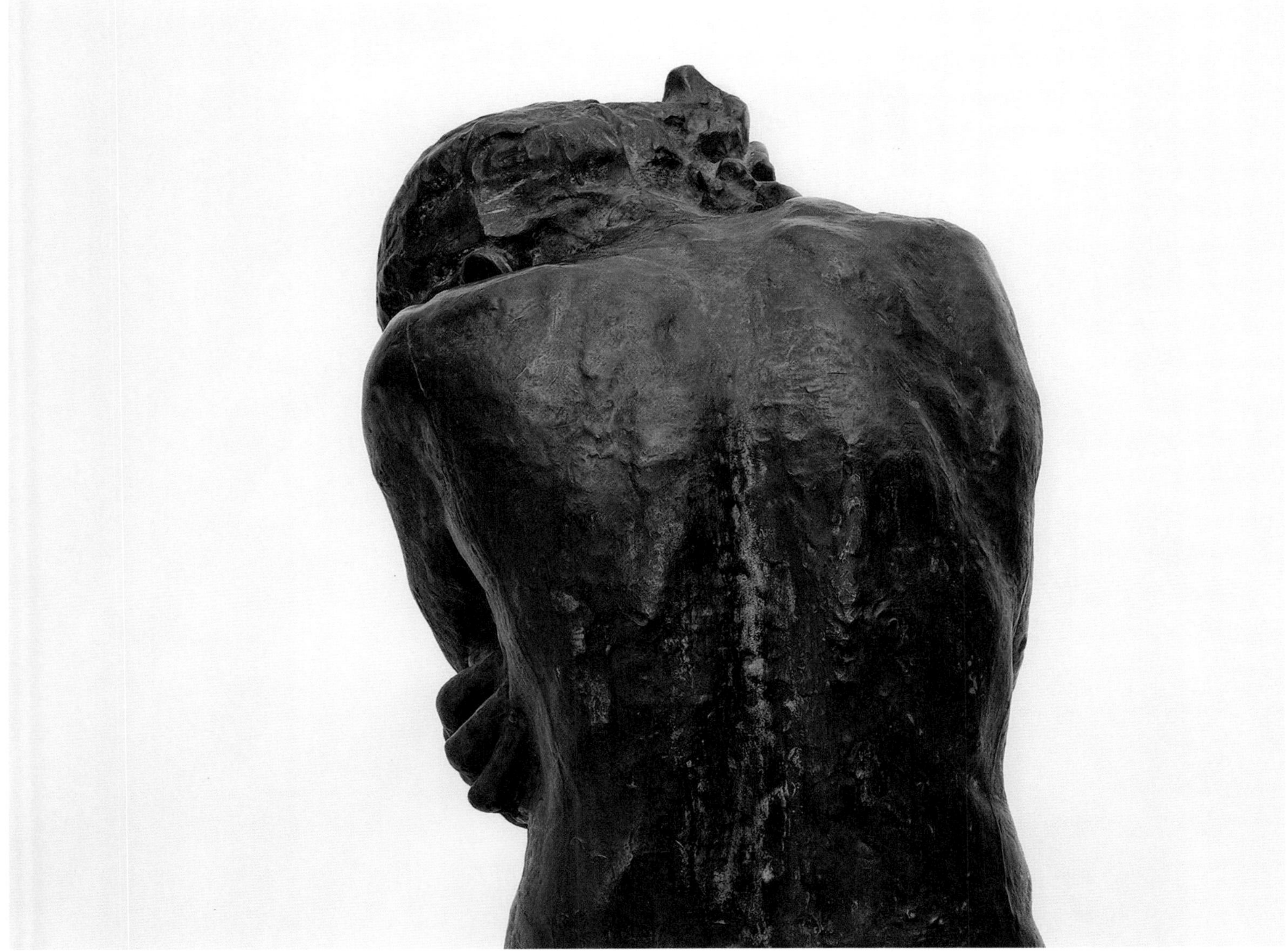

Cat. 95

1 Le Normand-Romain 2007, pp. 55–56.

2 Inv. cat. Philadelphia 1976, p. 148.

3 For detailed information on this sculpture, see inv. cat. Paris 2007a, vol. 1, pp. 114–119.

4 Le Normand-Romain 2007, p. 57.

5 Inv. cat. Paris 2007a, vol. 1, p. 345, references Paul Dubois's *Ève naissante* (1873, Petit Palais, Paris) and Alexandre Falguière's *Ève* (c. 1880, Musée d'Orsay, Paris). Further examples, including for portrayals of Eve after the Fall, can be found in inv. cat. Philadelphia 1976, p. 148 and figs. 8-1 to 8-3.

6 Le Normand-Romain 2010, p. 68.

7 Ibid., p. 70. The identification of the model was long contested; see inv. cat. Paris 2007a, vol. 1, p. 345; Le Normand-Romain 2007, p. 57.

8 "Je n'avais certainement pas pensé que, pour traduire Ève, il fallût prendre comme modèle une femme enceinte; un hasard, heureux pour moi, me l'a donné, et il a singulièrement aidé au caractère de la figure." Dujardin-Beaumetz [1913] 1992, p. 64; English quoted in: inv. cat. Paris 2007a, vol. 1, p. 345.

9 "C'est pour cela que mon Ève n'est pas finie." Dujardin-Beaumetz [1913] 1992, p. 64; English quoted in: ibid.

10 Le Normand-Romain 2010, p. 70.

11 Ibid., p. 73.

12 This is described, for instance, by De Fourcaud 1899, p. 251. Further contemporary commentaries on the sculpture's positioning are cited in inv. cat. Stanford 2003, pp. 189–190.

13 De Fourcaud 1899, p. 252. Paul Desjardins also criticised that the figure was "unpolished" and furthermore referred to it as "badly built"; Desjardins 1899, p. 286.

14 "L'Ève de Rodin est une des statues les plus magnifiquement inventées que je connaisse." De Fourcaud 1899, pp. 251–252; English quoted in: inv. cat. Paris 2007a, vol. 1, p. 347.

15 See inv. cat. Paris 2007a, vol. 1, pp. 338–348.

16 The cast on display in the exhibition stems from the Paris-based foundry of Alexis Rudier (1844–1897); his descendants continued to use the company "stamp" unchanged; inv. cat. Paris 2007a, vol. 1, pp. 28–29. Alexis's son Eugène Rudier (1878–1952) sold this cast to the art dealer Ludwig Gutbier in Munich. From there, it entered the possession of the Frankfurt-based entrepreneur Georg Hartmann in 1942, who donated it to the Städel Museum in 1953.

17 Letter from Rodin to the collector Philipp Sparkuhle, 10 October 1907, quoted in: inv. cat. Paris 2007a, vol. 1, p. 348.

18 Inv. cat. Paris 2007a, vol. 1, p. 345; Rodin had already considered having a bronze cast made as early as in 1886; ibid.

19 On the presentation of *Eve* in 1899 and 1900 in several exhibitions, see Gülicher 2011, pp. 76–95; see also the essay by the same author in this catalogue, pp. 276–282, esp. p. 278.

20 See Fontainas 1900, p. 401. On the significance of the *modelé* for the sculptor, see Rodin [1912] 1983, pp. 21–22, and Meier-Graefe 1904, vol. 1, p. 267.

21 Claris 1902a (German), pp. 20–21.

22 On Rodin's handling of the photograph, see also the essay by Juliane Betz in this catalogue, pp. 284–289.

Cat. 95

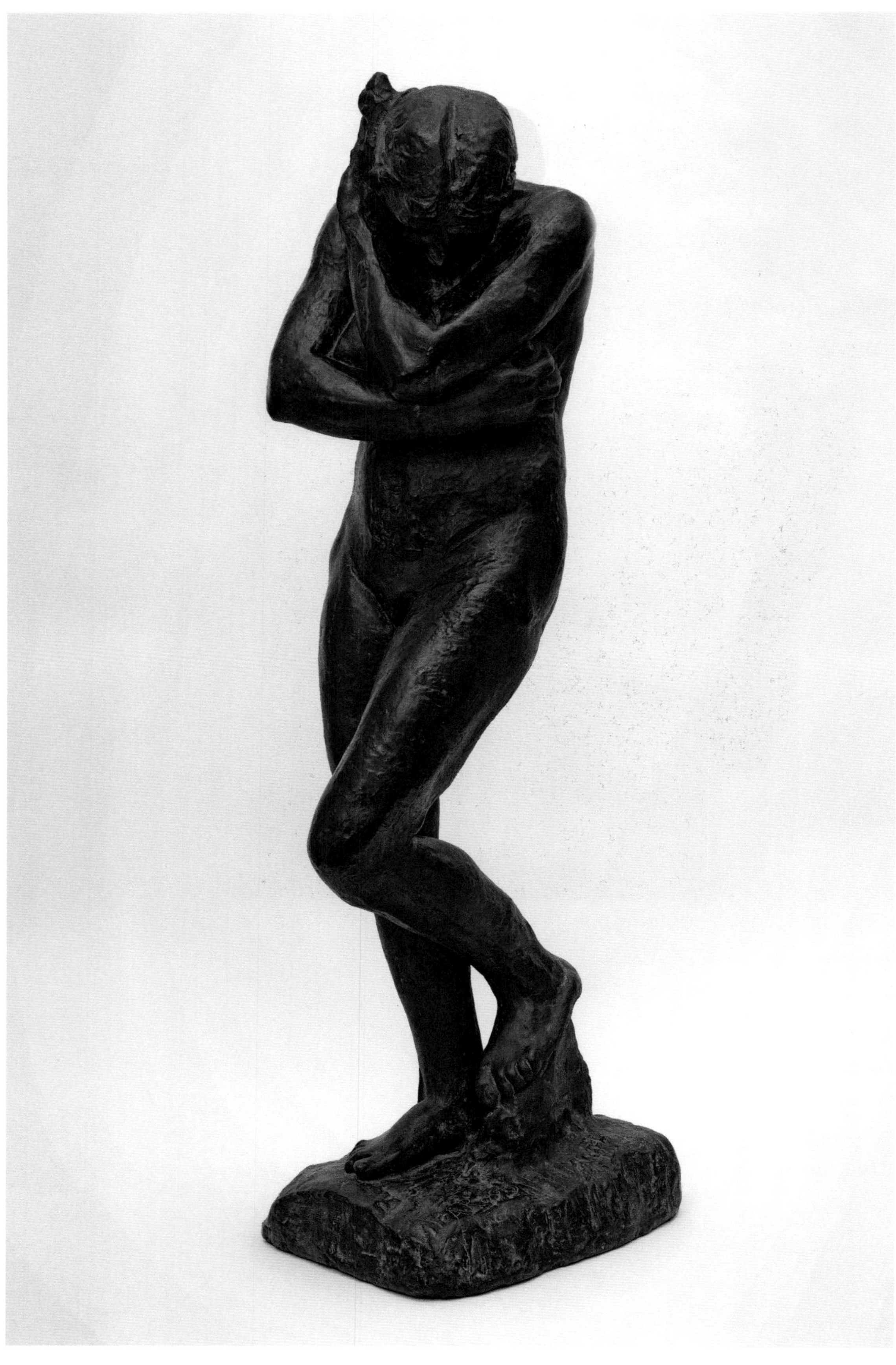

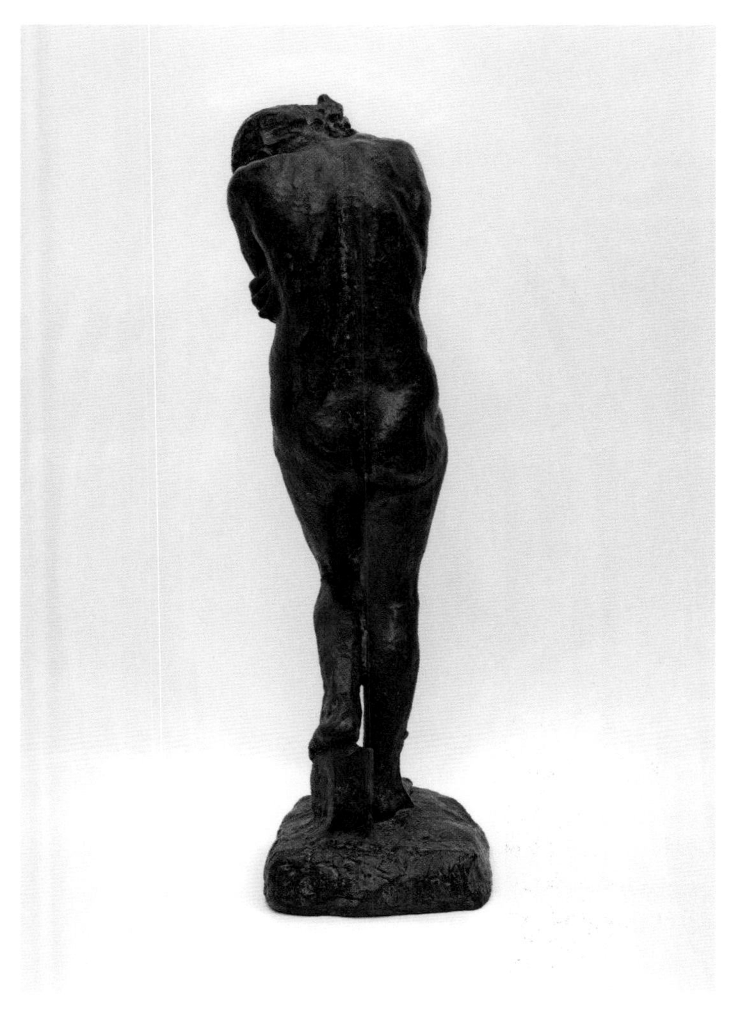

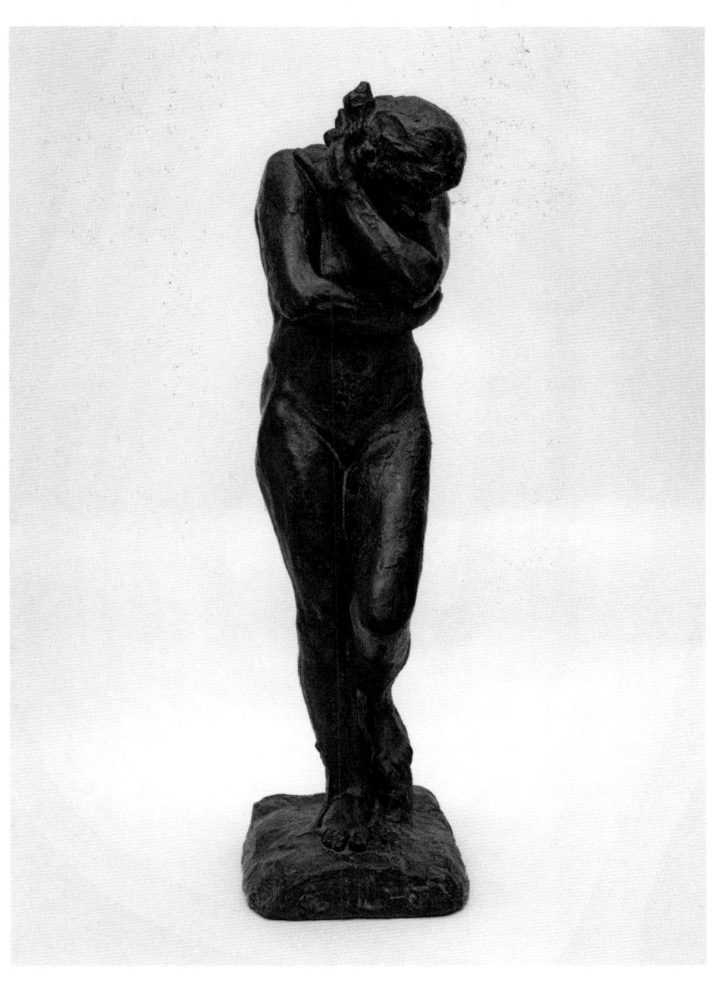

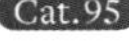
Cat.95

Cat.96 Eugène Druet, Eve in front of the Gates of Hell in the Studio at the Dépôt des Marbres, 1896–1900; photograph (vintage print) on gelatin silver paper, 29.7 × 39.6 cm; Staatliche Museen zu Berlin, Kunstbibliothek; inv. no. 2009,80/021
Cat.97 Jacques-Ernest Bulloz, Eve, c. 1903; carbon print, black (vintage print), 34.4 × 22.5 cm; Staatliche Museen zu Berlin, Kunstbibliothek; inv. no. 1905,354

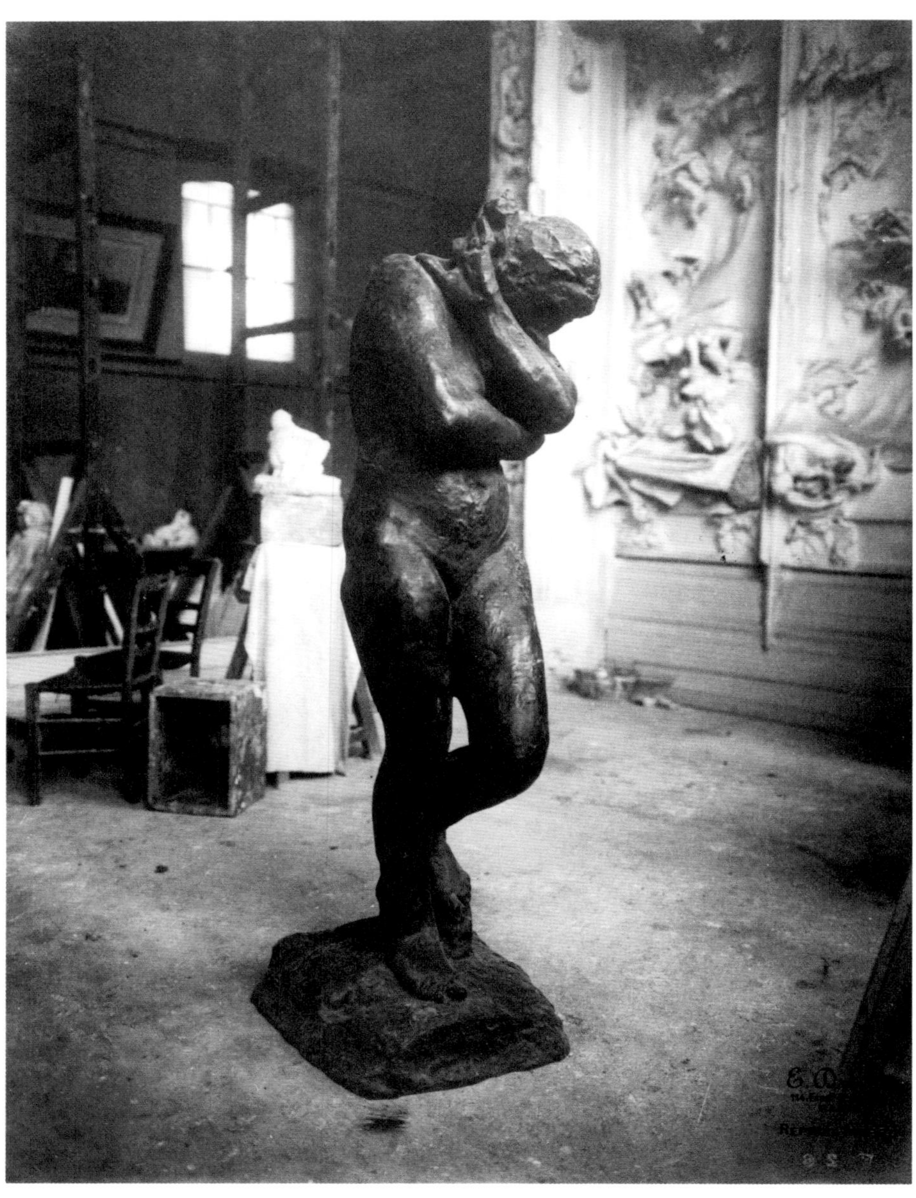

Cat.96

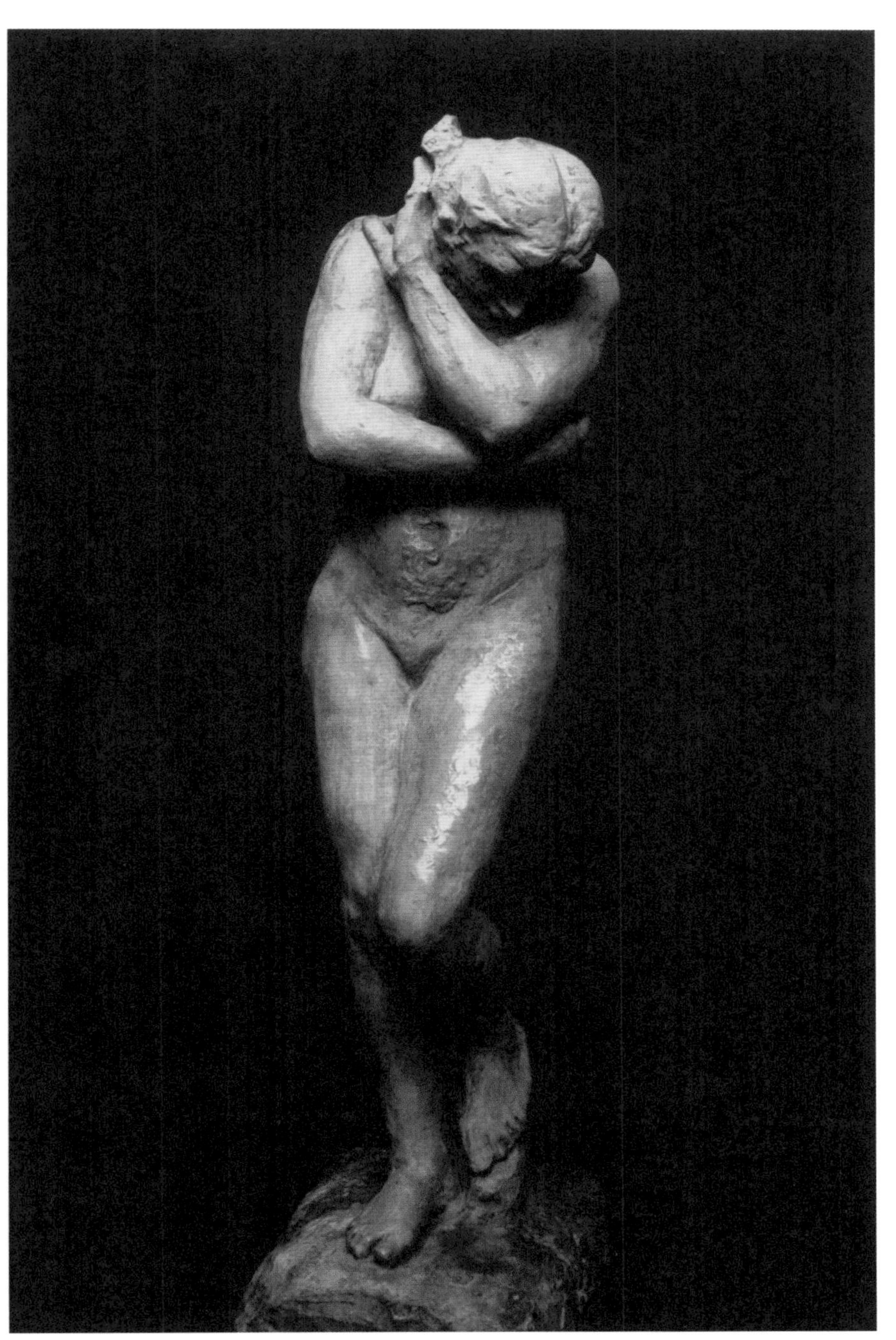

Cat. 97

 # Variations in works by Camille Claudel and Auguste Rodin

Camille Claudel presents her crouching woman, or rather the woman's torso, huddled up, her upper body pressed to her legs and her buttocks nearly touching the floor (cat. 100): it was presumably not until she had the plaster, which she had produced around 1884/85, cast after 1898, that she decided to lop off the arms, the head buried between them, as well as the left knee.[1] She transformed the conventional body study into a new type of work by means of its fragmentation.[2] The similarity with an ancient torso that resulted from the intervention puts it as well as the motif of a cowering women close to works by Auguste Rodin (see cat. 104), whose studio Claudel entered around 1884.[3] However, the surface of the *Torso* is in clear contrast to Rodin's *modelé* (see cat. 89–92, 95).[4] The smooth, cohesive contours are more reminiscent of his pencil drawings – for instance, his *Woman Sitting Cross-Legged with Her Arm Thrown over Her Head* (cat. 101). Rodin used the sharpened hard pencil to draw long lines over the thin wove paper, gradually shaping the figure by repeating the contours. He defined the volume of the woman's body in part by means of rubbed hatching, whose metallic lustre recalls bronze; however, he in turn broke through this effect by means of partial erasing. The study can be assigned to a group of drawings done after 1895/96 which Rodin – his eyes constantly fixed on the model – produced without looking at the sheet of paper he was drawing on.[5]

Also with respect to method, parallels with Rodin's oeuvre can be seen in Claudel's *Torso*. It concerns a subject that she would address throughout her creative work and that she realised in several versions. Her sculpture *The Waltz*, on which she worked from 1889 onwards, represents another form of the variation (cat. 99). In the original version, which has not survived, the two dancers embrace one another in the nude. Judged in 1892 by the responsible state censor Armand Dayot as too vulgar to be converted into marble, Claudel subsequently provided the female dancer with a robe.[6] In the first reworked version, the fabric envelops her and waves as a veil around the couple's heads, while in the second version exhibited here, it leaves her upper body bare and appears to grow out of her skin. This causes it to seem less decorative; instead it constitutes a crucial element of the composition and serves as a counterbalance to the bodies standing in an unstable diagonal.[7] At the same time, the composition of the fabric contrasts with that of the figures; in their dynamics, its untowelled grooves and ridges convey the actual motif: movement. The sculptural execution of dance was considered to be one of the greatest challenges, for which Claudel received much praise with *The Waltz*.[8] At the same time, she was concerned with the sculptural interpretation of music and rhythm as well as the movement of the viewer, who was only capable of comprehending the dancing couple by circumnavigating it completely and, in doing so, relating to the turning of the dancers (see cat. 80–84).

Claudel once again devoted herself to the *Waltz* sculpture around the turn of the century. She removed the male dancer and furnished his erstwhile partner with the attributes of Fortuna, thus reinterpreting the figure in terms of content.[9] While this separation of an individual figure from a couple or group composition was typical of Claudel's working process, Rodin proceeded in a contrary fashion when reusing sculptures that he had already developed, as demonstrated by the example of his *Faun* (cat. 98). Formally speaking, the work exhibits several common features with *The Waltz*. In this case as well, it is about a couple in motion struggling for balance, yet which could not be more different with respect to Claudel's dancers: a conspicuously small nymph jumps – according to contemporary critics like a frog[10] – around the neck of a gnarled faun, occasionally referred to as an "old tree".[11] Even at the time, due to the subject matter, the group of figures was judged to be a Symbolist work par excellence.[12] However, Rodin's interest might have been primarily of a formal nature. He addressed the subject of movement in numerous figurines of couples and, for this reason, frequently experimented with figures he had created earlier on. For the *Faun*, for instance, he used a *Mercury* he had developed for *The Gates of Hell* (see cat. 95) as well as a figure he had likewise designed for this context. Like a building set, Rodin used his sculptures as a repertoire for new combinations guided by formal interests.[13]

Rodin cultivated this handling of his own oeuvre across genres. Hence his works on paper also served as a field for experimentation. Besides preliminary drawings and the reproduction of preparatory etchings or pen-and-ink drawings for sculptures, they primarily involved variations of motifs whose context he constantly redefined by means of clipping and cutting out, collaging, retouching or annotating, like those of his continually reworked sculptural compositions.[14]

However, both Rodin's and Claudel's variations have little in common with the manner of working in series associated with Impressionism and exemplarily embodied by Claude Monet's paintings of the Cathedral of Rouen.[15] His repeated treatment of one-and-the-same motif at different times of day allowed the artist to lend vividness to the fleetingness of the momentary impression.[16] By contrast, Claudel and Rodin did not undertake a repeated study of the motif; rather, they reused existing sculptures or elements of the same (see cat. 84). Claudel's content-related reinterpretation of the female dancer to become Fortuna opposes Rodin's formally motivated assemblage, which as "l'art pour l'art" demonstrated new paths for the genre of sculpture.[17] — FR

Cat.98 Auguste Rodin, *Faun* (The Old Tree; The Old Oak [Le Vieil Arbre; Le Vieux Chêne]), c. 1885; bronze, 39.5 × 38.5 × 32 cm; signed on the back: "Rodin"; Städel Museum, Frankfurt am Main, inv. no. SGP6

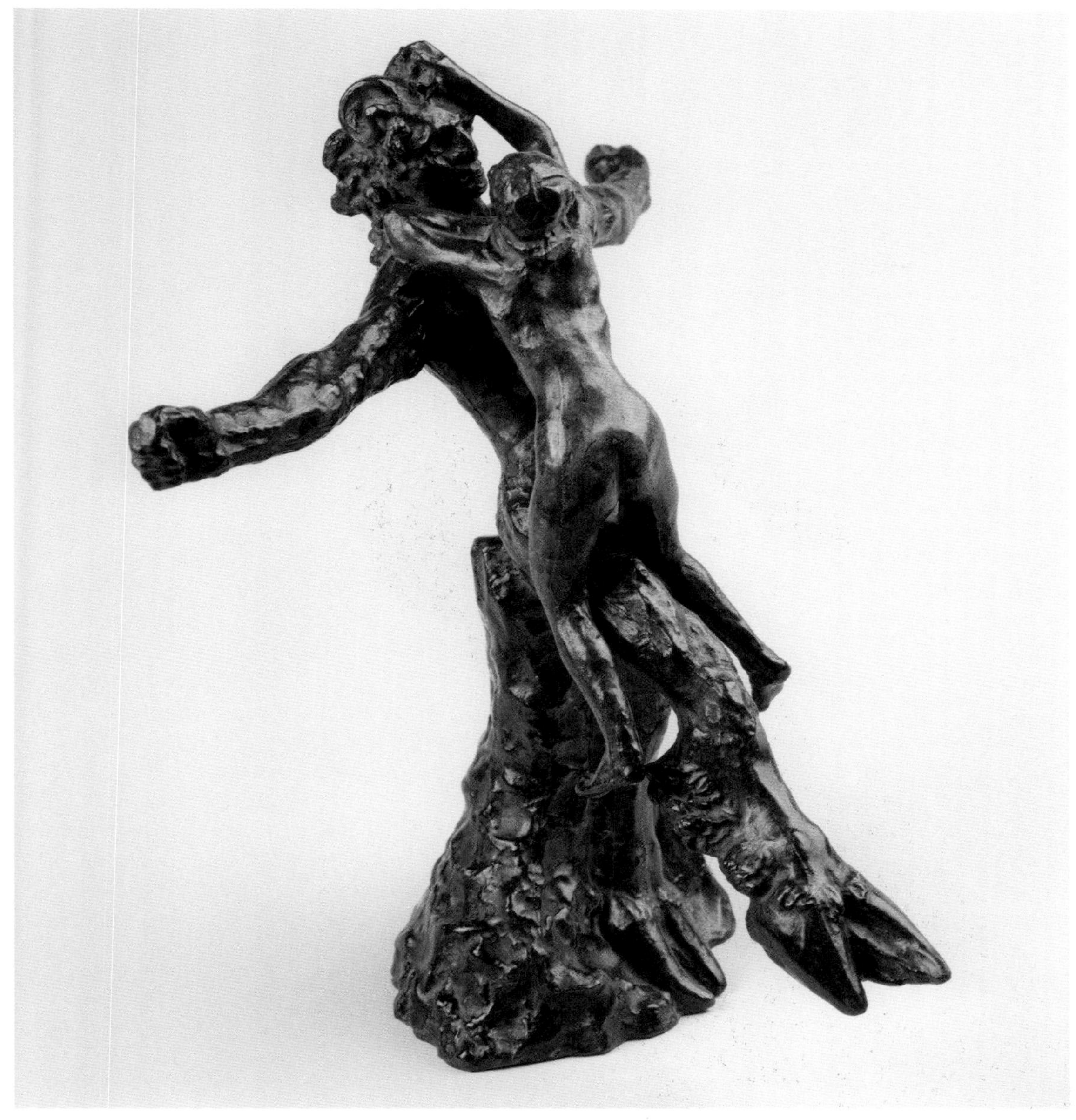

Cat.98

1   On the genesis of the work, see Rivière/Gaudichon/Ghanassia 2000, pp. 72–73, no. 14.
2   Ibid., p. 72.
3   See, for example, Rodin's *Femme accroupie* (Musée Rodin, Paris, inv. no. S.1,156), of which Claudel owned a copy; ibid.
4   Exh. cat. Paris/Poitiers 1984, pp. 31–32, no. 6, esp. p. 32 (Bruno Gaudichon).
5   On the phases of Rodin's drawing oeuvre, see Buley-Uribe 2005, p. 150.
6   On the genesis of the work, see Rivière/Gaudichon/Ghanassia 2000, pp. 113–117, no. 33.
7   For details on the different versions of *La Valse*, see exh. cat. Paris/de La Chapelle 1990, pp. 127–134, no. 27.
8   See ibid., p. 129, and the quotation there

by Octave Mirbeau, according to which Claudel took on this difficult task with flying colours. The sculptress had a marked interest in contemporary dance and music and maintained a close relationship with the composer Claude Debussy, who in turn had a small version of *La Valse* on his desk; see Rivière/Gaudichon/Ghanassia 2000, pp. 113–117, no. 33, esp. p. 114.
9   See ibid., pp. 173–175, no. 58.
10   "Un groupe de la plus grande originalité représente dans sa pensée l'amour physique, mais sans que la traduction de sa pensée soit obscène. C'est un mâle, un satyre, qui tient contre le haut de sa poitrine une faunesse contractée et les jambes ramassées dans un étonnant resserrement de grenouille qui s'apprête

à sauter." Edmond de Goncourt, entry from 17 April 1886, in De Goncourt 1894, pp. 121–124, esp. p. 124.
11   On the different titles of this work, see Mongi-Vollmer 2008, p. 5.
12   See inv. cat. Paris 2007a, vol. 2, p. 708 (with a reference to Fagus 1900: "l'œuvre directement et maitressement symbolique").
13   For details on Rodin's *Faun* and the figures he reused in it, see Mongi-Vollmer 2008.
14   On Rodin's collages and the fragmentation of works on paper as well as of sculptures, see exh. cat. Paris 2018b. On the aspect of metamorphosis in his works on paper, see Buley-Uribe 2005, pp. 147–149.
15   See, for example, exh. cat. Rouen 1994.

16   On this subject, see Joel Isaacson, who explains that the critic Ernest Chesneau, for instance, commented on Impressionism early on, initially insisting on the meaning of light and fleetingness, but later also emphasising the role of memory and the repeated examination of a motif; Isaacson 1986, pp. 382–383.
17   On the aspect of the assemblage in Rodin's work, see Barbier 1990; regarding *The Gates of Hell*, in particular, see Albert E. Elsen, chapter 5: "How Rodin Worked on Sculpture", in Elsen 1985, pp. 67–121, esp. pp. 82–84; regarding the *Faun*, see Mongi-Vollmer 2008. On the groundbreaking significance of this approach, see Rowell 1983.

Cat.99

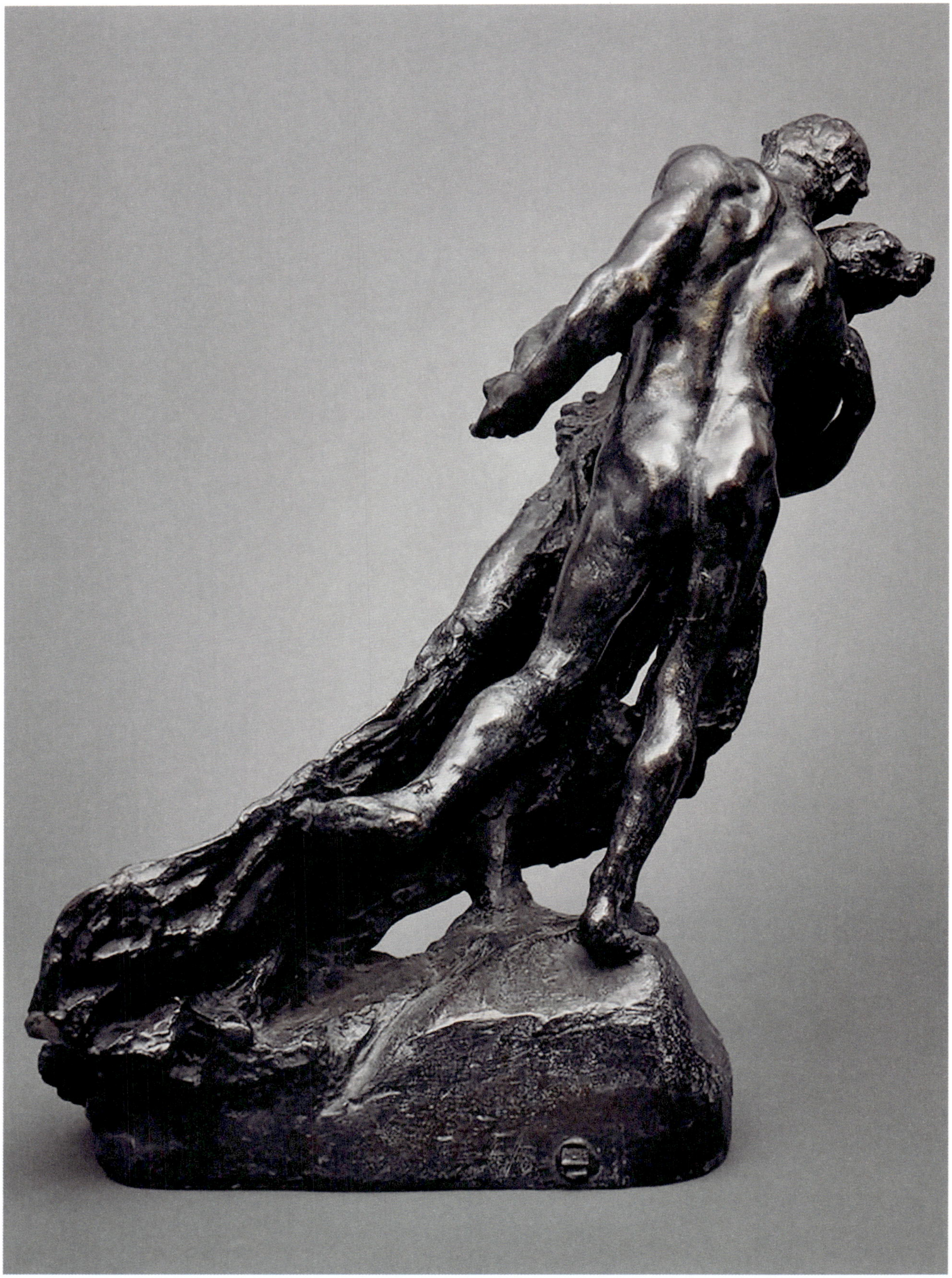

Cat. 99

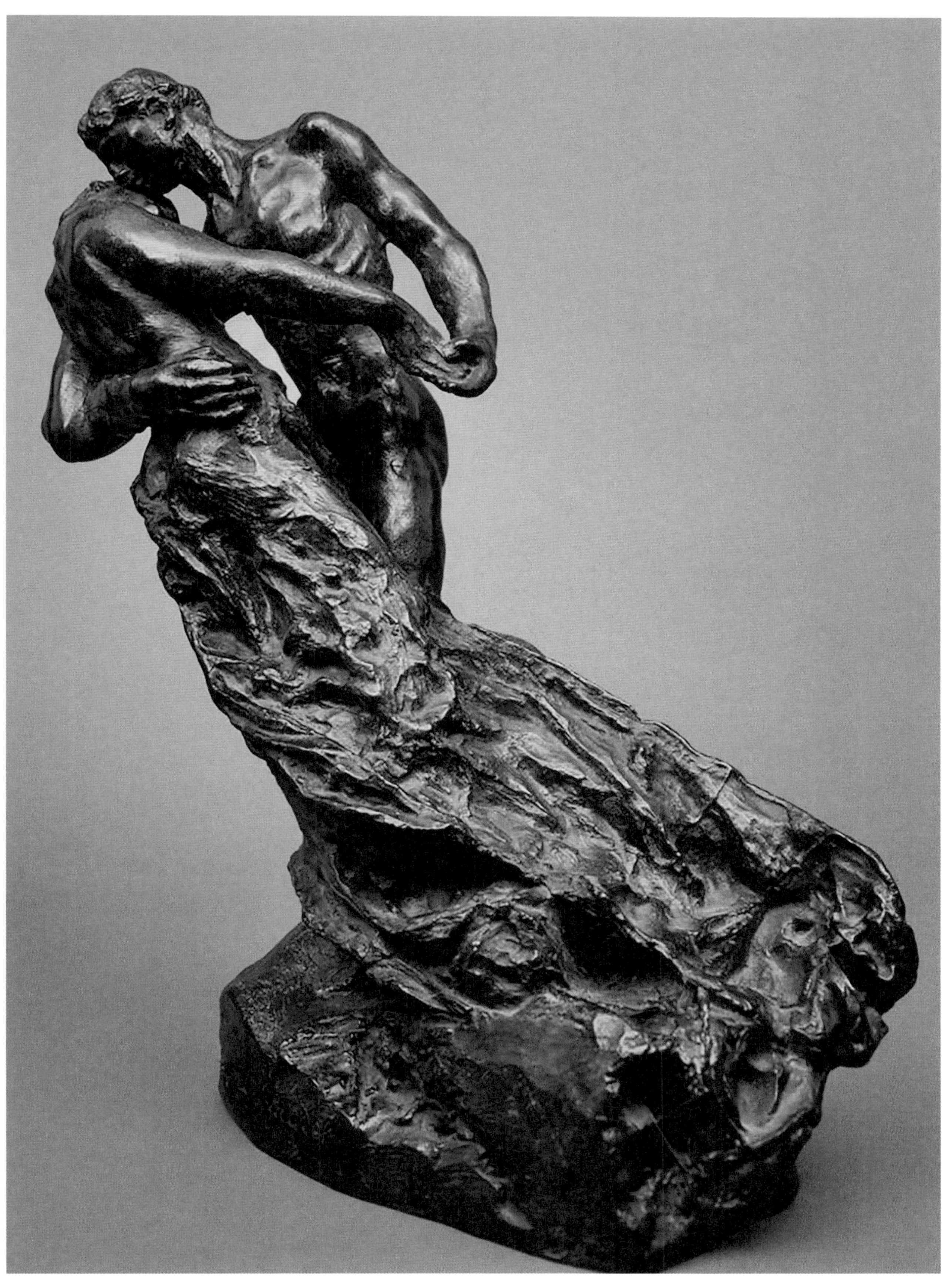

Cat. 100 Camille Claudel, **Torso of a Crouching Woman** (*Torse de Femme accroupie*), c. 1884/85; bronze, 44 × 27 × 26 cm; La Piscine – Musée d'art et d'industrie André Diligent, Roubaix, inv. no. 2007-14-1, Achat réalisé avec l'aide de la Société des Amis du musée, de l'État (fonds du patrimoine), du fonds régional d'acquisition des musées (État/Conseil Régional du Nord-Pas-de-Calais) et d'une souscription publique en 2007

Cat. 101 Auguste Rodin, **Woman Sitting Cross-Legged with Her Arm Thrown over Her Head**, c. 1900–1910; pencil, wiped and washed, on wove paper, 29.5 × 20 cm; signed lower right in pencil: "Aug Rodin"; Städel Museum, Frankfurt am Main, inv. no. SG 2402

Cat. 100

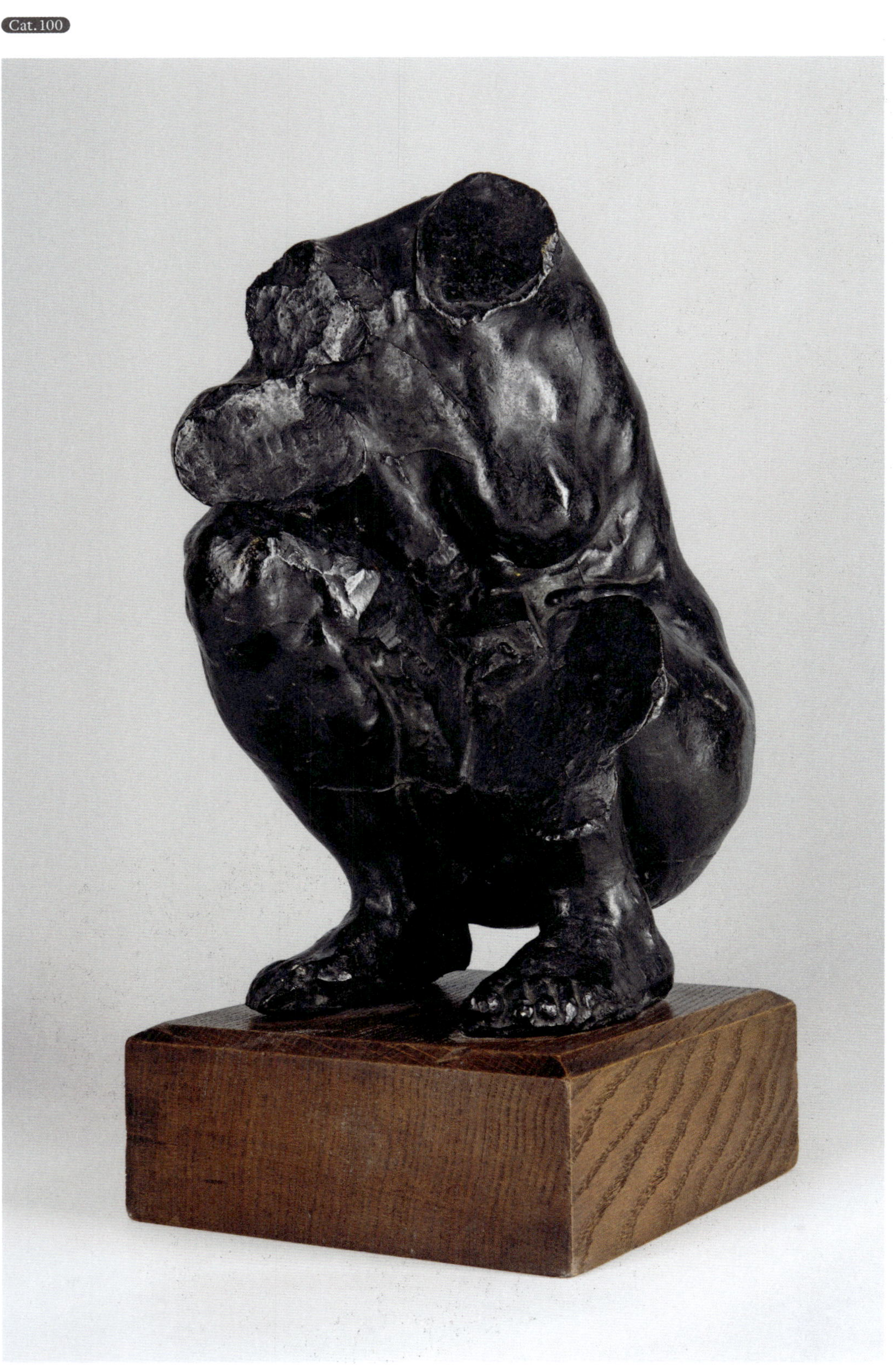

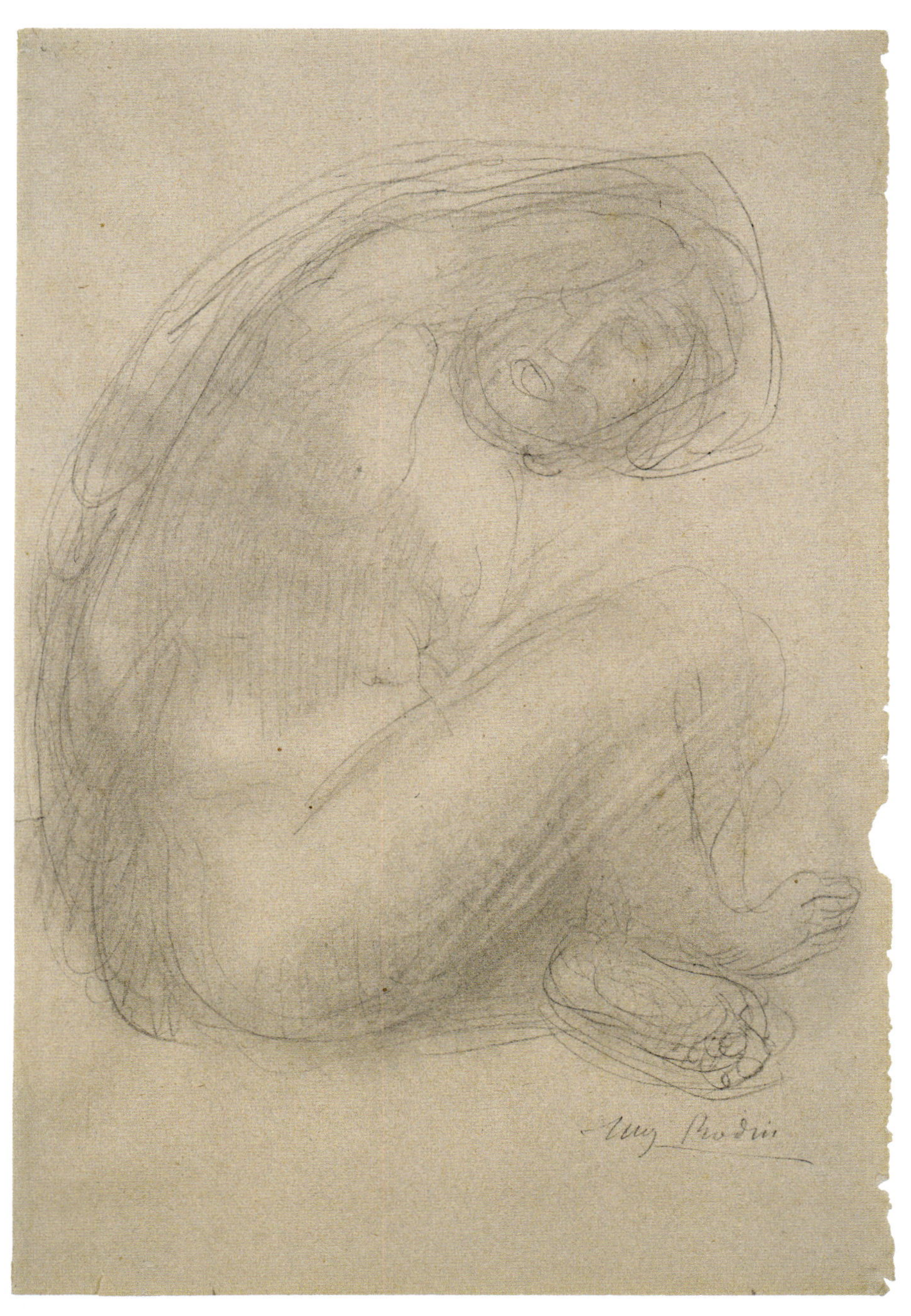

Cat. 101

In his early fifties, Auguste Rodin, already an extraordinarily renowned sculptor, stated that he could "only work with a model" and had "no good ideas" except when he "cop[ied] nature".[1] These statements explain why he was repeatedly referred to as a "naturalist" or "realist", two features that also played a role in the definition of Impressionism.[2] The sculpture *Saint John Preaching* (cat. 103), which Rodin presented for the first time at the Salon in 1880, can be regarded as a prime example of the method described:[3] The figure can be traced back to a visit in Rodin's studio by a man previously unknown to him who offered to pose as a model. At the sight of the peasant from Abruzzo, he "immediately thought of a Saint John the Baptist, in other words, a man of nature, a visionary, a believer, a precursor [...]."[4] The man's pose came about just as spontaneously, because the man named Pignatelli[5] planted himself with both feet on the floor, his legs wide apart and "open like a compass".[6] Rodin was persuaded by this posture and recognised "a man walking!"[7] At the same time, he was aware of the fact that, in the sense of balanced postures defined by the artist, he was disobeying all conventions with this completely free way of finding a pose. For this reason, and to protect himself from being accused of working dishonestly,[8] he wanted to create something credible, something that reproduced his "impression" as accurately as possible.[9] This meant that he modelled the muscular body[10] standing as described above, with the upper body turned slightly forward and to the left. The figure was praised repeatedly as being particularly expressive and full of life,[11] which Rodin explained as follows: "Now, the illusion of life is obtained in our art by good modelling and by movement."[12]

While developing the figure, several preliminary studies approximately one metre in height were produced as well as a true-to-scale bozzetto for the saint's head (cat. 102). The latter shows how Rodin sculpted Pignatelli's face framed by chin-length hair and a full beard. He first roughly modelled the form, then firmly pressed numerous small rolls or clots of light beige clay onto it, and spread the better part of the moist material with his fingers in such a way that it resulted in different structures and animated variations of light and shadow.[13] The modelling of this bust as well as the full-length figure invigorates the stature of the prophet gesticulating with his raised right hand and perhaps speaking as well. In this respect and in its ascetic appearance, the figure adheres to traditional iconography; yet the nakedness, the determined stride and the lack of any attributes testify to Rodin's new approach to the subject, which was a frequently chosen one in the late nineteenth century.[14] Despite some criticism of the realism of the figure,[15] the French state acquired the bronze cast of *Saint John* exhibited at the Salon of 1881. From 1884 onwards, it was presented at the Musée du Luxembourg, but in a place that was poorly lighted and too confined – in Rodin's view, this is all that mattered – with the consequence that visitors could not walk around the sculpture and view it from different sides.[16] When Eugène Druet (1867–1916) took a photograph of *Saint John* at the Musée du Luxembourg a good ten years later (cat. 105), it stood in a large hall full of paintings, surrounded by so much space that Rodin's trusted photographer at that time could take pictures of it from all sides, which was very much in keeping with the sculptor's concept.[17]

Shortly before his exhibition in the Pavillon de l'Alma (1900), Rodin combined parts of studies that he had modelled for *Saint John*, in this way creating a new sculpture (cat. 104) – a method of central importance for his oeuvre (see cat. 98–101). In this case, he placed a torso damaged during storage on two fairly well-preserved legs, without smoothing off the joints or aligning the surface design of the elements with one another.[18] The plaster figure created in this way was referred to in the exhibition catalogue as a "powerful study" for *Saint John*.[19] However, because the work's message is detached from any iconography due to the lack of head and arms, and because the work's message revolved around the supra-individual element of movement,[20] the title of *The Walking Man*, as it is commonly called today concurrent with Rodin's own perception of the pose (see above), established itself from 1907 onwards.[21] The figure illustrates Rodin's comment that a sculptor depicts movement by showing "the transition from one attitude to another", hence connecting past with future, in a highly demonstrative way.[22] Compared to *Saint John*, he intensified movement in *The Walking Man* by means of minor modifications: although both feet are standing flat on the floor and because this does not normally occur while walking, the viewer forms a mental picture of the raising of the one foot or the landing of the other that just occurred. In addition, this is emphasised by the turning of the upper body and the width of the stride, which from the side looks like it is directed markedly forwards. Viewed from the front, the figure seems somewhat more static and, moreover, unstable due to the arrangement of the feet one behind the other, and therefore as if it were in motion. Hence Rodin created a sculpture that captures something momentary, impermanent and, in his opinion, for the understanding of which a head is equally as unnecessary as arms.[23] The fact that he was concerned with the reproduction of walking itself may also be the reason why he presented the plaster in the Pavillon de l'Alma on a little over two-meter-high column, which is not visible however on the present cropped photograph by Druet (cat. 106; see p. 278, fig. 4).[24]

With *The Walking Man*, which Rodin himself called "one of my best things",[25] the sculptor succeeded in creating a seminal work: in view of the marked inclusion of both time and space as well as the "principle of the montage",[26] it is an entirely new type of sculpture. — JB

> "Now, the illusion of life is obtained in our art by good modelling and by movement."
>
> Auguste Rodin, 1912

Cat.102 Auguste Rodin, **The Head of Saint John the Baptist**, 1877/78; terracotta and oak, 30.5 × 23.7 × 21.1 cm; signed on the slope of the right shoulder: "A. Rodin"; Staatliche Kunsthalle Karlsruhe, inv. no. P 161

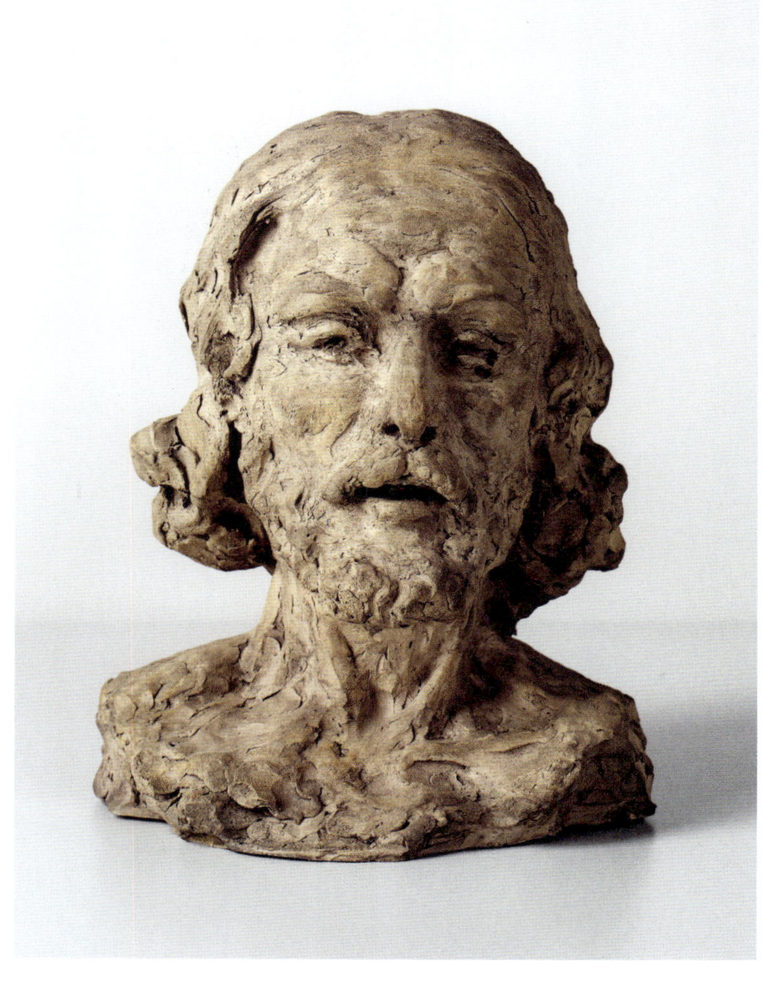

Cat.102

1 "Je ne puis travailler qu'avec un modèle. […] Je ne puis avoir des idées fortes que lorsque je copie la nature." Dujardin-Beaumetz [1913] 1992, pp. 63, 66.
2 On this, see the essays by Fabienne Ruppen, pp. 24–34, esp. pp. 29–30, and Dominik Brabant, pp. 174–183, esp. p. 180, in this catalogue.
3 Rodin exhibited a plaster in the Salon in 1880, and in 1881 a bronze cast.
4 "Je pensai immédiatement à un Saint Jean-Baptiste, c'est-à-dire à un homme de la nature, un illuminé, un croyant, un précurseur […]." Dujardin-Beaumetz [1913] 1992, p. 65; English quoted in: inv. cat. Paris 2007a, vol. 2, p. 642.
5 It is presumably Cesare Pignatelli, born in c. 1845; inv. cat. Paris 2007a, vol. 2, p. 642.
6 "[…] les deux jambes, ouvertes comme un compas." Dujardin-Beaumetz [1913] 1992, p. 65; English quoted in: inv. cat. Paris 2007a, vol. 2, p. 642.
7 "Mais c'est un homme qui marche!" Dujardin-Beaumetz [1913] 1992, p. 65; English quoted in: inv. cat. Paris 2007a, vol. 2, p. 642.

8 On the accusations surrounding *The Age of Bronze*, see the essay by Dominik Brabant in this catalogue, pp. 174–183, esp. pp. 178–179.
9 "[Q]ue je fisse quelque chose de bien; car, si je ne traduisais pas mon impression aussi exactement que je l'avais reçue, ma statue serait ridicule, et tout le monde se moquerait de moi." Dujardin-Beaumetz [1913] 1992, p. 66.
10 Photographs of Pignatelli from Rodin's estate are illustrated in exh. cat. Paris 1990, pp. 20, 26–28.
11 Rodin [1912] 1983, p. 32.
12 Ibid.
13 On this bust, see also exh. cat. Karlsruhe 2007, p. 289–292.
14 In a drawing reproduced in 1880 (Fogg Art Museum, Cambridge, inv. no. 1943.910), the saint is still holding a cross staff in his left hand, which is absent in a second drawing (Musée du Louvre, Paris, inv. no. RF 16079, recto) as well as in later illustrations. On this, see also inv. cat. Paris 2007a, vol. 2, p. 644.
15 See ibid., p. 643

16 See Gülicher 2011, p. 92.
17 A total of nine photographs of *Saint John* are known to exist in this particular setting (Fonds Druet-Vizzavona, Agence photo RMN-Grand Palais, Paris, inv. nos. DRUETB250–254, DRUETB257–259 and DRUETB2229). On the importance of transferring multiple views into photographs, see the essay by Juliane Betz in this catalogue, pp. 284–289, esp. p. 286.
18 Details on their origin and the current site of the parts can be found in inv. cat. Paris 2007a, vol. 2, p. 425. On the torso, see also inv. cat. Paris 2018, pp. 144–145.
19 "63. – Saint Jean-Baptiste. Une puissante étude pour la statue du musée du Luxembourg […]." Exh. cat. Paris 1900, p. 12. On the reasons for referring to it in this way, see Schnell 1980, p. 32.
20 The following frequently cited passage is exemplary of this: "He walks as if the whole wide world were in him, as if he were apportioning it as he walks. He walks. His arms speak of his walking, and his fingers stretch out, a sign of his stride

in the air." Rilke [1902] 2011, p. 43.
21 Inv. cat. Paris 2007a, vol. 2, p. 424.
22 Rodin [1912] 1983, p. 32 (italics in the original).
23 "Mais est-ce qu'on marche avec la tête?" Auguste Rodin, quoted in: Vollard 1937, p. 247.
24 The capital of the column can be seen on a less narrowly cropped print of the same photograph (Fonds Druet-Vizzavona, Agence photo RMN-Grand Palais, Paris, inv. no. DRUETC5011). In 1900, Rodin not only presented *The Walking Man* in this fashion; see the illustrations in exh. cat. Paris 2001, pp. 24–35. There is also evidence of the presentation of *The Walking Man* on a column for the years from 1901 to 1903; see Schnell 1980, p. 176, note 4.
25 Letter from Auguste Rodin to Henri Marcel, 1 January 1911, quoted in: inv. cat. Paris 2007a, vol. 2, p. 423.
26 See Schnell 1980, p. 32.

 Auguste Rodin, **Saint John Preaching (Saint Jean-Baptiste)**, 1878–1880, cast before 1906[1]; bronze, 206 × 54 × 124 cm; Ar fenthyg gan / Lent by Amgueddfa Cymru – National Museum Wales, Cardiff, inv. no. NMW A 2497 Auguste Rodin, **The Walking Man (L'Homme qui marche)**, c. 1900, cast before 1910[2]; bronze, 85 × 27.5 × 60 cm; signed on the plinth next to the left foot: "A. Rodin", on the back of the plinth: "ALEXIS RUDIER / FONDEUR PARIS"; Von der Heydt-Museum, Wuppertal, inv. no. P 54

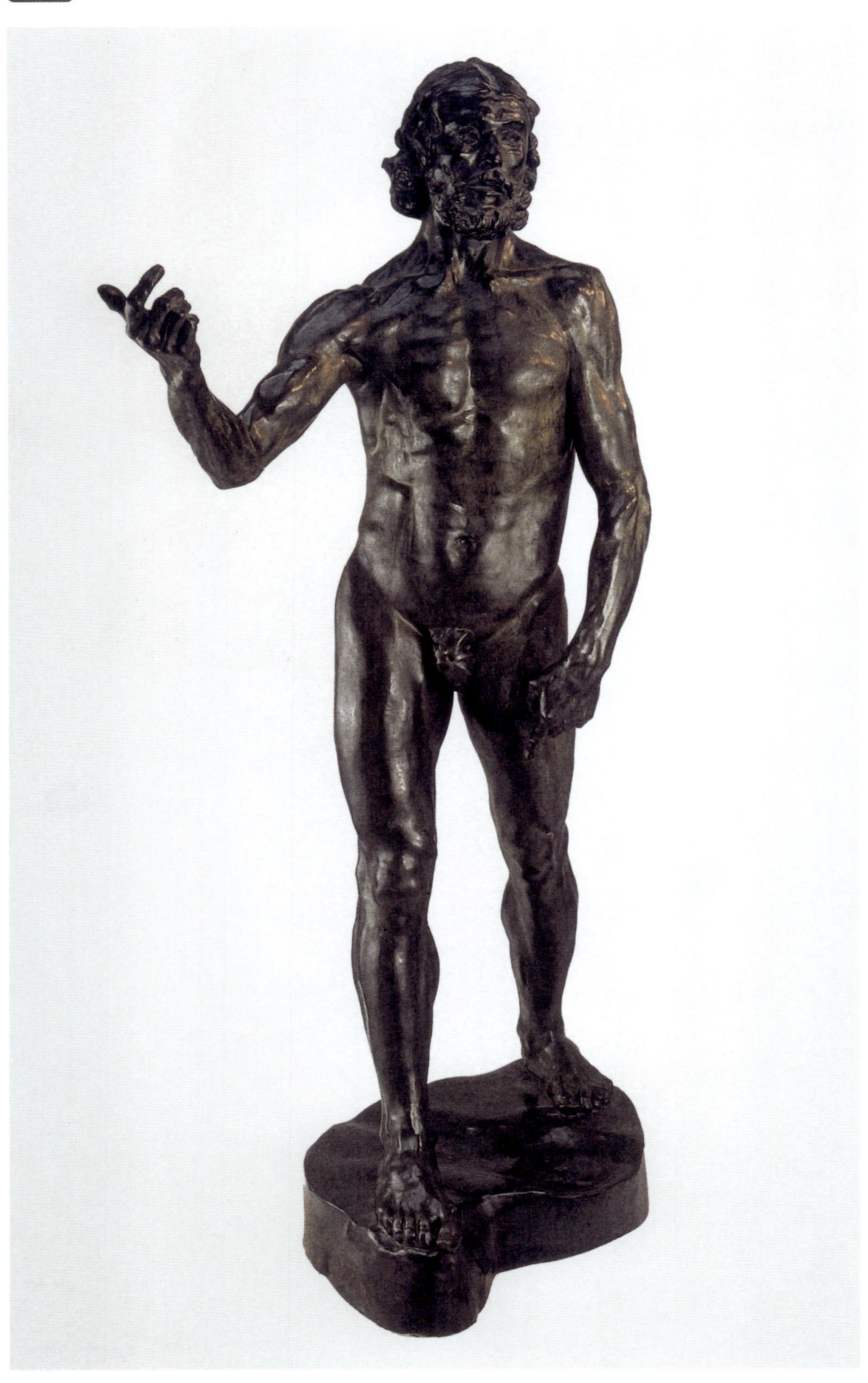

1   Inv. cat. Paris 2007a, vol. 2, p. 639.
2   Robert Wichelhaus donated this cast to the Von der Heydt-Museum in 1910.

Cat. 104

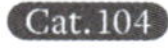

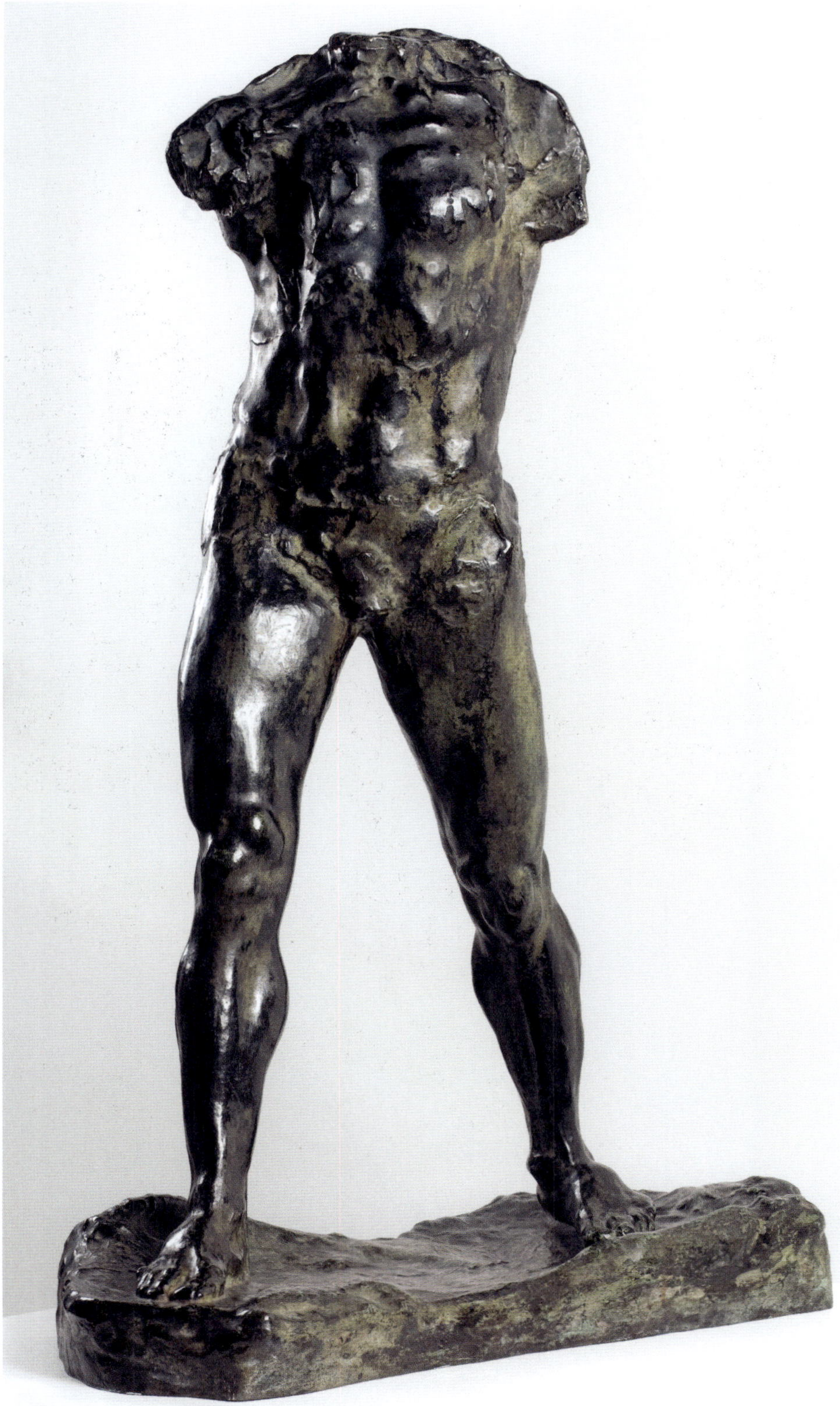

Cat.105 Eugène Druet, *Saint John the Baptist at the Musée du Luxembourg, Shadow of a Camera Tripod at the Left Edge*, 1896–1900; photograph (vintage print) on gelatin silver paper, 39.5 × 29.5 cm; Staatliche Museen zu Berlin, Kunstbibliothek, inv. no. 2009,80/011 Cat.106 Eugène Druet, *The Walking Man in the Pavillon de l'Alma, Oval Vignette*, 1896–1900; photograph (vintage print) on gelatin silver paper, 39.5 × 29.7 cm; Staatliche Museen zu Berlin, Kunstbibliothek, inv. no. 2009,80/124

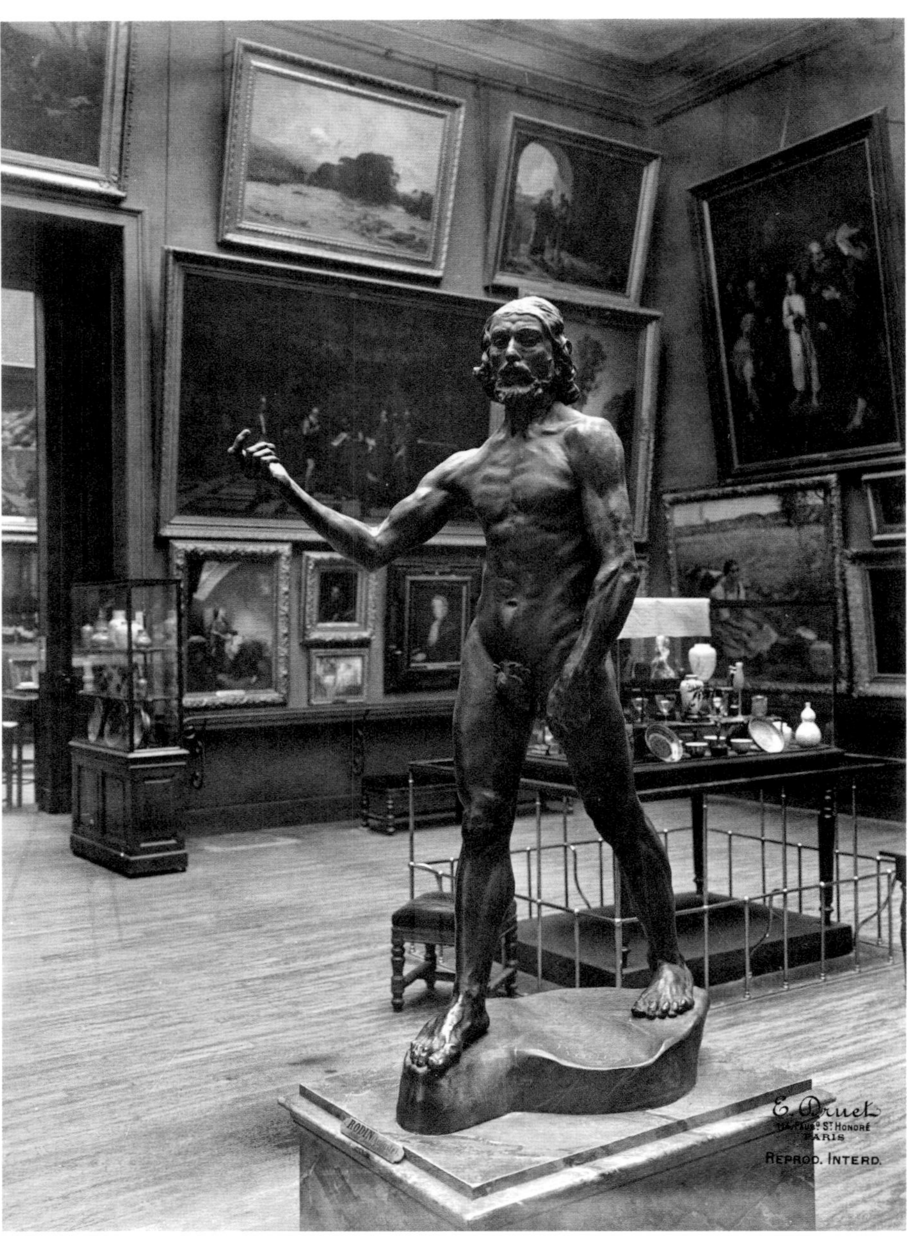

Cat.105

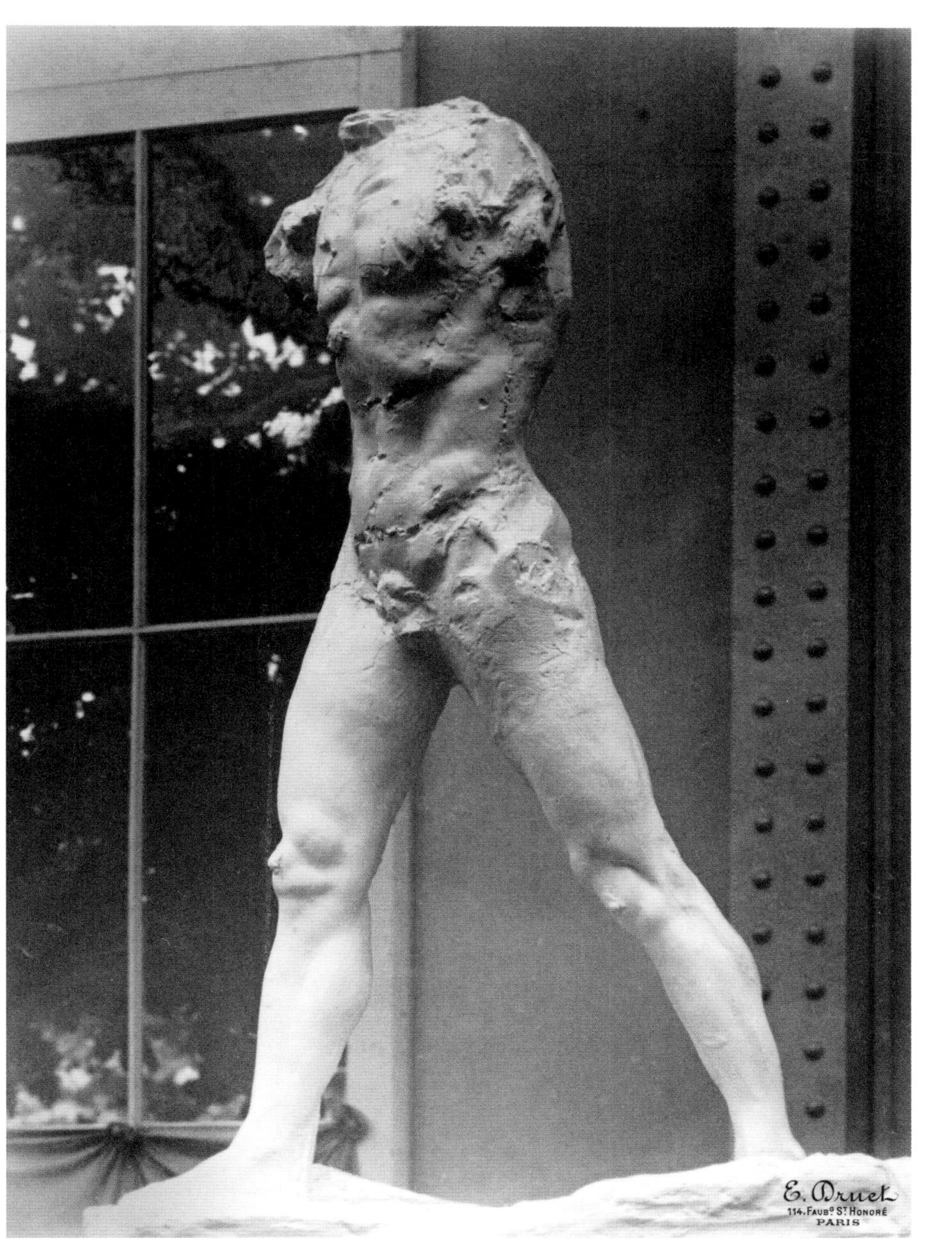

Cat. 106

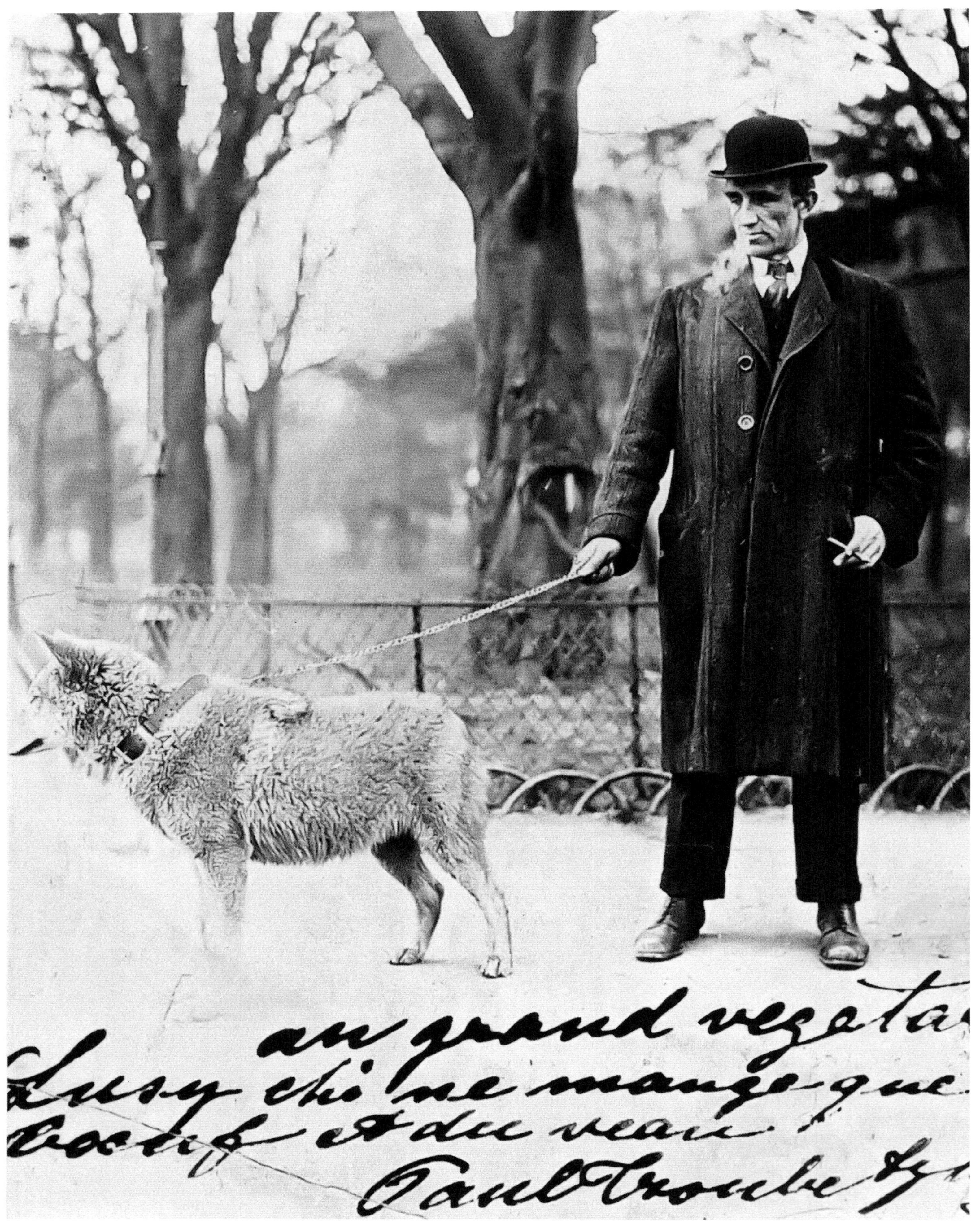
au grand végéta
Lusy qui ne mange que
boeuf et du veau
Paul Trouche fp

Paolo Troubetzkoy

Paolo Troubetzkoy

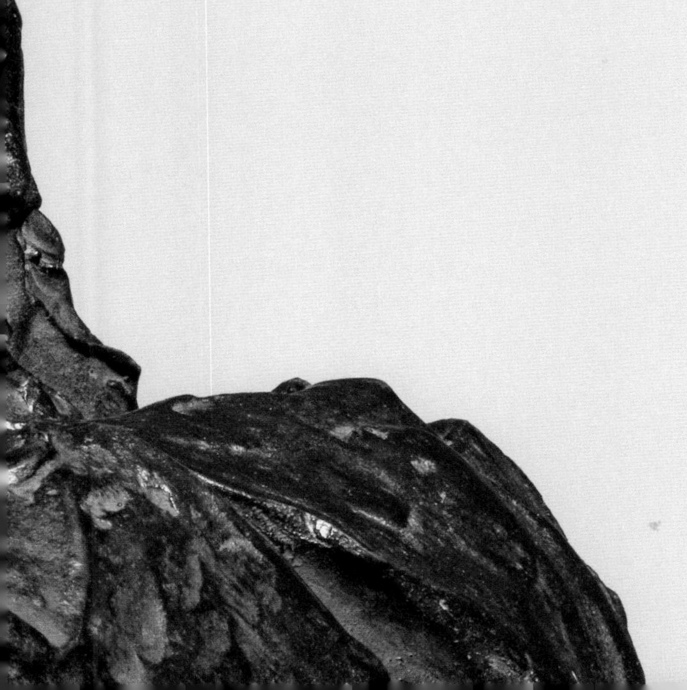

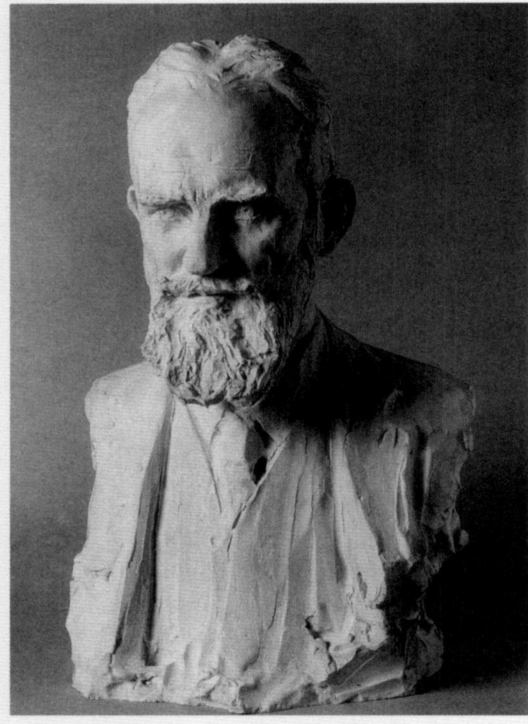

1 Paolo Troubetzkoy, *George Bernard Shaw*, 1908, plaster, patinated, 70 × 42 × 34 cm. Museo del Paesaggio, Verbania Pallanza

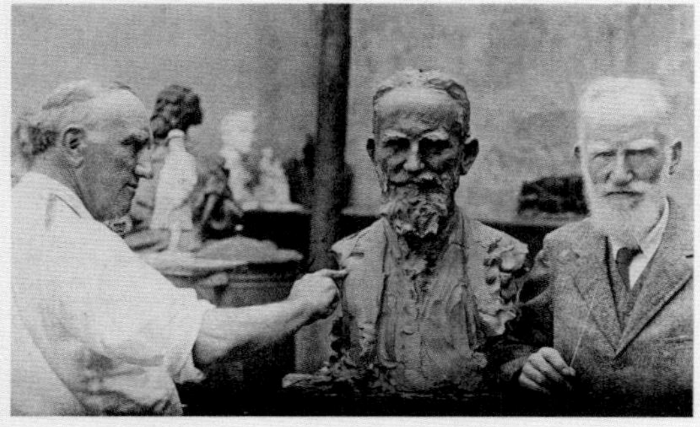

2 Paolo Troubetzkoy executing a bust of Bernard Shaw, undated, photograph, print from 1926

Yvette Deseyve

Paolo Troubetzkoy – "the most astonishing sculptor of modern times"

In 1931, no less a figure than the Irish writer George Bernard Shaw (figs. 1, 2) wrote the foreword for the sales exhibition Sculpture by *Prince Paul Troubetzkoy* at the Colnaghi art gallery in London.[1] Shaw's forceful remarks began with the observation that Troubetzkoy was one of the few geniuses about whom it was not only needed to speak of in superlatives, but even essential to do so – furthermore summing up that: "He is the most astonishing sculptor of modern times."[2] On the one hand, Shaw's praise made reference to Paolo Troubetzkoy's amazing ability to convincingly avail himself of any conceivable subject or genre in equal measure, be it animal sculptures, monuments as well as portrait sculpture. On the other hand, Shaw characterised him as a sculptor of modern times and, in doing so, alluded to Troubetzkoy's eccentric personality, to his role as both a part and a portraitist of cosmopolitan high society as well as the vegetarianism he militantly propagated in public (fig. 3),[3] from which some of his art critics had attempted to derive his emphatic gift of observation.

However, what makes him a truly modern sculptor is his rigorously lived mindset to study the external, natural appearance of things free of any academic traditions or instructions. With this artistic understanding, the name and oeuvre of the Italian sculptor is firmly embedded in the contemporary discourse on Impressionism.

Troubetzkoy in the contemporary debate on Impressionism

Proceeding from Charles Baudelaire's provocative demotion of sculpture to an inferior genre vis-à-vis painting,[4] a debate developed in 1902 that focused on a modern, Impressionist sculpture. Baudelaire's concept still corresponded with the academism of his time, which saw sculpture beholden to the classical ideal and did not accord it any means of expression whatsoever that were realistic and hence rooted in the present. What Baudelaire completely failed to recognise, however, was the painterly potential of the three-dimensional, with which sculptors, in particular, intensely dealt towards the end of the nineteenth century.[5] Hence the critic Edmond Claris published a broadly conceived survey among artists with regard to Baudelaire's dictum and discerned a resemblance to Impressionist painting in one group of sculptors: "And we can now establish the fact that a similar movement permeates sculpture: others artists tell us in their own material what Monet, Renoir, Degas, Pissarro, Rafaelli [sic!] announced in their language. With intrepid bravado, one is now attempting to deal a deathblow to cold nakedness and rigid academism, to break with traditional dogmas brought up by the schools – and to return to nature."[6] Following Auguste Rodin and Medardo Rosso, the artists in question include, amongst others, Antoine Bourdelle, Pierre-Félix Masseau, Félix Voulot, Ville Vallgren, Louis Eugène Dejean and Paolo Troubetzkoy.[7]

Although Troubetzkoy was not one of the artists that Claris queried, he nevertheless played an important part in his survey. Jean-François Raffaëlli, the French-born painter and sculptor of Italian origin, had not only presented his own definition of Impressionism to Claris, but illustrated it by example of Paolo Troubetzkoy and, in doing so, stylised him as the Impressionist sculptor par excellence: "Prince Troubetzkoy gave us [...] magnificent samples of Impressionist sculpture, e.g. sculpture where the vitality of the expression counts more than the accuracy of the form, the entire objects more than the detail, and in which harmony does not mean philistine and meticulous regularity as taught to us in museums and academies, but the simple and loving reproduction of impressions received from nature."[8] Claris also subscribed to Raffaëlli's assessment and commented: "Prince Troubetzkoy is a rebel. He accepts no conventions, he does not want to be inspired by anything other than nature and himself."[9] He is a sculptor who triumphs by virtue of his light effects, whose sculptural renderings full of intense life astound us, and, like the elegance of the animated forms, lends expression to what those being portrayed are feeling. Troubetzkoy's approach as framed by Raffaëlli and Claris is endorsed in numerous exhibition reviews in which contemporary critics described his art with the keywords "énergie"[10] or "vivacité"[11] and referred to him as an "improvisateur énergique"[12] who captured "snapshots in time"[13] or "momentary impressions".[14] At the same time, reviewers criticised his composition as "light-headed"[15] and "indefinite"[16] and "merely suggestive and delineative".[17] According to his critics, he was content with "quickly reproducing certain characteristic features instead of elaborating on the actual sculptural element of an aspect".[18] It is precisely these shortcomings that paraphrase the core sculptural content of Impressionism *ex negativo* – after all, its underlying idea was to capture the immediate impression, the fugitive moment, and to cause the plastic form, the constructive aspect, to recede into the background. In the second half of the nineteenth century, therefore, expression and form were placed in opposition to and played out against each other. It was not until after the turn of the century that these two poles in the history of sculpture would come together under the influence of form-focused tendencies towards abstraction as well as the so-called expressive sculptors.[19]

As already discernible in the remarks by Raffaëlli and Claris, the debate on Impressionist sculpture was closely accompanied by the rejection of traditional academic training, which culminated in Auguste Rodin's appeal "Away with the academies, back to nature!"[20] From then on, the concepts of proportion theory, nude study or an allegorical repertoire taught by the art academies were in opposition to the spontaneous orientation towards life that the Impressionists called for. Not least, as the much-admired father figure of modern sculpture, Rodin himself set an example for how one could be successful even without the academy, and thus Paolo Troubetzkoy also regarded the concept advocated by the academies as outdated and in need of reform.

Paolo, Pavel or Paul Troubetzkoy

Paolo Troubetzkoy was born in Intra on Lago Maggiore in 1866. As the son of a Russian diplomat stationed in Italy who stemmed from aristocratic circles and an American operatic diva, the artist, who at one time or another resided in Italy, Russia, France and the United States, signed his works with the various translations of his first name: Paolo, Pavel or Paul Troubetzkoy. Yet he was not only familiar with an urbane demeanour from his parental home: along with his two brothers, Paolo grew up in a home that was very appreciative of art.[21] Since the 1870s at the latest, the seat of the Troubetzkoy family on Lago Maggiore had developed into a

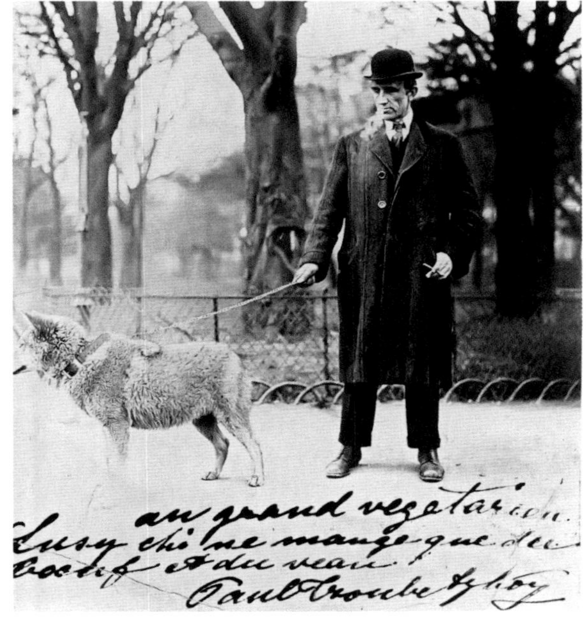

3 Paolo Troubetzkoy with one of his two tame wolves, c. 1905, photograph

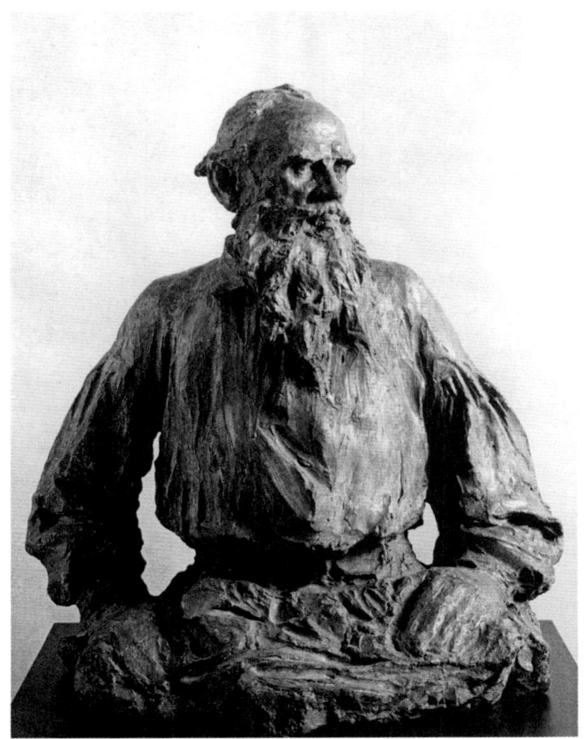

4 Paolo Troubetzkoy, *Leo N. Tolstoy*, 1898, plaster, patinated, 98 × 84 × 55 cm, photograph

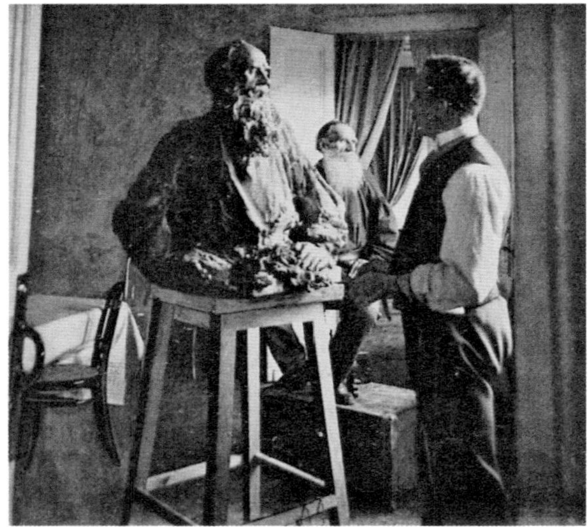

5 Paolo Troubetzkoy working on a bust of Tolstoy, c. 1898, photograph, from *Die Kunst für Alle* 17, no. 3 (1902), p. 49

meeting place for progressive Lombardian artists, musicians and writers, including members of the so-called Scapigliati such as the painters Tranquillo Cremona (cat. 115) and Daniele Ranzoni or the sculptor Giuseppe Grandi (p. 127, fig. 3). It was especially the latter who encouraged the young Paolo to do sculptural studies after nature and therefore reinforced his later decision to pursue an artistic career as a sculptor. In 1884, he began and, after only a few months, ended his training in the workshops of Donato Barcaglia and Ernesto Bazzaro (cat. 116) in Milan in favour of working autonomously in his own studio.[22] Contrary to the study of nudes that was compulsory for sculptor training and the customary copying of allegorical subjects, Troubetzkoy dedicated himself to animal studies from life. Looking back, he explained the approach that he already pursued at the time: "That which I strive to do is to convey as effectively as possible the impressions I receive from nature, without troubling myself about the artistic productions of either past or present, which could never give me the same intensity of feeling I obtain from direct observation."[23]

Thus in 1886, he also made his debut with a horse sculpture produced after life in an exhibition mounted at the Brera academy.[24] The very next year, he submitted two further animal studies for the *Esposizione artistica nazionale illustrata* taking place in Venice whose unconventional manner of representation met with an utter lack of understanding by the jury.[25] The novelty of the qualities of his sculpture, which were obviously not yet capable of being described adequately, becomes palpable in the uncertainly it evoked over whether one could even exhibit Troubetzkoy's works in the sculpture department in the first place, which the president of the jury tried to resolve with the words: "If this is not sculpture, then it is something better."[26]

A self-taught sculptor reforms the academic system

Troubetzkoy's sculptures aroused public attention wherever they were presented – sometimes accompanied by incomprehension, sometimes by curiosity. Whereas the Moscow audience initially anticipated the young sculptor with his first international exhibition experience, after that they were also shocked, however, by the revolutionary teaching methods with which Troubetzkoy turned the academic sculpture class inside out during his visiting professorship[27] at the local university of painting, sculpture and architecture in 1898/99.[28] He had all of the plaster copies removed from the working studios,[29] banned the compulsory study of nudes and called on his students to allow themselves to be guided by nature only: "Turn your intellect to nature, turn your abilities to reflection [...]. What you will find in sculpture is primarily a *universal mass*."[30] Troubetzkoy's sculptural mentality concentrates itself in this statement passed down by his students. Thus, what was essential to him was firstly turning to the absolutely visible, which meant to life or nature, and secondly the negation of a constructive style of sculpture that consists of individual forms, and this in favour of an understanding according to which body and space are to be conceived as a uniform mass. In doing so, the sculptor unavoidably shifted the carrier of a sculpture's essence – away from the form and towards the surface. This also constitutes the basis of his approach, thanks to which the surface is capable of developing its own artistic qualities as a carrier of meaning but also as material skin.

For the students in Moscow, who focused on copying classical forms, Troubetzkoy's approach meant the loss of any previously valid reference points. His Impressionist understanding of sculpture had nothing to do with proportion theory or the configuration of planes. There were no preparatory studies for his sculptures; they were process-dependent and intuitive. He relied on imagination, on surface structuring and on spontaneity in the production process – in other words, on skills that were only difficult to learn or communicate in a training workshop. In short, Troubetzkoy reformed the sculpture class by paradoxically abandoning any communicable contents, with the result that each individual was thrown back on himself. Besides nature, the students could only attempt to orientate themselves towards the teacher and imitate the artistic effects he strove for, such as the change of light and mass. In an essay on the artist from 1902, Vittorio Pica described this special technique – referred to as "scolpire à la Troubetzkoy"[31] – in detail: he is a "tireless worker who creates with enviable ease [...]. He not only took all of his models from daily goings-on around us, not only attempted to lend shape to the mental and emotional character of modern man, but also created very new and personal means of expression: that unique and at first sight odd technique that [...] causes his figures to seemingly come alive, to breathe, so to speak, under the eyes of the beholder. By beating the still soft clay with a rod needle [...] and, placing one wrinkle by the other, he creates a rough and fissured surface, [...] forms ridges that strangely contrast with other places that have been carefully smoothed, and in doing so produces those light and shadow effects that contribute so much to arousing the idea of the real in the beholder."[32]

The visible marks left by rod needles, brush and fingers continue to cover the entire surface of his works after they have been cast in bronze. They convey the uniqueness and thus the unrepeatability of a momentary artistic design. Copying the master was hence equally as impossible as a working process based on the division of labour, which was widely common in the nineteenth century. In the "personalisation" of his artistic production, Troubetzkoy went a step further and developed a material that allowed for his rapid production process and whose consistency accommodated the subtle surface design. The material – called "Trubeckoviano"[33] after its creator – was a mixture of clay, wax and mastic resin and, like the emergent plastic modelling paste in the second half of the nineteenth century, it was easy to shape and hardened only slowly.

Momentum versus *memoria* – the possibilities and limitations of the Impressionist portrait

For the portrait genre Paolo Troubetzkoy frequently employed, the sculptor's rapid method not only harboured the possibility of capturing multiple momentary impressions of the person being portrayed; at the same time, it called for the exemplary stability in expression and material attributed to a portrait in light of its memorial function. Thus, two poles – momentariness and memory independent of time – clearly mark the possibilities and limitations of Paolo Troubetzkoy's Impressionist portraiture.

In Russia, Leo N. Tolstoy (figs. 4, 5) became one of Troubetzkoy's close confidants. Between 1898 and 1900, the sculptor produced at least three portraits of him as well as two depictions of him on horseback, on whose execution in bronze he worked in his studio in Moscow.[34] For this purpose, he experimented with A. Robecchi, a caster who had followed him to Russia from Milan.[35] The caster and sculptor often left remnants of the original casting skin on Troubetzkoy's casts, contrasting these with polished and patinated places and documenting the artistic transformation process into bronze with unchased casting seams. It is precisely the early casts of which only few copies were executed, such as the portrayal of Giovanni Segantini (figs. 6, 7), that derive their unique quality not least from this.

Troubetzkoy had met Giovanni Segantini by way of the circle of Divisionists in Milan, and on a number of occasions in May 1896 he made unsuccessful attempts to portray him in conventional sessions.[36] It was the candid situation during Segantini's leave-taking from his friends that first conveyed the desired expression, which Troubetzkoy secured in only two hours as a life-sized portrait

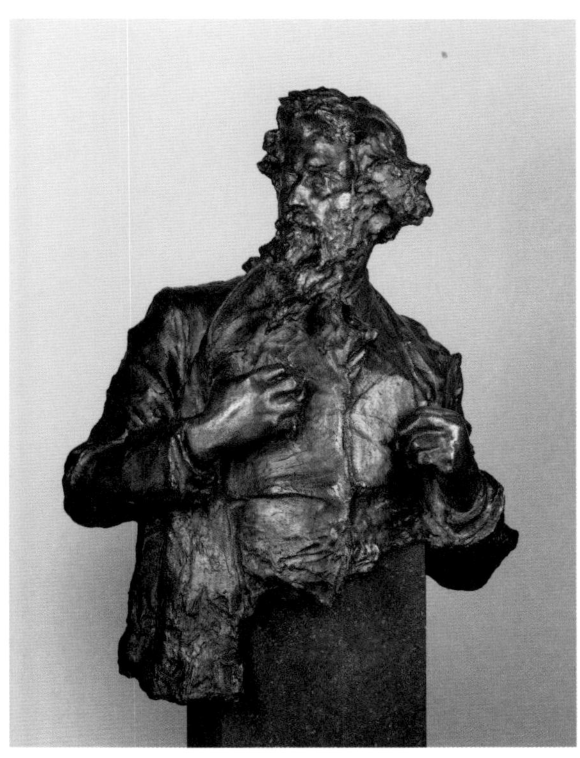

6 Paolo Troubetzkoy, *Giovanni Segantini*, 1896, bronze, 89 × 78 × 43 cm, Staatliche Museen zu Berlin, Nationalgalerie (cat. 109)

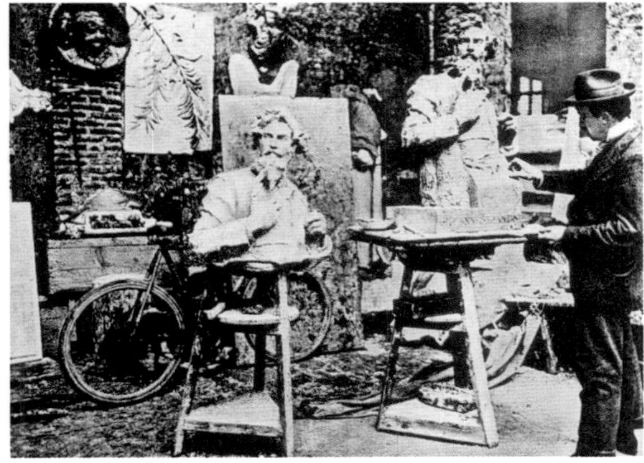

7 Paolo Troubetzkoy in his studio in Milan, c. 1896, photograph

"I don't want my pictures and statuettes to represent ideas such as the Symbolists strive to do. I don't wish them to tell stories."

Paolo Troubetzkoy, quoted in: Charles L. Borgmeyer, 1911

(fig. 7; cat. 109).[37] The sculptor achieved the impression of Segantini as a visionary artist at peace with himself not lastly by means of extending the portrait to produce a half-figure in which, besides the face, it is above all the bearing and the action of the hands that characterise him. Moreover, in some cases it is the period clothing, one example of which can be noticed in the portrait Adelaide Aurnheimer[38] (fig. 8; cat. 112), or the spatial situation suggested by the furniture that enrich Troubetzkoy's portraits and, at the same time, unintentionally inscribe a narrative element in the scene: "I don't want my pictures and statuettes to represent ideas such as the Symbolists strive to do. I don't wish them to tell stories."[39] Yet it is Troubetzkoy's full-figure portrait of Aurnheimer, the result of an offer of a prize during a costume competition at a social ball for the benefit of the Famiglia Artistica artists' association, that communicates the atmospheric situation "after the ball" par excellence. Many of the concavely driven, detailed areas in the manner of Troubetzkoy rupture the surface and create a shimmering carpet of light comprising dabs of light rigorously isolated from another; in doing so, they translate the dynamic, polychromatic reality into a static and initially monochromatic sculpture whose reflective surface, however, suggests a wide range of different colour values.[40] As a result, Troubetzkoy forced the penetration of the space into the sculptural mass. It is precisely this light-filled space that constitutes the specifically Impressionist composition of his sculptures.

The sculptor Paolo Troubetzkoy knew how to position himself as an observer of his own present, as a conveyor of modern life with his artistic approach and developed methods that were indeed revolutionary in order to achieve his personal impressions, largely divorced from art historical traditions, in the most direct way possible. His contemporaries therefore already perceived him as a most astonishing sculptor of modern times.

1 Troubetzkoy had already begun his first portrait studies of Shaw in the London studio of John Singer Sargent as early as in 1908; see Frezzotti 1990, p. 176.

2 Exh. cat. London 1931, no pagination.

3 See Anonymous 1904/05, p. 82: "He loves animals with a touching childishness and lives in his house in Petersburg with a bear, two wolves and a rabbit, all of which he raised to be vegetarians – which in the case of the rabbit, by the way, does not seem exactly wondrous." See also Borgmeyer 1911, pp. 5–6; exh. cat. London 2008, p. 15.

4 See the essay by Nina Schallenberg in this catalogue, pp. 276–282, esp. p. 276.

5 Also according to Julius Meier-Graefe in his chapter "Der Impressionismus in der Plastik" (Impressionism in Sculpture) in Meier-Graefe 1904, vol. 1, pp. 303–312. On Baudelaire's criticism of sculpture, see, among others, Hofmann 1959. For Baudelaire, a further point of criticism was sculpture's poly-perspectivity, which, compared to the painterly principle of "l'unité du point de vue", also presented the viewer with weaker views. However, it was precisely Impressionist sculpture that attempted to guide the viewer in the most precise way possible by means of deliberate stagings.

6 Claris 1902a (German), p. 6. The translation is a highly shortened version of Claris 1902 (French).

7 The list of names given in Meier-Graefe 1904, vol. 1, p. 305.

8 Claris 1902a (German), p. 36.

9 "Le prince Troubetskoï est un révolté. Il n'accepte pas les conventions. Il ne veut s'inspirer que de la nature et de lui." Claris 1902 (French), pp. 90–91.

10 Bidou 1910, p. 382.

11 Soulier 1903, p. 96.

12 René 1911, p. 386.

13 Anonymous 1898/99, p. 353.

14 A. H. 1904/05, p. 533.

15 "C'est de la sculpture à l'étourdie." Beaunier 1908, p. 490.

16 "[F]ormes indécises"; Rosenthal 1912, p. 411.

17 A. H. 1904/05, p. 533.

18 Ibid.

19 Exh. cat. Mannheim 1912; see Berger 2002.

20 Claris 1902a (German), p. 22.

21 On Troubetzkoy's artistic beginnings, in this case and in the following, see Rebora 1990.

22 Giuseppe Grandi had apparently refused to train Troubetzkoy in his workshop; cf. Cioffi 2013, p. 103.

23 Paolo Troubetzkoy, quoted in: Borgmeyer 1911, p. 7. He furthermore stated: "Nature is bigger than anything else; bigger than tradition, bigger than the individual; study nature. The Greeks expressed life as they saw it. To copy the Greek sculpture is to observe life through their eyes instead of, as it should be, through your own." Ibid., p. 6.

24 See Cioffi 2013, p. 103.

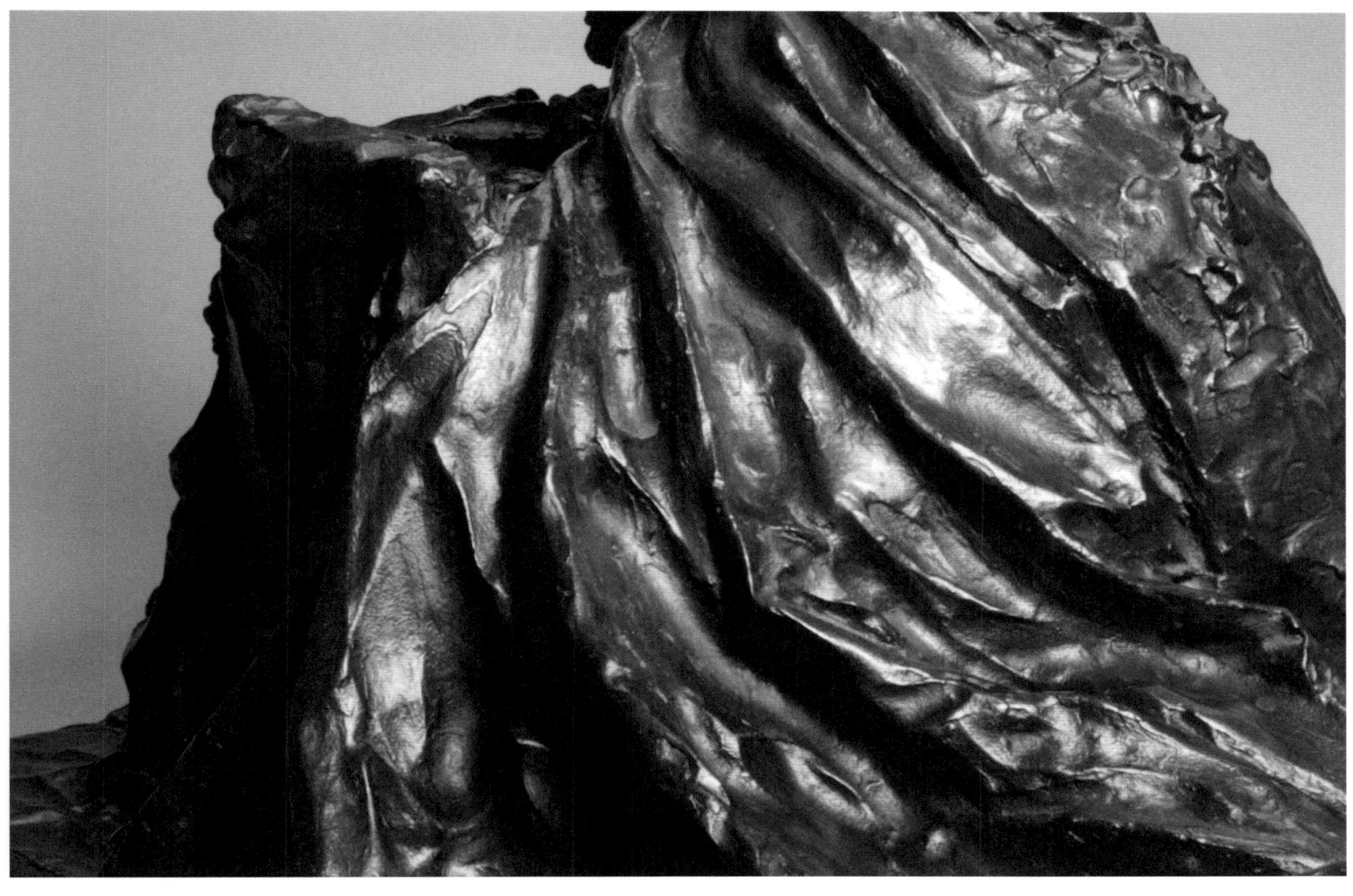

8   Paolo Troubetzkoy, *After the Ball* (*Adelaide Aurnheimer*) (detail), 1897, bronze, 45.5 × 52 × 53.5 cm, private collection, London (cat. 112)

25 See Frezzotti 1990a, p. 221.

26 "Se questa non è scultura allora è qualcosa di meglio." Antonio Fradeletto, quoted in: Frezzotti 1990a, p. 221.

27 On his own admission, Troubetzkoy initially declined the professor-ship on the grounds that he had never had a teacher and could hardly imagine teaching. However, he then accepted the position, because he believed he could spare the students conventional academic lessons. "I could effectually prevent some other professor from exercising his influence upon the pupils to the detriment of their natural gifts and instinctive freedom from convention." Paolo Troubetzkoy, quoted in:

Borgmeyer 1911, p. 9.

28 On Troubetzkoy and Russia, see Domogackaja 1990; Gavrilovich 1990.

29 Borgmeyer 1911, p. 9.

30 "Volgete alla natura il vostro intelletto, la vostra capacità di riflettere [...]. Scoprirete in scultura soprattutto una *masse généralle*." Paolo Troubetzkoy, quoted in: Domogackaja 1990, p. 60.

31 Ibid., p. 63.

32 Pica 1902, p. 50.

33 Domogackaja 1990, pp. 62–63.

34 On Troubetzkoy's portrayals of Tolstoy, see Wood 2016.

35 A. Robecchi, the brother of Carlo Robecchi from Milan, details of whose biography are not known; see "Notice Artiste no 37915: Robecchi",

https://www.musee-orsay.fr/fr/outils-transversaux/recherche/tout-le-site.html (accessed 18 November 2019). On this, see also Lebon 2003, pp. 216–217; exh. cat. London 2008, p. 11.

36 References to discarded nude studies have been passed down: "lo scultore [Troubetzkoy] lo aveva fatto posar nudo fino alla cintola." Giolli 1913, p. 13; quoted in: Rebora 1990, p. 109.

37 See Giolli 1913, p. 13.

38 The biographical identification is made on the basis of the alternating spelling of the name as "Madame Hoernheimer" or "Adelaide Aurnheimer" née "Rätzsch" or "Ratsch", which is not explained in more detail; see exh. cat. Verbania Pallanza 1990, p. 117; "Paolo (prince)

Troubetzkoy, Madame Adelaide Aurnheimer", https://www.musee-orsay.fr/fr/collections/catalogue-des-oeuvres/recherche-simple.html (accessed 18 November 2019). For the likewise alternating spelling as "Madame Anerheimer" or "Gertrud" or "Gertrud Anernheimer", see "Mme. Anerheimer, 1897", https://www.metmuseum.org/ (accessed 18 November 2019).

39 Paolo Troubetzkoy, quoted in: Borgmeyer 1911, p. 7.

40 On this, see Wootton 2016, esp. p. 64.

 # Stunning appearances

Like the sculptor Paolo Troubetzkoy, the painter Giovanni Segantini was part of a strong network in Milan's art scene, yet the origins and lifestyles of the two artists could not have been more different. Prince Troubetzkoy was born into an artistically inspired and, at least at times, affluent aristocratic, cosmopolitan family. By contrast, Giovanni Segantini's childhood and youth as a neglected and disenfranchised orphan seems to have been taken from a dismal, socio-critical novel. And whereas at the time the work was produced (cat. 109), Segantini had long since left Milan to live with his companion, Bice Bugatti, and their four children in the Canton of Grisons and later in Engadin, Troubetzkoy resided in the midst of the pulsating Lombardian capital. After several failed successes with designs for monuments, he carved out his way to recognition there – not last due to the portraits of his artist friends, including the one of Giovanni Segantini shown here.[1] Troubetzkoy portrayed the painter as a slightly larger-than-life half-figure as he was turning. Segantini dynamically pivots his head to the side whilst simultaneously slipping his thumbs under his vest. Legend has it that Segantini – during one of his rare visits to Milan[2] – sat several times, bare-chested, for Troubetzkoy, however without this having led to a satisfactory result. It was not until Segantini was saying his farewells that Troubetzkoy recognised it as the right moment, and he created the final version within two hours.[3] Whether or not Segantini actually held out half-naked in front of Troubetzkoy is anyone's guess; in any case, the sculptor masterfully reproduced the perfect moment.

Two aspects particularly strike the eye. On the one hand, the dynamic turning moment within the half-figure, which seems to convey not a pose but rather the painter's very own body language. The other aspect is the striking lower section of the figure. However, this varies in the different casts, as is also verified by a historical photograph (p. 225, fig. 7). Hence the artist subtly played with the relationship between the artistic portrait and the functional pedestal. In the sculpture in Berlin from the former collection of Felix Koenigs, he designed a stepped base to which a stepped wood pedestal was originally added.[4] This bronze cast was shown for the first time in 1896 on the occasion of a Segantini exhibition at the gallery of Felix Koenigs in Berlin. Segantini owned one in plaster, as he wrote to Koenigs: "I also own it as a plaster cast, and the longer I look at it, the more alive it seems to me."[5] Another cast was on display at the *International Art Exhibition* in Dresden in 1897, as reported in the press: "Paolo Troubetzkoy, Milan, with a dashing bust of Segantini and other works."[6] Like another bronze by Troubetzkoy, *After the Ball* (cat. 112), in Dresden the sculpture was installed in the much-lauded Great Hall, a feature of which was not only a tank inhabited by fish, but also fir branches along the walls and green gauze on the windows.[7] The *Segantini* continued to accompany Troubetzkoy on the international stage, such as in 1900 at the world's fair in Paris, where it was on view along with works by Medardo Rosso in the hall fitted out at short notice on the occasion of Segantini's sudden death.[8]

Troubetzkoy was awarded a gold medal at the world's fair, not for *Segantini* but for *Tolstoy on Horseback* (1899).[9] During his stay in Russia, he produced five portraits of the famous writer, including two on horseback, at Tolstoy's estate Yasnaya Polyana. After some hesitation, Leo Tolstoy, who had given up his title of nobility in 1882 and denied himself a variety of indulgences out of principle, let the aristocratic sculptor portray him (p. 224, fig. 5).[10] Like the portrait of Segantini, the block-like half-figure *Bust of Tolstoy* in particular (cat. 110) – represented here by a cast made for the American ambassador Charles R. Crane, who was on friendly terms with both artists, and bearing the inscription of its place of origin[11] – relies on the counter-directional, dynamic axes of the turned head and the flowing beard.[12] It is precisely the prominent beard that testifies to Troubetzkoy's dedication to cascade-like modelling, which he also demonstrated in Madame Aurnheimer's dress (cat. 112). Thus in 1904, the art critic Camille Mauclair praised Troubetzkoy's contributions to the Salon d'automne in Paris – one of which of this half-figure of Tolstoy – specifically because of its nervous modelling.[13]

In 1902, the author Robert de Montesquiou also spoke of "nervous impulses" in Troubetzkoy's works and compared this with the painting style of Giovanni Boldini (1842–1931).[14] The legendary Dandy de Montesquiou sat for numerous models.[15] As early as 1891/92, the American painter James McNeill Whistler (1834–1903) portrayed him as a full-figure in a narrow vertical format with a chinchilla cape casually hanging over his arm and standing in a diffuse, dark room (The Frick Collection, New York). Several lithographs originated in this context to which the essential elements of the monochromatic painting were transferred (cat. 107). The Boldini mentioned by de Montesquiou was already well known – and likewise admired as well as despised – in Paris in 1910. In 1937, the art dealer Ambroise Vollard recalled: "Boldini's colleagues believed they could ruin him by calling him the painter of the elegant world – the world of 1890."[16]

Having permanently lived in Paris since 1871, Boldini, who stemmed from Ferrara, was familiar with the Impressionist exhibitions, although he never received an invitation to any of the presentations himself.[17] This is surprising insofar as he maintained close contact with Edgar Degas; in 1892, they even undertook a trip together to Spain and Morocco. Boldini, however, made a sharp distinction: he praised Degas's art, yet set it apart from the "tailored banality" of the Impressionists.[18] Nevertheless, with his *plein-air* landscapes and views of Paris, his vibrating *fa presto* brushstroke, and his experimentation with the painterly *non-finito*, Boldini's works from the 1870s and the 1880s reflect the Impressionists that he did not hold in very high esteem.[19] This painting style characterises the 1902 portrait of his artist friend Georges Goursat in particular (cat. 108). Having lived in Paris since 1900, the caricaturist, who published under the name of "Sem", quickly captured a wide public. He was increasingly capable of affording himself a mundane lifestyle, which also included a decidedly British style of clothing. Outfitted accordingly with a bowler hat, a lined coat and distinctive laced boots, Boldini presented him as a self-confident man with arms akimbo and a direct, inviting gaze in this nearly monochromatic painting. Dispensing with perspectival spatial details, he embedded this colourful figure in a diffuse, brown colour sphere that contains free and partly arabesque elements that resemble enlarged details from the coat structure. Whereas Troubetzkoy's two artist's portraits intervene in real space through the axes of the body and the gaze, Boldini creates

Cat.107 James McNeill Whistler, *Comte de Montesquiou*, 1894; lithograph
on laid paper, 35.9 × 25 cm; Städel Museum, Frankfurt am Main, inv. no. 64711

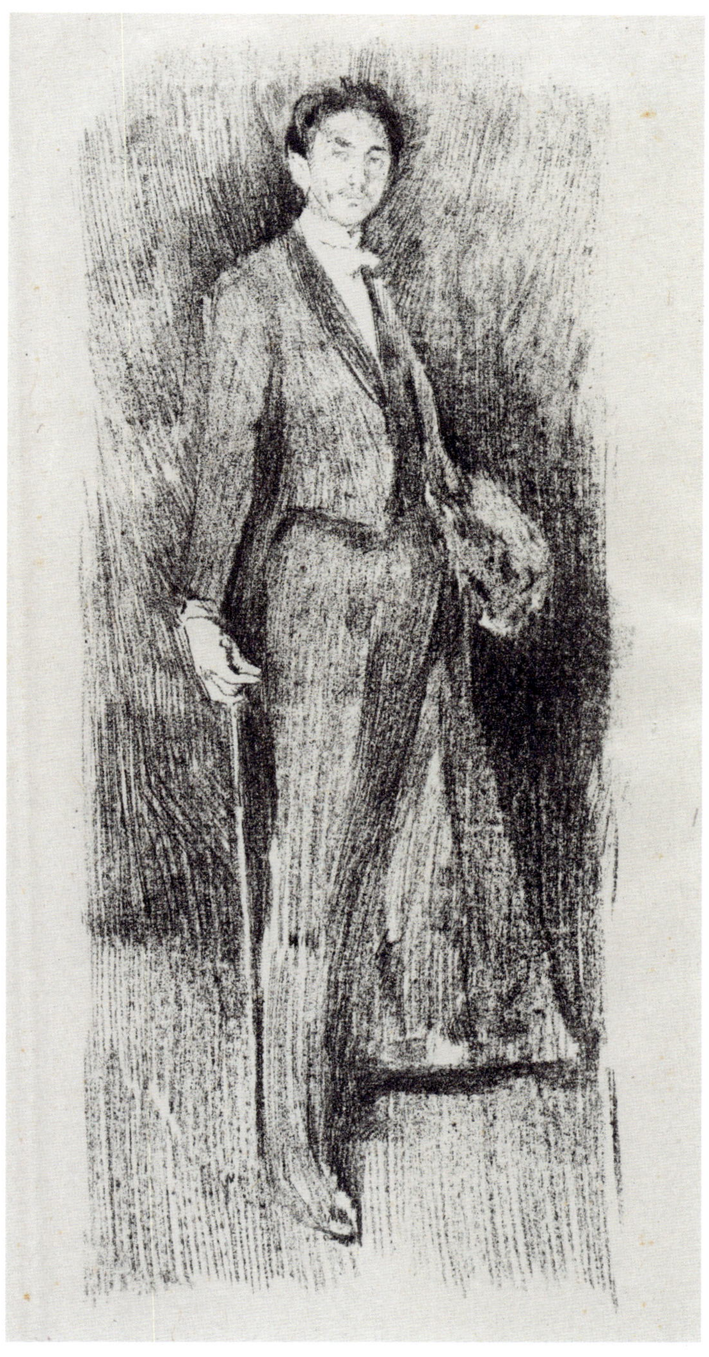

Cat. 107

space at his own discretion in the *Sem* portrait. If one calls to mind, for example, the purely aesthetically, compositionally motivated section of Troubetzkoy's *Segantini*, what he and Boldini share is both their artistic high-handedness as well as their "nervous impulses". For all the alleged spontaneity in capturing the moment being depicted, and for all the technical bravura in the simulation of rapid reproduction, these works of art testify to profound artistic reflection. — EM-V

1   Ginex 2014, p. 187.
2   Exh. cat. Verbania Pallanza 1990, p. 108.
3   Giolli 1913, p. 13; Quinsac 2009a, p. 250.
4   Maaz 2006, vol. 2, p. 817.
5   Letter from Giovanni Segantini to Fe ix Koenigs, undated, in Segantini 1912, p. 139.
6   Schumann 1896/97, p. 342.
7   Ibid., p. 338.
8   Quinsac 2011, p. 32.
9   Fles 1922, p. 29, sneered at this decision.

In his early years, Troubetzkoy allowed himself to be guided by Rosso. Whereas his statuettes "looked Impressionistic", he did not spare the viewer "a single tail-coat button, lorgnette or cuff".
10 Exh. cat. Naples 2003, p. 1
11 Wood 2016, p. 30. I would like to thank Michael D. Uva for making this text available to me.
12 Bossaglia/Castagnoli 1993, p. 148.

13 Mauclair 1904, p. 229, illustration of *Bust of Tolstoy*: p. 230.
14 "[U]ne meme somme d'influx nerveux"; Montesquiou 1902, quoted in: exh. cat. Verbania Pallanza 1990, p. 22.
15 Also including portraits of the count by Giovanni Boldini (1897) and Paolo Troubetzkoy (1907), both of which are now in the collection of Musée d'Orsay in Paris. Troubetzkoy's bust *Giovanni*

Boldini (1912/13) at Museo del Paesaggio, Verbania Pallanza, testifies to Boldini's and Troubetzkoy's mutual esteem.
16 Vollard [1937] 1980, p. 201.
17 Lees 2009, p. 27.
18 "[B]analità confezionata"; Giovanni Boldini, quoted in: Dumas 2003, p. 58.
19 Lees 2009. pp. 34–35.

 Giovanni Boldini, **Portrait of Sem** (Georges Goursat), 1902;
oil on canvas, 91.5 × 73 cm; Musée des Arts Décoratifs, Paris, inv. no. 37353
  Paolo Troubetzkoy, **Giovanni Segantini**, 1896, cast in 1896;
bronze, 98 × 78 × 43 cm; signed: "Paul Troubetzkoy / 1896"; Staatliche Museen
zu Berlin, Nationalgalerie, inv. no. B I 152

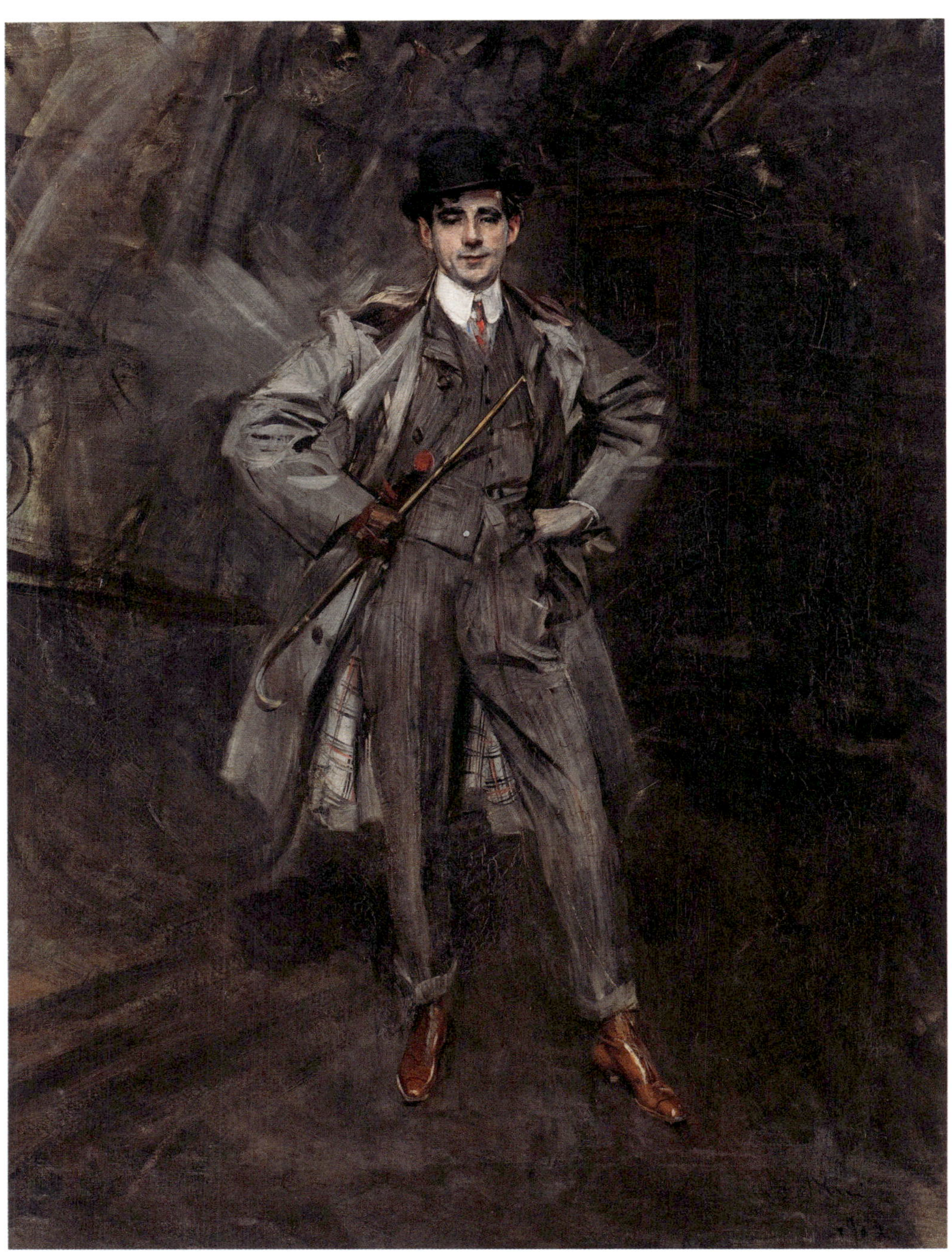

Cat.108

Cat. 109

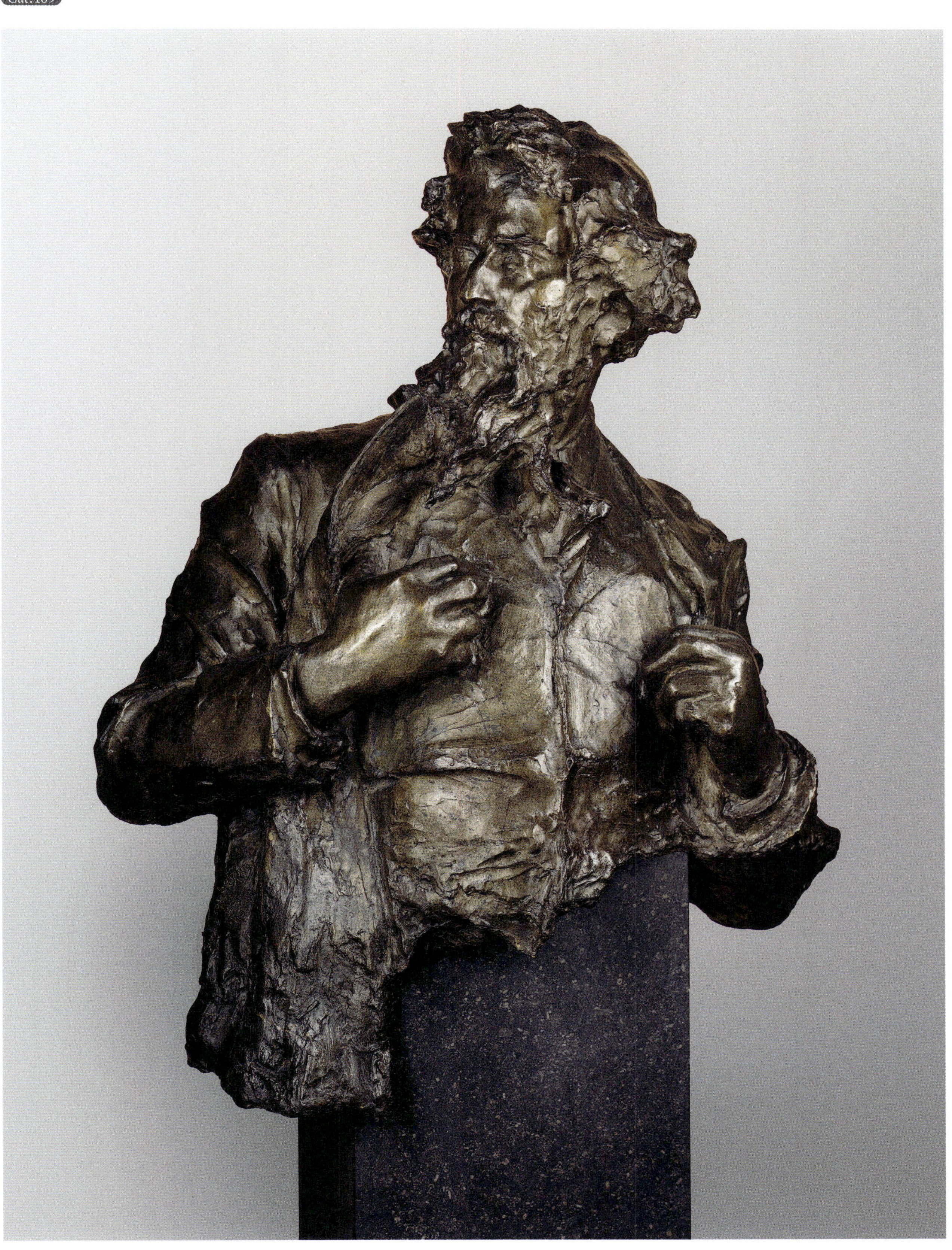

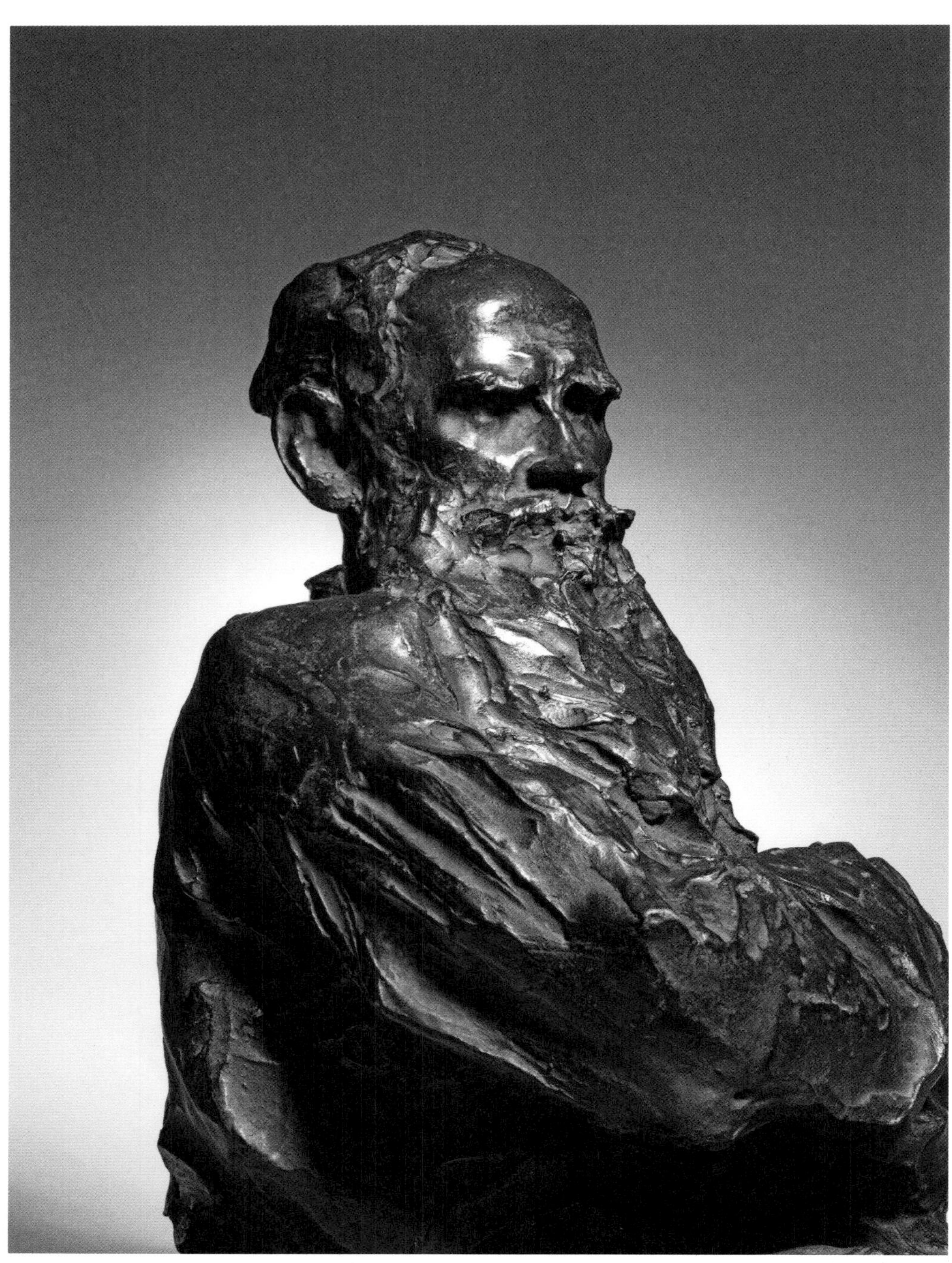

Cat.110

Cat.110

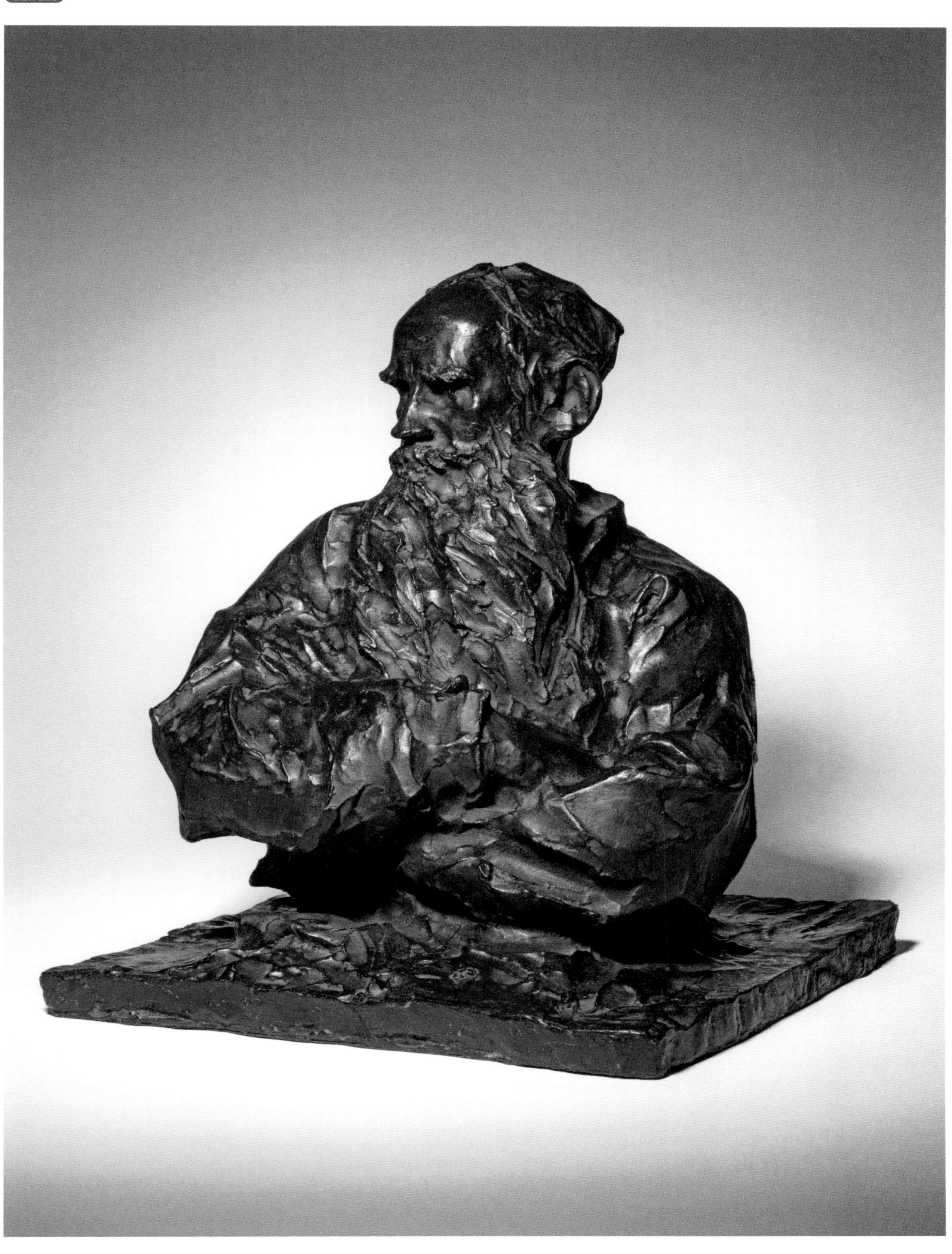

In 1893, London society lay at their feet. People raved about the sitter, Lady Agnew, as well as about the portraitist, John Singer Sargent (1856–1925). As the author Vernon Lee, who was on friendly terms with both of them, trenchantly wrote: "[A] very pretty woman whom John Sargent has just made into a society celebrity by a very ravishing portrait."[1] As a matter of fact: after the presentation of the painting at the Royal Academy, the young Lady Agnew became a darling of society, and Singer Sargent advanced to become a star portraitist.[2]

The portrait of the radiantly dressed lady casually sitting in a bergère, her subtly ironic gaze glancing slightly up from below, captivates the viewer – not only because she is undoubtedly an interesting and elegant person, but also because of the masterful and delicate painting style (cat. 111). The painter brilliantly renders the transparency and suppleness of the light fore- and background fabrics, the natural pallor of the ailing lady's complexion and the brilliance of her select jewellery. The warm light flows around or permeates each feature of the depiction – Sargent developed his paintings *alla prima* and never prepared a preliminary drawing, uniting it to create a splendid overall harmony. In the course of the universal praise, this aspect of Sargent's painting from 1893 may have led to referring to it as "Impressionistic painting": "as a portrait, a decorative pattern, or a piece of well-engineered impressionistic painting, it tops everything in the Academy [...]."[3] The fact that Singer Sargent was associated by, and for, the London public of the time with the French Impressionists was due, in particular, to the past. Not only had he begun his artistic training in Carolus-Duran's studio in Paris the same year of the first Impressionist exhibition (1874), but, during his residence there, which lasted until 1886, he was also acquainted with several of the participating artists, even though he never received an invitation to take part himself. In the French press, he was nevertheless referred to as an "Impressionist", as was the case on the occasion of the exhibition at the Galerie Georges Petit in 1883.[4]

Yet it was not until he relocated to London in 1886 that his examination of the Impressionists became more intense. It was especially his renewed visit to France in 1887 that led to a close artistic exchange with Claude Monet and culminated in a number of *plein-air* paintings that were closer than ever to the painting style of the French Impressionists.[5] At the same time, in 1886, Sargent was actively involved in the founding of the New English Art Club (NEAC) in London, which was also referred to as an "Impressionist club". The same critic that introduced the term "Impressionistic painting" in connection with the portrait of Lady Agnew subsequently described an interesting observation with respect to its execution: "His brushwork boldly challenges you by presenting a definite tone for every inch of surface [...] he never permits some pleasantly warmed juice to veil his view of air, colour and form."[6] They are indeed neatly separated tones carefully placed one alongside the other; only the colour white extends over the pictorial surface like a veil. This impression is heightened by the blurring in the area of the outlines. By alternately applying dry and wet paint, several levels were created that do not lie exactly one atop the other; in other places, transitions are slurred by means of outright superimposition. It is only when one looks at Lady Agnew's right side, from her arm up to her neck, that these masterly techniques become clearly apparent: last but not least, the care taken while creating a harmonious, literally fluid whole on the basis of numerous, nuanced internal decisions with respect to the choice of tone, brushstroke, lighting, spatial design; and the large and small sequences of movement allow comparing it with a sculptural work that found an international stage just five years later: Paolo Troubetzkoy's *After the Ball.*

This portrait of a woman was the main prize at a costume festival at the Famiglia Artistica artists' association in Milan in 1897. The best costume was rewarded with a portrait produced by Paolo Troubetzkoy, who was already widely known.[7] Adelaide Aurnheimer won the first prize for her costume of Manon Lescaut, the eponymous heroine of Puccini's opera that premiered in 1893. The German couple Carlo Federico and Adelaide Aurnheimer had lived in Milan since the 1880s and were active as patrons of the art.[8] That same year, 1897, *After the Ball* (cat. 112) was presented at the *International Art Exhibition* in Dresden, where it was awarded the silver medal and presented as a gift to the Royal Collections by Victor Hahn, the councillor of commerce.[9] In Dresden, people were pleased to see something new from Italy: "With their busts and statuettes by Prince Paolo Troubetzkoy, the Italians [prove] that they are also capable of creating something better than their popular, smooth marble products."[10]

A cast of *Madame Aurnheimer* was also shown in the Salon d'automne in Paris in 1904, along with another 45 works by Troubetzkoy.[11] The opulently dressed, seated figure turning within itself invites being viewed from different perspectives. Irrespective of from where one approaches it, one is surprised upon experiencing the dynamic verve with which the artist virtually chopped up the surface of the dress and even allows it to flow out over the plinth, while the only sparingly exposed body and the face are modelled in a smooth texture. The striking group *Mother and Child* (cat. 113) from 1898 also invites contemplation with a rotating, fluid gaze. The mother closely embraces not only the body of her daughter snuggling up against her, but leads to the two bodies and dresses almost dissolving into one another. The model for the mother was Troubetzkoy's future wife Elin, whom he had met just shortly before creating the sculpture. One version of this very emotional work was on display in the Russian Pavilion at the Paris world's fair in 1900, and once more at the Salon d'automne in Paris in 1905.[12]

> "His brushwork boldly challenges you by presenting a definite tone for every inch of surface [...] he never permits some pleasantly warmed juice to veil his view of air, colour and form."
>
> Robert Alan Stevenson, 1893

In the case of both the mother-and-child group as well as *After the Ball*, the detailed fissuring of the ample fabrics brings about not only a strongly animated play of light, but also of shadow.[13] Of even more appeal is the wealth of nuanced light-to-dark values that lie between the two extremes of light and shadow. For this reason, in 1902, Tristan Klingsor concluded that "this Impressionist [Troubetzkoy]" is the "colourist of sculpture."[14]

However, Troubetzkoy's technique of rupturing surfaces leads not only to an extraordinarily vital surface treatment, but also to a fragmented outline. Figure and space do not separate themselves into self-contained units; rather, they seem to fuse. The Scapigliati painters in Milan, whom Troubetzkoy was undoubtedly close to in his rare paintings, such as the *Portrait of a Girl* produced around 1905, also pursued this aim (cat. 114; see cat. 115). They created similar space–figure structures with their dark grounds and the dry, rather angular style of painting.[15] Yet it is worthwhile not only to look at these models but also to compare them with Sargent's painting of Lady Agnew. Both artists secure the necessary unity and harmony by means of the clear basic composition so as to then elaborate the textures in detailed steps in a highly nuanced way. At the same time, light plays a crucial role for both Troubetzkoy and Sargent. It dances on the surfaces just as it appears to permeate them. Sargent evokes light through his palette by repeatedly applying the light colours, which seem to almost radiate out of themselves in a transparent brushstroke. By contrast, Troubetzkoy refracts the light falling on – in the case of *Madame Aurnheimer* – the impermeable bronze surface through its fragmentation in such a way that the tonal values can vibrantly develop in the interplay between lit and shadowed zones, and the light even seems to partially disappear in the fissures of the dress. Both artists subtly blend their model with the surrounding space and astonish viewers through the demonstration of their virtuosity, also causing them to oscillate when it is a question of assessing the adequate distance to the work. Does looking at the work close up apply more than considering it from a distance? This question must be answered differently at any given moment, and the constant shift lies in the viewer themselves.

However, this inspiring proximity between painting and sculpture was not unanimously appreciated. In the *Mercure de France* in 1908, Charles Morice accused the artists Rosso and Troubetzkoy of causing confusion between painting and sculpture with their desire to translate the transitory nature of the moment into a permanent state – and, even more, of betraying the qualities of sculpture.[16] — EM-V

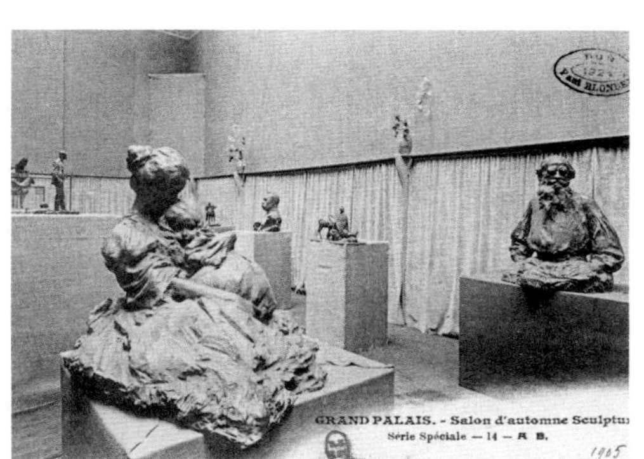

1 Salon d'Automne, Paris, 1905, with works by Paolo Troubetzkoy, photograph, Bibliothèque nationale de France, Département des Estampes et de la photographie, Paris

1 Vernon Lee, quoted in: Rayler Rolfe 1997, p. 28.

2 On the biography of Lady Agnew, see exh. cat. Edinburgh 1997; on the significance of the painting in the oeuvre of Singer Sargent and his appointment to Associate of the Royal Academy in 1894 based on its renown, see Ormond/ Kilmurray 2002, p. 64.

3 Stevenson 1893; quoted in: exh. cat. London 1998, p. 144.

4 Arthur Baignères on the occasion of the presentation of the portrait of Vernon Lee in the exhibition *Première exposition de la Société Internationale de Peintres et Sculpteurs*; Baignères 1883; quoted in: Kilmurray 1998, p. 105, note 7.

5 For more details, see Gerdts 1986.

6 Stevenson 1893; quoted in: exh. cat. London 1998, p. 144.

7 On the competition, see *Il Corriere della Sera*, 24/25 December 1897, p. 2; quoted in: exh. cat. Verbania Pallanza 1990, p. 118.

8 Exh. cat. London 2008, p. 66.

9 The work was destroyed in the Second World War. I extend my thanks to Astrid Nielsen at the Staatliche Kunstsammlungen Dresden for her friendly support and for making archival materials available.

10 Lier 1897, column 500.

11 Ginex 2014, p. 191.

12 Champy-Vinas 2014, p. 194.

13 Tristan Klingsor was the first one to describe this in detail; Klingsor 1902.

14 "C'est encore cette négligence volontaire de la connaissance acquise par l'analyse scientifique postérieure à l'impression artistique, qui fait de cet impressioniste le coloriste de la sculpture." Ibid., p. 33.

15 Exh. cat. Naples 2003, p. 110.

16 "On a dit, à propos de Rosso lui-même comme de Troubetzkoy, que ce désir n'est pas justifiable, qu'il trahit la statuaire et suppose entre elle et la peinture une confusion fâcheuse." Morice 1908. For more information on the connection between Rosso and Troubetzkoy, see Wootton 2016.

Cat. 111 John Singer Sargent, **Lady Agnew of Lochnaw**, 1892; oil on canvas, 127 × 101 cm; National Gallery of Scotland, Edinburgh, purchased with the aid of the Cowan Smith Bequest Fund 1925, Inv. Nr. NG 1656 **Cat. 112** Paolo Troubetzkoy, **After the Ball (Adelaide Aurnheimer)**, 1897; bronze, 45.5 × 52 × 53.5 cm; signed: "Paolo Troubetzkoy / Milano 1897"; private collection, London

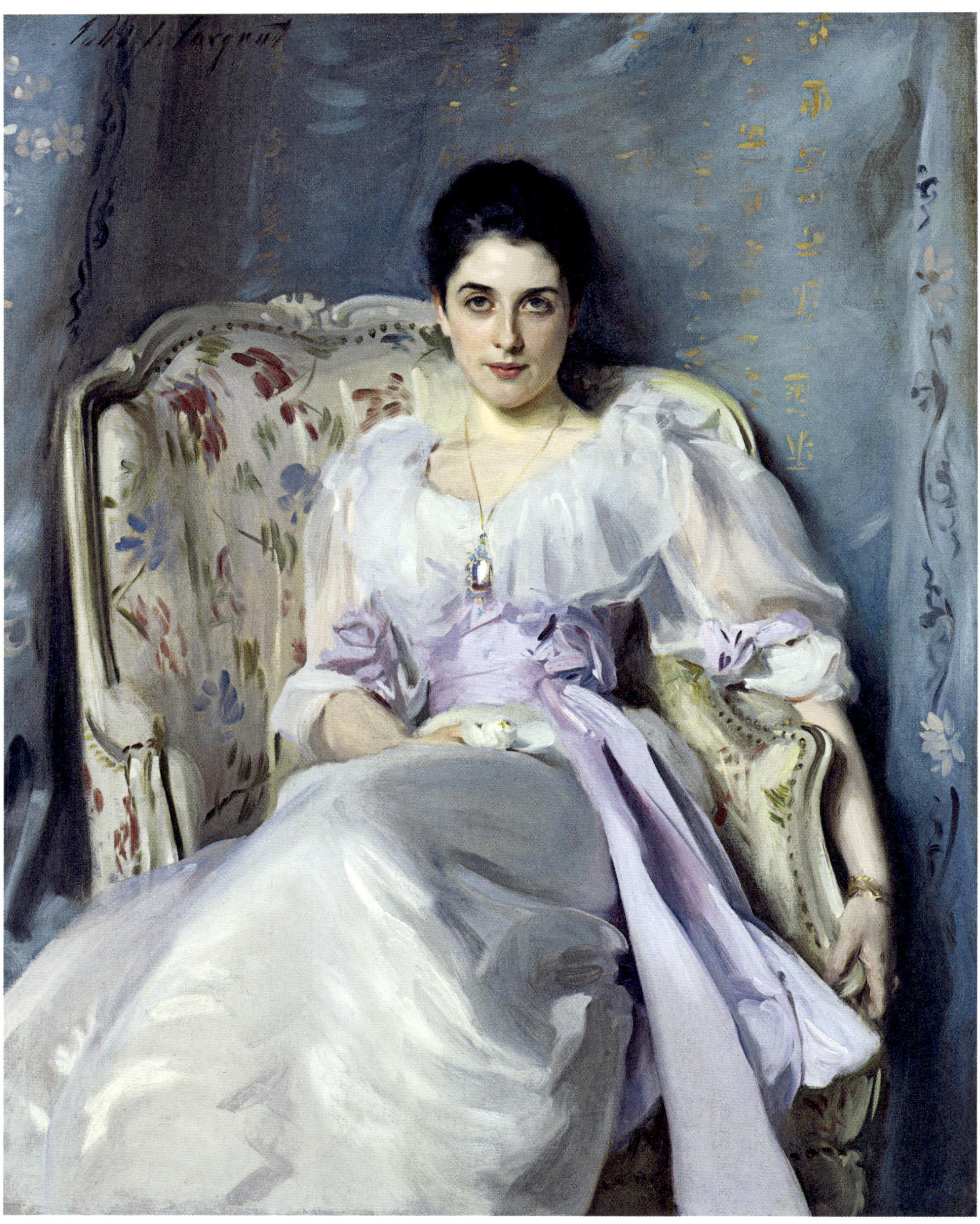

Cat. 111

Cat.112

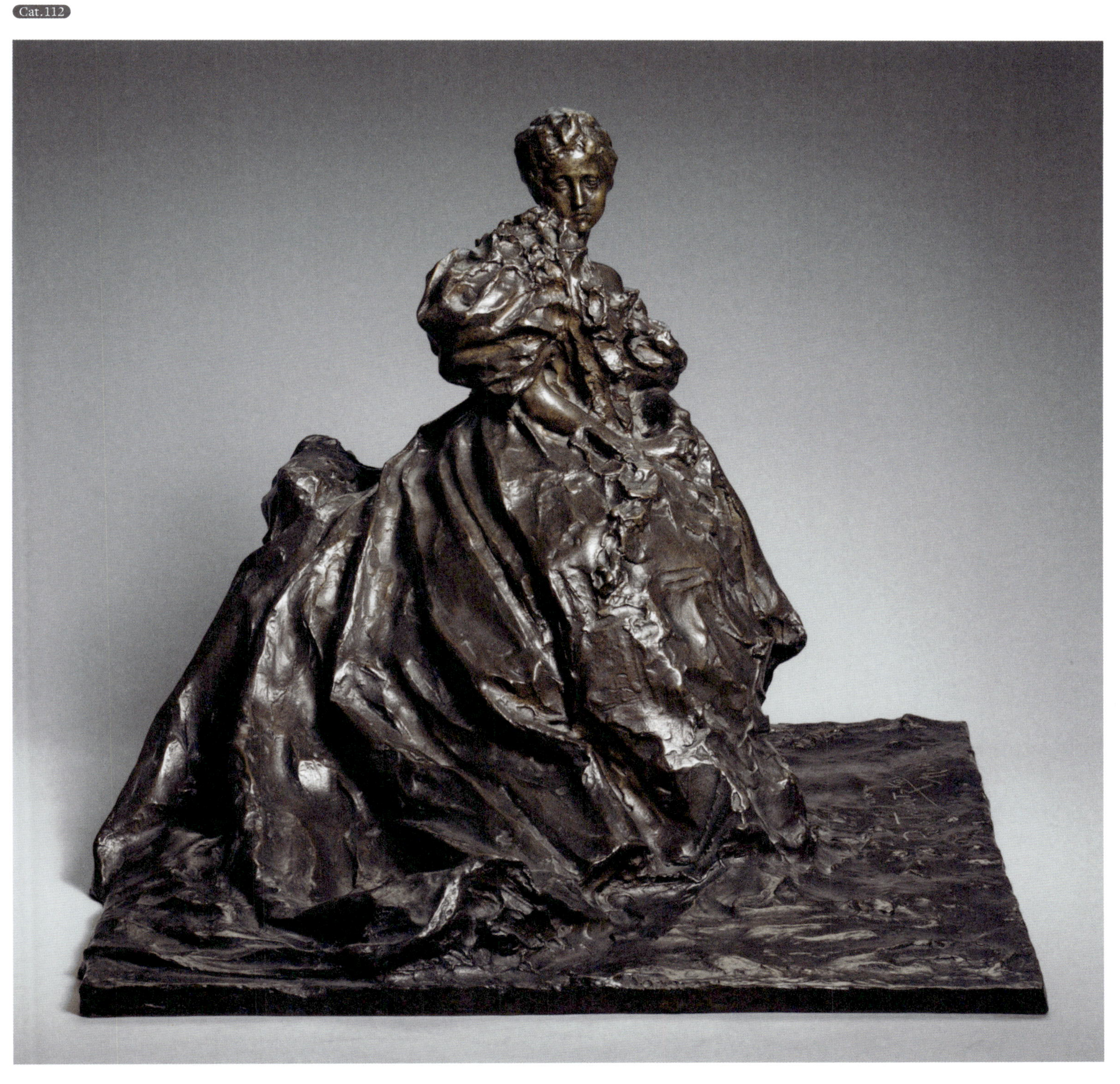

Cat. 113 Paolo Troubetzkoy, **Mother and Child**, 1898; plaster, 83 × 104 × 88 cm;
Petit Palais, Musée des Beaux-Arts de la Ville de Paris, inv. no. PPS2568
Cat. 114 Paolo Troubetzkoy, **Portrait of a Girl**, c. 1905; oil on canvas, 91 × 65 cm;
The Gilgore Collection, Dr Sheldon G. Gilgore and Irma H. Gilgore, Italian Art
1850–1925, Gilgore Museum, Naples, FL

Cat. 113

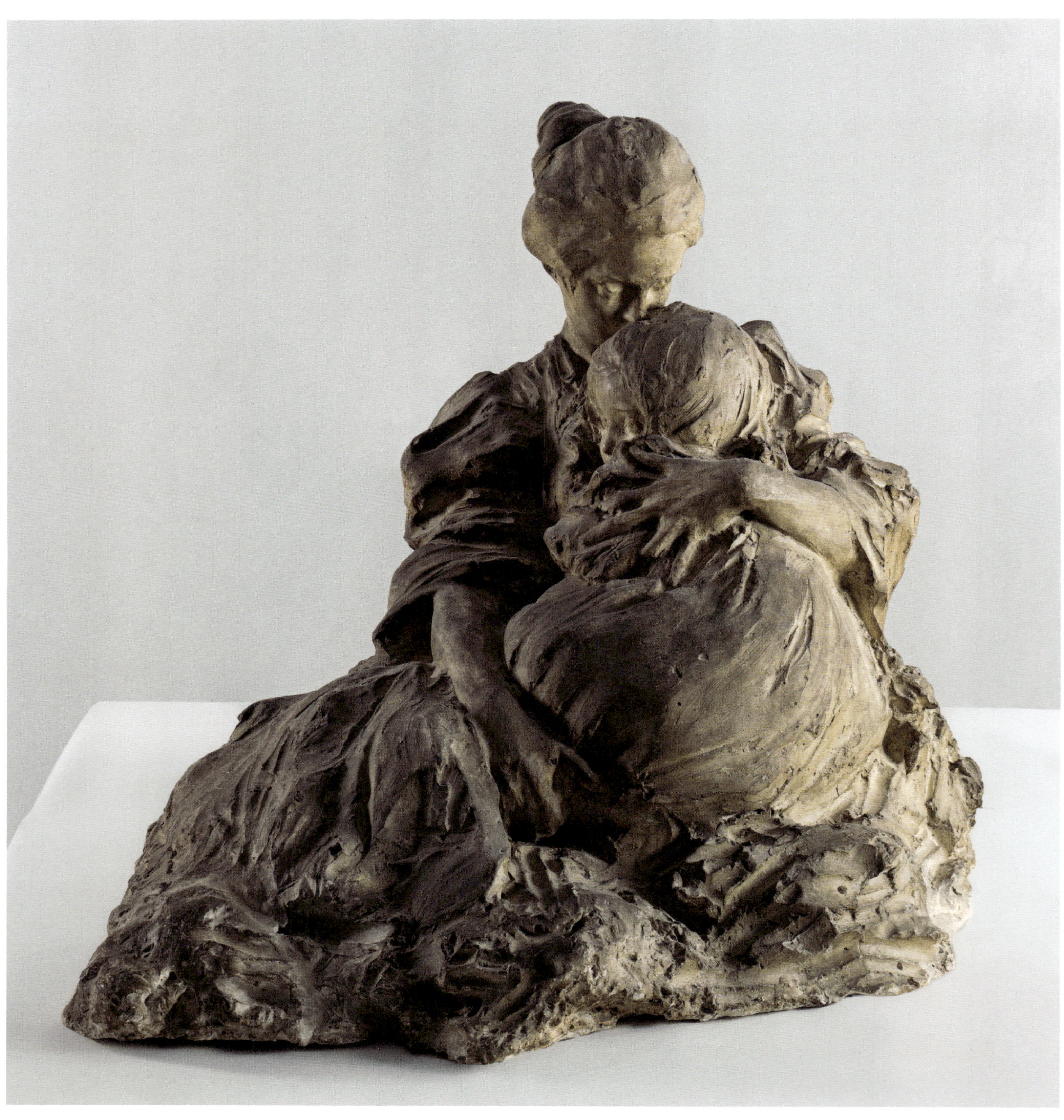

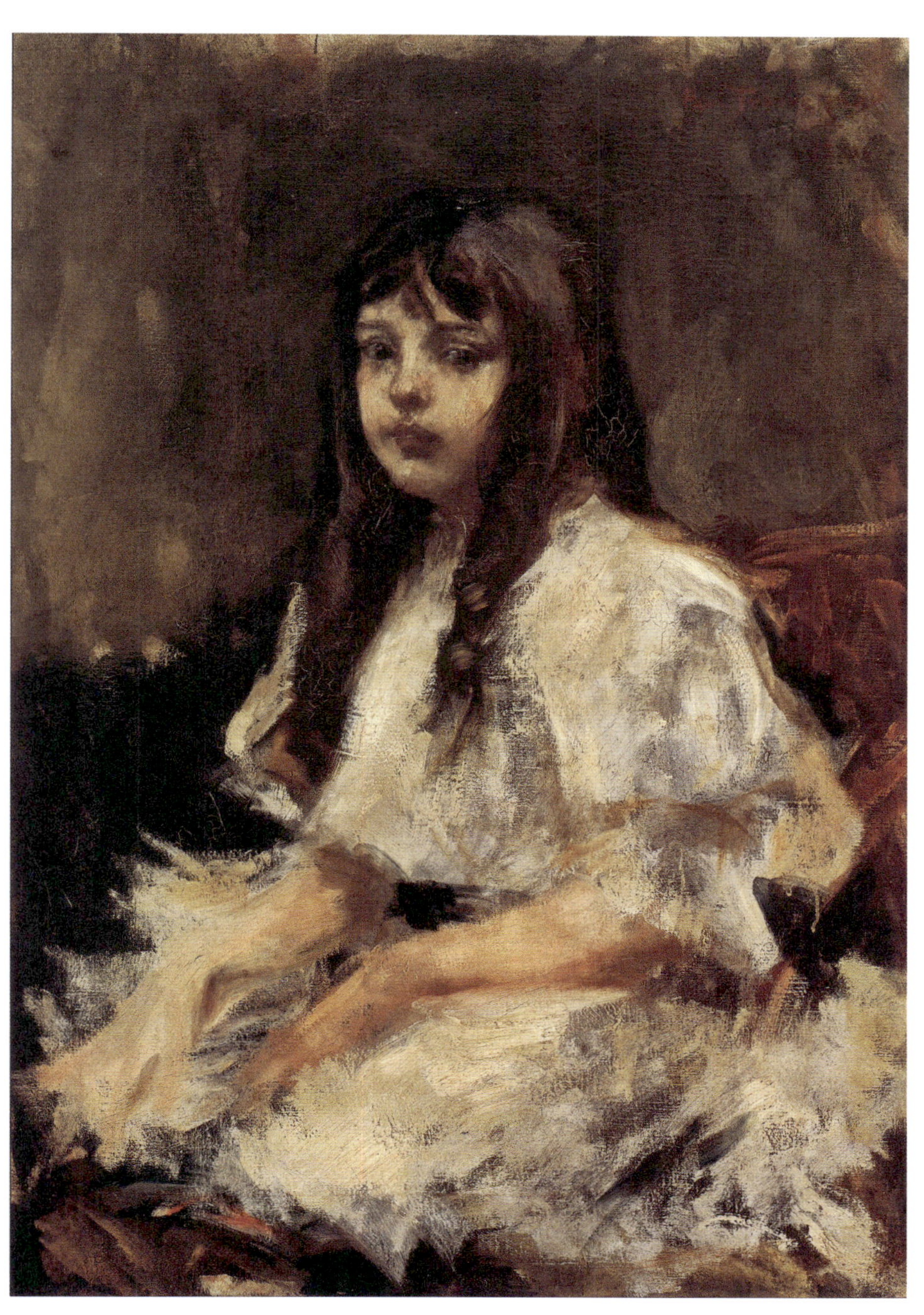

Cat.114

Tranquillo Cremona and the painting of the "Scapigliati"

Tranquillo Cremona (1837–1878) was a student of Giacomo Trécourt at the Civica Scuola di Pittura school of painting in Pavia before moving to Venice in 1852, where he attended the Accademia di Belle Arti. From 1859 onwards, he resided in Milan, where he studied painting under Giuseppe Bertini at the Accademia di Brera, and where he founded the artists' group La Scapigliatura along with the painter Daniele Ranzoni, the sculptor Giuseppe Grandi, and the writers Emilio Praga, Cletto Arrighi (the anagrammatic pseudonym of Carlo Righetti), Arrigo Boito and Carlo Dossi. The group's name – from *scapigliato*, dishevelled – derived from the title of a novel by Arrighi. Besides their friendship, what connected the group's members was their openly aired rebellion against middle-class conventions, the urge to violate rules and to break up academic hierarchies, and their delight in provocative digression and the scandalous, which also had an effect on their social behaviour. In artistic terms, the "scapligliati" stand for innovative, gossamer painting executed with soft brushstrokes that vibrate in direct light and, in some respects, are related to French Impressionism.

The Reader belongs to a group of works that Cremona produced between 1873 and 1878 and deliberately left unfinished. After his premature death on 10 June 1878, they remained in his studio. Some of them stand out due to their stylistic relatedness: *Visiting the College* (*La visita al collegio*, 1875–1878; private collection), *The Spanish Woman* (*La spagnola*, 1876–1878; private collection) and *Poor but Proud* (*Povero ma superbo*, 1877/78; Frugone Collection, Genoa). These works are characterised by the momentum in drawing and brushstroke with which the painter experimented from the early 1870s onwards. A new style emerged at the time, "[...] a strange approach to painting, everything behind a layer of veils, of things implied, in hues without contours, without any apparent use of line, with the most disparate colours, and with a certain flocculent touch that requires a distance of one hundred metres to obscure it," as the critic and writer

Filippo Filippi remarked in 1872.[1] It was a type of painting that was capable of dissolving forms – and likewise their traditional chiaroscuro structure – and merging them into the surrounding atmosphere in such a way that they became one. Paintings originated that communicated a vague idea of "[...] faces, melted and blurred beneath a feathery, hazy, indistinct layer"; paintings that "seem to have been hurled down out of spite, or else as a practical joke, having been finished in one day", but which were in fact "the fruit of repeated attempts and revisions, of spending not days but months on them."[2]

Cremona's new style, "stil novo", is of a complex nature, a unique form that cannot be traced back to another one. It is based in the extraordinary, subtle harmony of its colours and in its very distinct painting style. The result is highly sophisticated painting whose materiality features crystalline purity, comparable only with the great Netherlandish masters of the seventeenth century. This becomes particularly apparent when viewing *The Reader*, where the exploration of its outer appearance subordinates itself to purely painterly solutions, from the gentle bursts of light and shadow and the subtle connections between the shades of colour to the sophisticatedly constructed spatiality.

The painter played with breaking up the volumes by means of complicated dark–light effects, using the brush to place dabs of pure colour alongside one another and then rubbing them with his fingertips (a technique he preferred, which, according to contemporary sources, led to his death by lead poisoning) in order to vary and invigorate the colours. As a result, the figure completely immerses itself in space, in a holistic vision that becomes palpable thanks to the all-encompassing continuity of the fabric spun out of light. "[...] here painting has reached its furthest limits, beyond which music reigns," Carlo Dossi wrote in 1873 – and, in doing so, provided the viewer with an astute interpretative approach for the works that Cremona produced in the 1870s.[3] — SB

> "[...] faces, melted and blurred beneath a feathery, hazy, indistinct layer [...]."
>
> Filippo Filippi, 1872

---

1   "[...] una pittura strana, tutta a veli, a sottintesi, a sfumature senza contorri, senza disegno apparente, coi colori i più disparati, e con un certo tocco fioccoso che ha bisogno di cento metri di distanza per essere dissimulato." Filippi 1872.

2   "[...] di volti, fusa e confusa sotto uno strato piumoso, nebbioso, indefinibile [... tele] che sembrano gettate giù per dispetto, e fatte in un giorno [... ma che invece] sono il frutto di tentativi e di rifacimenti continui, da spenderci sopra non giorni ma mesi." Ibid.

3   "[...] qui la pittura è giunta ai suoi fini ultimi, di là dei quali regna la musica." Dossi 1873; quoted in: Dossi 2006. For additional information about the painting, see the following references: Bossaglia 1994, p. 160, no. 159 (Giovanni Dainotti; with older references); exh. cat. Brescia 2003, pp. 170, 236, no. 91; exh. cat. Novi Ligure 2007, p. 120, no. 65; exh. cat. Milan 2009, pp. 273, 295, no. 254; exh. cat. Milan 2015a, pp. 8, 62, no. 1.

 Tranquillo Cremona, *The Reader* (*La lettrice*), 1873–1878; oil on canvas,
105 × 85 cm; private collection, courtesy Galleria Bottegantica, Milan

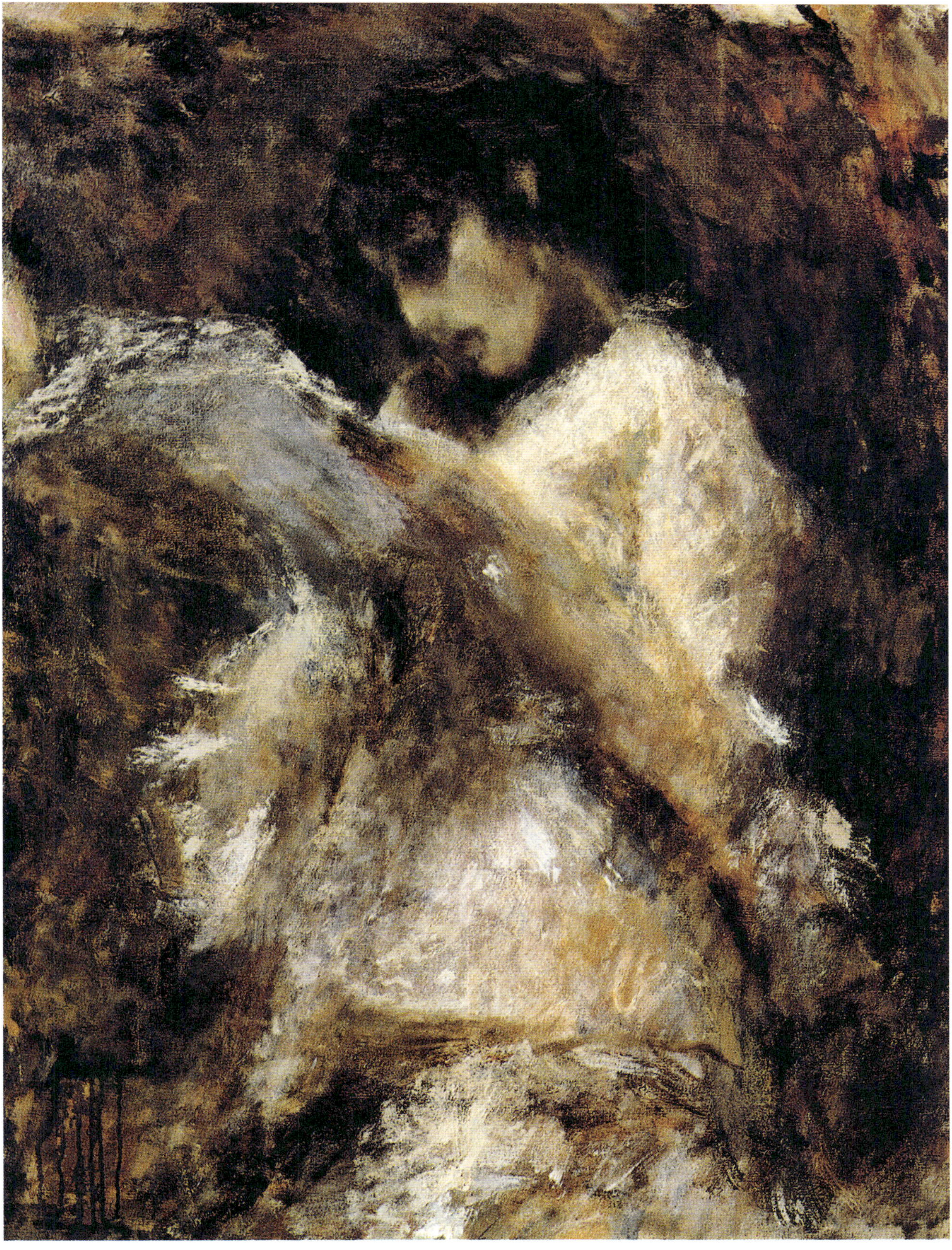

Ernesto Bazzaro – a "Scapigliatura" sculptor

Ernesto Bazzaro (1859–1937) lived and worked in Milan, where he was born and received his artistic training. His development as an artist is partially shrouded in darkness, since the period between 1875 and 1881 that he spent at the school of sculpture headed by Francesco Barzaghi and Ambrogio Borghi at the Accademia di Brera cannot be regarded as decisive. At the time, the paradigmatic model worked out in the previous decade by the painters of the Scapigliatura movement (see cat. 115) had numerous followers among those Lombardic artists who were in search of alternatives to academic role models. In addition, contemporary literature turned to the social conditions in society for the first time and began to take an interest in the "belly" of the city, in which life was marked by poverty and desperation. It was in the context of the Scapigliatura that Bazzaro's earliest works originated, the protagonists of which are the "little people" from Milan: street children (*The Foundling* [*La trovatella*], 1889, Staatliche Kunstsammlungen, Dresden), old men (*Exhaustion* [*Esaurimento*], 1894, Galleria d'Arte Moderna, Milan) and other actors in simple urban life (*The Widow* [*La vedova*], 1888, Galleria Nazionale d'Arte Moderna, Rome) – real models that were caught with a quick, hard gaze, free of any descriptive compromises and gradually converted into objects (out of plaster or bronze), their surfaces animated and restless due to having to constantly deal with the light.

Towards the end of the century, Bazzaro created the foundation for those models that characterise his mature work. His development proceeded from remnants of descriptive allusions to a progressive lack of interest in the importance of a work: Bazzaro increasingly concentrated on the examination of the object itself – namely, on the possibility of inscribing the visual impression recorded by the retina into the material along with the sensations that can be prompted by spatial distance, a form, a play of light or a gust of wind. These images are for the most part designed to develop typological sequences that Bazzaro repeated multiple times – never simply received but transformed, transposed and varied over the years and under the influence of the material used.

One example of this is *Study after Nature*, of which at least four versions are known in bronze and one – the first – in plaster, which then served as the model for the cast on display here. Two elegant women wearing hats and holding parasols are sitting on the left side of a bench. They are so immersed in conversation that they ignore the sad and miserable-looking old man next to them, whose posture resembles that of the protagonist of Bazzaro's sculpture *Exhaustion*. With great skill, the sculptor lends expression to a number of social and formal opposites: rich and poor, young and old come together; diagonals and vertical lines, a sloped posture and static pose are set against one another. One believes to perceive impressions in the composition as well as in the expressive figures that elude any urge to describe them: the light, which furrows the surfaces and raises them, enriches the group by so many allusions that an atmosphere develops that is detached from reality, yet in which the volumetric structure is accommodated. Maintaining a tag of verisimilitude in their facial feature, the figures live on the absolute presence of bodies shaped by gravity that pour out like a stream of magma from the heads downwards and accumulate on the base. The result is a crust of body parts, uneven, split, broken up by the countless puckerings of the material, through which a dialogue with light unfolds. — SB

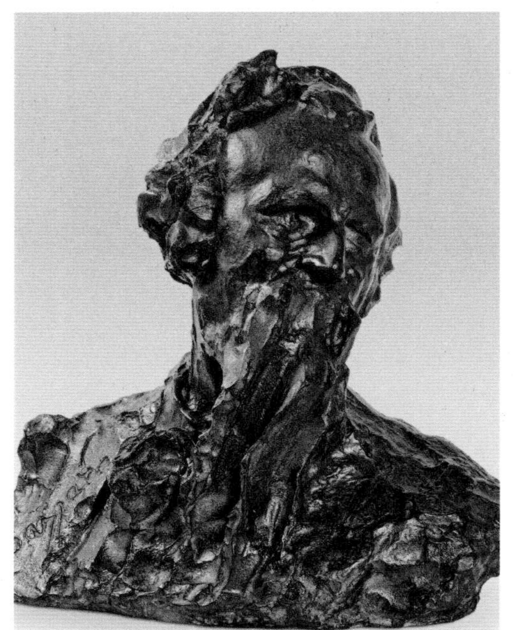

1 Ernest Bazzaro, *Self-portrait*, 1913, bronze, 50 × 48.5 × 29 cm, Galleria d'Arte Moderna, Milan

Cat.116 Ernesto Bazzaro, Study after Nature (Three Figures Seated on a Bench)
(Studio dal vero [Tre figure sedute su una panchina]), c. 1900–1910; bronze,
52 × 92 × 36 cm; stamped on the plinth: "Bazzaro"; private collection, courtesy Galleria
Bottegantica, Milan

Cat.116

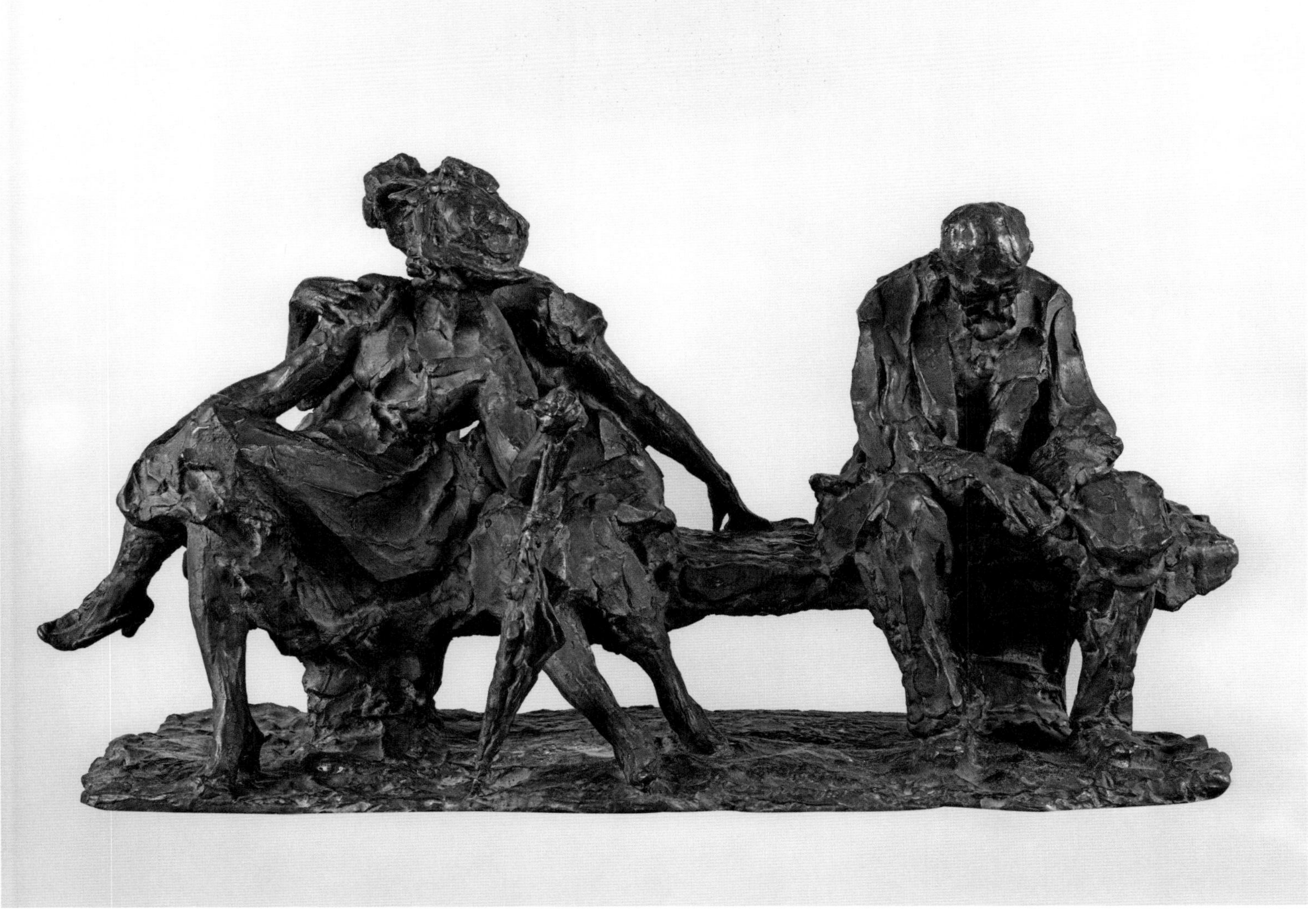

 # Outdoors

Around 1870, croquet was a popular leisure pursuit for sophisticated urban citizens.[1] In the context of the times, Édouard Manet's (1832–1883) painting *A Game of Croquet* (cat. 117) radiated a fresh spontaneity, depicting people of both sexes who have met in the garden to play game together. However, the arrangement is not as spontaneous as the motif suggests, but is rather rigorously composed: the two men, whose poses are markedly casual, frame the women equipped with wooden mallets (as well as the centrally placed watering can); together they progress evenly staggered along a diagonal extending into the depths of the pictorial space. Yet the space does not open up above a wide horizon, as dense leafage composed of numerous shades of green concludes the painting towards the back. Upon the urging of Berthe Moisot, Manet ventured outdoors for the first time in 1870 to paint works such as *A Game of Croquet*.[2] He captured the various textures as well as the natural play of light with a subtle, loose brushstroke.

The man and woman depicted in the sculpture by the Italian sculptor Leonardo Bistolfi (1859–1933) are also in a garden – not amusing themselves in bright daylight but, according to the title, in the romantic *Dusk* (cat. 118). The lady leans back closely against the gentleman sitting on a wall, formally merging with him to constitute a unity. The musing woman gazes into the distance, at the same time opening up the space to the left. The area in the foreground and middle ground of the plinth is also physically empty or open, whereas in the back the wall resolves the scene as rigorously as the leafage in Manet's painting. Due to this disposition, viewing the sculpture is geared towards a front or slight side view. The early influence of the Scapigliati artists (cf. cat. 115, 116) is visible here as is the anticipation of Bistolfi's further development towards Symbolism in the way it manifested in his famous marble monument for Giovanni Segantini (around 1904, Segantini Museum, St. Moritz).[3] The surface of the plaster on display here seems like the corresponding bronze casts, rough and unworked

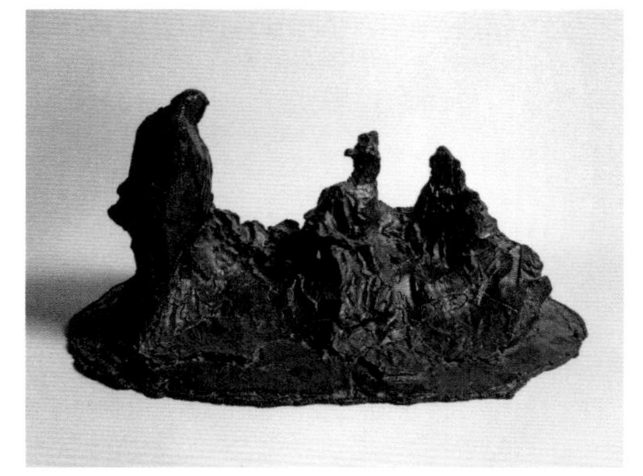

1 Medardo Rosso, *Conversation in the Garden*, 1899, bronze, 32 × 66.5 × 41.5 cm, Galleria Nazionale d'Arte Moderna, Rome

in particular in the area of the ground, the wall and the puff sleeves of the woman's dress; however, the smoothed body areas are only vaguely distinguishable, causing a latent obscurity of the volumes to be interpreted and the surface textures to be displayed. This obscurity underscores the vision of dusk, in whose diffuse light visual selectivity noticeably decreases.

Medardo Rosso's depiction of a *Conversation in the Garden* (fig. 1) also comes to mind in this respect. The group of small figures comprising a standing man and two seated women are difficult to make out as such, since the bodies are captured very summarily and at the same time also include the surrounding space. A spatial arrangement related to a clear perspective does not come about; even a front and a back are hard to identify. Rather, it appears as if Rosso assembled set pieces of spatial elements to produce a group. If the sculpture did not bear the title it does, it would hardly be able to imagine a conversation. According to the present state of knowledge, the sculptural group *Conversation in the Garden* was never presented in an exhibition during Rosso's lifetime, yet it was well known nevertheless: Edmond Claris published a photograph of the plaster in his book on Impressionist sculpture.[4]

For sculptors, groups in outdoor space are a particular challenge – above all when, as in these cases, they are more or less uneventful gatherings. No one fights, pushes, dies or dances. However, even without a definite outside influence, it is still about lending form to the relationship between the individual figures. In addition, the relation to the surrounding space plays a substantial role. Bistolfi, for example, works with the (emotional) density of the figures in contrast to the expanse surrounding them. In Rosso's work, on the other hand, the individual protagonists seem lost and as placeless as their environment. Alberto Giacometti (1901–1966) would rigorously pursue this aspect four decades later when he also further explored Rosso's precise analysis of the viewer's standpoint in relation to the object.[5] — EM-V

1   Rubin 1999; Conzen 2002, p. 70; exh. cat. Frankfurt 2006, p. 208.
2   Exh. cat. Frankfurt 2006, p. 208.
3   Exh. cat. Milan 1998, pp. 148 ff., which also includes more information about Bistolfi's biography; cf. exh. cat. Rome/Paris 2000; exh. cat. Milan 2017.
4   Claris 1902 (French), p. 119; not in Claris 1902a (German), cf. Lista 1994, pp. 90 ff.; exh. cat. Rovereto/Turin 2004, p. 168, with a discussion on the question of dates; Mola/Vittucci 2009, pp. 200 ff.
5   Lammert 2007.

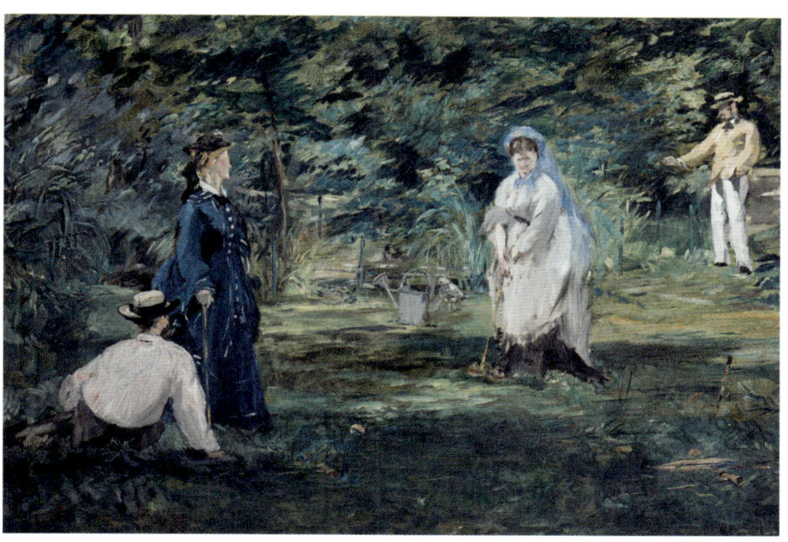

Cat. 117

Cat. 118

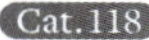

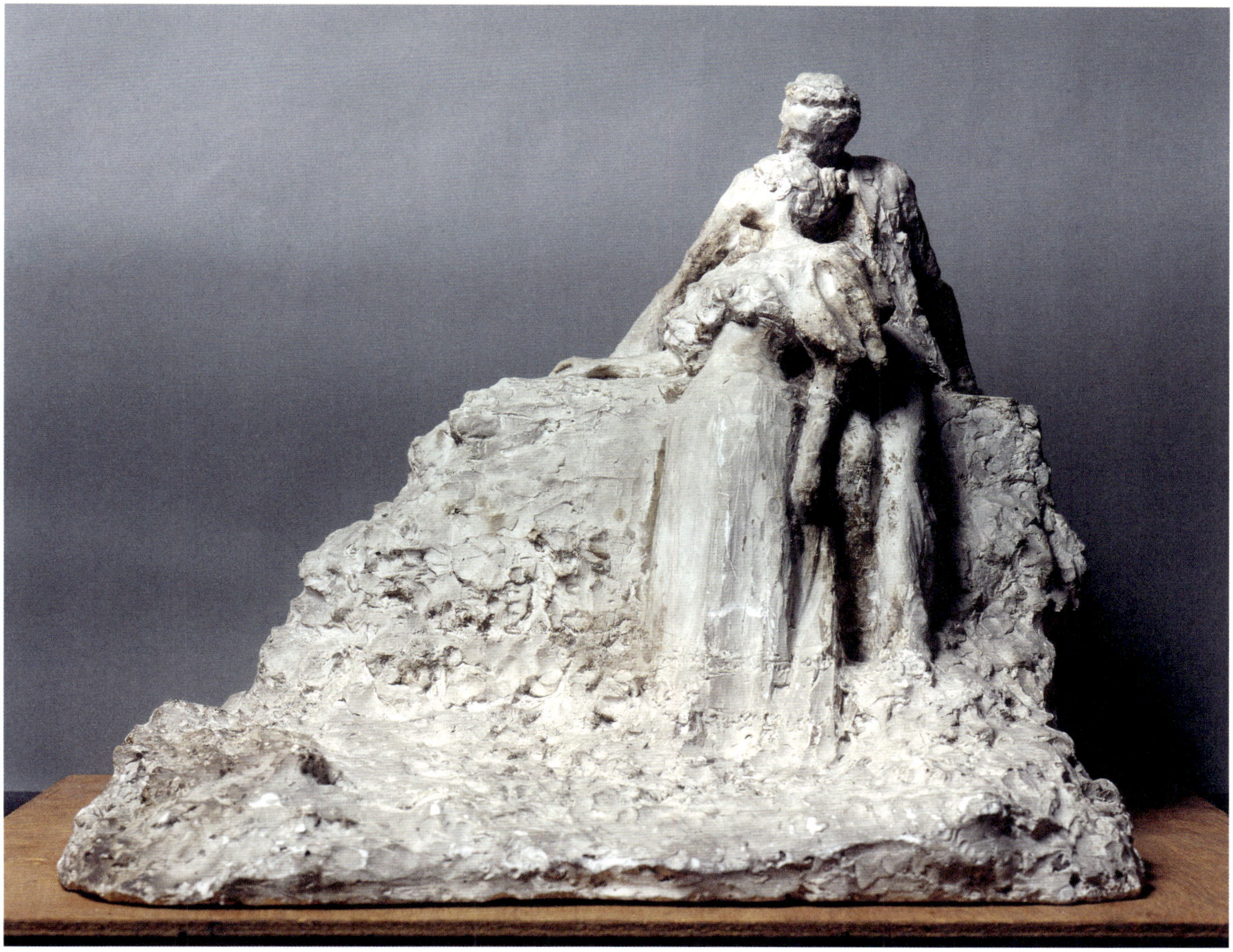

Cat. 119–123 Genre or caricature?

In paintings, drawings and paints, French Impressionism is essentially defined by scenes from everyday modern life, depictions of Parisian boulevards, people promenading along the Seine or performances on the stages of opera and theatre. In the sculpture at the close of the nineteenth century, however, these motifs have few equivalents either in France or elsewhere. The works presented here by Ferruccio Crespi (1861–1891; cat. 120), Paolo Troubetzkoy (1866–1938; cat. 121) and Antoine Bourdelle (1861–1929; cat. 119) constitute an exception in that they transpose genre scenes into the third dimension.

The figure group *After the Baths!* by the little-known Lombardian sculptor Ferruccio Crespi (cat. 120), who died at a young age, features a gaunt gentleman wearing clothes that are too large at the side of his heavily pregnant companion. The scene is characterised by intense interaction, which is related not only by their eye contact but also by their corresponding postures. What is striking is the noticeably animated surface both of the figures as well as of the plinth, on which the puzzling Italian title *Dopo i bagni!* is engraved; in this case, "bagni" has less to do with a public bath and more with the vernacular term for prison. The title thus suggests that the man has been "absent" for several months and now sees himself confronted with reality following his release from what was apparently a period of detainment full of hardship.[1] Besides the open modelling technique, the modernity of Crespi's sculpture lies primarily in the fact that it draws on a contemporary theme. It seems that he wanted to respond to the accusation of a lack of topicality in the area of sculpture – criticism that blemished the medium for decades.

Comparable with Crespi, his fellow countryman Paolo Troubetzkoy virtually created a modern antithesis to the heroic equestrian sculpture of the epoch with his *Fiacre in the Snow* (cat. 121) by having a coach being drawn by a decimated horse getting unceremoniously stuck in the mud. The coachman has alighted from the box seat and arduously battles his way through the adverse weather, which can only be surmised based on his stoop. As was already the case in Crespi's work, generally dispensing with smoothing the sculpture's surface is one of the most striking features in Troubetzkoy's work. The motif of snow permitted the artist to dissolve the sharp contours of wheels and coach. The mass lies over the entire ensemble like a gibbous mass, and the obscuration of the outlines underscores the impression of fugitiveness. In an early description from 1902, Tristan Klingsor (actually Arthur Justin Léon Leclère) referred to the work as a "Fiacre surpris par la neige à Milan", placing emphasis on Troubetzkoy's very own interest in reproducing an "impression".[2] According to the author, what appealed to the sculptor was not the accurate depiction of a coach *en miniature*, but rather of the numerous layers of the remaining snow. Troubetzkoy was "toujours impressionniste".[3] A cast – possibly this one – was presented at the Triennale di Brera in 1894.

The few contemporary reviews of the exhibit primarily describe the content of work as a successful depiction of the desolate social situation, illustrated by the resignating posture of the horse and the man.[4] Compared with the motifs of vibrant boulevards, on which carriages and passers-by appear as the epitome of the hustle and bustle of the big city, frequently found in paintings, drawings and prints, Troubetzkoy's sculpture is more evocative of hardship and destitution. Moreover, based on its overall appearance, from a formal point of view it was referred to as a "sketch" or "bozetto".[5] In the literature, one still reads of its "aspetto bozzettistico"[6] or more generally of its "bozzettismo"[7] to this day. What is meant by this is the fugitive method, which flirts, as it were, with how the supposed final work might have looked – although Troubetzkoy considered it to be in its finished state.

Antoine Bourdelle's sculpture *The Siesta* (cat. 119) is also defined by a sketchy modelling technique, which permits a marked play of light by means of multiple heightenings and depressions. The rendering of a man who has fallen asleep on the sofa reflects the artist's delight in playing with the shaping of the material. Unlike the works by Crespi and Troubetzkoy, this sculpture exhibits greater motif-related parallels with Impressionist paintings, drawings and prints. Numerous compositions of sleeping, reposing or weary individuals can be found in the circle around the Impressionists – in the work of Edgar Degas or Auguste Renoir, for example. The sleeping faun or Endymion of antiquity has become the ironing woman, the female dancer or a male labourer exhausted by the harshness of everyday life. By means of clothes and hat as well as the fashionable sofa, Bourdelle lends his figure a decidedly contemporary character.

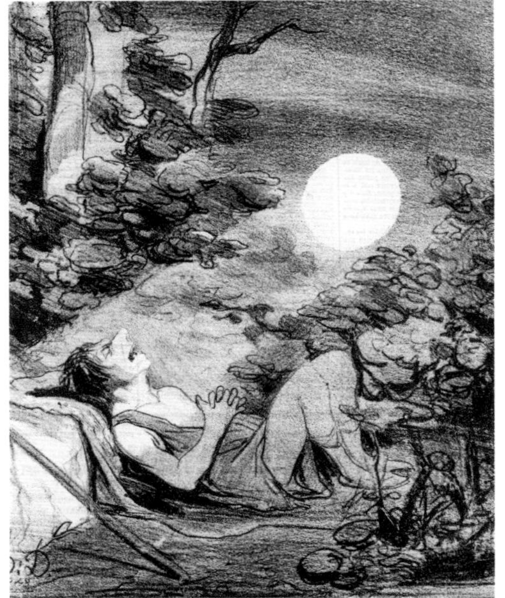

1 Honoré Daumier, *Endymion*, 1842, lithograph, Städel Museum, Frankfurt am Main

Besides their open modelling technique, what connects the three sculptures by Crespi, Troubetzkoy and Bourdelle is especially this content-related dimension, which appeals to the intellect and the moral conscience. In this respect, they are close to the caricature – above all, the works by Honoré Daumier (1808–1879), with which they share the formal stylistic means of exaggeration. Daumier's wide-ranging graphic oeuvre featured in both French and Italian print media. Among other things, between March 1850 and December 1851, he published about 30 lithographs of a figure in the satirical magazine *Le Charivari* that embodied "the shady agent, the indefatigable representative of Napoleonic propaganda": the *Ratapoil* (hairy rat).[8] As a staunch republican, Daumier used this political caricature to attack the looming Second French Empire. He modelled a corresponding figure (cat. 122) presumably in March 1851. However, the sculpture was withheld from the broad public during Daumier's lifetime;[9] it was not on view until 1892 at the Musée du Luxembourg in Paris.[10] The figure of *Ratapoil* lives on contradictions, as the exaggerated, imbalanced volumes seem at once fragile and powerful.

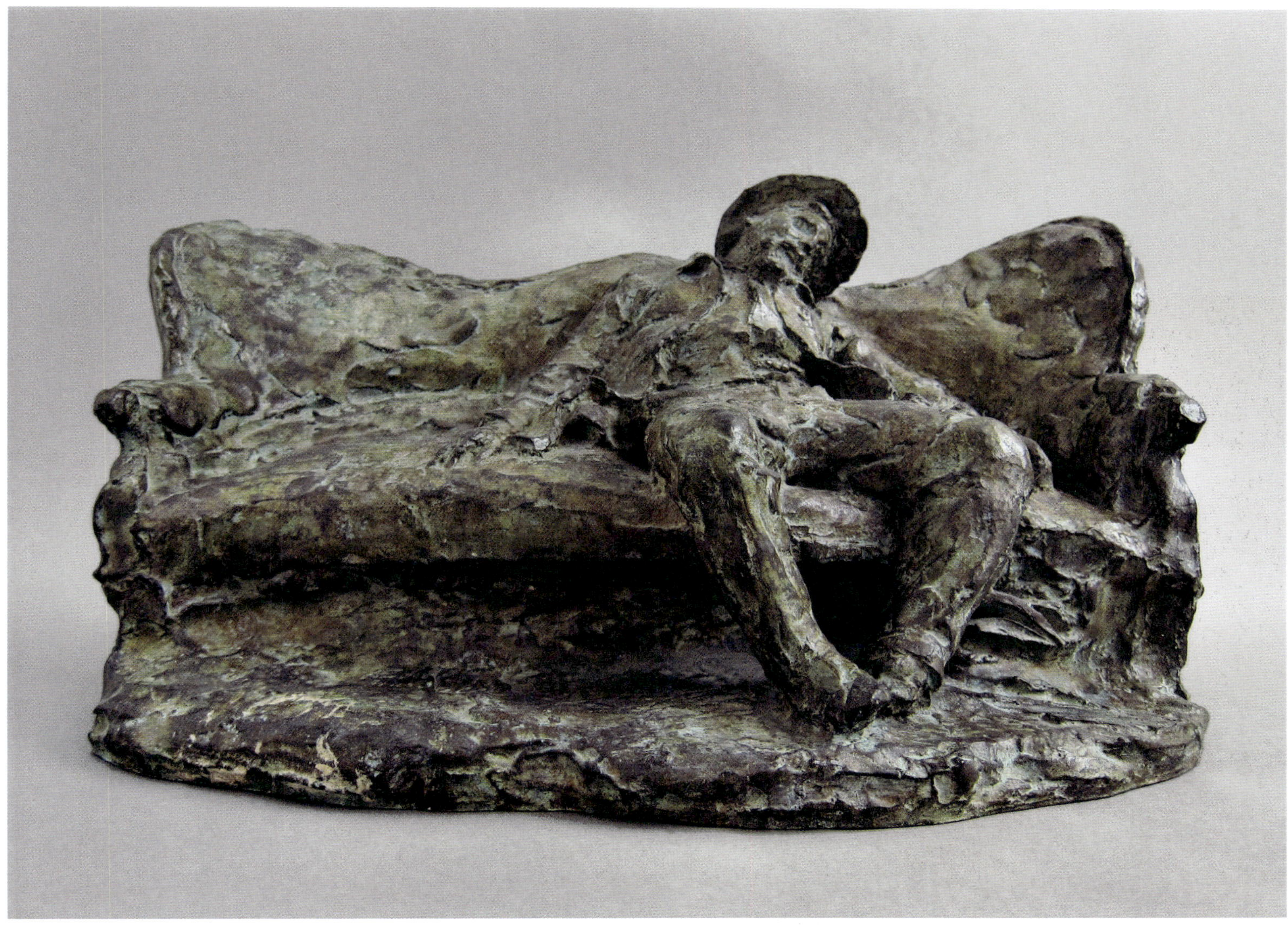

Cat.119

What is striking are the figure's oblique posture and the unusually animated surface. Whereas these two formal aspects exhibit parallels to later Impressionist sculpture, the latter only rarely took up the content-related dimensions of this politically motivated, caricaturing work. Yet in the context of the reception of Impressionism, reference is repeatedly made to the figure of *Ratapoil* – which attained inter-national prominence through Daumier's prints and drawings – in particular when it was a question of its decidedly slanted posture. The figure may have found a formal echo in Degas's works, as in his etching that features Mary Cassatt (1844–1926) in the paintings gallery of the Louvre (cat. 123) and in Medardo Rosso's *The Bookmaker* (see cat. 63).[11] — AE and EM-V

1 Exh. cat. Naples 2003, p. 52.
2 Klingsor 1902, p. 32.
3 Ibid., p. 43.
4 On the press commentaries, see exh. cat. Verbania Pallanza 1990, pp. 99–100;

exh. cat. Milan 2017, p. 208, no. 64 (Gianfranco Petriglieri).
5 *Lega Lombarda*, 24/25 June 1894, p. 2; quoted in: exh. cat. Verbania Pallanza 1990, p. 99.

6 Exh. cat. Milan 2017, p. 208, no. 64 (Gianfranco Petriglieri).
7 Licht 1994, p. 25.
8 "Honoré Daumier: *Ratapoil*", https://www.musee-orsay.fr/en/

collections/works-in-focus/ (accessed 12 December 2019).
9 Hecker 2017, p. 162.
10 Hofmann 2004, p. 50.
11 Hecker 2017, p. 162.

Cat.120 Ferruccio Crespi, After the Baths! (Dopo i bagni!), 1884–1891; bronze, 32.7 × 20.3 × 13 cm; The Gilgore Collection, Dr Sheldon G. Gilgore and Irma H. Gilgore, Italian Art 1850–1925, Gilgore Museum, Naples, FL Cat.121 Paolo Troubetzkoy, Fiacre in the Snow, 1894; bronze, 35 × 82 × 40 cm; Galleria d'Arte Moderna, Milan, inv. no. GAM 4362

Cat.120

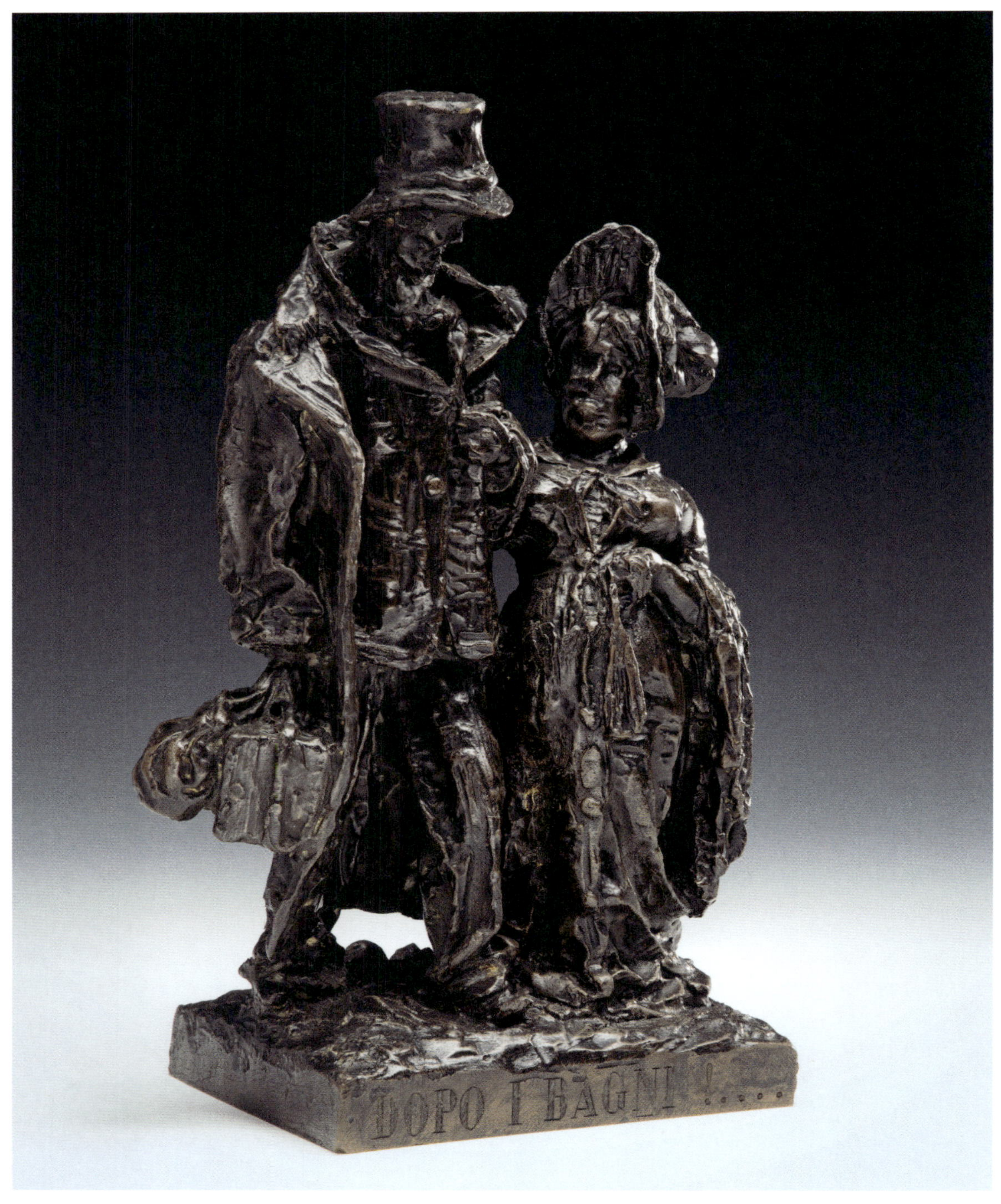
DOPO I BAGNI!

Cat.121

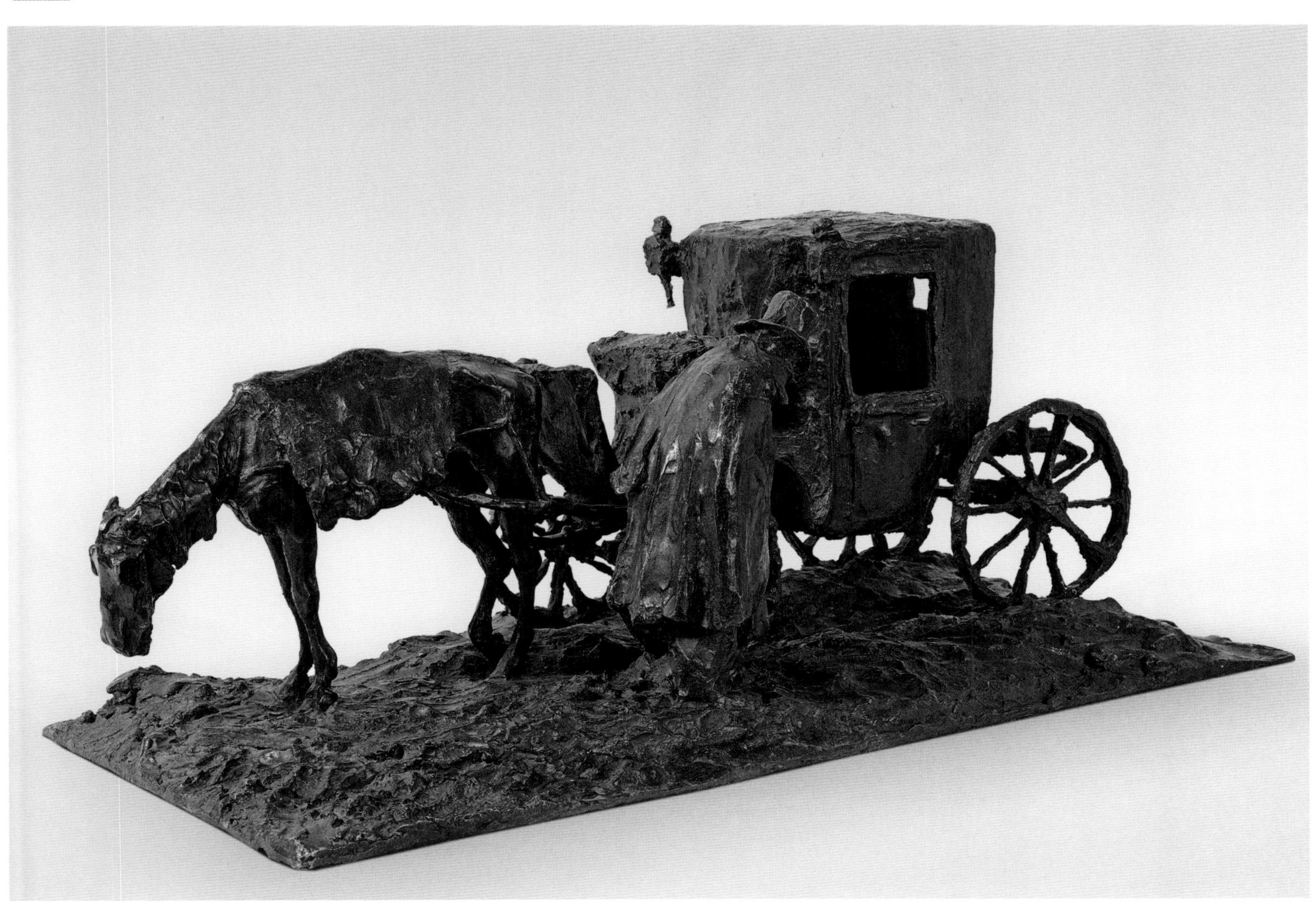

 Honoré Daumier, **Ratapoil**, 1851; bronze, 44.7 × 17 × 19 cm; stamped on the plinth: "Alexis Rudier / Fondeur PARiS", "9/20"; Städel Museum, Frankfurt am Main, inv. no. St.P 391 Edgar Degas, **Mary Cassatt at the Louvre: The Paintings Gallery**, 1879/80; etching, soft-ground etching, aquatint, drypoint and crayon électrique on paper, state: V/XX, 30.5 × 12.6 cm (plate), 35.9 × 26.5 cm (sheet); Museum Ulm, Ulm – Eigentum des Landes Baden-Württemberg, inv. no. BW 1961.12

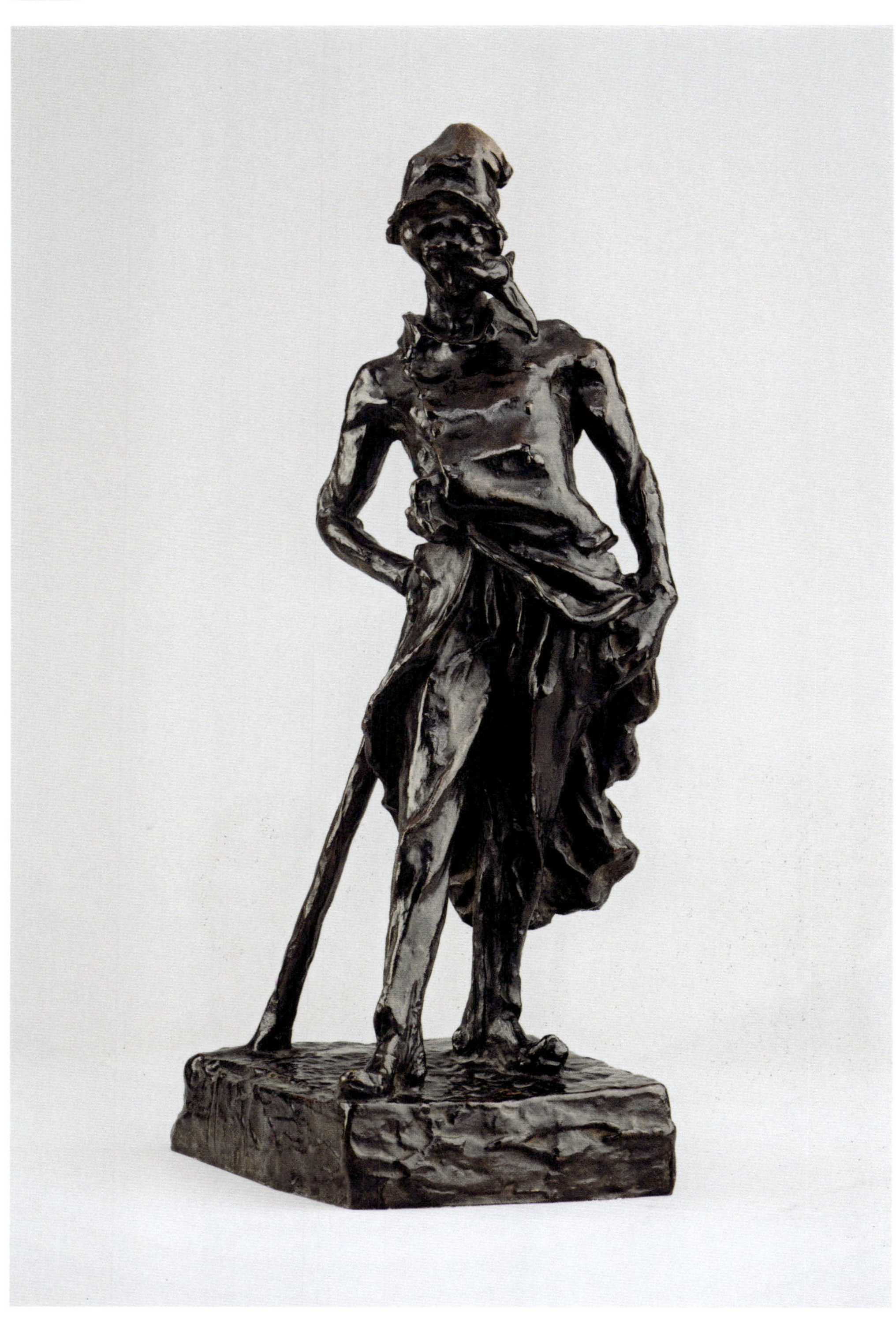

Cat. 123

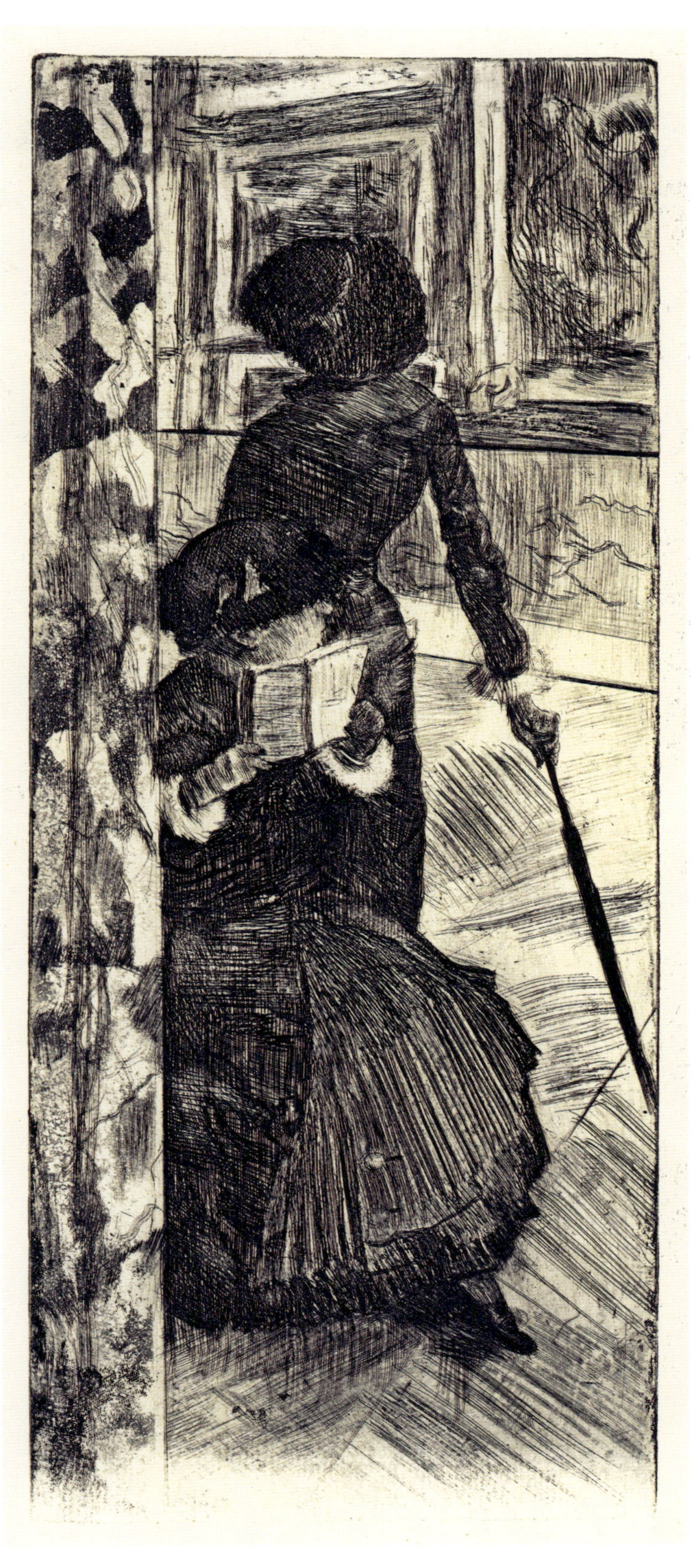

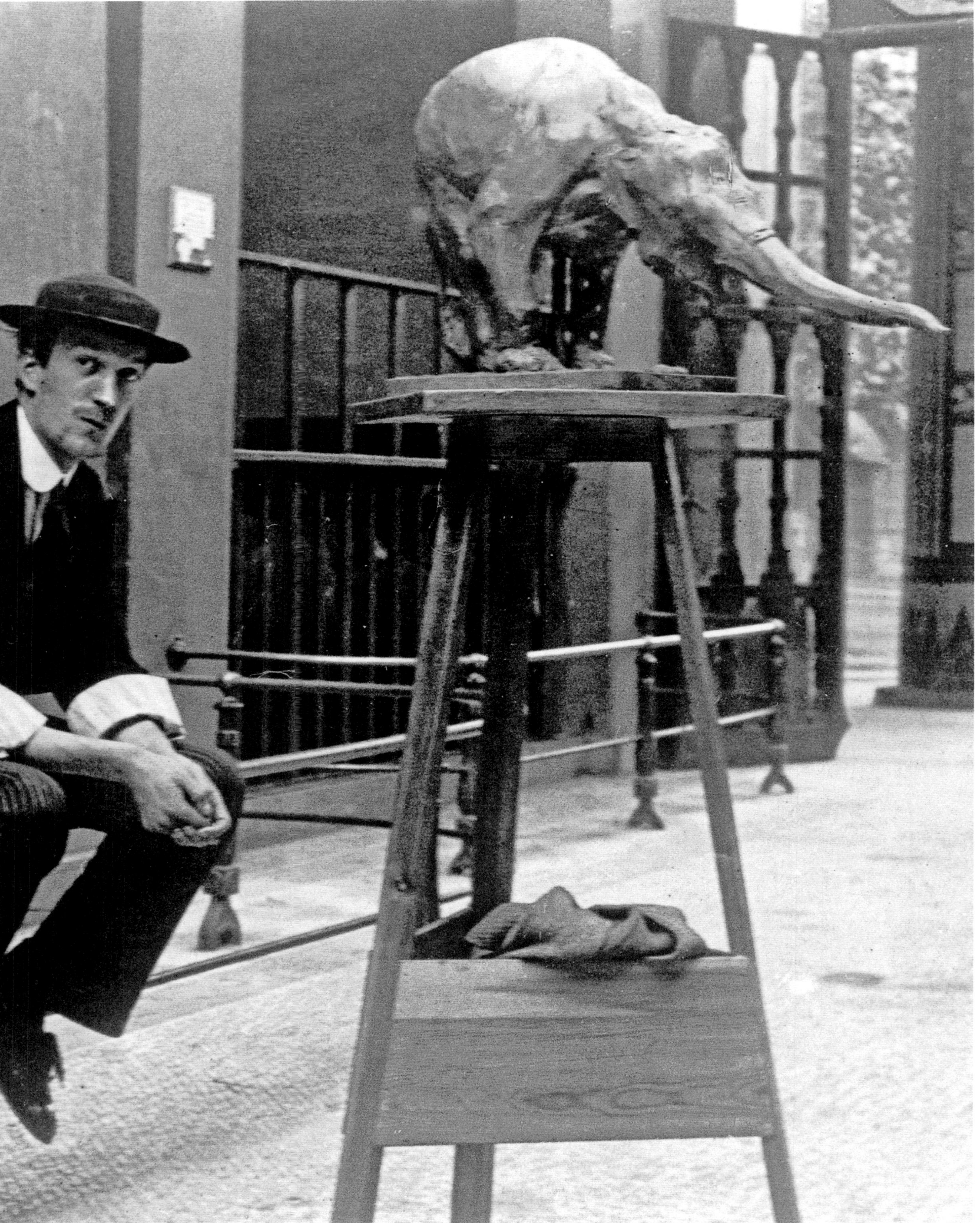

Rembrandt Bugatti

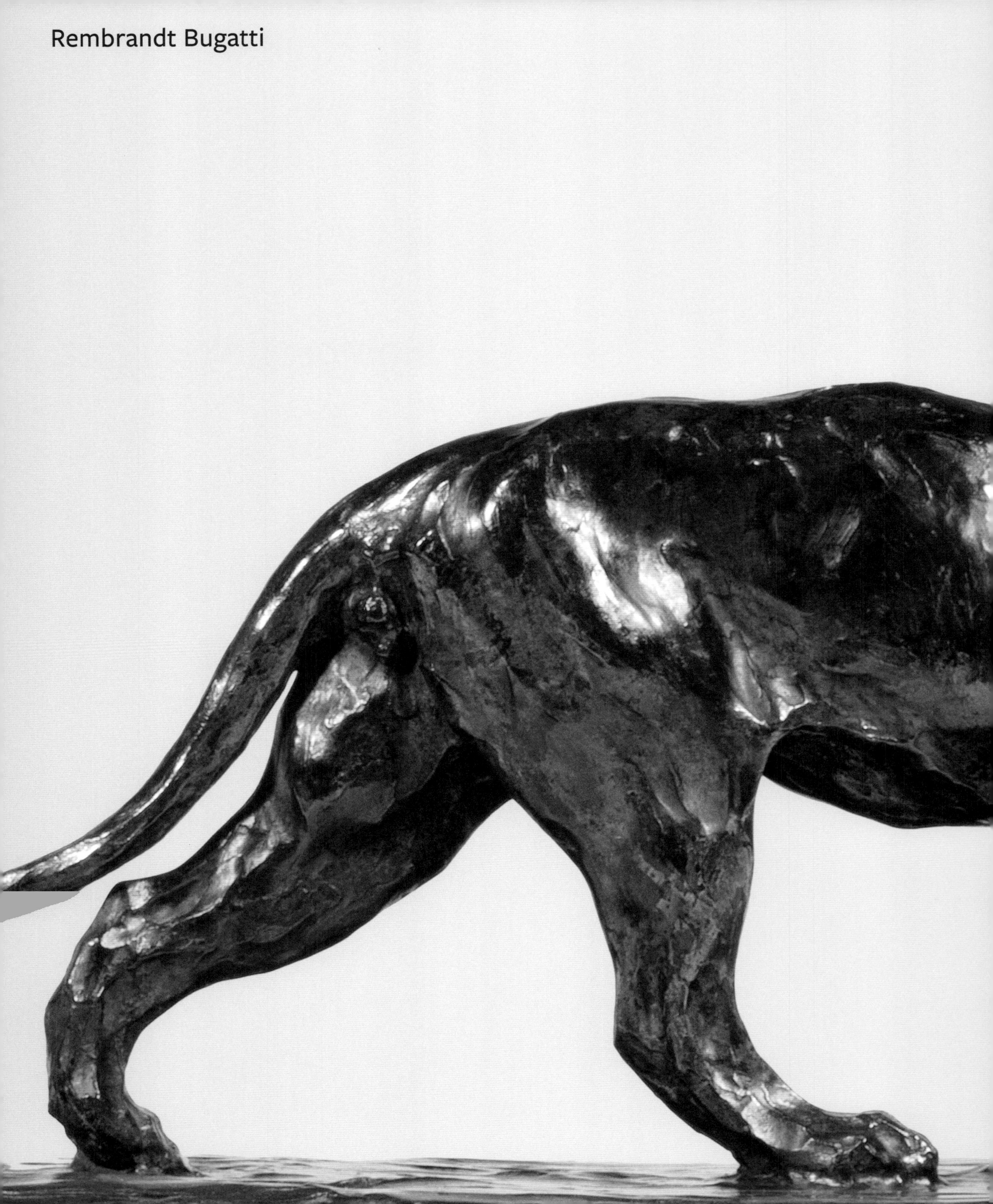
Rembrandt Bugatti

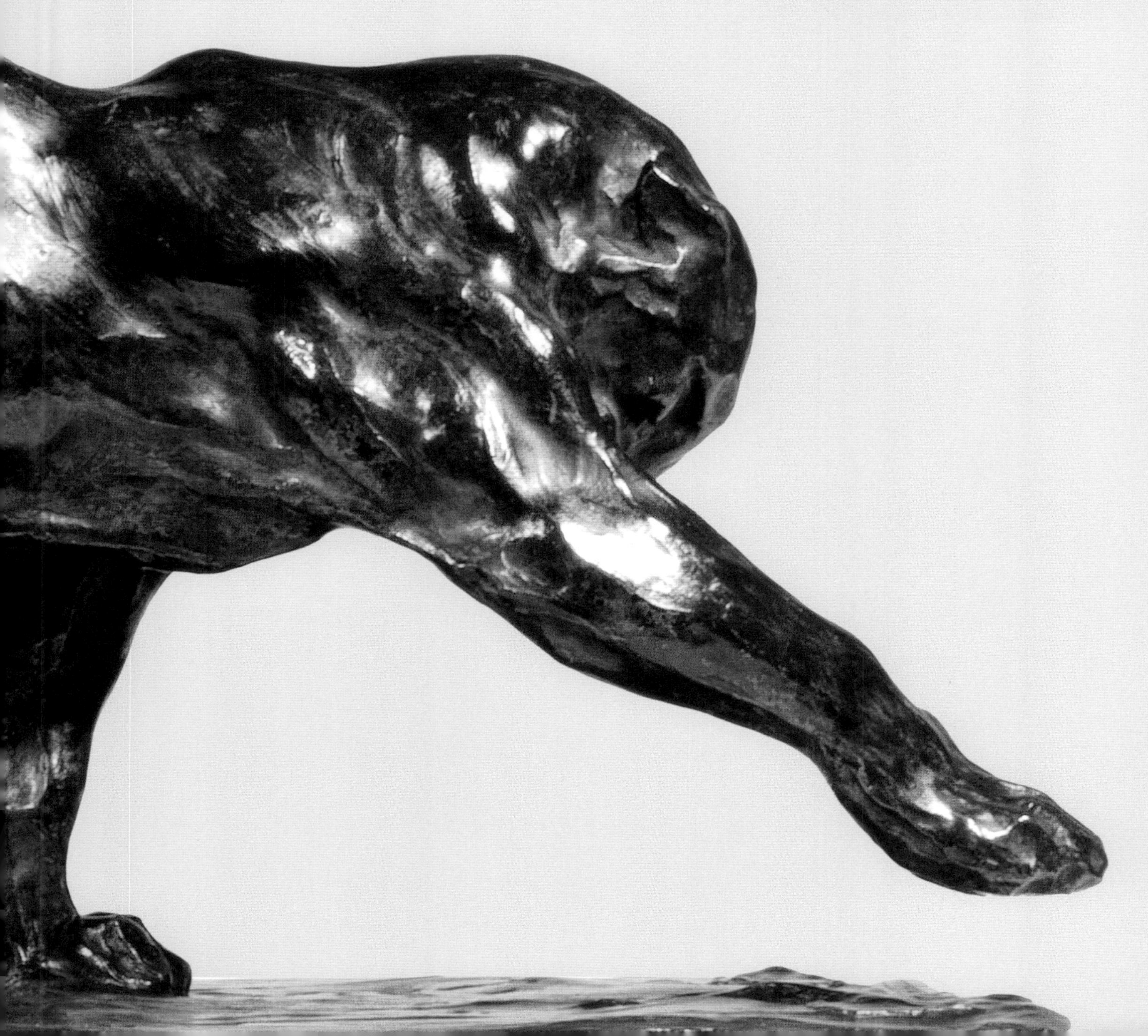

Rembrandt Bugatti

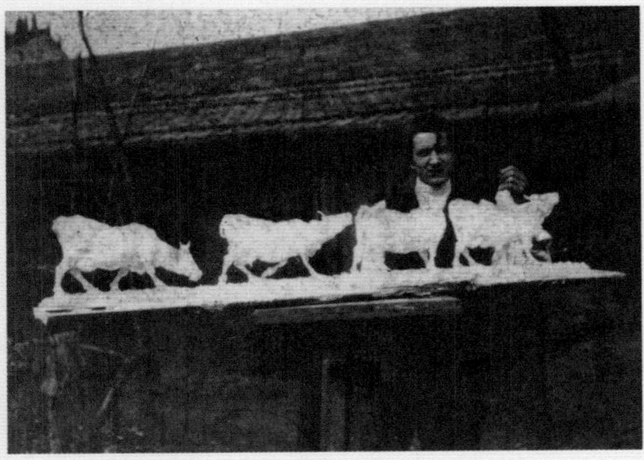

1 Rembrandt Bugatti with his sculpture *Return from the Pasture,*
c. 1901, photograph, Rembrandt Bugatti Conservatoire

Philipp Demandt

Rembrandt Bugatti – "the journalists call me the 'Segantini of sculpture'"

Rembrandt Bugatti (1884–1916) is one of the singular phenomena of the early twentieth century. Unable to be clearly assigned to either a nation, an artistic school or a specific style, the sculptor, who died at an early age, eludes unequivocal classification. Milanese by birth, then finding his way to Paris, and later continuing on to Antwerp, while his family settled in Alsace, which at the time belonged to the German empire, Bugatti is difficult to grasp if only based on his biography. His very individual social and artistic character as well as his oeuvre, which is as stringent as it is specific, potentiate the complexities of categorising him in terms of art history. And yet Bugatti's work can with some justification be viewed in the light of Impressionism – an Impressionism of extraordinary appearance.

Rembrandt Bugatti was born on 16 October 1884 in Milan; his later career as a sculptor is inseparably connected with the milieu in which he grew up. His unusual given name – Rembrandt – already makes reference to the creative environment of his childhood as well as the measure of freethinking that the Bugatti family permitted itself over several generations.[1]

The first influential figure in the life of Rembrandt Bugatti was his father, Carlo Bugatti (1856–1940), for his part son of the sculptor Giovanni Luigi Bugatti. Carlo Bugatti had – probably – studied architecture at the Accademia di Brera in Milan, where he met the painter Giovanni Segantini (1858–1899; cat. 125, 127), with whom he would form a life-long friendship. Beginning in the 1880s, Carlo called attention to himself with unique concepts for furniture, but later also designed entire interiors and items of everyday use such as a tea set made of silver and ivory. The imaginative eccentricity of his costly designs, which united Oriental, Moorish and Far Eastern stylistic elements, reflected itself in Bugatti's extroverted presence in self-styled clothing.

Carlo Bugatti and his wife Teresa entertained an open house in Milan that regularly hosted numerous artists: besides the above-mentioned Giovanni Segantini, who married (albeit not in legal terms) Carlo's sister Luigia and hence became Rembrandt's "uncle", these also included the sculptors Giuseppe Grandi and Ercole Rosa; the latter was Rembrandt's godfather. The composers Giacomo Puccini and Ruggero Leoncavallo were also among the guests in the Bugatti home. The surroundings of the young Rembrandt stimulated his artistic development accordingly.

However, it was another close friend of the family, the sculptor of Russian origin Paolo Troubetzkoy (1866–1938), who undoubtedly exercised the greatest influence on Rembrandt Bugatti.[2] The son of a Russian prince and an American opera singer rose to become the darling of the highest circles throughout Europe with his elegant, stupendously fugitive-seeming portrait sculptures. In his works,

Troubetzkoy cultivated an indifference that was as casual as it was calculated and in terms of style shifted him close to Joaquín Sorolla or John Singer Sargent (cat. 111), with whom the sculptor also socialised privately. Besides portraits of the beautiful people as well as numerous artist colleagues, Troubetzkoy devoted himself to animal sculpture with great abandon, in particular the depiction of dogs, with which he surrounded himself in his day-to-day life as a pacifist and staunch vegetarian. Sensitivity, non-violence and a love of animals as well as a penchant for elegance and eccentricity also later echoed in Troubetzkoy's protégé Bugatti, as did the outstanding sculptural talent that had already distinguished the Russian. In terms of style, one can hardly draw a distinction between Bugatti's early works and sculptures by Troubetzkoy.

Rembrandt and his older brother Ettore worked in their father's workshop early on. Whereas Ettore, the later legendary automobile constructor, was temporarily enrolled in the academy in Milan, except for the influences in his familiar surroundings, Rembrandt's artistic career proceeded autodidactically. According to family legend, Carlo Bugatti had discovered a group of three cows modelled in clay under a blanket in his workshop and, based on its degree of perfection, initially ascribed it to his older son Ettore; however, its creator turned out to be Rembrandt, who was just 15.[3]

It speaks not only for the great sculptural talent of the young man but also for the self-confidence of his father that the latter presented the plaster sculpture *Return from the Pasture* by his 16-year-old son at the spring exhibition in Milan as early as 1901 (fig. 1). One year later, Rembrandt was already represented in the exhibition with three works; he even had his father cast two of these in bronze. The following year, works by Bugatti were on display at the Venice Biennale, and in 1904 he then exhibited at the influential gallery run by Alberto Grubicy in Milan and at the Paris Salon.

Carlo Bugatti moved to Paris with his family in around 1903. This marked a turning point for Rembrandt, since his first works already attracted the attention of a bronze founder and art dealer who combined business savvy with a consummate casting technique like no other: Adrien-Aurélien Hébrard.

Hébrard had established his foundry in Paris in 1902. He would become as important for Impressionist sculpture as Paul Durand-Ruel was for Impressionist painting – Troubetzkoy and the heirs of Edgar Degas also had designs reproduced by Hébrard. Two years after establishing his foundry, in June 1904 Hébrard opened new, more impressive business premises not far from the Place de la Concorde. He devoted the first solo exhibition in the new spaces to the 19-year-old Rembrandt Bugatti. In view of its major success, the dealer signed an exclusive contract with the artist; he presented him in one to two exhibitions a year until 1913. Hébrard was one of the first founders that cast in numbered editions and, by doing so, regulated the exclusivity and price of their articles for sale accordingly.

Whereas Paris was nothing less than the world capital of art around 1900, all the same, productive contacts between Bugatti and other artists have not been passed down for those years. The artist was regarded as introverted; instead of frequenting the bars of Montmartre and Montparnasse, for instance, he visited the Jardin des Plantes – the zoological garden (fig. 2). With its big cats, antelopes, apes and birds, he found the fitting models there for his art: colours, forms, movement and morphologies offering late-nineteenth-century sculpture an entirely new range of subjects, an "experimental ground for modernity", as it were.[4] The sculptor Adolf von Hildebrand, who as a theorist exercised major influence, had already aptly remarked: "The animal is much newer, more unspoilt and fresher than the human figure, whereby everything that has already been done by others easily fits in between."[5]

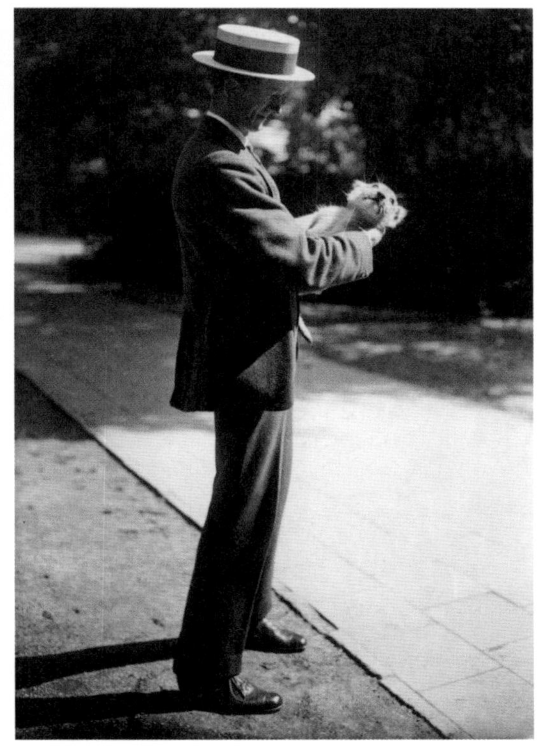

2 Rembrandt Bugatti with a lion cub at the Jardin des Plantes in Paris, c. 1905, photograph, Rembrandt Bugatti Conservatoire

Rembrandt Bugatti

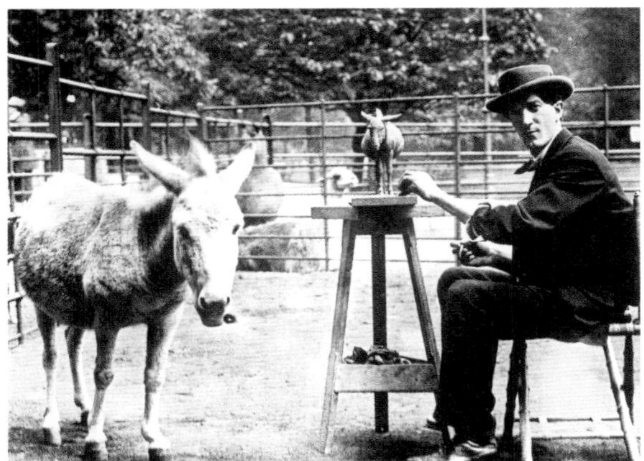

3 Rembrandt Bugatti with a donkey at the Royal Zoological Gardens in Antwerp, photograph, Rembrandt Bugatti Conservatoire

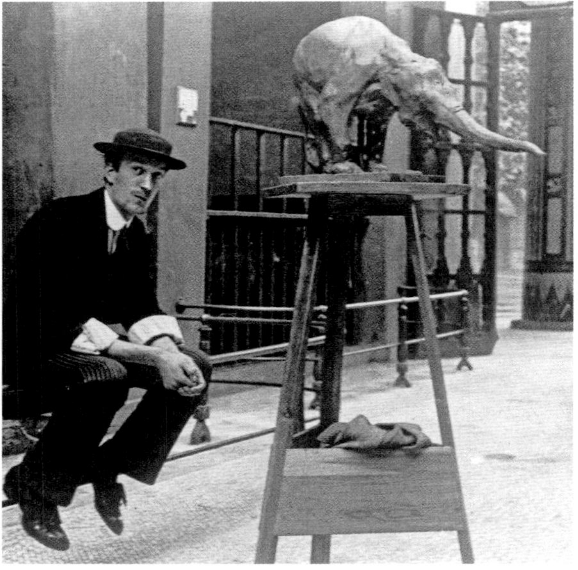

4 Rembrandt Bugatti at the Royal Zoological Gardens in Antwerp, c. 1907, photograph, Archive Josué Dupon

It is not without reason that the years between 1890 and 1920 became the heyday of animal sculpture, a development that in many ways was associated with that of middle-class society, which had taken the place of the clergy and aristocracy as a group of buyers for art – particularly paintings and sculptures in convenient formats. Colonialism, global commerce, international competition and the increasing systematisation of the sciences had advanced the founding of zoological gardens all over Europe. The driving force behind these undertakings were often initiatives or associations from the middle classes that congregated in zoos as sites of the communication of knowledge, social self-assurance and Sunday amusement. All of the major European zoos therefore also saw themselves as cultural organisations in which artists not only worked but also displayed their works (see cat. 129–131).

Towards the end of the nineteenth century, however, the exponential boom of modern depictions of animals, whose most important pioneer was the sculptor Antoine-Louis Barye (1795–1875), found little expression in the sculpture of Impressionism – which may be surprising in view of the modernity of said style. In fact, most of the French and German "animaliers" (such as François Pompon or August Gaul), were interested either in structural features or the basic forms of animal morphology, or they emphasised (such as Barye, Emmanuel Frémiet and Renée Sintenis) the charming, buoyant or dramatically existential qualities of the animal personality – the latter occasionally presented in fierce duels on one and the same plinth.

Significantly, however, the depiction of the autonomous animal played practically no role at all in the painting of French Impressionism, except for one or the other lapdog. Even in paintings and pastels by Edgar Degas, the centre of interest was the interaction between horse and equestrian. By contrast, he did address the horse on its own in the sculptural works that he never presented publicly (cat. 43–47). With its focus on city and cityscape, the human and the interpersonal, cultivated nature as well as recreational areas close to the city, French culture and society could take little pleasure in the autonomous animal figure.

The subject of the animal, nevertheless, looked very different in German Impressionism, which, like Impressionist sculpture, did not experience its breakthrough until one to two decades after French Impressionist painting. All of the main representatives of German Impressionism – Max Liebermann, Max Slevogt and Lovis Corinth – devoted themselves to the autonomous animal figure. Painters such as Heinrich von Zügel (fig. 6) even placed animals at the centre of their work, even though it was domestic livestock.

Bearing this observation in mind, for Rembrandt Bugatti at least an intellectual affinity to German Impressionism seems more plausible than to French, an inner connection that is extended by a geographical component given the fact that Bugatti spent a crucial period of his life as an artist in the Flemish city of Antwerp, and that the family of his brother, with whom he maintained close contact, lived in what was then German Alsace.

Rembrandt Bugatti never attended an art academy. There is no record of him ever having done anatomical studies, the foundation of animal sculpture from time immemorial. Even though the lack of academic training did not necessarily constitute his – Impressionism-associated – status as an anti-academic or even avant-gardist, his autonomous artistry, which cannot be clearly attributed to an academic school, is nevertheless rooted in this. This assessment receives further weight due to Bugatti's approach. His oeuvre is the result of an "absolute eye", a certitude when transferring what he had seen into three-dimensionality of which there are only few examples in art history.

Whereas Bugatti also portrayed human beings, usually friends and acquaintances, always as full figures, he had found another subject, his central subject, in the zoological gardens of Paris and Antwerp: the exotic animal. The artist – and this also places him in proximity to Impressionism – rarely worked in the studio but generally *en plein air,* thus directly in front of his models (fig. 3) or, in the case of dangerous animals, in front of their enclosures (fig. 4). Although Bugatti was a brilliant drawer, the drawing played no role for his sculptural work.

Bugatti observed the respective species, its movements, its behaviour and especially its interaction with fellow species for extended periods of time. Such an approach was all the more important, since the animal model, unlike the human model, normally does not hold still during the modelling process and hence poses exceptional challenges for the artist. Afterwards, the sculptor determined the composition in a supporting model made of wire and wood and began his work in front of the enclosure.

Like Troubetzkoy before him, Bugatti used plastiline, a new material that consisted of white clay, waxes and oils. Plastiline dries slower than clay, stays malleable longer and therefore guarantees a fresh, apparently unfinished, as it were, "Impressionist" expression. And in fact, for Bugatti, quick modelling in one go was an essential criterion for the success of a work, a process we are familiar with from Impressionist painters, who could by all means complete paintings within one day.

The visibility of traces of work were crucial for the effect of Bugatti's sculptures: the spreading, kneading and moulding of the material, the emphasis on handicraft and the sparing use of tools such as combs or styluses. Many a seated lady – in the work of Bugatti as well as of Troubetzkoy (cat. 112) – virtually oozes out of the material with sprawling garb, a fusion of figure and surroundings that seeks to avoid the contour and haptic selectivity in favour of a visual, phantasmal overall effect – and to that end relies not only on the play of light and shadow, but in particular on the relation between figure and plinth.

In Bugatti's work, the plinth defines the effectiveness of a sculpture – in its boundary as well as in the transgression thereof. In many cases, therefore, he has the plinth end directly with the seating or standing area of his animal models and leads extremities such as wings or tails far beyond the standing area (cat. 131). Other works feature the opposite – the plinth first ends there where a supposed negligibility like a full-length panther tail is rolled out on the plinth (fig. 5; cat. 129). Bugatti sometimes places his models asymmetrically on an overdimensional plinth and celebrates its relatively empty surface. All three compositional patterns aim towards taking up, including the space over or alongside the actual subject of the depiction; in this way, the space not occupied by the latter also becomes an integral part of the work. Thus, Impressionist sculpture – which cannot otherwise fall back on colour or an elaboration of the foreground, middle ground and background, indicating atmosphere and surroundings – once again approximates Impressionist painting.

Yet Bugatti's early attempt to advance even deeper into the area of Impressionist painting had to fail – his *Family of Goats* in a field of flowers from 1904 (cat. 128) appear as if they are standing ankle-deep in mud. Whereas the fusion of animal and landscape in painting, such as the atmospheric painting by Heinrich von Zügel from the collection of the Städel (fig. 6), still has major appeal, sculpture is stretched to its limits. From then on, the plinth took the place of the reproduction of landscape in Bugatti's work. He always directed particular attention to its elegant and animated painterly composition in all of his works.

While Bugatti had already been praised as an "Impressionist sculptor" in the review of his first solo exhibition in Paris in 1904 – because one saw a development "sur nature" in his works[6] – a look at the choice of motifs reveals a further relatedness between the artist and Impressionism: simple, observed and often even peripheral things were his dominant themes; by contrast, Bugatti for the most

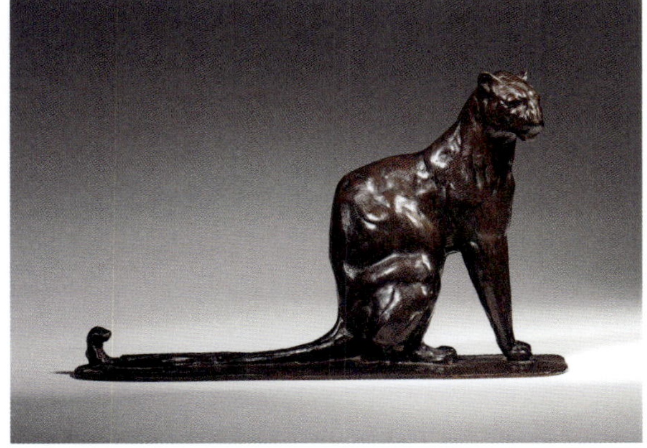

5 Rembrandt Bugatti, *Small Seated Panther*, c. 1912, bronze, 22 × 36 × 12 cm, private collection

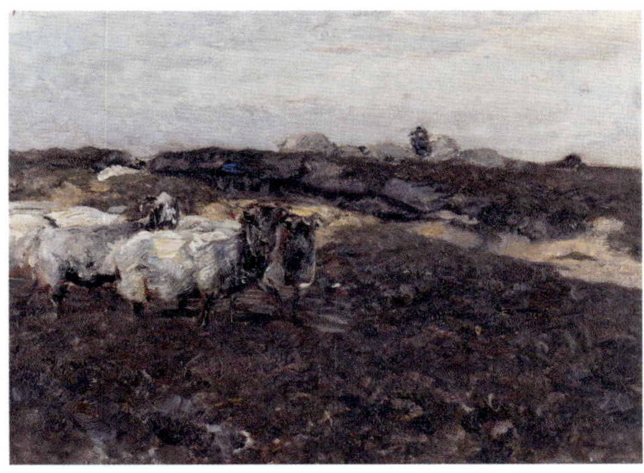

6 Heinrich von Zügel, *Sheeps in Moorland*, 1901, oil on canvas, 45 × 62 cm, Städel Museum, Frankfurt am Main

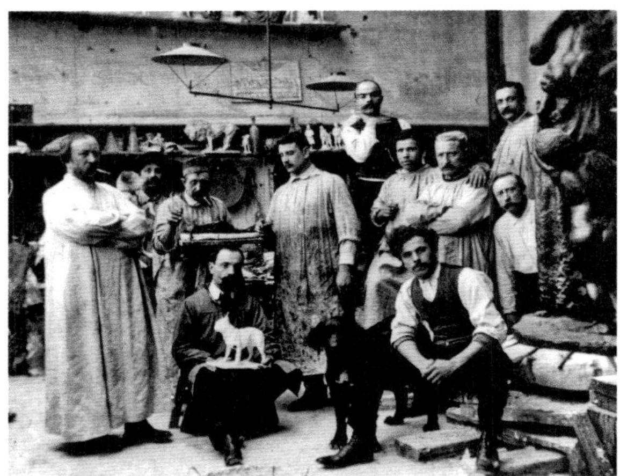

7   Marcello Valsuani and Albino Palazzolo with
the employees of the Hébrard foundry, c. 1906,
photograph, Rembrandt Bugatti Conservatoire

part excluded anything narrative, heroic, sacral or mythological. His approach was non-hierarchical; in the majority of cases, Bugatti even depicted his panthers, tigers and lions, which art usually presented in grand poses, in a realistic fashion – sleeping, eating or dozing away; he also addressed disease and injury (cat. 129). Specific poses appealed to him most of all – not beautiful ones. Like many Impressionist artists, Rembrandt Bugatti also had a range of compositional styles at his disposal – all the way to Realism – which he brought to bear depending on the surface character of his subject. With good reason, fashioning a smooth dachshund, an elephant or a rhinoceros "impressionistically" must have seemed contradictory to Bugatti.

Following the plaster casting of the fragile plastiline models, the artist sent these to his Parisian founder and gallerist Hébrard, where they were cast in bronze without the assistance or supervision of the artist. Hébrard's workshop manager, Albino Palazzolo, who like Bugatti came from Milan, was one of the most prominent bronze casters of the twentieth century (fig. 7). Using the lost wax technique, Palazzolo succeeded in converting Bugatti's models into thin-walled casts of unsurpassed quality. Palazzolo transposed even the smallest, most situational traces of Bugatti's work, such as the ridges of the dried material or fingerprints, to the permanent bronze; his casts do not exhibit a single millimetre of vapid surface. It was in this way that he eternalised the traces of fugitiveness in the working process as well as the desired *non-finito* of many a model – and hence two important characteristics of Impressionist sculpture.

Moreover, Palazzolo even had the ambition to cast Bugatti's large-format bronze groups, which other founders would have cast in segments, in one piece, something that once again enabled reducing the distance of the bronze to the original plastiline model. In Bugatti's works, there are no visible aspects of the casting process – such as casting seams that can be found in works by Auguste Rodin or Troubetzkoy. The artist also dispensed with fragmented compositions or busts, as was typical of other Impressionist sculptors like Rodin or Rosso. Incidentally, quite a few of Bugatti's works – yet another parallel with painting – were expressly not cast in editions but as unique pieces and consequently bear the cachet "pièce unique" on the plinth – a further possible signum of Impressionism, whose immediacy was able to reflect itself in supposed unrepeatability.w

Finally, the dark brown and lustrous patina that was typical of Hébrard casts ensured the specific play of light and shadow on the finished casts that was of such major importance for the "painterly" effect of Impressionist sculpture. The critic Édouard Sarradin wrote the following about Bugatti's works: "Owing to the quality of their movement and colour, to the particular emphasis on truth and life, their pleasantly sketchy appearance, they are, if you will, "Impressionistic."[7]

Rembrandt Bugatti concentrated on the peaceful depiction of the animal; dramatic or violent scenes, which were long characteristic of animal sculpture, do not exist in his oeuvre. Bugatti extended the accentuation of the phantasmal quality and essentiality of the animal by the consistently realistic reproduction of its morphology and sequences of movements.

Artistically, the motifs of the early years places Bugatti in close proximity to Giovanni Segantini, with whom he shared the penchant for an eremitic relationship with nature. Segantini was surely not only the inspiration for Bugatti's concept of form, which was initially very close to Italian Naturalism, but also for his tendency to compose his sculptures in what was occasionally an extreme and at the same time very painterly, two-dimensional way: in several works in bronze, Bugatti carried the metre-long trains of livestock, as one was familiar with in Segantini's paintings, to extremes (fig. 8). It was not by chance that, as he passed down himself, a journalist called him the "Segantini of sculpture" as early as in 1904.[8]

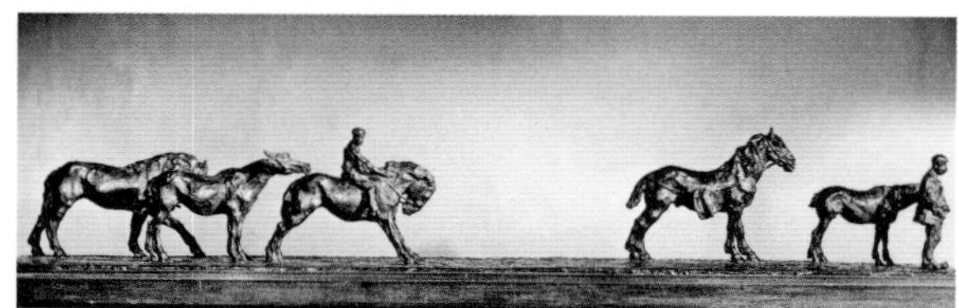

8 Rembrandt Bugatti, *The Horse Market*, c. 1903, bronze, 50 × 270 × 61 cm, private collection

Towards the end of his life, which was shaken from the outbreak of the First World War, bouts of depression as well as self-doubt, Bugatti altered his style. The artist now encased his models in almost armour-like shells and abstracted fur and surfaces – harbingers of art deco (fig. 9). Works from those years seem robot-like and martial; the focus is no longer on the nature and appearance of the creature, but rather on anatomy and muscular strength. Bugatti's big cats come across as skinned and dissected, so to speak. These sculptures are formed out of small pellets and rolls of plastiline, without however possessing a Bozzetto-like look that characterised works by Degas, who proceeded in a similar way. Bugatti's surfaces remained deliberate, graphic, constructed. And yet they are indeed extremely painterly, as they are reminiscent of the paintings by the second generation of Impressionism, Neo-Impressionism, in which brushstrokes were placed rigorously one alongside the other, not overlapping. Italian artists had developed this style into a very specific Divisionism, which already bears the separation and division of the individual brushstrokes and colour values in its name. No less a figure than Bugatti's uncle Giovanni Segantini was its most important representative.

The major share of Bugatti's works, approximately 300 sculptures, would be produced by 1914 at the zoo in Antwerp, at the time the largest of its kind on the continent. The artist's situation and disposition darkened with the outbreak of the First World War; he could find hardly any buyers for his works. Hébrard had closed his gallery, while Bugatti had to witness how the Antwerp zoo put down its animals due to a lack of food. Finally, Bugatti took his own life in Paris on 8 January 1916. Although he was the last-born in the league of Rosso, Degas, Rodin and Troubetzkoy, Bugatti was the first to leave this world again. He was only 31 years old.

9 Rembrandt Bugatti, *Royal Bengal Tiger*, c. 1913/14, bronze, 41 × 73 × 19.5 cm, private collection

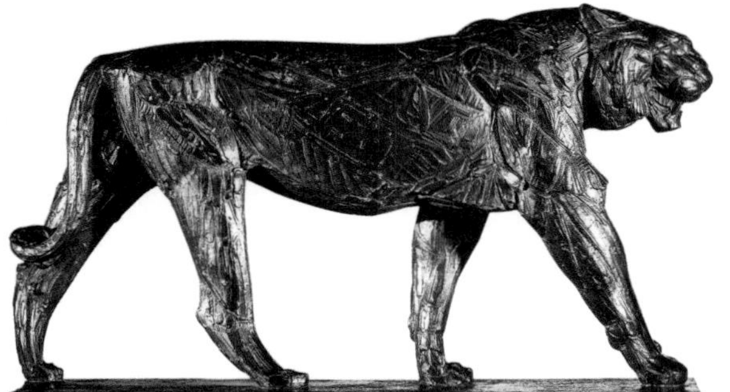

1 On the following remarks, see exh. cat. Berlin 2014, esp. Daemgen 2014.
2 On Paolo Troubetzkoy, see the essay by Yvette Deseyve in this catalogue, pp. 222–227.
3 Bugatti 1967, pp. 4–6.
4 Großkopf 2012, p. 8.
5 Von Hildebrand 1969, pp. 514.
6 Vauxcelles 1904.
7 Édouard Sarradin in: *Le Temps* quoted in: Horswell 2016, p. 64.
8 Postcard from Rembrandt Bugatti to Bianca Segantini, 16 July 1904, quoted in: Fromanger 2009, p. 45.

For Rembrandt Bugatti, everything began with the cows. According to family legend, he was just 15 years old when he modelled a peasant leading three cows by a rope.[1] Verifiable is the 17-year-old's participation in 1902 in the *Prima esposizione quadriennale* in Turin with three works, including the bronze *Return from the Pasture* (p. 256, fig. 1). For the young metropolitan – at the turn of the century, his hometown of Milan already had more than half a million inhabitants – such rural subjects were more likely to have been familiar to him through his uncle Giovanni Segantini and his painting than from his own everyday experiences.[2] The influence of various artist figures was symptomatic for Bugatti, since he did not learn his artistic craftsmanship in a systematic academic way but from role models and influences in his illustrious family home.[3]

Whereas the complete line of cows from *Return from the Pasture* (1901) unfortunately did not survive, there are casts of the individual animals as well as subgroups. These include the works *Cow Lowing* and *Bull and Cow* (cat. 124, 126). One still sees the apparently rapid kneading of the soft modelling clay even in the cast state. The sculptor succeeded in making the cow's prominent anatomic frame palpable through the protruding shoulder joints and the bony pelvis without foregoing playful, creative scope. Although his cows are symbols of austere peasant life in harmony with nature, their prominent and gentle forms are fascinating at the same time. Numerous depressions, ridges and craters on the surface are more likely to have resulted from the dynamics of the creative process than from observing the animal's physique. The sculptor even worked the irregularly shaped plinths in the same nervous style. Excellent in this respect is the observation that Richard Hamann made in connection with Auguste Rodin's portrait bust of Puvis de Chavannes: "[...] he also leaves all of the imperfections and indentations that occur when kneading the clay in the bronze, which resembles the form of a freshly ploughed field."[4] In this way, Bugatti creates not only the impression of standing or walking on furrowed soil, but also of an indissoluble union of animal and ground.

Family of Goats (cat. 128) also constitutes a seemingly peaceful union owing to the merging of their heads. Whereas the lush meadow growth reaches halfway up the legs of the adult animals, the kid seems to sink into it to its belly with a slightly humorous tone. In view of its height in the form of the tall, highly structured grasses and flowers, one can hardly speak of a classic plinth – in some places the meadow also extends beyond the plinth in the direction of the lower edge. With small holes, knots and drips, the sculpture also exhibits numerous traces of the casting process, which would have normally been removed by the chaser. Yet Bugatti decided to preserve these elements, hence consciously against the flawlessness of the cast.[5] The interrelationship of animal and landscape as depicted by Bugatti also influenced the painterly oeuvre of Giovanni Segantini in the 1880s and 1890s (see cat. 125). His *A Goat with Her Kid* (cat. 127) visualises the goat mother and her kid in the safe hands of nature. Segantini

> "[...] he also leaves all of the imperfections and indentations that occur when kneading the clay in the bronze, which resembles the form of a freshly ploughed field."
>
> Richard Hamann, 1907

produced the work during his successful period in Savognin in the Canton of Grisons (1886–1894), during which he was repeatedly acknowledged with gold medals at international exhibitions – although he had been stateless since childhood, had no travel documents and could therefore never visit the sites of his fame.[6] The painting's rather small format is possibly due to the fact that it (prior to 1903) was cut out of a larger work.[7] Whether conceived as such from the beginning or achieved through subsequent reduction, in any case, the surrounding space of both animals consists of nothing other than the ground. No depth space opens up, no horizon line, no sky. The depiction is immersed in a consistent crystalline light by means of small, light brushstrokes. The paint, systematically applied as fine dashes in ever-differing directions, produces a tactile structure. The only thing that lies flat over the fabric-like surface is the dark shadow of the animals cut by the right edge of the painting. Segantini began examining the prismatic breakdown of colours in 1886; in 1892, his works were presented during the first joint appearance of the Divisionists in the *Prima esposizione triennale di belle arti* at the Accademia di Brera in Milan. However, he did not approach this new form of artistic expression on the basis of the optical theory of colour to be applied purely and one separate from the other; rather, he was interested in colour and texture as carriers of emotional expression, making him move closer to Symbolism.[8]

Segantini also created a sensitive connection between the varying application of paint or brushstroke and motif in his painting *During the Thaw* (cat. 125). His keen observation and representation of the thawing ground and the reflexes of the dim light testify to a particular interest in the cyclic reawakening of nature, to which man and animal adapt in equal measure in their archaic, austere simplicity.[9] At the same time, the posture of the peasant, who is watching his cow drink, bears a striking resemblance to that of the animal; man, animal and sledge also constitute a unit along a diagonal through the composition.

When setting Bugatti's representations of the rustic animal world in relation to Segantini's paintings, a relatedness can be seen – not only in the respectful handling of this austere world of motifs, but also in the creation of an overarching structure and an overall harmony that, thanks to the characteristic style, never lapse into quaintness. Figure and space share their manner of representation equally and are intertwined not least by the unifying light. — EM-V

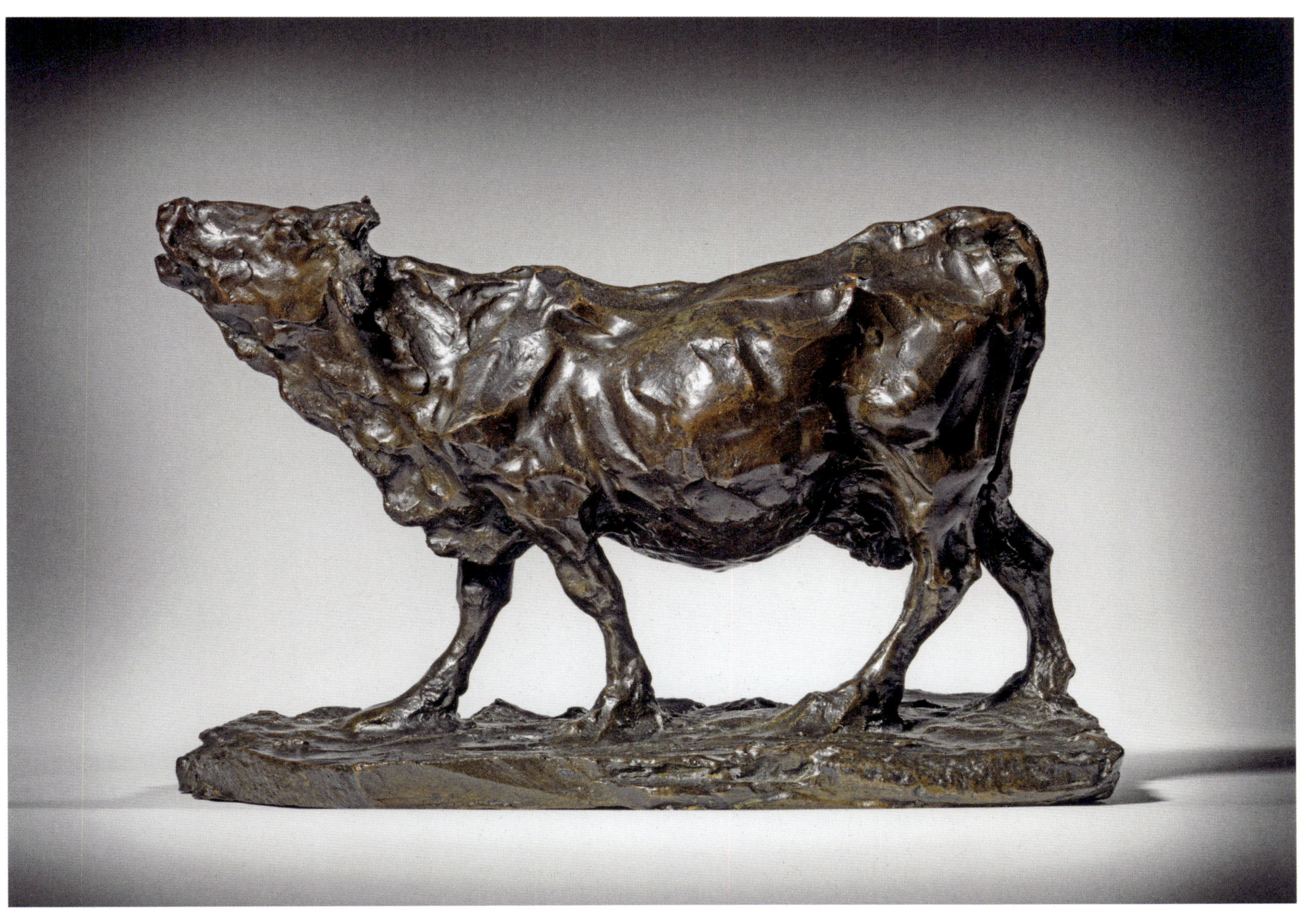

Cat.124

1   For general information on Bugatti's biography and the creation of legends, see Daemgen 2014; on *Cow Lowing*, see ibid., p. 27.

2   Ibid., p. 32; Ginex 2014, pp. 185–186.

3   Daemgen 2014, p. 30.

4   Hamann [1907] 1923, p. 34.

5   Horswell 2016, p. 65. The plaster cast of this group was on display in 1904 in the exhibition at the Hébrard foundry in Paris, an important milestone in Bugatti's artistic career; see Sedeyn 1904, fig. p. 65.

6   Quinsac 2011, p. 33.

7   It is worthwhile to compare this with a second painting of the same subject in a private collection in Italy; see exh. cat. Zurich 1990, p. 157.

8   Quinsac 2011, pp. 32–33.

9   Stutzer 2016, p. 114. I thank the author for his collegial support and for making the corresponding catalogue entry available.

Cat.125 Giovanni Segantini, **During the Thaw**, c. 1888; oil on canvas, 66 × 98 cm; Segantini Museum, St. Moritz, Depositum der Otto Fischbacher – Giovanni Segantini Stiftung Cat.126 Rembrandt Bugatti, **Bull and Cow**, 1902; bronze, 27 × 64 × 30 cm; signed: "R. Bugatti"; private collection

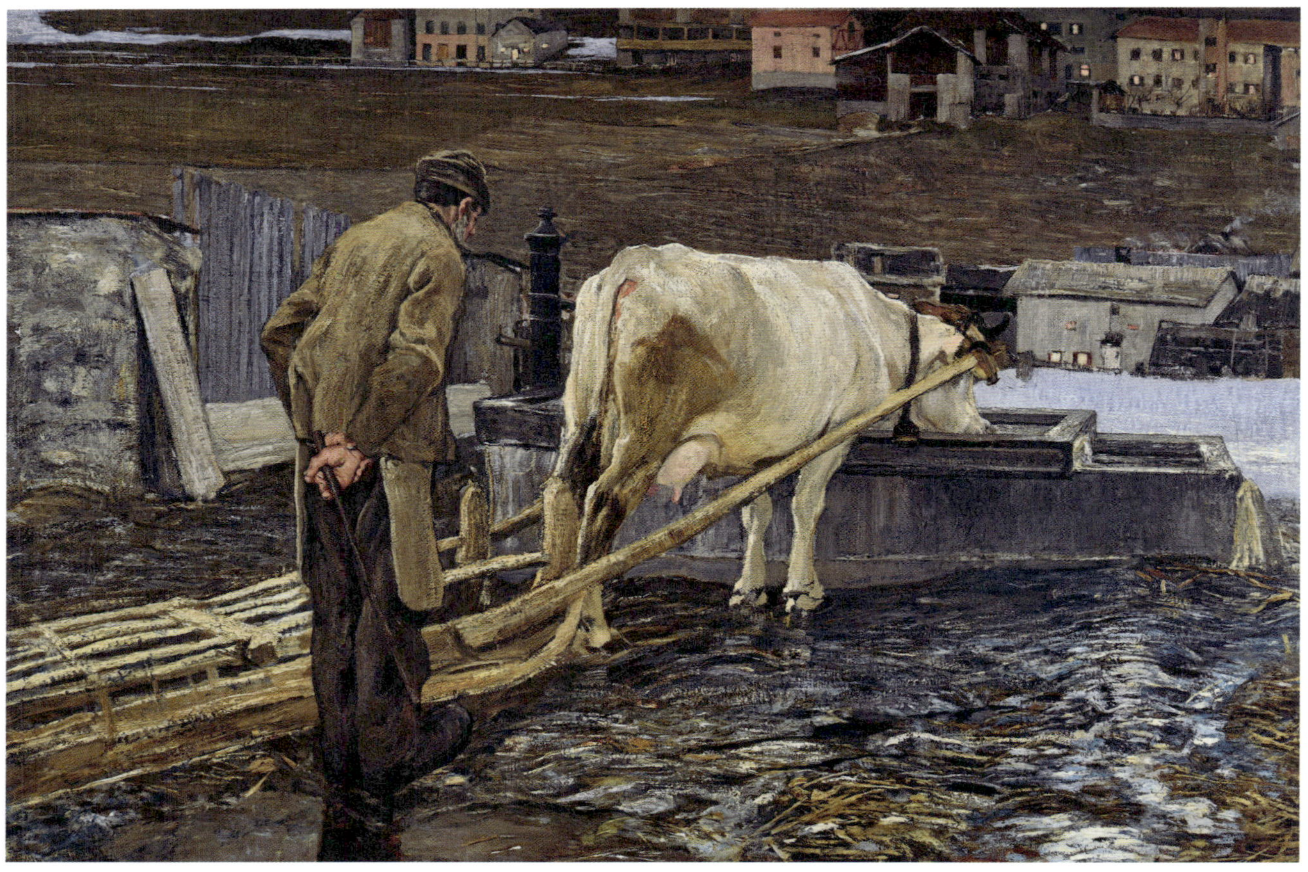

Cat.125

Cat.126

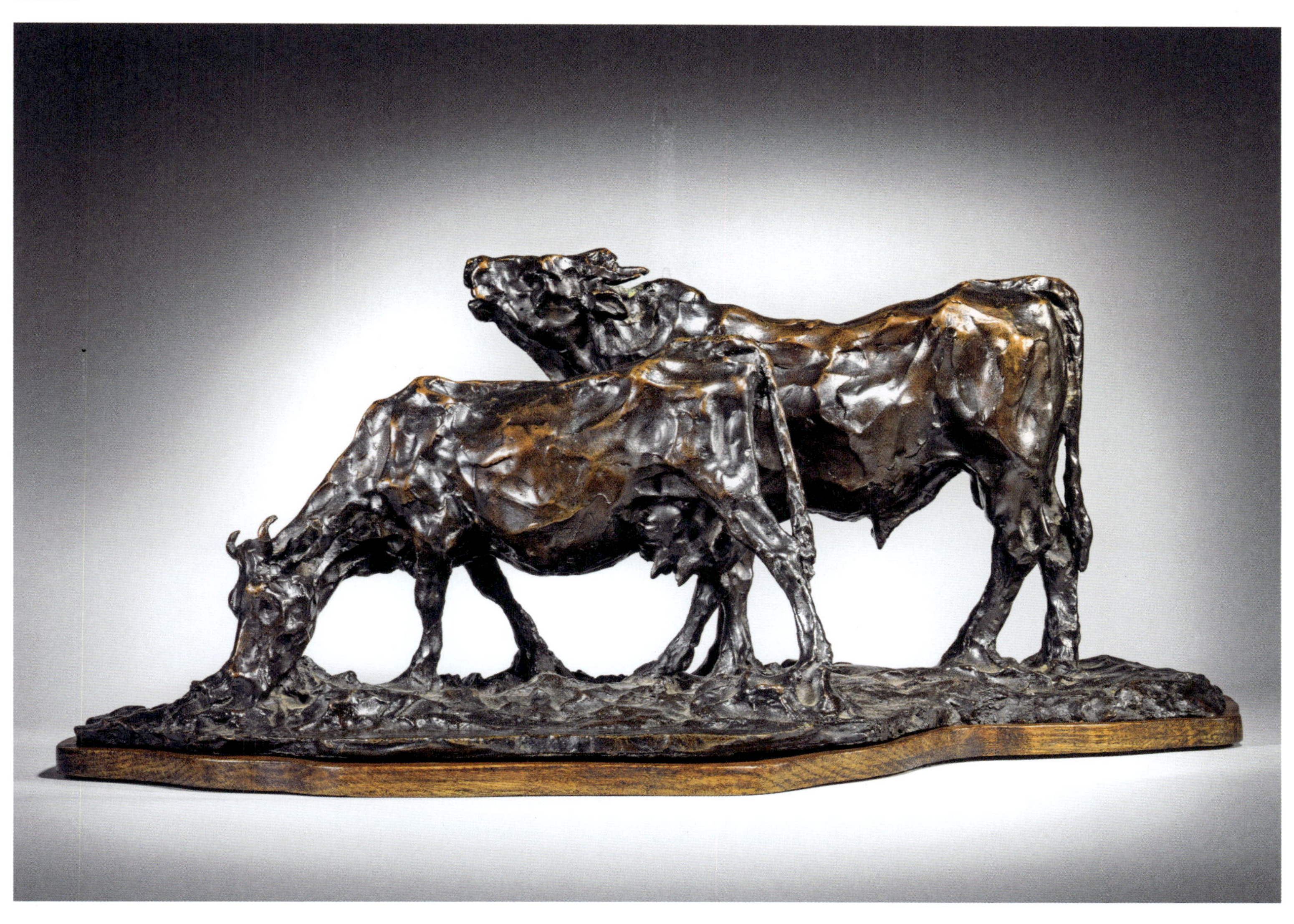

Cat.127 Giovanni Segantini, *A Goat with Her Kid*, 1890; oil on canvas, 42 × 71.5 cm; Rijksmuseum Amsterdam, Gift of Mr and Mrs Kessler-Hülsmann, Kapelle op den Bosch, inv. no. SK-A-3346 Cat.128 Rembrandt Bugatti, **Family of Goats**, 1904; bronze, 34.5 × 74 × 22 cm; signed: "R. Bugatti", stamped "C. VALSUANI"; Woburn Abbey Collection

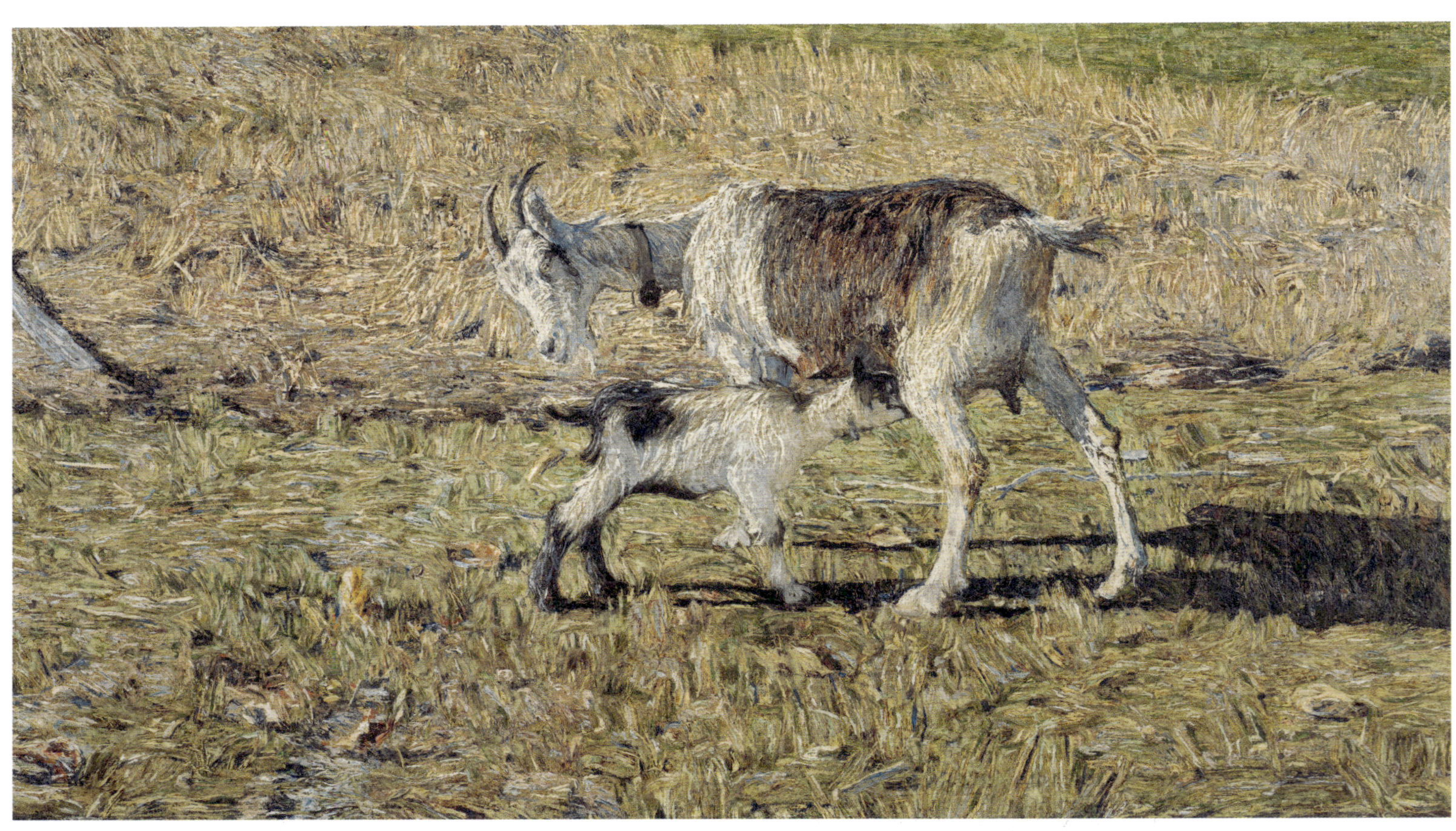

Cat.127

Cat.128

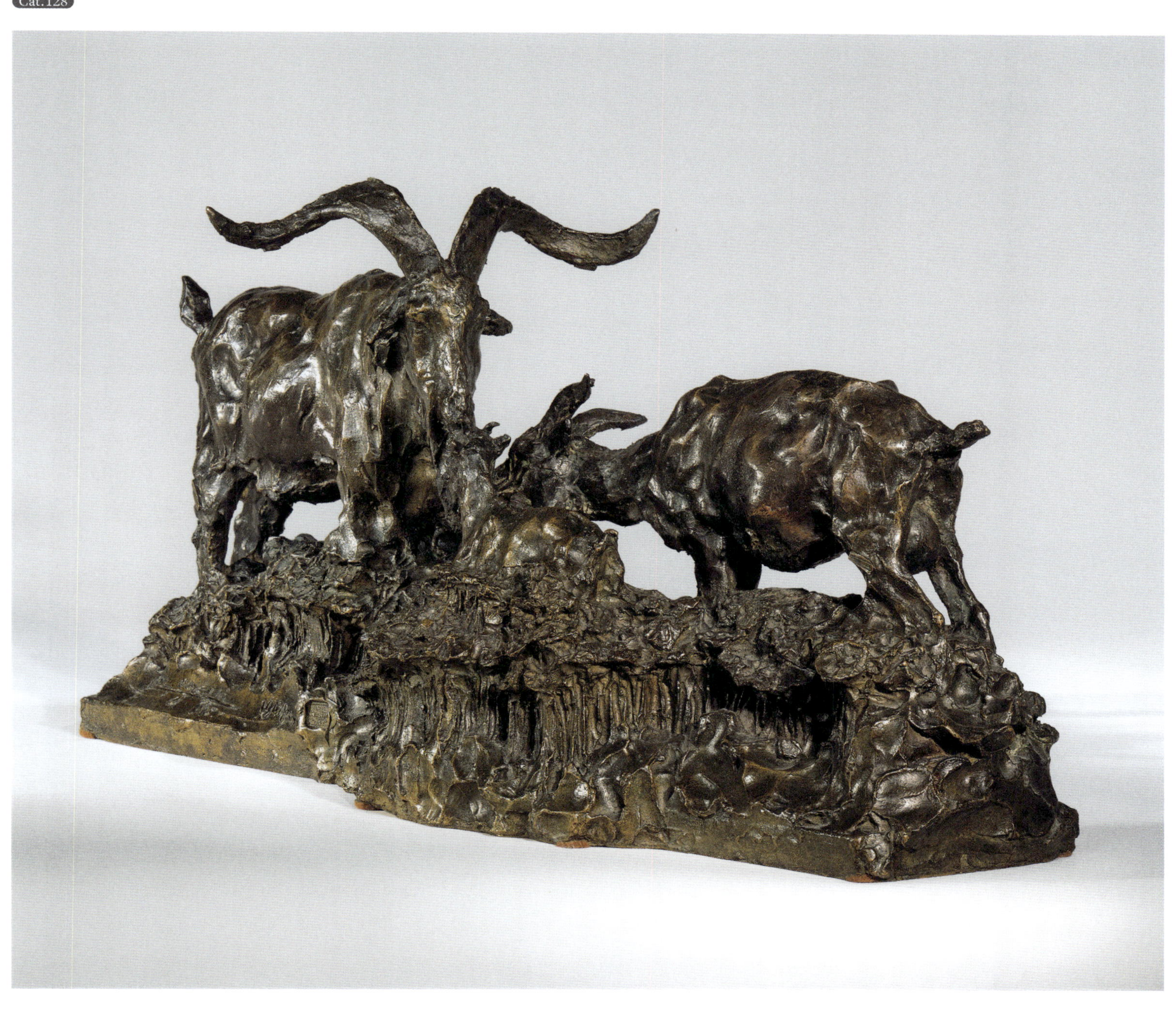

 # Observing animals: at the zoo

From the mid-nineteenth century onwards, zoological gardens had less to do with the natural environment of animals but instead with that of the urban middle classes. Popular as a learning environment and place of leisure, they were established in numerous European metropolises. Besides one's fellow humans, one could also observe indigenous, but in particular exotic animals – under ideal circumstances for the curious visitor, and from today's point of view rather questionable ones for the fenced-in occupants.[1] Since his move to Paris around 1903/04, the young Rembrandt Bugatti took advantage of the opportunity to visit the menagerie in the Jardin des Plantes. From 1906 onwards, he worked intensely in the zoological garden in Antwerp, which was characterised by a close connection of scientific institution and artistic site. One decided goal was to "provide live models for artists" – this idea was not least underscored by the fact that artists were exempt from the high entrance fee.[2] The zoo served as an open-air studio, and working "sur le vif" was popular amongst painters and sculptors.[3] As was already the case for his depictions of cows, in his sculptural rendering of zoo dwellers Bugatti also sought to capture the characteristic physical features and behavioural patterns of the respective species.

In doing so, he moved on a side track of animal depiction, as many of his colleagues strove to look at animals in the light of a human world order. The big cat, for example, firmly embedded in the iconography of domination, experienced a considerable reinterpretation in Bugatti's sculptures. Instead of placing emphasis on their wild, often brutal strength and force or visualising those virtues frequently assigned to human heroes, Bugatti's animals of prey represented nothing other than themselves.[4] Lacking heroic qualities, *Lioness Eating* (cat. 129), which he produced while still in Paris, opens itself up neither to the viewer nor to space. Instead, the recumbent animal, its head sunken and absorbed in eating, seems to nearly merge with its substrate. In no way does the depiction testify to a claim to power over a space to be conquered or, in the face of a rival, to be destroyed (the lioness is eating food and not prey), but on the contrary – to a denial of space. Similarly, one is attempted to speak of a deliberate denial of readability, as the feline predator's anatomy cannot be captured with a brief glance. By contrast, what is defining is the overall impression of a powerfully kneaded mass. One's eye therefore has to scan the animal's body in order to comprehend the object in the first place. And depending on the viewer's standpoint, different basic lines are disclosed. Viewed from the front, the S-shaped curve of the dorsal line dominates, whereas the sides emerge as mountain and valley landscapes. Thus, both artist and viewer are in the challenging situation of having to exercise patience and awareness in order to grasp the appearance and nature of the unstaged animal. In Bugatti's works, seeing therefore becomes a task to be completed individually, and not positive indulgence. Nevertheless, the highly animated surface and the approach meant for the careful and singular visual act resulted in Bugatti's niece L'Ébé referring to him as the "first Impressionist sculptor."[5]

The sculptor Rembrandt Bugatti was not the only one to spend time in the Jardin des Plantes; the poet Rainer Maria Rilke did so as well when he lived in Paris on the occasion of his studies of Rodin. It was here, in 1902, that a panther inspired him to write the powerful poem of the same name, "The Panther": "[...] The supple pace of powerful soft strides, / turning in the very smallest circle, / is like a dance of strength around a centre / in which a mighty will stands numbed." The tension between the power that has numbed in captivity and the still palpable, elegant suppleness is also rendered visible in Bugatti's sculpture *Two Panthers Walking* (cat. 131). With slightly lowered heads and opposing strides, the one walking closely behind the other, they are following a fictitious trail, with front paw or tail reaching beyond the narrow plinth and into the constricted space in what seems to be an endless repetition of their movement.

Besides animals of prey, birds play a special role in Bugatti's oeuvre. He created them individually, in pairs or in groups. During his time in Antwerp, he examined long-legged and long-necked birds multiple times. On the one hand, the extreme proportions of ostrich (cat. 130) and flamingo enable a stylisation of forms;[6] on the other hand, naked legs and feathered bodies present their vis-à-vis with a challenging surface contrast. Time and again, Bugatti's interest was drawn to the animals' poise in particular, whose high centre of physical gravity had to be balanced out on two thin legs, including with the aid of the wings. It is especially the ostrich with its head down that exhibits an almost tongue-in-cheek likeness to one or the other female dancer by Edgar Degas (see cat. 12–13) – the impending tilting moment seems close at hand should the pose have to be held for a longer period of time. Thus, the lapse of time in its smallest unit is accentuated: the moment. The figure is therefore rendered in a charged relationship between the depiction of movement and paralysis – a tension that is passed on to the viewer. — EM-V

---

1 Wessely 2014, p. 200.
2 Ibid., p. 200.
3 Champy-Vinas 2016, p. 132.
4 Ibid.
5 Quoted in: Ferlier 2014, p. 181.
6 Horswell 2016, p. 172.

Cat.129 Rembrandt Bugatti, **Lioness Eating**, 1903; bronze, 16.5 × 70 × 22 cm; signed: "R. Bugatti"; stamped: "A. A. HEBRARD"; The Sladmore Gallery, London
Cat.130 Rembrandt Bugatti, **Ostrich with Head Down**, 1909/10; bronze, 40.5 × 42 × 27 cm; signed: "R. Bugatti"; stamped: "CIRE / PERDUE / A. A. HEBRARD", "10"; The Sladmore Gallery, London

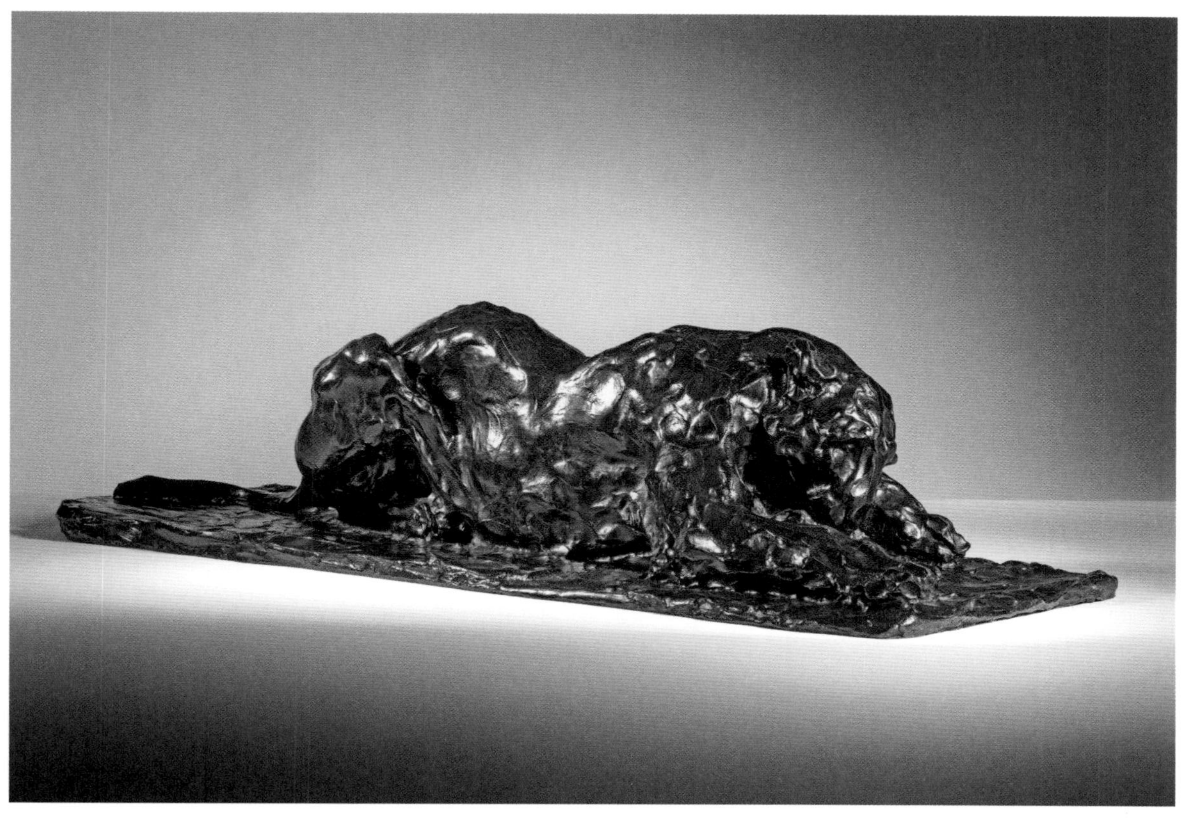

Cat.129

Cat.130

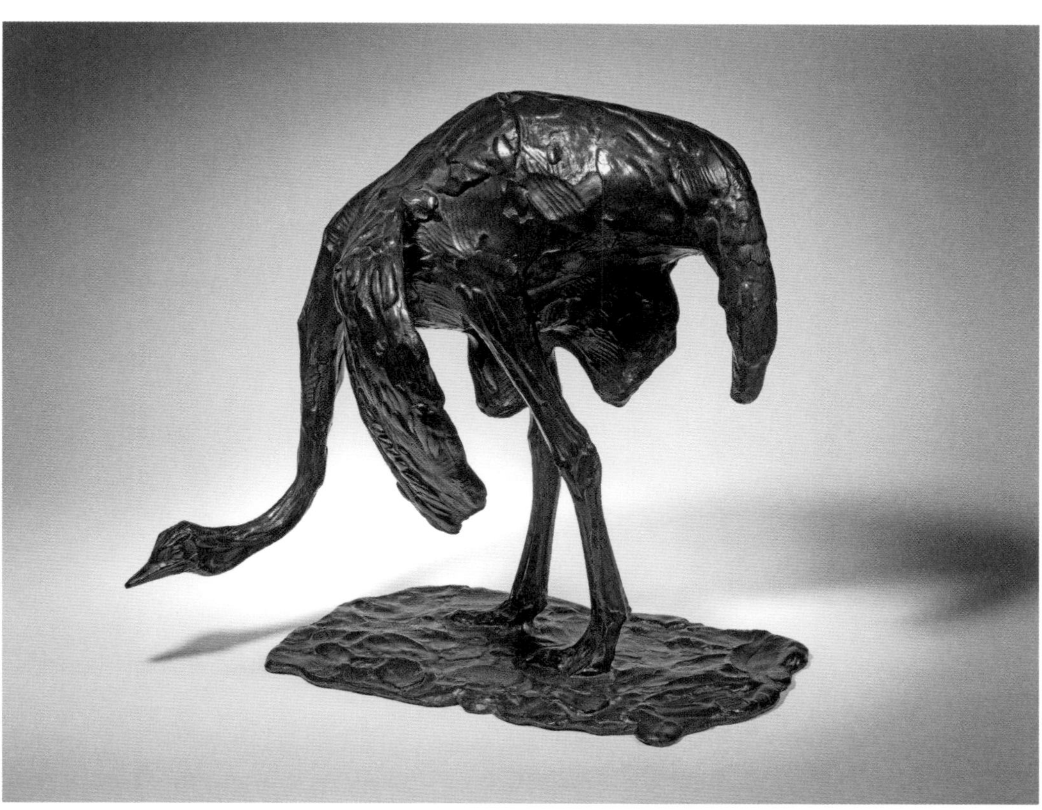

 Rembrandt Bugatti, Two Panthers Walking (no. 129), 1905;
bronze, 24.5 × 122.5 × 25 cm; signed: "R. Bugatti", stamped: "CIRE / PERDUE /
A. A. HEBRARD"; private collection

"The supple pace of powerful soft strides,
turning in the very smallest circle,
is like a dance of strength around a centre
in which a mighty will stands numbed."

Rainer Maria Rilke, 1903

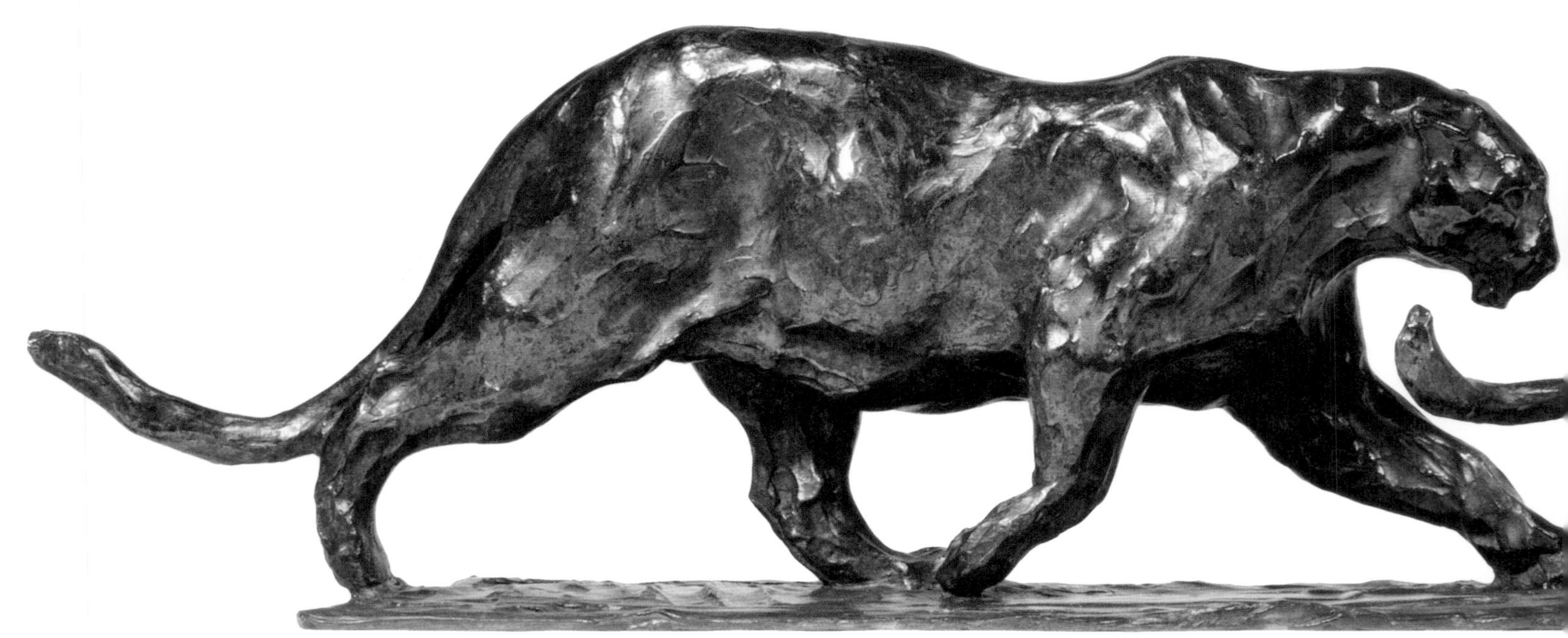

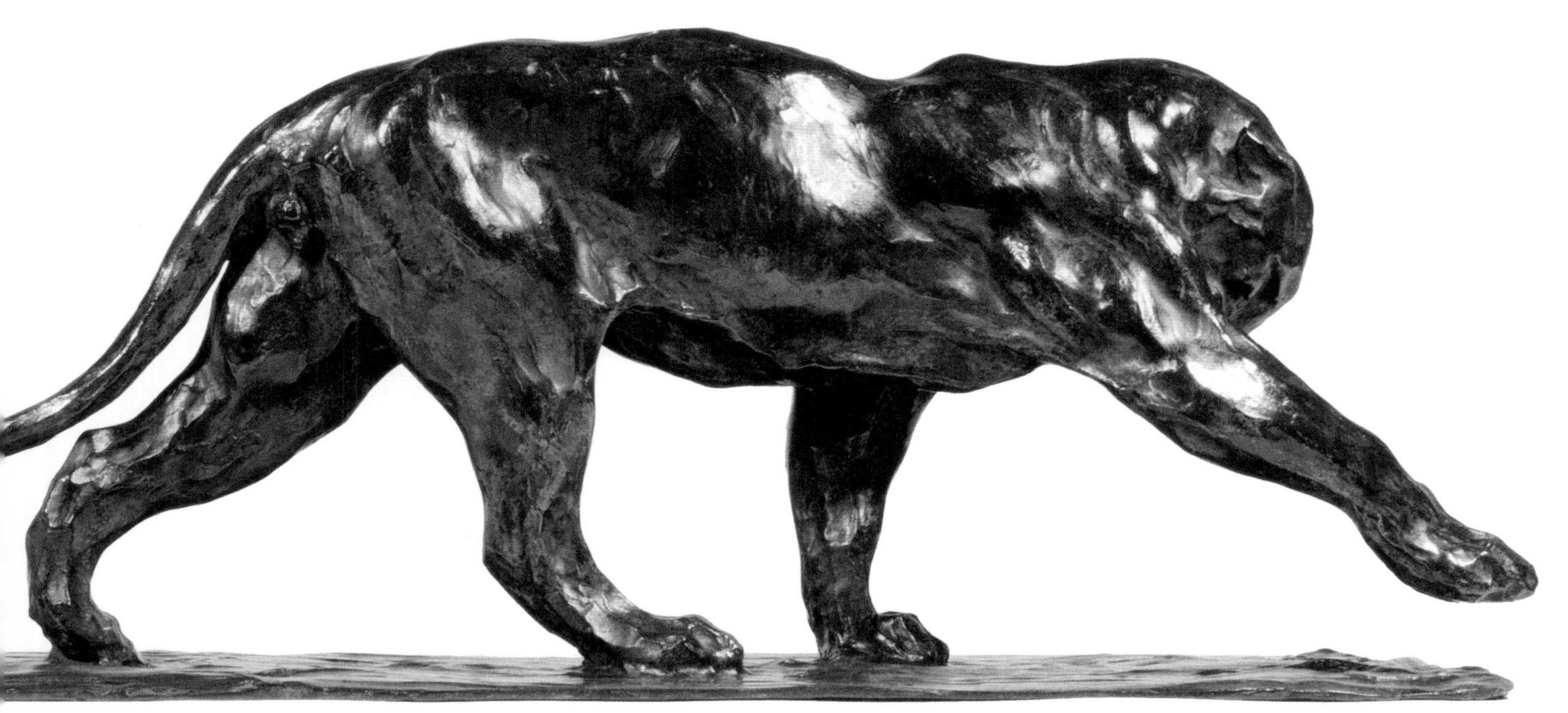

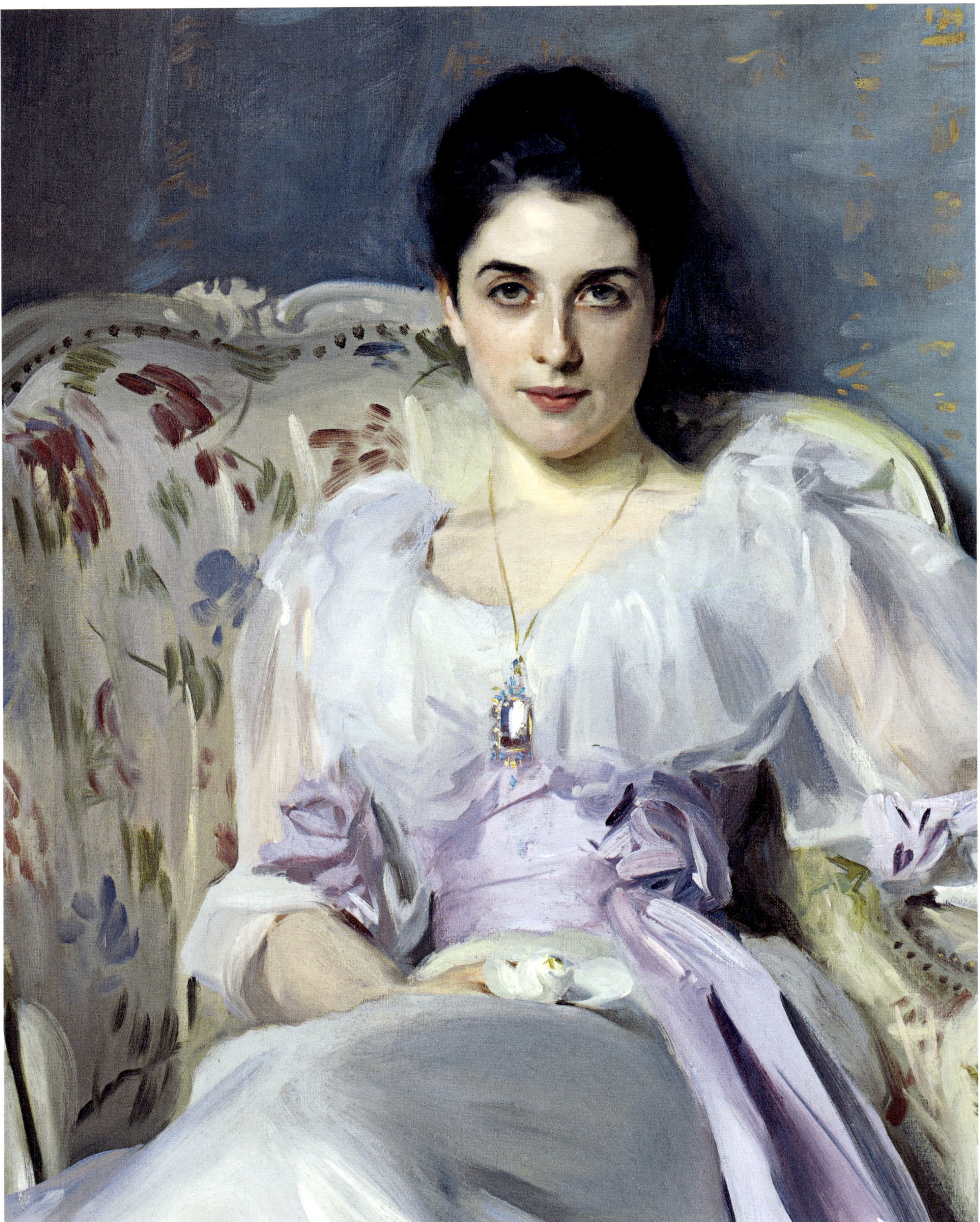

"Vainly does the sculptor
try to adopt one point of vision;
the viewer who walks round
the figures can choose a hundred
different positions without
finding the right one; and it often
happens, and this is humiliating
for the artist, that a chance
ray of light or the play of lamplight
throws into relief a beautiful
effect not intended by the artist."

Charles Baudelaire, 1846

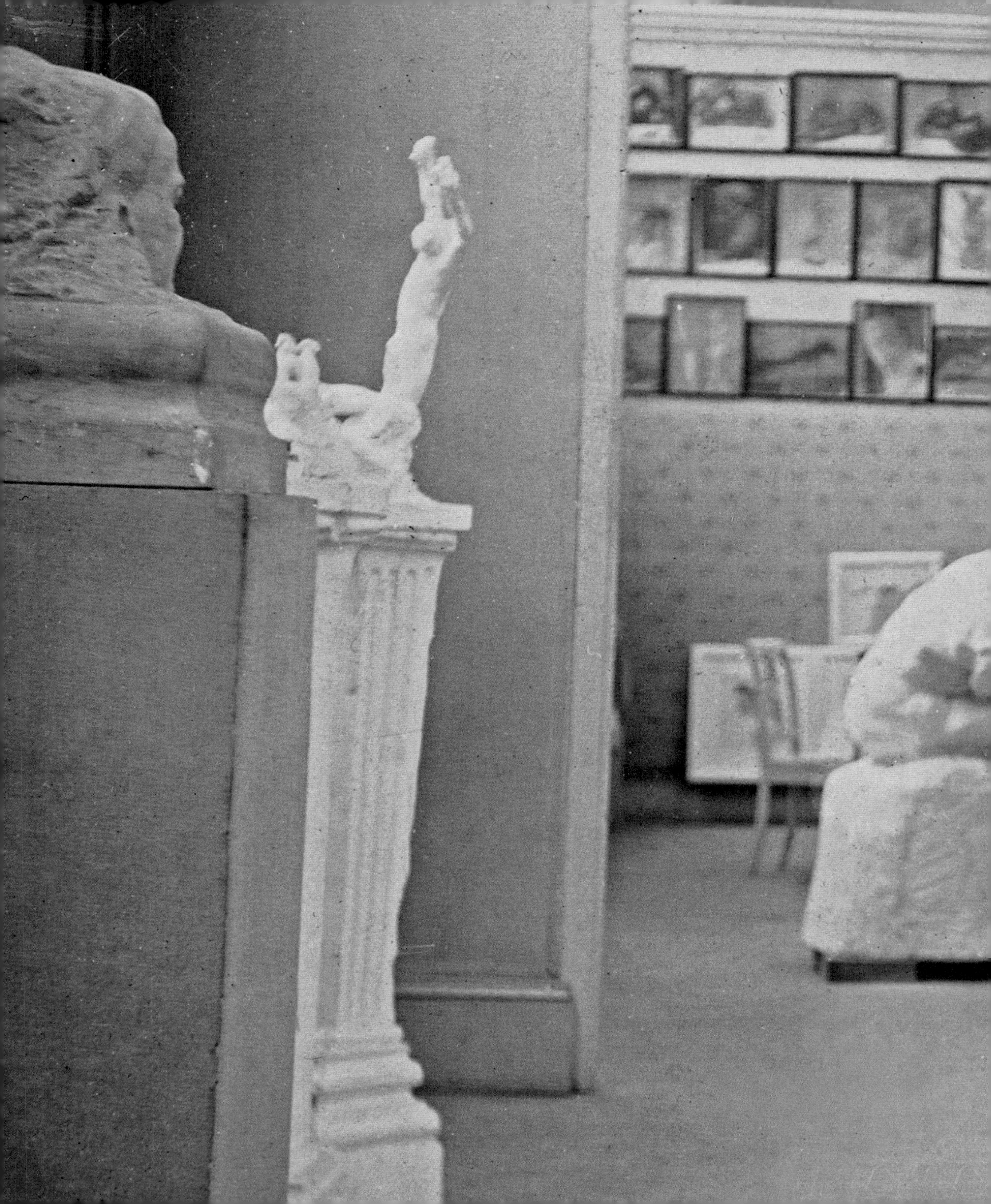

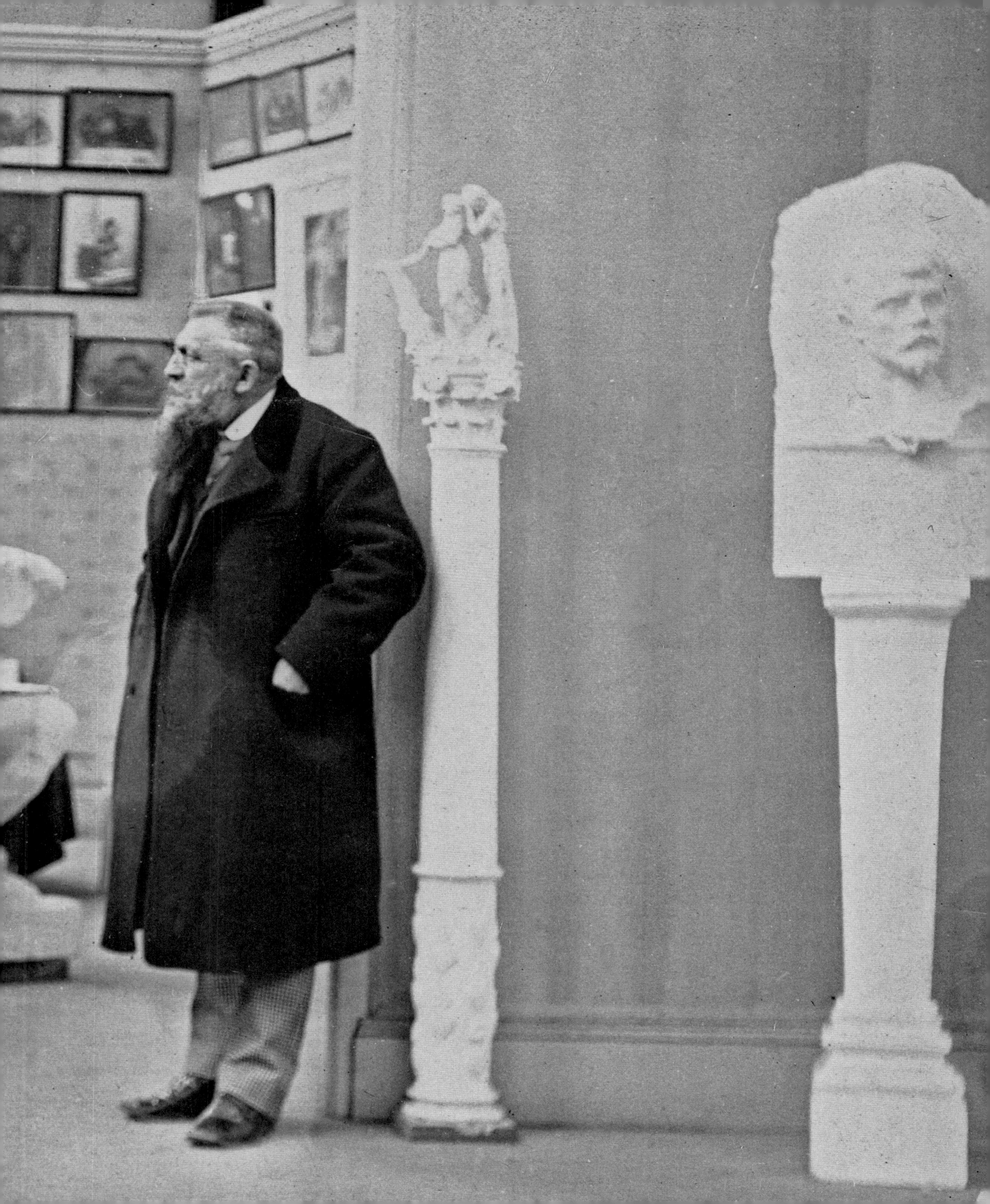

Stagings

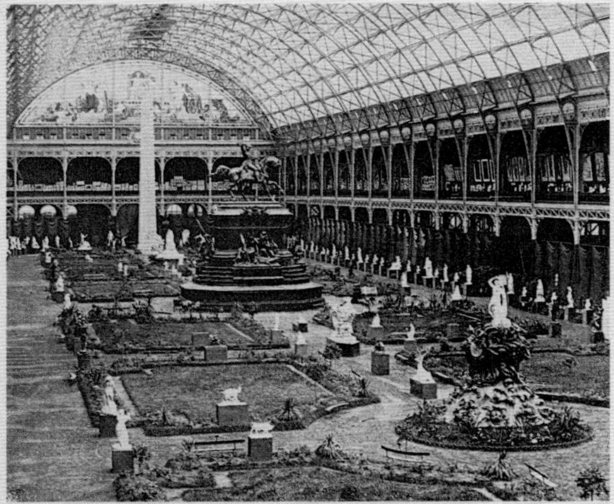

1 Salon de peinture et de sculpture, Paris, 1861, photograph

Nina Schallenberg

Air and light

On the presentation of Impressionist sculptures

In 1846, the French writer Charles Baudelaire published a review of the annual Salon exhibition in Paris in which he delivered a scathing opinion of the sculpture of his time. Under the heading of "Why sculpture is a bore?", he remarked that sculptures have "a number of disadvantages" due to their material facticity and their multifaceted nature: "Brutal and forthright like nature, sculpture is at the same time vague and elusive, because it displays too many facets at one and the same time. Vainly does the sculptor try to adopt one point of vision; the viewer who walks round the figures can choose a hundred different positions without finding the right one; and it often happens, and this is humiliating for the artist, that a chance ray of light or the play of lamplight throws into relief a beautiful effect not intended by the artist. A picture is nothing but what it intends to be. There is no way of looking at it except in its own light. Painting has only one point of view; painting is exclusive and despotic, and, in consequence, the painter's message is much more forceful."[1] For Baudelaire, what ensued from the vagueness of sculpture what that it "remained only a complementary art" whose aim was "to become the humble associate of painting and architecture and to serve their aims."[2]

In the mid-nineteenth century, sculptors had only limited opportunities in the official salons to present their works in keeping with their sculptural concepts. Sculptures were often placed jammed together in the middle of the spaces or were lined up like pearls on temporary pedestals along the aisles in the large halls (fig. 1). Grouped or positioned in such a way, they indeed lack the meaningful context that Baudelaire missed. It was not until the turn of the twentieth century that sculptors such as Auguste Rodin and Medardo Rosso succeeded in extending their sculptural concepts to include staging methods and hence integrating their works more closely into the surrounding space. The following will address this extension of sculptural practice.[3]

"Caractère" and "dominante": on the effect of sculptures

Rodin's and Rosso's staging practice was closely connected with the content-related approaches on which their works were based. As different as their sculptural concepts were, both of them left the attention to detail behind that had generally characterised the neoclassical sculpture of the nineteenth century. Their sculptures were not intended to be "brutal and forthright like nature", as Baudelaire had complained in his review, but should instead bear the animatedness and atmosphere of a motif that painting was capable of achieving.

Combining Impressionist and Symbolist theories, they were concerned with depicting those moments in which a truth has revealed itself behind the surfaces. Hence Rodin spoke of wanting to demonstrate the "caractère" of his motifs, by which he meant that energy determining an outward appearance from the inside. With this in mind, the art critic Camille Mauclair, one of Rodin's close confidants, described his artistic work with the following words: "[T]he primary characteristic of art is to discover, beneath fleeting appearances and expressions, those eternal characteristics and essential laws. [… R]odin brings to his times, which have barely emerged from the crisis of Impressionism – that is, from the impassioned study of the immediacy of light and gestures – the second truth, the recording of general and lasting feelings into a form which speaks as much to the mind as it does to the eyes […]."[4]

Rosso described a similarly profound moment of perception when he spoke of the occasion on which a motif suddenly revealed itself to him. On 17 October 1907, he published an article in the London newspaper *The Daily Mail* in which he stated: "The real visual truth of anything that meets our eye in nature can only strike us with full force in that short moment when the vision breaks upon us, as it were, as a surprise – that is to say, before our intellect, our knowledge of the material form of objects, have had time to come into play and to counteract and destroy that first impression."[5] According to Rosso, the emergence of a motif does not presuppose its real movement; instead, it is sufficient if a figure arouses attention due to external circumstances – for instance, a ray of light. Rosso refers to this moment of intense perception as "dominante": "There is no second or third plane. Only one is dominant."[6]

By virtue of their appreciation for the momentariness of the world of appearances and sensory perception, Rodin and Rosso were close to the Impressionist aesthetic. However, their pursuit of truthfulness and depth united them with the Symbolists, who assumed the existence of a hidden, lastingly valid order behind transitory modern life. What was questioned was how to lend visual expression to the existence of such principles. In this respect, two approaches developed in the context of Symbolism.[7] On the one hand, hidden realities were communicated by means of an enigmatic iconography and, on the other hand, on a formal level by centring on the aesthetic impact of the artistic means of composition. Recognition of the basic principles was to ensue – by way of the sensuous and emotional experience of the curve of a line, the nuance of a shadow or the presence of a volume. Rodin and Rosso took this formalist path. When working with the plastic material, they therefore oriented themselves not towards the faithful rendering of external reality but on the aesthetic effect that unfolded in the interplay between light and the surrounding elements. Besides the sculptural methods, therefore, modes of presentation also played an important role within their concepts.

Until far into the nineteenth century in France, the state-organised Salon was the central venue at which a broad public could view contemporary art. Because a committee was responsible for the arrangement of the works, the artists had little influence on the mode of presentation – correspondingly, numerous complaints poured in. Among other things, it was the demand for the improvement of these conditions that led to the differentiation of exhibition management in the second half of the nineteenth century. Artists' associations and private galleries were founded that offered alternative exhibition opportunities. In this context, Impressionist and Post-Impressionist painters developed methods of presentation in which the frames, wall colours and hanging style were specifically geared to the aesthetic of the paintings. Sculptors followed suit a bit later, including Rodin and Rosso.

"[T]he primary characteristic of art is to discover, beneath fleeting appearances and expressions, those eternal characteristics and essential laws."

Camille Mauclair, 1901

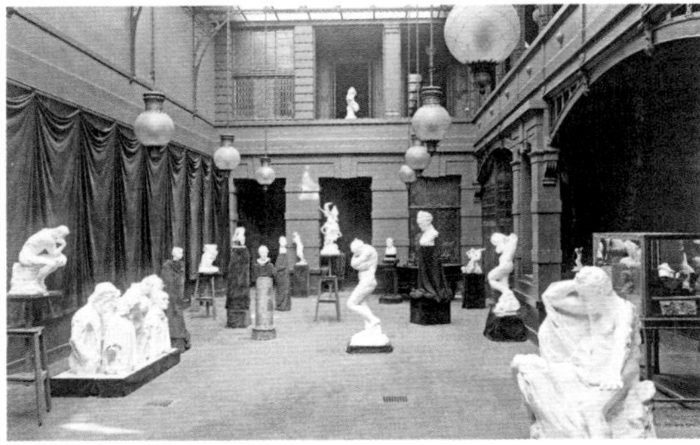

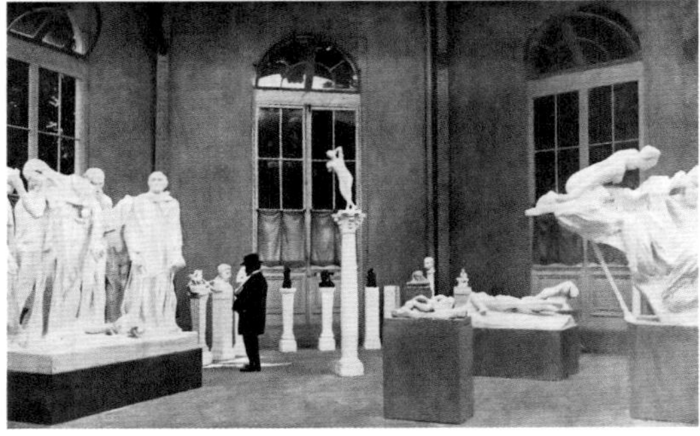

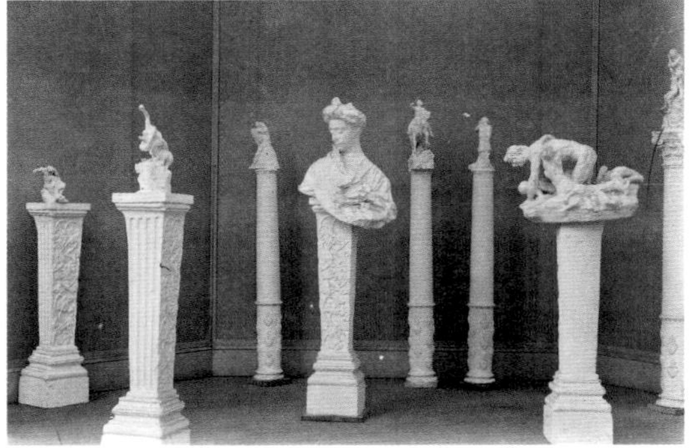

2 Salon de la Société nationale des Beaux-Arts et de la
Société des Artistes français, Palais des Machines, Paris,
1898, with Auguste Rodin's *Balzac* (at the left in the
foreground) and *The Kiss* (at the centre of the rotunda),
photograph, 22.9 × 29.2 cm, Rodin Archives, Iris & B.
Gerald Cantor Center for Visual Arts, Stanford University

3 *Exposition Rodin,* Maison d'Art, Brussels, 1899, photograph

4 *Exposition Rodin,* Place de l'Alma, Paris, 1900,
central exhibition space, photograph

5 *Exposition Rodin,* Place de l'Alma, Paris,
1900, cabinet, photograph

"Zone de liberté" – on Auguste Rodin's exhibition practice

For Rodin, the Société nationale des Beaux-Art (he was one of its cofounders) was of utmost importance for his exhibition practice.[8] In 1898, he presented his sculpture *The Kiss* in its Salon in the middle of a rotunda, and slightly outside the rotunda his design for the Balzac monument (fig. 2). The works were perfectly attuned to one another. The public first saw the rather conventional sculpture *The Kiss* and then caught sight of the towering *Balzac*. The presentation made for a scandal, during the course of which Rodin lost the commission for the monument, which is why he temporarily withdrew from the public sphere (see cat. 87). His next exhibitions took place a year later. He presented *Eve* (cat. 95) for the first time at the Salon of the Société nationale des Beaux-Arts, again in the rotunda.[9] He dispensed not only with a base, but also with the plinth by embedding the figure in the sand floor of the Salon, so that the biblical sinner dramatically stood at one level with the public. In harmony with a traditional iconography of shame, he depicted her withdrawn into herself; however, the long back area with its animated *modelé* opened itself up to the light and the surroundings. It was precisely this part of the sculpture, in which Rodin implemented his concept of an autonomous surface structure in a particularly radical way, that contemporary critics dismissed as an unfinished design. By contrast, others – for instance, Charles Morice – rated this incompleteness as Rodin's innovation.[10]

One week after the Salon, Rodin opened his first solo exhibition at the Maison d'Art in Brussels (fig. 3). *Eve* again occupied a central position in the main space. Hardly surprising, her back was turned towards the visitors entering the space. Rodin experimented with different pedestals during this show; he presented the monumental works *The Burghers of Calais* and *Victor Hugo* without pedestals, which some critics commented on by saying that one could see the tops of their heads.[11] Whereas the major share of the other works stood on pedestals covered with a dark cloth, sculptures such as *The Thinker* and *The Call to Arms,* for which Rodin favoured an elevated position, were presented on swivel studio stools. With respect to their placement in the space, Rodin made for wide clearances between the large-format sculptures, while smaller portraits and figures were arranged close to one another in one half of the space and supported each other. In doing so, with respect to positioning, he proceeded from the singularities of the works and did not followed an overriding symmetrical grid as otherwise common in the Salon.

Rodin continued this practice the following year, in 1900, when he had a pavilion for his *Exposition Rodin* built on a small parcel in Paris within walking distance of the world's fair. When positioning the works in the space, he adhered to principles similar to those he applied in Brussels. Smaller and medium-sized sculptures stood closer together, while the space around the monumental works remained open (fig. 4). He proved himself very innovative as regards the pedestals for the small- and medium-format sculptures (fig. 5). Some of them resembled columns with Corinthian capitals, while others exhibited a heart pattern or had a smooth shaft. At first, Rodin had ordered the latter, whose division into chapter, shaft and base took up the structure of antique columns, in the plaster-cast studio of the Louvre; he had purchased the model for the heart column from a private dealer. If he required further casts, he produced them in his own studio. In terms of style, Rodin's choice of pedestals drew on the style of Louis XVI, which already characterised the interior decoration of his exhibition pavilion, as well as on rococo, which was increasingly adopted around the turn of the century in the context of art nouveau. Irrespective of the influences, Rodin used these light architectural pedestals in an attempt to merge the sculptures with the interior space to create a unity. Even the extremely tall pedestals, which prompted derision by one or the other critic, did not cause the works to come across as isolated. Instead, their height

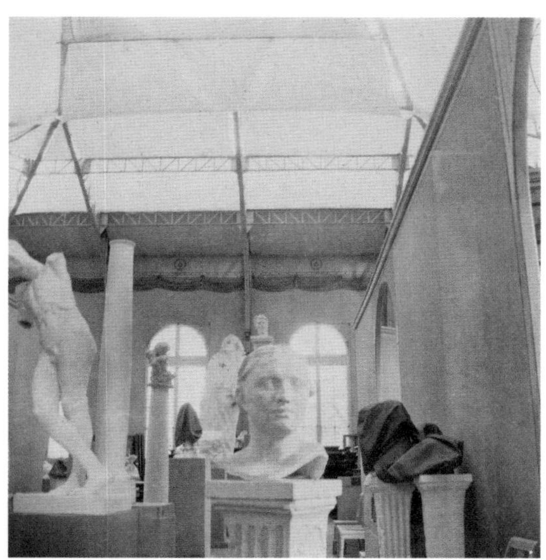

6 *Exposition Rodin*, Place de l'Alma, Paris, 1900,
view into the central aisle, photograph

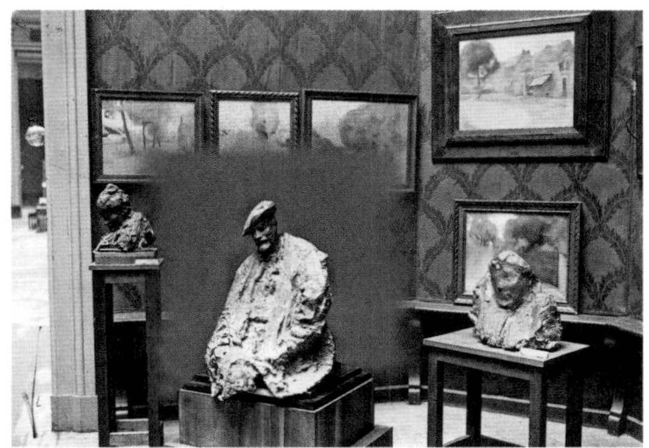

7 Salon d'Automne, Paris, 1904, with Medardo Rosso's
La Portinaia, 1883/84, *Henri Rouart*, 1890, and *Madame Noblet*,
1897, photograph, 16.2 × 23.2 cm, private collection

explains itself through their interaction with the rest of the spatial situation. By presenting the sculptures at different levels, Rodin achieved a much more vibrant impression of the ensemble than if they had stood at the same height – as was often the case in the Salon.

The lighting, which Rodin could, for the first time, specify entirely by himself during the planning of the pavilion, also supported this impression of vibrancy. He opted for lateral light, which made the most of the highly nuanced surface structure of the works. Moreover, he softened the daylight falling through the ceiling window into the space with the aid of taught lengths of fabric (fig. 6). The exhibition took place in July, and the extraordinary brightness of the spaces was reflected by what were the mostly white sculptural surfaces, resulting in the development of a kind of aureole of light around the works.

Rodin subsequently had even more large-scale solo exhibitions; however, he never again acquired the same degree of control than had been the case for his pavilion in Paris. There, he succeeded in creating a "zone de liberté"[12] for his sculptures in a very special way through their arrangement in space, the lighting and the interior architectural atmosphere in which they could find complete expression as those animated forms he had conceived them to be.

"Exhibition artist and lighting virtuoso" – on Medardo Rosso's exhibition practice

Rosso attempted to exercise more control than Rodin over the staging of his works, since the concentration of his motifs on the moment of the "dominante" meant that he did not develop them from all sides and that the figure being depicted could only be recognised if the light was precisely directed. However, he never had the position of power and the financial means that Rodin did, with the result that having his own exhibition pavilion built was inconceivable. Rosso likewise moved in alternative artistic circles – the Salon d'automne, established in 1903, played a particularly important role in this. Under the chairmanship of the painter Eugène Carrière, three solo exhibitions were organised within the scope of the 1904 Salon – namely, for Paul Cézanne, Pierre-Auguste Renoir and Medardo Rosso. For the latter, this was his first comprehensive show in France since his participation in the Salon de La Bodinière in 1893 and in the Salon des Champs-Élysées in 1895.[13] Under the overall title of *Impressions,* he presented 17 bronze and wax sculptures that stemmed from various working phases (fig. 7). They stood in the Grand Palais, where the Salon took place, in a niche-like compartment, if not even in a separate space.

In the nineteenth century, the endeavour to establish sculpture as a genre independent from architecture led to works being moved from the walls into the space of the Salons. Rosso brought his works back close to the walls in order to prevent them from being viewed from a different perspective other the one he intended. In the Salon d'automne, the *Portinaia* (cat. 53–54) could thus be approached from the front or from the right, whereas its left side was turned to the wall and was therefore not visible.

For Rosso's sculptures, the vertical perspective is also of importance, which manifested in his choice of pedestals of different heights. The portraits of Henri Rouart and Madame Noblet (cat. 70, 65) presented in the Salon d'automne seem to have been positioned relatively low. The previous year, in 1903, Rosso had participated in the exhibition *Development of Impressionism in Painting and Sculpture,* which was organised as the sixteenth show by the Vienna Secession. He informed the president of the Secession that the pedestal of a woman's portrait was to have a height of 53 centimetres; for *Sick Boy* and *The Bookmaker* (cat. 63), he recommended a height of 120 centimetres, and for *Child in the Sun* 110 centimetres

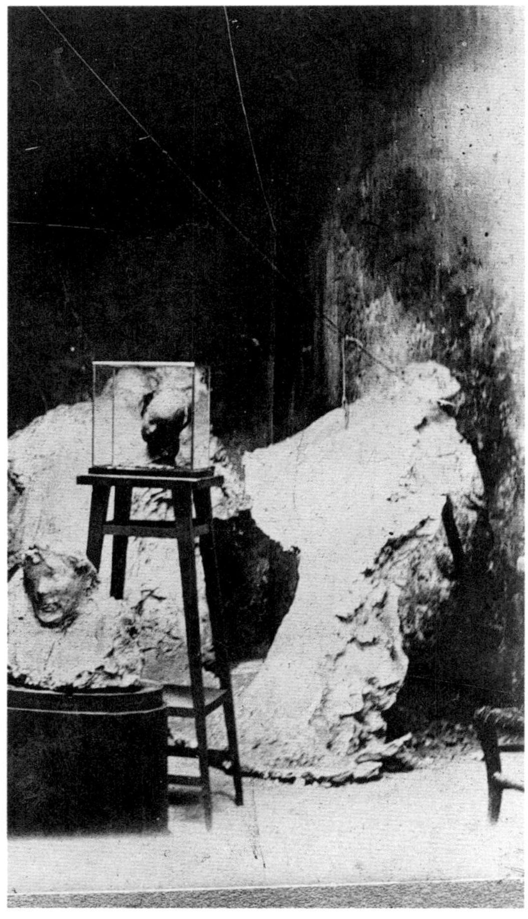

8 Medardo Rosso's studio on the Boulevard des Batignolles, c. 1899, with *Madame Noblet*, 1897, *Sick Boy* (*Bambino malato*), 1895, and *Paris la nuit*, 1896/97, photograph by Medardo Rosso (?), private collection

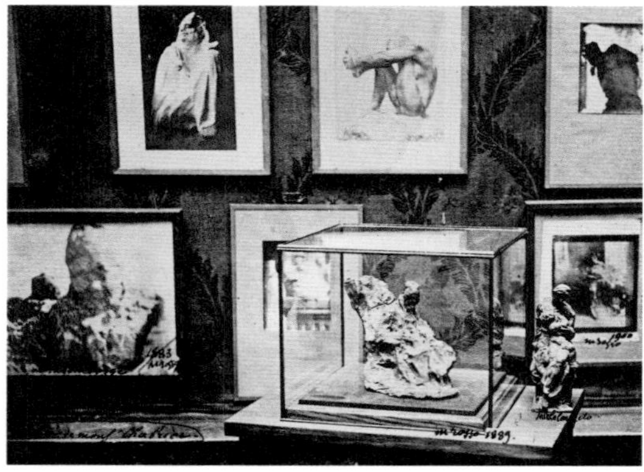

9 Salon d'Automne, Paris, 1904, with Medardo Rosso's *Malato all'ospedale* (*Sick Man in Hospital*), 1889, *Pietà after Michelangelo*, before 1904, and *Bambino al sole*, 1892, as well as photographs of sculptures by Rosso and Auguste Rodin, photograph, 17 × 22 cm, private collection

(cat. 73).[14] The pedestal for the woman's portrait was extremely low – an undated studio photograph features the bust of *Madame Noblet* in a similar position (fig. 8). Provided they wanted to see the face of the woman being depicted, viewers were forced to adopt a certain distance to the sculpture. At this juncture, a parallel can be drawn to the sculptural works by Edgar Degas, who Rosso became acquainted with in 1889 by way of Rouart. It was in *The Tub*, presumably from 1886 (cat. 29), in particular, that Degas united the plinth with the depiction of the tub in such a way that the bathing woman does not convincingly sink in the bathwater unless the sculpture is viewed diagonally from the top and from a distance.[15]

Rosso presented several works in glass vitrines, which he called "gabbia" (Italian for cage), for the first time in the Salon d'automne (fig. 9). Because the sculptures he placed in them were primarily made of wax, at first his main concern was apparently to protect the surfaces. With this in mind, the art critic Ludwig Hevesi made the following remark on the occasion of Rosso's solo exhibition at the Kunstsalon Artaria in Vienna in 1905: "The glass cages are useful to him if only because of his patina, since people like to touch the sculptures all over with their fingers and do not even notice that they smudge and discolour the main feature of the work."[16] In around 1900, vitrine-like exhibition furniture was frequently used in collections of antiquities and museums of applied arts for small-format, fragile exhibits. This was extremely rare for larger works, so that Rosso's increasingly systematic use of vitrines caused him to stand out. He even began including the corresponding vitrine in the delivery of sculptures he sold (p. 128, fig. 5).[17] Besides their protective function, several reasons shall be cited for this. The "gabbie" kept the sculptures at a physical distance from viewers, so that priority was given to the visual impression of the sculptures. Another reason was the restriction of the viewers' positions, as the cages limited the sides of the sculptures that could be viewed to four. Moreover, the dark metal edges of the vitrine had a framing effect, which blocked out the surrounding exhibition context and facilitated focusing on the motif. Both contemporary criticism as well as art historical research remarked that, as a result, the glass vitrines provided the sculptures with a self-contained space within a space.[18] However, such a separation of work and viewer space would have contradicted Rosso's notion of the world as a boundless animated continuum. Against this background, the mirror effect of the vitrine glass should be pointed out, which led to the superimposition of the sculptural figures with details from the surroundings (fig. 10). Thus, it appeared all the more as if the boundaries of the sculptural material dissolved and diffused it into the space.

Rosso assigned a crucial role to light for the prominence of a motif. "Light being of the very essence of our existence," he wrote in 1907, "a work of art that is not concerned with light has no right to exist. Without light, it must lack unity and spaciousness – it is bound to be small, paltry, wrongly conceived, based necessarily upon matter."[19] At the beginning of the twentieth century, exhibition spaces were illuminated either with daylight or gas lamps, so that the light could hardly be selectively directed at a sculpture. Whereas there were devices that concentrated beams of light, they had nothing in common however with today's spotlighting. The presentation at the Kunstsalon Artaria in 1905 provided one of the few opportunities for Rosso to influence the light in the exhibition spaces. Hevesi gave an account of the sculptor's time-consuming testing and determination of the light in several articles. According to Hevesi, Rosso mounted one or two electric light bulbs equipped with a shade above each of the vitrines. He characterised him as an "exhibition artist and lighting virtuoso" who knew how to "use air and light as sculptural material alongside bronze, clay, plaster and wax."[20]

In the case of Rosso's works, the appearance of movement as well as of the dissolution of the sculptural materials and motifs developed not only due

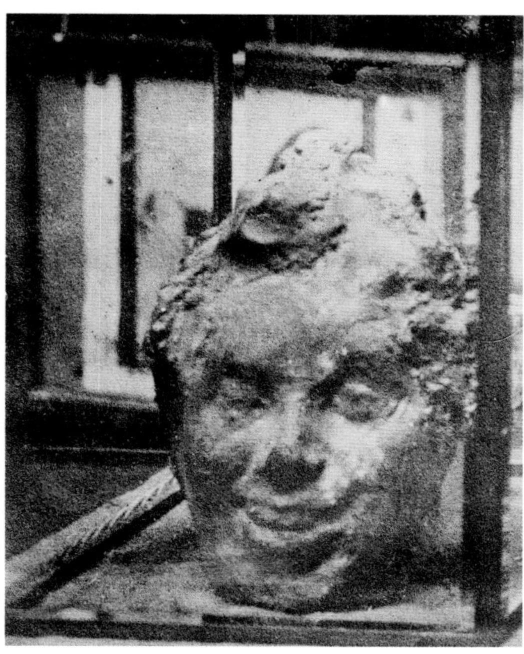

10 Salon d'Automne, Paris, 1904, with Medardo Rosso's
La Grande Rieuse, 1891, photograph, 11.2 × 9.4 cm,
private collection

to the precise arrangement of mood lighting, the surrounding colour nuances and the viewer's position. If these factors were not attuned to the sculptures, then their appearance was not far afield from the impression of "lumps of clay" that Paul Warncke described in his review of Rosso's exhibition at the Kunstsalon Keller und Reiner in Berlin in 1902.[21]

Decorative sculpture

With their practice of mise-en-scène, Rodin and Rosso strove for a close interplay between sculpture and the surroundings in terms of effect aesthetics. Such a shift of sculptural concepts from a free-standing to a space-related sculpture was reflected in a reassessment of the decorative around 1900. On behalf of the magazine *La Nouvelle Revue,* Edmond Claris conducted a survey on Impressionist sculpture in 1901 whose background was supplied by a dispute among critics over the dominating position of Rodin and Rosso that smouldered for several years. In the introduction to the survey, Claris brings two notions of sculpture in position against one another. On the one side and with reference to Baudelaire, he mentions a conventional understanding that is based on the realistic execution of a figure and which subordinates sculpture to architecture. On the other side, he confronts this with an understanding of sculpture involving the atmospheric aspects that are important when apprehending a motif: "With their courageous works, they [Rodin and Rosso] have borne the question of Impressionism into sculpture. They have posed this question: should sculpture remain subordinate to architecture and ornamentation? Can it only ever provide a rigid and exact cast of its model, executed according to arbitrarily fixed conventions, according to which the search for the line was to have been the sole concern? Or should it rather be the translation of impressions felt, taking into consideration everything which gives life to the subject: atmosphere, colour, perspective, feeling? In short, they have brought Impressionism into opposition with decorative art."[22] What is confusing is Claris's use of the term decorative, since it had been used in the opposite sense in the context of Impressionism and Symbolism. Works were referred to as decorative if their meaning revealed itself by way of the aesthetic impact of the formal compositional means. Claris's ambiguous use also attracted the attention of Ivanhoe Rambosson in his review of the book for the *Mercure de France:* "I only wonder why Monsieur Claris, who has written an interesting body of work, brings *Impressionist sculpture* into opposition with *decorative sculpture*. For him, decorative sculpture is the sculpture of the École des Beaux-Arts, and he rejects it. If decorative sculpture were this, he would be right in condemning it. But I must say, I do not understand the meaning of the word decorative in the same way. For me, decorative sculpture is that of Rodin, Pierre Roche and Charpentier. To me, the sculpture of Puech and of those under Puech does not seem to fulfil any decorative quality since it is devoid of precisely that characteristic, of that accuracy of modelling, of that balance of volumes, which make the forms sing in the atmosphere and confer upon them a greater beauty in the open air. It is not proper in an age in which the desire is precisely that of creating style and ornamentation that he should lend the word *decorative* a pejorative meaning. Is it not the aim alone of every true artistic creation to make of our existence a *decor* of all humanity, of majesty and of beauty?"[23] With "valeur", "modelé" and volume, Rambosson names those compositional means with which sculptors are capable of developing the effect aesthetics of their sculptures – and with his mentioning of atmosphere and making reference to the presentation of the sculptures outdoors, he emphasises that the works must necessarily be integrated into a spatial context. Half a century later, the "brutality" and vagueness of the sculpture that Baudelaire complained of had given way to a close interplay between sculptural and presentational elements. Thus, the sculptors around 1900 advanced an aesthetic development that continues to influence sculptural practice to this day: the development of expansive installative or situative approaches for which immaterial factors such as light, space and the viewer's position are just as important as the solid material.

"With their courageous works, they [Rodin and Rosso] have borne the question of Impressionism into sculpture."

Edmond Claris, 1902

1   Baudelaire [1846] 1972, p. 98.
2   Ibid.
3   This essay is based on my dissertation published under the name Gülicher; Gülicher 2011.
4   "[L]e premier trait de l'art est de découvrir, sous la fugacité des aspects et des expressions, les caractères permanentes, les lois vitales. [... R]odin apporte dans l'époque, à peine au sortir de la crise impressionniste, c'est-à-dire de l'étude passionnée de l'instantanéité des lumières et des gestes, la vérité seconde, la transcription des sentiments généraux et durables dans une forme qui parle autant à l'esprit qu'aux yeux […]." Mauclair 1901, p. 774.
5   Rosso 1907.
6   "Il n'y a pas: deuxième et troisième plan. Il y a une dominante." Medardo Rosso, quoted in: Aurel 1919, p. 175.
7   See Reynolds 1995, p. 27.
8   On Rodin's exhibition practice, see above all Beausire 1988; exh. cat. Paris 2001.
9   See the figure in Elsen 1974, p. 116.
10 Morice 1900, pp. 16–17.

11 P. L. 1899.
12 Auguste Rodin, quoted in: Schneider 1899.
13 In 1900, Rosso temporarily succeeded in presenting several works in the hall devoted to the painter Giovanni Segantini in the Italian pavilion of the world's fair. Alongside the large-format paintings, they looked like they had simply been deposited there; see the figure in Gülicher 2011, p. 105.
14 See Lista 1994, p. 173.
15 See Kerber 1990, p. 116–118.
16 Hevesi 1905a, S. 19.
17 Besides an illustration of the living room of the collector Etha Fles from 1913, this is also testified to by the delivery of a glass vitrine when the wax version of *Aetas Aurea* was purchased for the collection of the Musée du Petit Palais in Paris in March 1908; see Lista 1994a, p. 43.
18 Hevesi 1905b; Stix-Marget 1998, p. 56.
19 Rosso 1907.
20 Hevesi 1905a
21 Warncke 1902.
22 "Par des œuvres courageuses, ils [Rodin et Rosso] ont porté la question de

l'impressionisme en sculpture. Ils ont posé cette question: La sculpture doit-elle rester subordonnée à l'architecture et à l'ornementation; ne peut-elle donner seulement qu'un moulage rigide et exact du modèle, exécuté d'après des conventions fixées arbitrairement, dans lesquelles la recherche de la ligne ait été la préoccupation exclusive? Ou bien doit-elle être la traduction des impressions ressenties en tenant compte de tout ce qui donne la vie au sujet: atmosphère, couleur, perspective, sentiment? En résumé, ils ont opposé l'impressionnisme à l'art décoratif." Claris 1902 (French), pp. 27–28.
23 "Je me demande simplement pourquoi M. Claris, qui a fait œuvre intéressante, oppose la *sculpture impressionniste* à la *sculpture décorative*. Pour lui, la sculpture décorative c'est la sculpture de l'Ecole des Beaux-Arts et il la réprouve. Si la sculpture décorative était cela, il serait juste de la condamner. Mais je dois dire que je n'entends pas de la

même manière le sens du mot décoratif. Pour moi la sculpture décorative, c'est celle des Rodin, des Pierre Roche, des Charpentier. Celle des Puech et des sous-Puech ne me paraît réaliser aucune qualité décorative puisqu'elle est justement dénuée de ce sentiment des valeurs, de cette exactitude du modelé, de cet équilibre des volumes, qui font chanter les formes dans l'atmosphère et leur confèrent par le plein air une plus grande beauté. Ce n'est pas dans une époque dont le désir est justement d'arriver à la création d'un style et d'une ornementation qu'il siérait d'attribuer un sens péjoratif au mot *décoratif*. Est-ce que ce n'est point le but de toutes les vraies créations d'art que de faire à notre existence un *décor* de synthétique humanité, de noblesse, et de beauté?" Rambosson 1902, p. 253.

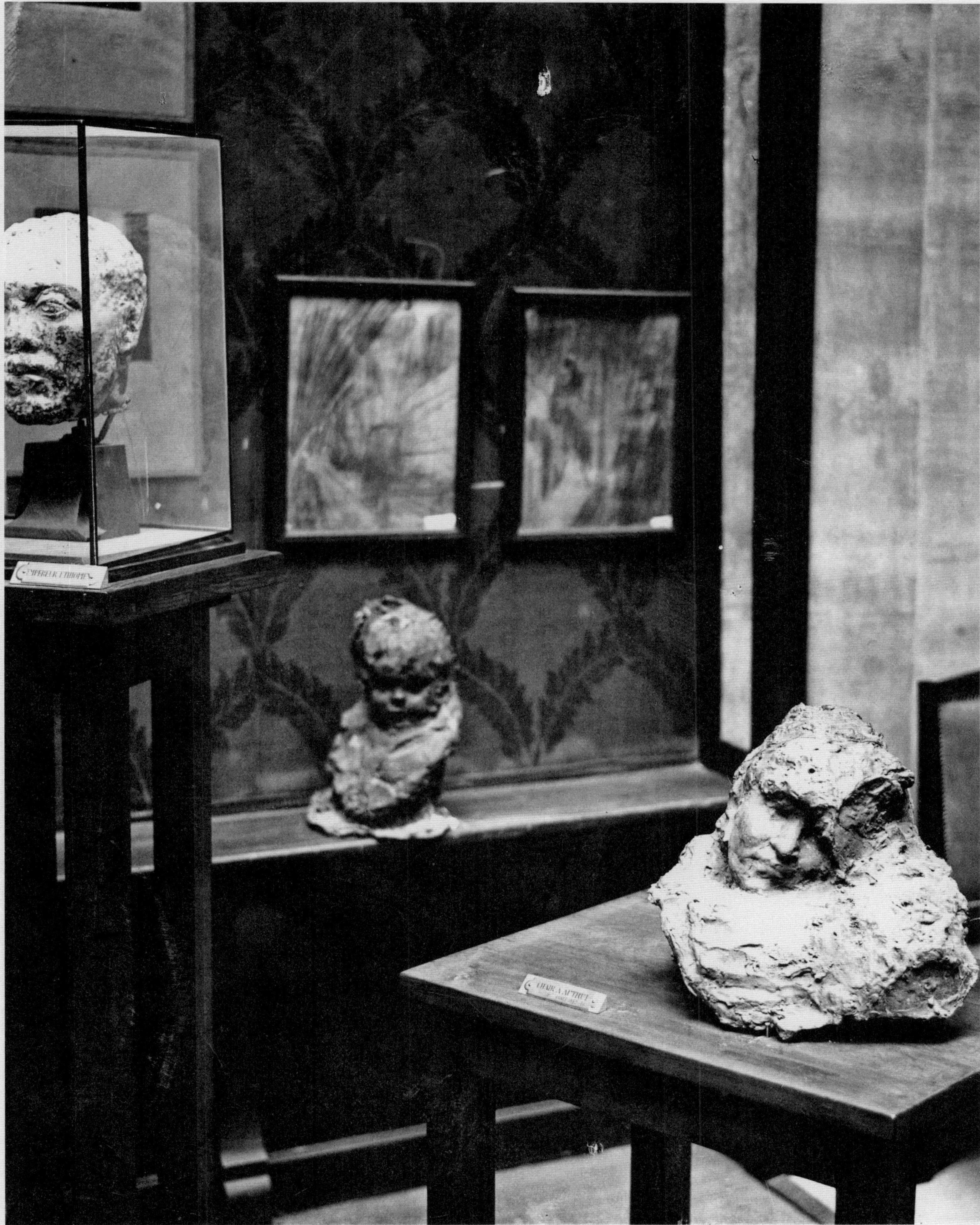

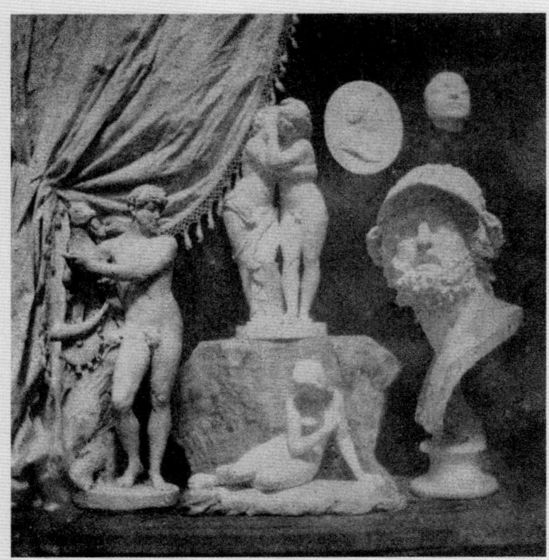

1 Hippolyte Bayard, *Still Life with Plaster Casts*, 1839/40, photograph, 12.2 × 12.5 cm, Musée d'Orsay, Paris

Juliane Betz

The directed gaze

Auguste Rodin, Medardo Rosso and
the art of photographing sculpture

It was in 1896/97 that the art historian Heinrich Wölfflin wrote his frequently cited essay on "how one should photograph sculpture".[1] His annoyance with the masses of "wrong" views of sculptures – that is, those showing them "from any arbitrary viewpoint" – had prompted him to write the text, which was published in two parts.[2] In it, he demands that sculpture be photographed from the vantage point that "corresponds to the artist's conception".[3] He then goes on to observe that, "these days", there were certainly sculptures "that simply leave it undecided as to what side they want to be viewed from, in that they do not present themselves exhaustively from any side at all, but only allow the beholder to arrive at complete clarity through a series of individual views".[4] When he wrote those particular words, he may have been thinking of his contemporary Auguste Rodin; to illustrate his overall point, however, he chose examples from the Italian Renaissance and antiquity. By suggesting that the sculptor's conception serve as orientation for the photographic reproduction (and, more fundamentally, the contemplation) of sculptures, he was offering a possible solution to the problem he had undertaken to discuss. Precisely that solution, however, was already being implemented. Auguste Rodin and Medardo Rosso were deliberately availing themselves of photography[5] to produce illustrations of their works entirely as they themselves saw fit – being the first sculptors to engage in such a practice. The aim of the following discussion is to shed light on their use of the photographic medium, an aspect that bears relevance for both artists' classification as Impressionist sculptors.

Early photography of sculpture

After the development of the photographic technique got underway in the 1820s, a conspicuously large number of sculptures, primarily small-scale plaster casts (fig. 1), were among the first objects illustrated with the new method.[6] This is easily explained: such casts were widespread, stationary, monochrome and not sensitive to light, which made them suitable for long exposure times, also in sunlight.[7] The market for these illustrations grew rapidly, stimulated and supplied from the 1860s onwards above all by professional photographers as well as art publishing houses such as Goupil & Cie., Adolphe Braun and the Alinari brothers.[8] Conventions for the illustration of sculpture had already become established in the early days of photography with the aim of making the three-dimensional objects experienceable in a single, clearly comprehensible view. One such practice was the homogeneously illuminated reproduction of light-coloured sculptures before a neutral, dark background, and of darker works before a light background – that is,

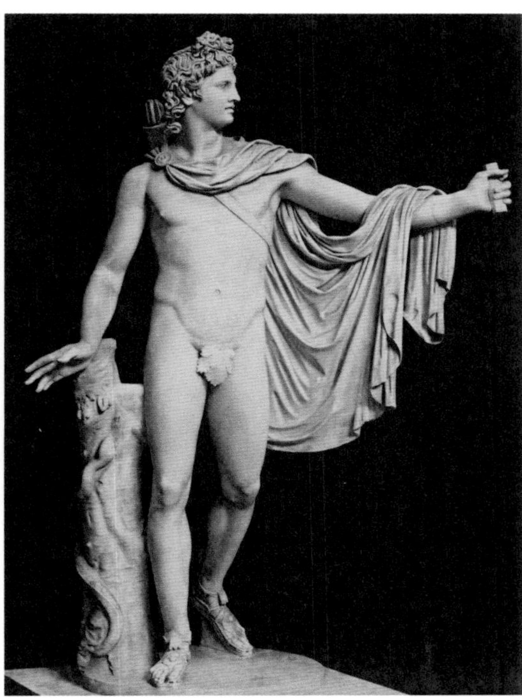

2 Alinari, *Apollo Belvedere*, 1880–1890, photograph,
24.9 × 19.2 cm, Städel Museum, Frankfurt am Main

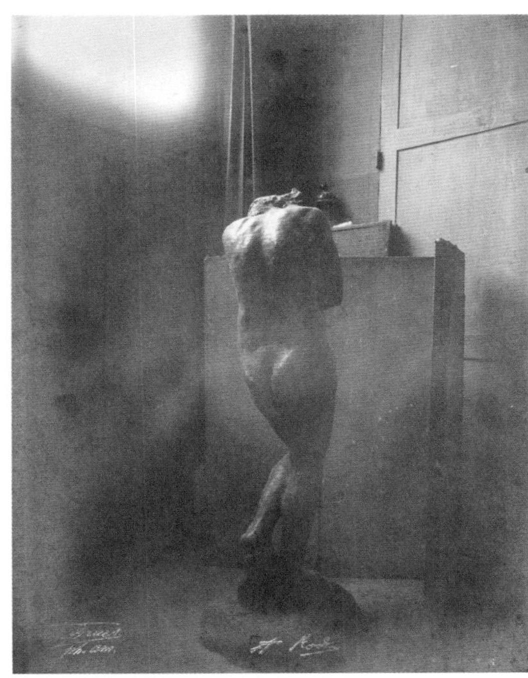

3 Eugène Druet, *Eve*, c. 1898, gelatin silver print,
39.8 × 30 cm, Musée Rodin, Paris

the creation of strong contrasts as a way of bringing out the objects' contours. The effect of this setup was to reduce, if not to negate entirely, the figure's relationship to space as a means of obscuring its scale (fig. 2).

What probably poses the greatest challenge in the photographic illustration of sculpture is the translation from three- to two-dimensionality and the accompanying necessity of choosing a single view of the work for each picture. If a sculptor attaches importance to the contemplation of a work from several sides, it is significantly more difficult both to capture the work photographically and to gain a proper impression of it in the photographic views. After all, the decisions taken by the photographer with regard to vantage point, lighting and "mise en scène"[9] and the procedure he follows in the production of the prints together determine how the beholder of the photograph – whose range of vision is perforce limited – will perceive the work. Photographs of sculpture must therefore be regarded per se as interpretations, even if, in comparison to manually produced illustrations (printmaking was the usual medium for the reproduction of artworks throughout the nineteenth century[10]), it had initially seemed objective, even "infallible". Indeed, within weeks of the announcement of the first photographic method by the Paris Academy of Sciences on 3 July 1839, an article in the *Kunst-Blatt* claimed that "statues and plaster casts" were reproduced in photographic views "not only entirely accurately, but to the highest degree of perfection in lighting and modelling".[11] The flip side of this accuracy was the authors' widely accepted assessment – that the technique possessed "a very high scientistic, but only a limited artistic value. The act of bringing forth the image itself comes about by purely physical means, and all that is left to the artistically practised eye is the choice of the favourable moment, with regard to the illumination, and of the angle of view for creating a pleasing image."[12] The opinion Wölfflin would state explicitly almost 60 years later – that the most expressive illustrations of sculptures were those produced by artists themselves or, as is to be inferred, at least under their direction – is thus already discernible in this early text. The exhibition at the Städel Museum features examples of both types of conception-oriented photography.

Illustrations for the public

The prime example of the photographic documentation of a sculptor's oeuvre directed by the sculptor himself – and a subject of frequent scholarly investigation over the past several decades – is the case of Auguste Rodin.[13] Rodin did not actually take the pictures but, from 1877 onwards,[14] cooperated with a number of photographers, as a consequence of which several thousand photos of his works have come down to us.[15] During the first 20 years, he used the photographic illustrations only in his studio. Apart from documenting the development of individual sculptures, the photos were also a basis for testing the sculptures' further – or alternative – development by drawing on the photographic prints and was thus partly also a means of conveying those ideas to his workshop employees. What is more, in many cases they served Rodin as a point of departure for drawings on paper or for newspaper illustrations in the printmaking medium.[16] The first public presentation of photographs of Rodin's sculptures took place in 1896 at Musée Rath in Geneva, where the majority of the photographic images represented three-dimensional works not on display.[17] The small-scale prints were the work of various little-known photographers and hardly suited to the purposes of such a presentation.[18]

That same year – which also saw the publication of the above-mentioned article by Wölfflin – Rodin, meanwhile a recognised sculptor, began collaborating with the photographer Eugène Druet (1867–1916), at the time still to be considered an amateur at the technique.[19] Within the framework of what was initially a

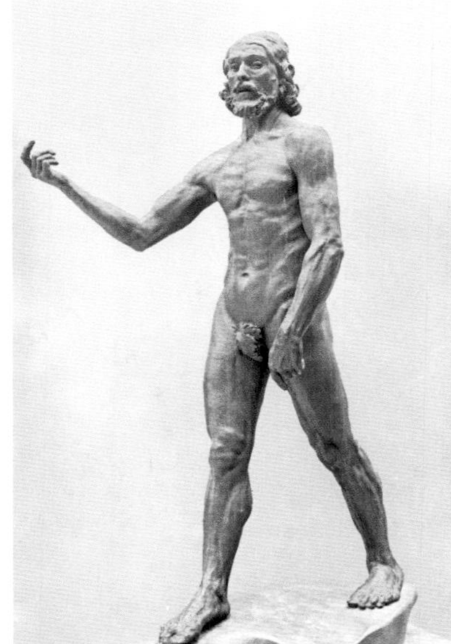

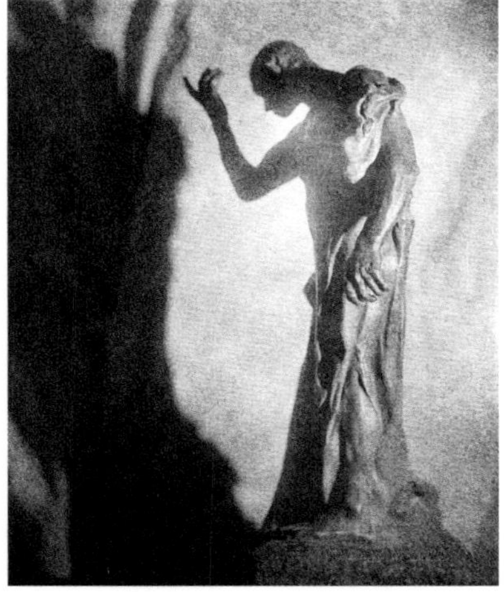

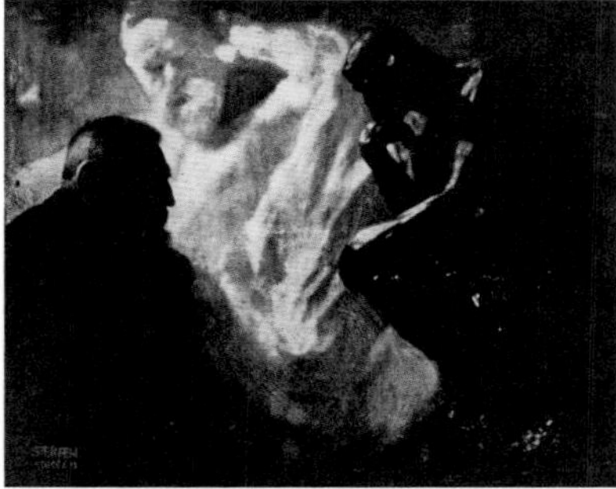

4 Jacques-Ernest Bulloz, *Saint John the Baptist*, after 1903, photograph, Musée Rodin, Paris

5 Stephen Haweis & Henry Coles, *Pierre de Wissant*, 1903/04, carbon print, 22.6 × 16.9 cm, Musée Rodin, Paris

6 Edward Steichen, *Rodin – Le Penseur*, 1905, half-tone print on Japanese paper, 14.8 × 18.5 cm, Städel Museum, Frankfurt am Main

cooperative arrangement based on mutual agreement, Rodin exerted an influence on the design of the photos to ensure the aesthetically pleasing illustration of his sculptures in a manner corresponding to his sculptural concept.[20] By 1900, when the two men quarrelled during the preparations for the exhibition at the Pavillon de l'Alma (1900), Druet had produced several hundred photos of the sculptor's plaster, marble and bronze sculptures.[21] Contemporaries regarded the results as an entirely "new" form of sculpture photography,[22] and already they recognised that the images' most striking feature was their unconventionality: Druet had deliberately "staged" the setting – often the artist's studio, complete with tools or other sculptures. Working indoors had moreover enabled him to control the incidence of the light, which frequently comes from one side in the photos and thus accentuates the figures' modelling (fig. 3; cat. 88). The prints, which Druet usually produced with the aid of a special enlargement method, were distinguished for the most part by a certain softness of focus as well as the avoidance of pure white and black values. These attributes were possible only because Druet made creative use of what were, at the time, the most advanced techniques for the production of images.[23] Another novelty was that he frequently moved around the sculptures with his camera, taking several pictures of them in the process, thus simulating the multi-perspectival contemplation Rodin premised as essential for grasping the works' meaning in its entirety (cat. 102–106).[24]

Particularly in view of the fact that Rodin had the photos made in part to meet the growing demand for illustrations of his works for publications, his insistence on having a say in how Druet proceeded shows that he must have been well aware of the power of the photographic image. Starting in 1897, Druet's photographs were frequently published in magazines and exhibition catalogues, and critics took them into account in their texts on Rodin's art; and from 1899 onwards, they were not only available for purchase, but also repeatedly appeared side by side with the sculptures in exhibitions, which effectively granted them the status of artworks in their own right.[25] Druet's photos had a lasting impact on how Rodin's art was seen at the time,[26] particularly by those viewers who had more access to the illustrations than to the originals. A review of 1899 provides evidence of how strongly the photos changed – and even competed with – people's perception of the sculptures: the text highlighted the photographs (and the drawings) by saying that they showed the "true" Rodin.[27] A standpoint much in the same vein was Julius Meier-Graefe's appraisal of the photos as indispensable for understanding Rodin's oeuvre: "This Druet saw Rodin in a manner – which, incidentally, the master himself had taught him – that can be referred to as nothing less than ingenious. If it didn't sound barbaric, you'd almost have to say that it wasn't until these photographs that we became acquainted with Rodin in all his greatness, his self-confident distribution of air."[28]

In 1903, when he no longer had Druet as much at his disposal as before,[29] Rodin decided to engage the services of a professional contract photographer capable not only of taking and printing the pictures, but also of marketing them and managing the image copyrights. He chose Jacques-Ernest Bulloz (1858–1942) for the task.[30] As in the case of Druet, Rodin was actively involved in the making of the photos. He prescribed the lighting, background and angle of view, even though he verifiably held Bulloz's work in high regard and the collaboration endured until the sculptor's death.[31] In this context it is remarkable how greatly the style of Bulloz's photos differed from that of Druet's. A photographer who had received his training from Adolphe Braun, Bulloz illustrated the sculptures in quite conventional manner: with emphasis on the contours, frontally or in three-quarter view, before neutral backgrounds, devoid of any indication of scale or location in space – in other words, his views were more prosaic than Druet's and "seemingly objective" (fig. 4; cat. 97).[32]

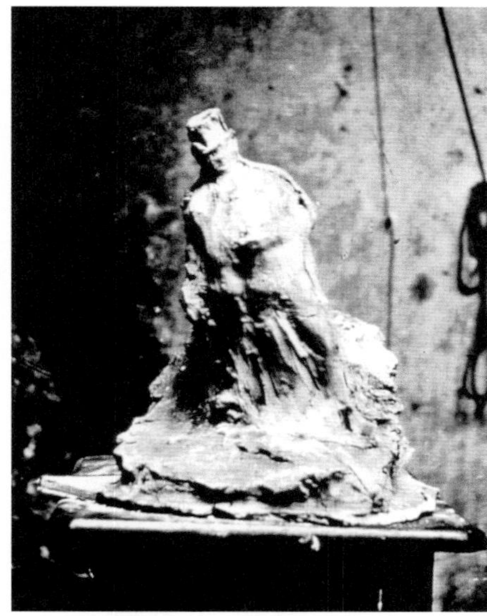

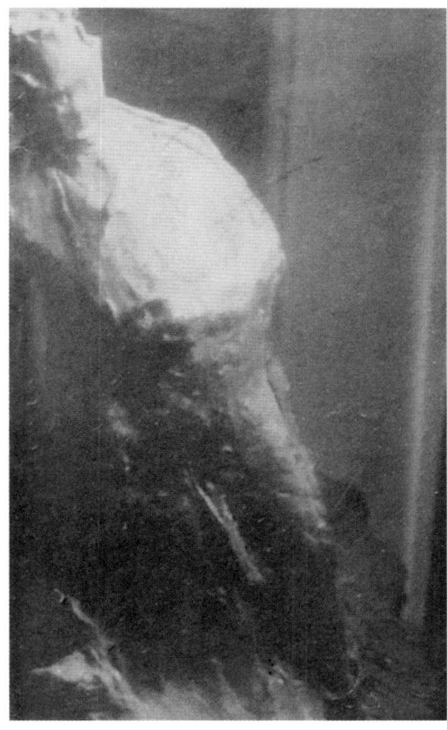

7 Medardo Rosso, *The Bookmaker* (1894), c. 1910–1920, photograph, 7.7 × 4.7 cm, private collection

8 Medardo Rosso, *The Bookmaker* (1894), c. 1901/02, photograph, 11.1 × 8.6 cm, private collection

Druet and Bulloz produced a large proportion of the published and marketed photographs of Rodin's works within just a few years. Their photos are distinguished by their technical quality, the size of the prints and the double signature of the sculptor and the photographer.[33] During the years of Rodin's collaboration with Bulloz, a number of other photographers also worked for the sculptor for relatively brief spans of time and on their own initiative. Adherents to the pictorialist current, they were seeking to prove that photography is a mode of artistic expression on a par with painting. In their approach, the retouching of the negative and intervention in the development of the prints played as important a role as the actual camera work. The photographs, for example, by Stephen Haweis & Henry Coles[34] and Edward Steichen[35] – some of which caused quite a sensation – are for the most part grainy and blurred. They bear a resemblance to works of printmaking and leave the viewer more or less in the dark as to the sculptures' actual appearance (fig. 5; p. 293, fig. 7). The photographers attached far more importance to their artistic claim than to the illustrative function of their works, for which reason Rodin's sculptures were a welcome, but essentially replaceable, "subject of interpretation".[36] At least in the case of Steichen, there was also the aspect of staging Rodin as an artistic genius, manifest in the combination of portrait and sculpture photography (fig. 6).

In summary, it can be said that the numerous photographs of Rodin's works are as disparate as the photographers themselves, their motivations and the conditions under which they worked. From 1896 onwards, if not before – that is, from the point in time when the images were meant for publication or at least intended to be suitable for that purpose – Rodin saw to it that they satisfied his own standards and wishes. Within those bounds, however, he was entirely capable of appreciating the interpretative endeavours of Druet and his successors.

Photographic intensification

Whereas Rodin worked with a whole series of photographers in his effort to control and promote the reception of his work, Medardo Rosso presumably photographed his works himself.[37] He began experimenting with photography in 1899,[38] varying the perspective, lighting and backgrounds, intervening in the development of the negatives and the exposure, and above all cropping and retouching the prints.[39] He differed from the pictorialists of the same period, however, in that he did not take these measures with the intent of producing artworks in their own right. On the contrary, his concern was to illustrate and explain what he considered to be the ideal perception of his works and thus his own sculptural conception so that he always had several photographs with him wherever he went.[40] We can therefore assume that he produced more than the approximately 400 prints housed in Museo Medardo Rosso in Barzio today, because he will certainly also have given some away as gifts, sent them to various addressees and destroyed those that had not turned out to his liking. The sculptural concept Rosso sought to convey aimed, in brief, at capturing the initial visual impression ("impressione") that comes even before the conscious perception of a thing. He was of the opinion that it is possible to comprehend even something three-dimensional "at a single glance", and established the viewing conditions accordingly: he stipulated how the work was to be lit, the height of its base, and even the one, single vantage point from which it was to be viewed. "You don't walk around a sculpture any more than you walk around a painting, because you don't walk around a form to gain an impression [of it]."[41] The suggestion here is that three-dimensionality is to be perceived for the most part pictorially, an approach that earned Rosso the epithet "painter without a brush".[42]

When Edgar Degas saw a photograph of Rosso's vegetable seller from the *Impressione d'omnibus* (p. 295, fig. 11), he reportedly exclaimed: "But this is a photograph of a painting?!"[43] On the one hand, this much-quoted reaction under-

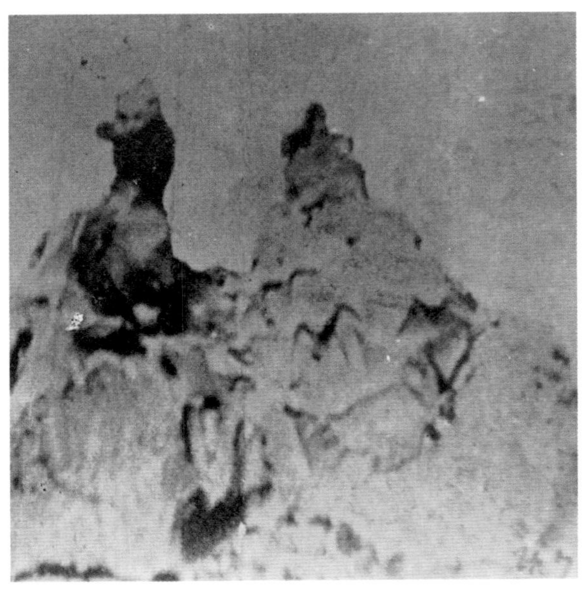

9 Medardo Rosso, *Conversation in the Garden*, c. 1904, photograph, 10 × 9.2 cm, private collection

scores what Charles Baudelaire characterised as a mode of depiction well wrought because it is clearly defined and permits only a single vantage point. On the other hand, it also reveals the viewer's disconcertment upon contemplating Rosso's photographs of his sculptures. As Werner Schnell rightly remarked, the images are distinguished by the tight framing of the subject, which leads to the removal of the surrounding space, enabling the viewer to fill in the rest with his own imagination, "as with a painting".[44] Further attributes are the small formats and the blurriness brought about by ever closer proximity to the sculpture in conjunction with the choice of a certain framing (figs. 7, 8; cat. 62–63). The numerous repetitions are also conspicuous: Rosso photographed sculptures such as the *Portinaia* (cat. 55–57) as many as 20 times,[45] yet he never published more than one or, at the most, two views of a given work.[46] This circumstance is clear evidence that he meant each shot to be viewed separately and – in keeping with the artist's specification of a clearly defined vantage point – regarded as one of a range of only slightly varied possible perspectives on the work and not, like Druet's series, as a fictive "circumambulation" of a sculpture by means of several mutually enhancing photographic views. In his endeavour to explain his sculptural intent with the aid of the photographs, Rosso insisted on the use of his own photos, in unchanged form, to illustrate his oeuvre in publications: "In short, I can't have photos made for me by others. I desire my own and no others. After all, those are the ones I believe are the best."[47]

Rosso's photos were first published in 1902, along with a statement by the artist himself, in Edmond Claris's *De l'Impressionnisme en sculpture*. It is for that reason that Nina Schallenberg underscored the significance of the "debate over impressionism in sculpture" as the driving force behind Rosso's sculpture-photographing activities.[48] It was presumably likewise in 1902[49] that he took to displaying his photographs as framed enlargements in exhibitions, where they were to help the visitors view his sculptures "correctly", although they could not replace the visual experience of the three-dimensional object in time and space.[50] The earliest presentation of his photographs for which we have a pictorial source is that at the Salon d'automne in 1904 (p. 280, fig. 9). There Rosso provoked comparison with the second impressionist sculptor, Rodin, by deliberately placing his own sculptures and photos in close proximity to the photos by Druet and by Haweis & Coles that represented Rodin's work on that occasion.[51]

A juxtaposition of Rosso's photographs with those of Rodin's works reveals the differences between the two sculptors' conceptions of how sculptures should be photographed. Rosso's images are virtual intensifications of the visual experience; they relentlessly focus the gaze on his sculptural works. What is more – as already noted in 1902 – their dissolution into partially undefinable black-and-white structures lends them a quality that, on account of their resemblance to a mode of painting that tends to dissolve the subject matter, makes his classification as an Impressionist seem plausible above and beyond the arguments pertaining purely to his sculptures. "Indeed, not everyone is capable of understanding this sculptural language, and many a visitor who contemplates the photographs hanging next to the sculptures will be inclined to mistake their contents for 'alpine landscapes'. In other words, one must learn to 'read' Rosso to understand 'Impressionism in sculpture', as whose representative he, along with Auguste Rodin, now appears" (fig. 9).[52]

To this day, the reception of Rodin's and Rosso's works has been influenced by the photographs they respectively designed or took. The very numerous and widely differing photographic images of Rodin's sculptures were primarily intended to facilitate the broadest possible perception of his oeuvre. At the same time, they contributed to categorical uncertainty regarding his classification as an Impressionist.[53] The foremost purpose of Rosso's photographs, by contrast, was to make his work comprehensible and to substantiate his status as *the* Impressionist sculptor par excellence.

"In short, I can't have photos made for me by others.
I desire my own and no others.
After all, those are the ones I believe are the best."

Medardo Rosso, presumably 1926

1   Wölfflin 1896/97. Before this text, there was "only simple instructional literature on photography", according to Bezzola 2010, p. 29. Some 20 years later, Wölfflin supplemented his deliberations with a discussion of the lighting; Wölfflin 1915.

2   Wölfflin 1896/97, 8, p. 224.

3   Ibid., p. 225.

4   Ibid.

5   Gülicher 2011, p. 161; with regard to Rosso, also see Brockhaus 1997, p. 81.

6   Surveys of the various motivations and reasons for photographing sculpture in the nineteenth and early twentieth centuries are found in: exh. cat. Geneva 1985; exh. cat. Paris 1991; exh. cat. Duisburg 1997; exh. cat. New York/Zurich 2010.

7   As far back as 1844, in The Pencil of Nature, William Henry Fox Talbot pointed out that sculptures like the plaster cast of an ancient Bust of Patroclus illustrated in his book lent themselves extremely well to good and rapid photographic reproduction because they are white and almost countless "effects" could be achieved by varying the incidence of the light; Talbot [1844] 2011, pls. V and XVII, text accompanying pl. V.

8   Hamber 1996, pp. 196–198.

9   The term refers to "the entire range of design decisions that determine the appearance of the motif in the photographic image"; Gülicher 2011, p. 165.

10 Betz 2016, pp. 116–119.

11 Schorn/Kolloff 1839, p. 307.

12 Ibid.

13 Since the archive in Musée Rodin opened in the late 1970s, Rodin's relationship to photography has been the subject of extensive research; see Pinet 2007, p. 12., also see exh. cat. Paris 1986 (with older literature) and further publications by Hélène Pinet; exh. cat. Berlin 1994; Philp 2000, pp. 15–75.

14 The first photographs by Gaudenzio Marconi show both the Age of Bronze and the model. They aided Rodin in defending himself against the accusation that he had, impermissibly, used a plaster cast of the live model to make

his sculpture; Pinet 2007b, p. 24. On this subject, also see the contribution by Dominik Brabant, pp. 174–183, here p. 178, in this catalogue.

15 The largest and, for Rodin, most important proportion of the approximately 7,000 photographs he commissioned or purchased show sculptures; Pinet 1997, pp. 71–72.

16 Ibid., pp. 72–74; Pinet 2007a.

17 Pinet 1997, p. 74. The 1896 exhibition featured works by Rodin, Eugène Carrière and Pierre Puvis de Chavannes. For a list of all exhibitions in which photographs of works by Rodin were on display, see: exh. cat. Paris 2007, pp. 218–219.

18 Pinet 2007b, p. 72.

19 For a discussion of Druet's biography, his work for Rodin and the disagreement between them, see Pinet 2007b. For an in-depth discussion of the Berlin Druet holdings, see Von Knobelsdorf 2004; exh. cat. Berlin 2005.

20 Gülicher 2011, p. 183.

21 Despite the differences between the two men, 71 photographs by Druet were on view in the exhibition; see exh. cat. Paris 2007, pp. 78–79.

22 Fagus 1899; Anet 1901, p. 217; Fontainas 1901, p. 218.

23 On Druet's technique, see Harich-Hamburger 2005, pp. 31–33.

24 In a letter he wrote in 1905, Rodin criticised the fact that a photograph could show only one quarter of a work. As his works were meant to be viewed from all sides, the photos were therefore incomprehensible; see exh. cat. Paris 2007, p. 11. On the series and how they related to the "profiles", see Philp 2000, pp. 25–37, esp. pp. 31–32.

25 Pinet 1997, p. 74.

26 Philp 2000, pp. 16, 45; Maaz 2005, esp. pp. 17, 24–26. Also see the section headed "Fotografie macht Plastik impressionistisch" in the lecture Bernhard Maaz gave on 31 January 2019 within the framework of the Passavant-Kolloquium "Impressionistische Skulptur. Flüchtigkeit in Wachs und Bronze" at the Städel Museum. The text will prospectively be published in 2020 in

the Münchner Jahrbuch der bildenden Kunst; see Maaz 2020.

27 "Des photographies et des croquis […] composent ce qu'il y a peut-être de plus intéressant dans ce déballage hétéroclite: bien mieux que les plâtres durs, il nous donnent le vrai Rodin, spontané, tel qu'il est dans la conception de son esprit inquiet et chercheur." Anonymous, in: Le Soir, April 1899, quoted in: exh. cat. Paris 2007, p. 218.

28 Meier-Graefe 1904a, p. 38.

29 After his dispute with Rodin in 1900/01 and the opening of his own art gallery in late 1903, Druet worked only sporadically for the sculptor. He continued to sell prints of his Rodin photographs, however, until his death in 1916; Philp 2000, pp. 38–41.

30 For a discussion of Bulloz's and his work for Rodin, see Pinet 2007c.

31 Ibid., p. 116.

32 Philp 2000, p. 47.

33 Pinet 1997, pp. 75–76.

34 In 1903/04, this photographer duo produced some 300 photographs of Rodin's in less than a year and a half. On that subject and in general, see Pinet 2007d, p. 153.

35 Steichen portrayed Rodin in 1901/02; he began photographing the sculptor's works in 1907; see Gülicher 2011, pp. 172–174. For a general discussion of Steichen's work for Rodin, see Pinet 2007f..

36 Pinet 2007g, p. 178 ("sujet d'interprétation").

37 The matter of whether Rosso took the pictures and/or made the prints himself has remained controversial to this day; see Gülicher 2011, pp. 190–191, with a summary of the state of research.

38 This issue is likewise controversial; on this subject, see ibid., p. 191, with an assessment I share.

39 Exh. cat. Santiago de Compostela 1996, p. 47; Stix-Marget 1998, pp. 118, 123–124; Gülicher 2011, pp. 199–200. Also see cat. 55–57, 64 in this catalogue.

40 Stix-Marget 1998, pp. 37, 118–119.

41 "On ne tourne pas autour d'une statue, pas plus qu'on ne tourne autour d'un tableau, parce qu'on ne tourne pas

autour d'une forme pour en concevoir l'impression." Medardo Rosso, 1902; original French quotation quoted in: Stix-Marget 1998, p. 49.

42 Stix-Marget 1998.

43 "Mais c'est la fotografie d'un tableau que vous m'apportez-là?" De Sainte-Croix 1896, p. 391. Degas's exclamation has been quoted frequently, for example, by: Claris 1902 (French), p. 21; Vauxcelles 1905; Hevesi 1905, p. 176; Hevesi 1909; reprinted in: exh. cat. Berlin 2013, n. p.

44 Schnell 1987, p. 293.

45 Brockhaus 2003, pp. 55–56; exh. cat. Santiago de Compostela 1996, figs. 23–39.

46 Gülicher 2011, p. 196.

47 "Insomma non posso farmi a lasciar fare altri fotografie. Le mie desidero e nessun altra. Sono quelle che poi credo meglio. Non ne voglio altre." Medardo Rosso in a letter he presumably wrote in 1926, original Italian quotation quoted in: Stix-Marget 1998, p. 156. On this subject, also see other quotations: ibid., pp. 118, 164.

48 Her dissertation was published under the name Gülicher; Gülicher 2011, here pp. 188, 201. Also see the contribution by Fabienne Ruppen, pp. 24–34, here pp. 31–32 in this catalogue.

49 Scholars disagree over the matter of when Rosso also began exhibiting photos: in 1886 (Lammert 2007, p. 501), 1889 (Stix-Marget 1998, pp. 161–162) or – most convincingly – 1902 (Gülicher 2011, p. 188).

50 Gülicher 2011, pp. 202–203.

51 "Et, cette année, au Salon d'Automne – où Rodin, dédaigneux, n'est représenté que par des photographies – Rosso pria la Commission de placement de mettre ses œuvres près de ces photographies, pour que le public pût confronter et juger!" Vauxcelles 1905.

52 V. M. 1902; quoted in: Gülicher 2011, pp. 188–189.

53 Rodin did not refer to himself as an "Impressionist"; see the contribution by Dominik Brabant in this catalogue, pp. 174–183.

Media and materiality

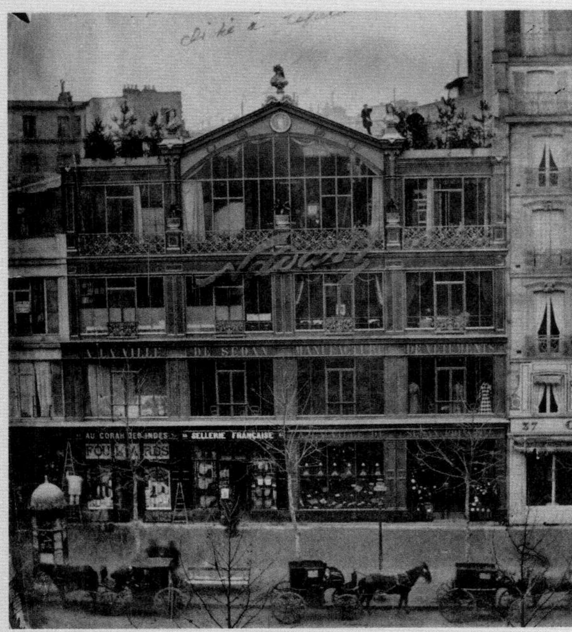

1 Studio of the photographer Nadar, 35 Boulevard des
Capucines, Paris, after 1850, photograph, 25 × 19.4 cm,
Bibliothèque nationale de France, Département des
Estampes et de la photographie, Paris

Dietmar Rübel

Dissolution of the solid and the permanent

On the interplay between Impressionist
sculpture and photography

"We are plays of a totality of all forms of fluidity –
light, colour, anything you want." Medardo Rosso[1]

In 1908, the philosopher and sociologist Georg Simmel illustrated the shifts in perception in modern metropolises using public transportation as an example: "Before
the appearance of omnibuses, railroads, and street cars in the nineteenth century,
men were not in a situation where for periods of minutes or hours they could or
must look at each other without talking to one another."[2] This passage recalls the
sculpture *Impressione d'omnibus (Impressions of an Omnibus)* of 1883/84 (cat. 57),
of which only a photograph has survived, by the sculptor Medardo Rosso, at the
time still in Milan and several years later in Paris. The experimental techniques
for which this sculpture stands with its striking working of the surface become
palpable in the photograph mounted on card. In addition, the artist undermines
or overcomes traditional notions of vision. Many contemporaries saw themselves
exposed to a cascade of momentary impressions that could only be observed with
difficulty – causing "perception oriented to perspective" to seem nearly impossible.[3]
In the hustle and bustle of big cities, when riding public transportation or amongst
crowds of people on the boulevards, details were no longer important for perception, but rather the overall impression, on which visually scanning the streets and
buildings had a determining influence. In the art of impressions, it was therefore
a matter of capturing exemplary moments from a multitude of interpenetrating
sensory impressions, which only possess anything like continuity in their permanent
transitions. In 1990, the art historian Jonathan Crary explained that new aesthetic
phenomena, such as Impressionism and the representational techniques of new
media like photography, marked the "passage" from geometrical to physiological
optics: vision was "taken out of the incorporeal relations of the camera obscura
and relocated in the human body."[4]

 Moreover, Rosso's *Impressione d'omnibus* illustrates central categories[5]
that are frequently consulted when identifying Impressionist sculptures: for one
thing, the reduced composition of the material in striving to render the impression of it being confined to the moment, and for another thing the attempt to
fuse the figure with its surroundings, with its – the word had just come in at the
time – "environment" by means of a non-Euclidian concept of space.[6] Focus was
placed on the creation of momentary situations, atmospheres and sensations –
Simmel described this as an "uninterrupted change of outer and inner stimuli".[7] In

subsequent decades, the term "impression" that Claude Monet cited in the title of his oil painting *Impression, soleil levant (Impression, Sunrise,* 1872; p. 13, fig. 3) increasingly approximated the concept of "impression" in perception theory – as the interface between internal perception and external world.[8] What role was assigned to Impressionist sculpture, especially in works in which an attempt was made to encounter this modernisation with animated and fugitive forms? In the following, this shall be illustrated by reference to the interplay between the materiality and the mediality of the sculptural and the photographic. Based on the various uses of photographic techniques, it will be shown how the photographic afforded a new plasticity, which in turn accelerated the emergence of Impressionist sculpture and fundamentally restructured the genre of sculpture that for centuries had been defined by dignity and ponderousness.[9]

The specific location at which the movement obtained its name "impressionnisme" in 1874 furnishes unmistakable evidence for the importance of photography for the "Société anonyme coopérative des artistes peintres, sculpteurs, graveurs, etc." It is well known that the group's first joint exhibition was made possible because a photographer, of all people, rented them his spaces located between Opéra and Madeleine: "Nadar" fashioned out of enormous, sweeping letters in the style of a handwritten signature was attached to the facade below the large studio window on the third and uppermost floor of building number 35 on the Boulevard des Capucines (fig. 1). This site marked a refiguring of sculpture, of this supposedly obsolete art form.[10] For with the introduction of photography in 1839, perception of the world changed, as from that point onwards a medium was available that was in a position to capture the endless transformations of the modern era by means of a reproduction process that was specific to the epoch. The photographic images of this epistemological turn led to the mutability and the relativity of all forms in the industrial age in a fascinating and clearly discernible way. At the same time, a seemingly insurmountable contradiction became apparent that certainly expedited the literal dissolution of the solid and the permanent.[11] It was precisely because sculpture was considered to be inconsistent with the acceleration, the unrest and the liquid, even form-dissolving aspect of modernity that it created unions with previously neglected materials and media, or those just being developed at the time.[12] Thus, beginning in the late nineteenth century, random documentary photographs encountered complex strategies of the interaction between photography and classic approaches in art.[13] Owing to the adventurous handling of its traditional material, paint, as well as to an intensified interest in abstraction, painting succeeded in bringing subject and compositional technique closer to one another to an increasingly stronger extent. It therefore speaks for itself that Claude Monet's work *Impression, soleil levant (Impression, Sunrise)* – a work produced in spring 1872 that visualised a transition in the port of Le Havre – gave the movement its name: a scene of the passage from night into day, from water into fog. In Impressionist works it is a question of, among other things, how objects and their transformational capacity are perceived and experienced.

The methodological dilemma in light of this *modernité* – in the age of the railway and photography as well as of motion pictures shortly thereafter – results from the day-to-day transformation of external as well as internal things and the artistic quest for adequate possibilities to respond to this – processes that opened up a comparable pace in the materials and media that were used. This particularly holds true for Medardo Rosso, whose *Impression de boulevard, le soir (Paris la nuit) (Impression of a Boulevard (Paris at Night)),* thus the materialisation of figures rushing by and their shadows, seemed like a three-dimensional photograph (fig. 2; cat. 64). Rosso therefore repeatedly accentuated the mutability inherent in sculptural materials such as clay – or in the case of *Impression de boulevard* the

2 Medardo Rosso's studio on the Boulevard des Batignolles in Paris, c. 1899, with *Madame Noblet,* 1897, *Sick Boy (Bambino malato),* 1895, and *Paris la nuit,* 1896/97, photograph by Medardo Rosso (?), private collection

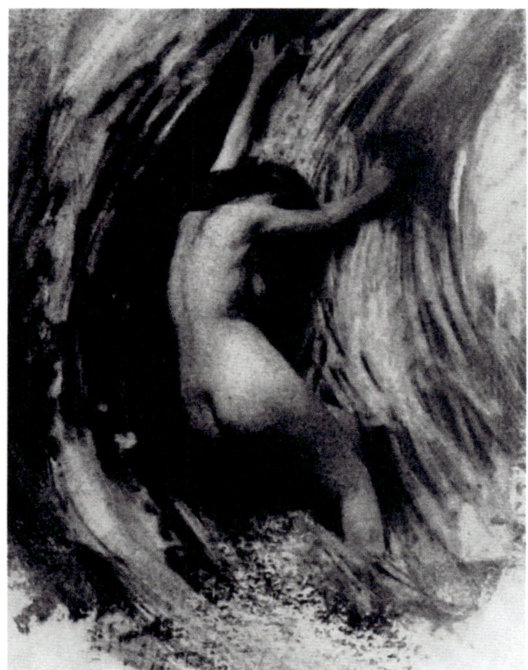

3   Robert Demachy, *Struggle*, c. 1904, from *Camera Work: A Photographic Quarterly* 5 (1904), p. 16

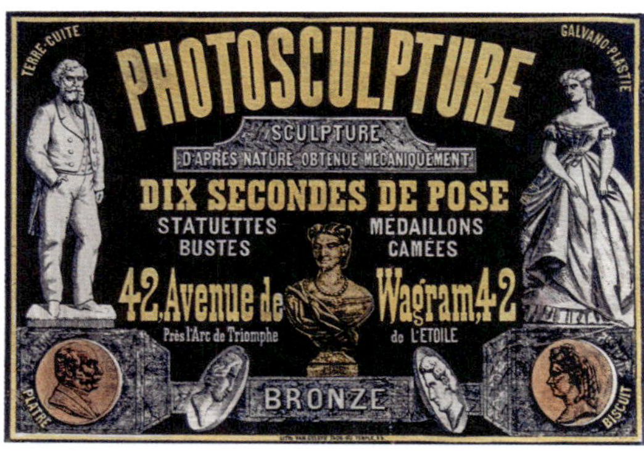

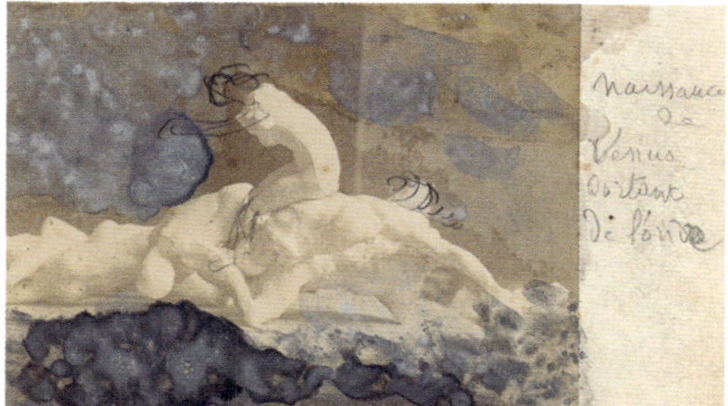

4   Poster for François Willème's photosculpture technique, Paris, 1860, lithograph, 75 × 106 cm, Bibliothèque nationale de France, Département des Estampes et de la photographie, Paris

5   Auguste Rodin, *Naissance de Vénus sortant de l'onde*, before 1889, photograph by an anonymous photographer, reworked by the artist with correction details, 10 × 14 cm, Musée Rodin, Paris

rougher plaster – by means of the noticeable manipulation of the sculptures' surfaces. Furthermore, his wax casts evoke the vigour applied when forming them and the change of the aggregate states that results during casting as well during the elaborate finishing process: fingerprints reflect reshaping, and tiny craters caused by small air bubbles and traces of soot indicate melting processes (see cat. 73). The sculpture in the context of Impressionism and the associated photographic practices reinforce the notion that works of art should be seen as enduring traces of artistic processes.

For sculpture, this meant a reconception of materiality in theory and practice: plasticity, which shows the masses as malleable and especially the surface finish of the sculptures as mutable, was demonstratively emphasised as a sensitive matrix for the impressions of modern life.[14] Since then, the plastic is no longer self-evidently on the side of the subjects and the subject *formation* – hence on that of a creator thought of as godlike and male – but it is also part of the obstinacy of objects and substances. It is precisely here that photographic methods emerged as agents of the fugitive and the malleable. In the context of Impressionist art, it is also the reason why the work of a sculptor like Medardo Rosso, as Wolfgang Kemp described it for the 1890s in general, increasingly shifted to "manipulating in the dark room". Sculptural practice was no longer the sole determining factor, but the "'elasticity' and 'plasticity' of the photographic and printing material".[15] In his famous essay "Impressionism in Photography" of 1890, the American photographer George Davison placed emphasis on the "extra rough surfaces", which he referred to as "the best printing material"; activity in the dark room therefore advanced to become the decisive artistic process.[16] This practice manifests itself in a work by the leading French proponent of pictorialism Robert Demachy, the photograph *Struggle*, printed on handmade paper, with its graphic wipe effects, which were achieved during printing and not on the negative (fig. 3). Owing to the artistic influence in the photo laboratory, the light-sensitive photo emulsion on the carrier material seems like a chalk drawing, and the figures seem to protrude into space – at the same time, the materiality of the photograph published in 1904 is rendered visible. Through the use and the revival of the gum bichromate process, which was patented in 1855 but found little use until the 1890s, for his plastic images, Demachy – similar to Rosso in his handling of wax – relied on processes that until then were considered alien to art or outdated.

Are canvas and marble still used to represent the modern world? Is the young medium of photography superseding the traditional genres of visual art? Such questions were discussed in artistic circles and at academies, and this, ensuing from the metropolis on the Seine, in numerous countries. The following was said in 1852 on the occasion of an artists' excursion to the forest of Fontainebleau by rail, established in 1849: "Today, one leaves Paris with a camera, a tripod and 25 or 30 primed paper negatives in a cardboard box, and nothing else! [...] There are virtually no limitations to what one [...] can photograph: [...] all of the motifs result in wonderful pictures."[17]

The pressure artists were under to be innovative can be concretised on the basis of two phenomena. The adverse reactions – particularly in France – to the wealth of detail in the photographic reproduction of natural phenomena are one example. In 1853, for example, Eugène Delacroix noted in his *Journal:* "The great artist concentrates interest by suppressing useless, repugnant, or stupid details [...]."[18] The aesthetic debate on capturing or neglecting details referred more strongly to the level of perception than to the modes of representation. Or as Charles Baudelaire worded it in his criticism of the Salon of 1846: "[A]rt being only an abstraction and a sacrifice of detail to the whole, the important thing is to concentrate attention particularly on the masses."[19] In the face of the new reproduction technologies, reduction began to predominate in the traditional methods of representation – including in sculpture.

This tendency towards abstraction – this is a further example – was accelerated by the emergence of a hybrid method that combined two different genres: so-called photosculpture. For many artists, the extremely accurate method, developed by François Willème, was a shock and the catalyst for striking new, above all Impressionist, paths.[20] The aim of this research project on the rationalisation of portrait sculpture, which was pursued from 1860 to 1868, was to use a device to coalesce several 360-degree photographs taken with different cameras and subsequently reproduce them semi-mechanically with the aid of a portrait modelled by projections (fig. 4). Two shifts in aesthetic theory and artistic practice can be recorded as the most important result of the debate on realistic representation and the reproduction of details: the concentration on the change of the media and transformation – this also includes work performed in the photo laboratory.

The complex of actions associated with the camera's arrival in sculptural practice becomes particularly apparent in Auguste Rodin's use of photographs, which is exemplary for the oscillation of the semi-mechanical medium between production and reception.[21] And yet different manners of using photography can be identified in the context of Impressionist sculpture: to start with, photographs that were produced in the studio. Rodin marked possible modifications (fig. 5) on these functional photographs – like on the sheet *Naissance de Vénus sortant de l'onde* (*The Birth of Venus*) of 1889. In addition, there are photographs that provide insight into the workshop, capturing the sculptures shortly after their completion, which is indicated by supposedly randomly placed tools or an arranged disorder – especially photographs by Eugène Druet, specifically those taken in 1898 of *Le Baiser* (*The Kiss*) with an embossing hammer on the floor (fig. 6).[22] These prints were also sold and presented in exhibitions of works by Rodin. This is in turn attested to by numerous installation views – for instance, of Rodin's own pavilion at the Place de l'Alma during the 1900 world's fair (figs. pp. 274–275).

The staged images taken by pictorialist photographers that were atmospherically enhanced in the laboratory constitute a further category. In late summer 1908, for example, the Luxembourg-born Edward J. Steichen took an outdoor photograph of the statue *Honoré de Balzac* (*Monument to Balzac*) in front of Rodin's studio in Meudon at four in the morning, because he had an aversion to the appearance of the calciferous plaster sculpture in daylight and instead preferred to take a picture of the figure in soft moonlight (fig. 7).[23] It is characteristic of Rodin's artistic strategy that he chose the pictorialist Steichen, and by doing so gave preference to a specific form of photography, and with the gum bichromate print on rough paper to a method that softened the modernity of the semi-mechanical medium and transported the photograph from its being confined to the moment into a state of timelessness.

Besides for documentary, functional photographs and staged art photography, there is yet another field of application in which focus is placed on the photographic as a transitional phenomenon. The materiality of the print constitutes the basis for the production of photographic phenomena that extend far beyond the atmospheric images of pictorialism. Over the years, it was above all Medardo Rosso who became increasingly interested in these traces of traces as disruptive residue. In his photographic experiments, which were probably performed under the artist's guidance or perhaps even single-handedly by Rosso himself, he was not only interested in documenting finished works; rather, the photos were geared towards making modern aesthetic, mental and visual experiences possible. Beginning in 1902 – Rodin had already been doing this since around 1896 – Rosso presented the results of these photographic experiments in conjunction with his sculptures

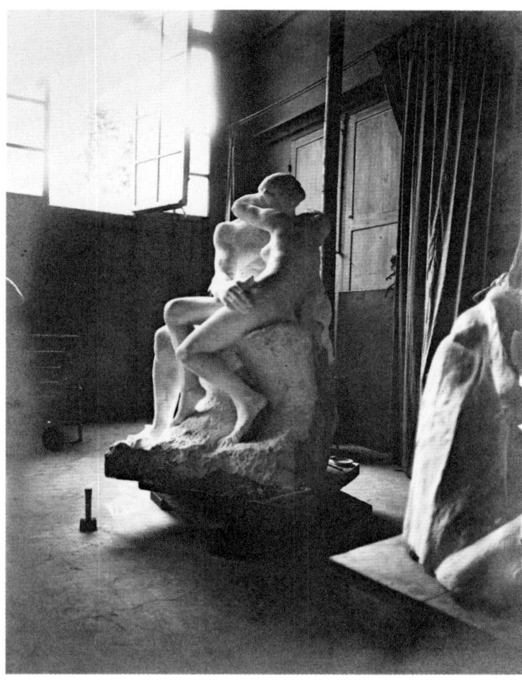

6 Eugène Druet, *Auguste Rodin's "Le Baiser"*, c. 1898, photograph, 39 × 30 cm, Musée Rodin, Paris

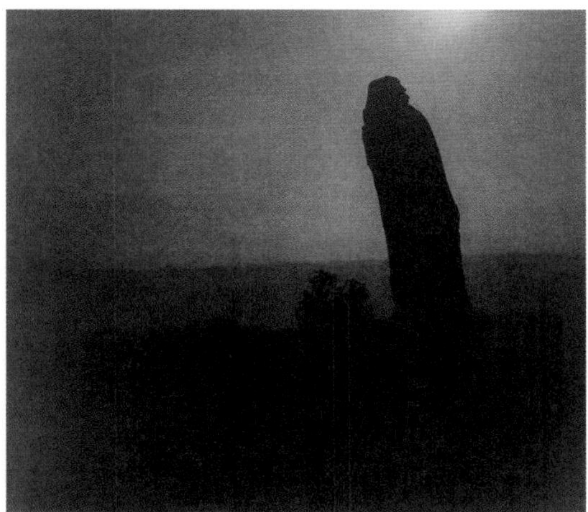

7 Edward J. Steichen, *Auguste Rodin's "Honoré de Balzac": The Silhouette – 4 A.M., Meudon*, 1908, photograph, 38 × 46 cm, The Metropolitan Museum of Art, New York ·

8 Medardo Rosso, *Madame X*,
1896, photograph, c. 1911, approx.
11.3 × 6.8 cm, private collection

9 Medardo Rosso, *Madame X*,
1896, photograph, c. 1900,
10.3 × 4.5 cm, private collection

10 Medardo Rosso, *Madame X*,
1896, photograph, c. 1900,
13.7 × 8.5 cm, private collection

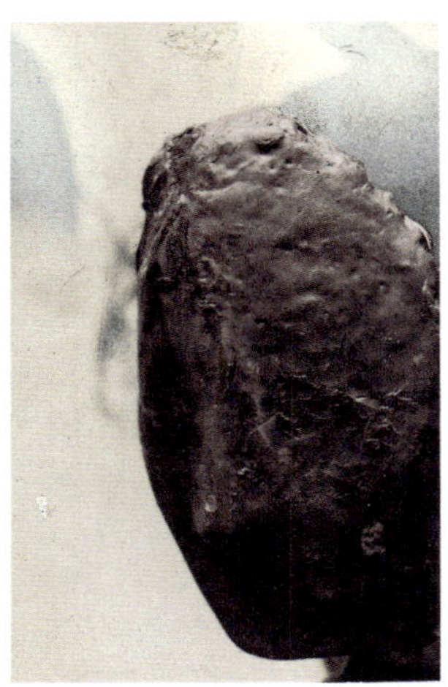

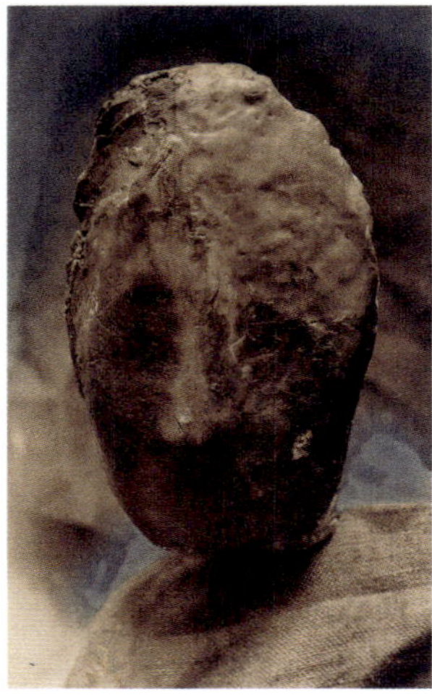

as ensembles. Hence these pictures intertwined the exhibition space with the processual working traces in the studio, thereby drawing on notions of authenticity that closely associated the artistic idea with the hand of the artist performing the work.[24] Beginning in 1902, entire photographic series of Rosso's sculptures were produced that he constantly captured with minimal changes to the camera setting, distance, detail and distribution of light (cat. 55–56). Moreover, each print was elaborately processed in the laboratory: "[…] the photo becomes the object itself."[25] Rosso attempted to bring photographic and sculptural methods closer to one another, as demonstrated, for example, by the photographic variations of *Madame X* (figs. 8–10). By means of pigmentation or deliberate impurifications, he achieved a surface texture on his sculptures, the porosity of which emphasises the materials' mutability.[26] This finds an equivalent in the unusual prints when the materiality of the photograph, the opacity of the paper, the particles and the chemical emulsions of the prints emerge as real materialities and concrete actors.[27] Beyond the impression and with the aid of his photographs, Rosso attempted to reveal and fix something with their materiality produced by the residual particles that the philosopher Walter Benjamin would refer to as the "optical unconscious" of the photographic several decades later.[28] A detailed view of *Impressione d'omnibus* reproduced as a large-format postcard heightens this effect. The granules and crystals on the photo paper highlighted by the print, which enable the production of the image in the first place, now appear as an unstable textural effect (fig. 11). They generate the picture and dissolve it at the same time.

Rosso's photographic variations are neither the expression of a cult of the original, nor do they indicate the pursuit of reproducing what is unique. Rather, it is a matter of serial imagery – which in turn corresponds with the large number of sculptures and their different versions. Rosso toned the prints in various colours as supplements to and extensions of his cast versions, or processed the surface additionally with chemicals, which is why corrosion can be detected on some prints – quasi photographic trace elements of residue.[29] As a sculptor, Rosso generally staged processes of blurring and dissolution and highlighted the processual character of the sculptures, which in this way merged with their surroundings. I would like to refer to what is made visible and set in motion in such works with their intermedia processes of the photographic as the "photogenesis of art".[30] This becoming-a-photograph illustrates the difficulties and possibilities of art under changed media-related conditions – what is interesting is that in the context of Impressionism, the individual processes were sometimes even applied post-medially, thus no longer media-specifically. The broken patterns and structures of the photograph as well as the sculptures point – this is illustrated by the detailed view of *Impressione d'omnibus* – to a world that is subject to permanent change, that does not fix but rather whose changes are to traced. These photosculptures simultaneously set a fluid perception in motion. A *"bloc of sensations, that is to say, a compound of percepts and affects"* developed through the combination of photographic and traditional methods that simultaneously perfected and dissolved the form(s) of the modern era.[31] In fact, not only at the macrolevel of perception in the accelerated metropolises of industrial societies, but also via what Gilles Deleuze – in his book on the "movement-image" – describes as "molecular perception" on the microlevel of the substances and particles: "a more than human perception, a perception not tailored to solids" is revealed in the photographs, "a more delicate and vaster perception, a molecular perception" so to speak.[32] What can be observed on photo sheets by Medardo Rosso is the communication between the substances themselves, by means of which, according to Michel Foucault, art becomes a "thoroughfare, an infinite transition" under photographic conditions.[33] This resulted in a mixture of relations that alternated back and forth between

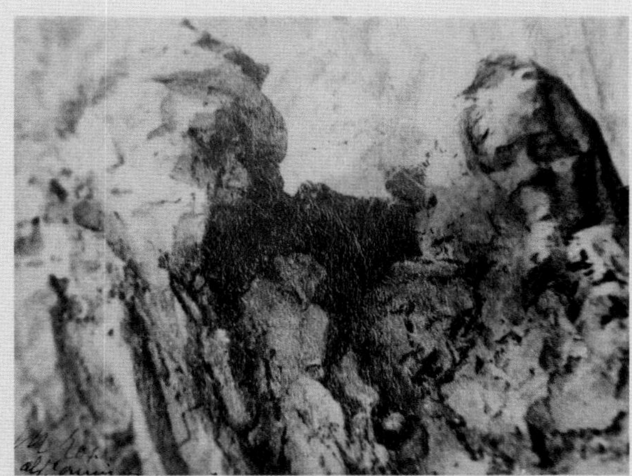

11 Medardo Rosso, *Impressione d'omnibus*, c. 1883/1884,
photo postcard, 21 × 26 cm, private collection, Busto Arsizio

studio and production as well as exhibition space and reception. At the same time, the category of materiality evolved out of a combination of science, technology, mass culture and art; and it was possible – this is the irritating thing about this restructuring – for the individual elements to change places or blend. Out of this arose art that traced the historical development of media-dependent changes in perception and inscribed this artistic research in the production process of one's own work. Or put differently: there is something in the photographic fixation of things in the context of Impressionism, including works of art, that is not resolved in the representation.

1 "Siamo scherzi di un tutto d'ogni genere liquido, luce colore tutto quanto vuoi." Letter from Medardo Rosso to Romolo Monti from around 1920; Italian original quoted in: exh. cat. Winterthur/Duisburg 2003, p. 74.
2 Simmel [1907] quoted in: Park and Burgess (eds) 1932, pp. 357–361, esp. p. 361. https://www.gutenberg.org/files/28496/28496-h/28496-h.htm#FNanchor_138_138 (accessed 14 November 2019).
3 Asendorf 1993, p. 92.
4 Crary 1990, p. 16.
5 Exh. cat. Lugano 1989; Rosso 1994.
6 Uexküll 1909.
7 Simmel [1903], "The Metropolis and Mental Life", quoted in: Wolff (trans. and ed.) 1950, pp. 409–424, esp. p. 410.
8 Cugini 2006.
9 Rübel 2005; Hecker 2017.
10 Müller 1996.
11 Rübel 2012.
12 Rübel 2014.
13 Bezzola 2010.
14 Rübel 2016.
15 Kemp 1980, p. 22.
16 Davison [1890], "Impressionism in Photography", quoted in: Hastings (ed.), *The Photographic Quarterly* (vol. 2 1891), pp. 171–173, esp. p. 173. https://archive.org/stream/photographicquar02unse/photographicquar02unse_djvu.txt (accessed 14 November 2019).
17 Noël Marie Paymal Lerebours, quoted in: Pohlmann 1996, p. 406.
18 Delacroix, quoted in: Badt 1965, p. 296.
19 Baudelaire [1846] 1972, esp. p. 56.
20 Gall 1997.
21 Exh. cat. Paris 2007; Schallenberg 2009.
22 Exh. cat. Berlin 2005.
23 Exh. cat. New York/Zurich 2010a, p. 86. On the occasion of these nocturnal photographs, Alflred Stieglitz devoted an issue of *Camera Work: A Photographic Quarterly* to Rodin (nos. 34/35 [April–July], 1911).
24 For more details on this in general, see Mongi-Vollmer 2004.
25 Schmedding 1997, p. 115.
26 Bacci 2006; Taylor 2019.
27 Kunze 2019.
28 Benjamin [1931] 2009, pp. 172–192, esp. p. 176.
29 For more details on this in general, see Dubois 1998, pp. 103 ff.
30 Rübel 2014; the author is currently working on a book with the working title of *Fotogenische Kunst* (Photogenic Art).
31 Deleuze and Guattari, *What Is Philosophy?*, Tomlinson and Burchell (trans.) 1994, p. 164 (italics in the original).
32 Deleuze, *Cinema*, vol. 1, Tomlinson and Habberjam (trans.) 1989, p. 80.
33 Foucault, quoted in: Shapiro 2014, pp. 327–333, esp. pp. 332–333.

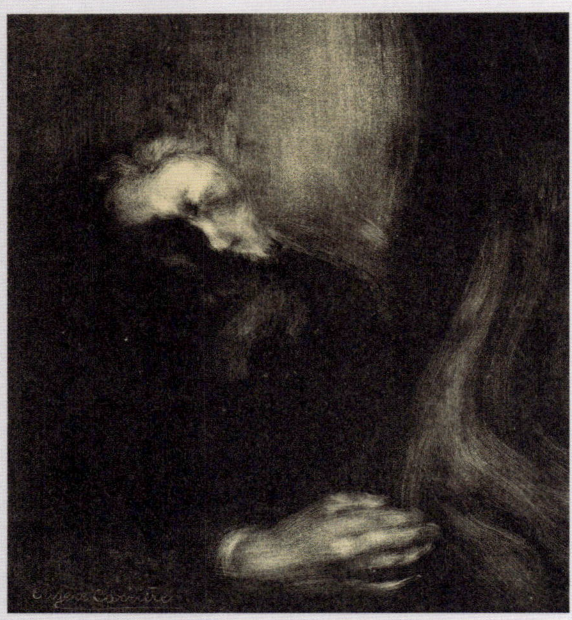

1 Eugène Carrière, *Rodin Sculptant* (detail), 1900 (cat. 94)

Astrid Reuter

Cross-media[1]

Graphic reproductions and sculpture in dialogue

In 1902, the art critic Camille Mauclair described the relationship between the artists Eugène Carrière and Auguste Rodin as two sides of the same artistic dream – "le Janus d'un même rêve" – a relationship that he had vividly characterised only a few lines earlier no less graphically with the words "Rodin paints in marble, and Carrière sculpts with shadow" (fig. 1).[2] This reference to the reciprocal kinship of their work is a common theme in contemporary assessments. In light of works by Carrière, the museum man Hugo von Tschudi, for instance, felt reminded of Rodin's marbles, and the philosophical historian Gabriel Séailles pointed out that Carrière's dimensional equilibrium corresponded with the sculptor's approach.[3] The named congruities between Rodin and Carrière apply to concrete subjects, questions of style and aesthetic concepts. Repeated reference has been made to the soft transitions between the forms (*sfumato*), the lightness and the resulting transparency of the material, the unfinished (*non-finito*) quality of the works, and their interiority.[4] However, it was Camille Mauclair who remarked: "They add an exceptional physical quality to modern art; they make painting and statuary into arts of psychological expression [...]."[5]

The artistic proximity of Eugène Carrière and Auguste Rodin manifests itself in an exceptional manner in a poster design for Rodin's presentation in the Pavillon de l'Alma (cat. 94) in Paris[6] that shows him working on a sculpture. The object only gradually appears to take shape under his hands, so that the process of composition becomes a kind of "act of creation". This visualisation of the genesis of the work is in keeping with Rodin's artistic understanding, who made the roughly worked, raw marble visible alongside carefully smoothened areas, declaring the creator's hand itself to be the motif. Carrière's lithography is akin to a translation of the creative sculptural process into a printmaking technique. He worked his motif out of the mysterious darkness of his ink-covered lithographic stone by means of wiping, scratching and grinding, causing the technique he used to visualise the transition from the unworked area to the image and thus from the abstract to the representational. As the Berlin-based art historian Curt Glaser formulated, his print acquired a sculptural quality, as it were, in the process: "For him [Carrière], the painting was painted sculpture, a sculpture fashioned in the softest material, like air itself, so to speak, which concentrates in varying densities. The immateriality of the lithographic print was the right medium for this art."[7]

The attempt to evoke sculptural effects using the creative means of planar art as described by Glaser finds a seemingly paradoxical equivalent in what

"Rodin paints in marble, and Carrière sculpts with shadow."

Camille Mauclair, 1901

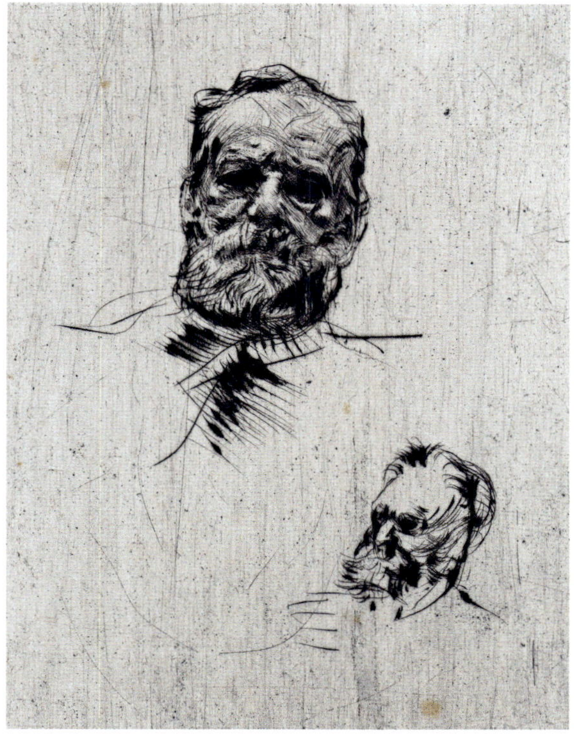

2 Auguste Rodin, *Victor Hugo*, 1885, drypoint, second state, 28.6 × 21.6 cm, The Metropolitan Museum of Art, New York, Rogers Fund, 1916

Medardo Rosso formulates as the desire for an immaterial effect of sculptural works. The native Italian, who was in close contact with Rodin at times and whose oeuvre numerous critics related to Carrière's, strove for a concentration of impressions that involved "making one forget" the subject matter. He sought liberation from the constraints of the boundaries between the genres: "Nothing is material in space. In this sense, art is indivisible. There is no painting at one end and sculpture at the other. Regardless of in what way, it is first and foremost imperative to strive to create an artwork that, through the life and the humanity that speak out of it, makes the viewer aware of all that would awaken the sublime play of almighty and powerful nature in him."[8]

The following considerations on the dialogue between sculpture and graphic reproductions are guided by this premise of cross-media thought. The genres are connected by what is traditionally a multistage production process in which the transfer between different materials (from plate to paper, from wax or plaster to bronze), the participation of various players, and the prospect of reproduction are of key importance. In the second half of the nineteenth century, both areas – sculpture as the supposed inanimate representation of nature and the print as the apparently less creative medium of reproduction – came under growing criticism. The departure from tradition and a move towards experimentation proved to be crucial stimuli in the search for new, modern forms of expression. Creative potential was expanded, visual habits were called into question, and traditional notions of execution and completion were abandoned in the unconventional handling of materials, tools and techniques. In the following, animation and individualisation shall be looked at as cross-genre categories of artistic creation. The basis for these considerations is the examination of the individual working steps involved in the evolution of a graphic reproduction – from handling the plate to the application of ink and printing.

Animation and individualisation

The contemporary discussion concerning a renewal of sculpture and graphic reproductions was geared towards animation, whose point of departure was the differentiated handling of the work's surfaces. Artists such as Medardo Rosso or Auguste Rodin frequently worked with animated forms, deliberately incorporated light and shadow in the composition, and left visible traces of the production process (see cat. 74, 90–91, 102). The critic Roger Marx found descriptive wording for the parallels between sculpture and graphic art when, in view of Rodin's drypoint etchings, he emphasises that he probed ("fouiller") and animated ("animer") clay as well as copper; he wielded the needle like a chisel and worked the copper plate in the same vigorous way as Carrara marble. The vitality ("accent de vie") and the veracity of the relief ("vérité du relief") created a contrast as well as a depth of the lines, and the refraction of light on the printed lines arising on the paper correspond with light reflections on marble. For Marx, Rodin's drypoint etchings became the mirror of his sculptural works and the sculptor himself the epitome of a "sculpteur-graveur" (fig. 2).[9]

Marx's observations, which were geared towards a physiognomy of the line, had numerous predecessors. As early as 1862, Charles Baudelaire spoke of the most intimate individuality ("individualité la plus intime") of the etching among the plastic arts ("l'art plastique") as most likely suitable for conveying the impression of spontaneity.[10] In his guide to the art of etching published in 1866, Maxime Lalanne also praised the unconstrained and vibrant expression of the etching needle, which was comparable to a spontaneously written letter. According to Lalanne, the etched lines achieve the highest degree of expressivity and even capture the transience of the light,[11] whereby their vibration and their vitality ("la chaleur pénétrante de

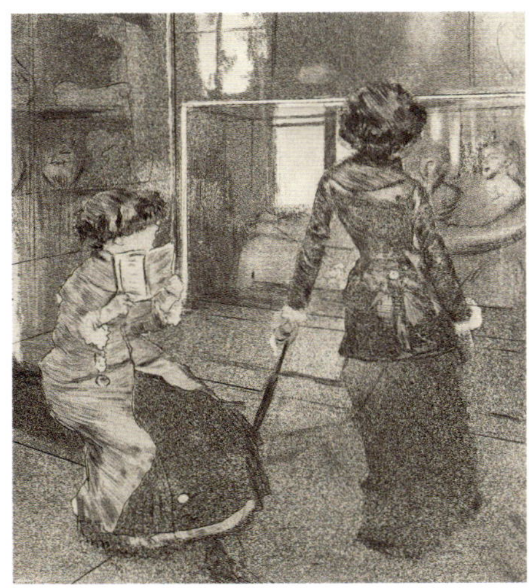

3 Edgar Degas, *Mary Cassatt at the Louvre: The Etruscan Gallery,* 1879–1880, soft-ground etching, drypoint, aquatint and etching, seventh state, 43.2 × 30.5 cm, The Metropolitan Museum of Art, New York, Rogers Fund, 1919

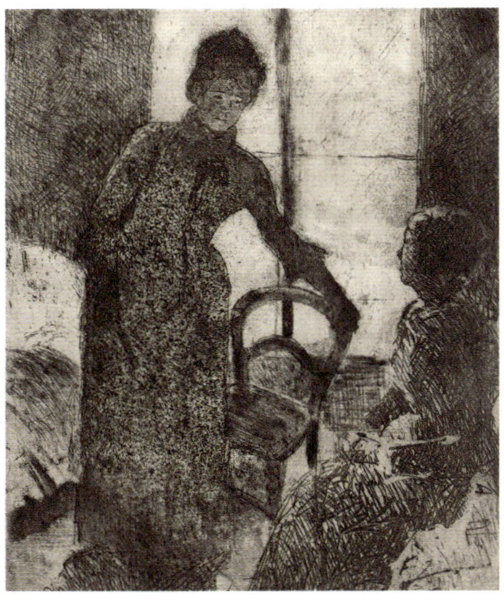

4 Mary Cassatt, *The Visitor,* c. 1881, soft-ground etching, aquatint, etching, drypoint and fabric texture, third state, 52.1 × 40 cm, The Metropolitan Museum of Art, New York, Rogers Fund, 1920 (cat. 133)

la vie") was owed to the acid.[12] Philippe Burty, the co-founder of the Société des peintres-graveurs français and an influential critic for the *Gazette des Beaux-Arts,* describes the etching process as a veritable erosion of the metal through the acid. The ink that enters the etched grooves of varying depth produced a relief in the print, the linear ridges of which refract light in various different ways. In microscopic observations of this kind, so to speak, the eye is directed towards the plastic formation of the printed lines, which turn them – similar to the restless surfaces of sculptures by Rodin or Rosso – into the carriers of light and shadow effects.[13]

Alongside the line, however, the ink was only one aspect of a wide palette of creative possibilities comprising the use of new tools and materials: combining and experimenting with different techniques such as soft-ground etching, the aquatint or the sugar lift; the manipulation of the etching process as well as the individual inking and printing of the plates and that involve chance in the process.[14] Edgar Degas was one of the artists for whom the unrestricted approach to various techniques became a challenging source of inspiration. A letter from a friend of his, the painter, graphic artist and author Marcellin Desboutin, gives an indication of the passion with which Degas explored printing: "Degas […] is no longer a friend, a man, an artist! At the moment, all he is a zinc or copper plate, blackened with printing ink, and this plate and this man are rolled out by his printing press, into whose wheelwork he has completely disappeared!"[15] Besides the conventional copper and zinc plates, Degas occasionally used daguerreotype plates. He experimented with the so-called "crayon électrique", the carbon rod of an arc lamp, which he used as a dry point, and worked with a grinding pencil, the "crayon à l'émeri", which produces softer lines.[16] In addition, he employed printing ink with different consistencies and experimented with the liquid aquatint technique and soft ground. As is the case for the monotype, it could be worked directly into the surface with tools or with the fingers.

Degas's etching *Mary Cassatt at the Louvre* (fig. 3), which he created for *Le Jour et la Nuit,* a journal that was planned for 1879/80 but ultimately failed, exemplifies his approach. It features his artist friend Cassatt, who maintained close contact with Degas who in turn owned various prints by her (fig. 4; cat.132–133, 135–136).[17] While the woman accompanying her, presumably her sister Lydia, holds a book in her hand, Mary supports herself on an umbrella and is immersed in contemplating an Etruscan sarcophagus. With the aid of etched lines and drypoint, of soft-ground etching as well as aquatint that varied in terms of granulation, density and tonality, Degas created a wealth of textures whose impressions range from soft to smooth, from frizzy to raw.[18] The overlapping of several levels and flecks of light obscures the spatial situation, whereby it remains open whether it is a case of real window openings, a reflection on the wall or of reflections in the display case glass. The light boundary lines of the vitrine encasing the Etruscan clay figures constitute a surprising marking. It could have served as a model for the presentation of his sculpture *Little Dancer Aged Fourteen.*[19] Moreover, it resembles the "gabbie" in which Medardo Rosso displayed his works. These vitrine-like cages served the sculptor, who precisely specified lighting and viewing angle, as a frame for the purpose of transferring his sculptures into two-dimensionality. He strove for unifying perception ("unité"), which he connected with light and air and which broke away from concentrating on the material and hence from touching or circling the works.[20] With this striving after an explicitly painterly effect of his sculptural works, Rosso is in keeping with the effort that becomes apparent in the luminous surface structures of the contemporary print.

For Degas and his contemporaries, the work process did not end with the first version. The material difference between printing plate and proof permitted the further processing of the motif in multiple stages, which was readily made use

5 Mary Cassatt, *In the Opera Box* (detail), c. 1880, soft-ground etching, aquatint and etching, third state, 36 × 26.5 cm, Museum of Fine Arts, Boston, Gift of Henri M. Petiet, confirmed by his estate

6 Mary Cassatt, *In the Opera Box* (detail), c. 1880, soft-ground etching, aquatint and etching, seventh state, 29.6 × 21.5 cm, Museum of Fine Arts, Boston, Gift of Henri M. Petiet, confirmed by his estate

7 Edgar Degas, *Self-Portrait* (detail), 1857, etching and drypoint, third state, 34.9 × 25.7 cm, The Metropolitan Museum of Art, New York, H.O. Havemeyer Collection, Bequest of Mrs. H.O. Havemeyer, 1929

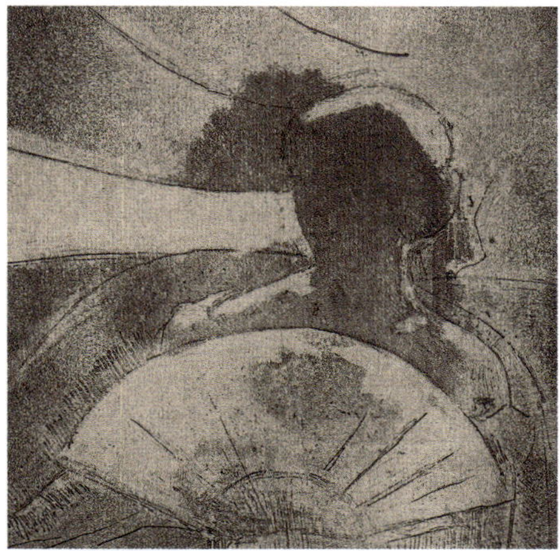

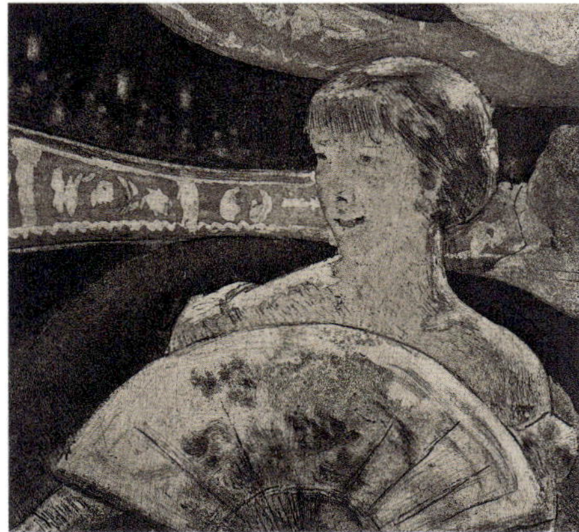

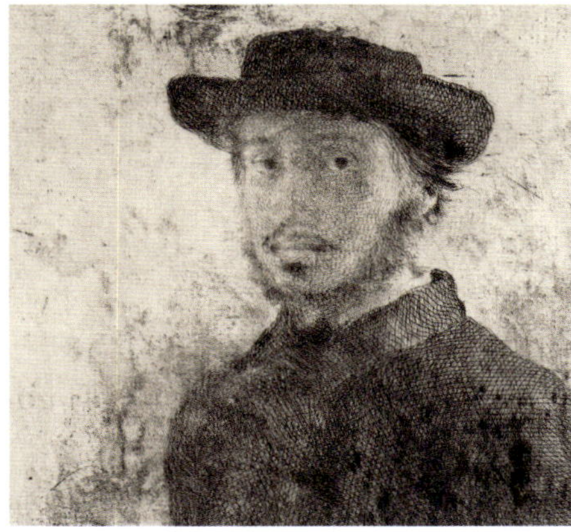

of. Degas varied his print *Mary Cassatt at the Louvre* across nine stages and used a section of the composition for another version, of which 20 different processing stages are known.[21] The diverse possibilities offered by the printing method also appealed to Cassatt. In the etching that she likewise designed for the journal *Le Jour et la Nuit,* Cassatt incorporated the eponymous theme of light and reversed the lighting situation in the course of the working process (figs. 5, 6). Whilst the lady with the fan is hardly discernible against the light in the first stage, the later versions suggest a direct source of light, which results in a differentiation of the figure as well as the festively lit hall visible behind her. The artist presented the first and the last stage of the etching at the fifth Impressionist exhibition in 1880, and by doing so followed Félix Bracquemond, who six years prior to that had also shown his portrait of Erasmus of Rotterdam after Hans Holbein the Younger in the first and last stage.[22] Whereas the hierarchy from beginning to completion in the depiction by Bracquemond, which he brought to perfection successively in ten stages, is unmistakable, in the case of Cassatt's radical transformation it is in no way a matter of a linear development of the motif, but of independent variations on the theme. The working proofs, which for a long time primarily served the purpose of controlling and correcting, therefore became works in their own right that could be presented alongside one another.[23] Her juxtaposition finds parallels in the presentation of sculptural works in multiple versions using differing materials.[24]

Modifications of a motif often did not limit themselves to the further processing of the printing plate itself. In addition to the use of different paper that varied in terms of colour, thickness and grammage, the specific application of ink and wiping, it played a special role as a means of manipulating the surface.[25] Both substantially contributed to making unique pieces out of the prints created with the aid of a printing method. Rembrandt – whose etchings are regarded as exemplary for the creation of light-and-dark effects, expression and atmosphere as well as for the use of different technical methods – already used the surface tone as a creative element for his etchings.[26] Emulating him, Degas also drew on the varying application of ink to produce a painterly effect, as his self-portrait created under the guidance of the engraver Joseph Tournay shows in an exemplary way (fig. 7).[27] Among the professional printers at the close of the nineteenth century, it was in particular Auguste Delâtre who was known for regulating the luminosity of the depictions by means of partially wiping the plate. The results of this *retroussage* were aptly called "épreuves monotypées".[28]

The increasing individualisation of prints eventually led to the demand for the independent implementation of the overall artistic process. Rembrandt, in whose estate two printing presses are listed, was regarded as the crucial reference for the artist undertaking the printing himself.[29] Unlike earlier publications on producing prints, guides such as the one published in 1866 by Maxime Lalanne now also provided information about the various working steps involved with inking and printing.[30] In addition, handy presses were available – for example, by the publisher Alfred Cadert.[31] They made for spatial independence from printing workshops and afforded artists greater autonomy in the production of prints. As early as at the beginning of the 1870s, Camille Pissarro belonged to the small circle of artists who printed on Dr Gachet's two presses in a private framework (fig. 8).[32] For his experiments with ink, he later repeatedly called on the support of his friend Degas, who owned his own press and furnished the prints with the handwritten addendum "imp. par E. Degas" (fig. 9).[33]

The high degree of independence in executing works not only enhanced the flexibility of artistic work; it was the condition for a creative process that incorporated experiment and chance and gave priority to the uniqueness of each individual print ("belle épreuve") over reproduction.[34] Medardo Rosso was

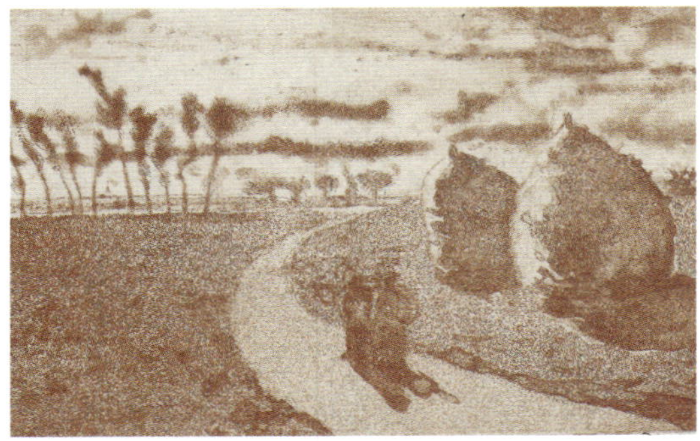

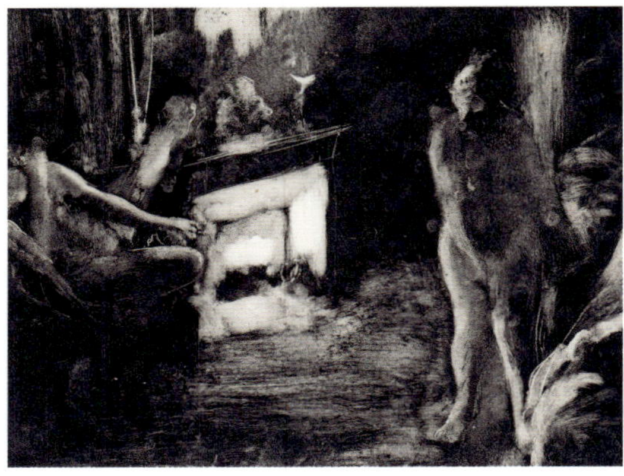

8   Camille Pissarro, *Twilight with Haystacks*, 1879,
aquatint with etching, third state, 12.7 × 20.3 cm, The Art
Institute of Chicago, Clarence Buckingham Collection

9   Edgar Degas, *The Fireside*, c. 1876/77, monotype,
50.2 × 64.8 cm, The Metropolitan Museum of Art,
New York, Harris Brisbane Dick Fund, The Elisha
Whittelsey Collection, The Elisha Whittelsey Fund,
and C. Douglas Dillon Gift, 1968

also convinced that the artist himself was the only one in a position to realise his own work.[35] He mastered the complex, physically demanding bronze method and also produced the wax cast,[36] whereby he used a markedly painterly material in the process that was considered particularly suited to the reproduction of the fluid effects of modern life.[37] Single-handed implementation permitted Rosso to modify the individual specimens during the work process. Like Rodin, he furthermore incorporated the casting seams or the remaining sprues into his works as artistic elements. Hence in prints as well as in sculpture, a new work aesthetic that renders the creative process visible took the place of perfection. In the area of graphic reproductions, the monotype marked both the climax and the endpoint of this development.

The special case of the monotype

It seems to be only a small step from the individual inking and wiping of the printing plate to the monotype, which completely dispenses with etched features. It is connected to the traditional printing method through the use of a printing plate, printing ink and a printing press, even though ordinarily just a single print is produced.[38] As in lithography, the depiction can either be painted or drawn directly on the plate or worked out of the surface that has been entirely covered with ink. At the same time, the creative process and the printing include chance as a deliberate means of composition.[39]

In technical terms, the monotype cannot be clearly defined. It shifts between print, drawing and painting. Edgar Degas described the works as "drawings executed and printed with fatty ink ("dessins faits à l'encre grasse et imprimés").[40] Suggestions for carrying it out can apparently be credited to his exchange with Ludovic-Napoléon Lepic, who in 1876 had explained the use of different tools, from a cloth to the finger, for the application and braying of the ink.[41] Degas's large-format monotype *The Fireside* provides a vivid example of the atmospheric effect that can be produced by working the motif out of the inked plate in this way (fig. 9). Only few places are completely free of ink; the lucent lines were partially scratched out with a pointed, thin tool, resulting in the impression of hard materials. The dissimilarly dense, grey areas exhibit varying surface structures, which, among other things, suggest extensive wiping or more detailed dabbing. The scene largely descends into mysterious darkness. The details of the bodies remain vague, and even the objects lined up on the mantelpiece can barely be identified. Degas suggests rather than describes. The monotype seems particularly suited for this mysterious play of light and conveys a sensuous experience of the various textures. At the same time, not only did the tools that were used leave marks on the plate, but the artist's hand also remains visible in the executed work.

For Degas, whose eyesight declined very early on, the tactile seems to have become increasingly important for his artistic work.[42] Since the 1860s, small-format sculptures fashioned out of wax, clay or plastic modelling paste constituted essential elements of his working process and with whose help he sought to achieve an accuracy that reflected a "sense of life".[43] The works themselves maintain traces of their processing that become indications of the pace as well as the intensity of the work, and in which faults or changes are also visible.[44] The composition has now inseparably inscribed itself into the executed sculpture or plastic object and continues to be readable not only in Degas's waxes, but also in Rodin's, Paolo Troubetzkoy's and Rembrandt Bugatti's bronzes in the form of thumb, modelling tool or knife. Degas, who was rather daunted by the permanence of the bronze, was interested in the open aspect of artistic work, which found a wealth of nourishment in the experimental handling of techniques and materials, of motifs and forms. At the same time, drawings printed with fatty ink presented him with an inspiring scope of action. The genres converged here unlike in almost any other technique; the experiment became the driving force in the search for new forms of design and expression. Contrary to the traditional work aesthetic, which aimed for perfection, attention was directed toward the origination process itself, in which the artist remained present as the "creator" of his work. In the use of viscous ink and to some extent in the obvious printing by hand, the haptic quality of the forming experiences a distinct markedness, approximating the plastic art of the sculptor. At the same time, the fingerprint, which is occasionally visible on prints and sculptures (figs. 10), is assigned particular importance. It is not only one of numerous traces of the working process, as frequently exhibited by the sculptures and prints of the time. As the epitome of personalisation, it is commensurate with a signature.

10   Edgar Degas, *Woman getting into Her Bed* (detail), 1880–1885 (cat. 36)

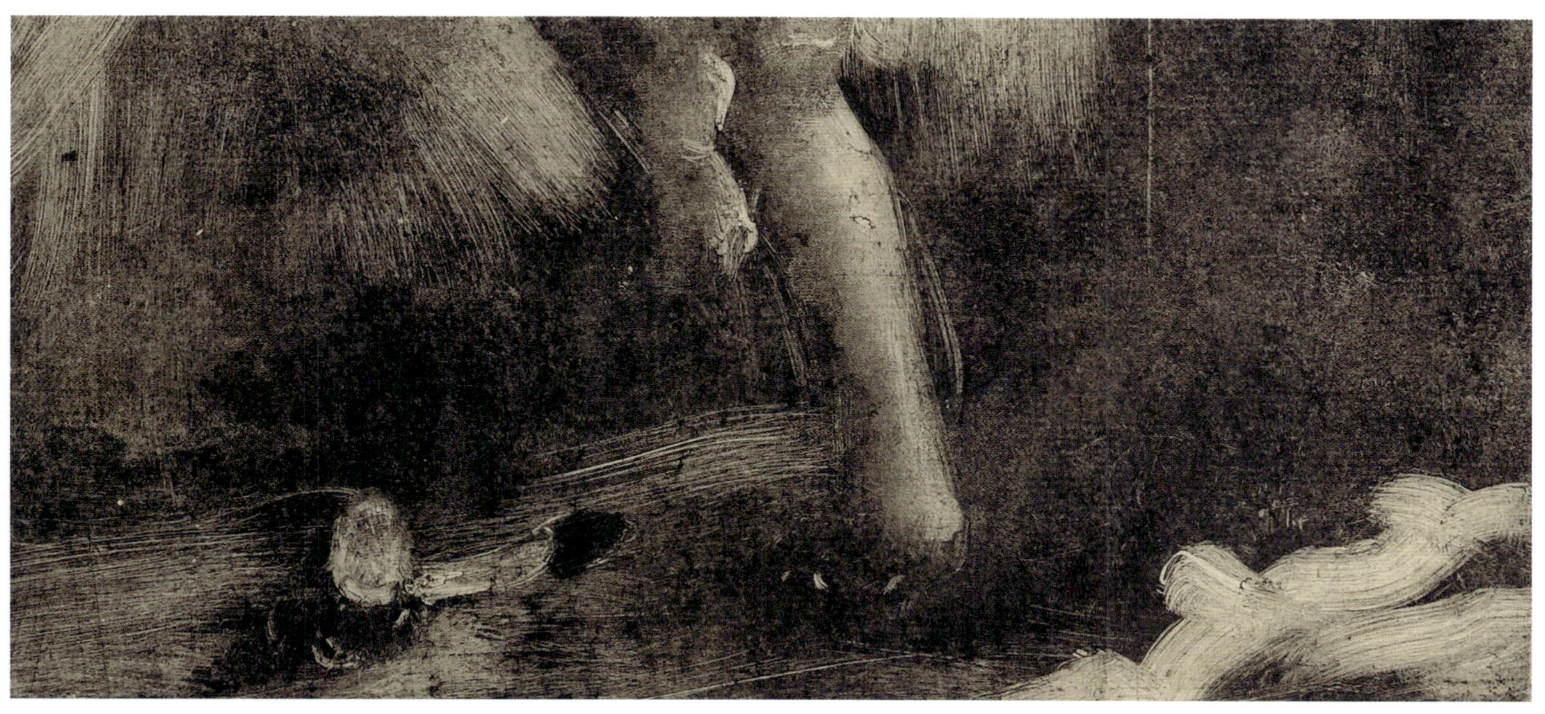

1 Jane R. Becker uses the term "cross-media kinship" to refer to the relationship between Rodin and Carrière in her 11 December 2017 blog on the Metropolitan Museum of Art home page; https://digi.ub.uni-heidelberg.de/diglit/art_decoratif1902/0086/image (accessed 10 October 2019).

2 "Rodin peint en marbre et Carrière sculpte en ombre [...]. Carrière et Rodin sont le Janus d'un même rêve." Mauclair 1902, p. 70.

3 See exh. cat. Bremen/Neuss 2006, pp. 47, 50.

4 On the similarities in works by Rodin and Carrière, see exh. cat. Tokyo/Paris 2006 and, extended by Rosso, Becker 1998. Jane R. Becker's seminal work describes the convergence of painting and sculpture in the oeuvres of the three artists, whereby she places emphasis on their common interest in light and shadow, colour and colour values, as well as movement.

5 "Ils mettent dans l'art moderne une qualité psychique exceptionnelle, ils font de la peinture et de la statuaire des arts d'expression psychologique [...]." Mauclair 1901; quoted in: exh. cat. Bremen/Neuss 2006, p. 50.

6 A variation of the motif was used as a catalogue cover; see exh. cat. Tokyo/Paris 2006, pp. 22–23, fig. 7, on the poster: p. 100, no. 19. The personal esteem of the two artists occasionally assumed concrete form in their exchange of works; Oya/Héran 2006, p. 17.

7 Glaser 1922, p. 378; see exh. cat. Bremen/Neuss 2006, pp. 69–70.

8 "Rien n'est materiel dans l'espace. / Ainsi conçu, l'art est indivisible. Il n'y a pas d'un côté la peinture, de l'autre la sculpture. Ce qu'il faut avant tout rechercher, c'est, par n'importe quels procécés, réaliser une œuvre qui, par la vie et l'humanité qui s'en dégagent, communique au spectateur tout ce qu'évoquerait en lui le spectacle grandiose de la puissance et saine nature." Claris 1902 (French), p. 55.

9 Roger Marx sees drypoint etchings as an expression of the artist's struggle with the material ("lutte de l'artiste avec la matière"); Marx 1902, esp. p. 207; see also Marx 1891, p. 260. On Rodin's drypoint etchings, see also Vilain 2008. In an essay, his son, Claude Roger-Marx, refers to the minor activity of sculptors in the area of graphic reproductions; Roger-Marx 1929, p. 155.

10 Charles Baudelaire, "L'eau-forte est à la mode", *Revue anecdotique* (April 1862), pp. 170–171, quoted in: McQueen, 2003, p. 174.

11 Lalanne 1866, p. 11. The etching becomes the reflection of the individual figure in art; see also Burty 1874, p. 13. In 1878, Philippe Burty speaks of the painter [-etcher] having enhanced the technique by the visibility of the "rapidité de leurs sensations, l'intimité de leurs rêves, l'émotion de leur pensée"; Burty 1878, pp. 10–11.

12 Lalanne 1866, p. 8. Lalanne supplies an in-depth description of all phases of the print and gives detailed advice for the handling of materials.

13 For Philippe Burty, it is also a matter of the distinction between etching and lithography. Burty 1874, p. 6.

14 On innovations in the area of graphic reproductions, see esp. Lees 2018; Sueur-Hermel 2010. Contemporaries repeatedly pointed out the intricacies of etching; Lalanne 1866, p. 9; Burty 1874, p. 6.

15 "Degas [...] n'est-ce plus un ami, n'est-ce plus un homme, n'est-ce plus un artiste? C'est une plaque de zinc ou de cuivre noircis à l'encre d'imprimer et cette plaque et cette homme sont laminés par sa presse dans l'engrenage de laquelle il a disparu tout entier!" Letter from Marcellin Desboutin to Léontine de Nittis, 17 July 1876.

16 On tools and methods, see the seminal essay Lees 2018, esp. pp. 28–56, here and in the following: pp. 36, 48–49; on Degas, see also Berger 2014, pp. 117–123.

17 Among other things, Degas owned all 13 prints of her large-format etching *The Visitor*, c. 1881; two copies from his estate are now at the Metropolitan Museum of Art, New York, Rogers Fund, 1920, inv. no. 20.1.3, and Rogers Fund, 1919, inv. no. 19.42.1; see Shapiro 1997, p. 240.

18 Christian Berger refers to the open areas of Degas's works and the correspondence between the presence of the support and the represented body; Berger 2018, esp. p. 100.

19 Theodore Reff speculates over whether this very same simple and yet elegant display case might have resembled that in which Degas presented his *Little Dancer Aged Fourteen*; Reff 1976, p. 242.

20 Medardo Rosso, "Konzeption – Grenze – Unendlichkeit", in exh. cat. Frankfurt 1984, pp. 61–66; see Lammert 2007. In view of his own portrait done by Rodin, George Bernard Shaw noted the luminosity of the stone. He speaks of the "curious glowing and flowing" of the marble, which prevented touching it; see Becker 1998, p. 64.

21 See Lees 2018, p. 39.

22 Ibid. 2018, pp. 15–16 with figs. 7–9, p. 40.

23 Degas and Cassatt were not the only ones to present their prints in several stages in 1880. Pissarro highlighted the cohesiveness of the four different stages of his *View of Forest* by presenting them in a violet frame; ibid., p. 18; see also Berger 2014, p. 93–97.

24 See the essay by Fabienne Ruppen in the present catalogue, pp. 24–34, here p. 28.

25 On the use of different kinds of paper and their effect, see, among others, Burty 1875, p. 10.

26 For details on the reception of Rembrandt, see McQueen 2003, esp. pp. 217–233.

27 On Degas and Rembrandt, see Reynaerts/Versluis-Van Dongen 2011.

28 Degas and Pissarro, however, rejected Delâtre's technique as too "saucy", even though they worked with wiping effects themselves; see Sueur-Hermel 2010, p. 26.

29 McQueen 2003, p. 225.

30 Parry Jannis 1980, p. 12.

31 Burty 1875, p. 7.

32 Pissarro did not possess his own press for a long time and had some of his prints produced in Auguste Delâtre's workshop in Paris; see Sueur-Hermel 2010, pp. 22, 25.

33 Prints in different ink are found, among other places, at the Museum of Fine Arts, Boston, and at The Art Institute of Chicago; see Lees 2018, figs. 57, 58.

34 Philippe Burty comments on the printing process in detail in his text on the "Belle épreuve"; Burty 1875. In 1875, the graphic artist Henri Guérard, who was extremely versed in the processing of the plates and in printing, also spoke out in favour of taking over the entire process as a condition for the "belle épreuve"; see Sueur-Hermel 2010, p. 25.

35 See exh. cat. Frankfurt 1984, p. 53.

36 On Rosso as a caster here and in the following, see Bushart 2016.

37 This is how Joris Karl Huysmans words it; see Becker 1998, p. 59. On the use of wax, see the essay by Alexander Eiling in the present catalogue, pp. 46–57, here p. 48.

38 Degas, who frequently went over his monotypes with pastel, often printed the plate multiple times, hence creating variations of one master; see Berger 2014, pp. 106–112; Munro 2017, p. 72.

39 On the playful aspect and on change in the monotype, see. Beyer 2014, pp. 143–158, 262–286.

40 Edgar Degas, quoted in: Berger 2014, p. 114.

41 Besides that of Degas, Lepic's signature is found on the monotype *The Ballet Master*, c. 1874, National Gallery of Art, Washington D.C., Rosenwald Collection, inv. no. 1964.8.1782. In *Comme je devins graveur à l'eau-forte*, in 1876 Lepic describes the technique of the "eau-forte mobile", in which the etched motifs are varied through the individual inking and processing of the plate; Lepic 1876. On Lepic, see, among others, Dinoia 2002.

42 Jane Munro establishes a connection to the monotypes; Munro 2017, p. 76.

43 For more detail on Degas's plastic works, see, most recently, exh. cat. Cambridge/Denver 2017, quote p. 192. For the original quote, see Thiébault-Sisson 1931, p. 3.

44 This is how Magdalena Bushart describes it with reference to Rodin; Bushart 2016, pp. 209–210.

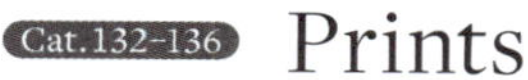

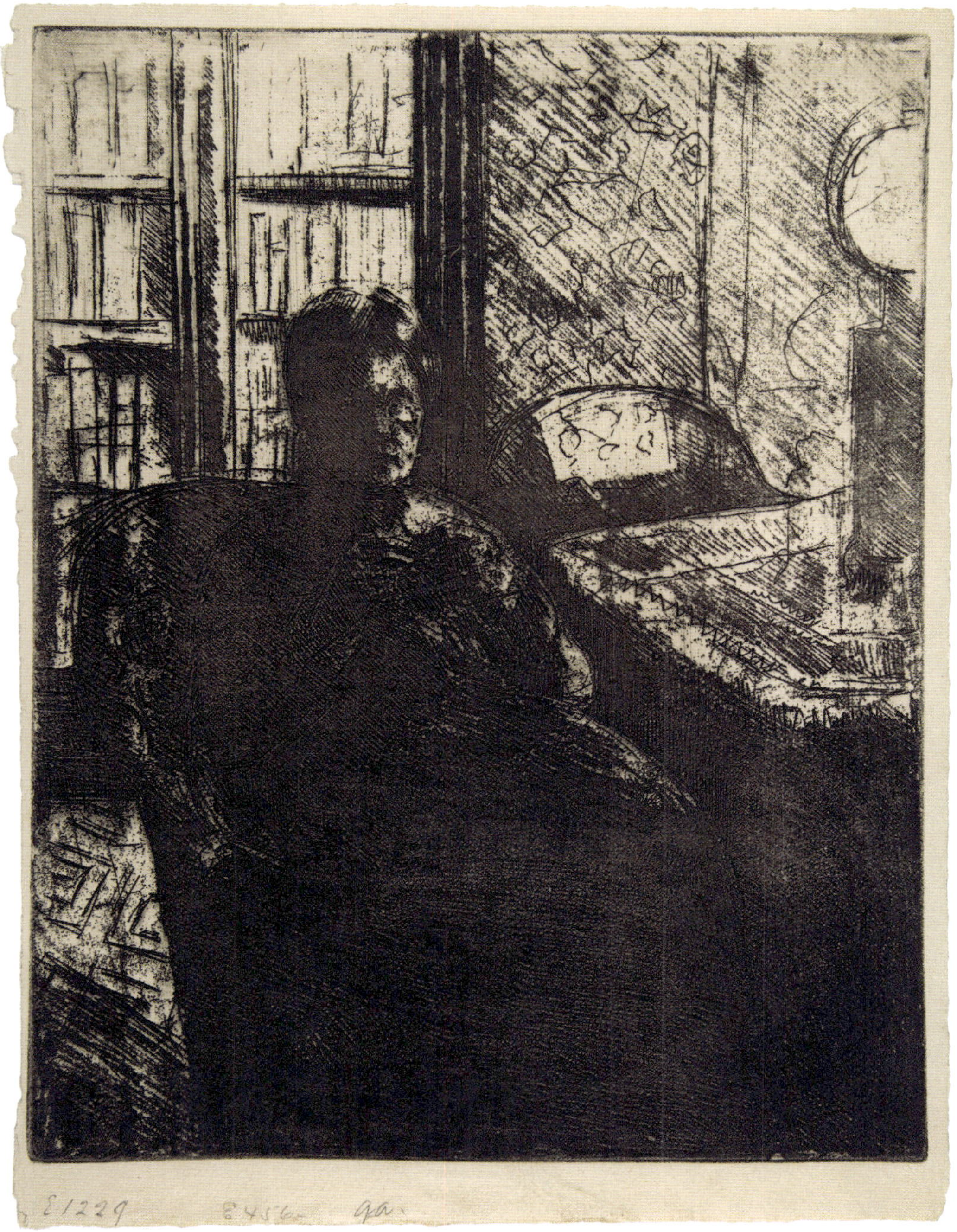

Cat.132

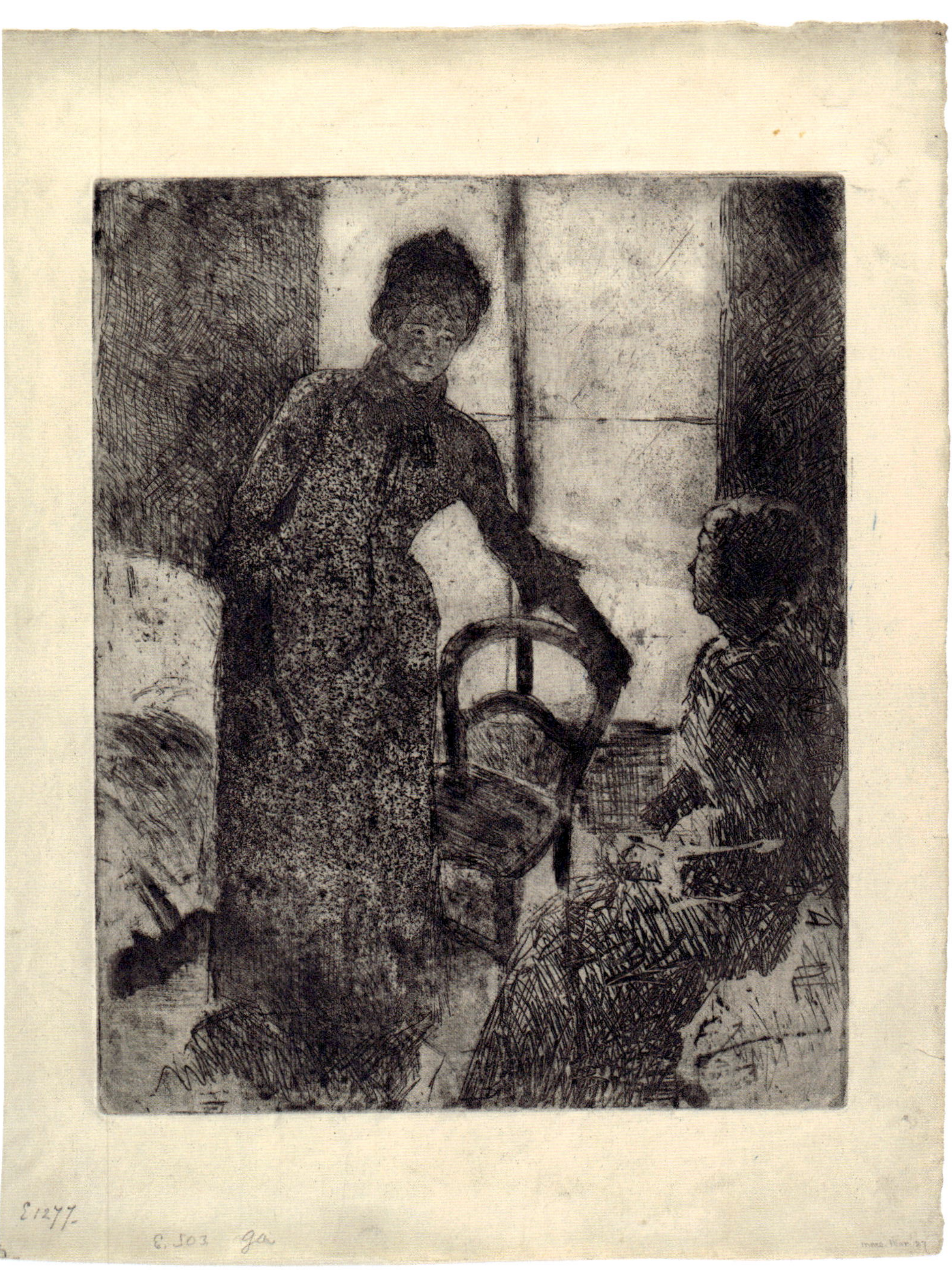

Cat. 133

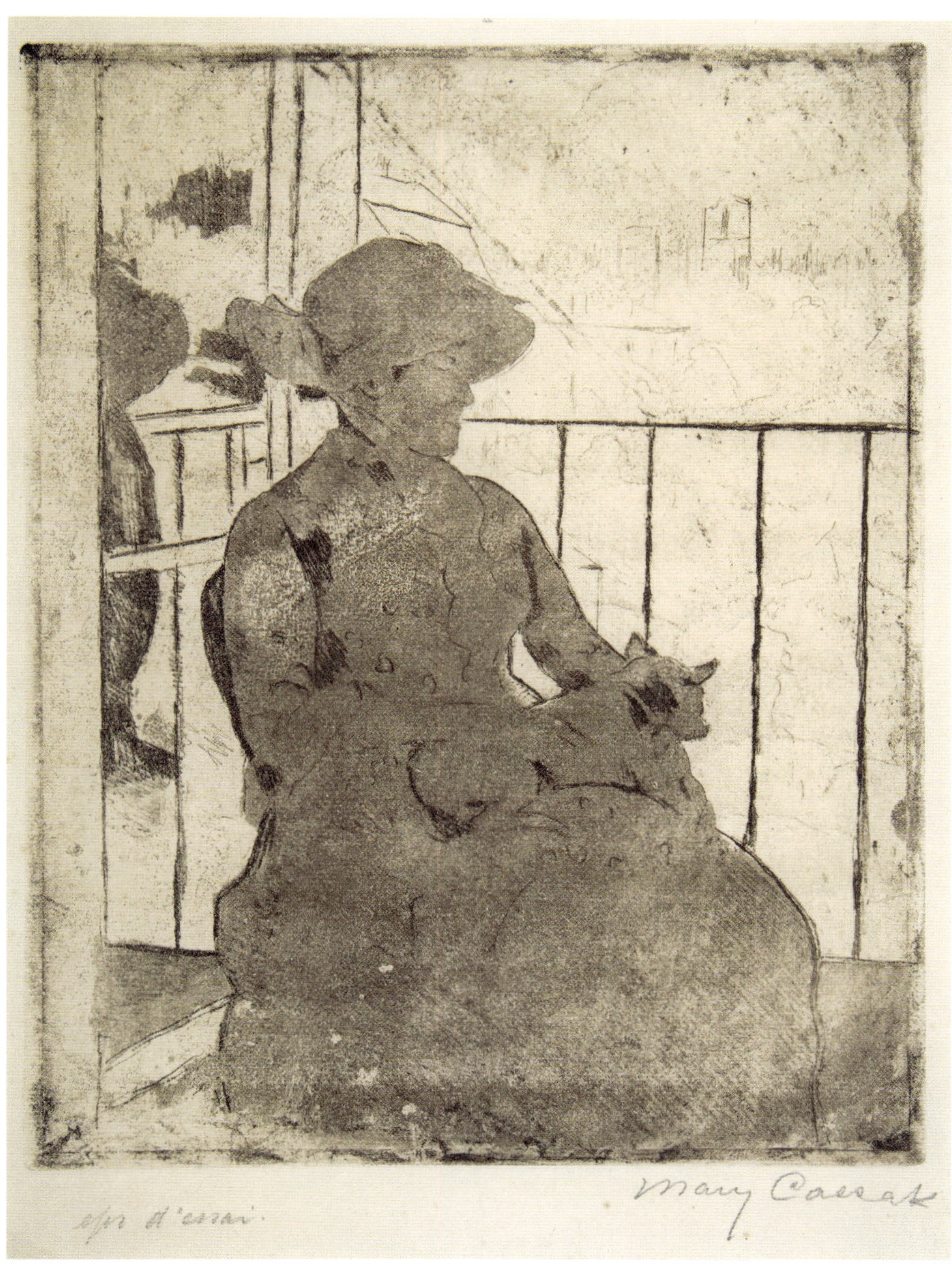

Cat.134

Cat.135 Mary Cassatt, **Knitting in the Library**, c. 1881; soft-ground etching and aquatint, second state of three, 27.8 × 21.6 cm (plate), 45.7 × 28.9 cm (sheet); The Metropolitan Museum of Art, New York, Rogers Fund, 1919, inv. no. 19.42.2
Cat.136 Mary Cassatt, **Waiting**, c. 1879; aquatint and soft-ground etching, second state of four, 21.7 × 14.6 cm (plate), 30.5 × 19.5 cm (sheet); The Metropolitan Museum of Art, New York, Rogers Fund, 1919, inv. no.19.42.3

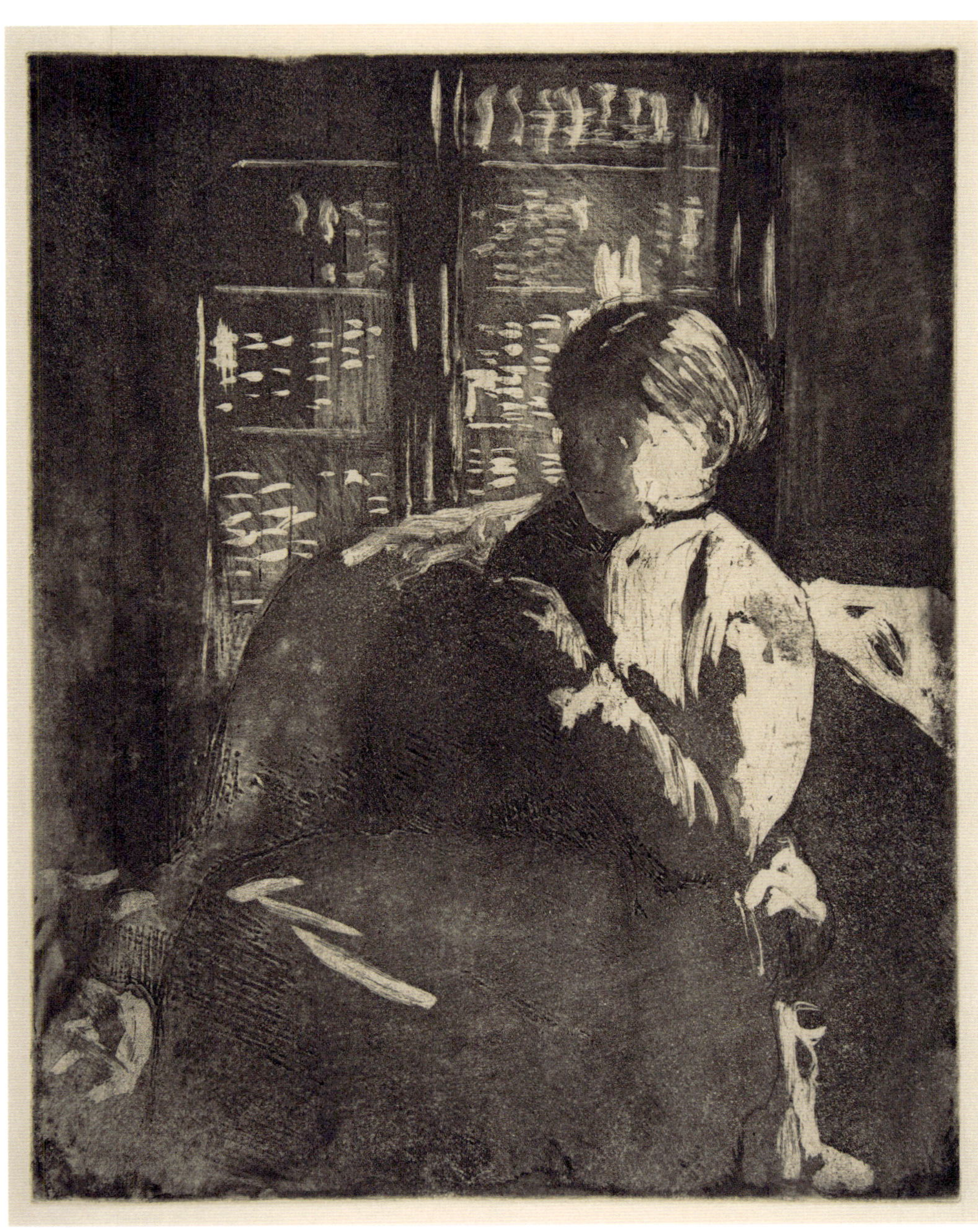

Cat.135

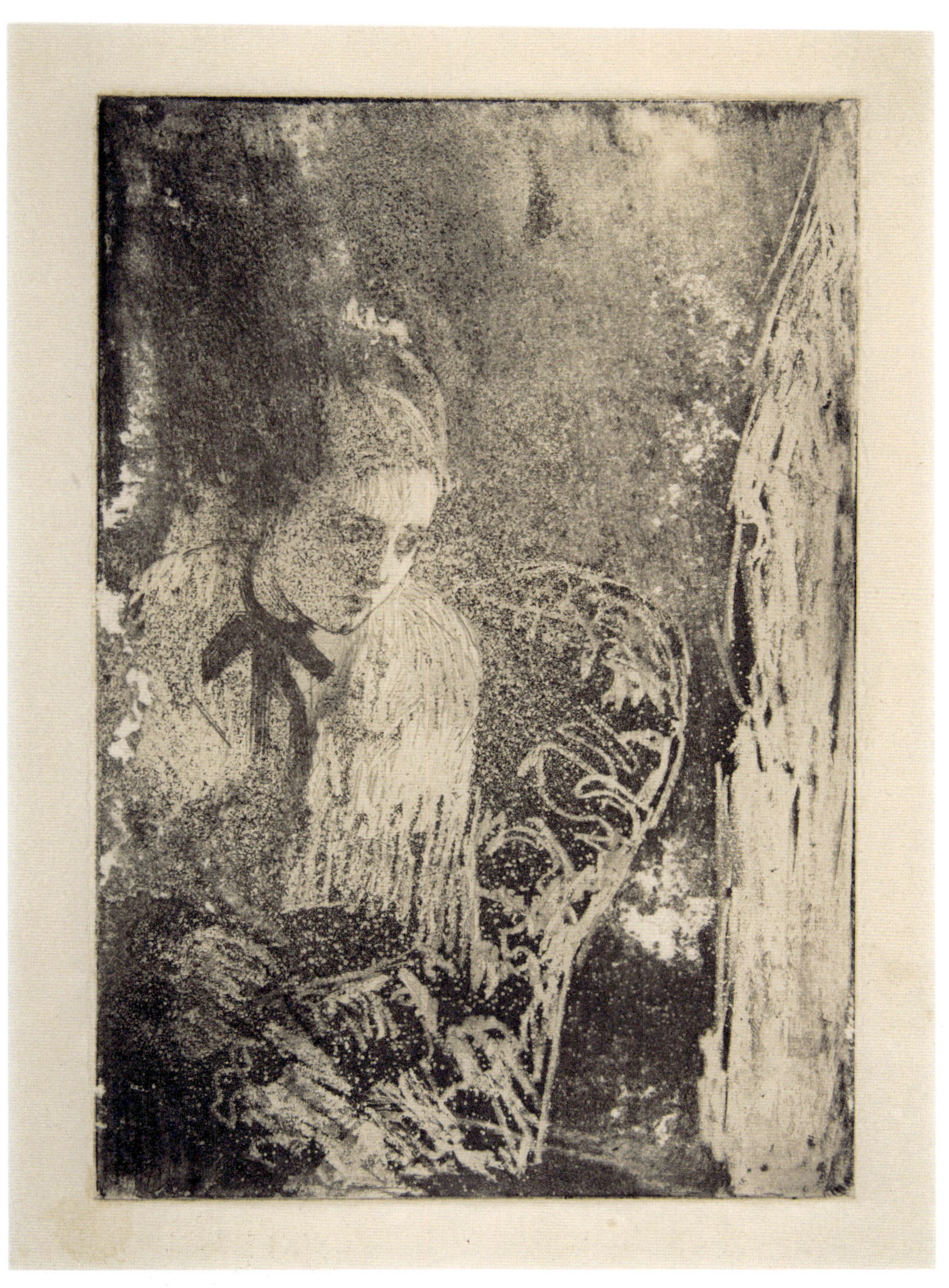

Cat. 136

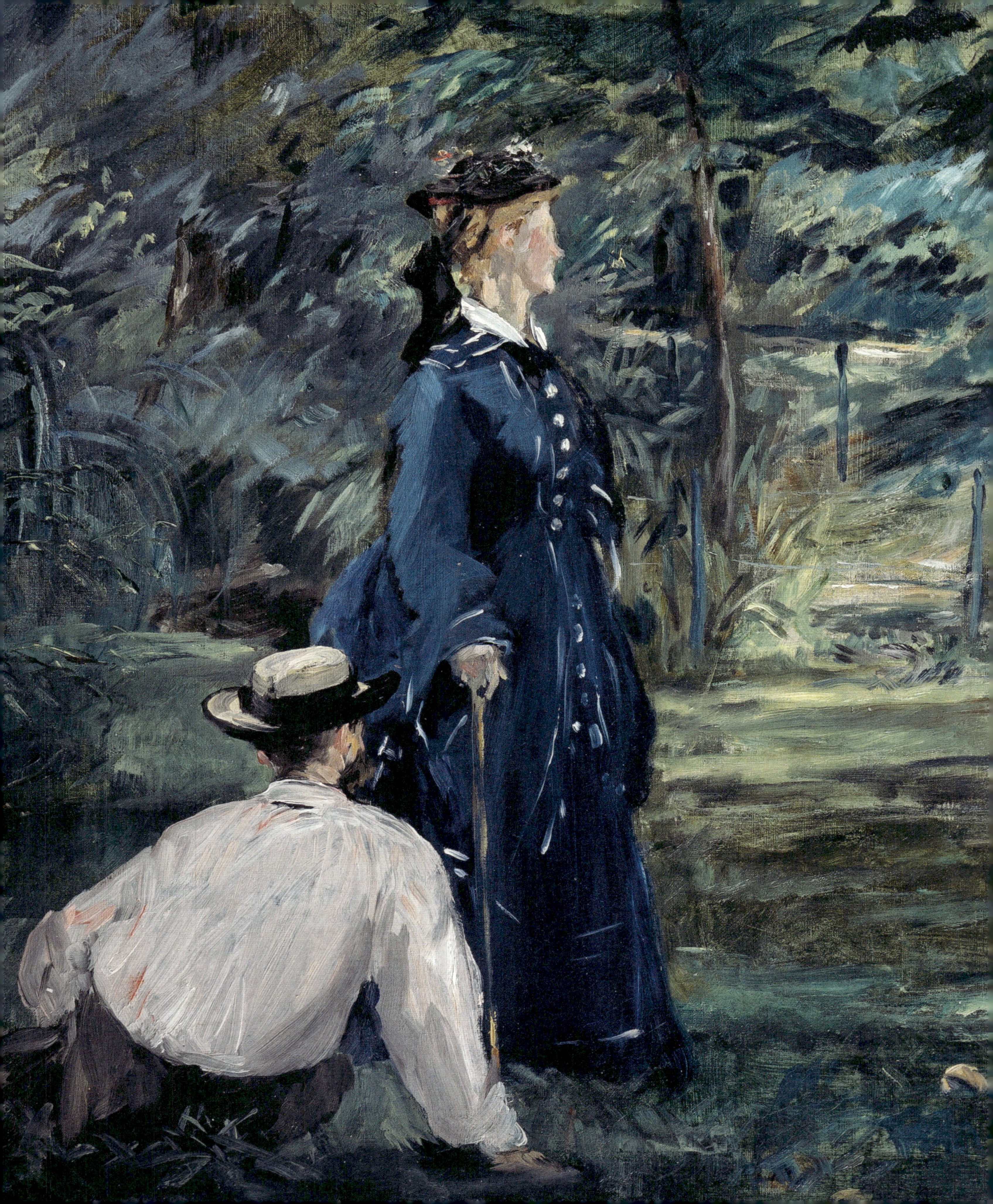

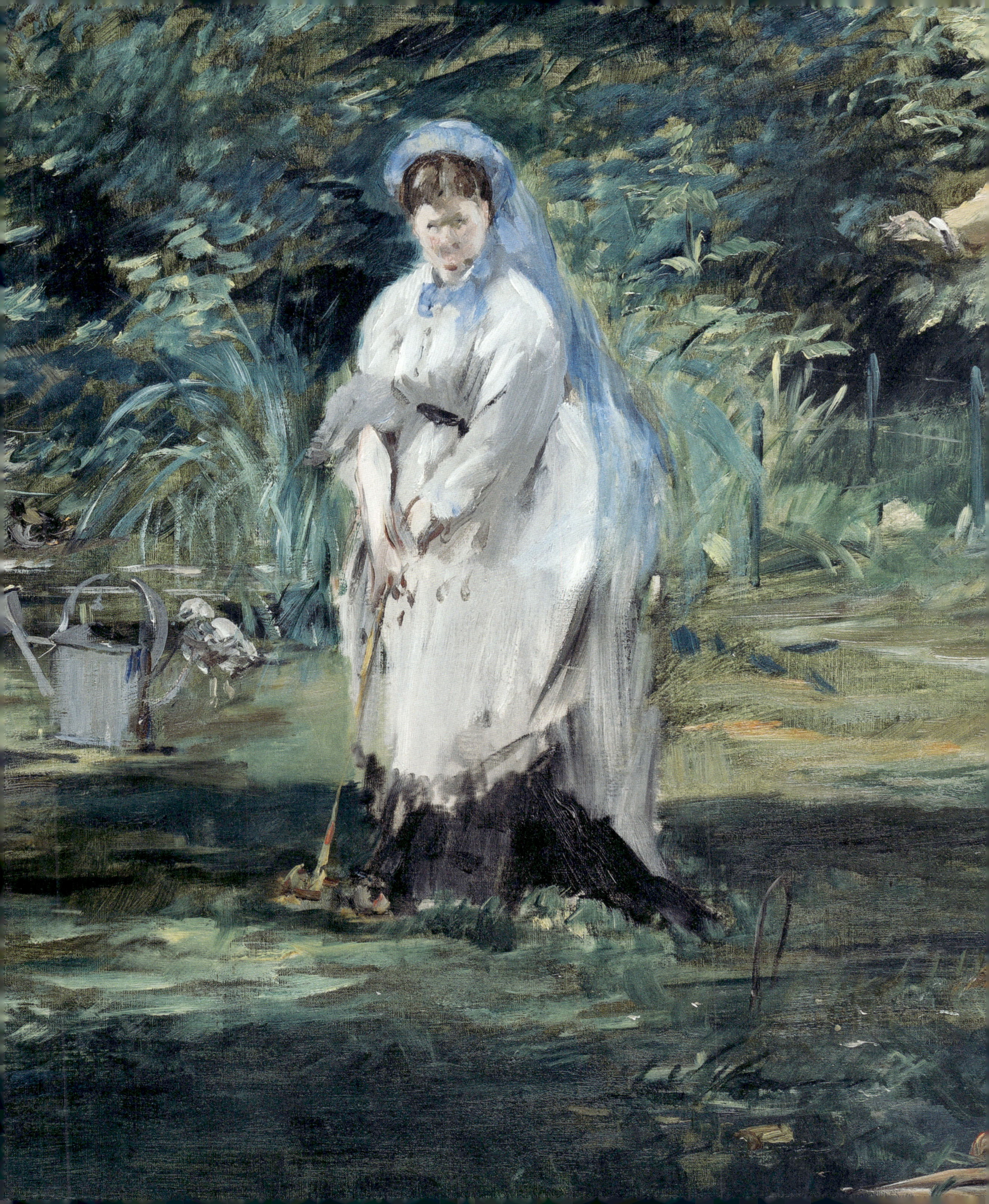

Bibliography

A

A. H. 1904/05: A.H.: "Von Ausstellungen und Sammlungen, Munich, Galerie Heinemann", in: *Die Kunst für Alle. Malerei, Plastik, Graphik, Architektur*, 20, 1904/05, pp. 533–536.

Adam 1886: Paul Adam: "Peintres impressionnistes", in: *La Revue Contemporaine. Littéraire, politique et philosophique*, 4, 4, 1886, pp. 541–551; reprinted in: Berson 1996, vol. 1, pp. 427–430.

Adhémar 1955: Jean Adhémar: "Before the Degas Bronzes", in: *Art News*, 54, 7, November 1955, pp. 34–35, 70.

Ajalbert 1886: Jean Ajalbert: "Le Salon des impressionnistes", in: *La Revue Moderne*, 20.06.1886, pp. 385–393; reprinted in: Berson 1996, vol. 1, pp. 430–434.

Ambrosini 1923: Luigi Ambrosini: "Parole di Medardo Rosso", in: *La Stampa*, 29.07.1923.

Anet 1901: Claude Anet: "La Photographie de l'œuvre de Rodin", in: *Revue Blanche*, 25, May–August 1901, pp. 216–217.

Anonymous 1874: Anonymous: "Société anonyme coopérative d'artistes-peintres, sculpteurs, etc., à Paris", in: *La Chronique des Arts et de la Curiosité (Supplément à la Gazette des Beaux-Arts)*, 3, 17.01.1874, p. 19; reprinted in: Berson 1996, vol. 1, p. 20.

Anonymous 1874a: Anonymous: "Nos Informations. Le Salon du boulevard des Capucines", in: *La Liberté*, 20.04.1874, p. 2; reprinted in: Berson 1996, vol. 1, pp. 26–27.

Anonymous 1877: Anonymous: "Rodin", in: *L'Étoile belge*, 29.01.1877.

Anonymous [Un peintre] 1877: Anonymous [Un peintre]: "L'Art Décoratif Contemporain", in: *L'Impressionniste*, 4, 28.04.1877, pp. 3–6.

Anonymous 1886: Anonymous: "L'Exposition des impressionnistes", in: *La République Française*, 17.05.1886, p. 3; reprinted in: Berson 1996, vol. 1, pp. 471–472.

Anonymous 1889: Anonymous: "Au jour le jour", in: *Le Journal de Rouen*, 21.06.1889; reprinted in: exh. cat. Paris 1989, p. 220.

Anonymous 1898/99: Anonymous: "Die Frühjahrs-Ausstellungen der Secession und des Künstlerhauses in Vienna", in: *Kunstchronik*, 10, 23, 1898/99, p. 353.

Anonymous 1904/05: Anonymous: "Ein vegetarischer Künstler", in: *Werkstatt der Kunst*, 4, 6, 1904/05, p. 82.

Anonymous 1907: Anonymous: "Twixt Rodin and Rosso. 'Let the Public Judge'", in: *Pall Mall Gazette*, 21.02.1907, p. 6.

Anonymous 1919: Anonymous: "Edgar Dégas [sic!], a Sculptor as Well as a Painter", in: *Vanity Fair*, March 1919, p. 50.

Anonymous 1925: Anonymous: "The Little Dancer. A Posthumous Sculpture by the Impressionist Painter, Edgar Degas", in: *Vanity Fair*, March 1925, p. 44.

Anonymous 1932: Anonymous: "Degas. Freude am Schaffen", in: *Das Kunstblatt. Gegenwartsfragen der Malerei und Plastik*, 17, 1932, pp. 13–14.

Armstrong 1991: Carol M. Armstrong: *Odd Man Out. Readings of the Work and Reputation of Edgar Degas*, Chicago 1991.

Armstrong 2012: Carol Armstrong: "Degas im Atelier. Verkörperndes Medium, Materialisierung des Körpers", in: exh. cat. Riehen 2012, pp. 23–32.

Arroyo Arce 2009: Nadja Arroyo Arce: "Degas, der Provokateur. Petite danseuse de quatorze ans", in: exh. cat. Hamburg 2009, pp. 59–63.

Asendorf 1993: Christopher Asendorf: *Batteries of Life: On the History of Things and Their Perception in Modernity*, Berkeley 1993.

Audeh 2002: Aida Audeh: *Rodin's Gates of Hell and Dante's Divine Comedy. An Iconographic Study*, Diss. Iowa City 2002.

Aurel 1919: Camille Aurel: *Rodin devant la femme. Fragments inédits de Rodin. La technique par lui-même*, Paris 1919.

Avery 2017: Victoria Avery: "The Sculpture of Degas. Production and Reproduction", in: exh. cat. Cambridge/Denver 2017, pp. 186–201.

B

Bacci 2006: Francesca Bacci: "Sculpting the Immaterial, Modelling the Light. Presenting Medardo Rosso's Photographic Œuvre", in: *Sculpture Journal*, 15, 2, December 2006, pp. 223–238.

Badt 1965: Kurt Badt: *The Art of Cézanne*, trans. Sheila Ann Ogilvie, Berkeley and Los Angeles 1965.

Baignères 1883: Arthur Baignères: "Première exposition de la société internationale de peintres et sculpteurs", in: *Gazette des Beaux-Arts*, 25, 2, 27, 01.02.1883, pp. 187–192.

Barbier 1987: Nicole Barbier: *Marbres de Rodin. Collection du Musée Rodin, Paris*, Paris 1987.

Barbier 1990: Nicole Barbier: "Rodins Assemblagen", in: *Das Fragment. Der Körper in Stücken*, compiled by Anne Pingeot et al., exh. cat. Musée d'Orsay, Paris/Schirn Kunsthalle Frankfurt, Frankfurt am Main, Marburg 1990, pp. 241–251.

Barbour/Sturman 2006: Daphne S. Barbour and Shelley G. Sturman: "The Modèle Bronzes", in: inv. cat. Pasadena 2006, pp. 51–67

Barbour/Sturman 2010: Daphne S. Barbour and Shelley G. Sturman: "Degas' Bronzes Analyzed", in: inv. cat. Washington 2010, pp. 23–31.

Barbour/Sturman 2010a: Daphne S. Barbour and Shelley G. Sturman: "Degas the Sculptor and His Technique", in: inv. cat. Washington 2010, pp. 35–45.

Bartlett 1899: Truman H. Bartlett: "Auguste Rodin, Sculptor", in: *The American Architect and Building News*, 25, 689, 1889; reprinted in: Elsen 1965, pp. 13–109.

Baudelaire [1857] 1954: Charles Baudelaire: "To a Passer-by", in: *Flowers of Evil*, trans. William Aggeler, Fresno, California, 1954, p. 311.

Baudelaire [1863] 1964: Charles Baudelaire: "The Painter of Modern Life", in: idem: *The Painter of Modern Life and Other Essays*, trans. and ed. Jonathan Mayne, London 1964, pp. 1–40.

Baudelaire [1846] 1972: Charles Baudelaire: "The Salon of 1846", in: idem: *Selected Writings on Art and Artists*, trans. P. E. Charvet, Cambridge etc. 1972, pp. 47–107.

Baudelaire [1846] 1977: Charles Baudelaire: "Pourquoi la sculpture est ennuyeuse / Warum die Bildhauerei langweilig ist / Warum die Bildhauerei ein Ärgernis ist" [1846], in: Baudelaire 1977 ff., vol. 1: *Juvenilia – Kunstkritik. 1832–1846*, Munich 1977, pp. 273–276.

Baudelaire [1863] 1989: Charles Baudelaire: "Der Maler des modernen Lebens" [1863], in: Baudelaire 1977 ff., vol. 5: *Aufsätze zur Literatur and Kunst. 1857–1860*, Munich 1989, pp. 213–258.

Baudelaire [1863] 1994: Charles Baudelaire: "Der Maler des modernen Lebens" [1863], in: idem: *Der Künstler and das moderne Leben. Essays, "Salons", intime Tagebücher*, edited by Henry Schumann, 2nd edition, Leipzig 1994, pp. 290–320.

Bauer 2018: Thomas Bauer: Die Vereindeutigung der Welt. Über den Verlust an Mehrdeutigkeit und Vielfalt, Ditzingen 2018.

Beaunier 1908: André Beaunier: "Les Salons de 1908", in: *Gazette des Beaux-Arts*, 3, 39, 1908, pp. 363–496.

Beausire 1988: Alain Beausire: *Quand Rodin exposait*, Paris 1988.

Beausire 1989: Alain Beausire: "La Galerie Georges Petit dans le courant des Sécessions", in: exh. cat. Paris 1989, pp. 40–46.

Becker 1998: Jane R. Becker: *"Only One Art". The Interaction of Painting and Sculpture in the Work of Medardo Rosso, Auguste Rodin, and Eugène Carrière, 1884–1906*, Diss. New York 1998.

Becker 1999: Jane R. Becker: "Medardo Rosso. Photographing Sculpture and Sculpting Photography", in: *The Artist and the Camera. Degas to Picasso*, edited by Dorothy Kosinski, exh. cat. San Francisco Museum of Modern Art etc., New Haven etc. 1999, pp. 159–175.

Bellonzi 1970: Fortunato Bellonzi: "Überblick über die Entwicklung der modernen italienischen Plastik", in: *Moderne italienische Bildhauer. Wanderausstellung von Bronze-Kleinplastiken in der Bundesrepublik Deutschland*, edited by Quadriennale d'Arte, Rome, exh. cat., Bonn 1970, pp. 11–51.

Benjamin [1931] 2009: Walter Benjamin: "Brief History of Photography" [1931], in: idem: *One-way Street and Other Writings*, trans. J. A. Underwood, London 2009, pp. 172–192.

Berger 2002: Ursel Berger: "Einführung", in: idem. (ed.): *Ausdrucksplastik (Bildhauerei im 20. Jahrhundert, Bd. 1)*, Berlin 2002, pp. 7–9.

Berger 2014: Christian Berger: *Wiederholung und Experiment bei Edgar Degas*, Diss. Berlin 2013, Berlin 2014.

Berger 2018: Christian Berger: "Edgar Degas' Bildoberflächen als Experimentierfelder", in: Magdalena Bushart and Henriette Haug (eds): *Spur der Arbeit. Oberfläche und Werkprozess*, Cologne etc. 2018, pp. 95–110.

Berson 1996: Ruth Berson: *The New Painting. Impressionism 1874–1886. Documentation*, 2 vols, vol. 1: *Reviews*, vol. 2: *Exhibited Works*, San Francisco 1996.

Bertall [d'Arnoux] 1881: Bertall [Charles-Albert d'Arnoux]: "Exposition. Des peintres intransigeants et nihilistes. 36, boulevard des Capucines", in: *Paris-Journal*, 21.04.1881, pp. 1–2; reprinted in: Berson 1996, vol. 1, pp. 320–332.

Bertelli 2004: Carlo Bertelli: "Medardo Rosso e la fotografia", in: exh. cat. Rovereto/Turin 2004, pp. 31–39.

Betz 2016: Juliane Betz: *Le Chant du Cygnet. Die "Gazette des Beaux-Arts" und die französische Reproduktionsgraphik in der zweiten Hälfte des 19. Jahrhunderts*, Diss. Heidelberg 2013, Merzhausen 2016.

Beyer 2014: Jonas Beyer: *Zwischen Zeichnung und Druck. Edgar Degas und die Wiederentdeckung der Monotypie im 19. Jahrhundert*, Diss. Berlin 2012, Paderborn 2014.

Bezzola 2010: Tobia Bezzola: "Von der Skulptur in der Fotografie zur Fotografie als Plastik", in: exh. cat. New York/Zurich 2010, pp. 28–35.

Bidou 1910: Henry Bidou: "Le Salon d'Automne", in: *Gazette des Beaux-Arts*, 4, 5, 1910, pp. 463–496.

Bierwirth 2018: Petra Bierwirth: *Bilder der Seele – Auguste Rodins Zeichnungen*, Hildesheim etc. 2018.

Black McCoy 2006: Claire Black McCoy: "'This Man is Michelangelo': Octave Mirbeau, Auguste Rodin and the Image of the Modern Sculptor", in: *Nineteenth Century Art Worldwide*, 5, 1, 2006; http://www.19thc-artworldwide.org/spring06/173-qthis-man-is-michelangeloq-octave-mirbeau-auguste-rodin-and-the-image-of-the-modern-sculptor (accessed 23 August 2019).

Blanc 1865: Charles Blanc: "Grammaire des arts du dessin. Architecture, sculpture, peinture", in: *Gazette des Beaux-Arts*, 7, 1, 18, 01.01.1865, pp. 42–65.

Blühm 2010: Andreas Blühm: "In Living Colour", in: *The Colour of Sculpture. 1840–1910*, exh. cat. Van Gogh Museum, Amsterdam/Henry Moore Institute, Leeds, Zwolle 2010, pp. 11–60.

Boehm 2003: Gottfried Boehm: "Die Intelligenz des Auges. Die Krise der Wahrnehmung im Impressionismus", in: Stauffer 2003, pp. 107–115.

Boehm 2017: Gottfried Boehm: *Die Sichtbarkeit der Zeit. Studien zum Bild in der Moderne*, edited by Ralph Ubl, Paderborn 2017.

Boehm [1977] 2017: Gottfried Boehm: "Plastik und plastischer Raum" [1977], in: Boehm 2017, pp. 37–56.

Boehm [1988] 2017: Gottfried Boehm: "Werk und Serie. Probleme des modernen Bildbegriffs seit Monet" [1988], in: Boehm 2017, pp. 137–145.

Boggs 1998: Jean Sutherland Boggs: "The Horse in Art and Legend", in: *Degas at the Races*, edited by idem, exh. cat. National Gallery of Art, Washington, D.C., New Haven etc. 1998, pp. 16–37.

Boras 1941: George Boras: "Il faut être de son temps", in: *The Journal of Aesthetics and Art Criticism*, 1, 1941, pp. 52–65.,

Borghi 1950: Mino Borghi: *Medardo Rosso*, Milan 1950.

Borgmeyer 1911: Charles L. Borgmeyer: "Prince Paul Troubetzkoy – Sculptor", in: *Fine Arts Journal*, 25, 1, 1911, pp. 2–34.

Bossaglia 1994: Rossana Bossaglia: *Tranquillo Cremona. Catalogo ragionato*, Milan 1994.

Bossaglia/Castagnoli 1993: Rossana Bossaglia and Piergiovanni Castagnoli: *Paolo Troubetzkoy – scultore (Verbania, 1866–1938)*, Verbania Intra 1993.

Bothner 1993: Roland Bothner: *Grund und Figur. Die Geschichte des Reliefs und Auguste Rodins Höllentor*, Munich 1993.

Bouret 1965: Jean Bouret: *Degas*, Paris 1965.

Bouret 1987: Jean Bouret: *Degas*, Paris 1987

Brabant 2009: Dominik Brabant: "Heraklitische Körper und die Bewegungsströme der Moderne: Zu Georg Simmels kunstphilosophischer Auseinandersetzung mit den Skulpturen und Plastiken Auguste Rodins", in: Marijana Erstic, Walburga Hülk and Gregor Schuhen (eds): *Körper in Bewegung. Modelle und Impulse der italienischen Avantgarde*, Bielefeld 2009, pp. 53–70.

Brabant 2017: Dominik Brabant: *Rodin-Lektüren. Deutungen und Debatten von der Moderne zur Postmoderne*, Cologne 2017.

Braunfels-Esche 1980: Sigrid Braunfels-Esche "Reliefs und Reliefauffassung von Adolf von Hildebrand", in: *Reliefs. Formprobleme zwischen Malerei und Skulptur im 20. Jahrhundert*, edited by Ernst-Gerhard Güse, exh. cat. Westfälisches Landesmuseum für Kunst und Kulturgeschichte, Münster/Kunsthaus Zürich, Berne 1980, pp. 23–34.

Brettell 2000: Richard R. Brettell: *Impression. Painting Quickly in France. 1860–1890*, in conjunction with the eponymous exhibition, National Gallery, London etc., New Haven and London 2000.

Brettell 2005: Richard R. Brettell: "Gauguin the Collector, Gauguin the Impressionist", in: exh. cat. Copenhagen/Fort Worth 2005, pp. 44–67.

Brettell 2005a: Richard R. Brettell: "Gauguin's Humiliation as an Impressionist. The 1886 Exhibition", in: exh. cat. Copenhagen/Fort Worth 2005, pp. 278–283.

Brettell 2017: Richard R. Brettell: "Charting New Territory. Impressionist and Post-Impressionist Drawing", in: *Drawn to Greatness*, edited by Jennifer Tonkovich, exh. cat. Morgan Library and Museum, New York/Clark Art Institute, Williamstown, New York 2017, pp. 164–189.

Brockhaus 1997: Christoph Brockhaus: "Vision statt Reproduktion", in: exh. cat. Duisburg etc. 1997, pp. 81–85.

Brockhaus 2003: Christoph Brockhaus: "La Portinaia in Skulptur und Photographie", in: exh. cat. Winterthur/Duisburg 2003, pp. 51–57.

Brunk 2003: Birgit Brunk: "Plastik für Sehende", in: exh. cat. Winterthur/Duisburg 2003, pp. 12–38

Bibliography

Brunk 2012: Birgit Brunk: *Medardo Rosso – Plastiker und Gusskünstler. Studien zur Struktur und Bedeutung der Variationen im plastischen Œuvre Medardo Rossos*, Diss. Gießen 2012.

Bugatti 1967: L'Ébé Bugatti: *The Bugatti Story*, Philadelphia 1967.

Buley-Uribe 2005: Christina Buley-Uribe: "Die 'Bildhauerzeichnung'. Ein ambivalenter Begriff", in: *Rodin. Skulpturen und Zeichnungen. Fotografien von Eugène Druet*, edited by Erik Stephan for Städtische Museen Jena, exh. cat. Kunstsammlung im Stadtmuseum Jena and Galerie der Jenoptik AG, Jena, 2005, pp. 147–153.

Burroughs 1932: Louise Burroughs: "Degas in the Havemeyer Collection", in: *The Metropolitan Museum of Art Bulletin*, 27, May 1932, pp. 141–146.

Burty 1874: *L'Eau-forte en 1874*, with an introduction by Philippe Burty, Paris 1874.

Burty 1874a: Philippe Burty: "The Paris Exhibitions. Les Impressionnistes", in: *The Academy*, 30.05.1874, pp. 616; reprinted in: Berson 1996, vol. 1, pp. 9–11.

Burty 1875: *L'Eau-forte en 1875*, with an introduction by Philippe Burty, Paris 1875.

Burty 1876: Philippe Burty: "Fine Art. The Exhibition of the 'Intransigeants'", in: *The Academy*, 15.04.1876, pp. 363–364; reprinted in: Berson 1996, vol. 1, pp. 64–66.

Burty 1878: *L'Eau-forte en 1878*, with an introduction by Philippe Burty, Paris 1878.

Burty 1882: Philippe Burty: "La Sculpture", in: *L'Exposition des Beaux-Arts*, Paris 1882, pp. 263–264.

Bushart 2016: Magdalena Bushart: "Das eigene Ding. Medardo Rosso und der Bronzeguss", in: Bushart/Haug 2016, pp. 209–224.

Bushart/Haug 2016: Magdalena Bushart and Henrike Haug (eds): *Formlos – formbar. Bronze als künstlerisches Material (Interdependenzen*, vol. 2), Cologne 2016.

Butler 1980: Ruth Butler: "Introduction", in: idem (ed.): *Rodin in Perspective*, Englewood Cliffs, New Jersey, 1980, pp. 1–31.

Butler 1993: Ruth Butler: *Rodin. The Shape of Genius*, New Haven and London 1993

C

C. E. [Ephrussi] 1881: C. E. [Charles Ephrussi]: "Exposition des artistes indépendants", in: *La Chronique des arts et de la curiosité*, 16.04.1881, pp. 126–127; reprinted in: Berson 1996, vol. 1, pp. 336–337.

Callen 1982: Anthea Callen: *Techniques of the Impressionists*, London 1982.

Callen 1989: Anthea Callen: "Anatomy and Physiognomy: Degas' Little Dancer of Fourteen Years", in: exh. cat. Liverpool 1989, pp. 10–17.

Callen 1995: Anthea Callen: *The Spectacular Body. Science, Method and Meaning in the Work of Degas*, New Haven and London 1995.

Callen 2000: Anthea Callen: *The Art of Impressionism. Painting Technique and the Making of Modernity*, New Haven etc. 2000.

Calvo Serraller 1996: Francisco Calvo Serraller: "Feeling Like Nothing", in: exh. cat. Santiago de Compostela 1996, pp. 59–84.

Camera Work 1911: *Camera Work. A Photographic Quarterly*, 34/35, April–July 1911.

Campbell 1998: Sara Campbell: "Une danseuse et trente tutus", in: Martine Kahane et al.: "Enquête sur la Petite Danseuse de quatorze ans de Degas", in: *48/14. La Revue du Musée d'Orsay*, 7, 1998, pp. 68–71.

Caramel 1984: Luciano Caramel, in: exh. cat. Frankfurt 1984, pp. 11–34.

Caruso/Schallmeiner 2014: Alexandra Caruso and Anneliese Schallmeiner: "Getrennt und gemeinsam: Die sammelnden Brüder Gottfried und Hermann Eissler", in: Eva Bimlinger and Heinz Schödl (eds) *Die Praxis des Sammelns. Personen und Institutionen im Fokus der Provenienzforschung*, Vienna etc. 2014, pp. 99–134.

Castagnary 1874: Jules-Antoine Castagnary: "Exposition du boulevard des Capucines. Les Impressionnistes", in: *Le Siècle*, 29.04.1874, p. 3; reprinted in: Berson 1986, vol. 1, pp. 15–17.

Caws 2001: Mary Ann Caws (ed.): *Manifesto: A Century of Isms*, Lincoln and London 2001.

Champy-Vinas 2014: Cécile Champy-Vinas: "Paris, capitale des arts", in: *Paris 1900. La ville spectacle*, edited by Christophe Leribault and Isabelle Collet, exh. cat. Petit Palais, Musée de Beaux-Arts de la Ville de Paris, Paris 2014, pp. 158–210.

Champy-Vinas 2016: Cécile Champy-Vinas: "Les Sculpteurs au Zoo: Sculpter les animaux sauvages, de Barye à Pompon", in: *Ligeia. Dossiers sur l'art*, 29, 145–148, January–June 2016, pp. 130–139.

Chevillot 2010: Catherine Chevillot: "La Sculpture Impressionniste", in: exh. cat. Roubaix 2010, pp. 52–61.

Chevillot 2017: Catherine Chevillot: "Les Jeunes Sculpteurs et Rodin: Une admiration universelle", in: exh. cat. Paris 2017, pp. 106–111.

Childs 2014: Elizabeth C. Childs: "Gauguin and Sculpture. The Art of the 'ultra-sauvage'", in: *Gauguin. Metamorphoses*, edited by Starr Figura et al., exh. cat. The Museum of Modern Art, New York, 2014, pp. 36–47.

Cioffi 2013: Rosanna Cioffi: "'L'estro' o 'la matta stranezza' di Troubetzkoy negli scritti di Mario De Micheli e Raffaello Giolli", in: Marta Nezzo and Giuliana Tomasella (eds): *Sotto la superficie visibile. Scrittore in onore di Franco Bernabei*, Treviso 2013, pp. 101–110.

Claretie 1881: Jules Claretie: "La Vie à Paris: les artistes indépendants", in: *Le Temps*, 05.04.1881, p. 3; reprinted in: Berson 1996, vol. 1, pp. 335–336.

Claris 1901 (French): Edmond Claris: "L'Impressionnisme en sculpture. Auguste Rodin et Medardo Rosso", in: *La Nouvelle Revue*, 10, 01.06.1901, pp. 321–336.

Claris 1902 (French): Edmond Claris: *De l'Impressionnisme en sculpture. Lettres et opinions de Rodin, Rosso, Constantin Meunier [...]*, Paris 1902.

Claris 1902a (German): Edmond Claris: *Der Impressionismus in der Skulptur. Auguste Rodin und Medardo Rosso*, trans. from French by Etha Fles, Utrecht 1902.

Claris 1902b (Spanish): Edmond Claris: "Renacimiento de la escultura", in: *La Lectura*, 1, 1902.

Claris 1929: Edmond Claris: "L'Impressionnisme en sculpture: Medardo Rosso", in: *La Nouvelle Revue*, 52, 4, 104, October/November 1929, pp. 131–134.

Clark 1985: Timothy J. Clark: *The Painting of Modern Life. Paris in the Art of Manet and his Followers*, London 1985.

Clark 1999: Timothy J. Clark: *The Painting of Modern Life. Paris in the Art of Manet and his Followers*, Princeton 1999.

Clausen Pedersen: Line Clausen Pedersen: "Degas' Method", in: exh. cat. Copenhagen 2013, pp. 13–125.

Clayson 1986: Hollis Clayson: "The Second Exhibition 1876. A Failed Attempt", in: exh. cat. Washington/San Francisco 1986, pp. 145–159.

Conzen 2002: Ina Conzen: "'Eine neue Welt'. Edouard Manet und die Impressionisten", in: exh. cat. Stuttgart 2002, pp. 13–157.

Cooper 2003: Harry Cooper: "Ecce Rosso!", in: *Medardo Rosso. Second Impressions*, edited by Harry Cooper and Sharon Hecker, exh. cat. Arthur M. Sackler Museum, Washington, D.C., etc., New Haven 2003, pp. 1–22.

Cortissoz 1919: Royal Cortissoz: "Degas as He was Seen by His Model. Intimate Notes on the Artist During his Last Phase", in: *New York Tribune*, 19.10.1919, section IV, p. 9.

Crary 1990: Jonathan Crary: *Techniques of the Observer: On Vision and Modernity in the Nineteenth Century*, Cambridge, Mass., and London 1990.

Cugini 2006: Carla Cugini: *"Er sieht einen Fleck, er malt einen Fleck." Physiologische Optik, Impressionismus und Kunstkritik*, Basle 2006.

Curtis 1999: Penelope Curtis: *Sculpture 1900–1945. After Rodin*, Oxford 1999.

Czestochowski 2002: Joseph S. Czestochowski: "Degas's Sculptures Re-examined: The Marketing of a Private Pursuit", in: Czestochowski/Pingeot 2002, pp. 11–25.

Czestochwoski/Pingeot 2002: Joseph S. Czestochwoski and Anne Pingeot (eds): *Degas Sculptures. Catalogue Raisonné of the Bronzes*, Memphis 2002.

D

Daemgen 2014: Anke Daemgen: "Rembrandt Bugatti: His Life, Family and Work", in: exh. cat. Berlin 2014, pp. 24–43.

Davison [1890]: George Davison: "Impressionism in Photography", in: Charles W. Hastings (ed.), *The Photographic Quarterly*, vol. II: October 1890 to July 1891, pp. 171–173.

De Charry 1882: Paul de Charry: "Beaux-Arts", in: *Le Pays*, 14.03.1882, p. 3; reprinted in: Berson 1996, vol. 1, pp. 383–384.

De Fourcaud 1882: Louis de Fourcaud: "Salon de Paris", in: *Le Gaulois*, 01.07.1882.

De Fourcaud 1899: Louis de Fourcaud: "Les Arts Décoratifs au Salon de 1889, La Sculpture à la Société Nationale des Beaux-Arts", in: *Revue des Arts décoratifs*, new series, 1, 19, 1899, pp. 247–257.

De Goncourt 1892: Edmond de Goncourt: "Préface", in: Gustave Geffroy: *La Vie Artistique*, vol. 1, Paris 1892, pp. I–XVI.

De Goncourt 1894: Edmond and Jules de Goncourt: *Journal. Mémoires de la vie littéraire*, 3rd series, vol. 1 (=7): *1885–1888*, Paris 1894.

De Goncourt 1959: Edmond de Goncourt: *Mémoires de la vie littéraire*, vol. 3: *1879–1890*, Paris 1959.

De Montagnac 1880: Elie de Mont. [Élisée-Louis Baron de Montagnac]: "Cinquième Exposition des impressionnistes, 10, rue des Pyramides", in: *La Civilisation*, 20.04.1880, p. 2; reprinted in: Berson 1996, vol. 1, pp. 301–302.

De Montagnac 1881: Elie de Mont. [Élisée-Louis Baron de Montagnac]: "L'Exposition du boulevard des Capucines", in: *La Civilisation*, 21.04.1881, p. 2; reprinted in: Berson 1996, vol. 1, pp. 360–362.

De Montifaud 1874: Marc de Montifaud: "Exposition du boulevard des Capucines", in: *L'Artiste*, 01.05.1874, pp. 307–313; reprinted in: Berson 1996, vol. 1, pp. 28–31.

De Sainte-Croix 1896: Camille de Sainte-Croix: "Medardo Rosso", in: *Mercure de France*, 17, 75, March 1896, pp. 378–391.

De Sainte-Croix 1898: Camille de Sainte-Croix: "La Bataille Artistique et littéraire", in: *La Petite République Socialiste*, 03.05.1898.

De Sanna 1985: Jole De Sanna: *Medardo Rosso o la creazione dello spazio moderno*, Milan 1985.

Degas 1931: Edgar Degas: *Lettres de Degas*, edited by Marcel Guérin, Paris 1931.

Degas 1945: Edgar Degas: *Lettres de Degas*, edited by Marcel Guérin, Paris 1945.

Degas 1985: *The Notebooks of Edgar Degas. A Catalogue of the Thirty-Eight Notebooks in the Bibliothèque Nationale and Other Collections*, edited by Theodore Reff, vol. 1, New York 1985.

Deleuze 1989: Gilles Deleuze: *Cinema*, vol. 1, trans. Hugh Tomlinson and Barbara Habberjam, Minneapolis 1989.

Deleuze/Guattari 1994: Gilles Deleuze and Félix Guattari: *What Is Philosophy?*, trans. Hugh Tomlinson and Graham Burchell, New York and Chichester 1994.

Denis 1920: Maurice Denis: *Théories. 1890–1919. Du symbolisme et de Gauguin vers un nouvel ordre classique*, 4th edition, Paris 1920.

Deschamps 1828: Émile Deschamps: "Préface", in: idem: *Études françaises et étrangères*, Paris 1828, p. XVI.

Desjardins 1899: Paul Desjardins: "Les Salons de 1889, II, Sculpture", in: *Gazette des Beaux-Arts*, 41, 3, 22, 01.10.1899, pp. 283–292.

DeWitte 2017: Deborah DeWitte: 'Drawings on View in State-funded Venues and Artists' Societies in Paris. 1860–90", in: *Master Drawings*, special issue: *Nineteenth-Century Draftsmen and Collectors*, 55, 2, 2017, pp. 225–248.

Dinoia 2002: Rosalba Dinoia: "L'Eau-forte 'Mobile' dans l'évolution de l'estampe originale à la fin du XIXe siècle. Epériences françaises et italiennes", in: *Histoire de l'art*, 50, 2002, pp. 95–108.

Doetsch 2007: Hermann Doetsch: "Momentaufnahmen des Flüchtigen. Skizzen zu einer Lektüre von *Le peintre de la vie modern*", in: Karin Westerwelle (ed.): *Charles Baudelaire. Dichter und Kunstkritiker*, Würzburg 2007, pp. 139–162.

Domogackaja 1990: Svetlana Petrovna Domogackaja: "L'arte di Paolo Troubetzkoy in Russia", in: exh. cat. Verbania Pallanza 1990, pp. 54–67.

Dossi 1873: Carlo Dossi: "Tranquillo Cremona e G useppe Grandi all'Esposizione di Belle Arti nell'anno 1873", in: *Le tre arti*, Milan 1873; reprinted in: Dossi 1906, pp. 5–12.

Dossi 1906: Carlo Dossi: *Fricassea. Critica di arte, storia e letteratura*, Como 1906.

Droth 2017: Martina Droth: "Medardo Rosso", in: *The Burlington Magazine*, 1370, April 2017, pp. 349–350.

Druick 1989: Douglas Druick: "La Petite Danseuse et les criminels: Degas moraliste?", in: *Degas inédit. Actes du Colloque Degas, Musée d'Orsay, 18–21 avril 1988*, Paris 1989, pp. 224–250.

Druick 1998: Douglas Druick: "Framing the Little Dancer Aged Fourteen", in: exh. cat. Omaha etc. 1998, pp. 77–96.

Drumont 1874: E. [Édouard] Drumont: "L'Exposition du boulevard des Capucines", in: *Le Petit Journal*, 19.04.1874, p. 2; reprinted in: Berson 1996, vol. 1, pp. 20–21.

Dubois 1998: Philippe Dubois: *Der fotografische Akt. Versuch über ein theoretisches Dispositiv*, Amsterdam etc. 1998.

Dujardin-Beaumetz [1913] 1992: [Henri-Charles-Étienne] Dujardin-Beaumetz: *Entretiens avec Rodin* [1913], edited by François Dujardin-Beaumetz, Paris 1992.

Dumas 2002: Ann Dumas: "Degas: Painter/ Sculptor", in: Czestochowski/Pingeot 2002, pp. 39–47.

Dumas 2003: Ann Dumas: "Degas e gli italiani a Parigi", in: exh. cat. Ferrara 2003, pp. 21–66.

Dunn 1978: Roger Terry Dunn: *The Monet – Rodin Exhibition at the Galerie Georges Petit in 1889. A Study of the Significance of the Exhibition and its Setting, the Work of the Two Artists at Mid-Career, and their Artistic and Social Relationship*, Diss. Evanston 1978.

Duranty 1867: Edmond Duranty: "Sur la physionomie", in: *Revue libérale*, 2, 25.07.1867, pp. 499–523.

Duranty 1879: Louis Edmond Duranty: "La Quatrième Exposition faite par un groupe d'artistes indépendants", in: *La Chronique des arts et de la curiosité*, 19.04.1879, pp. 126–128; reprinted in: Berson 1996, vol. 1, pp. 218–219.

Duranty [1876] 1946: Edmond Duranty: *La Peinture Moderne. Á propos du groupe d'artistes qui expose dans les Galeries Durand-Ruel* [1876], edited by Marcel Guérin, Paris 1946.

Bibliography

E

E. d'H. [d'Hervilly] 1874: E. d'H. [Ernest-Marie d'Hervilly]: "L'Exposition du boulevard des Capucines", in: *Le Rappel*, 17.04.1874, p. 2; reprinted in: Berson 1996, vol. 1, pp. 23–24.

E. de M. [De Montagnac] 1889: E. de M. [Elisée-Louis Baron de Montagnac], in: *La Liberté*, 26.06.1889; reprinted in: exh. cat. Paris 1989, pp. 226.

Eiling 2014: Alexander Eiling: "Klassik und Experiment im Werk von Edgar Degas", in: exh. cat. Karlsruhe 2014, pp. 16–29.

Eiling 2016: Alexander Eiling: "'Il faut copier et recopier les maîtres …'. Degas und die Kopie", in: exh. cat. Wuppertal 2016, pp. 117–127.

Eiling et al. 2014: Alexander Eiling et al.: "Von Sparta nach Paris. Historie und Bühne", in: exh. cat. Karlsruhe 2014, pp. 157–199.

Eisenman 1986: Stephen F. Eisenman: "The Intransigent Artist or How the Impressionists Got Their Name", in: exh. cat. Washington/San Francisco 1986, pp. 51–59.

Elliott 2014: Patrick Elliott: "Capturing the Fleeting Moment: Impressionism and Sculpture", in: exh. cat. Berlin 2014, pp. 206–217.

Elliott 2016: Patrick Elliott: "Beeldhouwkunst en Impressionisme: Degas, Rodin, Rosso", in: exh. cat. The Hague 2016, pp. 23–25.

Elliott 2017: Patrick Elliott: "Rodin's Burghers of Calais: A New Image of Man", in: *Rodin's Burghers of Calais. Under the Spotlight*, exh. cat. The Sladmore Gallery, London, 2017, pp. 42–49.

Elsen 1965: Albert E. Elsen: *Auguste Rodin. Readings on His Life and Work*, Englewood Cliffs 1965.

Elsen 1974: Albert E. Elsen: *Origins of Modern Sculpture. Pioneers and Premises*, New York 1974.

Elsen 1985: Albert E. Elsen: *The Gates of Hell by Auguste Rodin*, Stanford 1985.

Eremite 1893: Kalophile Eremite [Alphonse Germain]: "Chroniques. IV. Les arts: Les expositions: La Bodinière", in: *L'Ermitage*, December 1893, p. 373.

Exh. cat. Aarhus 2015: *Monet – Lost in Translation. Corot, Courbet, Diaz de la Peña, Rousseau, Boudin, Pissarro, Degas, Sisley, Morisot, Guillaumin, Renoir, Gauguin*, edited by Suzanne Greub, exh. cat. ARoS Aarhus Kunstmuseum, Munich 2015.

Exh. cat. Amsterdam 1991: *Degas. Sculptor*, edited by Ronald Pickvance and Charlotte van Rappard-Boon, exh. cat. Rijksmuseum Vincent van Gogh, Amsterdam, Zwolle 1991.

Exh. cat. Berlin 1994: *Licht und Schatten. Rodin-Photographien von Eugène Druet*, exh. cat. Georg-Kolbe-Museum, Berlin 1994.

Exh. cat. Berlin 2005: *Druet sieht Rodin. Photographie & Skulptur*, edited by Bernhard Maaz, exh. cat. Alte Nationalgalerie, Berlin 2005.

Exh. cat. Berlin 2013: *Medardo Rosso. 12 Skulpturen. Le sculpteur de la lumière*, exh. cat. Kunsthandel Wolfgang Werner Berlin, Bremen etc. 2013.

Exh. cat. Berlin 2014: *Rembrandt Bugatti: The Sculptor, 1884–1916*, edited by Philipp Demandt and Anke Daemgen, exh. cat. Alte Nationalgalerie Berlin – Staatliche Museen zu Berlin, Munich 2014.

Exh. cat. Berlin/Vaduz 2014: *Lens-based Sculpture. Die Veränderung der Skulptur durch die Fotografie*, edited by Bogomir Ecker, exh. cat. Akademie der Künste, Berlin/Kunstmuseum Liechtenstein, Vaduz, Cologne 2014.

Exh. cat. Boston/Paris 2012: *Degas and the Nude*, compiled by George T. M. Shackelford and Xavier Rey, exh. cat. Museum of Fine Arts, Boston/Musée d'Orsay, Paris, London 2012.

Exh. cat. Bremen/Neuss 2006: *Intimität der Gefühle. Eugène Carrière zum 100. Todestag*, compiled by Anne Röver-Kann, edited by Kunstverein in Bremen and Kunsthalle Bremen, exh. cat. Kunsthalle Bremen/Clemens-Sels-Museum Neuss, Bremen 2006.

Exh. cat. Brescia 2003: *Impressionismo italiano*, edited by Renato Barilli, exh. cat. Palazzo Martinengo, Brescia, Milan 2003.

Exh. cat. Calais/Paris 1977: *Auguste Rodin. Le monument des Bourgeois de Calais (1884–1895) dans les collections du Musée Rodin et du Musée des Beaux-Arts de Calais*, compiled by Claudie Judrin, Monique Laurent and Dominique Viéville, exh. cat. Musée des Beaux-Arts de Calais/Musée Rodin, Paris, Paris and Calais 1977.

Exh. cat. Cambridge/Denver 2017: *Degas. A Passion for Perfection*, edited by Jane Munro, exh. cat. The Fitzwilliam Museum, Cambridge/Denver Art Museum, New Haven and London 2017.

Exh. cat. Chicago 1984: *Degas in The Art Institute of Chicago*, compiled by Richard R. Brettell and Suzanne Folds McCullagh, exh. cat. The Art Institute of Chicago, New York 1984.

Exh. cat. Cologne/Florence 2008: *Impressionismus. Wie das Licht auf die Leinwand kam*, compiled by Iris Schaefer et al., exh. cat. Wallraf-Richartz-Museum and Fondation Corboud, Cologne/Palazzo Strozzi, Florence, Milan 2008.

Exh. cat. Copenhagen 1988: *Rodin. La collection du Brasseur Carl Jacobsen à la Glyptothèque – et œuvres apparentés*, compiled by Anne-Birgitte Fonsmark, exh. cat. Ny Carlsberg Glyptothek, Copenhagen 1988.

Exh. cat. Copenhagen 2013: *Degas' Method*, edited by Line Clausen Pedersen, exh. cat. Ny Carlsberg Glyptotek, Copenhagen 2013.

Exh. cat. Copenhagen/Fort Worth 2005: *Gauguin and Impressionism*, compiled by Richard R. Brettell and Anne-Birgitte Fonsmark, exh. cat. Ordrupgaard, Copenhagen/Kimbell Art Museum, Fort Worth, New Haven and London 2005.

Exh. cat. Duisburg 2016: *An der Oberfläche. Von Rodin bis De Bruyckere. Die Oberfläche als Bedeutungsträger in der Skulptur*, edited by Söke Dinkla, exh. cat. Lehmbruck Museum, Duisburg, Cologne 2016.

Exh. cat. Duisburg etc. 1997: *Skulptur im Licht der Fotografie. Von Bayard bis Mapplethorpe*, edited by Erika Billeter, exh. cat. Wilhelm-Lehmbruck-Museum, Duisburg etc., Wabern-Berne 1997.

Exh. cat. Edinburgh 1997: *The Portrait of a Lady. Sargent and Lady Agnew*, compiled by Julia Rayer Rolfe, exh. cat. National Gallery of Scotland, Edinburgh 1997.

Exh. cat. Edinburgh 2003: *Degas and the Italians in Paris*, compiled by Ann Dumas, exh. cat. National Galleries of Scotland, Edinburgh 2003.

Exh. cat. Ferrara 2003: *Degas e gli italiani a Parigi*, edited by Ann Dumas, exh. cat. Palazzo dei Diamanti, Ferrara 2003.

Exh. cat. Ferrara/Williamstown 2009: *Giovanni Boldini in Impressionist Paris*, edited by Sarah Lees, exh. cat. Palazzo dei Diamanti, Ferrara/Sterling and Francine Clark Institute, Williamstown, New Haven etc. 2009.

Exh. cat. Frankfurt 1984: *Medardo Rosso 1858–1928*, edited by Peter Weiermair on behalf of Frankfurter Kunstvereins, exh. cat. Kunstverein Frankfurt, Steinernes Haus am Römerberg, Frankfurt am Main, Münsterschwarzach 1984.

Exh. cat. Frankfurt 2006: *Gärten. Ordnung – Inspiration – Glück*, edited by Sabine Schulze, exh. cat. Städel Museum, Frankfurt am Main, Ostfildern 2006.

Exh. cat. Geneva 1985: *Pygmalion photographe. La sculpture devant la caméra, 1844–1936*, compiled by Rainer Michael Mason, exh. cat. Cabinet des Estampes, Musée d'Art et d'Histoire, Geneva 1985.

Exh. cat. Giverny 2015: *Degas. Un peintre impressionniste?*, edited by Maria Ferretti Bocquillon and Xavier Rey, exh. cat. Musée des Impressionnismes Giverny, Paris 2015.

Exh. cat. The Hague 2016: *Van Rodin tot Bourgeois. Sculptuur in de 20ste eeuw*, edited by Patrick Elliott, exh. cat. Het Gemeentemuseum, The Hague 2016.

Exh. cat. Hamburg 2009: *Degas. Intimität und Pose*, edited by Hubertus Gaßner, exh. cat. Hamburger Kunsthalle, Munich 2009.

Exh. cat. Karlsruhe 2007: *Elegant/expressiv. Von Houdon bis Rodin. Französische Plastik des 19. Jahrhunderts*, edited by Staatliche Kunsthalle Karlsruhe, exh. cat. Staatliche Kunsthalle Karlsruhe, Heidelberg 2007.

Exh. cat. Karlsruhe 2014: *Degas. Klassik und Experiment*, edited by Alexander Eiling, exh. cat. Staatliche Kunsthalle Karlsruhe, Munich 2014.

Exh. cat. Karlsruhe 2018: *Sehen. Denken. Träumen. Französische Zeichnungen aus der Staatlichen Kunsthalle Karlsruhe*, edited by Dorit Schäfer and Astrid Reuter, exh. cat. Staatliche Kunsthalle Karlsruhe, Berlin 2018.

Exh. cat. Liverpool 1989: *Degas. Images of Women*, edited by Richard Kendall, exh. cat. Tate Gallery, Liverpool, London 1989.

Exh. cat. London 1906: *Medardo Rosso. Impressions*, exh. cat. Eugene Cremetti Gallery, London 1906.

Exh. cat. London 1931: *Sculpture by Prince Paul Troubetzkoy, with a Word by Bernard Shaw*, exh. cat. P. & D. Colnaghi & Co. London, London 1931, unpaginated.

Exh. cat. London 1990: *Art in the Making. Impressionism*, compiled by David Bomford et al., exh. cat. The National Gallery, London, New Haven etc. 1990.

Exh. cat. London 1998: *John Singer Sargent*, edited by Elaine Kilmurray and Richard Ormond, exh. cat. Tate Gallery, London 1998.

Exh. cat. London 2008: *Prince Paul Troubetzkoy. The Belle Epoque Captured in Bronze*, compiled by Oliver Wootton, exh. cat. The Sladmore Gallery, London 2008.

Exh. cat. London 2011: *Degas and the Ballet. Picturing Movement*, compiled by Richard Kendall and Jill DeVonyar, exh. cat. Royal Academy of Art, London 2011.

Exh. cat. London 2017: *Medardo Rosso. Sight Unseen and His Encounters with London*, exh. cat. Galerie Thaddaeus Ropac, London 2017.

Exh. cat. London etc. 1994: *Medardo Rosso*, exh. cat. Whitechapel Art Gallery, London etc., London 1994.

Exh. cat. London/Chicago 1996: *Degas. Beyond Impressionism*, edited by Richard Kendall, exh. cat. National Gallery, London/The Art Institute of Chicago, New Haven 1996.

Exh. cat. Louviers 2016: *Portraits impressionnistes. Le visage d'une nouvelle société*, edited by Michel Natier and Philippe Piguet, exh. cat. Musée de Louviers 2016.

Exh. cat. Lugano 1989: *L'impressicnismo nella scultura*, edited by Luciano Caramel, exh. cat. Galleria Pieter Coray, Lugano, Milan 1989.

Exh. cat. Lyon 1998: *Rodin. Les Métamorphoses de Mme F.: Auguste Rodin, Maurice Fenaille et Lyon*, edited by Philippe Durey and Antoinette Le Normand-Romain, exh. cat. Musée des Beaux-Arts de Lyon 1998.

Exh. cat. Madrid 1990: *Medardo Rosso. Los dibujos – I disegni*, edited by Luciano Caramel, exh. cat. Istituto Italiano di Cultura, Palacio de Abrantes, Madrid, Milan 1990.Exh. cat. Manchester/Cambridge 1987: *The Private Degas*, compiled by Richard Thomson, exh. cat. Withworth Art Gallery, Manchester/The Fitzwilliam Museum, Cambridge, London 1987.

Exh. cat. Mannheim 1912: *Ausdrucks-Plastik. IV. Ausstellung des Freien Bundes zur Einbürgerung der bildenden Kunst in Mannheim*, edited by Freie Bund zur Einbürgerung der bildenden Kunst, exh. cat. Kunsthalle Mannheim, Mannheim 1912.

Exh. cat. Milan 1979: *Mostra di Medardo Rosso*, exh. cat. Palazzo della Permanente, Milan 1979.

Exh. cat. Milan 1998: *Da Vela a Medardo Rosso. I grandi scultori italiani dell'Ottocento*, exh. cat. Museo Minguzzi, Milan 1998.

Exh. cat. Milan 2009: *Scapigliatura. Un "pandemonio" per cambiare l'arte*, edited by Annie-Paule Quinsac, exh. cat. Palazzo Reale, Milan, Venice 2009.

Exh. cat. Milan 2015: *Medardo Rosso. La luce e la materia*, edited by Paola Zatti, exh. cat. Galleria d'Arte Moderna, Milan 2015.

Exh. cat. Milan 2015a: *Dalla Scapigliatura al Divisionismo. Le origini della modernità*, edited by Stefano Bosi and Enzo Savoia, exh. cat. Bottegantica, Milan 2015.

Exh. cat. Milan 2017: *100 anni. Scultura a Milano 1815–1915*, edited by Omar Cucciniello et al., exh. cat. Galleria d'Arte Moderna, Milan 2017.

Exh. cat. Naples 2003: *Winds of Change. From the Gilgore Collection: The Milanese Avant-Garde 1860–1900*, exh. cat. Gilgore Collection, Naples, Florida, 2003.

Exh. cat. New York 1963: *Medardo Rosso*, edited by Margaret Scolari Barr, exh. cat. The Museum of Modern Art, New York 1963.

Exh. cat. New York/Chicago 1986: *John Singer Sargent*, edited by Patricia Hills, exh. cat. Whitney Museum of American Art, New York/The Art Institute of Chicago, New York 1986.

Exh. cat. New York/Edinburgh 2009: *Raphael to Renoir. Drawings from the Collection of Jean Bonna*, edited by Stijn Alsteens et al., exh. cat. The Metropolitan Museum of Art, New York/National Gallery of Scotland, Edinburgh, New Haven etc. 2009.

Exh. cat. New York/Zurich 2010: *Foto-Skulptur. Die Fotografie der Skulptur 1839 bis heute*, exh. cat. The Museum of Modern Art, New York/Kunsthaus Zürich, Ostfildern 2010; English edition: exh. cat. New York and Zurich 2010a.

Exh. cat. New York/Zurich 2010a: *The Original Copy. Photography of Sculpture, 1839 to Today*, exh. cat. The Museum of Modern Art, New York/Kunsthaus Zürich, New York 2010 (English edition: exh. cat. New York/Zurich 2010).

Exh. cat. Nice/Paris 2009: *Matisse – Rodin*, edited by Jean-Baptiste Chantoiseau, exh. cat. Musée Matisse, Nice/Musée Rodin, Paris, Paris 2009.

Exh. cat. Novi Ligure 2007: *L'altra metà della vita. Interni nell'arte da Pellizza a De Chirico. 1865–1940*, edited by Nicoletta Colombo and Giuliana Godio, exh. cat. Museo dei Campionissimi, Novi Ligure 2007.

Exh. cat. Omaha etc. 1998: *Degas and the Little Dancer*, edited by Richard Kendall, exh. cat. Joslyn Art Museum, Omaha etc., New Haven and London 1998.

Exh. cat. Paris 1874: *Société anonyme des artistes peintres, sculpteurs, graveurs, etc. Première exposition*, exh. cat. 35, boulevard des Capucines, Paris 1874.

Exh. cat. Paris 1876: *Catalogue de la 2e exposition de peinture par MM. Béliard – Legros – Pissarro – Bureau – Lepic – Renoir – Caillebotte – Levert – Rouart – Cals – Millet (J.-B.) – Sisley – Degas – Monet (Claude) – Tiliot – Desboutin – Morisot (Berthe) – François (Jacques) – Ottin fils*, exh. cat. 11, rue Le Peletier, Paris 1876.

Exh. cat. Paris 1886: *Catalogue de la 8me Exposition de Peinture*, exh. cat. 1, rue Laffitte, Paris 1886.

Exh. cat. Paris 1889: *Claude Monet – Auguste Rodin*, exh. cat. Galerie Georges Petit, Paris, 1889; reprinted in: exh. cat. Paris 1989, pp. 48–70.

Exh. cat. Paris 1900: *Exposition de 1900. L'œuvre de Rodin*, exh. cat. Pavillon Place de l'Alma, Paris 1900.

Exh. cat. Paris 1986: *Les Photographes de Rodin. Jacques-Ernest Bulloz, Eugène Druet, Stephen Haweis et Henry Coles, Jean-François Limet, Eduard Steichen*, compiled by Hélène Pinet, exh. cat. Musée Rodin, Paris 1986.

Bibliography

Exh. cat. Paris 1986a: *La Sculpture Française au XIXe siècle*, compiled by Anne Pingeot, exh. cat. Galeries nationales du Grand Palais, Paris 1986.

Exh. cat. Paris 1989: *Claude Monet – Auguste Rodin. Centenaire de l'exposition de 1889*, edited by Jacques Vilain, exh. cat. Musée Rodin, Paris 1989.

Exh. cat. Paris 1990: *Rodin et ses modèles. Le portrait photographié*, compiled by Hélène Pinet, exh. cat. Musée Rodin, Paris 1990.

Exh. cat. Paris 1991: *Photographie/Sculpture*, compiled by Dominique Païni, exh. cat. Palais de Tokyo, Paris 1991.

Exh. cat. Paris 1999: *Six chefs-d'œuvre français prétés par Francfort/Impressionisten. 6 französische Meisterwerke*, exh. cat. Musée d'Orsay, Paris, Frankfurt am Main 1999.

Exh. cat. Paris 2001: *Rodin en 1900. L'exposition de l'Alma*, edited by Antoinette Le Normand-Romain and Josette Grandazzi, exh. cat. Musée du Luxembourg, Paris 2001.

Exh. cat. Paris 2007: *Rodin et la photographie*, edited by Hélène Pinet, exh. cat. Musée Rodin, Paris 2007.

Exh. cat. Paris 2010: *Monet, Rodin. Rien que vous et moi*, edited by Nadine Lehni and Véronique Mattiussi, exh. cat. Musée Rodin, Paris 2010.

Exh. cat. Paris 2010a: *Gustave Moreau. L'Homme aux figures de cire*, edited by Marie-Cécile Forrest and Anne Pingeot, exh. cat. Museé National Gustave Moreau, Paris, Somogy etc. 2010.

Exh. cat. Paris 2012: *Rodin. La chair, le marbre*, edited by Aline Magnien, exh. cat. Musée Rodin, Paris 2012.

Exh. cat. Paris 2017: *Rodin. Le livre du centenaire*, edited by Catherine Chevillot and Antoinette Le Normand-Romain, exh. cat. Grand Palais, Paris 2017.

Exh. cat. Paris 2017a: *Degas, danse, dessin. Hommage à Degas avec Paul Valéry*, edited by Leïla Jarbouai and Marine Kisiel, exh. cat. Musée d'Orsay, Paris 2017.

Exh. cat. Paris 2018: *Rodin et la danse*, edited by Catherine Chevillot and Jean-Baptiste Chantoiseau, exh. cat. Musée Rodin, Paris 2018.

Exh. cat. Paris 2018a: *La Sculpture Polychrome en France, 1850–1910*, edited by Édouard Papet, exh. cat. Museé d'Orsay, Paris 2018.

Exh. cat. Paris 2018b: *Rodin. Dessiner, découper*, compiled by Sophie Biass-Fabiani, exh. cat. Musée Rodin, Paris 2018.

Exh. cat. Paris 2019: *Degas à l'Opéra*, edited by Henri Loyrette, exh. cat. Musée d'Orsay, Paris 2019.

Exh. cat. Paris etc. 1988: *Degas*, edited by Jean Sutherland Boggs et al., exh. cat. Galeries Nationales du Grand Palais, Paris etc., Paris 1988 (English edition).

Exh. cat. Paris/Caen 2010: *L'Estampe Impressionniste de Manet à Renoir. Trésors de la Bibliothèque Nationale de France*, edited by Caroline Joubert, Michel Melot and Valérie Sueur-Hermel, exh. cat. Bibliothèque Nationale de France, Paris/Musée des Beaux-Arts de Caen, Paris 2010.

Exh. cat. Paris/Poitiers 1984: *Camille Claudel (1864–1943)*, compiled by Monique Laurent and Bruno Gaudichon, exh. cat. Musée Rodin, Paris/Musée Sainte-Croix, Poitiers, Paris 1984.

Exh. cat. Potsdam 2017: *Impressionismus – Die Kunst der Landschaft*, edited by Ortrud Westheider and Michael Philipp, exh. cat. Museum Barberini, Potsdam, Munich etc. 2017.

Exh. cat. Riehen 2011: *Segantini*, edited by Beyeler Museum AG etc., exh. cat. Fondation Beyeler, Riehen/Basle, Ostfildern 2011.

Exh. cat. Riehen 2012: *Edgar Degas. Das Spätwerk*, edited by Schwander, exh. cat. Fondation Beyeler, Riehen/Basle, Ostfildern 2012.

Exh. cat. Rodez 2000: *Maurice Fenaille. Les secrets d'un mécène*, edited by Laurence Imbernon and Annie Philippon, exh. cat. Musée Denys-Puech, Rodez 2000.

Exh. cat. Rome/Paris 2000: *Italie 1880–1910. Arte alla prova della modernità*, exh. cat. Galleria Nazionale d'Arte Moderna, Rome/Musée d'Orsay, Paris, Turin 2000.

Exh. cat. Roubaix 2010: *Degas sculpteur. Un exceptionnel Orsay hors les murs*, edited by Bruno Gaudichon and Catherine Chevillot, exh. cat. La Piscine – Musée d'Art et d'Industrie André-Diligent, Roubaix, Paris 2010.

Exh. cat. Rouen 1994: *Rouen, les cathédrales de Monet*, edited by Gilles Grandjean, exh. cat. Musée des Beaux-Arts, Rouen 1994.

Exh. cat. Rovereto/Turin 2004: *Medardo Rosso. Le origini della scultura moderna*, exh. cat. Museo di Arte Moderna e Contemporanea, Rovereto/Galleria Civica d'Arte Moderna e Contemporanea, Turin, Milan 2004.

Exh. cat. Santiago de Compostela 1996: *Medardo Rosso*, edited by Gloria Moure, exh. cat. Centro Galego de Arte Contemporánea, Santiago de Compostela 1996.

Exh. cat. St. Louis 2018: *Medardo Rosso. Experiments in Light and Form*, exh. cat. Pulitzer Arts Foundation, St. Louis, Missouri 2018.

Exh. cat. Stuttgart 2001: *Von Rodin bis Baselitz. Der Torso in der Skulptur der Moderne*, edited by Kathrin Elvers-Švamberk and Wolfgang Brückle, exh. cat. Staatsgalerie Stuttgart, Ostfildern 2001.

Exh. cat. Stuttgart 2002: *Edouard Manet und die Impressionisten*, exh. cat. Staatsgalerie Stuttgart, Ostfildern 2002.

Exh. cat. Tokyo/Paris 2006: *Auguste Rodin – Eugène Carrière*, edited by Mina Oya, exh. cat. The National Museum of Western Art, Tokyo/Musée d'Orsay, Paris, Paris 2006.

Exh. cat. Verbania Pallanza 1990: *Paolo Troubetzkoy. 1866–1938*, edited by Giovanni Piantoni and Paolo Venturoli, exh. cat. Museo del Paesaggio, Palazzo Viani Dugnani, Verbania Pallanza, Turin 1990.

Exh. cat. Vienna 1903: *Entwicklung des Impressionismus in Malerei und Plastik*, edited by Vereinigung Bildender Künstler Österreichs, Secession Vienna, exh. cat. Viennaer Secession, Vienna 1903.

Exh. cat. Washington 1984: *Degas. The Dancers*, edited by George T. M. Shackelford, exh. cat. National Gallery of Art, Washington, D.C., 1984.

Exh. cat. Washington/San Francisco 1986: *The New Painting. Impressionism 1874–1886*, edited by Charles S. Moffett, exh. cat. National Gallery of Art, Washington, D.C./The Fine Arts Museum of San Francisco, Oxford 1986.

Exh. cat. Winterthur/Duisburg 2003: *Medardo Rosso*, edited by Dieter Schwarz, exh. cat. Kunstmuseum Winterthur/Stiftung Wilhelm Lehmbruck Museum Duisburg, Zentrum Internationaler Skulptur, Düsseldorf 2003.

Exh. cat. Wuppertal 2016: *Degas – Rodin. Wettlauf der Giganten zur Moderne*, edited by Gerhard Finckh, exh. cat. Von der Heydt-Museum, Wuppertal 2016.

Exh. cat. Zurich 1990: *Giovanni Segantini. 1858–1899*, edited by Daniela Tobler, exh. cat. Kunsthaus Zürich 1990.

F

Fagioli/Minnuno 1993: Marco Fagioli and Lucia Minnuno (eds): *Medardo Rosso. Catalogo delle sculture*, Florence 1993.

Fagus 1899: Félicien Fagus [= Georges-Eugène Faille]: "Ses collaborateurs", in: *La Revue des Beaux-Arts et des Lettres*, 01.01.1899, p. 13.

Fagus 1900: Félicien Fagus [= Georges-Eugène Faille]: "Salon de la Plume, 2: Le Vieux Chêne, par Rodin", in: *La Revue Blanche*, 15.07.1900; reprinted in: *La Revue Blanche, 1889–1903*, 30 vols, Geneva 1968, vol. 22: May/June/July/August 1900, p. 465.

Fénéon 1886: Félix Fénéon: "Les Impressionnistes", in: *La Vogue*, 13–20.06.1886, pp. 261–275; reprinted in: Berson 1996, vol. 1, pp. 441–445.

Ferlier 2014: Ophélie Ferlier: "Fur and Feather. Animaliers in Paris – Animal Sculpture from Barye to Pompon", in: Exh. cat. Berlin 2014, pp. 177–183.

Filippi 1872: Filippo Filippi: "Esposizione nazionale di Belle Arti. X. Pittori milanesi", in: *La Lombardia*, 251, 11.09.1872.

Finckh 2016: Gerhard Finckh: "Vorwort", in: exh. cat. Wuppertal 2016, pp. 11–43.

Fleckner 2010: Uwe Fleckner: "Karl Ernst Osthaus und die französische Moderne. Über das widersprüchliche Selbstverständnis eines Sammlers", in: Hartwig Fischer and Uwe M. Schneede (eds): *"Das schönste Museum der Welt". Museum Folkwang bis 1933. Essays zur Geschichte des Museum Folkwang*, Göttingen 2010, pp. 47–69.

Fles 1922: Etha Fles: *Medardo Rosso. Der Mensch und der Künstler*, Freiburg im Breisgau 1922.

Flor 1882: Charles Flor: "Deux Expositions", in: *Le National*, 03.03.1882, p. 2; reprinted in: Berson 1996, vol. 1, pp. 387–389.

Foa 2019: Michelle Foa: "The Making of Degas: Duranty, Technology, and the Meaning of Materials in Later Nineteenth-Century Paris", in: *nonsite.org*, 27, 2019, pp. 1–27; https://nonsite.org/article/the-making-of-degas (accessed 27 September 2019).

Fonsmark 2005: Anne-Birgitte Fonsmark: "Gauguin's Debut as a Sculptor", in: exh. cat. Copenhagen/Fort Worth 2005, pp. 70–73.

Fonsmark 2005a: Anne-Birgitte Fonsmark: "Gauguin and 'Impressionist Sculptors'", in: exh. cat. Copenhagen/Fort Worth 2005, pp. 126–133.

Fonsmark 2005b: Anne-Birgitte Fonsmark: "The Sculpture Mania. 1882", in: exh. cat. Copenhagen/Fort Worth 2005, pp. 190–193.

Fonsmark 2005c: Anne-Birgitte Fonsmark: "A Painter-Sculptor Makes Ceramics", in: exh. cat. Copenhagen/Fort Worth 2005, pp. 286–297.

Fontainas 1900: André Fontainas: "L'Exposition Centennale", in: *Mercure de France*, 35, 127, July 1900, pp. 388–412.

Fontainas 1901: André Fontainas: "Art modern", in: *Mercure de France*, 39, 139, July 1901, pp. 215–219.

Förschl 2006: Eve Förschl: "Medardo Rosso", in: *Nationalgalerie Berlin. Das XIX. Jahrhundert, Bestandskatalog der Skulpturen*, edited by Bernhard Maaz, inv. cat. Nationalgalerie, Berlin, 2 vols, Leipzig 2006, vol. 2, pp. 633–634.

Foucault [1975] 2002: Michel Foucault: "Die fotogene Malerei" [1975]: in: idem: *Schriften in vier Bänden. Dits et Écrits*, vol. 2, Frankfurt am Main 2002, pp. 871–882.

France 1900: Anatole France: "La Porte de l'Enfer", in: *Le Figaro*, 07.06.1900.

Franz 2003: Erich Franz: "Emotion der Entgrenzung. Zu den Zeichnungen vor Medardo Rosso", in: exh. cat. Winterthur/Duisburg 2003, pp. 180–187.

Frezzotti 1990: Stefania Frezzotti: "George Bernard Shaw", in: exh. cat. Verbania Pallanza 1990, pp. 174–176.

Frezzotti 1990a: Stefania Frezzotti: "Paolo Troubetzkoy. Regesto biografico", in: exh. cat. Verbania Pallanza 1990, pp. 220–223.

Fromanger 2009: Véronique Fromanger: *Rembrandt Bugatti. Sculpteur. Une trajectoire foudroyante. Répertoire monographique*, Paris 2009.

G

G. G. [Geffroy] 1881: G. G. [Gustave Geffroy]: "L'Exposition des artistes indépendants", in: *La Justice*, 04.04.1881, p. 3; reprinted in: Berson 1996, vol. 1, pp. 341–342.

Gall 1997: Jean-Luc Gall: "Photo/sculpture. L'invention de François Willème", in: *Études photographiques*, 3, November 1997, pp. 64–81; https://journals.openedition.org/etudesphotographiques/95 (accessed 4 November 2019)

Gaudichon 1983: Bruno Gaudichon: "Ottin, Auguste-Louis-Marie", in: *Catalogue des sculptures des XIXe et XXe siècles dans les collections des musées de la ville de Poitiers et de la société des antiquaires de l'ouest*, compiled by Blandine Chavanne et al., inv. cat. Musées de la Ville de Poitiers, Société des Antiquaires de l'Ouest, Poitiers 1983, p. 101.

Gaudichon 2010: Bruno Gaudichon: "Et moi qui veux faire de la sculpture", in: exh. cat. Roubaix 2010, pp. 13–42.

Gauguin 1983: Paul Gauguin: *45 lettres à Vincent, Théo et Jo van Gogh*, edited by Douglas Cooper, 's-Gravenhage 1983.

Gauguin 1984: Paul Gauguin: *Correspondance de Paul Gauguin. Documents, témoignages*, edited by Victor Merlhès, Paris 1984.

Gavrilovich 1990: Donatella Gavrilovich: "Troubetzkoy nei circoli artistici della Russia di fine secolo", in: exh. cat. Verbania Pallanza 1990, pp. 44–53.

Geffroy 1889: Gustave Geffroy: "Auguste Rodin", in: exh. cat. Paris 1889, pp. 46–84; reprinted in: exh. cat. Paris 1989, pp. 59–68.

Geffroy 1889a: Gustave Geffroy: "Chronique. L'exposition Monet – Rodin", in: *La Justice*, 21.06.1889; reprinted in: exh. cat. Paris 1989, pp. 219–220.

Geffroy 1922: Gustave Geffroy: *Claude Monet. Sa vie, son temps, son œuvre*, Paris 1922.

Gerdts 1986: William Gerdts: "'The Arch-Apostle of the Dab-and-Spot-School': John Singer Sargent as an Impressionist", in: exh. cat. New York/Chicago 1986, pp. 111–145.

Gerstein 1982: Marc Gerstein: "Degas's Fans", in: *The Art Bulletin*, 64, 1, 3, 1982, pp. 105–118.

Getsy 2010: David J. Getsy: *Rodin. Sex and the Making of Modern Sculpture*, New Haven etc. 2010.

Giedion-Welcker 1955: Carola Giedion-Welcker: *Plastik des 20. Jahrhunderts. Volumen und Raumgestaltung*, Stuttgart 1955.

Ginex 2014: Giovanna Ginex: "From Milan to Paris. Rembrandt Bugatti's Beginnings within the Art Environment of His Home City", in: exh. cat. Berlin 2014, pp. 185–193.

Giolli 1913: Raffaello Giolli: *P. Troubetzkoy*, Milan [1913].

Glaser 1922: Curt Glaser: *Die Graphik der Neuzeit. Vom Anfang des XIX. Jahrhunderts bis zur Gegenwart*, Berlin 1922.

Glaser 1922a: Curt Glaser: "Degas als Bildhauer", in: *Kunst und Künstler. Illustrierte Monatsschrift für bildende Kunst und Kunstgewerbe*, 20, 1922, pp. 123–128.

Gloor 2016: Lukas Gloor: "Das Tutu der *Kleinen vierzehnjährigen Tänzerin* von Edgar Degas – ein flüchtiges Gewebe", in: exh. cat. Wuppertal 2016, pp. 301–307.

Göthe 2014: Anett Göthe: "Degas und der Japonismus", in: exh. cat. Karlsruhe 2014, pp. 54–65.

Goetschy 1880: Gustave Goetschy: "Indépendants et impresionistes [sic]", in: *Le Voltaire*, 06.04.1880, p. 2; reprinted in: Berson 1996, vol. 1, pp. 282–285.

Graber 1942: Hans Graber (ed.): *Edgar Degas. Nach eigenen und fremden Zeugnissen*, Basle 1942.

Gray 1963: Christopher Gray: *Sculpture and Ceramics of Paul Gauguin*, Baltimore 1963.

Bibliography

Großkopf 2012: Anna Großkopf: "Das Tier im Blick. Der Bildhauer Anton Puchegger", in: *Das Tier im Blick. Der Bildhauer Anton Puchegger (1878–1917)*, edited by Ingeborg Becker, exh. cat. Bröhan-Museum, Berlin, 2012, pp. 5–16.

Growe 1981: Bernd Growe: *Zur Bildkonzeption Edgar Degas'*, Frankfurt am Main 1981.

Gruetzner Robins 2007: Anna Gruetzner Robins: *A Fragile Modernism. Whistler and his Impressionist Followers*, New Haven and London 2007.

Gruetzner Robins 2011: Anna Gruetzner Robins: *Degas. The Painter of Modern Life. Memories of Degas by George Moore and Walter Sickert*, London 2011.

Gsell 1918: Paul Gsell: "Edgar Degas Statuaire", in: *La Renaissance de l'art français et des industries de luxe*, December 1918, pp. 373–378.

Gülicher 2011: Nina Gülicher: *Inszenierte Skulptur. Auguste Rodin, Medardo Rosso und Constantin Brancusi*, Diss. Berlin 2008, Munich 2011.

H

Halévy 1995: Daniel Halévy: *Degas parle*, Paris 1995.

Hamann [1907] 1923: Richard Hamann: *Der Impressionismus in Leben und Kunst* [1907], Marburg 1923.

Hamber 1996: Anthony Hamber: *"A higher branch of the art". Photographing the Fine Arts in England 1839–1880 (Documenting the Image*, vol. 4), Amsterdam 1996.

Hammacher 1973: Abraham Marie Hammacher: *Tradition und Erneuerung. Die Entwicklung der modernen Skulptur*, Berlin 1973.

Hargrove 2007: June Hargrove: "Against the Grain. The Sculpture of Paul Gauguin in the Context of his Contemporaries", in: *Current Issues in 19th-Century Art (Van Gogh Studies*, vol. 1), Zwolle and Amsterdam 2007, pp. 73–111.

Harich-Hamburger 2005: Gisela Harich-Hamburger: "Eugène Druets Photographien nach Rodin, technisch betrachtet und historisch bewertet", in: exh. cat. Berlin 2005, pp. 29–38.

Hatt 2004: Michael Hatt: "Substance and Shadow: Conceptions of Embodiment in Rodin and the New Sculpture", in: Claudine Mitchell (ed.): *Rodin. The Zola of Sculpture*, Aldershot 2004, pp. 217–235.

Hauptman 2018: Jodi Hauptman: "Scrap Drawings", in: exh. cat. St. Louis 2018, pp. 71–85.

Hausenstein 1921: Wilhelm Hausenstein: "Degas als Plastiker", in: *Ganymed. Blätter der Marées-Gesellschaft*, 4, 1922, pp. 273–276.

Havemeyer 1961: Louisine Havemeyer: *Sixteen to Sixty. Memoirs of a Collector*, New York 1961.

Hecker 2010: Sharon Hecker: "An 'Enfant malade' by Medardo Rosso from the Collection of Louis Vauxcelles", in: *The Burlington Magazine*, 152, November 2010, pp. 727–753.

Hecker 2015: Sharon Hecker: "Everywhere is nowhere: Medardo Rosso and the Cultural Cosmopolitan in Fin-de-Siècle Paris" in: Karen L. Carter and Susan Waller (eds): *Foreign Artists and Communities in Modern Paris 1870–1914. Strangers in Paradise*, Farnham etc. 2015.

Hecker 2016: Sharon Hecker: "Technical Experiments and Serial Sculpture", in: exh. cat. St. Louis 2016, pp. 30–37.

Hecker 2017: Sharon Hecker: *A Moment's Monument. Medardo Rosso and the International Origins of Modern Sculpture*, Oakland, California, 2017.

Hecker 2017a: Sharon Hecker: "The Afterlife of Sculptures: Posthumous Casts and the Case of Medardo Rosso (1858–1928)", in: *Journal of Art Historiography*, 16, June 2017, pp. 1–18; https:// arthistoriography.files.wordpress.com/2017/06/hecker.pdf (accessed 22 July 2019).

Hecker 2018: Sharon Hecker: "Born in a Train. The Impact of Medardo Rosso's Internationalism on his Legacy", in: *Sculpture Journal*, 27.01.2018, pp. 105–116.

Hecker 2018a: Sharon Hecker: "Subjects of the Exhibition", in: exh. cat. St. Louis 2018, pp. 93–122.

Heinrich 2017: Christoph Heinrich: "Das Gleiche ist immer anders. Monets Serien und die Arbeit an der Abstraktion", in: exh. cat. Potsdam 2017, pp. 74–87.

Herbert 1988: Robert L. Herbert: *Impressionism. Art, Leisure, and Parisian Society*, New Haven etc. 1988.

Hevesi 1905: Ludwig Hevesi: "Medardo Rosso", in: *Kunst und Kunsthandwerk*, 8, 1905, pp. 174–182, 184 (fig.).

Hevesi 1905a: Ludwig Hevesi: "Medardo Rosso. Kunsthaus Artaria", in: *Fremden-Blatt*, 41, 10.02.1905, p. 19.

Hevesi 1905b: Ludwig Hevesi: "Medardo Rosso. Ein impressionistischer Bildhauer", in: *Pester Lloyd*, 19.02.1905.

Hevesi 1909: Ludwig Hevesi: "Medardo Rosso", in: idem: *Altkunst – Neukunst. Vienna 1894–1908*, Vienna 1909, pp. 554–558, reprinted in: exh. cat. Berlin 2013, non-paginated.

Höcherl 2003: Heike Höcherl: *Rodins Gipse. Ursprünge moderner Plastik (Schriften zur Bildenden Kunst*, edited by Jürg Meyer zur Capellen, vol. 12), with a foreword by Josef A. Schmoll genannt Eisenwerth, Frankfurt am Main etc. 2003.

Hofmann 1959: Werner Hofmann: "Das Material in der neuen Plastik", in: *Das Werk. Architektur und Kunst*, 46, 3, 1959, pp. 101–105.

Hofmann 2004: Werner Hofmann: *Daumier und Deutschland*, Munich and Berlin 2004.

Holsten 2007: Siegmar Holsten: "Vorwort", in: exh. cat. Karlsruhe 2007, pp. 7–18.

Horswell 2016: Edward Horswell: *Rembrandt Bugatti. Life in Sculpture*, 5th revised edition, London 2016.

Huysmans 1883: Joris-Karl Huysmans: *L'Art Moderne*, Paris 1883.

Huysmans 1883a: Joris-Karl Huysmans: "L'Exposition des indépendants en 1881", in: Huysmans 1883, pp. 225–257; reprinted in: Berson 1996, vol. 1, pp. 348–355.

I

Inv. cat. Paris 2007: *Rodin et le bronze. Catalogue des œuvres conservées au Musée Rodin*, compiled by Antoinette Le Normand-Romain, inv. cat. Musée Rodin, Paris, 2 vols, Paris 2007.

Inv. cat. Paris 2007a: *The Bronzes of Rodin. Catalogue of Works in the Musée Rodin*, compiled by Antoinette Le Normand-Romain, inv. cat. Musée Rodin, Paris, 2 vols, Paris 2007.

Inv. cat. Paris 2018: *La Galerie des sculptures du Petit Palais*, edited by Cécile Champy-Vinas, inv. cat. Petit Palais, Paris 2018.

Inv. cat. Pasadena 2006: *Degas in the Norton Simon Museum (Nineteenth-Century Art*, 2 vols), compiled by Sara Campbell et al., inv. cat. Norton Simon Museum, Pasadena, New Haven 2006.

Inv. cat. Philadelphia 1976: *The Sculpture of Auguste Rodin. The Collection of the Rodin Museum, Philadelphia*, compiled by John L. Tancock, inv. cat. Rodin Museum, Philadelphia 1976.

Inv. cat. Stanford 2003: *Rodin's Art. The Rodin Collection of the Iris & B. Gerald Cantor Center for Visual Arts at Stanford University*, compiled by Albert E. Elsen, inv. cat. Iris & B. Gerald Cantor Center for Visual Arts, Stanford University, New York 2003.

Inv. cat. Washington 2010: *Edgar Degas Sculpture* (*The Collections of the National Gallery of Art Systematic Catalogue*), compiled by Suzanne Glover Lindsay, Daphne S. Barbour and Shelley G. Sturman, inv. cat. National Gallery of Art, Washington, D.C., Princeton 2010.

Isaacson 1986: Joel Isaacson: "The Seventh Exhibition 1882. The Painters Called Impressionists", in: exh. cat. Washington/San Francisco 1986, pp. 375-393.

J

Janson 1985: Horst W. Janson: *Nineteenth-Century Sculpture*, New York 1985.

Jacques 1889: Edmond Jacques: "Rodin et Monet, in: *L'Intransigeant*, 07.07.1889; reprinted in: exh. cat. Paris 1989, p. 237.

Jarbouai 2019: Leïla Jarbouai: "Les petites danseuses", in: exh. cat. Paris 2019, pp. 253-261.

Jarrassé 1993: Dominique Jarrassé: *Rodin. Faszination der Bewegung*, trans. from French by Beatrice Löbl-Irmey, Paris 1993.

Jeanniot 1933: Georges Jeanniot: "Souvenirs sur Degas", in: *La Revue Universelle*, 55, 15, November 1933, pp. 280-304.

K

Kemp 1980: Wolfgang Kemp (ed.): *Theorie der Fotografie*, vol. 1: *1839-1912*, Munich 1980.

Kendall 1995: Richard Kendall: "Who Said Anything about Rodin? The Visibility and Contemporary Renown of Degas' Late Sculpture", in: *Apollo*, 142, August 1995, pp. 72-77.

Kendall 1996: Richard Kendall: "The Role of Sculpture", in: exh. cat. London/Chicago 1996, pp. 254-256.

Kendall 1998: Richard Kendall: "Can Art Descend Lower?", in: exh. cat. Omaha etc. 1998, pp. 45-75.

Kerber 1990: Bernhard Kerber: "Skulptur und Sockel: Probleme des Realitätsgrades", in: *Giessener Beiträge zur Kunstgeschichte*, vol. 8, 1990, pp. 113-193.

Kilmurray 1998: Elaine Kilmurray: "Impressionism", in: exh. cat. London 1998, p. 105.

Kisiel 2019: Marine Kisiel: "Mise en scène et mise en toile", in: exh. cat. Paris 2019, pp. 141-149.

Kjellberg 2005: Pierre Kjellberg: "Ottin, Auguste Louis Marie", in: idem: *Les Bronzes du XIXe siècle. Dictionnaire des sculptures*, 2nd edition, Paris 2005, p. 556.

Klingsor 1902: Tristan Klingsor: "L'Art Russe. Le Prince Troubetzkoy", in: *La Revue*, 40, 1902, pp. 30-45.

König 1997: Alexandra König: "Henri Matisse. 'Ich habe Skulpturen gemacht wie ein Maler'", in: *Die Maler und ihre Skulpturen. Von Edgar Degas bis Gerhard Richter*, edited by Gerhard Finckh, exh. cat. Museum Folkwang, Essen, Cologne 1997, pp. 81-86.

Kolberg 1990: Gerhard Kolberg: "Wer erfand die schräge Figur? Ein Disput um Auguste Rodin und Medardo Rosso, den 'Bildhauer des Lichts'", in: *Cologneer Museums-Bulletin. Berichte und Forschungen aus den Museen der Stadt Cologne*, 2, April–June 1990, pp. 4-11.

Kopp 1999: Michaela Kopp: *Rilke und Rodin. Auf der Suche nach der wahren Art des Schreibens* (*Heidelberger Beiträge zur deutschen Literatur*, vol. 3), Frankfurt am Main 1999.

Kramer 2001: Kolja Kramer: "Eine Dreiecksbeziehung für den französischen Impressionismus. Die Impressionisten-Ausstellung 1903 in der Viennaer Sezession", in: *Belvedere. Zeitschrift für Bildende Kunst*, 7, 2, 2001, pp. 48-65, 101-112.

Krauss 1977: Rosalind E. Krauss: *Passages in Modern Sculpture*, London and New York 1977.

Krauss 1981: Rosalind E. Krauss: "The Originality of the Avant-Garde. A Postmodernist Repetition", in: *October*, 18, 1981, pp. 47-66.

Kunze 2019: Franziska Kunze: *Opake Fotografien. Das Sichtbarmachen fotografischer Materialität als künstlerische Strategie*, Berlin 2019.

L

La Fare [Chaulieu] 1882: La Fare [Armand Chaulieu]: "Chez les impressionnistes", in: *Le Gaulois*, 23.02.1882, pp. 1-2; reprinted in: Berson 1996, vol. 1, pp. 399-400.

Lafond 1918/19: Paul Lafond: *Degas*, 2 vols, Paris 1918/19.

Lalanne 1866: Maxime Lalanne: *La Gravure à l'eau-forte*, with a foreword by Charles Blanc, Paris 1866.

Lami 1921: Stanislas Lami: "Ottin (Auguste-Louis-Marie)", in: idem: *Dictionnaire des sculpteurs de l'école française*, 4 vols, Nendeln 1914-1921, vol. 4, 1921, pp. 27-32.

Lammert 2007: Angela Lammert: "Paragone bei Medardo Rosso und Alberto Giacometti", in: Hannah Baader et al. (ed.): *Im Agon der Künste. Paragonales Denken, ästhetische Praxis und die Diversität der Sinne*, Paderborn and Munich 2007, pp. 491-517.

Le Fustec 1889: Jean Le Fustec: "L'Exposition Monet-Rodin", in: *La République Française*, 28.06.1889; reprinted in: exh. cat. Paris 1989, pp. 229-230.

Le Men 2010: Ségolène Le Men: *Monet*, Paris 2010.

Le Normand 1981: Antoinette Le Normand: *La Tradition Classique et l'esprit romantique. Les sculpteurs de l'Académie de France à Rome de 1824 à 1840* (*Collection Académie de France à Rome*, vol. 3), Rome 1981.

Le Normand-Romain 1998: Antoinette Le Normand-Romain: "Un 'mécène aussi généreux que discret'. Les commandes de sculptures de Maurice Fenaille à Rodin", in: exh. cat. Lyon 1998, pp. 14-33.

Le Normand-Romain 2000: Antoinette Le Normand-Romain: "Un 'mécène aussi généreux que discret'. Les commandes de sculptures de Maurice Fenaille à Rodin", in: exh. cat. Rodez 2000, pp. 51-77.

Le Normand-Romain 2007: Antoinette Le Normand-Romain: "Das Höllentor – ein Schmelztiegel", in: *Rodin*, compiled by David Breuer, exh. cat. Royal Academy of Arts, London/Kunsthaus Zürich, Ostfildern and Zurich 2007, pp. 55-63.

Le Normand-Romain 2009: Antoinette Le Normand-Romain: "Balzac et Bourdelle", in: Henry-Claude Cousseau, Christina Buley-Uribe and Véronique Mattiussi (eds): *Naissance de la modernité. Mélanges offerts à Jacques Vilain*, Paris 2009, pp. 235-241.

Le Normand-Romain 2009a: Antoinette Le Normand-Romain: "Matisse, Rodin, Bourdelle: *Le Serf* et *L'Homme qui marche*", in: exh. cat. Nice/Paris 2009, pp. 25-30.

Le Normand-Romain 2010: Antoinette Le Normand-Romain: "'Eine der schönsten Inkarnationen der ersten Frau.' Die Figur der Eva", in: *Rodin and Vienna*, edited by Agnes Husslein-Arco, exh. cat. Österreichische Galerie Belvedere, Vienna, Munich 2010, pp. 67-80.

Le Normand-Romain 2013: Antoinette Le Normand-Romain: *Rodin*, Paris 2013.

Le Normand-Romain/Haudiquet 2001: Antoinette Le Normand-Romain and Annette Haudiquet: *Rodin. Les Bourgeois de Calais*, Paris 2001.

Lebon 2003: Élisabeth Lebon: *Dictionnaire des fondeurs de bronze d'art. France 1890-1950*, Perth 2003.

Lees 2009: Sarah Lees: "Giovanni Boldini in Impressionist Paris", in: exh. cat. Ferrara/Williamstown 2009, pp. 19-67.

Bibliography

Lees 2018: Sarah Lees: "Innovative Impressions. Cassatt, Degas and Pissarro as Painter-Printmaker", in: *Innovative Impressions. Prints by Cassatt, Degas and Pissarro*, edited by idem and Richard R. Brettell, exh. cat. Philbrook Museum of Art, Tulsa, Oklahoma, Munich 2018, pp. 17–103.

Lemoisne 1946–1949: Paul-André Lemoisne: *Degas et son œuvre*, 4 vols, vol. 1: *Degas et son œuvre*, Paris 1946; vol. 2: *Peintures et pastels. 1853–1882*, Paris 1946; vol. 3: *Peintures et pastels. 1883–1908*, Paris 1947; vol. 4: *Tables des illustrations*, Paris 1949.

Lemoisne 1919: Paul-André Lemoisne: "Les Statuettes de Degas", in: *Art et Décoration*, 214, September/October 1919, pp. 109–117.

Lepic 1876: Ludovic-Napoléon Lepic: *Comme je devins graveur à l'eau-forte*, Paris 1876.

Leroi 1882: Paul Leroi: "Salon de 1882", in: *L'Art*, 4, 1882, p. 188.

Leroy 1874: Louis Leroy: "L'Exposition des impressionnistes", in: *Le Charivari*, 25.04.1874; reprinted in: Berson 1996, vol. 1, pp. 25–27.

Licht 1994: Fred Licht: "Origins of Modern Sculpture – The Italian Contribution", in: *Chiseled with a Brush. Italian Sculpture 1860–1925 from the Gilgore Collections*, edited by Ian Wardropper and Fred Licht, exh. cat. Art Institute of Chicago 1994, pp. 15–31.

Licht 2003: Fred Licht: "The Milanese Avant-Garde. An Introduction to the Scapigliatura", in: exh. cat. Naples 2003, pp. 11–29.

Lier 1897: H. A. [Hermann Arthur] Lier: "Die Internationale Kunstausstellung in Dresden", in: *Kunstchronik*, 8, 32, 19.08.1897, col. 498–504.

Lindsay 2010: Suzanne Glover Lindsay: "Degas' Sculpture after His Death", in: inv. cat. Washington 2010, pp. 15–21.

Lindsay 2010a: Suzanne Glover Lindsay: "Dancers", in: inv-cat. Washington 2010, pp. 112–115.

Lista 1994: Giovanni Lista: *Medardo Rosso. Destin d'un sculpteur 1858–1928*, Paris 1994.

Lista 1994a: Giovanni Lista: *Medardo Rosso. La Sculpture Impressionniste*, Paris 1994.

Lista 2003: Giovanni Lista: "Die Ursprünge des 'italienischen Impressionismus' von Medardo Rosso", in: exh. cat. Winterthur/Duisburg 2003, pp. 39–49.

Loyrette 1999: Henri Loyrette: "Edgar Degas. Orchestermusiker", in: exh. cat. Paris 1999, pp. 58–65.

M

Maaz 2005: Bernhard Maaz: "Druet sieht Rodin. Spuren und Bedeutung einer Zusammenarbeit", in: exh. cat. Berlin 2005, pp. 9–28.

Maaz 2006: Bernhard Maaz: "Troubetzkoy", in: *Nationalgalerie Berlin. Das XIX. Jahrhundert, Bestandskatalog der Skulpturen*, edited by idem, inv. cat. Nationalgalerie, Berlin, 2 vols, Leipzig 2006, vol. 2, pp. 817–818.

Maaz 2010: Bernhard Maaz: *Skulptur in Deutschland zwischen Französischer Revolution und Erstem Weltkrieg*, 2 vols, Berlin and Munich 2010.

Maaz 2020: Bernhard Maaz: "Was ist und zu welchem Ende studieren wir 'impressionistische' Plastik?", in: *Münchner Jahrbuch der bildenden Kunst*, 3rd series, vol. 70, Munich 2019 (published in 2020).

Maheux 1992: Anne Maheux: "Looking Into Degas's Pastel Technique", in: Jean Sutherland Boggs and idem: *Degas Pastels*, New York 1992, pp. 19–38.

Mallarmé [1876] 2002: Stéphane Mallarmé: "Die Impressionisten und Edouard Manet", in: exh. cat. Stuttgart 2002, pp. 191–202 (German translation after: *The Art Monthly Review*, 30.09.1876; here in English after lost French original).

Malon 1890: Benoît Malon: "Nécrologie. A. Ottin", in: *La Revue Socialiste*, 12, 1890, pp. 736–737.

Mannoni 2017: Laurent Mannoni: "Un siècle en movement", in: exh. cat. Paris 2017a, pp. 66–72.

Mantz 1881: Paul Mantz: "Exposition des œuvres des artistes indépendants", in: *Le Temps*, 23.04.1881; reprinted in: Berson 1996, vol. 1, pp. 356–358.

Marques 2002: Luiz Marques: "Mechanism and Classical Tradition in Degas's Bronzes", in: Czestochowski/Pingeot 2002, pp. 109–115.

Marx 1891: Roger Marx: "Simples notes sur le salon des Peintres-Graveurs", in: *L'Artiste*, 123, 1891, pp. 259–265.

Marx 1902: Roger Marx: "Les Pointes sêches de M. Rodin", in: *Gazette des Beaux-Arts*, 44, 3, 27, 01.03.1902, pp. 204–208.

Mauclair 1895: Camille Mauclair: "Choses d'art", in: *Mercure de France*, 16, 72, December 1895, pp. 410–413.

Mauclair 1901: Camille Mauclair: "Auguste Rodin. Son œuvre, son milieu, son influence", in: *Revue Universelle*, 17.08.1901, pp. 769–774.

Mauclair 1901a: Camille Mauclair: "La Psychologie du mystère", in: *Les Maîtres Artistes*, 2, December 1901, p. 45.

Mauclair 1902: Camille Mauclair: "L'Âme d'Eugène Carrière (À propos d'un livre sur lui)", in: *L'Art Décoratif*, 1902, pp. 58–70.

Mauclair 1904: Camille Mauclair: "La Peinture et la sculpture au salon d'automne", in: *L'Art Décoratif*, 1904, pp. 222–230.

Maufrigneuse [De Maupassant] 1882: Maufrigneuse [Guy de Maupassant]: "Notes d'un démolisseur", in: *Gil Blas*, 17.05.1882, pp. 1–2.

McQueen 2003: Alison McQueen: *The Rise of the Cult of Rembrandt. Reinventing an Old Master in Nineteenth-Century France*, Amsterdam 2003.

Meier-Graefe 1904: Julius Meier-Graefe: *Entwickelungsgeschichte der modernen Kunst. Vergleichende Betrachtung der bildenden Künste, als Beitrag zu einer neuen Aesthetik*, 3 vols, Stuttgart 1904.

Meier-Graefe 1904a: Julius Meier-Graefe: "Pariser Bericht", in: *Kunst und Künstler*, 2, 1, 1904, p. 38.

Meier-Graefe 1915: Julius Meier-Graefe: *Entwicklungsgeschichte der modernen Kunst. Vergleichende Betrachtung der bildenden Künste, als Beitrag zu einer neuen Aesthetik*, 3 vols, 2nd expanded edition, Munich 1915.

Melot 2010: Michel Melot: "Les Impressionnismes", in: exh. cat. Paris/Caen 2010, pp. 9–14.

Merkel 1995: Ursula Merkel: *Das plastische Porträt im 19. und frühen 20. Jahrhundert. Ein Beitrag zur Geschichte der Bildhauerei in Frankreich und Deutschland*, Berlin 1995.

Michel 1919: Alice Michel: "Degas et son modèle", in: *Mercure de France*, 131, 496, 16.02.1919, pp. 623–639.

Millard 1976: Charles W. Millard: *The Sculpture of Edgar Degas*, Princeton 1976.

Mirbeau 1885: Octave Mirbeau: "Auguste Rodin", in: *La France*, 18.02.1885.

Mirbeau 1889: Octave Mirbeau: "Claude Monet" [1889], in: exh. cat. Paris 1889, pp. 48–53; reprinted in: exh. cat. Paris 1889, pp. 4–26.

Mirbeau 1889a: Octave Mirbeau: "Auguste Rodin", in: *L'Echo de Paris*, 25.06.1889; reprinted in: exh. cat. Paris 1989, pp. 225–226.

Mola 2007: Paola Mola: "The Work and the Series", in: *Rosso. The Transient Form*, exh. cat. Peggy Guggenheim Collection, Venice, Milan 2007, pp. 45–127.

Mola 2009: Paola Mola: "La noia di Baudelaire", in: Mola/Vittucci 2009, pp. 9–21.

Mola 2009a: Paola Mola: "La forma instabile", in: Mola/Vittucci 2009, pp. 23–41.

Mola/Vittucci 2009: Paola Mola and Fabia Vittucci: *Medardo Rosso. Catalogo ragionato della scultura*, Milan 2009.

Mongi-Vollmer 2004: Eva Mongi-Vollmer: *Das Atelier des Malers. Die Diskurse eines Raums in der zweiten Hälfte des 19. Jahrhunderts*, Berlin 2004.

Mongi-Vollmer 2008: Eva Mongi-Vollmer: "Fokus auf Auguste Rodin. Faun/Le vieil arbre/Le vieux chêne, um 1885 (SGP 6)", in: *Fokus auf Auguste Rodin. Faun/Le vieil arbre/Le vieux chêne, um 1885 (SGP 6)*, compiled by idem: exh. cat. Städel Museum, Frankfurt am Main 2008, pp. 1–15.

Montesquiou 1902: Robert de Montesquiou: "Au Prince Troubetzkoy", in: *Les Modes*, June 1902.

Moore 1890: George Moore: "Degas. The Painter of Modern Life", in: *The Magazine of Art*, 13, October 1890, pp. 416–425.

Moore 1942: George Moore: "Gedanken zu Degas", in: Graber 1942, pp. 157–163.

Morice 1895: Charles Morice: "Les Passants. Medardo Rosso", in: *Le Soir*, 29.09.1895.

Morice 1900: Charles Morice: *Rodin*, Paris 1900.

Morice 1908: Charles Morice: "L'Exposition de M. Troubetzkoy (Galerie Hébrard)", in: *Mercure de France*, 73, 264, 16.06.1908, p. 734.

Moure 1996: Gloria Moure: "Medardo Rosso: The Contemporary Turning Point in Sculpture", in: exh. cat. Santiago de Compostela 1996, pp. 13–50.

Müller 1990: Lothar Müller: "Impressionistische Kultur. Zur Ästhetik von Modernität und Großstadt um 1900", in: Thomas Steinfeld and Heidrun Suhr (eds): *In der großen Stadt. Die Metropole als kulturtheoretische Kategorie*, Frankfurt am Main 1990, pp. 41–69.

Müller 1996: Lothar Müller: "Jenseits des Transitorischen: zur Reflexion des Plastischen in der Ästhetik der Moderne", in: Hartmut Böhme and Klaus R. Scherpe (eds): *Literatur und Kulturwissenschaften. Positionen, Theorien, Modelle*, Reinbek bei Hamburg 1996, pp. 134–160.

Munro 2017: Jane Munro: "Degas' Greasy Ink Drawings", in: exh. cat. Cambridge/Denver 2017, pp. 70–77.

Muybridge 1887: Eadweard Muybridge: *Animal Locomotion. An Electro-Photographic Investigation of Consecutive Phases of Animal Movements, Commenced 1872 – Completed 1885*, New York 1887.

N

Nicolson 1994: Vanessa Nicolson: "Rosso's Drawings", in: exh. cat. London etc. 1994, pp. 45–57.

O

Ormond/Kilmurray 2002: Richard Ormond and Elaine Kilmurray: *John Singer Sargent. Complete Paintings*, vol. 2: *Portraits of the 1890s*, New Haven 2002.

Osborn 1905: Max Osborn, *Moderne Plastik*, Berlin 1905.

Ottin 1868: Auguste Ottin: *Méthode élémentaire du dessin. Ouvrage accompagné de 66 modèles de dessin*, Paris 1868.

Ottin 1870: Auguste Ottin: *Organisation des arts du dessin. Expositions publiques, encouragements, commandes officielles*, Paris 1870.

Oya/Héran 2006: Mina Oya and Emmanuelle Héran: "Rodin et Carrière: une amitié", in: exh. cat. Tokyo/Paris 2006, pp. 16–29.

P

P. L. 1899: P. L.: "Notes d'art. Exposition Rodin à la Maison d'art", in: *Flandre Libérale*, 15.05.1899.

Papet 2018: Édouard Papet: "La Sculpture Polychrome en France 1850–1910", in: exh. cat. Paris 2018a, pp. 17–32.

Paradise 1985: JoAnne Paradise: *Gustave Geffroy and the Criticism of Painting*, Diss. Stanford 1982, New York and London 1985.

Paris/de La Chapelle 1990: Reine-Marie Paris and Arnaud de La Chapelle: *L'Œuvre de Camille Claudel. Catalogue raisonné*, Paris 1990.

Parry Janis 1980: Eugenia Parry Janis: "Setting the Tone – The Revival of Etching, The Importance of Ink", in: *The Painterly Print. Monotypes from the Seventeenth to the Twentieth Century*, edited by John Philip O'Neill, exh. cat. The Metropolitan Museum of Art, New York/The Museum of Fine Arts, Boston, New York 1980, pp. 9–28.

Pfisterer/Tauber 2018: Ulrich Pfisterer and Christine Tauber: *Einfluss, Strömung, Quelle. Aquatische Metaphern in der Kunstgeschichte*, Bielefeld 2018.

Philp 2000: Annette Philp: *Photographie interpretiert Skulptur. Auguste Rodin, Constantin Brancusi, Alberto Giacometti*, Diss. Braunschweig 1997, Berlin 2000.

Pica 1902: Vittorio Pica: "Paul Troubetzkoy", in: *Die Kunst für Alle. Malerei, Plastik, Graphik, Architektur*, 17, 3, 1902, pp. 49–53.

Pickvance 1986: Ronald Pickvance: "The Fourth Exhibition 1879. Contemporary Popularity and Posthumous Neglect", in: exh. cat. Washington/San Francisco 1986, pp. 243–265.

Pinet 1997: Hélène Pinet: "Das Wichtigste ist, zu zeigen", in: exh. cat. Duisburg etc. 1997, pp. 71–79.

Pinet 2007: Hélène Pinet: "Histoire d'une collection", in: exh. cat. Paris 2007, pp. 10–13.

Pinet 2007a: Hélène Pinet: "Dans l'atelier. L'œil du photographe. Le regard de Rodin", in: exh. cat. Paris 2007, pp. 24–29.

Pinet 2007b: Hélène Pinet: "'Rodin ne voit que par de lui.' Eugène Druet", in: exh. cat. Paris 2007, pp. 72–77.

Pinet 2007c: Hélène Pinet: "Jacques-Ernest Bulloz. Une maison artistique d'éditions photographiques", in: exh. cat. Paris 2007, pp. 112–119.

Pinet 2007d: Hélène Pinet: "Stephen Haweis et Henry Coles. Une association éphémère", in: exh. cat. Paris 2007, pp. 152–154.

Pinet 2007e: Hélène Pinet: "À la recherche de la couleur. Jean Limet", in: exh. cat. Paris 2007, pp. 176–179.

Pinet 2007f: Hélène Pinet: "'Vos photographies feront comprendre au monde mon Balzac.' Edward Steichen et Rodin", in: exh. cat. Paris 2007, pp. 190–195.

Pinet 2009: Hélène Pinet: "Bevilaqua et (ou) Pignatelli", in: exh. cat. Nice/Paris 2009, pp. 85–87.

Pingeot 1991: Anne Pingeot: *Degas. Sculptures*, Paris 1991.

Pingeot 2000: Anne Pingeot: "La risposta di Medardo Rosso", in: exh. cat. Rome/Paris 2000, pp. 159–170.

Pingeot 2010: Anne Pingeot: "Les Sculptures des cire et l'air du temps", in: exh. cat. Paris 2010a, pp. 29–43.

Pingeot/Le Normand-Romain/Lemaistre 1982: Anne Pingeot, Antoinette Le Normand-Romain and Isabelle Lemaistre: *Sculpture française. XIXe siècle (Notices d'histoire de l'art, vol. 6)*, Paris 1982.

Pissarro 1980: Camille Pissarro: *Correspondance de Camille Pissarro*, edited by Janine Bailly-Herzberg, 5 vols, Paris 1980–1991, vol. 1: *1865–1885*, Paris 1980.

Pohlmann 1996: Ulrich Pohlmann: "Barbizon und die Photographie", in: *Corot, Courbet und die Maler von Barbizon. "Les amis de la nature"*, edited by Christoph Heilmann, exh. cat. Haus der Kunst, Munich, Munich etc. 1996, pp. 403–416.

Bibliography

Potts 2000: Alex Potts: *The Sculptural Imagination. Figurative, Modernist, Minimalist*, New Haven and London 2000.

Pullen 1994: Derek Pullen: "Rosso's Sculpture Technique", in: exh. cat. London etc. 1994, pp. 59–63.

Pulvenis de Seligny 2009: Marie-Thérèse Pulvenis de Seligny: "Un métier pour immortels. Métamorphose des forms", in: exh. cat. Nice/Paris 2009, pp. 37–49.

Q

Quinsac 2009: Annie-Paule Quinsac: "Dal 'pandemonio per cambiare l'arte' all'accademismo", in: exh. cat. Milan 2009, pp. 27–49.

Quinsac 2009a: Annie-Paule Quinsac: "L'accademismo scapigliato in scultura", in: exh. cat. Milan 2009, p. 250.

Quinsac 2011: Annie-Paule Quinsac: "Über den Divisionismus hinaus – Segantini und die Ästhetik des 'Fin de Siècle'", in: exh. cat. Riehen 2011, pp. 32–36.

R

Raimondi 1958: Riccardo Raimondi: *Degas e la sua famiglia in Napoli. 1793–1917*, Naples 1958.

Rambosson 1902: Yvanhoë Rambosson: "L'Impressionnisme en sculpture?", in: *Mercure de France*, 43, July 1902, pp. 253–354.

Rayler Rolfe 1997: Julia Rayler Rolfe: "Sargent and Lady Agnew", in: exh. cat. Edinburgh 1997, pp. 11–33.

Read 1966: Herbert Read: *Die Geschichte der modernen Plastik*, Munich and Zurich 1966.

Rebora 1990: Sergio Rebora: "Giovanni Segantini", in: exh. cat. Verbania Pallanza 1990, pp. 108–109.

Reff 1972: Theodore Reff: "Degas and the Literature of his Time", in: Ulrich Finke (ed.): *French 19th Century Painting and Literature*, Manchester 1972, pp. 182–231.

Reff 1976: Theodore Reff: *Degas. The Artist's Mind*, London 1976.

Reff 1995: Theodore Reff: "The Morbid Content of Degas's Sculpture", in: *Apollo*, 142, 402, 1995, pp. 64–71.

René 1911: Jean René: "Le Salon d'Automne", in: *Gazette des Beaux-Arts*, 53, 4, 6, 1911, pp. 375–393.

Rewald 1956: John Rewald: *Degas. Sculpture. The Complete Works*, New York 1956.

Rewald 1973 [1946]: John Rewald: *The History of Impressionism* [1946], 4th expanded edition, New York 1973.

Rey 2015: Xavier Rey: "Degas et l'impressionnisme", in: exh. cat. Giverny 2015, pp. 15–25.

Reynaerts/Versluis-Van Dongen 2011: Jenny Reynaerts and Stella Versluis-Van Dongen: "A Portrait of the Artist as a Young Man: Edgar Degas Inspired by Rembrandt", in: *The Rijksmuseum Bulletin*, 59, 2011, pp. 102–133.

Reynolds 1995: Dee Reynolds: *Symbolist Aesthetics and Early Abstract Art. Sites of Imaginary Space*, Cambridge etc. 1995.

Rilke 1924: Rainer Maria Rilke: *Auguste Rodin*, Leipzig 1924.

Rilke [1902] 2011: Rainer Maria Rilke: *Auguste Rodin*, [1902], 2nd ed., trans. Victoria Charles, New York 2011.

Rodin [1912] 1983: Auguste Rodin: *Rodin on Art and Artists: Conversations with Paul Gsell* [1912], trans. Romilly Fedden, New York 1983.

Rilke [1913] 1984: Rainer Maria Rilke: *Auguste Rodin* [1913], Frankfurt am Main [1913] 1984.

Rivière 1877: Georges Rivière: "L'Exposition des Impressionnistes", in: *L'Impressionniste*, 2, 14.04.1877, pp. 1–6.

Rivière 1877a: Georges Rivière: "Explications", in: *L'Impressionniste*, 3, 21.04.1877, pp. 3–4.

Rivière/Gaudichon/Ghanassia 2000: Anne Rivière, Bruno Gaudichon and Danielle Ghanassia: *Camille Claudel. Catalogue raisonné. Nouvelle édition revue et augmentée*, Paris 2000.

Rodin 1911: Auguste Rodin: *L'Art. Entretiens réunis par Paul Gsell*, Paris 1911.

Rodin 1912: Auguste Rodin: *Die Kunst. Gespräche des Meisters gesammelt von Paul Gsell*, 2nd edition, Leipzig 1912.

Roger-Marx 1929: Claude Roger-Marx: "Engraving by Sculptors in France", in: *The Print Collector's Quarterly*, 16, 1929, pp. 145–164.

Rosenthal 1912: Léon Rosenthal: "Les Salons de 1912. Le Salon d'Automne", in: *Gazette des Beaux-Arts*, 54, 4, 8, November 1912, pp. 405–419.

Rosso 1907: Medardo Rosso: "Impressionism in Sculpture: An Explanation", in: *The Daily Mail*, 17.10.1907.

Rosso 1994: Medardo Rosso: *La Sculpture Impressionniste*, edited by Giovanni Lista, Paris 1994.

Rouart 1930: Eugène Rouart: "En souvenir de Medardo Rosso", in: *L'Archer*, 4, April 1930, pp. 281–285.

Rousseau 1877: Jean Rousseau: "Revue des Arts", in: *Echo du Parlement*, Brussels, 11.04.1877.

Rowell 1983: Margit Rowell: "Fragments, Assemblages, Bricolages", in: *Rodin et la sculpture contemporaine. Compte-rendu du colloque organisé par le musée Rodin du 11 au 15 octobre 1982 au musée Rodin*, edited by Musée Rodin, Paris 1983, pp. 119–124.

Rubin 1999: James Rubin: "Edouard Manet. Croquer le croquet – Manets Gartenpartie", in: exh. cat. Paris 1999, pp. 66–83.

Rübel 2005: Dietmar Rübel: "Plastizität. Fließende Formen und flexible Materialien in der Plastik um 1900", in: Thomas Strässle and Caroline Torra-Mattenklott (eds): *Poetiken der Materie. Stoffe und ihre Qualitäten in Literatur, Kunst und Philosophie*, Zurich 2005, pp. 283–306.

Rübel 2012: Dietmar Rübel: *Plastizität. Eine Kunstgeschichte des Veränderlichen*, Munich 2012.

Rübel 2014: Dietmar Rübel: "Die Fotogenese der Skulptur (molekulare Gemeinschaften)", in: exh. cat. Berlin/Vaduz 2014, pp. 110–125.

Rübel 2016: Dietmar Rübel: "Eine Vielzahl von Oberflächen. Skulpturen zwischen Handarbeit und Maschinenästhetik", in: exh. cat. Duisburg 2016, pp. 28–37.

S

Salbert 1963: Janine Salbert: "Gustave Geffroy et Rodin", in: *Annales de Bretagne*, 70, 1, 1963, pp. 105–121.

Salmon 1919: André Salmon: *La jeune sculpture française*, Paris 1919.

Schaefer/Saint-George/Lewerentz 2008: Iris Schaefer, Caroline von Saint-George and Katja Lewerentz: "Womit malten die Impressionisten?", in: exh. cat. Cologne/Florence 2008, pp. 42–67.

Schallenberg 2009: Nina Schallenberg: "Auguste Rodin et la photographie. La valeur artistique de la reproduction photographique", in: Herbert Molderings and Gregor Wedekind (eds): *L'Évidence Photographique*, Paris 2009, pp. 351–376.

Schallenberg 2017: Nina Schallenberg: "Schockmomente. Rezeptionsästhetische Strategien von Medardo Rosso und Constantin Brancusi", in: Guido Reuter and Ursula Ströbele (eds): *Skulptur und Zeit im 20. und 21. Jahrhundert*, Cologne etc. 2017, pp. 33–48.

Schenkenberg 2018: Tamara H. Schenkenberg: "'You cannot divide or stop the air'. Dimensions of Space in Medardo Rosso's Sculpture", in: exh. cat. St. Louis 2018, pp. 37–55.

Schmedding 1997: Anne Schmedding: "'Rien n'est matériel dans l'espace' – Die Fotografien des Bildhauers Medardo Rosso", in: *Daidalos*, 66 (*Fotografie als Argument*), December 1997, pp. 112–117.

Schmoll genannt Eisenwerth 1976: Josef A. Schmoll genannt Eisenwerth: "Simmel und Rodin", in: Hannes Böhringer and Karlfried Gründer (eds): *Ästhetik und Soziologie um die Jahrhundertwende. Georg Simmel*, Frankfurt am Main 1976, pp. 18–39.

Schmoll genannt Eisenwerth 1983: Josef A. Schmoll genannt Eisenwerth: *Rodin-Studien. Persönlichkeit, Werke, Wirkung, Bibliographie*, Munich 1983.

Schmoll genannt Eisenwerth 1983a: Josef A. Schmoll genannt Eisenwerth: "Rodins 'Le Masque de l'Homme au nez cassé'", in: Schmoll genannt Eisenwerth 1983, pp. 163–214.

Schmoll genannt Eisenwerth 1983b: Josef A. Schmoll genannt Eisenwerth: "Neue Aspekte zu Rodins 'Höllenpforte'", in: Schmoll genannt Eisenwerth 1983, pp. 215–232.

Schmoll genannt Eisenwerth 1994: Josef A. Schmoll genannt Eisenwerth: *Rodin und Camille Claudel*, Munich and New York 1994.

Schneider 1899: Gustave Schneider: "L'Exposition Privée de Rodin", in: *Le Petit Bleu de Paris*, 19.07.1899.

Schnell 1980: Werner Schnell: *Der Torso als Problem der modernen Kunst*, Berlin 1980.

Schnell 1987: Werner Schnell: "Apparition als Skulptur. Medardo Rosso und Alberto Giacometti auf der Suche nach dem Erscheinungsbild des Menschen", in: *Städel-Jahrbuch*, N.F., 11, 1987, pp. 291–310.

Schnell 2016: Werner Schnell: "Warum Rodin Bronze brauchte – und auch mit Marmor Erfolg hatte", in: Bushart/Haug 2016, pp. 185–207.

Schopenhauer [1888] 1919: Arthur Schopenhauer: *Parerga und Paralipomena* [1888], vol. 2 (*Arthur Schopenhauer's Sämmtliche Werke*, vol. 6), 2nd edition, Leipzig 1919.

Schorn/Kolloff 1839: Ludwig Schorn and Eduard Kolloff: "Der Daguerrotyp", in: *Kunst-Blatt*, 20, 77, 24.09.1839, pp. 305–308.

Schumann 1896/97: Paul Schumann: "Die Dresdner Kunstausstellung", in: *Die Kunst für Alle. Malerei Plastik, Graphik, Architektur*, 12, 1896/97, pp. 338–344.

Schuon 2016: Cornelia Schuon: *Wahrnehmung und Darstellung von Wirklichkeit in der Krise. Exemplarische Analysen zu Realismuskonzepten von Édouard Manet und Edgar Degas*, Bonn 2016.

Schwarz 2003: Dieter Schwarz: "'Rouart aime son portrait – un peu tard mais enfin'. Zu Medardo Rossos *Ritratto di Henri Rouart*", in: Stauffer 2003, pp. 155–172.

Schwarz 2003a: Dieter Schwarz: "'L'emozione è un instante.' Reflexe von Medardo Rossos Werk", in: exh. cat. Winterthur/Duisburg 2003, pp. 58–68.

Scott 1998: David Scott: "Matter for Reflexion. Nineteenth-Century French Art Critics' Quest for Modernity in Sculpture", in: Richard Hobbs (ed.), *Impressions of French Modernity. Art and Literature in France. 1850–1900*, Manchester and New York 1998, pp. 99–117.

Sedeyn 1904: Emile Sedeyn: "Rembrandt Bugatti", in: *L'Art Décoratif*, 71, August 1904, pp. 61–66.

Segantini 1912: Giovanni Segantini: *Giovanni Segantinis Schriften und Briefe*, edited by Bianca Zehder-Segantini, Leipzig 1912.

Seidel 1913: Curt Seidel: "Rosso – Rodin", in: *Der Sturm*, 4, 154/155, March 1913, p. 2.

Selz 1963: Jean Selz: *Modern Sculpture: Origins and Evolution*, trans. Annette Michelson, New York 1963.

Sfeir-Semler 1992: Andrée Sfeir-Semler: *Die Maler am Pariser Salon 1791–1880*, Frankfurt am Main etc. 1992.

Shapiro 1997: Barbara Stern Shapiro: "A Printmaking Encounter", in: *The Private Collection of Edgar Degas. A Summary Catalogue*, edited by Ann Dumas et al., exh. cat. The Metropolitan Museum of Art, New York 1997, pp. 235–245.

Shapiro 2014: Gary Shapiro, "Painting and Photography", in: Leonard Lawler and John Nale (eds): *The Cambridge Foucault Lexicon*, Cambridge 2014, pp. 327–333.

Shiff 1984: Richard Shiff: *Cézanne and the End of Impressionism. A Study of the Theory, Technique, and Critical Evaluation of Modern Art*, Chicago 1984.

Shiff 1986: Richard Shiff: "The End of Impressionism", in: exh. cat. Washington/San Francisco 1986, pp. 61–89.

Sickert 1917: Walter Sickert: "Degas", in: *The Burlington Magazine*, 31, 176, November 1917, pp. 183–191.

Sickert 1923: Walter Sickert: "The Sculptor of Movement", in: *Exhibition of the Works in Sculpture of Edgar Degas*, exh. cat. Leicester Galleries, London, London 1923; reprinted in: Sickert 2000, pp. 455–457.

Sickert 2000: Walter Sickert: *The Complete Writings on Art*, edited by Anna Gruetzner Robins, Oxford etc. 2000.

Simmel [1902] 1995: Georg Simmel: "Rodins Plastik und die Geistesrichtung der Gegenwart" [1902], in: idem: *Aufsätze und Abhandlungen 1901–1908 (Gesamtausgabe, vol. 7.1)*, edited by Rüdiger Kramme et al., Frankfurt am Main 1995, pp. 92–100.

Simmel [1903] 1950: Georg Simmel: "The Metropolis and Mental Life" [1903], in; *The Sociology of Georg Simmel*, trans. and ed. Kurt H. Wolff, New York and London 1950, pp. 409–424.

Simmel [1907] 1932: Georg Simmel: "Sociology of the Senses: Visual Interaction" [1907], in: Robert E. Park and Ernest W. Burgess (eds), *Introduction to the Science of Sociology*, Chicago 1932, pp. 357–361.

Soulier 1903: Gustave Soulier: "La Cinquième Exposition Internationale d'Art à Venise", in: *L'Art Décoratif*, 5, 2, 1903, pp. 81–120.

Stauffer 2003: Christine E. Stauffer (ed.): *Festschrift für Eberhard W. Kornfeld zum 80. Geburtstag*, Berne 2003.

Stevenson 1893: Robert Alan Stevenson, in: *The Art Journal*, 1893, p. 242.

Stix-Marget 1998: Gabriele Stix-Marget: *Maler ohne Pinsel. Der Bildhauer und Fotograf seiner Werke. Medardo Rosso 1858–1928*, Diss. Kiel 1998, Munich 1998.

Stutzer 2016: Beat Stutzer: *Giovanni Segantini*, Zurich 2016.

Sueur-Hermel 2010: Valérie Sueur-Hermel: "Trésor impressionnistes de la Bibliothèque Nationale de France", in: exh. cat. Paris/Caen 2010, pp. 21–29.

T

Talbot [1844] 2011: William Henry Fox Talbot: *The Pencil of Nature* [1844], Chicago 2011.

Tardieu 1877: Charles Tardieu: "Le Salon de Paris – 1877 – La Sculpture", in: *L'Art*, 3, 10, 1877, pp. 100–108.

Taylor 2015: Damian Taylor: *'Busy Working with Materials'. Transposing Form, Re-exposing Medardo Rosso*, Diss. Oxford 2015.

Taylor 2019: Damian Taylor: "Casting Negatives: Medardo Rosso's Ecce Puer in Light of the Darkroom", in: *Sculpture Journal*, 28, 1, 2019, pp. 55–74.

Thiaudière 1886: Edmond Thiaudière: "Au salon: La sculpture – Les bustes, II, Medardo Rosso", in: *L'Opinion*, 02.06.1886, p. 2.

Thiébault-Sisson 1921: François Thiébault-Sisson: "La Vie Artistique: Degas Sculpteur", in: *Le Temps*, 25.05.1921, p. 3.

Bibliography

Thiébault-Sisson 1931: François Thiébault-Sisson: "Degas sculpteur raconté par lui-même", in: *Le Temps*, 11.08.1931, p. 3.

Thomson 1981: Richard Thomson: "Degas's Torse de Femme and Titian", in: *Gazette des Beaux-Arts*, 123, 6, 98, July/August 1981, pp. 45–48.

Thomson 1983: Richard Thomson: "The Sculpture of Camille Pissarro", in: *Source. Notes in the History of Art*, 2, 4, summer 1983, pp. 25–28.

Thomson 1988: Richard Thomson: *Degas. The Nudes*, London 1988.

Thomson 1995: Richard Thomson: *Edgar Degas: Waiting*, Malibu 1995.

Thomson 2009: Richard Thomson: "Degas. Sequenzen und Wiederholungen (1880–1910)", in: exh. cat. Hamburg 2009, pp. 65–79.

Timbal 1877: Charles Timbal: "La Sculpture au Salon", in: *Gazette des Beaux-Arts*, 19, 2, 16, 01.07.1877, pp. 30–47.

Treydel 2017: Renate Treydel: "Ottin, Auguste-Louis-Marie", in: *Allgemeines Künstlerlexikon. Die Bildenden Künstler aller Zeiten und Völker*, edited by Andreas Beyer, Bénédicte Savoy and Wolf Tegethoff, vol. 94, Berlin and Boston 2017, pp. 23–24.

Trianon 1880: Henry Trianon: "Cinquième exposition par un groupe d'artistes indépendants (10, rue des Pyramides)", in: *Le Constitutionnel*, 08.04.1880, pp. 2–3; reprinted in: Berson 1996, vol. 1, pp. 312–314.

Trianon 1881: Henry Trianon: "Sixième exposition de peinture par un groupe d'artistes. 35, boulevard des Capucines", in: *Le Constitutionnel*, 24.04.1881, pp. 2–3; reprinted in: Berson 1996, vol. 1, pp. 366–369.

Tucker 1974: William Tucker: *Early Modern Sculpture. Rodin, Degas, Matisse, Brancusi, Picasso, Gonzalez*, New York 1974.

Tucker 1974a: William Tucker: *The Language of Sculpture*, London 1974.

Tucker 1986: Paul Tucker: "The First Impressionist Exhibition 1874. The First Impressionist Exhibition in Context", in: exh. cat. Washington/San Francisco 1986, pp. 93–117.

Tucker [1973] 2009: William Tucker: "Schwere bei Rodin und Degas" [1973], in: exh. cat. Hamburg 2009, pp. 95–105.

U

Uexküll 1909: Jakob von Uexküll: *Umwelt und Innenwelt der Tiere*, Berlin 1909.

Ullrich 2002: Wolfgang Ullrich: *Die Geschichte der Unschärfe*, Berlin 2002.

V

V. M. 1902: V. M.: "Aus dem Kunstgewerbe-Museum", in: *Leipziger Tageblatt*, 08.07.1902.

Valabrègue 1881: Antony Valabrègue: "Beaux-Arts. L'Exposition des impressionnistes", in: *La Revue Littéraire et artistique*, 15.04.1881, pp. 180–181; reprinted in: Berson 1996, vol. 1, pp. 369–370.

Vauxcelles 1904: Louis Vauxcelles: "Exposition Rembrandt Bugatti", in: *Gil Blas*, 03.07.1904, p. 1.

Vauxcelles 1905: Louis Vauxcelles: "Au Salon d'Automne. – Le sculpteur Medardo Rosso", in: *Gil Blas*, 31.10.1905, p. 1.

Vilain 2008: Jacques Vilain: "Rodin graveur à la pointe sèche", in: Aurore de Neuville (ed.): *La Sulpture au XIXe siècle*, Paris 2008, pp. 284–293.

Vollard 1924: Ambroise Vollard: *Degas (1834–1917)*, Paris 1924.

Vollard 1925: Ambroise Vollard: *Renoir. An Intimate Record*, New York 1925.

Vollard 1925a: Ambroise Vollard, *La Vie & l'œuvre de Pierre-Auguste Renoir*, Paris 1925.

Vollard 1925b: Ambroise Vollard: "Degas", in: *Kunst und Künstler. Illustrierte Monatsschrift für bildende Kunst und Kunstgewerbe*, 23, 2, 1925, pp. 60–67.

Vollard 1937: Ambroise Vollard: *Souvenirs d'un marchand de tableaux*, Paris 1937.

Vollard: 1938: Ambroise Vollard: *En écoutant Cézanne, Degas, Renoir*, Paris 1938.

Vollard [1937] 1980: Ambroise Vollard: *Erinnerungen eines Kunsthändlers* [1937], Zurich 1980.

Von Hildebrand 1969: Adolf von Hildebrand: "Über die Gründung eines zoologischen Gartens in Munich" [unpublished], in: idem: *Gesammelte Schriften zur Kunst*, compiled by Henning Bock, Cologne and Opladen 1969, pp. 514–515.

Von Knobelsdorf 2004: Juliana von Knobelsdorf: "Zum Berliner Konvolut der Fotografien Eugène Druets nach Werken von Auguste Rodin", in: *Jahrbuch der Berliner Museen*, vol. 46, 2004, pp. 197–226.

Von Matt/Rewald 1957: Leonard von Matt and John Rewald: *Degas. Das plastische Werk*, Zurich 1957.

W

Waldmann 1990: Susann Waldmann: *Die lebensgroße Wachsfigur. Eine Studie zur Funktion und Bedeutung der keroplastischen Porträtfigur vom Spätmittelalter bis zum 18. Jahrhundert*, Munich 1990.

Ward 1991: Martha Ward: "Impressionist Installations and Private Exhibitions", in: *The Art Bulletin*, 73, 4, 12.1991, pp. 599–622.

Warncke 1902: Paul Warncke: "Berliner Kunstausstellungen", in: *Kunstchronik*, 13, 18, 1902, col. 273–277.

Wessely 2014: Christina Wessely: "The Art of Looking Closely: Zoological Gardens around 1900 at the Interface of Science, Art and Spectacle", in: exh. cat. Berlin 2014, pp. 194–205.

White/White 1965: Harrison C. and Cynthia A. White: *Canvases and Careers. Institutional Change in the French Painting World*, New York 1965.

Wissman 1986: Fronia E. Wissman: "The Sixth Exhibition 1881. Realists among the Impressionists", in: exh. cat. Washington/San Francisco 1986, pp. 337–352.

Witkovsky 2018: Matthew S. Witkovsky: "A Matter of Time", in: exh. cat. St. Louis 2018, pp. 57–69.

Wölfflin 1896/97: Heinrich Wölfflin: "Wie man Skulpturen aufnehmen soll", in: *Zeitschrift für bildende Kunst*, N.F., 7, 1896, pp. 224–228; 8, 1897, pp. 294–297.

Wölfflin 1915: Heinrich Wölfflin: "Wie man Skulpturen aufnehmen soll? (Probleme der italienischen Renaissance)", in: *Zeitschrift für bildende Kunst*, N.F., 26, 1915, pp. 237–244.

Wölfflin 1915a: Heinrich Wölfflin, *Kunstgeschichtliche Grundbegriffe. Das Problem der Stilentwickelung in der neueren Kunst*, Munich 1915.

Wohlrab 2016: Christiane Wohlrab: *Non-finito als Topos der Moderne. Die Marmorskulpturen von Auguste Rodin*, Paderborn 2016.

Wood 2016: Jon Wood: "Troubetzkoy, Tolstoy and the Art of Portrayal", in: *Society of Portrait Sculptors*, 2016, pp. 26–33.

Wootton 2016: Oliver L. Wootton: "Troubetzkoy and Rosso. Searching for Light", in: *Society of Portrait Sculptors*, 2016, pp. 58–67.

Z

Zimmermann 1998: Michael F. Zimmermann: "Ardengo Soffici und der Fall Medardo Rosso: Der Impressionismus in Italien", in: Wolfgang Liebenwein and Anchise Tempestini (eds): *Gedenkschrift für Richard Harprath*, Munich 1998, pp. 517–527.

Zimmermann 2016: Michael F. Zimmermann (ed.): *Vision in Motion. Streams of Sensation and Configurations of Time*, Zurich and Berlin 2016.

Zola 1880: Émile Zola: *Le Roman Expérimental*, Paris 1880.

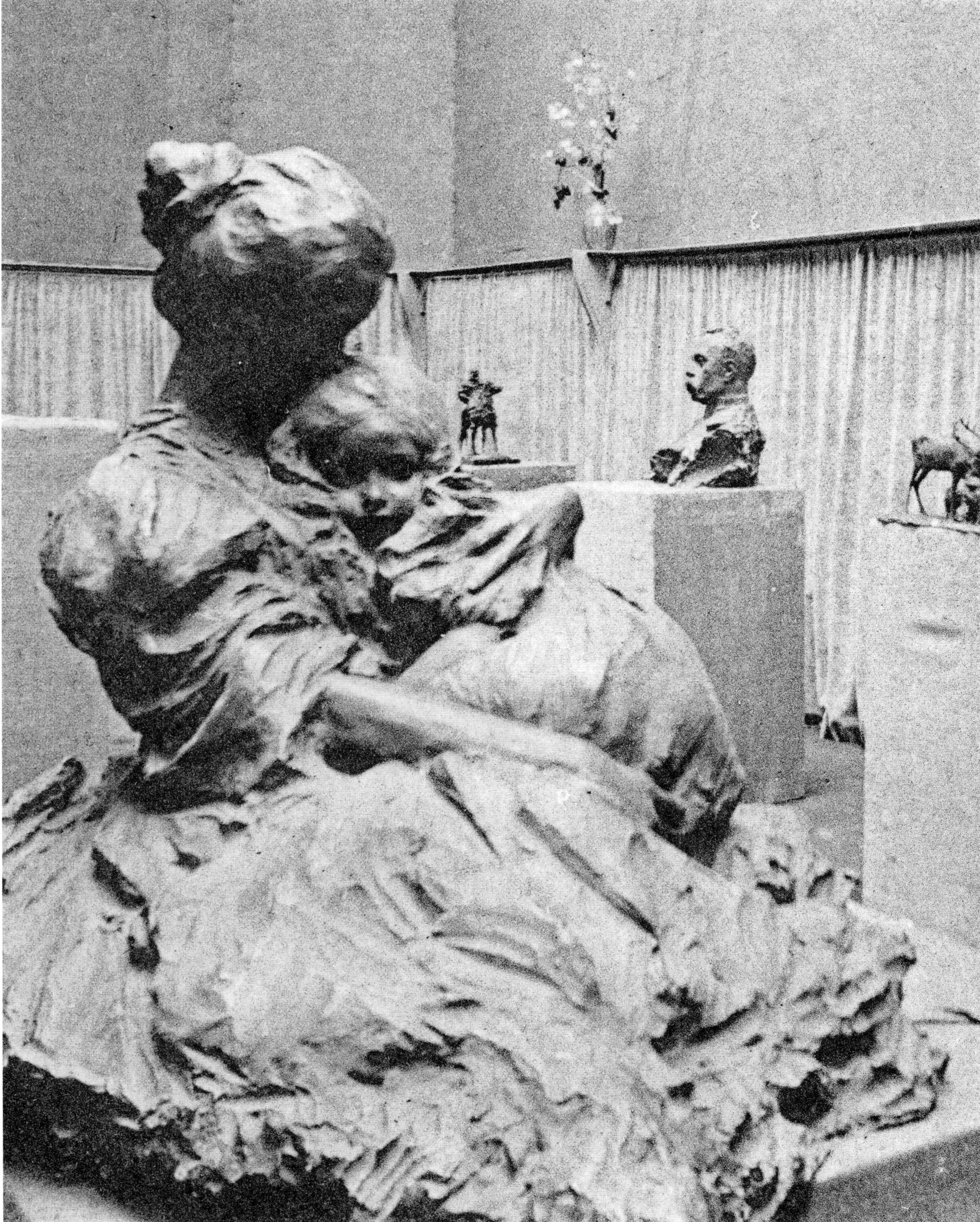

Colophon

This catalogue has been published in conjunction with the exhibition
en passant. Impressionism in sculpture
Städel Museum, Frankfurt am Main, 19 March to 28 June 2020

Editors
Alexander Eiling, Eva Mongi-Vollmer

Editing
Juliane Betz, Fabienne Ruppen

Picture editing
Marie-Luise Geißler

Catalogue management
Eva Mongi-Vollmer

Graphics/corporate design
Martin Kaufmann

Graphic design and typesetting
Tonique, Frankfurt am Main
Alexander Horn, Lukas Schmidt,
Tim Schötensack

Project supervisor, Prestel Verlag
Markus Eisen

Copy-editing
Ariane Kossack

Translation from German
Judith Rosenthal (essays by JB,
ES, EM-V, ES/EM-V, FR)
Rebecca van Dyck (greetings,
foreword, essays by PD, AR, DR,
NS and all catalogue entries)

Translation from French and Italian
José Enrique Macián

Pre-press and reproduction
Helio Repro, Munich

Production
Cilly Klotz

Printing and binding
Printer Trento, Trento

Typefaces
Freight Sans, Freight Display

Paper
150 g/qm Amber Graphic white

Overall production
Prestel Verlag
Munich · London · New York
A member of Verlagsgruppe
Random House GmbH
Neumarkter Strasse 28
81673 Munich

© 2020 Städel Museum,
Frankfurt am Main,
Prestel Verlag,
Munich · London · New York,
and the authors

Trade edition
ISBN 978-3-7913-5960-1 (German)
ISBN 978-3-7913-5961-8 (English)

Museum edition
ISBN 978-3-941399-98-3 (German)
ISBN 978-3-941399-99-0 (English)

A CIP catalogue record for this book is
available from the British Library

In respect to links in the book,
Verlagsgruppe Random House expressly
notes that no illegal content was
discernible on the linked sites at the time
the links were created. The publisher
has no influence at all over the current
and future design, content or authorship
of the linked sites. For this reason,
Verlagsgruppe Random House expressly
disassociates itself from all content
on linked sites that has been altered since
the link was created and assumes no
liability for such content.

Prestel Publishing Ltd.
16–18 Berners Street
London W1T 3LN

Prestel Publishing
900 Broadway, Suite 603
New York, NY 10003

www.prestel.com
www.prestel.de

Städel Museum

Director
Philipp Demandt

Assistants of the director
Jutta Pfister, Johanna Schick

Curators
Alexander Eiling and Eva Mongi-Vollmer
in collaboration with Juliane Betz and
Fabienne Ruppen

Modern art
Alexander Eiling; Juliane Betz, Marie-Luise
Geißler, Ira Haller, Alina Happ, Eva Höllerer,
Kristina Lemke, Fabienne Ruppen, Elena
Schroll, Philipp von Wehrden

Exhibition organisation
Katja Hilbig-Bergmann, Sven Lubinus;
Dominik Auvermann, Nora Becker,
Beatrice Drengwitz, Barbara Noeske-Winter,
Hannah Vietoris, Albrecht Wild

Conservation
Paintings and sculptures:
Stephan Knobloch; Eva-Maria Bader,
Lilly Becker, Mareike Gerken
Papierarbeiten: Ruth Schmutzler; Sabine
Protze

Technical department/installation crew
Thomas Pietrzak, Nils Jahnke; Michael
Götz, Thorsten Knapp, Thomas König,
Ralf Lappe, Ted Obermann

External partners/international relations
Johanna Schick, Freya Schlingmann

Education department
Chantal Eschenfelder, Anne Sulzbach;
Janine Burnicki, Anne Dribbisch,
Anna Huber, Antje Lindner, Annabell Manz,
Natalie Marie Meyer, Saskia Volk

Marketing
Bernadette Mildenberger, Linda Herrmann,
Annabell Hurle; Diana Hillesheim,
Katalin Várdai, Rebekka Zajonc

Graphics/corporate design
Sandra Adler-Krause,
Martin Kaufmann; Anna Voß

Press/public relations
Pamela Rohde; Theresa Franke, Susanne
Hafner, Jannikhe Möller, Sarah Omar,
Franziska von Plocki, Vanessa Tron

Engagement (Sponsoring)
Julia Lange; Martina Marcone,
Jasmin Guette

Engagement (Fundraising)
Stefanie Jerger; Corinna Fröhling

Administration
Heinz-Jürgen Bokler, Iris Sauer;
Laura Eversmeier, Adelheid Felsing,
Letizia Franco, Elisabeth Graczyk,
Jutta Okos, Anja Pontoriero, Annika Sauer,
Vanessa Schäfer, Susann Schürer,
Weronika Szarafin, Sophie Voß

IT department
Sebastian Heine; Tihomir Kukic,
Benjamin Schiller

Events
Kerstin Schultheis; Vivia Hirschfeld,
Jan Filip Kleiner, Hannah Krämer,
Chiara Lucchese

Museum shop/cafe
Anke Gordon, Ruth Endter, Sarah Seefelder;
Chaula De los Santos, Maria del Pilar
Espinosa Suarez, Philipp Fiehl, Magdalena
Kaluza, Sabine Kreutzer, Tanja Neumann,
Cassandra Nicolaus, Willi Probst, Anette
Riede

Supervisory service/cashier desk
Thomas Hruschka, Jolanta Radtke,
Catrin Röttinger-Zengel,
Richard Silaghi, Ruzica Skrijelj

Library
Elena Ganzlin; Michael Mohr

Provenance research/archives
Iris Schmeisser

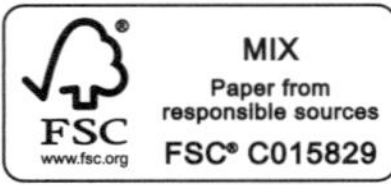

Publishing group Random House
FSC® N001967

Printed in Italy

Photo credits and artists' copyrights

Rijksmuseum Amsterdam/Rene den Engelsman: cat. 127

Photo Courtesy of Archivio Medardo Rosso: cat. 60; 62

Photo Courtesy of Archivio Medardo Rosso/ Luca Carrà: cat. 66

Museum of Fine Arts, Boston: cat. 50; p. 76, fig. 1; p. 299, fig. 6

bpk/Kunstbibliothek, SMB/Eugène Druet: cat. 88; 96; 97; 105; 106; p. 20, fig. 17

bpk/Kupferstichkabinett, SMB/Dietmar Katz: cat. 93; 94

bpk/Nationalgalerie, SMB/Andres Kilger: cat. 61; 109; p. 174, fig. 1

bpk/Nationalgalerie, SMB/Karin März: cat. 15; 44

bpk/Staatliche Kunstsammlungen Dresden/ Jürgen Karpinski: cat. 89

bpk/Staatliche Kunstsammlungen Dresden/ Werner Lieberknecht: p. 181, fig. 8

bpk/Hamburger Kunsthalle/Elke Walford: cat. 11

bpk/Sprengel Museum Hannover/ Eadweard Muybridge: p. 54, fig. 12

bpk/Staatliche Kunsthalle Karlsruhe/Wolfgang Pankoke: cat. 7; 102; p. 182, fig. 9

bpk/The Metropolitan Museum of Art, New York/Edward Steichen: p. 20, fig. 18; p. 293, fig. 7

bpk/BnF, Dist. RMN – GP/Félix Nadar: p. 290, fig. 1

bpk/RMN – Grand Palais/Bayard Hippolyte (1801–1887): p. 284, fig. 1

bpk/RMN – Grand Palais/Bellot, Michèle | Schormans, Jean: cat. 29

bpk/RMN – Grand Palais/Adrien Didierjean: p. 179, fig. 5, 6

bpk/RMN – Grand Palais/Louis Emile Durandelle: p. 16, fig. 7

bpk/RMN – Grand Palais/Gauthier: p. 47, fig. 4; p. 48, fig. 5; p. 49, fig. 7; p. 54, fig. 13

bpk/RMN – Grand Palais/Hervé Lewandowski: cat. 45; p. 77, fig. 2; p. 91, fig. 2

bpk/RMN – Grand Palais/Tony Querrec: p. 18, fig. 13

bpk/Staatsgalerie Stuttgart: cat. 67

Richard Borek Stiftung, Braunschweig/ Peter Sierigk: cat. 35

Bridgeman Images: p. 13, fig. 3; p. 29, fig. 6

Museum of Fine Arts, Budapest: cat. 53

Amgueddfa Cymru – National Museum Wales, Cardiff: cat. 103

Museo Civico e Gipsoteca Bistolfi, Casale Monferrato – Archivio fotografico: cat. 118

The Art Institute of Chicago: p. 300, fig. 8

Ny Carlsberg Glyptotek, Copenhagen: cat. 9; 17; 20; 25; 27; 28

Ny Carlsberg Glyptotek, Copenhagen/Ole Haupt: p. 30, fig. 7

National Galleries of Scotland, Edinburgh/ John McKenzie: cat. 111

Museum Folkwang, Essen/ARTOTHEK: cat. 73

Gallerie degli Uffizi, Galleria d'arte moderna di Palazzo Pitti, Florence: p. 159, fig. 2

Städel Museum, Frankfurt am Main: cat. 5; 8; 16; 37; 40; 46; 51; 52; 58; 59; 86; 95; 98; 101; 107; 117; 122; p. 15, fig. 6; p. 17, fig. 10; p. 246, fig. 1; p. 259, fig. 6; p. 285, fig. 2; p. 286, fig. 6

Städel Museum, Frankfurt am Main/ Fabienne Ruppen: p. 28, fig. 4

Collection Jean Bonna, Geneva/Patrick Goetelen: cat. 23; 39

Google Arts & Culture: p. 110, fig. 2

Museum für Kunst und Gewerbe, Hamburg: p. 90, fig. 1

Universitätsbibliothek Heidelberg, L'art français: revue artistique hebdomadaire, 3, 1889–1890 (Nr. 105–107), p. "az": p. 185, fig. 1

The Sladmore Gallery, London: cat. 14; 72; 124; 126; 129; 130

Archive Josue Dupon, courtesy The Sladmore Gallery, London: p. 258, fig. 4

Tate, London: cat. 12

Victoria and Albert Museum, London: p. 67, fig. 2

Digital image courtesy of the Getty's Open Content Program, Los Angeles: p. 91, fig. 3

Lyon MBA/Alain Basset: cat. 18

Colección Carmen Thyssen-Bornemisza en depósito en el Museo Nacional Thyssen-Bornemisza, Madrid: cat. 22

Musei Civici, Comune di Mantova, Mantua: cat. 32

Civico Archivio Fotografico, Castello Sforzesco, Milan: p. 126, fig. 1

Courtesy Galleria Bottegantica SRL, Milan / Bruno Bani, Milan: cat. 31

Courtesy Galleria Bottegantica SRL, Milan / Andrea Parisi, Reggio Emilia: cat. 115

Courtesy Galleria Bottegantica SRL, Milan / Stefano Martelli, Crevalcore (Bo): cat. 116

Galleria d'Arte Moderna, Milan/Luca Carrà: cat. 121; p. 127, fig. 3; p. 242, fig. 1

Musée Ingres, Montauban: cat. 1

The Gilgore Collection, Dr. Sheldon G. Gilgore and Irma H. Gilgore, Italian Art 1850–1925, Gilgore Museum, Naples, FL/Jennifer Dana Deane: cat. 114; 120

The Metropolitan Museum of Art, New York, NY: cat. 132–136; p. 28, fig. 5; p. 296, fig. 2; p. 298, fig. 3, 4; p. 299, fig. 7; p. 300, fig. 9

The Morgan Library and Museum, New York: p. 59, fig. 3

Musée Camille Claudel, Nogent-sur-Seine/Yves Bourel: cat. 99

Bibliothèque nationale de France, Paris: p. 24, fig. 1; p. 26, fig. 2; p. 36, fig. 1; p. 37, fig. 2; p. 66, fig. 2; p. 235, fig. 1; p. 292, fig. 4

MAD, Paris/Jean Tholance: cat. 108

Musée Bourdelle, Paris: cat. 119

Petit Palais, Musée des Beaux-Arts de la Ville de Paris: cat. 113

Musée Rodin, Paris: p. 170; p. 274; p. 278, fig. 4; p. 286, fig. 5

Musée Rodin, Paris/Christian Baraja: cat. 33; p. 175, fig. 2

Musée Rodin, Paris/Jean de Calan: p. 278, figs. 3, 5; p. 279, fig. 6; p. 285, fig. 3; p. 286, fig. 4; p. 292, fig. 5; p. 293, fig. 6

Musée Rodin, Paris/Pauline Hisbacq: p. 177, fig. 3

Musée Rodin, Paris/Hervé Lewandowski: cat. 68

Musée Rodin, Paris/Jerome Manoukian: cat. 91

Norton Simon Art Foundation, Pasadena: p. 50, fig. 10

Philadelphia Museum of Art: p. 91, fig. 4

Galleria d'Arte Moderna Ricci Oddi, Piacenza: cat. 65

Musées de Poitiers/Christian Vignaud: cat. 2

Private collection: cat. 43; 47; 49

Private collection, Photo Courtesy of Archivio Medardo Rosso/Serge Domingie: cat. 71

Private collection, Berlin/Roman März: cat. 19

Private collection, Europe/Städel Museum, Frankfurt am Main/Horst Ziegenfusz: cat. 4

Private collection, Frankfurt am Main: cat. 48

Private collection, Marie Anne Krugier-Poniatowski: cat. 42

Private collection, London: cat. 24

Private collection, London/Ken Adlard: cat. 13; 30; 34; 110

Private collection, London/Steve Russell: cat. 87

Private collection, London/Heini Schneebeli: cat. 85; 112

Private collection, Scotland/John McKenzie: p. 102, fig. 1

Private collection, Ewen Spencer/Ken Adlard: cat. 10

Collection PCC, Switzerland: cat. 54

Collection PCC, Switzerland/Junita Arneld: cat. 74; 75; 77–79

Private collection/Ken Adlard: cat. 80–84

Private collection/Volker Naumann: cat. 26

Private collection/Klaus Ruland: cat. 36

Rembrandt Bugatti Répertoire: cat. 131; p. 11; p. 256, fig. 1; p. 257, fig. 2; p. 258, fig. 3; p. 259, fig. 5; p. 260, fig. 7; p. 261, fig. 8, 9

Virginia Museum of Fine Arts, Richmond: p. 110, fig. 1

Galleria Nazionale d'Arte Moderna, Rome: p. 17, fig. 9; p. 244, fig. 1

La Piscine, Roubaix/Alain Leprince: cat. 92; 100

Réunion des Musées Métropolitains Rouen Normandie/C. Lancien, C. Loisel: cat. 6

Archivio Fotografico e Mediateca MART, Rovereto: cat. 63

Pulitzer Arts Foundation and Alise O'Brien Photography, St. Louis: p. 159, fig. 3

Segantini Museum, St. Moritz/Stephan Schenk: cat. 125

Photo Musées de Strasbourg/M. Bertola: cat. 3

RKD – Netherlands institute for art history, The Hague: p. 128, fig. 5

Musée des Augustins, Toulouse/Daniel Martin: p. 180, fig. 7

Museum Ulm, Ulm – Eigentum des Landes Baden-Württemberg: cat. 123

National Gallery of Art, Washington, D.C.: p. 12, fig. 1; p. 46, fig. 1; p. 48, fig. 6; p. 49, fig. 8; p. 52, fig. 11; p. 58, fig. 2; p. 178, fig. 4

Albertina, Vienna: cat. 41

Belvedere, Vienna: cat. 90

Kunst Museum Winterthur, SIK-ISEA, Zurich/ Jean-Pierre Kuhn: cat. 70

Woburn Abbey and Gardens/Peter John Gates: cat. 128

Von der Heydt-Museum, Wuppertal/Antje Zeis-Loi, Medienzentrum Wuppertal: cat. 104

Museum de Fundatie, Zwolle and Heino/Wijhe: cat. 38; 69